The Films of

VOLUME 2

The Films of the Nineties

A Complete, Qualitative Filmography
of 3,268 Feature-Length English Language
Films, Theatrical and Video-Only,
Released Between January 1, 1990,
and December 31, 1999

ROBERT A. NOWLAN *and*
GWENDOLYN L. NOWLAN

Volume 2 : Matrix–Z
(entries 1901–3268, index)

McFarland & Company, Inc., Publishers
Jefferson, North Carolina, and London

Volume 2

LIBRARY OF CONGRESS CATALOGUING-IN-PUBLICATION DATA

Nowlan, Robert A.
   The films of the nineties : a complete qualitative filmography
of over 3000 feature-length English language films, theatrical and
video-only, released between January 1, 1990, and December 31,
1999 / by Robert A. Nowlan and Gwendolyn L. Nowlan.
      p.   cm.
   Includes index.

   ISBN 978-0-7864-4700-8
   softcover : 50# alkaline paper ∞

   1. Motion pictures — Catalogs.   I. Nowlan, Gwendolyn Wright,
1945– . II. Title.
PN1998.N784   2011
016.79143'75'09049 — dc21   2001020241

BRITISH LIBRARY CATALOGUING DATA ARE AVAILABLE

On the cover: Julia Roberts as Vivian Ward in *Pretty Woman*, 1990
(Photofest)

Manufactured in the United States of America

McFarland & Company, Inc., Publishers
  Box 611, Jefferson, North Carolina 28640
    www.mcfarlandpub.com

Table of Contents

1901. *The Matrix* (1999, Warner Bros., 136m, c). D & W Wachowski Brothers, P Joel Silver, PH Bill Pope, ED Zach Staenberg*, M Don Davis, PD Owen Paterson, AD Hugh Bateup & Michelle McGahey, SD Sarah Light, Jacinta Leong, Godric Cole, Judith Harvey, Andrew Powell & Deborah Riley.

LP Keanu Reeves (Neo), Laurence Fishburne (Morpheus), Carrie-Anne Moss (Trinity), Hugo Weaving (Agent Smith), Gloria Foster (Oracle), Joe Pantoliano (Cypher), Marcus Chong (Tank).

This comic book feature has 20th-century hacker Reeves joining cult leader and terrorist Fishburne to prevent an all-out war scheduled for the 21st century between humans and a society of advanced computers. The story stinks but the special effects are very impressive.

1902. *A Matter of Degrees* (1991, Prism Ent., 100m, c). D W.T. Morgan, P Randall Poster & Roy Kissin, W Poster, Jack Mason & Morgan, PH Paul Ryan, ED Curtiss Clayton & Charlie Mullin, M Jim Dunbar, PD Mark Friedberg, AD Ginger Tourgas, SD Bonita Flanders.

LP Ayre Gross (Maxwell Glass), Judith Hoag (Kate Blum), Tom Sizemore (Zeno), Wendell Pierce (Wells), John Doe (Peter Downs), Christina Haag (Isabelle Allen).

Students revolt when a college changes its campus radio program from its progressive format to one of more laid-back easy-listening music.

1903. *Maverick* (1994, Warner Bros., 129m, c). D Richard Donner, P Donner & Bruce Davey, W William Goldman, PH Vilmos Zsigmond, ED Stuart Baird & Mike Kelly, M Randy Newman, PD Tom Sanders, AD Daniel Dorrance, SD Lisa Dean.

LP Mel Gibson (Bret Maverick), Jodie Foster (Annabelle Bransford), James Garner (Zane Cooper), Graham Greene (Joseph), Alfred Molina (Angel), James Coburn (Commodore), Dub Taylor (Room Clerk), Geoffrey Lewis (Matthew Wicker), Paul L. Smith (Archduke), Dan Hedaya (Twitchy).

Many former TV series have received the big screen treatment this decade, and most of them stunk up the theaters. Not so this one. Gibson's pleasant impersonation of Garner's old character is lots of fun. On the other hand, it'll never make anyone's list of classic Westerns. The peg the movie hangs on is for both Gibson and comely female gambler Foster to come up with the $10,000 entry fee in a winner-take-all poker contest. Garner's too old to play Maverick, but he's not too old to show the youngsters why he was so appealing in it and other roles, which he played with less than dead seriousness.

1904. *Maximum Risk* (1996, Columbia, 126m, c). D Ringo Lam, P Moshe Diamant, W Larry Ferguson, PH Alexander Gruszynski, ED Bill Pankow, M Robert Folk, PD Steven Spence, AD Leslie Thompkins & Damien Lanfranchi, SD Christian Calviera.

LP Jean-Claude Van Damme (Alain/Mikhail), Natasha Henstridge (Alex), Jean-Hughes Anglade (Sebastien), Zach Grenier (Ivan), Paul Ben-Victor (Pellman), Frank Senger (Loomis).

Once again Van Damme stars as twin martial arts experts. Unfortunately, two for one doesn't make him twice the actor. French cop Van Damme impersonates his dead twin brother, a Russian mobster in Little Odessa, the Russian emigre neighborhood of New York City. He must deal with the Russian Mafia and corrupt FBI agents.

1905. *Maximum Security* (1996, Royal Oaks Ent., 80m, c). D Fred Olen Ray, P Alan Bursteen, W Sean O'Bannon, PH Gary Graver, ED Jeffrey Schwarz, M David Lawrence, PD Bryce Holtshousen, AD Amie Brockway, SD Kenneth Robeson.

LP Paul Michael Robinson (Mason Richter), Landon Hall (Tracy Quinn), George Franklin (Glenn Jackson), John Lazar (Murdock), Bob Johnson (Harrison O'Reilly III), Steve Scionti (Jesus Gonzales).

An Arab prince is taken hostage aboard his jet in Los Angeles by terrorists led by Lazar. City cop Robinson talks his way aboard the plane and single-handedly routs the terrorists. He's forced to kill the prince, who had staged his own kidnapping to get money from his family. Robinson becomes the fall guy and is sentenced to a new high tech prison. Now Lazar and the remainder of his gang resurface, planning to start a war between the U.S. and Arab states by planting and setting off a thermonuclear bomb ... guess where? That's right, at the prison where Robinson in serving time, which is conveniently located in the heart of L.A. Need we go on?

1906. McBain (1991, Shapiro/Glickenhaus, 103m, c). D & W James Glickenhaus, P J. Boyce Harman, Jr., PH Robert M. Baldwin, Jr., ED Jeffrey Wolf, M Christopher Franke, PD Charles C. Bennett.

LP Christopher Walken (McBain), Maria Conchita Alonso (Christina), Michael Ironside (Frank Bruce), Steve James (Eastland), Jay Patterson (Doctor Dalton), Thomas G. Waites (Gill), Chick Vennera (Santos).

Walken heads a mercenary team of Vietnam buddies who join with beautiful revolutionary Alonso to overthrow an evil Central American dictator.

1907. McHale's Navy (1997, Universal, 109m, c). D Bryan Spicer, P Sid Sheinberg, Bill Sheinberg & Jon Sheinberg, W Peter Crabbe (based on a story by Crabbe and Andy Rose), PH Buzz Feitshans IV, ED Russell Denove, M Dennis McCarthy, PD Gene Rudolf, AD Kim Hix, SD Patrice Laure.

LP Tom Arnold (McHale), David Alan Grier (Parker), Dean Stockwell (Binghampton), Debra Messing (Carpenter), Tim Curry (Vladakov), Ernest Borgnine (Cobra), Bruce Campbell (Virgil), French Stewart (Happy).

TV's McHale's Navy was a pretty lame comedy, notable only for bringing Tim Conway to the public's attention. There is absolutely no reason to pay homage to the series by once again bringing it to the big screen. Apparently the filmmakers must have subconsciously agreed because the story is stupid and the cast inept. For the record, Arnold, as McHale, and the crew of his PT boat rout psychotic terrorist Curry, who knows only one way to play a role: way, way over the top.

1908. Me & Veronica (1993, Arrow Ent., 97m, c). D Don Scardino, P Nellie Nugiel, Leslie Urdang, Max Mayer & Mark Linn-Baker, W Leslie Lyles, PH Michael Barrow, ED Jeffrey Wolf, PD John Arnone, SD Karin Wiesel.

LP Elizabeth McGovern (Fanny), Patricia Wettig (Veronica), Michael O'Keefe (Michael), John Heard (Frankie), Robert Leeshock (Jimmy), Will Hare (Red).

Divorced waitress McGovern is visited by her sister Wettig. Sis announces that she is headed to jail for welfare fraud and wants McGovern to take care of her two kids. While visiting Wettig in prison, McGovern discovers that her sister is mentally ill and suicidal.

1909. Me Myself I (1999, Australian/France, Sony Pictures–Gaumont, 104m, c). D & W Pip Karmel, P Fabien Liron, PH Graeme Lind, ED Denise Haratzis, M Charlie Chan, PD Murray Picknett.

LP Rachel Griffiths (Pamela Drury), David Roberts (Robert Dickson), Sandy Winton (Ben), Yael Stone (Stacey), Shaun Loseby (Douglas), Trent Sullivan (Rupert).

In this often hilarious dramatic comedy, Griffiths believes she's "missed the boat" of life. But then she confronts her double and sees herself as the woman she might have been had she married her dream man Dickson 13 years earlier. Naturally, her alternate life isn't all she imagined it would be.

1910. Mean Guns (1997, Filmwerks, 110m, c). D Albert Pyun, P Tom Karnowski & Gary Schmoeller, W Andrew Witham & Nat Whitcomb, PH George Mooradian, ED Ken Morrisey, M Tony Riparetti.

LP Christopher Lambert (Lou), Ice T (Vincent Moon), Michael Halsey (Marcus), Kimberly Warren (Dee), Deborah Van Valkenburgh (Cam), Hunter Doughty (Lucy), Yuji Okumoto (Hoss), Thom Mathews (Crow).

Sometime in the future, a hundred violent felons are taken into an abandoned prison and given baseball bats and guns. They are informed that $10 million will be divided among the last three survivors.

1911. Meatballs 4 (1992, Moviestore Ent., 91m, c). D & W Bob Logan, P Donald P. Borchers, PH Vance Burberry, ED Peter H. Varity, M Steve Hunter, PD Dorian Vernacchio & Deborah Raymond.

LP Corey Feldman (Ricky Wade), Jack Nance (Neil Peterson), Sarah Douglas (Monica), Bojesse Christopher (Wes), Johnny Cocktails (Victor).

Water skier Feldman is hired as recreation director at a Water Skiing Camp. He must deal with Douglas, who wants to buy the camp and use the land for a real estate development scheme. Other than water skiing stunts, the film is about as interesting as a punctured life jacket.

1912. Medicine Man (1992, Hollywood Pictures–Buena Vista, 104m, c). D John

McTiernan, P Andrew G. Vajna & Donna Dubrow, W Tom Schulman & Sally Robinson (based on the story by Schulman), PH Donald McAlpine, ED Michael R. Miller, M Jerry Goldsmith, PD John Krenz Reinhart, Jr., AD Don Diers & Jesus Buenrostro, SD Enrique Estevez.

LP Sean Connery (Dr. Robert Campbell), Lorraine Bracco (Dr. Rae Crane), Jose Wilker (Dr. Miguel Ornega), Rodolfo DeAlexandre (Tanaki), Francisco Tsirene Rereme (Jahausa).

Bracco's voice is so shrill and annoying that it is difficult to give this disappointing film a fair evaluation. Connery is an eccentric botanist laboring in the Venezuelan rain forest. He is joined by Brooklyn scientist Bracco. They disagree about her being there. They disagree about Connery's work. They disagree about everything. So naturally love develops. Another annoying feature about the movie is that the audience is clued early on into the secret of a cancer cure that Connery and Bracco can't replicate. This makes the two scientists look like dim-witted and unobservant quacks.

1913.   Meet Joe Black   (1998, Universal, 180m, c). D & P Martin Brest, W Ron Osborn, Jeff Reno, Kevin Wade & Bo Goldman (based on the play *Death Takes a Holiday* by Alberto Casella, adapted by Walter Ferris, and the screenplay by Maxwell Anderson & Gladys Lehman), PH Emmanuel Lubezki, ED Joe Hutshing & Michael Tronick, M Thomas Newman, PD Dante Ferretti, AD Robert Guerra, SD Leslie Bloom.

LP Brad Pitt (Joe Black/Young Man in Coffee Shop), Anthony Hopkins (William Parrish), Claire Forlani (Susan Parrish), Jake Weber (Drew), Marcia Gay Harden (Allison), Jeffrey Tambor (Quince).

New York tycoon Hopkins knows he's dying but makes a deal with Death to postpone it by being Death's guide on earth. It seems the Grim Reaper is curious about why humans fear him. Death shows some good sense in choosing Brad Pitt's body for his personification. Too bad the filmmakers couldn't have been as choosey with the script and direction. At three hours the film's length causes some in the audience to beg death to wrap up things and take all concerned across the River Styx. But as Pitt, Death is too busy making time with Hopkins' physician daughter Forlani. The same ground was covered by Fredric March in *Death Takes*

a Holiday (1934), but he only took 78 minutes to satisfy his curiosity and convince Evelyn Venable to go willingly with him.

1914.   Meet the Applegates   (1991, Triton Pictures, 82m, c). D Michael Lehmann, P Denise DiNovi, W Lehmann & Redbeard Simmons, PH Mitchell Dubin, ED Norman Hollyn, M David Newman, PD Jon Hutman, AD Kara Lindstrom & Adam Lustig, SD Nancy Nye.

LP Ed Begley, Jr. (Dick Applegate), Stockard Channing (Jane Applegate), Cami Cooper (Sally Applegate), Dabney Coleman (Aunt Bea), Glenn Shaddix (Greg Samson), Adam Biesk (Vince Samson).

A family of gigantic South American insects disguise themselves as humans and take up residency in U.S. suburbia, where they stalk human prey.

1915.   Meet the Deedles   (1998, Walt Disney Pictures–Buena Vista, 92m, c). D Steve Boyum, P Dale Pollock & Aaron Meyerson, W Jim Herzfeld & Pollock, PH David Hennings, ED Alan Cody, M Steve Bartek, PD Stephen Storer, AD Linden Snyder, SD Robin Peyton.

LP Steve Van Warner (Stew Deedle), Paul Walker (Phil Deedle), A.J. Langer (Lt. Jesse Ryan), John Ashton (Capt. Douglas Pine), Dennis Hopper (Frank Slater), Eric Braeden (Elton Deedle).

When his fraternal twin sons Van Warner and Walker, surfers and frequent troublemakers, are in danger of being expelled from their school, their disappointed father Braeden decides that a summer at a Wyoming camp will be just the thing to straighten them out. There's considerable culture shock all around when the Hawaii-based boys arrive in Wyoming.

1916.   Meet Wally Sparks   (1997, Trimark, 105m, c). D Peter Baldwin, P Leslie Greif, W Rodney Dangerfield & Harry Basil, PH Richard H. Kline, PD Bryan Jones, AD Steve Karman, SD Jacqui.

LP Rodney Dangerfield (Wally Sparks), Burt Reynolds (Mr. Spencer), Debi Mazar (Sandy), David Ogden Stiers (Governor Floyd Preston), Cindy Williams (Emily Preston), Alan Rachins (Judge Williams), Ton Danza (Tony "Boom Boom" Banta).

Dangerfield, the crude and obnoxious host of TV's most offensive talk show, invades polite society and just about destroys it. There are too few good one-liners for Dangerfield to offset the lack of a funny story.

1917. Meeting Daddy (1998, Todd Hoffman Production, 92m, c). D & W Peter Gould, P Matt Salinger & Todd Hoffman, PH Mike Mayels, ED Samuel Craven, M & PD Aaron Osborne, AD Erin Cochran.

LP Josh Charles (Peter), Alexandra Wentworth (Melanie), Lloyd Bridges (Col. Branson), Beau Bridges (Larry), Kristy Swanson (Laura Lee).

The fun in this black comedy is supposed to be based on the widely- different backgrounds of Manhattan-born Jew Charles and southern belle Wentworth. The two return to Savannah to tend to her ailing and eccentric father, Lloyd Bridges. Wentworth's father makes the Addams family seem normal. Unfortunately, the promised humor is seldom delivered.

1918. Meeting Venus (1991, U.K., Warner Bros., 119m, c). D Istvan Szabo, P David Puttnam, W Szabo & Michael Hirst, PH Lajos Koltai, ED Jim Clark, M Richard Wagner, PD Attila Kovacs, AD Lorand Javor.

LP Glenn Close (Karin Anderson), Niels Arestrup (Zoltan Szanto), Marian Labuda (Von Schneider), Maite Nahyr (Maria Krawiecki), Victor Poletti (Stefano Del Sarto), Johara Racz (Dancer).

Here's a nice effort from award-winning Hungarian director Szabo. World-renown conductor Arestrup is tapped to mount a multinational production of Wagner's *Tannhauser*. At the same time he's having an affair with his temperamental diva Close. The best thing about Close's performance is that when she opens her mouth to sing, Kiri Te Kanawa's voice comes out.

1919. Melting Pot (1998, Melting Pot Prods., 104m, c). D Tom Musca, P Richard Abramowitz & Adam Brightman, W Musca & Mark Kemble, PH Arturo Smith, ED Christopher Koefoed, M Stan Ridgway, PD Elizabeth Burhop.

LP Paul Rodriguez (Gustavo Alvarez), CCH Pounder (Lucinda Davis), Cliff Robertson (Jack Durman), Una Damon (Chungmi Kong), Annette Murphy (Gustavo's wife).

East L.A. working stiff Rodriguez is bullied by his much smarter wife Murphy into running for a council seat when longtime incumbent Robertson retires. The social satire makes some amusing points about the U.S. electoral system.

1920. Memoirs of an Invisible Man (1992, Warner Bros., 102m, c). D John Carpenter, P Bruce Bodner & Dan Kolsrud, W Robert Collector, Dana Olsen & William Goldman (based on the novel by H.F. Saint), PH William A. Fraker, ED Marion Rothman, M Shirley Walker, PD Lawrence G. Paull, AD Bruce Crone, SD Rick Simpson.

LP Chevy Chase (Nick Halloway), Daryl Hannah (Alice Monroe), Sam Neill (David Jenkins), Michael McKean (George Talbot), Stephen Tobolowsky (Warren Singleton), Jim Norton (Dr. Bernard Wachs).

San Franciso businessman Chase falls asleep during a business meeting, survives a nearby nuclear fusion accident, and awakens invisible. CIA agent Neill chases Chase, whose invisibility he'd like to exploit in the old spy game. Being invisible complicates Chase's romance with Hannah. If you want to see a good invisible man film, rent the 1933 original with Claude Rains. It wasn't funny, but then neither is this one.

1921. Memphis Belle (1990, Warner Bros., 106m, c). D Michael Caton-Jones, P David Puttnam & Catherine Wyler, W Monte Merrick, PH David Watkin, ED Jim Clark, M George Fenton, PD Stuart Craig, AD John King & Alan Tompkins, SD Ian Giladjian.

LP Matthew Modine (Dennis Dearborn), John Lithgow (Col. Bruce Derringer), Eric Stoltz (Danny Daly), Sean Astin (Richard "Rascal" Moore), Harry Connick, Jr. (Clay Busby), Reed Edward Diamond (Virgil), Tate Donovan (Luke Sinclair), D.B. Sweeney (Phil Rosenthal), Billy Zane (Val Kozlowski).

A fine young cast recreates the last mission of a WWII American bomber crew stationed in England. The crew of the *Memphis Belle* was the first to survive and complete a 25-mission tour.

1922. Men (1997, A-Pix Ent., 96m, c). D Zoe Clarke-Williams, P Paul Williams, W Clark-Williams, Karen Black & James Andronica (based on the novel by Margaret Diehl), PH Susan Emerson, ED Annamaria Szanto &

Stephen Eckelberry, M Mark Mothersbaugh, PD Clovis Chambaret.

LP Sean Young (Stella James), John Heard (George), Dylan Walsh (Teo), Richard Hillman (Frank), Karen Black (Alex), Beau Starr (Tony), Shawnee Smith (Clara).

Fiercely independent Young's experiences with a series of casual affairs and semipermanent arrangements with other men turns her into a strong and mature woman. Well, that's one way of doing it.

1923. ***Men at Work*** (1990, Triumph, 98m, c). D & W Emilio Estevez, P Cassian Elwes, PH Tim Suhrstedt, ED Craig Bassett, M Stewart Copeland, PD Dins Danielsen, AD Patricia Klawonn, SD Will Combs.

LP Charlie Sheen (Carl Taylor), Emilio Estevez (James St. James), Leslie Hope (Susan Wilkins), Keith David (Louis Fedders), Dean Cameron (Pizza Man), John Getz (Maxwell Potterdam, III).

Garbage collectors Sheen and Estevez find themselves involved in a political murder when they find a body in the trash.

1924. ***Men Don't Leave*** (1990, Warner Bros., 115m, c). D Paul Brickman, P Jon Avnet, W Barbara Benedek (based on the film *La Vie Continue* written by Moshe Mizrahi), PH Bruce Surtees, ED Richard Chew, M Thomas Newman, PD Barbara Ling, AD John Mark Harrington, SD William Arnold.

LP Jessica Lange (Beth Macauley), Chris O'Donnell (Chris Macauley), Charlie Korsmo (Matt Macauley), Arliss Howard (Charles Simon), Tom Mason (John Macauley), Joan Cusack (Jody), Kathy Bates (Lisa Coleman).

After the accidental death of her husband Mason, suburban mother Lange is forced to sell the family's home and move to Baltimore to find a job to support herself and her two boys, O'Donnell and Korsmo. O'Donnell is bitter and cruel enough to say that the wrong parent has died. Korsmo hasn't dealt with his father's death. Lange isn't trained for much, but she has talent in cooking and gets a job working in a gourmet shop for bitchy Bates. Teenager O'Donnell is tapped by x-ray technician Cusack as her lover — a situation which Lange can neither deal with nor end. Not yet ready for any romantic entanglements, Lange nevertheless appreciates the friendship of musician Howard. The movie ends without clearing up all the loose ends in the lives of the three — that's what makes it realistic.

1925. ***Men in Black*** (1997, Columbia Tri-Star, 98m, c). D Barry Sonnenfeld, P Walter F. Parkes & Laurie MacDonald, W Ed Solomon (based on the Malibu Comic *The Men in Black* by Lowell Cunningham), PH Don Peterman, ED Jim Miller, M Danny Elfman†, PD Bo Welch†, AD Thomas Duffield, SD Cheryl Carasik†.

LP Tommy Lee Jones (Agent K), Will Smith (Agent J), Linda Fiorentino (Dr. Laurel Weaver), Vincent D'Onofrio (Edgar), Rip Torn (Agent Zed), Tony Shalhoub (Jeebs), Siobhan Fallon (Beatrice), Mike Nussbaum (Gentle Rosenberg), Jon Gries (Van Driver).

In one of the biggest hits of the year, Jones and Smith star in a science-fiction comedy. They are two agents of a supersecret organization whose mission is to monitor the activity of extraterrestrials on Earth — and suppress the evidence of alien existence. Their major assignment is to "deal with" a giant bug that disguises itself as farmer D'Onofrio. It heads off to New York City in search of "the universe," which will give its race the power to conquer earth and other worlds.

1926. ***Men in Love*** (1990, Movie Visions, 87m, c). D Marc Huestis, P Scott Catamas, W Catamas & Emerald Starr, PH Fawn Yacker & Marsha Kahn, ED Frank Christopher, M Donald James Regal, AD Vola Ruben.

LP Doug Self (Steven), Joe Tolbe (Peter), Emerald Starr (Robert), Kutira Descosterd (Christiana), Vincent Schwickert (B.S.), James A. Taylor (Jonathan).

It is an amateurish but honest story of a gay man who travels to Hawaii to throw the ashes of his lover, who has died of AIDS, into the ocean.

1927. ***Men of Respect*** (1991, Grandview Films–Columbia, 107m, c). D & W William Reilly (based on the play *Macbeth* by William Shakespeare), P Efraim Horowitz, PH Bobby Bukowski, ED Elizabeth Kling, M Misha Segal, PD William Barclay.

LP John Turturro (Mike Battaglia), Katherine Borowitz (Ruthie), Rod Steiger (Charlie D'Amico), Graeme Ferguson (Duffy), Dennis Farina (Bankie Como), Lila Skala (Lucia).

The story is an updated version of Shakespeare's *Macbeth*. Turturro is an ambitious gangster nagged by his real life wife Borowitz to take out the mob boss and realize his criminal destiny.

1928. *Menace II Society* (1993, New Line Cinema, 90m, c). D Allen Hughes & Albert Hughes, P Darin Scott, W Tyger Williams (based on a story by Williams & Allen and Albert Hughes), PH Lisa Rinzler, ED Christopher Koefoed, M QD III, PD Penny Barrett, SD Adel A. Mazen.

LP Tyrin Turner (Caine), Larenz Tate (O-Dog), Samuel L. Jackson (Tat Lawson), Glenn Plummer (Pernell), Khandi Alexander (Karen Lawson), Jada Pinkett (Ronnie), Vonte Sweet (Sharif), Charles S. Dutton (Mr. Butler).

This is a frightening film because audiences know it represents things as they are on urban streets. There young men must abide by the code of kill-or-be-killed. Lacking either heroes or real villains, the young actors brilliantly expose the horrors of inner- city life and death.

1929. *Mercury Rising* (1998, Universal, 112m, c). D Harold Becker, P Brian Grazer & Karen Kehala, W Lawrence Konner & Mark Rosenthal (based on the novel *Simple Simon* by Ryne Douglas Pearson), PH Michael Seresin, ED Peter Honess, M John Barry, PD Patrizia von Brandenstein, AD Jim Truesdale & Steve Saklad, SD Jeff Adams, Karen Fletcher & Andrew Menzies.

LP Bruce Willis (Art Jeffries), Alec Baldwin (Nicholas Kudrow), Miko Hughes (Simon), Chi McBride (Tommy B. Jordan), Kim Dickens (Stacey), Robert Stanton (Dean Crandell).

Autistic nine-year-old Hughes cracks a top-secret government code. Bureaucrat Baldwin orders the boy eliminated. FBI agent Willis jumps in to protect the boy. The film is milked for all the sentimentality it can get but fails to deliver a credible story.

1930. *Mercy* (1996, Unapix Films, 85m, c). D & W Richard Shepard, P Rolfe Kent, Rocky Collins & Shepard, PH Sarah Cawley, ED Adam Lichtenstein, M Kent, PD Anne Ross, AD Leanne Sharpton.

LP John Rubinstein (Frank Kramer), Amber Kain (Ruby), Sam Rockwell (Matty), Jane Lanier (Carol), Novella Nelson (Angela), Phil Brock (Phil Kline), Rhea Silver-Smith (Nicole).

New York society lawyer Rubinstein discovers he hasn't much control of his life and world when his young daughter, Silver-Smith, is kidnapped. The kidnappers, Kain and Rockwell, send Rubinstein on a wild goose chase from phone booth to phone booth all over the city. With each call he must agree to more demands.

1931. *Mermaids* (1990, Orion, 110m, c). D Richard Benjamin, P Lauren Lloyd, Wallis Nicita & Patrick Palmer, W June Roberts (based on the novel by Patty Dann), PH Howard Atherton, ED Jacqueline Cambas, M Jack Nitzsche, PD Stuart Wurtzel, AD Steve Saklad & Evelyn Sakash, SD Deborah Kanter & Philip Wurtzel.

LP Cher (Mrs. Flax), Bob Hoskins (Lou Landsky), Winona Ryder (Charlotte Flax), Michael Schoeffling (Joe), Christina Ricci (Kate Flax), Caroline McWilliams (Carrie), Jan Miner (Mother Superior).

Cher portrays the mother of two girls, Ryder and Ricci. She hits the road whenever any man seems to be getting too serious about his relationship with her. She's an unconventional single mother who prefers it that way. Now living in a small New England town, adolescent Ryder develops a crush on hunk Schoeffling, who will take her virginity but not in the beautiful way she had hoped for. Cher allows local shoe merchant Hoskins to get close, but not too close. Ricci almost drowns. While this summary doesn't sound too exciting, the cast, especially Cher, makes the most of the story, and audiences are rewarded with a heartwarming comedy.

1932. *A Merry War* (1997, U.K., First Look Pictures, 101m, c). D Robert Bierman, P Peter Shaw, W Alan Plater (based on the novel *Keep the Aspidistra Flying* by George Orwell), PH Giles Nuttgens, ED Bill Wright, PD Sarah Greenwood, AD Philip Robinson.

LP Richard E. Grant (Gordon Comstock), Helena Bonham Carter (Rosemary), Jim Carter (Erskine), Harriet Walter (Julia Comstock), Lill Roughley (Mrs. Trilling), Julian Wadham (Ravelston).

Grant works as a copywriter for an advertising firm in London during the 1930s. He quits his job to become a poet. This doesn't sit well with his girlfriend Bonham Carter, who wants the two to marry, something he is unable to afford. Then she becomes pregnant. He becomes a changed man, and returns to his former job, and the two marry. The message seems to be that having no money is worse than having responsibilities.

1933. *Message in a Bottle* (1999, Warner Bros., 132m, c). D Luis Mandoki, P Denise Di Novi, Jim Wilson & Kevin Costner, W Gerald DiPego (based on the novel by Nicholas Sparks), PH Caleb Deschanel, ED Steven Weisberg, M Gabriel Yared, PD Jeffrey Beecroft, AD Steve Saklad & Mark Zuelzke, SD Masako Masuda, Andrea Dopaso, Mike Cukers & Nancy Deren.

LP Kevin Costner (Garret Blake), Robin Wright Penn (Theresa Osborne), Paul Newman (Dodge Blake), John Savage (Johnny Land), Illeana Douglas (Lina Paul), Robbie Coltrane (Charlie Toschi).

Heartbroken shipbuilder Costner writes a letter to his dead wife, puts it in a bottle and throws the bottle into the ocean near his home on the Outer Banks of North Carolina. The bottle and the message, addressed to "Catherine," is found by Wright Penn, a researcher for the *Chicago Tribune*, while she jogs along the shore. She decides she has to meet the man who expressed such tender sentiments. She does and romance develops, as you might expect. It's sad to see Newman in his first real old codger role as Costner's crusty but loveable father.

1934. *The Messenger: The Story of Joan of Arc* (1999, Sony Pictures–Columbia Pictures, 148m, c). D Luc Besson, P Patrice Ledoux, W Andrew Birkin & Besson, PH Thierry Arbogast, ED Sylvie Landra, M Eric Serra, PD Hughes Tisandier, AD Alain Paroutaud, SD Alain Pitrel & Robert Le Corre.

LP Milla Jovovich (Joan of Arc), John Malkovich (Charles VII), Faye Dunaway (Yolande D'Aragon), Dustin Hoffman (The Conscience), Pascal Greggory (The Duke of Alencon), Vincent Cassel (Gilles de Rais), Tcheky Karyo (Dunois).

French director Besson presents his now-estranged wife Jovovich in the familiar role of the illiterate French peasant girl picked by God to lead France in battle with its enemies and crown the Dauphin (Malkovich) King Charles VII. Too otherwordly for the more sophisticated temporal and religious leaders, she must endure the agony of being accused of being in league with Satan and go to the stake for her faith. In this version of the oft-filmed story, the battle scenes are the most effective; those in which the lead must show emotional range and power are less so.

1935. *Metamorphosis: The Alien Factor* (1993, Vidmark, 95m, c). D & W Glenn Takakjian, P Ted A. Bohus & Scott Morette, PH John A. Corso, ED Janice Keunelian, M John Gray, PD John Paino.

LP Tara Leigh (Sherry Griffen), Tony Gigante (Mitchell), Dianna Flaherty (Kim Griffen), Katherine Romaine (Nancy Kane), Marcus Powell (Doctor Viallini), Allen Lewis Rickman (Doctor Stein), George Gerard (Dr. Michael Foster).

Genetic engineer Gerard has been working with strange alien spores, growing slimy creatures from them. One of them bites the doctor and he undergoes a grotesque transformation into a slimy monster who goes on a killing rampage.

1936. *Meteor Man* (1993, MGM, 100m, c). D & W Robert Townsend, P Loretha C. Jones, PH John A. Alonzo, ED Adam Bernardi, Richard Candib, Andrew London & Pam Wise, M Cliff Eidelman, PD Toby Corbett, AD Greg Papalia, SD Kathryn Peters, William J. Newmon, II & Stephanie J. Gordon.

LP Robert Townsend (Jefferson Reed), Marla Gibbs (Mrs. Reed), Eddie Griffin (Michael), Robert Guillaume (Mr. Reed), James Earl Jones (Mr. Moses), Bill Cosby (Marvin), Frank Gorshin (Mr. Byers), Sinbad (Malik).

Urban idealist Townsend is hit by a meteor, giving him supernatural powers that allow him to rid his neighborhood of drug dealers. Unfortunately, it seems that to really get rid of the crime related to drugs in our innercities, it will take a miracle at least as preposterous.

1937. *Metro* (1997, Buena Vista, 117m, c). D Thomas Carter, P Roger Birnbaum, W Randy Feldman, PH Fred Murphy, ED Peter E. Berger, M Steve Porcaro, PD William Elliott, AD Greg Papalia, SD Jerie Kelter.

LP Eddie Murphy (Scott Roper), Michael Rapaport (Kevin McCall), Michael Wincott (Michael Korda), Carmen Ejogo (Ronnie Tate), Kim Miyori (Detective Kimura), Art Evans (Lt. Sam Baffert).

In this formalistic thriller, Murphy is back in a cop role, but it doesn't remind audiences of his hits with the *Beverly Hills Cop* series. It does make them yearn for his return to his role in *The Nutty Professor*.

1938. *Metropolitan* (1990, New Line, 98m, c). D Whit Stillman, P Stillman, Brian Greenbaum & Peter Wentworth, W Stillman†, PH John Thomas, ED Chris Tellefsen, M Mark Suozzo.

LP Carolyn Farina (Audrey Rouget), Edward Clements (Tom Townsend), Christopher Eigeman (Nick Smith), Taylor Nichols (Charlie Black), Allison Rutledge-Parisi (Jane Clarke), Dylan Hundley (Sally Fowler), Isabel Gillies (Cynthia McClean), Bryan Leder (Fred Neff), Will Kempe (Rick Von Sloneker).

We began watching this movie several times on cable and something always interrupted before it was finished. Finally, one day we got far enough into the film that we would tolerate no interruptions. A cast of talented unknowns portrays a group of preppie students who gather together for meaningless social events. It's a rare treat to look into the empty lifestyles of well-to-do kids with little to do.

1939. *Miami Blues* (1990, Orion, 97m, c). D & W George Armitage (based on the novel by Charles Willeford), P Jonathan Demme & Gary Goetzman, PH Tak Fujimoto, ED Craig McKay, PD Maher Ahmad.

LP Fred Ward (Sgt. Hoke Moseley), Alec Baldwin (Frederick J. "Junior" Frenger), Jennifer Jason Leigh (Susie "Pepper" Waggoner), Nora Dunn (Ellita Sanchez), Obba Babatunde (Blink Willie).

Recently paroled killer and pathological liar Baldwin poses as a cop so he can have potential crime victims to himself. He hooks up with gullible prostitute Leigh and they play house. She cooks and cleans and he sets out each morning for a day's work of crime. Ward is a slow-witted cop who, after losing his gun and false teeth to Baldwin, makes it his mission to end Alec's crime career.

1940. *Miami Rhapsody* (1995, Hollywood Pictures–Buena Vista, 95m, c). D & W David Frankel, P Barry Jossen & Frankel, PH Jack Wallner, ED Steven Weisberg, M Mark Isham, PD J. Mark Harrington, SD Barbara Peterson.

LP Sarah Jessica Parker (Gwyn), Gil Bellows (Matt), Antonio Banderas (Antonio), Mia Farrow (Nina), Paul Mazursky (Vic), Kevin Pollak (Jordan), Barbara Garrick (Terri), Carla Gugino (Leslie), Bo Eason (Jeff), Naomi Campbell (Kaia), Kelly Bishop (Zelda), Jeremy Piven (Mitchell).

As Parker prepares for her wedding, she casts an eye on the marital problems of her parents and brother. Not liking what she finds — they are all cheating on their spouses — she calls off her wedding and takes up with her mother's lover, Banderas.

1941. *Michael* (1996, New Line, 105m, c). D Nora Ephron, P Sean Daniel, Nora Ephron & James Jacks, W Nora Ephron, Delia Ephron, Peter Dexter & Jim Quinlan, PH John Lindley, ED Geraldine Peroni, M Randy Newman, PD Dan Davis, AD James Tocci, SD Tracey Doyle.

LP John Travolta (Michael), William Hurt (Frank Quinlan), Andie MacDowell (Dorothy Winters), Robert Pastorelli (Huey Driscoll), Jean Stapleton (Pansy Milbank), Bob Hoskins (Vartan Malt), Teri Garr (Judge Esther Newberg).

Angel Travolta is sent from heaven for one last assignment: set straight a pair of cynical journalists, Hurt and MacDowell. Don't expect anything like Cary Grant in *The Bishop's Wife* or Henry Travers in *It's a Wonderful Life*. Travolta is a bit of a slob, with habits not what one would expect of a heavenly messenger.

1942. *Michael Collins* (1996, U.S./U.K., Warner Bros., 117m, c). D & W Neil Jordan, P Stephen Woolley, PH Chris Menges†, ED J. Patrick Duffner & Tony Lawson, M Elliot Goldenthal†, PD Anthony Pratt, AD Arden Gantly, Jonathan McKinstry & Cliff Robinson, SD Josie MacAvin.

LP Liam Neeson (Michael Collins), Aidan Quinn (Harry Borland), Stephen Rea (Ned Broy), Alan Rickman (Eamon De Valera), Julia Roberts (Kitty Kiernan), Charles Dance (Soames), Ian Hart (Joe O'Reilly).

Neeson is outstanding as the 1920s IRA leader Michael Collins; that is, unless you happen to be English and don't fancy seeing your country and its soldiers as the bad guys. The film is very violent, although the background of the struggle is given little attention. The romantic triangle of Neeson, Quinn and Roberts seems a contrivance to pull in female viewers and adds very little to the story.

1943. Mickey Blue Eyes (1999, Warner Bros.–Castle Rock, 103m, c). D Kelly Makin, P Elizabeth Hurley & Charles Mulvehill, W Adam Scheinman & Robert Kuhn, PH Donald E. Thorin, ED David Freeman, M Basil Poledouris, PD Gregory Keen, AD Tom Warren, SD Susan Kaufman & Andrea Fenton.

LP Hugh Grant (Michael Felgate), James Caan (Frank Vitale), Jeanne Tripplehorn (Gina Vitale), Burt Young (Vito Graziosi), James Fox (Philip Cromwell), Joe Viterelli (Vinnie), Gerry Becker (Agent Connell).

Grant is once again his loveable, bungling self—a fish out of water in a mafia story. He's a very proper British auctioneer who falls for schoolteacher Tripplehorn before discovering that she is actually a Mafia princess, daughter of wiseguy Caan. She's afraid that if she accepts his proposal of marriage, her family, headed by her uncle Young, will suck Grant into the business. He feels he's up to the task, but indeed Young sees how he can use Grant's talents in a money laundering scheme. It's good predictable fun.

1944. Middelton's Changeling (1998, U.K., High Times Pictures, 97m, c). D, P & W Marcus Thompson (based on the drama *The Changeling* by Thomas Middleton & William Rowley), PH Richard K.J. Butland, ED Thompson, M Brian Gray & Gary Moore, AD Rob Swinburne.

LP Ian Drury (De Flores), Amanda Ray-King (Beatrice Joanna), Colm O Maonlai (Alsemero), Richard Mayes (Vermandero), Guy Williams (Alonso), Billy Connolly (Alibius).

In this 17th century–set drama, a young man from Valencia is in love with the daughter of the most powerful man in Alicante. She feels the same but is unfortunately intended for another. She asks her father's servant to murder her fiancé, which he does; but lusting for his mistress, he demands the right to deflower her on her wedding night. Things get very bloody.

1945. Midnight Blue (1997, MPCA, 95m, c). D Scott Snider, P Brad Krevoy, Steve Stabler & Jeremy Kramer, W Douglas Brode, PH Mark Vicente, ED Christopher Cibelli, M Eric Allaman, PD Brian Spencer Kasch, AD Robert Joseph, SD Katie Lipsitt.

LP Damian Chapa (Martin), Annabel Schofield (Martine/Georgine), Dean Stockwell (Detective), Harry Dean Stanton (Eric), Steve Kanaly (Collier), Jennifer Jostyn (Barbara).

It's a tolerable soft-core film starring Chapa as a banker attending a conference in New Orleans. While there he becomes obsessed with call girl Schofield — enough to want to dump his loyal girlfriend Jostyn for her. His search for the missing hooker puts him into trouble with the law.

1946. A Midnight Clear (1992, A&M Films, 107m, c). D & W Keith Gordon (based on the novel by William Wharton), P Bill Borden & Dale Pollock, PH Tom Richmond, ED Donald Brochu, M Mark Isham, PD David Nichols, AD David Lubin, SD Janis Lubin.

LP Peter Berg (Bud Miller), Kevin Dillon (Mel Avakian), Ayre Gross (Stan Shutzer), Ethan Hawke (Will Knott), Gary Sinise ("Mother" Wilkins), Frank Whaley ("Father" Mundy).

The time is near the end of WWII. A group of war-weary American GIs come into contact with a group of equally war-weary German soldiers in the Ardennes Forest. The two sides cautiously move towards their own cease-fire and a brief respite from the horrors of war. It is an eloquent statement.

1947. Midnight Edition (1994, Shapiro Glickenhaus, 98m, c). D Howard Libov, P Jonathan Cordish, Ehud Epstein & Libov, W Libov, Yuri Zeltser & Michael Stewart (based on the autobiography *Escape of My Dead Man* by Murray Attaway), PD Guy Tuttle, SD Karen Young.

LP Will Patton (Jack Travers), Michael DeLuise (Darryl Weston), Clare Wren (Sarah Travers), Judson Vaughn (Will Jenkins), Ji-Tu Cumbuka (Reginald Brown), Sarabeth Tucek (Becky Gallagher).

Investigative reporter Patton becomes obsessed with the story of DeLuise, a 19-year-old Georgia drifter who, for no apparent reason, massacred a local family and has been sentenced to die.

1948. Midnight in the Garden of Good and Evil (1997, Warner Bros., 155m, c). D Clint Eastwood, P Eastwood & Arnold Stiefel,

W John Lee Hancock (based on the novel by John Berendt), PH Jack N. Green, ED Joel Cox, M Lennie Niehaus, PD Henry Bumstead, AD Jack G. Taylor, Jr. & James J. Murakami, SD Richard Goddard & John Anderson.

LP Kevin Spacey (Jim Williams), John Cusack (John Kelso), Jack Thompson (Sonny Seiler), Jude Law (Billy Hanson), The Lady Chablis (Chablis Deveau), Alison Eastwood (Mandy Nichols), Irma P. Hall (Minerva), Paul Hipp (Joe Odom), Dorothy Loudon (Serena Dawes), Anne Haney (Margaret Williams), Kim Hunter (Betty Harty), Geoffrey Lewis (Luther Driggers).

New York writer Cusack travels to Savannah, Georgia, to write a magazine article about the legendary annual Christmas party given by wealthy socialite Spacey. He finds himself in the middle of a murder trial when Spacey shoots and kills his hot-tempered houseboy and sometime lover Law. There are memorable performances all around. In addition to the excellent work of Spacey and Cusack, applause must go to Thompson as Spacey's very savvy lawyer and director Eastwood's grown-up daughter Alison, looking her lovely best. Among the character actors portraying "real" characters, top marks go to Hall as a voodoo priestess and Deveau playing himself, a flamboyant and deliciously ladylike transvestite entertainer.

1949. *Midnight Tease* (1994, Concorde–New Horizons, 85m, c). D & P Scott Levy, W Daniella Purcell, PH Dan E. Toback, ED Roderick Davis, M Chris Lennertz, PD Trae King.

LP Cassandra Leigh (Samantha), Rachel Reed (Amy), Edmund Halley (Doctor Saul), Ashlie Rhey (Mantra), Todd Joseph (J.J.), Nicole Grey (Dusty).

This film offers gruesome murders, stripteases and nightmares driven by incest. On the negative side, there is no suspense, no plot and no acting. Leigh, who works at a nudie club, has visions of childhood abuse, which add to her concern about assaults on her co-workers.

1950. *A Midwinter's Tale* (1996, U.K., Sony Pictures Classics, 98m, b&w). D & W Kenneth Branagh, P David Barron, PH Roger Lanser, ED Neil Farrell, M Jimmy Yuill, PD Tim Harvey.

LP Richard Briers (Henry Wakefield), Hetta Charnley (Molly), Joan Collins (Margaretta D'Arcy), Nicholas Farrell (Tom Newman), Mark Hadfield (Vernon Spatch), Julia Sawalha (Nina), Gerard Horan (Carnforth Greville), Michael Maloney (Joe Harper).

A largely unknown cast of actors portrays a crew of actors squabbling as they rehearse an alternate version of *Hamlet*, which they plan to stage in a small English country church.

1951. *The Mighty* (1998, Miramax, 100m, c). D Peter Chelsom, P Jane Startz & Simon Fields, W Charles Leavitt (based on the book *Freak the Mighty* by Rodman Philbrick), PH John De Borman, ED Martin Walsh, M Trevor Jones, PD Caroline Hanania, AD Dennis Davenport, SD Cal Loucks.

LP Sharon Stone (Gwen Dillon), Elden Henson (Maxwell Kane), Kieran Culkin (Kevin Dillon), Gena Rowlands (Gram), Harry Dean Stanton (Grim), Gillian Armstrong (Loretta Lee), James Gandolfini (Kenny Kane).

Narrator Henson, seemingly a dimwit, tells audiences that the "Freak" next door neighbor, Culkin, changed his life. Culkin suffers from a progressive degenerative disease that has left him physically deformed. Bright and fearless, Culkin tutors Henson, who is nearly illiterate, in reading, with stories of the Arthurian legend. The two virtual outcasts imagine themselves to be one brave and chivalrous hero with dying prankster Culkin perched on Henson's back. Ian Michael Smith, of *Simon Birch*, was considered for the Culkin role. Stone, who gets top billing, has a secondary role as Culkin's grieving mother.

1952. *Mighty Aphrodite* (1995, Miramax, 95m, c). D Woody Allen, P Robert Greenhut, W Allen†, PH Carlo DiPalma, ED Susan E. Morse, M Dick Hyman, PD Santo Loquasto, AD Tom Warren, SD Susan Bode.

LP Woody Allen (Lenny Weinrib), Helena Bonham Carter (Amanda Weinrib), F. Murray Abraham (Leader), Claire Bloom (Amanda's Mother), Olympia Dukakis (Jocasta), Michael Rapaport (Kevin), Mira Sorvino* (Linda Ash), David Ogden Stiers (Laius), Jack Warden (Tiresias), Peter Weller (Jerry Bender).

When Allen and his wife Bonham Carter are unable to have a child of their own, they adopt one. After a few years, and despite the warnings of an ever present Greek chorus, Allen is determined to learn something about the actual mother of his son. His search leads him to Sorvino, a porn star and prostitute. Allen can't prevent himself from trying to help his child's mother help herself by finding her a good man and getting her away from her sordid life. It's a delightful comedy, with Sorvino priceless in her Oscar-winning performance. The voice she's chosen for her character is in itself a master stroke, but it's not the limit of her special contributions to this very satisfying film.

1953. *The Mighty Ducks* (1992, Walt Disney Prods.–Buena Vista, 100m, c). D Stephen Herek, P Jon Avnet & Jordan Kerner, W Steven Brill & Brian Hohlfield, PH Thomas Del Ruth, ED Larry Bock & John F. Link, M David Newman, PD Randy Ser, AD Tony Fanning, SD Julie Kaye Fanton.

LP Emilio Estevez (Gordon Bombay), Joss Ackland (Hans), Lane Smith (Coach Reilly), Heidi Kling (Casey), Josef Sommer (Gerald Ducksworth), Joshua Jackson (Charlie Conroy), Elden Ratliff (Fulton Reed).

Estevez is a high-powered lawyer, the kind all the negative jokes are about. He's arrested for D.W.I. and is sentenced to community service as the coach of a public league hockey team in Minneapolis' poorest neighborhood. It's a formula piece, so the script is predictable, as his team teaches him the important lesson (not usually associated with sports nowadays, more's the pity) that "winning isn't everything."

1954. *Mighty Joe Young* (1998, Walt Disney–Buena Vista, 114m, c). D Ron Underwood, P Ted Hartley & Tom Jacobson, W Mark Rosenthal & Lawrence Konner (based on a screenplay by Ruth Rose and a story by Merian C. Cooper), PH Don Peterman & Oliver Wood, ED Paul Hirsch, M James Horner, PD Michael Corenblith, AD Dan Webster & Charlie Dahoub, SD Merideth Boswell.

LP Charlize Theron (Jill Young), Bill Paxton (Gregg O'Hara), Rade Sherbedgia (Strasser), Peter Firth (Garth), David Paymer (Harry Ruben), Regina King (Cicily Banks), Robert Wisdom (Kweli), John Alexander (Mighty Joe Young).

This Disney remake of the 1949 post–*King Kong* film starring Terry Moore, has beautiful scientist Theron, dressed for Rodeo Drive, discovering a 15-foot-tall ape in a remote African jungle. Wishing to save the beast from poachers, she arranges to move him to a California game preserve, which only makes the ape's prospects worse.

1955. *Mighty Morphin Power Rangers: The Movie* (1995, 20th Century–Fox, 95m, c). D Bryan Spicer, P Haim Saban, Shuki Levy & Suzanne Todd, W Arne Olsen (based on a story by John Kamps & Olsen), PH Paul Murphy, ED Wayne Wahrman, M Graeme Revell, PD Craig Stearns, AD Colin Gibson, SD Tim Ferrier.

LP Karan Ashley (Aisha/Yellow Ranger), Johnny Yong Bosch (Adam/Black Ranger), Steve Cardenas (Rocky/Red Ranger), Jason David Frank (Tommy/White Ranger), Amy Jo Johnson (Kimberly/Pink Ranger), David Yost (Billy/Blue Ranger), Paul Freeman (Ivan Ooze), Mark Ginther (Lord Zedd).

TV's six teenage super heroes with super powers and super attitudes are brought to the big screen to save Earth from the clutches of evil Freeman. Only kids will think it super.

1956. *Mikey* (1992, Tapestry Films, 92m, c). D Dennis Dimster-Denk, P Peter Abrams, Robert Levy & Natan Zahavi, W Jonathan Glassner, PH Tom Jewett, ED Zahavi & Omer Tal, M Tim Truman, PD Nigel Clinker & Marcia Calosio.

LP Josie Bisset (Jessie), Lyman Ward (Mr. Jenkins), John Diehl (Neil), Ashley Laurence (Gilder), Mimi Craven (Rachel), Brian Bonsall (Mikey).

The one constant in a series of dreadful accidents that have taken place in several foster homes and schools is sweet little Bonsall. But he couldn't be responsible — or could he?

1957. *Milk* (1999, U.K., Sky Pictures, 94m, c). D & W Bill Brookfield, P George Duffield, Galt Niederhoffer & Meg Thomson, PH Peter Hannan, ED Peter Hollywood, M Jools Holland, PD Laurence Dorman, AD Harry James Woodward.

LP James Fleet (Adrian), Phyllida Law (Veronica), Joss Ackland (The Vicar), Clotilde Coureau (Ilaria), Peter Jones (Harry), Francesca Annis (Harriet), Dawn French (Virginia), Richard Johnson (John).

This irreverent black comedy details the actions of the family and friends of a 75-year-old woman in the days after her death. It seems she lived life sexually to the fullest extent, and her passing is not mourned by her 45-year-old son Fleet, who had grudgingly been caring for his mum on a rural dairy farm. The gathering of the various mourners is an excuse for unforgivable — but amusing — behavior.

1958. Milk Money (1994, Paramount, 110m, c). D Richard Benjamin, P Kathleen Kennedy & Frank Marshall, W John Mattson, PH David Watkin, ED Jacqueline Cambas, M Michael Convertino, PD Paul Sylbert, SD Casey Hallenbeck & Antoinette J. Gordon.

LP Melanie Griffith (V), Ed Harris (Tom Wheeler), Michael Patrick Carter (Frank Wheeler), Malcolm McDowell (Waltzer), Anne Heche (Betty), Casey Siemaszko (Cash), Philip Bosco (Jerry the Pope), Brian Christopher (Kevin Clean), Adam Lavorgna (Brad).

Twelve-year-old Carter and two of his friends travel to the city in search of a prostitute. They come across good-natured Griffith who, due to some circumstances hardly worth mentioning, is forced to move in with Carter and his widower father Harris in their suburban home. The best scene is when Carter takes Griffith to school to illustrate his sex education project.

1959. Miller's Crossing (1990, 20th Century–Fox, 115m, c). D Joel Coen, P Ethan Coen, W Joel Coen & Ethan Coen, PH Barry Sonnenfeld, ED Michael R. Miller, M Carter Burwell, PD Dennis Gassner, AD Leslie McDonald, SD Kathleen McKernin.

LP Gabriel Byrne (Tom Reagan), Marcia Gay Harden (Verna), John Turturro (Bernie Bernbaum), Jon Polito (Johnny Caspar), J.E. Freeman (Eddie Dane), Albert Finney (Leo), Mike Starr (Frankie).

In 1929, Byrne's boss Finney is in a struggle with arch-rival Polito over control of the town. Finney and Byrne's friendship is severed when both fall for hard-as-nails Harden. Turturro is a small-time hood trying to weasel in on both gangs. He is also Harden's brother. It's an excellent atmospheric piece, filled with underworld codes of ethics, unexpected twists and double-crosses.

1960. Milo (1998, Treehouse Films–Filmwave Pictures, 90m, c). D Pascal Franchot, P Jeff Kirshbaum & Hans Bauer, W Craig Mitchell, PH Yuri Neyman, ED Donn Aron & Ross Guidici, M Kevin Manthei, PD Frank Bollinger, AD Angela Trujillo & Terri Phillips, SD Eden Barr.

LP Jennifer Jostyn (Claire Mullins), Antonio Fargas (Mr. Kelso), Paula Cale (Marian), Maya McLaughlin (Abigail), Vincent Schiavelli (Dr. Matthew Jeeder), Asher Metchik (Milo).

In this *Halloween* knock-off, Jostyn returns after sixteen years to her hometown where she and four other young girls were lured by Metchik to his gynecologist father's office, where he murdered one and wounded another. Supposedly, Metchik died by drowning years ago, but Jostyn starts seeing him everywhere.

1961. Mimic (1997, Miramax, 102m, c). D Guillermo Del Toro, P Bob Weinstein, B.J. Rack & Ole Bornedal, W Matthew Robbins, Del Toro, Matt Greenberg & John Sayles (based on the short story by Donald A. Wolheim), PH Dan Laustsen, ED Patrick Lussier & Peter Devaney Flanagan, M Marco Beltrami, PD Carol Spier, AD Tamara Deverell, SD Elinor Rose.

LP Mira Sorvino (Dr. Susan Tyler), Jeremy Northam (Dr. Peter Mann), Josh Brolin (Josh Maslow), Giancarlo Giannini (Manny), Alexander Goodwin (Chuy), Alix Koromzay (Remy), F. Murray Abraham (Dr. Gates), Charles S. Dutton (Leonard).

Entomologist Sorvino develops a breed of genetically enhanced cockroaches to wipe out roaches causing a plague in Manhattan. Having done their job, the new cockroaches are destroyed — or are they?

1962. Mindwalk (1991, Triton Pictures, 112m, c). D Bernt Capra, P Adriana A.J. Cohen, W Fritjof Capra & Floyd Byars (based on a story by Bernt Capra, and the book *The Turning Point* by Fritjof Capra), PH Karl Kases, ED Jean-Claude Piroue, M Philip Glass.

LP Liv Ullman (Sonia Hoffman), Sam Waterston (Jack Edwards), John Heard (Thomas Harriman), Ione Skye (Kit), Emmanuel Montes (Romain).

After failing in his try for the presidency, liberal American politician Waterston travels to Paris to visit his old friend, poet Heard. The two meet Norwegian quantum physicist Ullman, who lectures them on the history of physics. The film is not quite the thing for moviegoers who prefer smart dialogue playing a second fiddle to action and violence.

1963. *The Minus Man* (1999, TSG Picture, 115m, c). D & W Hampton Fancher (based on the novel by Lew McCreary), P Fida Attich & David L. Bushell, PH Bobby Bukowksi, ED Todd Ramsey, M Marco Beltrami, PD Andrew Laws, AD Austin Gorg.

LP Owen Wilson (Vann Siegert), Brian Cox (Doug), Mercedes Ruehl (Jane), Janeane Garofalo (Ferrin), Dwight Yoakam (Blair).

Drifter Wilson is a serial killer. His weapon of choice is a flask of poison-laced Amaretto.

1964. *The Miracle* (1991, U.K., Miramax, 96m, c). D & W Neil Jordan (based on the story "Night in Tunisia" by Jordan), P Stephen Woolley & Redmond Morris, PH Phillipe Rousselot, ED Joke Van Wijk, M Anne Dudley, PD Gemma Jackson, AD David Wilson.

LP Beverly D'Angelo (Renee), Donal McCann (Sam), Niall Byme (Jimmy), Lorraine Pilkington (Rose), J.G. Devlin (Mr. Beausang), Catherine Delaney (Miss Strange), Tom Hickey (Tommy).

Bright but bored Irish teens Pilkington and Byme become intrigued with D'Angelo, a mysterious American who suddenly turns up in their town.

1965. *Miracle on 34th Street* (1994, 20th Century–Fox, 74m, c). D Les Mayfield, P John Hughes, W Hughes (based on the 1947 film by George Seaton, from a story by Valentine Davies), PH Julio Macat, ED Raja Gosnell, M Bruce Broughton, PD Doug Kraner, AD Steve Arnold, SD John Berger, Nancy Mickelberry & Carl Stensel.

LP Richard Attenborough (Kriss Kringle), Elizabeth Perkins (Dorey Walker), Dylan McDermott (Bryan Bedford), J.T. Walsh (Ed Collins), James Remar (Jack Duff), Jane Leeves (Alberta Leonard), Simon Jones (Shellhammer), William Windom (C.F. Cole), Mara Wilson (Susan Walker), Robert Prosky (Judge Harper).

Who was consulted to determine if there was any need for a remake of a Christmas classic which is shown on television every year at the holidays? That's what we thought. Other than the dubious advantages of color over black and white, there appears to be nothing

going for this new version of the story of an old man who believes himself to be the real Santa Claus. Wilson is cute as the little girl whose faith in him is seen by Attenborough as a test of whether Santa Claus is still relevant in people's lives.

1966. *The Mirror Has Two Faces* (1996, TriStar, 126m, c). D Barbra Streisand, P Streisand & Arnon Milchan, W Richard LaGravenese (based on s stogy by LaGravenese and the screenplay *Le Miroir a Deux Faces* by Andre Cayatte & Gerard Oury), PH Dante Spinotti & Andrzej Bartkowiak, Ed Jeff Werner, M Marvin Hamlisch, PD Tom John, AD Teresa Carriker-Thayer, SD John Alan Hicks & Pamela Turk.

LP Barbra Streisand (Rose Morgan), Jeff Bridges (Gregory Larkin), Lauren Bacall† (Hannah Morgan), George Segal (Henry Fine), Mimi Rogers (Claire), Pierce Brosnan (Alex), Brenda Vaccaro (Doris), Austin Pendelton (Barry), Elle Macpherson (Candy).

How shall we put this? Wouldn't it be wonderful to hear Streisand's glorious singing voice without having to watch her play the ugly duckling who turns into a beautiful swan? She's a professor at Columbia, and a big hit with her students but not with men. Bridges is a mathematics professor without a clue as to how to interest his students. Bridges, however, has no trouble getting women into his bed. In fact, he sees his success in this regard as a problem. He's thrown together with Streisand and suggests a platonic marriage, so he can concentrate on his work without all that sexual nonsense. Barbra agrees because she loves the dumb lug and hopes he'll eventually come to his senses and her bed. She makes herself over into what passes for a very desirable woman, but even this doesn't quite do the trick. Still, by the end of the movie the two are dancing down the street to the sound of Streisand singing the title song. By the way, Lauren Bacall was quite good as Streisand's mom and was thought to be a shoo-in for an Oscar, but not everyone voted on the basis of a long career, we guess.

1967. *Mirror Images* (1992, Academy Ent., 94m, c). D Alexander Gregory Hippolyte, P Andrew Garroni, W Rick Marx, PH Paul Desatoff, ED Kent Smith, M Joseph Smith, PD Blair Martin, AD Mike Shaw.

LP Delia Sheppard (Kaitlin/ Shauna), Jeff Conaway (Jeff Blair), Julie Strain (Gina Kaye), Nels Van Patten (Joey Zoom), Korey Mall (Gil), Ricard Arbolino (Carter Sayles).

Sheppard plays sexy twins, one a bored housewife and the other a stripper. They find their lives filled with passion and danger due to an encounter with a handsome madman.

1968. *Mirror, Mirror* (1991, Academy Ent., 103m, c). D Marina Sargenti, P & M Jimmy Lifton, W Annette Cascone & Gina Cascone (based on the story by Yuri Zeltser & Sargenti), PH Robert Brinkman, ED Glen Morgan & Barry Dresner, AD Stuart Blatt.

LP Karen Black (Mrs. Gordon), William Sanderson (Mr. Veze), Rainbow Harvest (Megan Gordon), Kristen Dattilo (Nikki), Ricky Paull Goldin (Ron).

Awkward highschooler Harvest uses black magic, gained from an old mirror, to take revenge on her cruel classmates.

1969. *The Misadventures of Margaret* (1998, U.K./France, TF1 Intl. and Granada, 105m, c). D & W Brian Skeet (based on the novel *Rameau's Niece* by Cathleen Schine), P Ian Benson, PH Romain Winding, ED Claire Douglas, M St. Etienne, PD Martin Childs, SD John McFarlane & Jennifer Halpern.

LP Parker Posey (Margaret Nathan), Jeremy Northam (Edward Nathan), Craig Chester (Richard Lane), Elizabeth McGovern (Till Turner), Brooke Shields (Lily), Corbin Bernsen (Art Turner).

This film is meant to recreate classic Hollywood Romantic comedies, but those worked because of humorous situations and appealing people. This film trys to get by with sexual frankness, nudity and horny women.

1970. *The Misadventures of Mr. Wilt* (1990, U.K., Rank, 93m, c). D Michael Tuchner, P Brian Eastman, W Andrew Marshall & David Renwick (based on the novel by Tom Sharpe), PH Norman Langley, ED Chris Blunden, M Anne Dudley, PD Leo Austin, SD Steve Hedinger.

LP Griff Rhys (Henry Wilt), Mel Smith (Inspector Flint), Alison Steadman (Eva Wilt), Diana Quick (Sally), Jeremy Clyde (Hugh), Roger Allam (Dave), David Ryall (Rev. Froude).

Rhys is delightful as a hapless community college English teacher who fantasizes about killing his wife Steadman. When the latter disappears, he's a prime suspect. To add to his problems, on the night of his wife's disappearance, he was observed having a sexual encounter with an anatomically correct doll.

1971. *Les Misérables* (1998, Columbia Pictures–Sony Pictures, 131m, c). D Bille August, P Sarah Radclyffe & James Gorman, W Rafael Yglesias (based on the novel by Victor Hugo), PH Jorgen Pearson, ED Janus Billeskov-Jansen, M Basil Poledouris, PD Anna Asp, AD Peter Grant.

LP Liam Neeson (Jean Valjean), Geoffrey Rush (Javert), Uma Thurman (Fantine), Claire Danes (Cosette), Hans Matheson (Marius), Reine Brynolfsson (Captain Beauvais), Peter Vaughan (Bishop), Mimi Newman (Young Cosette).

The story of Hugo's classical tale of the conflict between ex-convict Neeson, who wants nothing more than to forget his past and forge a new life, and Rush, the relentless lawman constantly pursuing him, should be familiar to most (especially those who have been thrilled by Alain Boublil and Claude-Michel Schonberg's legendary musical). This third English version of the story is a lavish production. Neeson looks like one might imagine Jean Valjean to look, and Rush is awesome as the obsessive Javert. Thurman, as Fantine, has a fine death scene, but the work of Danes, as Cosette, and Matheson, as Marcus, is too 20th century to make their characters credible.

1972. *Misery* (1990, Castle Rock–Columbia, 107m, c). D Rob Reiner, P Reiner, Andrew Scheinman, Steve Nicolaides & Jeffrey Scott, W William Goldman (based on the novel by Stephen King), PH Barry Sonnenfeld, ED Robert Leighton, M Marc Shaiman, PD Norman Garwood, AD Mark Mansbridge, SD Stan Tropp.

LP James Caan (Paul Sheldon), Kathy Bates* (Annie Wilkes), Richard Farnsworth (Buster, Sheriff), Frances Sternhagen (Virginia), Lauren Bacall (Marcia Sindell).

When best-selling novelist Caan has an automobile accident he is rescued by one of his greatest fans, nurse Bates. She takes him to her home where she keeps him as a prisoner after she discovers that in his newest novel he has killed off her favorite romantic character. In her Oscar-winning performance Bates is superb as a fanatic fan who is intent on dictating how Caan is to write his novels.

1973. *Miss Julie* (1999, U.K., MGM/UA, 103m, c). D Mike Figgis, P Figgis & Harriet Cruickshank, W Figgis & Helen Cooper (based on the play by August Strindberg), PH Benoit Delhomme, ED Matthew Wood, M Figgis, PD Michael Howells.

LP Saffron Burrows (Miss Julie), Peter Mullan (Jean), Maria Doyle Kennedy (Christine).

Director Figgis offers a powerful film adaptation of the Strindberg play about the doomed relationship of a turn-of-the-century Swedish noblewoman and her servant. The former is played effectively by Burrows, and the latter played broodingly by Mullan.

1974. *Missing Pieces* (1996, Orion Pictures, 92m, c). D & W Leonard Stern, P Aaron Russo, PH Peter Stein, ED Evan Lottman, M Marvin Hamlisch, PD Michael Hanan, AD Mark Zuelske, SD Doug Mowat.

LP Robert Wuhl (Lou Wimpole), Eric Idle (Wendell Dickens), Lauren Hutton (Jennifer), Bob Gunton (Gabor), Richard Belzer (Baldisari), Bernie Koppel (Dr. Gutman), Kim Lankford (Sally).

An ancient riddle sends Wuhl and Idle on a quest for fame and fortune. This road picture has very little to recommend it. Best leave its pieces missing.

1975. *Mission Impossible* (1996, Paramount, 110m, c). D Brian De Palma, P Tom Cruise & Paula Wagner, W David Koepp & Robert Towne (based on a story by Koepp & Steven Zaillian, and the television series by Bruce Geller), PH Stephen H. Burum, ED Paul Hirsch, M Danny Elfman & Lalo Schifrin, PD Norman Reynolds, AD Frederick Hole, SD Peter Howitt.

LP Tom Cruise (Ethan Hunt), Jon Voight (Jim Phelps), Emmanuelle Beart (Claire), Henry Czerny (Kittridge), Jean Reno (Krieger), Ving Rhames (Luther), Kristin Scott Thomas (Sarah Davies), Vanessa Redgrave (Max), Emilio Estevez (Jack Harmon — uncredited).

As we recall it, the *Mission Impossible* series was quite enjoyable. Each week a team of experts was gathered together by Peter Graves, who cleverly helped the villain of the week bring his own evil ways to an end. Too bad they didn't make a movie like that. Some who are not familiar with the TV series might find this film, starring Cruise, to be of some interest (and even suspenseful), but why call it *"Mission Impossible"*?

1976. *Mississippi Masala* (1992, U.S./U.K., Samuel Goldwyn Company, 118m, c). D Mira Nair, P Michael Nozik & Nair, W Sooni Taraporevala, PH Edward Lachman, ED Roberto Silvi, M L. Subramaniam, PD Mitch Epstein, AD Jefferson Sage, SD Jeanette Scott.

LP Denzel Washington (Demetrius), Sarita Choudhury (Mina), Roshan Seth (Jay), Sharmila Tagore (Kinnu), Charles S. Dutton (Tyrone), Joe Seneca (Williben), Ranjit Chowdhry (Anil).

In a modern day *Romeo and Juliet* story, African-American Washington and Indian Choudhury fall in love. Her family fled Idi Amin's Uganda and settled in the American South. Both families oppose the relationship, and the racism on both sides makes the lovers outcasts.

1977. *Mr. and Mrs. Bridge* (1990, Miramax, 124m, c). D James Ivory, P Ismail Merchant, W Ruth Prawer Jhabvala (based on the novels *Mrs. Bridge* and *Mr. Bridge* by Evan S. Connell), PH Tony Pierce-Roberts, ED Humphrey Dixon, M Richard Robbins, PD David Gropman.

LP Paul Newman (Walter Bridge), Joanne Woodward† (India Bridge), Robert Sean Leonard (Douglas Bridge), Margaret Welsh (Carolyn Bridge), Kyra Sedgwick (Ruth Bridge), Blythe Danner (Grace).

This film leisurely examines the lives of an American middle-class couple during the time between the two world wars. Newman and Woodward give outstanding performances as WASPs who don't care for changes in their orderly existence.

1978. *Mr. Baseball* (1992, Universal, 109m, c). D Fred Schepisi, P Schepisi, Doug Claybourne & Robert Newmyer, W Gary Ross, Kevin Wade & Monte Merrick (based on the story by Theo Pelletier & John Junkerman), PH Ian Baker, ED Peter Honess, M Jerry Goldsmith, PD Ted Haworth.

LP Tom Selleck (Jack Elliot), Ken Takakura (Uchiyama), Aya Takanashi (Hiroko Uchiyama), Dennis Haysbert (Max "Hammer" Dubois),

Toshi Shioya (Yoji Nishimura), Kohsuke Toyohara (Toshi Yamashita).

American baseball player Selleck's contract is sold to a team in Japan. He hopes to use the experience as his ticket back to the big leagues. Expect all the usual problems of a "fish out of water."

1979. *Mr. Destiny* (1990, Silver Screen Partners IV–Buena Vista, 110m, c). D James Orr, P & W Orr & Jim Cruickshank, PH Alex Thomson, ED Michael R. Miller, M David Newman, PD Michael Seymour, AD Catherine Hardwicke, SD Kathleen McKernin.

LP James Belushi (Larry Burrows), Linda Hamilton (Ellen Burrows), Michael Caine (Mike), Jon Lovitz (Clip Metzler), Hart Bochner (Niles Pender), Bill McCutcheon (Leo Hansen), Rene Russo (Cindy Jo), Jay O. Sanders (Jacki Earle).

Twenty years earlier Belushi struck out in a crucial baseball game and believes it was the cause of his meaningless life and lack of luck. Mysterious Caine slips him a potion that allows Belushi to see what would have happened to his life if he had gotten a hit.

1980. *Mr. Frost* (1990, U.K./France, Triumph, 104m, c). D Philippe Setbon, W Setbon & Brad Lynch, PH Dominique Brenguier, ED Ray Lovejoy, M Steven Levine, AD Max Berto, SD Patrick Weibel.

LP Jeff Goldblum (Mr. Frost), Alan Bates (Inspector Detweiler), Kathy Baker (Dr. Sarah Day), Roland Giraud (Raymond Reynhardt), Francois Negret (Christophe Kovac).

English detective Bates succeeds in arresting icy killer Goldblum. The latter has committed twenty-four murders and has refused to speak for three years. Psychiatrist Baker sets out to find out why.

1981. *Mr. Holland's Opus* (1996, Buena Vista, 142m, c). D Stephen Herek, P Ted Field, Michael Nolin & Robert W. Cort, W Patrick Sheane Duncan, PH Oliver Wood, ED Trudy Ship, M Michael Kamen, PD David Nichols, AD Dina Lipton, SD Jan Bergstrom.

LP Richard Dreyfuss† (Glenn Holland), Glenne Headly (Iris Holland), Jay Thomas (Bill Meister), Olympia Dukakis (Principal Jacobs), William H. Macy (Vice Principal Wolters), Alicia Witt (Gertrude Lang), Terence Howard (Louis Russ), Damon Whittaker (Bobby Tidd), Jean Louisa Kelly (Rowena Morgan), Alexandra Boyd (Sarah Olmstead), Nicholas John Renner (Cole at 6 Years Old), Joseph Anderson (Cole at 15 Years Old), Anthony Natale (Cole at 28 Years Old), Joanna Gleason (Adult Gertrude).

In a film which unashamedly plays with the audience's emotions, Dreyfuss is a musician and would-be composer. He reluctantly enters the teaching profession to pay the bills. At first he isn't much interested in his minimally talented students, but over the years he becomes the kind of teacher that Mr. Chips could only aspire to be. While helping countless students to learn many more important things than just music, Dreyfuss fails with his son, born deaf. In a finale bound to bring a tear to one's eyes, laid-off after nearly thirty years, Dreyfuss is given the opportunity to conduct his symphony, played by an orchestra of former students, including the governor of the state. It's corny, yes, but the emotions one feels are real, and Dreyfuss deserves all the credit for that.

1982. *Mr. Jealousy* (1998, Lions Gate Films, 105m, c). D & W Noah Baumbach, P Joel Castleberg, PH Steven Bernstein, ED J. Kathleen Gibson, M Luna & Robert Een, PD Anne Stuhler, AD Roswell Hamrick, SD Candis Heiland.

LP Eric Stoltz (Lester Grimm), Annabella Sciorra (Ramona Ray), Chris Eigeman (Dashiell Frank), Carlos Jacott (Vince), Marianne Jean-Baptiste (Lucretia), Brian Kerwin (Stephen).

Stoltz has had a long history of jealousy where girls are concerned. At 30, he begins a relationship with Sciorra but becomes obsessed with thoughts of her past boyfriends, especially young writer Frank. Stoltz begins following Frank around and even joins his therapy group. His jealousy contributes to bringing Sciorra and Frank back together.

1983. *Mister Johnson* (1991, Avenue Ent., 101m, c). D Bruce Beresford, P Michael Fitzgerald & Kathy Fitzgerald, W William Boyd & Beresford (based on the novel by Joyce Cary), PH Peter James, ED Humphrey Dixon, M Georges Delerue, PD Herbert Pinter, AD Fabian Adibe, SD Graham Summer.

LP Maynard Eziashi (Mister Johnson), Pierce Brosnan (Harry Rudbeck), Edward Woodward (Sargy Gollup), Beatie Edney (Celia Rudbeck),

Denis Quilley (Bulteen), Nick Reding (Tring), Bella Enahoro (Bamu).

In the African bush in the 1920s, Eziashi is a black clerk who desperately wishes to be accepted as a proper Englishman. His means of achieving his aim include manipulating, lying and stealing. In the process, he turns his back on his own people, becoming just another annoying cog in British colonialism.

1984. Mr. Jones (1993, TriStar, 114m, c). D Mike Figgis, P Alan Greisman & Debra Greenfield, W Eric Roth & Michael Cristofer (based on a story by Roth), PH Juan Ruiz Anchia, ED Tom Rolf, M Maurice Jarre, PD Waldema Kalinowksi, AD Larry Fulton, SD Gae Buckley & Florence Fellman.

LP Richard Gere (Mr. Jones), Lena Olin (Libbie), Anne Bancroft (Dr. Catherine Holland), Tom Irwin (Patrick), Delroy Lindo (Howard), Bruce Altman (David), Lauren Tom (Amanda).

Manic-depressive Gere attempts suicide and is hospitalized under the care of psychiatrist Olin. The two become romantically involved, a no-no in doctor-patient relationships upon which the film takes no stand.

1985. Mr. Magoo (1997, Walt Disney Pictures–Buena Vista, 97m, c). D Stanley Tong, P Ben Myron, W Pat Proft & Tom Sherohman (based on the character "Mr. Magoo" owned by the UPA Productions of America), PH Jingle Ma, ED Stuart Pappe, David Rawlins & Michael R. Miller, M Michael Tavera, PD John Willett, AD Doug Byggdin, SD Elizabeth Wilcox.

LP Leslie Nielsen (Quincy Magoo), Kelly Lynch (Luanne Leseur), Ernie Hudson (Agent Gus Anders), Stephen Tobolowsky (Agent Chuck Stupack), Nick Chinlund (Bob Morgan), Matt Keeslar (Waldo), Jennifer Garner (Stacey Sampanahoditra), Miguel Ferrer (Ortega Peru), Malcolm McDowell (Austin Cloquet).

Leslie Nielsen once was a serious actor before he found fame and fortune playing bungling, foolish characters for laughs. His appearance in a live-action version of the old UFA cartoon, as the nearsighted Mr. Magoo, is so trite as to suggest that maybe it's time to once again look for a straight role.

1986. Mr. Nanny (1993, New Line Cinema, 84m, c). D Michael Gottlieb, P Bob Engelman, W Gottlieb & Ed Rugoff, PH Peter Stein, ED Earl Ghaffari & Michael Ripps, M David Johansen & Brian Koonin, PD Don DeFina, AD Jose Duarte.

LP Terry "Hulk" Hogan (Sean Armstrong), Sherman Hemsley (Bert Wilson), Austin Pendelton (Alex Mason), Robert Gorman (Alex, Jr.), Madeline Zima (Kate), Mother Love (Corinne).

Retired professional wrestler Hogan seeks employment as a bodyguard but settles for a job baby-sitting two neglected kids.

1987. Mr. Saturday Night (1992, Columbia, 119m, c). D & P Billy Crystal, W Crystal, Lowell Ganz & Babaloo Mandell, PH Donald Peterman, ED Kent Beyda, M Marc Shaiman, PD Albert Brenner, AD Carol Winstead Wood, SD Kathe Klopp.

LP Billy Crystal (Buddy Young, Jr.), David Paymer (Stan Yankelman), Julie Warner (Elaine), Helen Hunt (Annie), Mary Mara (Susan), Jerry Orbach (Phil Gussman), Ron Silver (Larry Meyerson), Sage Allen (Mom).

Crystal is a very amusing performer; but Crystal as writer and director is something else. This story of a legendary Catskills comedian, who is something of a bastard, never catches fire. Oh, Crystal gives himself some funny lines, but the story of this man's life is almost meaningless.

1988. Mr. Stitch (1996, U.S./France, WarnerVision, 98m, c). D & W Roger Avary, P Rutger Hauer & Avary, PH Tom Richmond, ED Sloane Klevin, M Tomandandy, PD Damien LaFranche, AD Kevin White & Richard Louderback.

LP Rutger Hauer (Dr. Rue Wakeman), Wil Wheaton (Lazarus), Nia Peeples (Dr. Elizabeth English), Ron Perlman (Dr. Frederick Texarian), Taylor Negron (Dr. Al Jacobs).

In a secret underground lab, a team of scientists, led by Hauer, have created a patchwork man, stitched together from the bodies of 88 different men and women. The resulting creature has flashbacks to events in the lives of those who contributed to his being.

1989. Mr. Wonderful (1993, Warner Bros., 109m, c). D Anthony Minghella, P Marianne Moloney, W Minghella, Amy Schor & Vicki Polon, PH Geoffrey Simpson, ED John Tintori, M Michael Gore, PD Doug Kraner, AD

Steve Saklad, SD Alyssa Winter & Sylvia Cedeno.

LP Matt Dillon (Gus DeMarco), Annabella Sciorra (Lee), Mary Louise Parker (Rita), William Hurt (Tom), Bruce Altman (Mr. Wonderful), Vincent D'Onofrio (Dominic), James Gandolfini (Mike), Jessica Harper (Funny Face).

Working class stiff Dillon finds that his alimony payments to his ex-wife Sciorra are preventing him from having much of a life. To resolve this problem he is determined to find a new husband for his ex and thus get off the hook of supporting her.

1990. *Mr. Write* (1994, Shapiro Glickenhaus Ent., 90m, c). D Charlie Loventhal, P Joan Fishman & Rick Herrington, W Howard J. Morris (based on his play), PH Elliot Davis, ED Eric L. Beason, M Miles Roston, PD Pamela Woodbridge, AD Carey Meyer, SD Marty Huyette.

LP Paul Reiser (Charlie), Jessica Tuck (Nicole), Martin Mull (Dan), Tom Wilson (Billy), Doug Davidson (Roger), Jane Leeves (Wylie), Wendy Jo Sperber (Roz).

Would-be writer Reiser hopes to support his ambition by appearing in commercials. He falls in love with advertising executive Tuck, but to win her he has to deal with Davidson, her stupid boy friend, and Mull, her obnoxious father.

1991. *Mr. Wrong* (1996, Touchstone–Buena Vista, 92m, c). D Nick Castle, P Marty Katz, W Kerry Ehrin, Chris Matheson & Craig Munson, PH John Schwartzman, Ed Patrick Kennedy, M Craig Safan, PD Doug Kraner, AD Nancy Patton, SD Cloudia.

LP Ellen DeGeneres (Martha Alston), Bill Pullman (Whitman Crawford), Joan Cusack (Inga), Dean Stockwell (Jack Tramonte), Joan Plowright (Mrs. Crawford), John Livingston (Walter).

DeGeneres probably should have come out of the closet before making her film debut in this unamusing comedy. A thirtysomething woman, she is pressured by her parents and friends to find Mr. Right and settle down. A likely candidate shows up in the person of Pullman, but he's a romantic nut who drives her crazy with his various declarations of love.

1992. *Mistress* (1992, Tribeca Prods.–Rainbow Releasing, 108m, c). D Barry Primus,

P Meir Teper & Robert De Niro, W Primus & J.F. Lawton (based on the story by Primus), PH Sven Kirsten, ED Steven Weisberg, M Galt MacDermot, PD Phil Peters, AD Randy Grickson, SD K.O. Fox.

LP Robert Wuhl (Marvin Landisman), Martin Landau (Jack Roth), Jace Alexander (Stuart Stratland, Jr.), Robert De Niro (Evan M. Wright), Laurie Metcalf (Rachel Landisman), Eli Wallach (George Lieberhoff), Danny Aiello (Carmine Rasso), Sheryl Lee Ralph (Beverly Dumont), Jean Smart (Patricia Riley), Tuesday Knight (Peggy Pauline), Christopher Walken (Warren Zell).

Studio hack producer Landau finds an old script of screenwriter Wuhl's and together the two approach money men for the funds to make the film. Each of the fat cats, De Niro, Aiello and Wallach, have a mistress they want to star in the film.

1993. *Mrs. Brown* (1997, U.K./Ireland, Miramax, 103m, c). D John Madden, P Sarah Curtis, W Jeremy Brock (based on an idea by George Rosie), PH Richard Greatrex, ED Robin Sales, M Stephen Warbeck, PD Martin Childs, AD Charlotte Watts.

LP Judi Dench† (Queen Victoria), Billy Connolly (John Brown), Geoffrey Palmer (Henry Ponsonby), Antony Sher (Disraeli), Gerald Butler (Archie Brown), Richard Pasco (Doctor Jenner), David Westhead (Bertie, Prince of Wales), Bridget McConnel (Lady Ely), Georgie Glen (Lady Churchill).

Here's a marvelous film with outstanding performances by Dench, as Victoria, and Connolly, as the de facto head of her staff, who helps her survive without her beloved Albert. Her long absences from public view encourage enemies in Parliament to push for the abolition of the monarchy, much to the distress of Sher, portraying Prime Minister Disraeli. Speculation that her relationship with the charming Scot Connolly is more than that of monarch and servant doesn't help the matter. Through a series of misunderstandings, Dench withdraws her friendship from Connolly until he is on his deathbed, when she visits him and apologizes for not being a loyal friend.

1994. *Mrs. Dalloway* (1997, U.K./Netherlands, First Look Pictures, 97m, c). D Marleen Gorris, P Lisa Katselas Pare & Stephen Bayly, W Eileen Atkins (based on the novel by

Virginia Woolf), PH Sue Gibson, ED Michiel Reichwein, M Ilona Sekacz, PD David Richens, AD Alison Wratten & Nik Callan, SD Carlotta Barrow & Jeanne Vertigan.

LP Vanessa Redgrave (Mrs. Clarissa Dalloway), Natascha McElhone (Young Clarissa), Rupert Graves (Septimus Warren Smith), Michael Kitchen (Peter Walsh), Alan Cox (Young Peter), Sarah Badel (Sally Seton, Lady Rosseter), Lena Headey (Young Sally), John Standing (Richard Dalloway), Robert Portal (Young Richard), Amelia Bullmore (Rezia Warren Smith), Robert Hardy (Sir William Bradshaw).

On the night of a grand social event, Redgrave, the wife of a British M.P., thinks back to her youth when she chose between a safe and secure life over a more daring existence with the one she really loved. McElhone is brilliant as the young Clarissa, who chooses dashing Portal rather than be with Headey, the woman with whom she is hopelessly in love. Redgrave is superb, maintaining her composure even when Badel, as the mature Headey, arrives at her party with her husband.

1995. *Mrs. Doubtfire* (1993, 20th Century–Fox, 120m, c). D Chris Columbus, P Marsha Garces Williams, Robin Williams & Mark Radcliffe, W Randi Mayem Singer & Leslie Dixon (based on the novel *Alias Madame Doubtfire* by Anne Fine), PH Donald McAlpine, ED Raja Gosnell & Alexandra Fitzpatrick, M Howard Shore, PD Angelo Graham, AD W. Steven Graham, SD Garrett Lewis, Steve Saklad, Steve Wolff, Robert Goldstein & Harold Fuhrman.

LP Robin Williams (Daniel Hillard/Mrs. Imphegenia Doubtfire), Sally Field (Miranda Hillard), Pierce Brosnan (Stu), Harvey Fierstein (Frank), Polly Holliday (Gloria), Lisa Jakub (Lydia Hillard), Matthew Lawrence (Chris Hillard), Mara Wilson (Natalie Hillard), Robert Prosky (Mr. Lundy).

Williams is just a big kid. But his wife Field is tired of having four kids, with her husband the least responsible of the bunch. She sues for divorce and wins custody of the children. Williams lives for his kids so he takes advantage of his ex's search for a housekeeper by impersonating a sixty-ish English nanny. No one can resist the old dear.

1996. *Mrs. Parker and the Vicious Circle* (1994, Fine Line, 125m, c). D Alan Rudolph,

P Robert Altman, W Rudolph & Randy Sue Coburn, PH Jan Kiesser, ED Suzy Emilger, M Mark Isham, PD Francois Seguin, AD James Fox, SD Frances Calder.

LP Jennifer Jason Leigh (Dorothy Parker), Campbell Scott (Robert Benchley), Matthew Broderick (Charles MacArthur), Andrew McCarthy (Eddie Parker), Peter Gallagher (Alan Campbell), Jennifer Beals (Gertrude Benchley), Gwyneth Paltrow (Paula Hunt), Sam Robards (Harold Ross), Martha Plimpton (Jane Grant), Tom McGowan (Alexander Woolcott).

This is a not-very-interesting look at the Algonquin Round Table wits of the 1920s. Most of the time audiences familiar with the literary lights being impersonated in the film are too busy trying to keep track of who is who to pay too much attention to the slow-paced story. As usual, Leigh disappears into her part as the acerbic and brilliant Dorothy Parker; and although her performance can't be faulted, it's not enough to make the film memorable.

1997. *Mrs. Winterbourne* (1996, TriStar, 104m, c). D Richard Benjamin, P Dale Pollock, Rose Canter & Oren Koules, W Phoef Sutton & Lisa-Maria Radano (based on the novel *I Married a Dead Man* by Cornell Woolrich), PH Alex Nepomniaschy, ED Jacqueline Cambas & William Fletcher, M Patrick Doyle, PD Evelyn Sakash, AD Dennis Davenport, SD Casey Hallenbeck.

LP Shirley MacLaine (Grace Winterbourne), Ricki Lake (Connie Doyle), Brendan Fraser (Bill/Hugh Winterbourne), Miguel Sandoval (Paco), Loren Dean (Steve DeCunzo), Peter Gerety (Father Brian), Jane Krakowski (Christine).

Lake is pregnant and unwed. On a train she meets a young married couple on the way to introduce the wife to her in-laws for the very first time. For reasons meant to advance the plot, the bride has Lake try on her wedding ring. About this time there is a train wreck, the young couple are killed, and Lake goes into labor and delivers a baby. She is mistaken for the wife of the dead son of the Winterbourne family. Guess what? The dead scion of the family had a twin brother, Fraser. Can you see through the haze where all this is heading?

1998. *Mixed Nuts* (1994, TriStar, 97m, c). D Nora Ephron, P Tony Thomas, Paul Junger Witt & Joseph Hartwick, W Nora Ephron &

Delia Ephron (based on the film *Le Pere Noel Est un Ordure*), PH Sven Nykvist, ED Robert Raitano, M George Fenton, PD Bill Groom, AD Dennis Bradford, SD George DeTitta, Jr.

LP Steve Martin (Philip), Rita Wilson (Catherine), Madeleine Kahn (Mrs. Munchnik), Robert Klein (Mr. Lobel), Anthony LaPaglia (Felix), Juliette Lewis (Gracie), Rob Reiner (Dr. Kinsky), Adam Sandler (Louie), Liev Schreiber (Chris).

In one of the worst films of the year, Martin and a bunch of kooks look for humor at a suicide prevention center on Christmas Eve — and find none.

1999. *Mo' Better Blues* (1990, Universal, 127m, c). D, P & W Spike Lee, PH Ernest Dickerson, ED Sam Pollard, M Bill Lee, PD Wynn Thomas, AD Pam E. Stephens, SD Ted Glass.

LP Denzel Washington (Bleek Gilliam), Spike Lee (Giant), Wesley Snipes (Shadow Henderson), Giancarlo Esposito (Left Hand Lacey), Robin Harris (Butterbean Jones), Jolie Lee (Indigo Downes), Bill Nunn (Bottom Hammer), John Turturro (Moe Flatbush), Dick Anthony Williams (Big Stop Gilliam), Cynda Williams (Clarke Betancourt), Nicholas Turturro (Josh Flatbush), Samuel L. Jackson (Madlock).

Lee offers a tribute to black jazz musicians. The film features Washington as a moderately successful trumpet player and singer, and Snipes as his saxophone playing rival.

2000. *Mo' Money* (1992, Columbia, 98m, c). D Peter Macdonald, P Michael Rachmil, W Damon Wayans PH Don Burgess, ED Hubert C. De La Bouillerie, M Jay Gruska, PD William Arnold, SD Michael Claypool.

LP Damon Wayans (Johnny Stewart), Stacey Dash (Amber Evans), Joe Santos (Lt. Raymond Walsh), John Diehl (Keith Heading), Harry J. Loomis (Tom Dilton), Marlon Wayans (Seymour Stewart), Evan Lionel Smith (Detective Mills), Gordon McClure (Reverend Pimp Daddy).

Con man Damon Wayans, looking to go legit, finds himself in the middle of a credit card scam. Marlon Wayans makes his film debut and does a nice turn as his brother's brother.

2001. *Mobsters* (1991, Universal, 104m, c). D Michael Karbelnikoff, P Steve Roth, W Nicholas Kazan & Michael Mahern (based on Mahern's story), PH Lajos Koltai, ED Scott Smith & Joe D'Augustine, M Michael Small, PD Richard Sylbert, AD Peter Lansdown Smith, SD George R. Nelson.

LP Christian Slater (Charles "Lucky" Luciano), Patrick Dempsey (Meyer Lansky), Richard Grieco (Benny "Bugsy" Siegel), Costas Mandylor (Frank Costello), F. Murray Abraham (Arnold Rothstein), Anthony Quinn (Don Masseria), Lara Flynn Boyle (Mara Motes).

This film provides a fictional history of the beginning of national organized crime. It is the story of some very infamous mobsters-to-be when they were just young wild and crazy guys. It will please fans of bloody shoot-em-ups.

2002. *The Mod Squad* (1999, MGM, 94m, c). D Scott Silver, P Ben Myron, Alan Riche & Tony Ludwig, W Stephen Kay, Silver & Kate Lanier (based upon characters created by Buddy Ruskin), PH Ellen Kuras, ED Dorian Harris, M B.C. Smith, PD Patrick Sherman, AD Andrew Max Cahn, SD Cat Smith.

LP Claire Dancs (Julie Barnes), Giovanni Ribisi (Pete Cochrane), Omar Epps (Linc Hayes), Dennis Farina (Capt. Adam Greer), Josh Brolin (Billy Waites), Steve Harris (Detective Briggs), Richard Jenkins (Detective Mothershed).

This revisiting of the 1968–73 TV series won't do much for the careers of Danes, Ribisi and Epps. They portray three young social misfits who escape prison by agreeing to become undercover cops with attitudes. Wonder what TV series remake Hollywood will come up with next — *My Mother, the Car*?

2003. *Model by Day* (1994, U.S./Canada, Academy Ent., 120m, c). D Christian Duguay, P Ken Gord, W Matthew Weisman, PH David Franco, ED Patrick Lussier, PD Linda Del Rosario.

LP Famke Janssen (Lex), Shannon Tweed (Shannon), Stephen Shellen (Eddie Walker), Sean Young (Mercedes), Kim Coates (Tommy), Nigel Bennett (Nicolai).

When model Janssen's father is murdered, she takes martial arts training and, posing as "Lady X," seeks revenge. She becomes a suspect in a murder case and falls for the investigating detective.

2004. *A Modern Affair* (1996, Tribe Prods., 91m, c). D Vern Oakley, P Oakley, Melanie Webber & Jennifer Wilkinson, W Paul Zimmerman (based on a story by Oakley & Zimmerman), PH Rex Nicholson, ED Suzanne Pillsbury, M Jan Hammer, PD Cathy T. Marshall, SD Janna Fournier.

LP Lisa Eichhorn (Grace Rhodes), Stanley Tucci (Peter Kessler), Caroline Aaron (Elaine), Mary Jo Salerno (Lindsay), Tammy Grimes (Dr. Gresham).

In this lightweight comedy, successful businesswoman Eichhorn gets pregnant by artificial insemination and develops a yen to learn about the donor father.

2005. *Modern Love* (1990, Triumph, 109m, c). D, P & W Robby Benson, PH Christopher G. Tufty, ED Gib Jaffe, M Don Peake, PD Carl E. Copeland, AD Nancy Harvin.

LP Robby Benson (Greg), Karla De Vito (Billie), Rue McClanahan (Evelyn), Burt Reynolds (Col. Parker), Frankie Valli (Mr. Hoskins), Louise Lasser (Mom).

Benson and his real-life wife De Vito star in this modest production, which is the story of a poor slob whose life isn't all he had hoped for. He tries to improve its quality with fantasies, which get out of hand.

2006. *Mojave Moon* (1997, Trimark, 95m, c). D Kevin Dowling, P Matt Salinger, W Leonard Glasser, PH James Glennon, ED Susan Crutcher, M Johnny Caruso & Craig Stuart Garfinkle, PD Charles Dwight Lee, AD Sandi J. Cook, SD Alain Briere.

LP Danny Aiello (Al McCord), Anne Archer (Julie), Michael Biehn (Boyd), Angelina Jolie (Ellie), Alfred Molina (Sal), Jack Noseworthy (Kaiser), Zack Norman (Terry).

Recently divorced L.A. car salesman Aiello is so desperate for love that he allows nubile young Jolie to convince him to drive her to her home in the Mojave desert. Not getting what he wants from the Lolita-like youngster, he turns his attention to her mom Archer. The latter's wacky live-in lover Biehn stands in the way of Aiello's happiness.

2007. *Moll Flanders* (1996, MGM/UA, 123m, c). D & W Pen Densham (based on a story by Densham, and on the character of the novel by Daniel Defoe), PH David Tattersall,

ED Neil Travis & James R. Symons, M Mark Mancina, PD Caroline Hanania, AD Steve Simmonds, SD Fiona Daly.

LP Robin Wright (Moll Flanders), Morgan Freeman (Hibble), Stockard Channing (Mrs. Allworthy), Brenda Fricker (Mrs. Mazzawatti), John Lynch (Jonathan), Geraldine James (Edna).

Orphan Wright works in a brothel run by greedy Channing. Her only friend is Channing's servant Freeman. She falls for impoverished artist Lynch and has a brief period of happiness.

2008. *Molly* (1999, MGM–Cockamamie/Absolute Ent., 89m, c). D John Duigan, P William J. Macdonald, W Dick Christie, PH Gabriel Beristain, ED Humphrey Dixon, M Trevor Jones, PD Sharon Seymour, AD Bruce Alan Miller, SD Maggie Martin.

LP Elisabeth Shue (Molly McKay), Aaron Eckhart (Buck McKay), Jill Hennessy (Susan Brookes), Thomas Jane (Sam), D.W. Moffett (Mark Cottrell).

In a terribly sentimental and poorly cut film, Shue portrays a woman who undergoes a brain operation that transforms her from a frightened quasi-autistic near-child to a poised woman — but one with the curiosity of a child. However, things are not meant to last, and when her immune system begins to reject her new brain cells, she reverts. Sounds a bit like *Charly* (1968), doesn't it?

2009. *Mom and Dad Save the World* (1992, Warner Bros., 87m, c). D Greg Beeman, P Michael S. Phillips, W Ed Solomon & Chris Matheson, PH Jacques Haitkin, ED Okuwah Garrett, M Jerry Goldsmith, PD Craig Stearns, AD Randy Moore, SD Dorree Cooper.

LP Teri Garr (Marge Nelson), Jeffrey Jones (Dick Nelson), Jon Lovitz (Tod Spengo), Dwier Brown (Sirk), Kathy Ireland (Semage), Thalmus Rasulala (General Afir), Wallace Shawn (Sibor), Eric Idle (Raff).

Garr and Jones are celebrating 20 years of marriage when Lovitz, the petty dictator of a faraway planet of imbeciles, kidnaps them. He plans to make Garr his wife.

2010. *Money for Nothing* (1993, Buena Vista, 100m, c). D Ramon Menendez, P Tom Musca, W Menendez, Musca & Carol Sobieski,

PH Tom Sigel, ED Nancy Richardson, M Craig Safan, PD Michelle Minch, AD Beth Kuhn, SD Susan Raney.

LP John Cusack (Joey Coyle), Debi Mazar (Monica Russo), Michael Madsen (Det. Pat Laurenzi), Benicio Del Toro (Dino Palladino), Michael Rapaport (Kenny Kozlowski), Maury Chaykin (Vincente Goldoni).

Cusack is an average working stiff who finds $1.2 million that falls out of an armored car on its way to a casino. To say that the find changes his life puts it mildly. It's based on a real event.

2011. *Money Talks* (1997, New Line, 92m, c). D Brett Ratner, P Walter Coblenz & Tracy Kramer, W Joel Cohen & Alec Sokolow, PH Russell Carpenter & Robert Primes, ED Mark Helfrich, M Lalo Schifrin, PD Robb Wilson King, AD John Marshall, SD Lance Lombardo.

LP Charlie Sheen (James Russell), Chris Tucker (Franklin Hatchett/ Vic Damone, Jr.), Paul Sorvino (Guy Cipriani), Heather Locklear (Grace Cipriani), Gerard Ismael (Raymond Villard), Paul Gleason (Officer Pickett).

Street hustler Tucker is unwittingly involved in a bloody jailbreak in which several cops and prisoners are killed. Tucker seeks help from TV newsman Sheen to find evidence to clear his name. It's another *48 Hours* ripoff.

2012. *Money Train* (1995, Columbia, 103m, c). D Joseph Ruben, P Jon Peters & Neil Canton, W Doug Richardson & David Loughery (based on a story by Richardson), PH John W. Lindley, ED George Bowers & Bill Pankow, M Mark Mancina, PD Bill Groom, AD Dennis Bradford & Sarah Knowles, SD Beth Rubino.

LP Wesley Snipes (John), Woody Harrelson (Charlie), Robert Blake (Patterson), Jennifer Lopez (Grace Santiago), Chris Cooper (Torch), Joe Grifasi (Riley), Scott Sowers (Mr. Brown).

Foster brothers Snipes and Harrison are two transit cops who decide to rob the money train — a subway car that collects the cash from the transit system. The duo have been having nothing but trouble with their sadistic supervisor Blake, and both love the same girl, Lopez, so they figure what the heck.

2013. *Monkey Trouble* (1994, New Line, 106m, c). D Franco Amurri, P Mimi Polk & Heidi Rufus Isaacs, W Amurri & Stu Krieger,

PH Luciano Tovoli, ED Ray Lovejoy & Chris Peppe, M Mark Mancina, PD Les Dilley, AD Nathan Crowley, SD Denise Pizzini.

LP Thora Birch (Eva), Harvey Keitel (Azro), Mimi Rogers (Amy), Christopher MacDonald (Tom), Kevin Scannell (Peter), Finster (Dodger).

Kleptomaniac chimp Finster runs away from drunken Gypsy thief Keitel. He ends up with young Birch, who's desperate to find a pet. As is usual, Keitel is marvelous, but so then are Birch and the monkey.

2014. *Monster High* (1990, Catapult/ Lightyear, 84m, c). D Rudiger Poe, P Eric Bernt, W Roy Langsdon & John Platt, PH Eric Goldstein, ED Warren Chadwick, M Richard Lyons, PD Gigi Lorick.

LP David Marriott (Mr. Armageddon), Dean Iandoli (Norm Median), Diana Frank (Candice Cain), Kevin Dominguez (Paul Smith), David Fuhrer (Mel Anoma), D.J. Kerzner (Orson "O.D." Davis).

You'd have to be pretty hard up for violence and gore to watch this tasteless trash about an alien who preys on high school kids.

2015. *Montana* (1998, Zeta Ent., 99m, c). D Jennifer Leitzes, P Sean Cooley, Zane W. Levitt & Mark Yellen, W Erich Hoeber & Jon Hoeber, PH Ken Kelsch, ED Norman Buckley, M Cliff Eidelman, PD Daniel Roth, AD Mark Ricker.

LP Kyra Sedgwick (Claire), Stanley Tucci (Nick), Robbie Coltrane (The Boss), Robin Tunney (Kitty), Philip Seymour Hoffman (Duncan), John Ritter (Dr. Wexler).

About the only thing different in this film from many other stories of modern gangsters and hitmen is that the meanest of the bunch is Sedgwick.

2016. *A Month by the Lake* (1995, Miramax, 92m, c). D John Irvin, P Robert Fox, W Trevor Bentham (based on the novel by H.E. Bates), PH Pasqualino De Santis, ED Peter Tanner, M Nicola Piovani, PD Gianni Giovagnoni, SD Mauro Passi.

LP Vanessa Redgrave (Miss Bentley), Edward Fox (Major Wilshaw), Uma Thurman (Miss Beaumont), Alida Valli (Mrs. Fascioli), Alessandro Gassman (Vittorio), Carlo Carter (Mr. Bonizzoni).

At an Italian resort prior to the start of WWII, middle-aged spinster Redgrave vies with young American governess Thurman for the affection of stuffy retired army major Fox.

2017. *Monument Ave.* (1998, Lions Gate Films, 93m, c). D Ted Demme, P Jim Serpico, Nicolas Clermont & Elie Samaha, W Mike Armstrong, PH Adam Kimmel, ED Jeffrey Wolf, PD Ruth Ammon.

LP Denis Leary (Bobby O'Grady), Martin Sheen (Hanlon), Billy Crudup (Teddy), Jeanne Tripplehorn (Annie), Jason Barry (Seamus), Lenny Clarke (Skunk), John Diehl (Digger), Noah Emmerich (Red).

Leary grew up in Charleston, an Irish ghetto of Boston. He begins to question his life of drinking, drugs, hanging out at local bars and criminal activity. What are his other choices?

2018. *Moonlight and Valentino* (1995, Gramercy, 107m, c). D David Anspaugh, P Alison Owen, Eric Fellner & Tim Bevan, W Ellen Simon (based on her play), PH Julio Macat, ED David Rosenbloom, M Howard Shore, PD Robb Wilson King, AD David Ferguson, SD Carol Lavoie.

LP Elizabeth Perkins (Rebecca Trager Lott), Whoopi Goldberg (Sylvie Morrow), Gwyneth Paltrow (Lucy Trager), Kathleen Turner (Alberta Russell), Jon Bon Jovi (The Painter), Shadia Simmons (Jenny Morrow), Peter Coyote (Paul — uncredited).

Having great difficulty dealing with her recent widowhood, Perkins seeks and receives the help of her neighbor Goldberg, her sister Paltrow and her stepmother Turner. The four sit and talk, and talk, and talk. It seems to do some good.

2019. *Morning Glory* (1993, Academy Ent., 90m, c). D Steven Hilliard Stern, P Michael Viner & Stern, W Charles Jarrott & Deborah Raffin (based on the novel by LaVyrle Spencer), PH Laszlo George, ED Rick Benwick, M Jonathan Elias, AD David Hiscox, SD Barry Kemp.

LP Christopher Reeve (Will Parker), Deborah Raffin (Elly Dinsmore), Lloyd Bochner (Bob Collins), Nina Foch (Miss Beasley), Helen Shaver (Lula Peaks), J.T. Walsh (Sheriff Reese Goodloe).

During the Depression, pregnant widow Raffin advertises for a husband to help her run her poor farm. Ex-con Reeve, trying to put his life right, answers the ad. When a local "good-time-had-by-all" is killed, Sheriff Walsh thinks Reeve looks like a fine one to hang the killing on.

2020. *Mortal Kombat* (1995, New Line, 101m, c). D Paul Anderson, P Lawrence Kasanoff, W Kevin Droney, PH John R. Leonetti, ED Martin Hunter, M George S. Clinton, PD Jonathan Carlson, AD Jeremy Cassells, SD Susan L. Degus.

LP Christopher Lambert (Lord Rayden), Bridgette Wilson (Sonya Blade), Linden Ashby (Johnny Cage), Talisa Soto (Princess Kitana), Cary-Hiroyuki Tagawa (Shang Tsung), Robin Shou (Liu Kang).

This contest of martial arts experts debuted straight from the video game to the big screen. In it, three human heroes and a variety of (human and otherwise) evil monsters and sorcerers clash.

2021. *Mortal Kombat: Annihilation* (1997, New Line, 93m, c). D John R. Leonetti, P Lawrence Kasanoff, W Brent V. Friedman & Bryce Zabel (based on a story by Kasanoff, Joshua Wexler & John Tobias, and the video-game created by Ed Boon & Tobias), PH Matthew F. Leonetti, ED Peck Prior, M George S. Clinton, PD Charles Wood, AD Nathan Schroeder, SD Simon R.S. Wakefield.

LP Robin Shou (Liu Kang), Talisa Soto (Kitana), Lynn Red Williams (Jax), Sandra Hess (Sonya Blade), James Remar (Rayden), Litefoot (Nightwolf), Irina Pantaeva (Jade), Brian Thompson (Shao Kahn).

In this second feature derived from the kung-fu video game, defenders of Earth must defeat a crew of evil minions from a parallel dimension, the Outworld.

2022. *Mortal Thoughts* (1991, Rufglen Films–Columbia Pictures, 104m, c). D Alan Rudolph, P John Fiedler & Mark Tarlov, W Claude Kerven & William Reilly, PH Elliot Davis, ED Tom Walls, M Mark Isham, PD Howard Cummings, AD Robert K. Shaw, Jr., SD Beth Kushnick.

LP Demi Moore (Cynthia Kellogg), Glenne Headly (Joyce Urbanski), Bruce Willis (James Urbanski), Stuart Pankow (Arthur Kellogg), Harvey Keitel (Detective John Woods), Billie Neal (Detective Linda Nealon), Frank Vincent (Dominic Marino).

Moore and Headly are lifelong friends and

business partners. Headly is married to abusive Willis. The latter is killed in an accident, and the women attempt to cover up his death. Police detective Keitel wonders if it really was an accident.

2023. Mortuary Academy (1992, Landmark Films, 85m, c). D Michael Schroeder, P Dennis Winfrey & Chip Miller, W William Kelman, PH Roy H. Wagner, ED Ellen Keneshea, M David Spear, PD Jon Rothschild, AD Gary New.

LP Paul Bartel (Dr. Paul Truscott), Mary Woronov (Mary Purcell), Perry Lang (Sam Grimm), Tracey Walter (Dickson), Christopher Atkins (Max Grimm), Lynn Danielson (Valerie).

To earn their inheritance, brothers Lang and Atkins must attend the family's mortuary school. Hoping for some of the same sick success Bartel and Woronov had with *Eating Raoul*, the cast instead settles for lame jokes about necrophilia.

2024. Most Wanted (1997, New Line, 99m, c). D David Glenn Hogan, P Eric L. Gold, W Keenan Ivory Wayans, PH Marc Reshovsky, ED Michael J. Duthie & Mark Helfrich, M Paul Buckmaster, PD Jean-Philippe Carp, AD Arlan Jay Vetter, SD Alex Carle.

LP Keenan Ivory Wayans (Sgt. James Dunn), Jon Voight (General Adam Woodward/Lt. Col. Grant Casey), Jill Hennessy (Dr. Victoria Constantini), Paul Sorvino (CIA Deputy Director Kenny Rackmill), Eric Roberts (Assistant Deputy Director Spencer), Robert Culp (Donald Bickhart).

In this so-so action flick with an elaborate but not tightly written story, Marine sniper Wayans is on death row for killing his unhinged superior during the Gulf War. He is recruited by covert operations chief Voight to help hunt down the survivors of a top secret criminal group. Instead, he is set up for the assassination of the First Lady. He will get his revenge.

2025. Mother (1994, Triboro, 90m, c). D Frank Laloggia, P Patrick Peach, W Michael Angelella, PH Gerry Lively, ED Bette Jane Cohen, M Peter Bernstein, PD Jonathan Carlson, AD Jeremy Cassells, SD Susan Degas.

LP Diane Ladd (Olivia Hendrix), Olympia Dukakis (Mrs. Jay), Morgan Weisser (Tom Hendrix), Ele Keats (Audrey), Matt Clark (Ben Wilson), Scott Wilson (Dr. Chase).

Possessive mother Ladd is willing to kill to keep her nineteen-year-old son Weisser tied to her apron strings.

2026. Mother (1996, Paramount, 104m, c). D Albert Brooks, P Scott Rudin & Herb Nanas, W Brooks & Monica Johnson, PH Lajos Koltai, ED Harvey Rosenstock, M Marc Shaiman, PD Charles Rosen, AD Charles Butcher, SD Anne D. McCulley.

LP Albert Brooks (John Henderson), Debbie Reynolds (Beatrice Henderson), Rob Morrow (Jeff Henderson), Lisa Kudrow (Linda), Isabel Glasser (Cheryl Henderson), Peter White (Charles).

Debbie Reynolds returns to the screen as fortysomething Brooks' loving and ever helpful mother. She about drives him crazy with her constructive criticism and constant searching for some sign of improvement in her baby boy.

2027. Mother Night (1996, Fine Line, 113m, c). D Keith Gordon, P Gordon & Robert B. Weide, W Weide (based on the novel by Kurt Vonnegut), PH Tom Richmond, ED Jay Rabinowitz, M Michael Convertino, PD Francois Seguin, AD Zoe Sakellaropoulo, SD Simon LaHaye.

LP Nick Nolte (Howard Campbell), Sheryl Lee (Helga Noth), Alan Arkin (George Kraft), John Goodman (Frank Wirtanen — uncredited), Kirsten Dunst (Resi Noth), Ayre Gross (Abraham Epstein).

American spy Nolte poses as a German propaganda minister during WWII. He fears that he's too convincing and is doing too fine a job for the Nazis.

2028. Mother's Boys (1994, Miramax, 114m, c). D Yves Simoneau, P Jack E. Freedman, Wayne S. Williams & Patricia Herskovic, W Barry Schneider & Richard Hawley (based on the novel by Bernard Taylor), PH Elliot Davis, ED Michael Ornstein, M George Clinton, PD Peter Paul Raubertas, AD David Bomba.

LP Jamie Lee Curtis (Jude), Peter Gallagher (Robert), Joanne Whalley-Kilmer (Callie), Vanessa Redgrave (Lydia), Luke Edwards (Kes), Colin Ward (Michael).

Having abandoned her husband Gallagher

and children years earlier, Curtis suddenly reappears and tries to reestablish her dominance over her family. Curtis does a well-bred sociopath very nicely.

2029. *Motorama* (1993, Planet Prods., 90m, c). D Barry Shils, P Donald R. Borchers, W Joseph Minion, PH Joseph Yacoe, ED Peter Verity, M Andy Summers, PD Vincent Jefferds & Cathlyn Marshall.

LP Jordan Christopher Michael (Gus), Martha Quinn (Bank Teller), Susan Tyrell (Bartender), John Diehl (Phil), Robert Picardo (Jerry the Policeman), Garrett Morris (Andy), Michael J. Pollard (Lou), Sandy Baron (Kidnapping Husband), Mary Woronov (Kidnapping Wife).

Ten-year-old Michael becomes obsessed with winning a gas station contest that involves collecting game cards. He steals a car and hits the road in a quest for winning cards. He encounters "older woman" Barrymore while on his bizarre trip.

2030. *Mountains of the Moon* (1990, Tri-Star, 135m, c). D Bob Rafelson, P Daniel Melnick, W Rafelson & William Harrison (based on his book, and on original journals of Richard Burton & John Hanning Speke), PH Roger Deakins, ED Thom Noble, M Michael Small, PD Norman Reynolds, AD Maurice Fowler & Fred Hole, SD Harry Cordwell.

LP Patrick Bergin (Capt. Richard Francis Burton), Iain Glen (Lt. John Hanning Speke), Richard E. Grant (Laurence Oliphant), Fiona Shaw (Isabel Arundell Burton), John Savident (Lord Murchison), James Villiers (Lord Oliphant), Delroy Lindo (Mabruki), Bernard Hill (Dr. David Livingstone).

Nineteenth century explorers Burton and Speke, nicely impersonated by Bergin and Glen, work together and at odds to discover the source of the Nile.

2031. *The Mouse* (1997, Strand Releasing, 98m, c). D & W Daniel Adams, P Hank Blumenthal, Harris Tulchin & John Savage, PH Denise Brassard, ED Victoria Street, M Johnathan Edwards, PD Gay Studebaker, AD Richard Devine.

LP John Savage (Bruce "The Mouse" Strauss), Angelica Torn (Mary Lou Strauss), Rip Torn (trucker — God), Charles Bailey-Gates (Joe), Irina Cashen (Jamie Strauss), Tim Williams (Frank "The Gator" Lux).

This film is served up as a comical biography of a real-life and over-the-hill boxer, played by Savage. Apparently, he is the biggest all-time loser in the history of the sport. It isn't particularly funny.

2032. *Mouse Hunt* (1997, DreamWorks SKG, 97m, c). D Gore Verbinski, P Alan Riche, Tony Ludwig & Bruce Cohen, W Adam Rifkin, PH Phedon Papamichael, ED Craig Wood, M Alan Silvestri, PD Linda DeScenna, AD James Nedza, SD Ric McElvin.

LP Nathan Lane (Ernie Smuntz), Lee Evans (Lars Smuntz), Christopher Walken (Caesar), Vicki Lewis (April Smuntz), Maury Chaykin (Alexander Falko), Eric Christmas (The Lawyer).

Brothers Lane and Evans inherit their father's string factory and an old mansion. The boys see a way to make a fortune by fixing up the dilapidated architectural treasure, but all their efforts to do so are thwarted by the house's sole inhabitant, a *Home Alone*–like mouse. It's a moderately funny film, worth one free TV viewing.

2033. *Much Ado About Nothing* (1993, Samuel Goldwyn Company, 111m, c). D & W Kenneth Branagh (based on the play by William Shakespeare), P Stephen Evans, David Parfitt & Branagh, PH Roger Lanser, ED Andrew Marcus, M Patrick Doyle, PD Tim Harvey, AD Martin Childs.

LP Emma Thompson (Beatrice), Kenneth Branagh (Benedick), Robert Sean Leonard (Claudio), Keanu Reeves (Don John), Denzel Washington (Don Pedro), Michael Keaton (Dogberry), Kate Beckinsale (Hero), Richard Briers (Leonato).

The performances in this screening of Shakespeare's bawdy comedy of love that does not run smoothly are mixed. The Brits turn in a fine job, but the American stars, with the exception of Keaton in a very funny turn as Dogberry, seem quite wooden. The main romantic story is of the reluctant pairing of acerbic lovers Branagh and Thompson.

2034. *Mulan* (1998, Walt Disney–Buena Vista, 88m, c). D Barry Cook & Tony Bancroft, P Pam Coats, W Rita Hsiao, Jodu Ann Johnson & Alan Ormsby (from a story by

Chris Sanders) M Jerry Goldsmith†, Matthew Wilder† & David Zippel†, PD Hans Bacher, AD Ric Sluiter.

LP Voices: Ming-Na Wen (Mulan), Lea Salonga (Mulan singing), Eddie Murphy (Mushu), B.D. Wong (Shang), Donny Osmond (Shang singing), Harvey Fierstein (Yao), Jerry S. Tondo (Chien-Po).

Reportedly based on Chinese legends, this is the tale of a young Chinese maiden who disguises herself as a man and enlists in the army to fight the invasion of marauding Huns. She not only saves the prince but the emperor as well. Technically the film is excellent — but this is one occasion where the "cute" Disney touches are less successful. Comedy is supplied by a small dragon, voiced by Murphy, which seems very much out of place in the story.

2035. Mulholland Falls (1996, MGM/ UA, 107m, c). D Lee Tamahori, P Richard D. Zanuck & Lili Fini Zanuck, W Pete Dexter (based on a story by Floyd Mutrux & Dexter), PH Haskell Wexler, ED Sally Menke, M Dave Grusin, PD Richard Sylbert, AD Gregory William Bolton, SD Claire Jenora Brown.

LP Nick Nolte (Hoover), Melanie Griffith (Katherine), Chazz Palminteri (Coolidge), Michael Madsen (Eddie Hall), Chris Penn (Relyea), Treat Williams (Fitzgerald), Jennifer Connelly (Allison Pond), Daniel Baldwin (McCafferty), Andrew McCarthy (Jimmy Fields), John Malkovich (Timms).

Nolte heads up the Hat squad, an elite group of Los Angeles police detectives who are out to rid the City of Angels of mobsters. When Nolte's former mistress is murdered, the squad comes across corrupt government officials and a cover-up.

2036. Multiplicity (1996, Columbia, 110m, c). D Harold Ramis, P Trevor Albert & Ramis, W Chris Miller, Mary Hale, Lowell Ganz & Babaloo Mandel (based on the short story by Miller), PH Laszlo Kovacs, ED Pam Herring & Craig Herring, M George Fenton, PD Jackson DeGovia, AD Geoff Hubbard, SD K.C. Fox.

LP Michael Keaton (Doug Kinney), Andie MacDowell (Lauren Kinney), Zack Duhame (Zack Kinney), Katie Schlossberg (Jennifer Kinney), Harris Yulin (Dr. Leeds), Richard Masur (Del King).

With far too many business and personal responsibilities for one man, Keaton decides to have himself cloned and farm out the work to himself. The process is not quite perfected, and each clone of Keaton has something of its own personality, which causes great confusion to Keaton's wife MacDowell.

2037. Mumford (1999, Buena Vista–Touchstone, 112m, c). D & W Lawrence Kasdan, P Charles Okun & Kasdan, PH Ericson Core, ED Carol Littleton & William Steinkamp, M James Newton Howard, PD Jon Hutman, AD Wray Steven Graham, SD Dawn Swiderski.

LP Loren Dean (Mumford), Hope Davis (Sofie Crisp), Jason Lee (Skip Skipworth), Alfre Woodard (Lily), Mary McDonnell (Althea Brockett), Pruitt Taylor Vance (Henry Follett), Zooey Deschanel (Nessa Watkins), Martin Short (Lionel Dillard), David Paymer (Dr. Ernest Delbanco).

Dean shows up in a small town and opens a psychiatric practice. Problem is, he has no degrees, experience or education in the field. However, he is very good at what he does. The comedy has many fine moments, and Dean, who lacks the big name necessary to put across a film such as this at the box office, shows up quite well.

2038. The Mummy (1999, Universal, 124m, c). D & W Stephen Sommers (screenplay by Sommers, Lloyd Fonvielle & Kevin Jarre), P James Jacks & Sean Daniel, PH Adrian Biddle, ED Bob Ducsay, M Jerry Goldsmith, PD Allan Cameron, AD Tony Reading, Giles Masters, Clifford Robinson & Peter Russell, SD Peter Howitt.

LP Brendan Fraser (Rick O'Connell), Rachel Weisz (Evelyn), John Hannah (Jonathan), Arnold Vosloo (Imhotep), Kevin J. O'Connor (Beni), Jonathan Hyde (The Egyptologist), Oded Fehr (Ardeth Bey).

Among the cheesy horror films of the 1930s was the truly frightening 1932 version of The Mummy starring Boris Karloff. He was the Egyptian priest revived after thousands of years, believing that Zita Johann was the reincarnation of the beloved princess for whom he committed sacrilege and suffered being mummified alive. Another version of the story was the stylish British film made in 1959 with Christopher Lee as the lovesick high priest and reincarnated mummy. The latest version has the likeable Fraser, as a soldier-explorer, and bumbling antiquities librarian Weisz unleashing Vosloo, whose sin and fate is presented in a seven minute prologue. Played for laughs and chills, it's modest fun, but it won't leave the lasting impressions made by the far simpler productions of the story.

2039. Munchie (1992, Concorde, 80m, c). D Jim Wynorski, P Mike Elliott, W Wynorski & R.J. Robertson, PH Don E. Fauntleroy, ED Rich Gentner, M Chuck Cirino, PD Staurt Blatt, AD Carey Meyer.

LP Loni Anderson (Cathy), Dom DeLuise (Voice of Munchie), Andrew Stevens (Elliott), Jaime McEnnan (Gage Dobson), Arte Johnson (Professor Cruikshank), Mike Simmrin (Leon).

Munchie is a forgotten alien discovered in a mine shaft by young McEnnan. He turns out to be McEnnan's best friend, protecting him from bullies and things.

2040. Munchie Strikes Back (1994, New Horizons, 89m, c). D Jim Wynorksi, P Mike Elliott, W Wynorski & R.J. Robertson.

LP Andrew Stevens (Elliott), Lesley-Anne Down (Linda McClelland), Dom DeLuise & Howard Hesseman (Voice of Munchie), Angus Scrimm (Kronus), Trenton Knight (Chris).

The magical imp is back, but who cares. Even the kids won't eat up this silly sequel.

2041. Muppet Treasure Island (1996, Walt Disney–Buena Vista, 99m, c). D Brian Henson, P Henson & Martin G. Baker, W Jerry Juhl Jim Hart & Kirk Thatcher, PH John Fenner, ED Michael Jablow, M Hans Zimmer, PD Val Strazovec, AD Alan Cassie, SD Simon Wakefield.

LP Tim Curry (Long John Silver), Kevin Bishop (Jim Hawkins), Billy Connolly (Billy Bones), Jennifer Saunders (Mrs. Bluveridge), Frederick Warder (Calico Jerry), Peter Greeves (Black Eyed Pea).

As the title says, it's the Muppets' version of Robert Louis Stevenson's classic story of a young boy who searches for buried treasure and encounters pirates. Curry is a scream, but that's not meant as a compliment. All the favorite Muppet characters, Fozzie Bear, Kermit, Miss Piggy, Sam Eagle, the Swedish Chef, Rizzo the Rat and The Great Gonzo, make their appearances.

2042. The Muppet Christmas Carol (1992, Buena Vista, 85m, c). D Brian Henson, P Henson & Martin G. Baker, W Jerry Juhl, PH John Fenner, ED Michael Jablow, M Miles Goodman, PD Val Strazovec, AD Alan Cassie & Dennis Bosher, SD Michael Ford.

LP Michael Caine (Scrooge), David Goelz (The Great Gonzo/Robert Marley/Bunsen Honeydew/Betina Cratchit), Steve Whitmire (Rizzo the Rat/Bean Bunny/Kermit the Frog/Breaker/Belinda Cratchit), Jerry Nelson (Tiny Tim Cratchit/Jacob Marley/Ma Bear/Ghost of Christmas Present), Frank Oz (Miss Piggy/Fozzie Bear/Sam Eagle/Animal).

Jim Henson's son Brian carries on his father's inspired work in this telling of Dickens' classic Christmas tale, with Caine as a mean and nasty Scrooge and the muppets playing the other familiar roles.

2043. Muppets from Space (1999, Sony Pictures–Columbia, 88m, c). D Tim Hill, P Brian Henson & Martin G. Baker, W Jerry Juhl, Joseph Mazzarino & Ken Kaufman, PH Alan Caso, ED Michael A. Stevenson & Richard Pearson, M Jamshied Sharifi, PD Stephen Marsh, AD William Glenn Davis.

Voices: Dave Goelz (Gonzo), Steve Whitmore (Kermit the Frog), Bill Barretta (Pepe the Prawn), Jerry Nelson (Robin), Kevin Clash (Clifford), Frank Oz (Miss Piggy, Fonzie Bear).

LP Jeffrey Tambor (K. Edgar Singer), F. Murray Abraham (Noah), Rob Schneider (TV Producer), Ray Liotta (Gate Guard), David Arquette (Dr. Tucker), Andie MacDowell (Shelley Snipes).

Can pigs fly? Not Miss Piggy and the other muppets in this lame vehicle. In the past, muppet productions have been clever and entertaining up to a point, but this one falls on its face. The story centers on Gonzo, who decides the source of all his troubles is that he is an alien from outer space. Government types become convinced of the same thing and plan to remove his brain for study. It's up to the rest of the muppet family to rescue him.

2044. Murder and Murder (1997, Zeitgeist Films, 113m, c). D, P, W & ED Yvonne Rainer, PH Stephen Kazmierski, M Frank London, PD Stephen McCabe, AD Cathy Cook.

LP Joanna Merlin (Doris), Kathleen Chalfant (Mildred), Catherine Kellner (Teenage Mildred), Isa Thomas (Jenny).

This film is the story of an aging lesbian couple. Merlin is a part-time art teacher and grandmother, while Chalfant is a tenured professor who lectures on lesbian and feminist issues. Unseen by these two are Kellner (Chalfant as a teen) and Thomas (Merlin's long dead mother), who comment on Merlin and Chalfant. The film preaches about the alarming number of women who die from breast cancer, the location of toxic dumps and the number of Americans who are without health insurance.

2045. *Murder at 1600* (1997, Warner Bros., 107m, c). D Dwight Little, P Arnold Kopelson & Arnon Milchan, W Wayne Beach & David Hodgin, PH Steven Bernstein, ED Billy Weber, M Christopher Young, PD Nelson Coates, AD Dan Yarhi, SD Tedd Kuchera.

LP Wesley Snipes (Detective Harlan Riggs), Diane Lane (Nina Chance), Alan Alda (Alvin Jordan), Daniel Benzali (Nick Spikings), Ronnie Cox (President Jack Neil), Dennis Miller (Detective Stengel), Charles Rocket (Jeffrey), Diane Baker (Kitty Neil), Tate Donovan (Kyle Neil), Douglas O'Keefe (John Kerry — Assassin), Harris Yulin (General Clark Tully).

When the corpse of a beautiful young White House employee is found at the first family's home, Washington, D.C. cop Snipes heads up the investigation. It sure looks like the murderer is the president's son Donovan, known for abusing his lovers, one of whom was the deceased. Someone doesn't want the case to be solved. Secret Service agent Lane is assigned to the case by the agency's head, Benzali. The more the two dig, the more dangerous things become for them.

2046. *Murder by Numbers* (1990, Magnum, 91m, c). D, W & ED Paul Leder, P Ralph Tornberg & Leder, PH Francis Grumman, M Bob Summers, SD Robert Holcombe.

LP Sam Behrens (Lee Bolger), Shari Belafonte (Lisa), Ronee Blakley (Faith), Stanley Kamel (George), Jayne Meadows (Pamela), Debra Sandlund (Leslie), Dick Sargent (Patrick Crain), Cleavon Little (David Shelby), Wlad Cembrowicz (Walter).

Lawyer Behrens is convinced to look into the disappearance of wealthy homosexual Cembrowicz. He's dead, but why, who and how are among the questions that need to be answered. The mystery is intriguing and suspenseful, but the production is so carelessly done that the film has to be classified as a major disappointment.

2047. *Murder in Mind* (1998, U.S./U.K., Live Ent.–Lakeshore Intl., 89m, c). D Andrew Morahan, P Vicki Slotnik & Jeremy Paige, W Michael Cooney (based on his play), PH John Aronson, ED Andrea MacArthur, M Paul Buckmaster, PD Ben Morahan, AD Stephen Sinclair.

LP Nigel Hawthorne (Dr. Ellis), Mary-Louise Parker (Caroline), Jimmy Smits (Peter), Jason Scott Lee (Halloway), Gailard Sartain (Charlie), Jon Ceda (Superior Officer).

Detective Scott Lee arrests Parker for the gruesome murders of her wealthy husband Smits and their handyman Sartain. She claims to have no memory of the crime, although there is a 911 recording of her confessing to the crime. Psychiatrist Hawthorne is brought in to use hypnosis to help her recall the events of that night.

2048. *Murder in the First* (1995, Warner Bros., 122m, c). D Marc Rocco, P Marc Frydman & Mark Wolper, W Dan Gordon, PH Fred Murphy, ED Russell Livingstone, M Christopher Young, PD Kirk M. Petruccelli, AD Michael Rizzo, SD Greg Grande.

LP Christian Slater (James Stamphill), Kevin Bacon (Henri Young), Gary Oldman (Associate Warden Glenn), Embeth Davidtz (Mary McCasslin), Bill Macy (William McNeil), Stephen Tobolowsky (Mr. Henkin), Brad Dourif (Byron Stamphill), R. Lee Emrey (Judge Clawson), Kyra Sedgwick (Blanche).

In 1937, a botched escape try wins Bacon three years of living naked in solitary confinement deep in the bowels of Alcatraz. When he gets the chance he murders the stool pigeon who turned him in. Public defender Slater is given the job of defending Bacon in an open-and-shut case, but the young attorney digs into the reason for his client's behavior, discovering the pattern of hideous and continuous brutality and torture Bacon has suffered at the hands of Associate Warden Oldman.

2049. *Murdered Innocence* (1996, Columbia TriStar, 88m, c). D Frank Coraci, P Phyllis Alia & Fred Carpenter, W Steven Peros, Coraci & Carpenter, PH William Francesco, ED Thomas Lewis & Suzanne Pillsbury, M Alan Pasqua, AD & SD Jack Parente.

LP Jason Miller (Detective Rollins), Fred Carpenter (Scott), Jacqueline Macario (Lauren), Gary Aumiller (William "Teach" Spencer), Ellen Green (Mrs. Baron), Donna Bostany (Detective Leone), Craig Morris Weintraub (Young Scott).

Ex-con Carpenter and escaped con Aumiller must finish something that began twenty years earlier when Spencer killed Aumiller's lover, Greene, Carpenter's mother.

2050. *Muriel's Wedding* (1995, Australia, Miramax, 105m, c). D & W P.J. Hogan, P Lynda House & Jocelyn Moorhouse, PH Martin McGrath, ED Jill Bilcock, M Peter Best, PD Patrick Reardon, AD Hugh Bateup, SD Jane Murphy & Glen W. Johnson.

LP Toni Collette (Muriel), Bill Hunter (Bill), Rachel Griffiths (Rhonda), Jeane Drynan (Betty), Gennie Nevinson (Deidre), Matt Day (Brice), Daniel Lapaine (David Van Arkle).

It's an "ugly duckling" tale with overweight and unpopular Collette handling the role brilliantly and with great good humor. To fit in with the crowd she aspires to be a member of, she steals money from her father so she can join them on vacation at a fancy resort. When the theft is discovered, she leaves home, moves to Sydney and shares an apartment with very popular Griffiths. Muriel's relationships with men prove disappointing, and she finally settles on marriage to a South African swimmer who needs Australian citizenship to compete in the Olympics.

2051. *The Muse* (1999, USA Films, 97m, c). D Albert Brooks, P Herb Nanas, W Brooks & Monica Johnson, PH Thomas Ackerman, ED Peter Teschner, M Elton John, PD Dina Lipton, AD Marc Dabe, SD Christopher S. Nushawg.

LP Albert Brooks (Steven Phillips), Sharon Stone (Sarah), Andie MacDowell (Laura Phillips), Jeff Bridges (Jack Warrick), Mark Feuerstein (Josh Martin), Steven Wright (Stan Spielberg).

Having been told he's lost his "edge" and fired by young Paramount executive Feuerstein, screenwriter Brooks is desperate. He encounters his friend Bridges, a highly successful writer in the company of beautiful Stone. He learns that Stone is, in fact, one of the nine daughters of Zeus and acts as muse to many of the top writers in Hollywood. Eager to get back his edge, he enlists the aid of Stone, who is very demanding of material things in exchange for her tidbits of creativity. When Brooks' wife MacDowell finds out about Stone, she is naturally outraged, but Stone shares her talents and launches MacDowell on a very successful gourmet cookie career. The trouble with the film is that going up the hill of the story is so much more clever and amusing than the ride down to the end.

2052. *Music from Another Room* (1998, Orion Pictures, 104m, c). D & W Charlie Peters, P Brad Krevoy, Stephen Stabler, John Bertolli & Bradley Thomas, PH Richard Crudo, ED Tim O'Meara, PD Charles Breen, AD Chris Gorak, SD Denise Pizzini.

LP Brenda Blethyn (Grace), Jude Law (Danny), Jennifer Tilly (Nina), Martha Plimpton (Karen), Gretchen Mol (Anna), Jon Tenney (Eric), Jeremy Piven (Billy).

As a boy, Law helped his father deliver a baby girl, whom he swore he would marry when they both grew up. Years later he meets the girl again, in the person of Mol. He wishes to keep his promise, but she has her hands full with her dying mother Blethyn and the rest of her dysfunctional family.

2053. *The Music of Chance* (1993, IRS Media, 98m, c). D Philip Haas, P Frederick Zollo & Dylan Sellers, W Philip Haas & Belinda Haas (based on the novel by Paul Auster), PH Bernard Zitzermann & Jean DeSegonzac, ED Belinda Haas, M Philip Johnston, PD Hugo Luczyc-Wyhowski, AD Ruth Ammon, SD Christy Belt.

LP James Spader (Jack Pozzi), Mandy Patinkin (James Nashe), M. Emmet Walsh (Calvin Marks), Joel Grey (Willy Stone), Samantha Mathias (Tiffany), Charles Durning (Bill Fowler), Christopher Penn (Floyd Murks).

Cardsharp Spader and his partner Patinkin travel to the home of millionaires Grey and Durning, intent on fleecing the two rich marks. Things don't go quite according to plan.

2054. *Music of the Heart* (1999, Miramax, 124m, c). D Wes Craven, P Marianne Maddalena, Susan Kaplan, Alan Miller & Walter Scheuer, W Pamela Gray (based on the documentary film *Small Wonders* by Allen and

Lana Miller), PH Peter Deming, ED Patrick Lussier, M Mason Daring, PD Bruce Miller, AD Beth Kuhn.

LP Meryl Streep† (Roberta Guaspari), Aidan Quinn (Brian Sinclair), Angela Bassett (Janet Williams), Cloris Leachman (Assunta Guaspari), Josh Pais (Dennis), Jay O. Sanders (Dan).

In an unusual film for director Craven, Streep stars in the true story of a deserted wife who makes a fresh start by taking a job teaching violin to underprivileged kids in East Harlem. When, as so often happens, the music programs of the school are cut, she doesn't give up easily. She takes her fight so far that she sees her kids play alongside the likes of Isaac Stern and Itzhak Perlman at Carneige Hall. Yeah, it plays on your emotions, but just sit back and enjoy the tune.

2055. *Mutant Species* (1995, LIVE Ent., 100m, c). D David A. Prior, P Robert Willoughby & Michael W. Evans, Jr., W William Virgil & Prior, PH Carlos Gonzalez, ED Tony Malinowski, M William T. Stromberg, PD Andrew Menzies.

LP Leo Rossi (Hollinger), Ted Prior (Trotter), Denise Crosby (Carol Anne), Grant Gelt (Jordie), Powers Boothe (Frost), Wilford Brimley (Devro), Grant James (Senator Roberts).

A team of mercenaries search for an alien symbiont/weapon. One of the soldiers is accidentally exposed to the alien's DNA and mutates into a killing machine.

2056. *Mutator* (1991, Prism Ent., 89m, c). D John R. Bowey, P Russell D. Markowitz, W Lynn Rose Higgins (based on the story by Higgins & Gerald A. Rose), PH Lynton Stephenson, ED Dean Vermaak, M Rene Veldsman, AD Patricia Urquhart & Dimitri Repanis.

LP Brion James (David Allen), Carolyn Clark (Ann Taylor), Milton Raphael Murrill (Travers), Neil McCarthy (Adam), Brian O'Shaughnessy (Axelrod), Embeth Davidtz (Jennifer).

Something goes wrong and a firm creates a new life form, a demonic pussycat who is anything but the cat's meow.

2057. *My Best Friend's Wedding* (1997, Columbia Tri-Star, 105m, c). D P.J. Hogan, P Jerry Zucker & Ronald Bass, W Bass, PH Laszlo Kovacs, ED Garth Craven & Lisa Frucht-

man, M James Newton Howard†, PD Richard Sylbert, AD Karen Fletcher Trujillo, SD William Kemper Wright.

LP Julia Roberts (Julianne Potter), Dermot Mulroney (Michael O'Neal), Cameron Diaz (Kimmy Wallace), Rupert Everett (George Downes), Philip Bosco (Walter Wallace), M. Emmet Walsh (Papa Joe O'Neal), Rachel Griffiths (Samantha Newhouse), Carrie Preston (Amanda Newhouse).

When her ex-flame and closest friend Mulroney invites New York City career woman Roberts to his wedding to Diaz, Julia goes into a panic. Mulroney and Roberts had made a pact to marry each other someday. She took it seriously; he apparently did not. Roberts flies off to Chicago four days before the scheduled nuptials, intent on breaking up the romance. She doesn't count on Diaz's beguiling innocence being a formative, if unaware, adversary. Her plans not going well, she induces gay Everett to show up as her fiancé, hoping to make Mulroney jealous enough to call off the wedding. This and other dirty tricks pulled by Roberts succeed — but does it make Roberts happy? No way! While the main cast is excellent, Everett steals the show.

2058. *My Blue Heaven* (1990, Warner Bros., 97m, c). D Herbert Ross, P Ross & Anthea Sylbert, W Nora Ephron, PH John Bailey, ED Stephen A. Rotter, M Ira Newborn, PD Charles Rosen, AD Richard Berger, SD Jim Bayliss, Robert Maddy & Nick Navarro.

LP Steve Martin (Vinnie Antonelli), Rick Moranis (Barney Coopersmith), Joan Cusack (Hannah Stubbs), Melanie Mayron (Crystal Rybak), Carol Kane (Shaldeen), Bill Irwin (Kirby), William Hickey (Billy Sparrow).

Martin is an ex-mobster who has given evidence against his former associates and must enter the witness-protection program. Moranis is the FBI agent with the job of keeping an eye on Martin, who lives up to the saying, "once a crook, always a crook."

2059. *My Boyfriend's Back* (1993, Buena Vista, 84m, c). D Bob Balaban, P Sean S. Cunningham, W Dean Lorey, PH Mac Ahlberg, ED Michael Jablow, M Harry Manfredini, PD Michael Hanan, AD Charles Lagola, SD Douglas Mowat, John A. Frick & Jonathan Short.

LP Andrew Lowery (Johnny Dingle), Traci

Lind (Missy McCloud), Danny Zorn (Eddie), Edward Herrmann (Mr. Dingle), Mary Beth Hurt (Mrs. Dingle), Jay O. Sanders (Sheriff McCloud), Cloris Leachman (Maggie).

In a very strange black comedy, teen Lowery looks forward to taking Lind, the prettiest girl in the school, to the senior prom. The only problem is that nerdish Lowery has been shot while saving Lind's life and is now a zombie who has trouble keeping all his body parts. The only way he's going to last long enough to go to the dance is by eating human flesh.

2060. *My Brother's Wife* (1994, A-Pix Ent., 120m, c). D Jack Bender, P Philip Kleinbart & Paul Lussier, W Percy Granger (based on the play *The Middle Ages* by A.R. Gurney), PH Neil Roach, ED Robert Florio, M Laura Karpman, PD Stephen Storer, SD Sharon Viljoen.

LP John Ritter (Barney Rusher), Mel Harris (Eleanor Gilbert Rusher), Polly Bergen (Myra Gilbert), Dakin Matthews (Charles Rusher), David Byron (Billy Rusher).

For two decades Ritter has pursued his sister-in-law Harris, the woman of his dreams. She is married to Matthews, whom Ritter despises.

2061. *My Cousin Vinny* (1992, 20th Century–Fox, 119m, c). D Jonathan Lynn, P Dale Launer & Paul Schiff, W Launer, PH Peter Deming, ED Tony Lombardo, M Randy Edelman, PD Victoria Paul, AD Randall Schmook & Michael Rizzo, SD Michael Seirton.

LP Joe Pesci (Vincent La Guardia Gambino), Ralph Macchio (Bill Gambini), Marisa Tomei* (Mona Lisa Vito), Mitchell Whitfield (Stan Rothenstein), Fred Gwynne (Judge Chamberlain Haller), Lane Smith (Jim Trotter, III), Austin Pendelton (John Gibbons).

In a very funny movie, Pesci is a fish out of water. He is a New York lawyer, who has never tried a case, hired by his cousin Macchio when he and a buddy are accused of a holdup and murder in a small community in the deep South. Even more fun than Pesci, who is a scream, is Tomei as his longtime fiancée and motor vehicle expert, a talent which will eventually save the day. Gwynne (in his final film appearance) gives a charming performance as the judge.

2062. *My Family: Mi Familia* (1995, New Line, 125m, c). D Gregory Nava, P Anna Thomas, W Nava & Thomas (based on a story by Nava), PH Edward Lachman, ED Nancy Richardson, M Pepe Avila & Mark McKenzie, PD Barry Robison, AD Troy Myers, SD Suzette Sheets.

LP Jimmy Smits (Jimmy Sanchez), Esai Morales (Chucho), Eduardo Lopez Rojas (Jose Sanchez), Jenny Gago (Maria Sanchez), Elpidia Carrillo (Isabel Magana), Lupe Ontiveros (Irene Sanchez), Edward James Olmos (Paco, the Narrator).

It's the intriguing but not totally satisfying epic story of a Mexican-American family, told from the time the immigrant founder of the family arrives in Los Angeles until his last grandchild leaves home. The family survives much heartache and tragedy, which will surely touch viewers' hearts.

2063. *My Father, the Hero* (1994, France/U.S., Buena Vista, 90m, c). D Steve Miner, P Jacques Bar & Jean-Louis Livi, W Francis Veber & Charlie Peters (based on the screenplay *Mon Pere, Ce Heros* by Gerard Lauzier), PH Daryn Okada, ED Marshall Harvey, M David Newman, PD Christopher Nowak, AD Patricia Woodbridge, SD Don K. Ivey & Claudette Didul.

LP Gerard Depardieu (Andre), Katherine Heigl (Nicole), Dalton James (Ben), Lauren Hutton (Megan), Faith Prince (Diana), Stephen Tobolowsky (Mike), Ann Hearn (Stella), Emma Thompson (Isabelle — uncredited).

Fourteen-year-old Heigl is on a vacation with her father Depardieu on an island paradise. To impress James, she passes off Dad as her lover. Everyone becomes aware of this imaginary relationship except Depardieu. You can imagine the reaction he gets when he sings for other guests "Thank Heaven for Little Girls."

2064. *My Favorite Martian* (1999, Walt Disney–Buena Vista, 93m, c). D Donald Petrie, P Robert Shapiro, Jerry Leider & Mark Toberoff, W Sherri Stoner & Deanna Oliver (based on the television series created by John L. Greene), PH Thomas Ackerman, ED Malcolm Campbell, M John Debney, PD Sandy Veneziano, AD Christopher Burian-Mohr.

LP Christopher Lloyd (Uncle Martin), Jeff Daniels (Tim O'Hara), Elizabeth Hurley (Brace Channing), Daryl Hannah (Lizzie), Wallace Shawn (Coleye), Christine Ebersole

(Mrs. Lorelei Brown), Michael Lerner (Mr. Channing), Ray Walston (Armitan).

Those not nostalgic for the 1950s TV show about alien Walston, who settled in with the late Bill Bixby and was in danger weekly of having his true identity discovered, will not care for this film.

2065. My Fellow Americans (1996, Warner Bros., 101m, c). D Peter Segal, P Jon Peters, W E. Jack Kaplan, Richard Chapman & Peter Tolan, PH Julio Macat, ED William Kerr, M William Ross, PD James Bissell, AD Gae Buckley, SD Gary Fettis.

LP Jack Lemmon (Russell P. Kramer), James Garner (Matt Douglas), John Heard (Ted Matthews), Dan Aykroyd (William Haney), Sela Ward (Kaye Griffin), Wilford Brimley (Joe Hollis), Everett McGill (Col. Paul Tanner), Bradley Whitford (Carl Witnaur), Lauren Bacall (Margaret Kramer).

Longtime political rivals Republican Lemmon and Democrat Garner, both ex-presidents of the United States, are forced to become an odd couple when Aykroyd, the reigning president, decides the country would be better off if the two were dead.

2066. My Giant (1998, Sony Pictures–Columbia Pictures, 103m, c). D Michael Lehmann, P Billy Crystal, W David Seltzer, PH Michael Coulter, ED Stephen Semel, M Marc Shaiman, PD Jackson DeGovia, AD Tom Reta, SD Kathe Klopp.

LP Billy Crystal (Sammy Kanin), Kathleen Quinlan (Serena Kanin), Gheorghe Muresan (Max), Joanna Pacula (Lillianna), Zane Carney (Nick Kanin), Rider Strong (Justin Allen).

Hey guys, here's a corker of an idea for a film. Team a little guy like Crystal with a great big guy like seven-foot, seven-inch Romanian basketball player Muresan. Just think of all the clever quips Billy can make at the expense of Gheorghe. The latter does not seem to note the humor as he moves through the movie with the same dangerously awkward movement he uses on the court. Crystal is a talent agent who believes he can exploit the big man's size, and what he does is exploit a sensitive man.

2067. My Girl (1991, Imagine Films–Columbia, 102m, c). D Howard Zieff, P Brian Glazer, W Laurice Elehwany, PH Paul Elliott, ED Wendy Greene Bricmont, M James New-ton Howard, PD Joseph T. Garrity, AD Pat Tagliaferro.

LP Dan Aykroyd (Harry Sultenfuss), Jamie Lee Curtis (Shelly DeVoto), Macaulay Culkin (Thomas J. Sennett), Anna Chlumsky (Vada Sultenfuss), Richard Masur (Phil Sultenfuss), Griffin Dunne (Mr. Bixler), Ann Nelson (Gramoo Sultenfuss).

Chlumsky is charming as an 11-year-old girl living with her funeral director father. During her summer vacation she befriends Culkin and sees her father fall in love with beautician Curtis. It's a cute, sad and sentimental story, made all the more so by the death of and open casket wake for, Culkin.

2068. My Girl 2 (1994, Columbia, 99m, c). D Howard Zieff, P Brian Grazer, W Janet Kovalcik (based on characters created by Laurice Elehwany), PH Paul Elliott, ED Wendy Greene Bricmont, M Cliff Eidelman, PD Charles Rosen, AD Diane Yates, SD Mary Olivia McIntosh & Harold Fuhrman.

LP Dan Aykroyd (Harry Sultenfuss), Jamie Lee Curtis (Shelly Sultenfuss), Anna Chlumsky (Vada Sultenfuss), Austin O'Brien (Nick Zsigmond), Richard Masur (Phil Sultenfuss), Christine Ebersole (Rose Zsigmond).

Now a young teen, Chlumsky seeks information about the deceased mother she never knew. This film is not a worthy vehicle for the talented youngster, and Aykroyd's and Curtis' performances don't help matters.

2069. My Grandfather Is a Vampire (1992, New Zealand, Tucker Prods., 90m, c). D David Blyth, P Murray Newey, W Michael Heath, PH Kevin Hayward, ED David Huggett, M Jim Manzie, PD Kim Sinclair, AD Kirsten Shouler.

LP Al Lewis (Vernon T. Cooger), Justin Gocke (Lonny), Milan Borich (Kanziora), Pat Evison (Leah), Noel Appleby (Ernie), David Weatherley (Sgt. Dicky Ticker), Ian Watkin (Father Vincent).

Vampire Lewis isn't such a bad guy, and what's all that nonsense about not being able to survive the sunrise and the need to suck blood?

2070. My Heroes Have Always Been Cowboys (1991, Samuel Goldwyn Company, 106m, c). D Stuart Rosenberg, P Anthony Poll, W Joel Don Humphreys, PH Bernd Heinl,

ED Dennis M. Hill, M James Horner, PD Ted Haworth, AD Richard Johnson, SD George Toomer.

LP Scott Glenn (H.D. Dalton), Kate Capshaw (Jolie Meadows), Ben Johnson (Jessie Dalton), Tess Harper (Cheryl Hornby), Balthazar Getty (Jud Meadows), Gary Busey (Clint Hornby), Mickey Rooney (Junior).

After an accident leaves him injured, aging rodeo bullrider Glenn returns to his home town to attempt to pick up the pieces of his life and to care for his aging father Johnson.

2071. *My Life* (1993, Columbia, 112m, c). D & W Bruce Joel Rubin, P Jerry Zucker, Rubin & Hunt Lowry, PH Peter James, ED Richard Chew, M John Barry, PD Neil Spisak, AD Larry Fulton, SD Anne McCulley & Gina Cranham.

LP Michael Keaton (Bob Jones), Nicole Kidman (Gail Jones), Haing S. Ngor (Mr. Ho), Bradley Whitford (Paul), Queen Latifah (Theresa), Michael Constantine (Bill), Rebecca Schull (Rose).

Successful L.A. executive Keaton is dying of cancer. His wife Kidman is pregnant with their first child. He decides to videotape his final months to leave as a legacy of his life for the child he will probably never see. It is a compelling examination of the dying process and how it affects both the afflicted and those who will live on.

2072. *My Life So Far* (1999, U.K., Miramax, 93m, c). D Hugh Hudson, P David Putnam & Steve Norris, W Simon Donald (based on the book *Son of Adam* by Sir Denis Forman), PH Bernard Lutic, ED Scott Thomas, M Howard Blake, PD Andy Harris, AD John Frankish, SD Gillie Delap.

LP Colin Firth (Edward Pettigrew), Rosemary Harris (Gamma Macintosh), Irene Jacob (Heloise), Tcheky Karyo (Gabriel Chenoux), Mary Elizabeth Mastrantonio (Moria Pettigrew), Malcolm McDowell (Morris Macintosh), Kelly Macdonald (Elspeth Pettigrew), Robbie Norman (Fraser Pettigrew).

This childhood memoir is told from the point of view of 10-year-old Norman. It charmingly examines growing up in a time of innocence as a member of an eccentric and well-to-do family during the period between the two world wars.

2073. *My Life's in Turnaround* (1994, Arrow Releasing, 84m, c). D & W Eric Schaeffer & Donal Lardner Ward, P Daniel Einfeld, PH Peter Hawkins, Ed Susan Graff, M Red Hays, PD Mischa Petrwo.

LP Eric Schaeffer (Splick Featherstone), Donal Lardner Ward (Jason Little), Lisa Gerstein (Sarah Hershfeld), Dana Wheeler-Nicholson (Rachael), Debra Clein (Amanda).

Would-be filmmakers Schaeffer and Ward, who know nothing about making a movie, make a movie about two would-be filmmakers, who know nothing of making a film, making a film. It works for us.

2074. *My New Gun* (1992, IRS Media, 99m, c). D & W Stacy Cochran, P Michael Flynn, PH Edward Lachman, ED Camilla Toniolo, M Pat Irwin, PD Toby Corbett, SD Catherine Davis.

LP Diane Lane (Debbie Bender), James LeGros (Skippy), Stephen Collins (Gerald Bender), Tess Harper (Kimmy), Bill Raymond (Andrew), Bruce Altman (Irwin), Maddie Corman (Myra).

When suburban housewife Lane is given a .38 revolver by husband Collins to protect herself, she gives it to her wacky neighbor LeGros, who claims he needs it to protect his mother. His behavior is so strange that Lane becomes intrigued with finding out more about him and his plans.

2075. *My Own Private Idaho* (1991, Fine Line Features, 102m, c). D & W Gus Van Sant, P Laurie Parker, PH Eric Alan Edwards & John Campbell, ED Curtiss Clayton, PD David Brisbin, AD Ken Hardy, SD Melissa Stewart.

LP River Phoenix (Mike Waters), Keanu Reeves (Scott Favor), James Russo (Richard Waters), William Richert (Bob Pigeon), Rodney Harvey (Gary), Chiara Caselli (Carmella), Michael Parker (Digger), Jessie Thomas (Denise).

It's an interesting road movie about two street hustlers. Pheonix is a male prostitute who suffers from narcolepsy. Reeves is a troubled bisexual from an affluent family. Director Van Sant weaves the story of Shakespeare's *Henry IV, Part II* into the film.

2076. *My Very Best Friend* (1996, Viacom, 92m, c). D Joyce Chopra, P Laurette

Hayden, Richard Davis & Sandra Saxon Brice, W Lindsay Harrison & John Robert Bensink, PH James Glennon, ED Paul Dixon, M Patrick Williams, PD Perri Gorrara, SD Ane Christensen.

LP Jaclyn Smith (Dana Griffin), Jill Eikenberry (Barbara Wilkins), Tom Irwin (Alex Wilkins), Tom Mason (Ted Marshall), Mary Kay Place (Molly Butler), Kimberly Warnat (Kate Wilkins).

Eikenberry is relieved when her glamorous friend Smith becomes engaged to Mason. Smith tricks him into marriage by telling him she's pregnant when, as Eikenberry is aware, she actually is sterile. When Mason discovers the truth, he threatens to divorce her. Smith pushes him off his yacht and watches him drown. Fearful that she might be accused of murder, she waives rights to an inheritance. Then she sets her cap for Eikenberry's more and more distant husband Irwin. He is killed while skydiving, shortly after Eikenberry catches him in bed with Smith. What will become of these two friends?

2077. *Mystery, Alaska* (1999, Buena Vista–Hollywood Pictures, 118m, c). D Jay Roach, P David E. Kelley & Howard Baldwin, W Kelley & Sean O'Byrne, PH Peter Deming, ED Jon Poll, M Carter Burwell, PD Rusty Smith, AD Andrew Neskoromny, SD Elizabeth Wilcox.

LP Russell Crowe (John Biebe), Hank Azaria (Charles Danner), Mary McCormack (Donna Biebe), Burt Reynolds (Judge Walter Burns), Colm Meaney (Mayor Scott Pitcher), Lolita Davidovich (Mary Jane Pitcher), Maury Chaykin (Bailey Pruitt), Ron Eldard ("Skank" Marden), Ryan Northcott (Stevie Weeks), Judith Ivey (Joanne Burns).

Take one part of a very good film, *Hoosiers*, one part of a very bad film, *John Goldfarb, Please Come Home*, and one part of TV's *Northern Exposure* and you have this film. Reynolds portrays a judge who coaches a pickup hockey team made up of the inhabitants of a remote Alaskan town who, for reasons that need not be explained here, are to play the New York Rangers on their home ice. Makes sense that the pros will scrape up the ice with parts of the locals, doesn't it? But the good ol' northern boys have a "phenom" in the person of Northcott. The film may appeal to hockey lovers and fans of Davids against Goliaths.

2078. *Mystery Date* (1991, Orion, 110m, c). D Jonathan Wacks, P Cathleen Summers, W Terry Runte & Parker Bennett, PH Oliver Wood, ED Tina Hirsch, M John DuPrez, PD John Willett, AD Willie Heslup, SD Kim MacKenzie.

LP Ethan Hawke (Tom McHugh), Teri Polo (Geena Matthews), Brian McNamara (Craig McHugh), Fisher Stevens (Dwight), B.D. Wong (James Lew), Tony Rosato (Sharpie), Don Davis (Doheny).

While on a dream date, confused, unhappy teen Hawke is mistaken for McNamara, his older handsome and suave brother. He finds his world turned upside down.

2079. *Mystery Men* (1999, Universal, 120m, c). D Kinka Usher, P Lawrence Gordon, Mike Richardson & Lloyd Levin, W Neil Cuthbert (based on the Dark Horse comic book series created by Bob Burden), PH Stephen H. Burum, ED Conrad Buff, M Stephen Warbeck, PD Kirk M. Petruccelli, AD Barry Chusid, SD Victor Zolfo.

LP Hank Azaria (Blue Raja), Janeane Garofalo (Bowler), William H. Macy (Shoveler), Kel Mitchell (Invisible Boy), Paul Reubens (Spleen), Ben Stiller (Furious), Wes Studi (Sphinx), Greg Kinnear (Captain Amazing), Lena Olin (Dr. Anabel Lee), Geoffrey Rush (Casanova Frankenstein), Tom Waits (Doc Heller).

Here's the gist: Superhero Kinnear is held captive by his evil nemesis Rush. It's up to a septet of superhero wannabees, the mystery men (one of whom is a female), to come to his rescue. The super seven are none too super, except in their own minds. There are some fine bits and pieces showing off the talents of the cast, but not enough to make this send-up of comic books leap tall buildings with a single bound.

2080. *Mystery Science Theater 3000: The Movie* (1996, Gramercy Pictures, 74m, c). D & P Jim Mallon, W Michael J. Nelson, Trace Beaulieu, Mallon, Kevin Murphy, Mary Jo Pehl, Paul Chaplin & Bridget Jones (based on the the TV show *Mystery Science Theater 3000* created by Joel Hodgson), PH Jeff Stonehouse, ED Bill Johnson, M Billy Barber, PD Jef Maynard, SD Blakesley Clapp.

LP Trace Beaulieu (Dr. Clayton Forrester/ Voice of Crow T. Robot), Michael J. Nelson

(Mike Nelson), Jim Mallon (Voice of Gypsy), Kevin Murphy (Voice of Tom Servo), John Brady (Benkitnorf).

Cable-TV's Comedy Central production comes to the big screen. A human and two robots make fun of a popular sci-fi film, in this case 1955's *This Island Earth*.

2081. The Myth of Fingerprints (1997, Sony Pictures Classics, 90m, c). D & W Bart Freundlich, P Mary Jane Skalski, Tim Perell & Freundlich, PH Stephen Kazmierski, ED Kate Williams & Ken J. Sackheim, M David Bridie & John Phillips, PD Susan Bolles, AD John McFarlane, SD Catherine Pierson.

LP Noah Wyle (Warren), Julianne Moore (Mia), Hope Davis (Margaret), Blythe Danner (Lena), Roy Scheider (Hal), Michael Vartan (Jake), Laurel Holloman (Leigh), Brian Kerwin (Elliott), James LeGros (Cezanne).

The Thanksgiving holiday is a ticking bomb for the modern dysfunctional New England family of father Scheider, mother Danner, their two sons Wyle and Vartan, and daughters Moore and Holloman. It will remind audiences of the 1995 comedy *Home for the Holidays*, which was superior.

2082. Nadja (1995, October Films, 92m, c). D & W Michael Almereyda, P Mary Sweeney & Amy Hobby, PH Jim DeNault, ED David Leonard, M Simon Fisher Turner, PD Kurt Ossenfort.

LP Elina Lowensohn (Nadja), Suzy Amis (Cassandra), Peter Fonda (Dr. Van Helsing/Dracula), Martin Donovan (Jim), Galaxy Craze (Lucy), Karl Geary (Renfield), Jared Harris (Edgar).

In a modern take on the vampire tale, Lowensohn is the bloodsucking daughter of now deceased Count Dracula. She seduces and falls in love with Craze, which brings Fonda (in a humorous portrayal of the old family nemesis Van Helsing) to the rescue.

2083. Naked (1993, U.K., First Line Features, 131m, c). D & W Mike Leigh, P Simon Channing, PH Dick Pope, ED John Gregory, M Andrew Dickinson, PD Alison Chitty, AD Eve Stewart.

LP David Thewlis (Johnny), Katrin Cartlidge (Sophie), Greg Cruttwell (Jeremy), Lesley Sharp (Louise), Claire Skinner (Sandra), Peter Wright (Brian), Elizabeth Berrington (Giselle).

Foulmouthed and brutal Thewlis exchanges philosophies and dialogues with an assortment of 1990s London characters. Thewlis is very abusive to a string of female characters. It is a violent comedy love story, if you can buy that.

2084. The Naked Gun 2½: The Smell of Fear (1991, Paramount, 85m, c). D David Zucker, P Jerry Zucker, Jim Abrahams & Gil Netter, W David Zucker & Pat Proft (based on the characters created by Zucker for the TV series *Police Squad!*), PH Robert Stevens, ED James Symons & Chris Greenbury, M Ira Newborn, PD John J. Lloyd, SD Mickey S. Michaels.

LP Leslie Nielsen (Lt. Frank Drebin), Priscilla Presley (Jane Spencer), George Kennedy (Ed Hocken), O.J. Simpson (Nordberg), Robert Goulet (Quentin Hapsburg), Richard Griffiths (Earl Hacker/Dr. Meinheimer), Jacqueline Brookes (Commissioner Brumford).

This typically dumb and crass comedy has Nielsen investigating an energy scam. As in the original, the fun is the sight gags and the seriousness the characters maintain in the face of every absurdity. We have chosen to place this film before the next one, as it comes first in time, if not by alphabet. Getting things wrong is in keeping with the nature of the series.

2085. Naked Gun 33⅓: The Final Insult (1994, Paramount, 83m, c). D Peter Segal, P Robert K. Weiss & David Zucker, W Pat Proft, Zucker & Robert LoCash, PH Robert Stevens, ED James R. Symons, M Ira Newborn, PD Lawrence G. Paull, AD Bruce Crone, SD Kathe Klopp.

LP Leslie Nielsen (Lt. Frank Drebin), Priscilla Presley (Jane Spencer-Drebin), George Kennedy (Capt. Ed Hocken), O.J. Simpson (Nordberg), Fred Ward (Rocco), Kathleen Freeman (Muriel), Anna Nicole Smith (Tanya), Ellen Greene (Louise).

Nielsen is retired from the force. He is not happy as the little man of the house to wife Presley, who is out making her mark. He's called back to the force due to a series of terrorist activities. The jokes were dated even before the release of the film. By this time the creators were really struggling.

2086. Naked in New York (1994, Fine Line, 91m, c). D Dan Algrant, P Frederick Zollo, W Algrant & John Warren, PH Joey

Forsyte, ED Bill Pankow, M Angelo Badalamenti, PD Kalina Ivanov.

LP Eric Stoltz (Jake Briggs), Mary-Louise Parker (Joanne White), Ralph Macchio (Chris), Jill Clayburgh (Shirley Briggs), Tony Curtis (Carl Fisher), Timothy Dalton (Elliot Price), Lynne Thigpen (Helen), Kathleen Turner (Dana Coles), Roscoe Lee Browne (Mr. Reid), Whoopi Goldberg (Tragedy Mask).

When their respective careers start taking off, playwright Stoltz and photographer Parker find their relationship being put to the test. It's the story of a neurotic romance. The film is graced, for better or worse, by a slew of celebrities in cameo appearances.

2087. *Naked Lies* (1998, Magic Hour Pictures, 93m, c). D Ralph Portillo, P Portillo & James Elliott, W Jalee Baily, Michael Edwards & D. Avelo, PH Keith Hullard, ED Nicholas Zennaiter, AD Gabriela Paredes.

LP Shannon Tweed (Cara Landry), Fernando Allende (Damian Medina), Jay Baker (Mitch Kendall), Salvador Pineda (Lt. Rivas), Steven Bauer (Kevin).

Too bad Tweed's acting talent doesn't match her remarkable body. Here Tweed does what she does best in her various films — take off her clothes. The only real differences in her movies are her reasons for taking off her clothes. Here her motivation is to get the goods on Mexican crime king Allende, with whom she begins a torrid affair.

2088. *Naked Lunch* (1991, U.K./Canada, 20th Century–Fox, 115m, c). D & W David Cronenberg (based on the novel by William S. Burroughs), P Jeremy Thomas, PH Peter Suschitzky, ED Ronald Sanders, M Howard Shore, PD Carol Spier, AD James McAteer, SD Elinor Rose Galbraith.

LP Peter Weller (William Lee), Judy Davis (Joan Frost/Joan Lee), Ian Holm (Tom Frost), Julian Sands (Yves Cloquet), Roy Scheider (Dr. Benway), Monique Mercure (Fadela).

This film is based on William S. Burroughs autobiographical account of drug abuse, homosexuality, violence and general weirdness set in the drug-inspired land called Interzone. It isn't for everyone. Those interested in making an attempt to understand the Beat Generation and its key figures may find it revealing.

2089. *Naked Souls* (1996, Vanguard Ent., 90m, c). D Lyndon Chubbuck, P Lyndon & Ivana Chubbuck, W Frank Dietz, PH Eric J. Goldstein, ED Rebecca Ross, M Nigel Holton, PD Elisabeth Scott.

LP Pamela Anderson (Britanny "Brit" Clark), Brian Krause (Edward Adams), David Warner (Everett Longstreet), Clayton Rohner (Jerry), Justina Vail (Amelia), Dean Stockwell (Duncan Ellis).

Baywatch's Anderson and her pumped-up body are supposed to be the draw in this film, but she isn't on the screen much of the time. This is a case of good news-bad news. For those who can't take their eyes off her body, it's bad news; those who expect other talents from her, such as acting, will conclude it's good news. As for the plot: Krause must save Anderson from evil Warner.

2090. *Narrow Margin* (1990, Tri-Star, 97m, c). D & W Peter Hyams (based on the screenplay by Earl Fenton, from a story by Martin Goldsmith & Jack Leonard), P Jonathan A. Zimbert, PH Hyams, ED James Mitchell, M Bruce Broughton, PD Joel Schiller, AD David Willson, Kim Mooney & Eric Orbom, SD Kim MacKenzie.

LP Gene Hackman (Robert Caulfield), Anne Archer (Carol Hunnicut), James B. Sikking (Nelson), J.T. Walsh (Michael Tarlow), M. Emmet Walsh (Sgt. Dominick Benti), Susan Hogan (Kathryn Weller), Nigel Bennett (Jack Wootton).

Archer, a reluctant witness against the mob, is being brought back to L.A. on a train under the protection of D.A. Gene Hackman. The bad guys plan to prevent her from ever reaching her destination alive. It's no *The Lady Vanishes*, but it has its moments.

2091. *National Lampoon's Loaded Weapon 1* (1993, New Line Cinema, 105m, c). D Gene Quintano, P Suzanne Todd & David Willis, W Quintano & Don Holley (based on the story by Holley & Tori Tellem), PH Peter Deming, ED Christopher Greenbury, M Robert Folk, PD Jaymes Hinkle, AD Alan E. Muraoka, SD Sarah B. Stone.

LP Emilio Estevez (Jack Colt), Samuel L. Jackson (Wes Luger), Jon Lovitz (Becker), Tim Curry (Mr. Jigsaw), Kathy Ireland (Destiny Demeanor), Frank McRae (Captain Doyle),

William Shatner (General Curtis Mortars), Whoopi Goldberg (Sergeant York).

In a send-up of the *Lethal Weapon* films, Estevez and Jackson clown their way through the story of two cops seeking a microfilm that contains the formula for turning cocaine into cookies.

2092. *National Lampoon's Senior Trip* (1995, New Line, 94m, c). D Kelly Makin, P Wendy Grean, W Roger Kumble & I. Marlene King, PH Francis Protat, ED Stephen Lawrence, PD Gregory Keen, AD John Dondertman, SD Jeff Fruitman.

LP Matt Frewer (Principal Moss), Valerie Mahaffey (Miss Tracy Milford) Lawrence Dane (Senator John Lerman), Tommy Chong (Red), Jeremy Renner (Mark "Dags" D'Agostino), Rob Moore (Reggie), Fiona Loewi (Lisa Perkins).

A Midwestern high school class takes a bus trip to Washington, D.C., to meet the President. Funny, we thought we'd never laugh.

2093. *Natural Born Killers* (1994, Warner Bros., 120m, c). D Oliver Stone, P Jane Hamsher, Don Murphy & Clayton Townsend, W David Veloz, Richard Rutowski & Stone (based on a story by Quentin Tarantino), PH Robert Richardson, ED Hank Corwin & Brian Berdan, M Trent Reznor, PD Victor Kempster, AD Alan R. Tomkins & Margery Zweizig, SD Meredith Boswell.

LP Woody Harrelson (Mickey Knox), Juliette Lewis (Mallory Knox), Robert Downey, Jr. (Wayne Gale), Tommy Lee Jones (Dwight McClusky), Tom Sizemore (Jack Scagnetti), Rodney Dangerfield (Mallory's Dad), Russell Means (Old Indian), Edie McClurg (Mallory's Mom).

In another controversial Oliver Stone movie, Harrelson and Lewis are lovey-dovey white trash who kill for kicks. Thanks to reporter Downey, their cruelty and killing is given folkhero attention. The two dimwits just love all the attention and are happy to oblige with more bloodletting. It's definitely a film for fans of gratuitous violence. Some blame the film for copycat killers.

2094. *Navajo Blues* (1997, A-Pix Ent., 87m, c). D Joey Travolta, P Travolta & George Yager, W Richard Dillon, PH Dan Heigh, ED Sue Clark, M Scott Haynes, PD Bill Rosies.

LP Steven Bauer (Nicholas Epps), Irene Bedard (Audrey Wyako), Charlotte Lewis (Elizabeth Wyako), Barry Donaldson (Robert), Ed O'Ross (Not Lightning Struck), George Yager (Stevens).

Scheduled to testify against a crime boss, Bauer's superiors want to put him on ice until the trial. They decide that he should hide out on a Navajo reservation. There he will have to contend with a series of ritual murders.

2095. *Navy Seals* (1990, Orion, 104m, c). D Lewis Teague, P Brenda Feigen & Bernard Williams, W Chuck Pfarrer & Gary Goldman, PH John A. Alonzo, ED Don Zimmerman, M Sylvester Levay, PD Guy J. Comtois & Veronica Hadfield, AD Ed Williams & Vaughn Edwards, SD Malcolm Stone & Debra Schutt.

LP Charlie Sheen (Lt. Dale Hawkins), Michael Biehn (Lt. James Curran), Joanne Whalley-Kilmer (Claire Verens), Rick Rossovich (Leary), Cyril O'Reilly (Rexer), Bill Paxton (Dane), Dennis Haysbert (Graham).

Macho Navy commandos, trained to rescue hostages from Middle Eastern underground organizations, are intent on destroying an arsenal of deadly weapons.

2096. *Necessary Roughness* (1991, Paramount, 108m, c). D Stan Dragoti, P Mace Neufeld & Robert Rehme, W Rick Natkin & David Fuller, PH Peter Stein, ED John Wright & Steve Mirkovich, M Bill Conti, PD Paul Peters, SD Lynn Wolverton-Parker.

LP Scott Bakula (Paul Blake), Robert Loggia (Coach Wally Riggendorf), Hector Elizondo (Coach Ed Gennero), Harley Jane Kozak (Suzanne Carter), Sinbad (Andre Krimm), Larry Miller (Dean Elias).

The fortunes of a once dominating college football program have fallen on hard times. Hope for a turnaround arrives on campus in the person of Bakula, a 34-year-old farmer who sure can pass that pigskin.

2097. *Needful Things* (1993, Castle Rock–Columbia, 96m, c). D Fraser C. Heston, P Jack Cummins, W W.D. Richter & Lawrence Cohen (based on the novel by Stephen King), PH Tony Westman, ED Rob Kobrin, M Patrick Doyle, PD Douglas Higgins, SD Dominique Fauquet-Lemaitre & Jim Burrage.

LP Max Von Sydow (Leland Gaunt), Ed

Harris (Sheriff Alan Pangborn), Bonnie Bedelia (Polly Chambers), Amanda Plummer (Nettie Cobb), J.T. Walsh (Danforth Keeton, III), Ray McKinnon (Deputy Norris Ridgewick), Duncan Fraser (High Priest).

A strange curio shop, run by mysterious salesman Von Sydow, springs up out of nowhere in a small New England town. All hell breaks loose.

2098. *The Negotiator* (1998, Warner Bros., 138m, c). D F. Gary Gray, P David Hoberman & Arnon Milchan, W James DeMonaco & Kevin Fox, PH Russell Carpenter, ED Christian Wagner, M Graeme Revell, PD Holger Gross, AD Kevin Ishioka, SD Todd Holland, Richard Reynolds & Barbara-Anne Spencer.

LP Samuel L. Jackson (Danny Roman), Kevin Spacey (Chris Sabian), David Morse (Commander Adam Beck), Ron Rifkin (Commander Frost), John Spencer (Chief Al Travis), J.T. Walsh (Terence Niebaum), Regina Taylor (Karen Roman).

Jackson, top hostage negotiator of the Chicago police, is falsely accused of a crime and is forced to break the law to prove his innocence. In this taut suspense thriller Jackson finds himself on the other side of negotiation when he refuses to give his terms to anyone other than fellow police negotiator Spacey.

2099. *The Neighbor* (1993, Canada, Academy Ent., 93m, c). D Rodney Gibbons, P Tom Berry, W Kurt Wimmer, PH Ludek Bogner, ED Robert Newton, PD Claude Pare.

LP Rod Steiger (Myron Hatch), Linda Kozlowski (Mary Westhill), Ron Lea (John Westhill), Bruce Boa (Mr. Bishop), Sean McCann (Lt. Crow), Frances Bay (Sylvia).

Pregnant Kozlowski can't convince her husband Lea that next door neighbor Steiger is much more sinister than he appears. He'll learn.

2100. *Neil Simon's Lost in Yonkers* (1993, Rastar Prods.–Columbia, 112m, c). D Martha Coolidge, P Ray Stark, W Neil Simon (based on his play), PH Johnny E. Jensen, ED Steven Cohen, M Elmer Bernstein, PD David Chapman, AD Mark Haack, SD Marvin March, Thomas H. Paul & Mark Garner.

LP Richard Dreyfuss (Louie), Mercedes Ruehl (Bella), Irene Worth (Grandma), Brad Stoll (Jay), Mike Damus (Arty), David Strath-

airn (Johnny), Guy Miranda (Hollywood Harry), Jack Laufer (Eddie).

This filmed play never quite comes to life. The story begins when their father is forced to leave young Stoll and Damus with their tyrannical grandmother Worth. She runs a candy store — and her family — with an iron hand. Ruehl is the simple-minded but loveable daughter who lives with her mother and under her thumb. Dreyfuss is a son who is in trouble with mobsters and uses the old family home as a hiding place. Nothing seems to get resolved and the circumstances aren't really laughable.

2101. *Nell* (1994, 20th Century–Fox, 112m, c). D Michael Apted, P Jodie Foster & Renee Missel, W William Nicholson & Mark Handley (based on his play *Idioglossia*), PH Dante Spinotti, ED Jim Clark, M Mark Isham, PD Jon Hutman, AD Tim Galvin, SD Samara Hutman.

LP Jodie Foster† (Nell), Liam Neeson (Gerome Lovell), Natasha Richardson (Paula Olsen), Richard Libertini (Alexander Paley), Nick Searcy (Todd Peterson), Robin Mullins (Mary Peterson).

"Wild child" Foster is discovered living in the backwoods of North Carolina by physician Neeson. She speaks a language unknown to anyone else. Neeson and his romantic interest, Richardson, learn to understand and care for Foster and must defend her from efforts to institutionalize her.

2102. *Nemesis* (1993, Imperial Ent. Corp., 94m, c). D Albert Pyun, P Ash R. Shah, Eric Karson & Tom Karnowski, W Rebecca Charles, PH George Morradian, ED David Kern & Mark Conte, M Michael Rubini, PD Colleen Saro, AD Phil Zarling.

LP Olivier Gruner (Alex Rain), Tim Thomerson (Farnsworth), Deborah Shelton (Julian), Marjorie Monaghan (Jared), Brion James (Maritz), Jackie Earle Haley (Einstein), Merele Kennedy (Max Impact), Cary-Hiroyuki Tagawa (Angie Liv).

Sometime in the not too distant future, Japan and the U.S. have merged politically and economically. Semi-retired cyber-cop Gruner is set the task of battling corrupt government officials who want to take over the world.

2103. *The Neon Bible* (1996, U.K./U.S., Miramax Intl., 88m, c). D & W Terence

Davies (based on the novel by John Kennedy Toole), PH Mick Coulter, ED Charles Rees, M Robert Lockhart, PD Christopher Hobbs, AD Phil Messina, SD Kristin Messina.

LP Gena Rowlands (Aunt Mae), Diana Scarwid (Sarah), Denis Leary (Frank), Jacob Tierney (David, Age 15), Leo Burmester (Bobbie Lee Taylor), Frances Conroy (Miss Scover).

In the American South of the 1940s, Rowlands is a radio singer who does her best to boost the morale of her nephew Tierney. He is desperate for affection and some hope of escaping his family's poverty.

2104.   Neon City   (1992, Canada, Kodiak Films–Vidmark Ent., 107m, c). D Monte Markham, P Schmidt Wolf, Jeff Begun & John Schouweiler, W Buck Finch, Begun & Markham, PH Timothy Galfas, ED David Hagar, PD Fu Ding Cheng, SD Steven Lee.

LP Michael Ironside (Harry Stark), Vanity (Reno), Lyle Alzado (Bulk), Nick Klar (Tom), Richard Sanders (Dickie Devine), Valerie Wildman (Sandy).

Travelers attempting to reach fabled Neon City must risk crossing a barren wasteland where they are in danger from mutant bandits.

2105.   The Nephew   (1998, Ireland, CLT-UFA, 106m, c). D Eugene Brady, P Pierce Brosnan & Beau St. Clair, W Jacqueline O'Neill & Sean P. Steele, PH Jack Conroy, ED J. Patrick Duffner, M Stephen McKeon.

LP Hill Harper (Chad), Aislin McGuckin (Aislin), Pierce Brosnan (Joe Brady), Donal McCann (Tony Egan), Sinead Cusack (Brenda O'Boyce), Niall Tobin (Sean).

Brosnan's producing bow is the unlikely tale of the effects on a small Irish community when it discovers that they have a young American cousin, Harper, who is talented, handsome and black.

2106.   Nervous Ticks   (1993, Grandview Ave. Pictures, 95m, c). D Rocky Lang, P Arthur Goldblatt, W David Frankel, PH Bill Dill, ED Carie Coughlin, M Jay Ferguson, PD Naomi Shohan, AD Dan Whifler, SD Amy Wells.

LP Bill Pullman (York Daley), Julie Brown (Nancy), Peter Boyle (Ron Rudman), Brent Jennings (Cole), James Le Gros (Rusty), Paxton Whitehead (Cheshire), Josh Mostel (Sol Warshaw).

Shot in real time, this film is the wacky story of airline employee Pullman who attempts to run off to Rio with married Brown.

2107.   The Net   (1995, Columbia, 118m, c). D Irwin Walker, P Walker & Rob Cowan, W John Brancato & Michael Ferris, PH Jack N. Green, ED Richard Halsey, M Mark Isham, PD Dennis Washington, AD Tom Targownik, SD Anne D. McCulley.

LP Sandra Bullock (Angela Bennett), Jeremy Northam (Jack Devlin), Dennis Miller (Dr. Alan Champion), Diane Baker (Mrs. Bennett), Wendy Gazelle (Ruth Marks/Imposter), Ken Howard (Bergstrom).

Lonely computer whiz Bullock innocently becomes involved in a high tech conspiracy. The villains erase her identity to make it easier to do away with her. Bullock is a charmer, but this computer mish-mash isn't.

2108.   Netherworld   (1992, Full Moon Ent.–Paramount, 91m, c). D David Schmoeller, P Thomas Bradford, W Billy Chicago (based on the idea by Charles Band), PH Adolfo Bartoli, ED Carol Oblath, M David Bryan, AD Billy Jett & James Fraser, SD Elizabeth Shannon.

LP Michael Bendetti (Corey Thornton), Holly Floria (Dianne), Denise Gentile (Delores), Anjanette Comer (Mrs. Palmer), Robert Burr (Mr. Yates), Robert Sampson (Noah).

The heir to a Louisiana mansion must bring his father back from the dead in this voodoo story.

2109.   Neurotic Cabaret   (1991, Kipp Productions, 85m, c). D & P John Woodward, W Woodward & Tammy Stones, PH Danny Anaya, ED Woodward, M John Mills, PD John Perdichi.

LP Tammy Stones (Terri), Edwin Neal (Nolan), Dennis Washington (Nick), Colleen Keegan (Annette), Pat Kelly (Pat), Paul Vasquez (Cheo).

Aspiring actress-screenwriter Stones and her boyfriend Neal want to film a sci-fi script *Space Pirates*. To finance their efforts, she dances at a girlie club where lots of bills are stuck in her panties; but it's not enough. What else will she do for her art?

2110.   Nevada   (1998, Cineville, 107m, c). D & W Gary Tieche, P Kathryn Arnold, PH

Nancy Schreiber, ED Rebecca Ross, M Robert Perry, PD Bryce Perrin, AD Dawn Ferry.

LP Amy Brenneman (Chrysty Bucks), Ben Browder (Shelby), James Wilder (Rip), Keith Anthony Bennett (Nate), Bridgette Wilson (Jane), Gabrielle Anwar (Linny), Kirstie Alley (McGill).

The message of this movie is that a woman should have the right to desert her husband and children to seek her own identity. Perhaps so, but couldn't it had been done more interestingly?

2111. *Never Been Kissed* (1999, 20th Century–Fox/Fox 2000, 107m, c). D Raja Gosnell, P Sandy Isaac & Nancy Juvonen, W Abby Kohn & Marc Silverstein, PH Alex Nepomniaschy, ED Debra Chiate & Marcelo Sansevieri, M David Newman, PD Steven Jordan, AD William Hiney, SD Suzette Sheets.

LP Drew Barrymore (Josie Geller), David Arquette (Rob Geller), Michael Vartan (Sam Coulson), Molly Shannon (Anita), John C. Reilly (Gus), Garry Marshall (Rigfort).

Nerdy 25-year-old copy editor Barrymore is handed a dream assignment. Enroll in high school to get the inside dope on what's happening with today's teenagers. Trouble is Barrymore is an awkward misfit, not likely to be invited to get to know the school's really "important" and cool kids. Viewers are treated to some flashbacks to Drew's first encounter in high school where she was dubbed "Josie Grossie." When her brother Arquette enrolls in her new school to give her reputation a boost, she finds some newfound popularity. She will have to make an ethical decision when her editor Marshall insists she write an exposé of student-teacher relationships.

2112. *Never Talk to Strangers* (1995, TriStar, 102m, c). D Peter Hall P Andras Hamori, Jeffrey R. Neuman & Martin J. Wiley, W Lewis Green & Jordan Rush, PH Elemer Ragalyi, ED Roberto Silvi, M Pino Donaggio, PD Linda Del Rosario, SD Richard Paris.

LP Rebecca De Mornay (Dr. Sarah Taylor), Antonio Banderas (Tony Ramirez), Dennis Miller (Cliff Raddison), Len Cariou (Henry Taylor), Harry Dean Stanton (Max Cheski), Eugene Lipinski (Dudakoff).

Criminal psychologist De Mornay meets Banderas in a grocery store. He is alternatively charming and dangerous. She hires a private detective to trail Banderas and learn more about his true identity. De Mornay has problems from her past which further complicate her romance with her creepy lover.

2113. *The Neverending Story II: The Next Chapter* (1991, Germany/U.S., Warner Bros., 89m, c). D George Miller, P Dieter Geissler, W Karin Howard (based on the novel *The Neverending Story* by Michael Ende), PH David Connell, ED Peter Hollywood & Chris Blunden, M Robert Folk & Hans Zimmer, PD Robert Laing & Goetz Weidner.

LP Jonathan Brands (Bastian), Kenny Morrison (Atreyu), Clarissa Burt (Xayide), Alexandra Johnes (Childlike Empress), Martin Umbach (Nimbly).

Brands is a new actor in the role of Bastian, the young reader/hero who must save the magical world of Fantasia.

2114. *The New Age* (1994, Warner Bros., 110m, c). D & W Michael Tolkin, P Keith Addis & Nick Wechsler, PH John J. Campbell, ED Suzanne Fenn, M Mark Mothersbaugh, PD Robin Standefer, AD Kenneth A. Hardy, SD Claire Jenora Bowen.

LP Peter Weller (Peter Witner), Judy Davis (Katherine Witner), Patrick Bauchau (Jean Levy), Rachel Rosenthal (Sarah Friedberg), Adam West (Jeff Witner), Paula Marshall (Alison Gale).

Weller and Davis are a materialistic couple whose world falls apart, forcing them to search for some deeper meaning to their lives. This leads them to taking new lovers and seeking the wisdom of new age gurus. It's meant to be a comedy about spiritual emptiness. West does a nice turn as Weller's playboy father.

2115. *New Blood* (1999, U.K./Canada, Lions Gate/Screenland Pictures, 98m, c). D & W Michael Hurst, P Jason Piette & Andy Emilio, PH David Pelletier, ED Michael Doherty, M Jeff Danna, PD Ian Hall.

LP John Hurt (Alan White), Nick Moran (Danny White), Carrie-Anne Moss (Leigh), Shawn Wayans (Valentine), Joe Pantoliano (Hellman), Eugene Robert Glazer (Mr. Ryan).

In this thriller, Moran offers his father Hurt a proposition. Moran's twin sister is dying and urgently needs a heart transplant. Moran offers his heart if Hurt will impersonate a man who

Moran was to kidnap and deliver to mysterious Glazer. It's almost certain that Hurt won't survive in this bloody affair.

2116. New Jack City (1991, Warner Bros., 97m, c). D Mario Van Peebles, P Doug McHenry & George Jackson, W Barry Michael Cooper & Thomas Lee Wright, PH Francis Kenny, ED Steven Kemper, M Michael Colombier, PD Charles C. Bennett, AD Barbra Matis & Laura Brock, SD Elaine O'Donnell.

LP Wesley Snipes (Nino Brown), Ice-T (Scotty Appleton), Allen Payne (Gee Money), Chris Rock (Pookie), Mario Van Peebles (Detective Stone), Michael Michele (Selina), Bill Nunn (Duh Duh Duh Man), Russell Wong (Kim Parks), Judd Nelson (Nick Peretti).

In a story inspired by *Scarface*, Snipes is a vicious black crack dealer clawing his way to the top of New York's drug underworld. Renegade cops Ice-T and Nelson take him and his crime empire down.

2117. New Jersey Drive (1995, Gramercy, 96m, c). D & W Nick Gomez (based on a story by Gomez & Michel Marriott), P Larry Meistrich, PH Adam Kimmel, ED Tracy S. Granger, PD Lester Cohen, SD Lynn-Marie Nigro.

LP Sharron Corley (Jason Petty), Gabriel Casseus (Midget), Saul Stein (Roscoe), Gwen McGee (Renee Petty), Andre Moore (Ritchie), Donald Adeosun Faison (Tiny Dime), Conrad Meertins, Jr. (P-Nut).

In a gritty film, ghetto youth Corley's main joy in life is stealing cars and riding around in them. Things get pretty repetitive without going anywhere.

2118. Newsies (1992, Walt Disney Prods.–Buena Vista, 125m, c). D Kenny Ortega, P Michael Finnell, W Bob Tzudiker & Noni White, PH Andrew Laszlo, ED William Reynolds, M Alan Menken, Danny Troob & J.A.C. Redford, AD Nancy Patton, SD Robert Gould.

LP Christian Bale (Jack Kelly/Francis Sullivan), David Moscow (David Jacobs), Luke Edwards (Les Jacobs), Max Casella (Racetrack), Marty Belafsky (Crutchy), Robert Duvall (Joseph Pulitzer), Michael Lerner (Weasel), Kevin Tighe (Snyder), Ele Keats (Sarah Jacobs).

In this musical, a bunch of newsboys take on a corrupt newspaper mogul. The exuberance of the young talent doesn't make up for the lack of an interesting story between songs.

2119. The Newton Boys (1998, 20th Century–Fox, 122m, c). D Richard Linklater, P Anne Walker-McBay, W Linklater, Claude Stanush & Clark Lee Walker (based on Stanush's book), PH Peter James, ED Sandra Adair, M Edward D. Barnes, PD Catherine Hardwicke, AD Andrea Dopaso & John Frick, SD Jeanette Scott.

LP Matthew McConaughey (Willis Newton), Skeet Ulrich (Joe Newton), Ethan Hawke (Jess Newton), Vincent D'Onofrio (Doc Newton), Julianna Margulies (Louise Brown), Dwight Yoakam (Brentwood Glasscock).

This film tells the story of four real-life brothers who achieved almost mythical status when they became some of the most famous bank robbers in American history.

2120. The Next Karate Kid (1994, Columbia, 104m, c). D Christopher Cain, P Jerry Weintraub, W Mark Lee (based on characters created by Robert Mark Kamen), PH Laszlo Kovacs, ED Ronald Roose, M Bill Conti, PD Walter P. Martishius, SD Tracey A. Doyle.

LP Noriyiki "Pat" Morita (Mr. Miyagi), Hilary Swank (Julie Pierce), Michael Ironside (Colonel Dugan), Constance Towers (Louisa), Chris Conrad (Eric), Arsenio "Sonny" Trinidad (Abbott Monk), Michael Cavalieri (Ned).

Ralph Macchio has been replaced by Swank in this story which is almost a clone of the original *Karate Kid* movie. The idea is becoming too boring to watch.

2121. Next Stop, Wonderland (1998, Miramax, 104m, c). D Brad Anderson, P Mitchell B. Robbins, W Anderson & Lyn Vaus, PH Uta Brieswitz, ED Anderson, M Claudio Ragazzi, PD Chad Detweiler.

LP Hope Davis (Erin Castleton), Alan Gelfant (Alan Montiero), Victor Argo (Frank), Jon Benjamin (Eric), Cara Buono (Julie), Philip Seymour Hoffman (Sean), Holland Taylor (Piper Castleton).

This film presents two lonelyhearts, Davis, a Boston nurse in her thirties, and Gelfant, a 35-year-old man who has quit his family's plumbing business to go to college to study marine biology. Before they can mesh, she has to sort out the respondents to a personal ad placed by her mother Taylor on her behalf. Then, too, she must deal with the return of her politically correct boyfriend Hoffman.

2122. Nick and Jane (1997, CFP Distribution, 96m, c). D Richard Mauro, P Bill McCutchen III, W Mauro, Peter Quigley & Neil William Alumkal, PH Chris Norr, ED Wendey Stanzler & Mauro, M Mark Suozzo, PD Mark Helmuth, AD Stacey Tanner, SD Adam Glickman.

LP Dana Wheeler-Nicholson (Jane Whitmore), James McCaffrey (Nick Miller), Gedde Watanabe (Enzo), David Johansen (Carter), Clinton Leupp (Miss CoCo Peru), Saundra Santiago (Stephanie), John Dossett (John Price).

This film only partially succeeds in trying to recapture the charm of romantic comedies of Hollywood's Golden Age. High-powered businesswoman Wheeler-Nicholson and cabbie McCaffrey are unlikely lovers. But after fate (or the screenwriters) throws them together in two chance encounters, she offers him a thousand dollars to pose as her new beau to make her former boyfriend, Dossett, jealous. Sound familiar?

2123. Nick of Time (1995, Paramount, 89m, c). D & P John Badham, W Patrick Sheane Duncan, PH Roy H. Wagner, ED Frank Morriss & Kevin Stitt, M Arthur B. Rubinstein, PD Philip Harrison, AD Eric Orbom, SD Julia Badham.

LP Johnny Depp (Gene Watson), Courtney Chase (Lynn Watson), Charles S. Dutton (Huey), Christopher Walken (Mr. Smith), Roma Maffia (Ms. Jones), Marsha Mason (Governor Eleanor Grant), Peter Strauss (Brendan Grant).

When his daughter is kidnapped, devoted father Depp is forced to become an unwilling assassin of Mason, the governor of California. It's a fast-paced thriller with an improbable plot that's filmed in real time.

2124. Nickel & Dime (1990, Columbia/TriStar, 96m, c). D Ben Moses, P Lynn Danileson & Moses, W Eddy Pollon & Seth Front, PH Henry M. Lebo, ED Joan E. Chapman, M Stephen Cohn, PD George Costello, SD Damon Medlen.

LP C. Thomas Howell (Jack Stone), Wallace Shawn (Everett Willis), Lise Cutter (Cathleen Markson), Roy Brocksmith (Sammy Thornton), Lynn Danielson (Destiny Charm), Kathleen Freeman (Judge Lechter).

Teaming Howell and Shawn works, but the film is a mediocre effort. Con man and lawyer Howell specializes in locating missing heirs. He engages the assistance of straight-arrow accountant Shawn to find the lost scion and heir to the estate of a murdered millionaire.

2125. Night and the City (1992, 20th Century-Fox, 98m, c). D Irwin Winkler, P Jane Rosenthal & Winkler, W Richard Price & Jo Eisinger (based on his screenplay and the original screenplay by Jules Dassin, and the novel by Gerald Kersh), PH Tak Fujimoto, ED David Brenner, M James Newton Howard, PD Peter Larkin, AD Charley Beal, SD Robert J. Franco.

LP Robert De Niro (Harry Fabian), Jessica Lange (Helen Nasseros), Cliff Gorman (Phil), Alan King ("Boom-Boom" Grossman), Jack Warden (Al Grossman), Eli Wallach (Peck), Barry Primus (Tommy Tessler), Gene Kirkwood (Resnick).

This film is a remake of a 1950 movie of the same name, which starred Richard Widmark and Gene Tierney. Sleazy lawyer De Niro is having an affair with Lange, wife of bar owner Gorman. At the same time he is trying to promote a major boxing match. His big mouth and big ideas set him up for quite a fall.

2126. Night Angel (1990, Paragon Arts, 90m, c). D Dominique Othenin-Girard, P Joe Augustyn & Jeff Geoffray, W Joe Augustyn & Walter Josten, PH David Lewis, ED Jerry Brady, M Cory Lerios, PD Ken Aichele.

LP Isa Andersen (Lilith), Karen Black (Rita), Linden Ashby (Craig), Debra Feuer (Kirstie), Helen Martin (Sadie), Doug Jones (Ken), Gary Hudson (Rod).

It's a predictable and quite ordinary story, based on the Lilith legend of Jewish folklore, of murderous, demonic Anderson, a seductress who poses as a fashion model. The film is seething with grotesque sex and violence, but even this is not done well.

2127. A Night at the Roxbury (1998, Paramount, 81m, c). D John Fortenberry, P Lorne Michaels & Amy Heckerling, W Steve Koren, Will Ferrell & Chris Kattan, PH Francis

Kenny, ED Jay Kamen, M David Kitay, PD Steve Jordan, AD Carl Stensel, SD John Philpotts.

LP Will Ferrell (Steve Bubati), Chris Kattan (Doug Bubati), Molly Shannon (Emily), Dan Hedaya (Mr. Bubati), Richard Grieco (Himself), Loni Anderson (Mrs. Bubati), Elisa Donovan (Cambi).

Those who are not devotees of *Saturday Night Live* may not be familiar with Ferrell and Kattan's skits as two hair-gelled, silver-chained, satin-blazered brothers. Such folks may not be interested in following 81 minutes of the boys' routine as they try to open their own club, modeled on the Roxbury, the top local discotheque.

2128. *Night Breed* (1990, 20th Century–Fox, 102m, c). D & W Clive Barker (based on the novel *Cabal* by Barker), P Gabriella Martinelli, PH Robin Vidgeon, ED Richard Marden & Mark Goldblatt, M Danny Elfman, PD Steve Hardie.

LP Craig Sheffer (Boone), Anne Bobby (Lori), David Cronenberg (Decker), Charles Haid (Capt. Eigerman), Hugh Quarshie (Detective Joyce).

A serial killer is sought in the Canadian wilderness. What is found is a tribe of monsters called the Night Breed.

2129. *Night Falls on Manhattan* (1997, Paramount, 113m, c). D & W Sidney Lumet (based on the novel *Tainted Evidence* by Robert Daley), P Thom Mount & Josh Kramer, PH David Watkin, ED Sam O'Steen, M Mark Isham, PD Philip Rosenberg, AD Robert Guerra, SD Carolyn Cartwright.

LP Andy Garcia (Sean Casey), Richard Dreyfuss (Sam Vigoda), Lena Olin (Peggy Lindstrom), Ian Holm (Liam Casey), Ron Leibman (DA Morgenstein), James Gandolfini (Joey Allegretto), Sheik Mahmud-Bey (Jordan Washington), Colm Force (Elihu Harrison).

When the police try to arrest notorious Harlem drug lord Mahmud-Bey, three policemen are killed. Publicity conscious D.A. Leibman appoints inexperienced lawyer Garcia, an ex-cop, to prosecute Mahmud-Bey. Garcia's cop father Holm had been seriously wounded in the raid, which would seem reason enough to disqualify Garcia from prosecuting. But, never mind. As he pleads the case, Garcia finds himself sifting through the police's dirty laundry.

2130. *Night Fire* (1994, Triboro Ent. Group, 93m, c). D & P Mike Sedan, W Catherine Tavel & Helen Haxton (based on a story by Sedan), PH Zoran Hochstatter, ED Thomas Meshelski, M Miriam Cutler.

LP Shannon Tweed (Lydia), John Laughlin (Barry), Rochelle Swanson (Gwen), Martin Hewitt (Cal), Alma Beltran (Maria).

Wealthy businesswoman Tweed's plans for a romantic weekend alone with her husband are spoiled when a strange couple show up at their country home. It's not a bad film, and then it's always a pleasure to ogle Tweed.

2131. *Night of the Living Dead* (1990, 21st Century–Columbia, 96m, c). D Tom Savini, P John A. Russo & Russ Steiner, W George Romero (based on the screenplay by Romero & Russo), PH Frank Prinzi, ED Tom Dubensky, M Paul McCollough, PD Cletus Anderson, AD James Feng, SD Brian J. Stonestreet.

LP Tony Todd (Ben), Patricia Tallman (Barbara), Tom Towles (Harry Cooper), McKee Anderson (Helen Cooper), William Butler (Tom), Katie Finnerman (Judy Rose), Bill Mosley (Johnnie), Heather Mazur (Sarah).

This remake of the 1968 black-and-white horror classic is virtually shot-for-shot the same, but this time in vivid color. If you liked the original, you'll like this one.

2132. *Night of the Running Man* (1994, Vidmark Prods., 93m, c). D Mark L. Lester, P Dana Dubrovsky, George Perkins & Lester, W Rodney Vaccaro (based on the novel by Lee Wells), PH Mark Irwin.

LP Scott Glenn (David Eckhart), Andrew McCarthy (Jerry Logan), John Glover (Derek Mills), Janet Gunn (Chris Altman).

When Las Vegas cab driver McCarthy finds $1 million stolen from a casino, he takes off, trailed by hitman Glenn, hired to recover the cash.

2133. *Night of the Warrior* (1991, Trimark Ent., 100m, c). D Rafal Zielinski, P Mike Erwin & Thomas Ian Griffith, W Griffith, PH Edward Pei, ED Jonas Thaler, M Ed Tomney, PD Michael Helmy.

LP Lorenzo Lamas (Miles Keane), Anthony Geary (Lynch), Kathleen Kinmont (Katherine Pierce), Ken Foree (Oliver), Felicity Waterman (Joy), Arlene Dahl (Edie Keane).

Lamas makes it a family affair, starring with his wife Kinmont and his mom Dahl. He's an exotic dance club owner who pays the bills by fighting in illegal, underground blood matches.

2134. Night on Earth (1992, Fine Line Features, 130m, c). D, P & W Jim Jarmusch, PH Frederick Elmes, ED Jay Rabinowitz, M Tom Waits, SD Johan LeTenoux.

LP Gena Rowlands (Victoria Snelling), Winona Ryder (Corky), Lisanne Falk (Rock Manager), Armin Mueller-Stahl (Helmut Grokenberger), Giancarlo Esposito (YoYo), Rosie Perez (Angela).

Jim Jarmusch casts some friends as cab drivers and their passengers on the same night in different countries. Interesting, but not memorable.

2135. Night Train (1998, Ireland, Alternative Cinema Co., 94m, c). D John Lynch, P Tristan Lynch, W Aodhan Madden, PH Seamus Deasy, ED J. Patrick Duffner, M Adam Lynch, PD Alan Farquaharson.

LP John Hurt (Michael Poole), Brenda Blethyn (Alice Mooney), Pauline Flanagan (Mrs. Mooney), Rynagh O'Grady (Winnie), Peter Caffrey (Walter).

After serving time for keeping the wrong kind of account books, Hurt finds that a gangster thinks he owes him money. Hurt hides out in a Dublin rooming house run by Flanagan and her timid daughter Blethyn. It's a bit of a lonelyhearts drama from this point.

2136. Night Visitor (1990, Premier/MGM-UA, 93m, c). D Rupert Hitzig, P Alain Silver, W Randal Visovich, PH Peter Jansen, ED Glenn Erickson, M Parmer Fuller, PD Jon Rothschild.

LP Elliott Gould (Ron Devereaux), Richard Roundtree (Capt. Crane), Allen Garfield (Zachary Willard), Michael J. Pollard (Stanley Willard), Derek Rydall (Billy Colton), Teresa Van Der Woude (Kelly Fremont), Shannon Tweed (Lisa Grace).

Compulsive liar Rydall witnesses the Satanic murder of Tweed, the beautiful whore who lives next door, committed by none other than his history teacher Garfield. But he can't get anyone to believe him.

2137. The Night We Never Met (1993, Miramax, 99m, c). D & W Warren Leight, P

Michael Peyser, PH John Thomas, ED Camilla Toniolo, M Evan Lurie, PD Lester Cohen, AD Daniel Talpers, SD Jessica Lanier.

LP Matthew Broderick (Sam Lester), Annabella Sciorra (Ellen Holder), Kevin Anderson (Brian McVeigh), Justine Bateman (Janet Beehan), Jeanne Tripplehorn (Pastel), Michael Mantell (Aaron Holder), Christine Baranski (Lucy).

In a romantic comedy short on comedy, soon to be married yuppie Anderson sublets his apartment for alternate days to Broderick and Sciorra. Broderick's trying to get over his breakup with Tripplehorn, and Sciorra wants a place to paint, away from her non-supportive husband Mantell. What happens when they show up on the same day?

2138. Nightwatch (1998, Dimension Films–Miramax, 101m, c). D Ole Bornedal, P Michael Obel, W Steven Soderbergh & Bornedal (based on the film Nattevagten by Bornedal), PH Dan Lausten, ED Sally Menke, M Joachim Holbek, PD Richard Hoover, AD Kathleen McKernin & Adam Scher, SD Brian Kasch.

LP Ewan McGregor (Martin Bells), Nick Nolte (Inspector Thomas Cray), Josh Brolin (James Gallman), Patricia Arquette (Katherine), Alix Koromzay (Joyce), Lauren Graham (Marie), John C. Reilly (Inspector Bill Davis).

This advertised psychological thriller begins with a pre-credit sequence of the brutal murder of a prostitute. It doesn't improve on this sequence. McGregor, a night watchman at a morgue, is suspected of being a serial killer, but the audience can point to better candidates than him.

2139. Nil by Mouth (1997, U.K./U.S., Sony Pictures Classics, 128m, c/b&w). D & W Gary Oldman, P Luc Besson, Douglas Urbanski & Oldman, PH Ron Fortunato, ED Brad Fuller, M Eric Clapton, PD Hugo Luczyc-Wyhowski, AD Luanna Hanson.

LP Ray Winstone (Raymond), Kathy Burke (Valerie), Charlie Creed-Miles (Billy), Laila Morse (Janet), Edna Dore (Kath), Chrissie Cotterill (Paula), Jon Morrison (Angus).

Oldman makes his directorial debut with this story of the hopeless lives of the members of a London working-class family. Loutish Winstone is fueled by alcohol and hatred. He lives with his pregnant and often abused wife

Burke, their six-year-old daughter and Creed-Miles, Burke's drug-addicted younger brother. It's a shocking and primitive slice-of-life film.

2140. Nina Takes a Lover (1995, Triumph Releasing, 100m, c). D & W Alan Jacobs, P Jane Hernandez & Jacobs, PH Phil Parmet, ED John Nutt, M Todd Boekelheide, PD Don De Fina, SD Victoria Lewis.

LP Laura San Giacomo (Nina), Paul Rhys (Photographer), Michael O'Keefe (Journalist), Cristi Conaway (Friend), Fisher Stevens (Paulie).

Tabloid journalist O'Keefe is writing a series on adultery. San Giacomo tells about her affair, now ended, with Rhys. She took a lover when she felt the passion had gone out of her marriage because her husband was on the road so often.

2141. Nine Months (1995, 20th Century–Fox, 103m, c). D & W Chris Columbus, P Anne Francois, Columbus, Mark Radcliffe & Michael Barnathan, PH Donald McAlpine, ED Raja Gosnell & Stephen Rivkin, M Hans Zimmer, PD Angelo P. Graham, AD W. Steven Graham, SD Garrett Lewis.

LP Hugh Grant (Samuel Faulkner), Julianne Moore (Rebecca Taylor), Tom Arnold (Marty Dwyer), Joan Cusack (Gail Dwyer), Jeff Goldblum (Sean Fletcher), Robin Williams (Dr. Kosevich), Mia Cottet (Lily).

When Grant's girlfriend Moore announces she's pregnant, he goes ballistic. She doesn't feel his attitude is very supportive. You just know that after milking the premise dry for all the humor possible, charming Grant will do the right thing. Most of the laughs are supplied by the brief scenes with Williams as an obstetrician. The picture is based on the popular 1994 French film *Neuf Mois*.

2142. Ninth Street (1999, Hodcarrier Films, 95m, b&w). D Tim Rebman & Kevin Willmott, P & W Willmott (based on his play), PH Troy Paddock, ED Michael Brendt, M Wayne Hawkins & Isaac Hayes, PD Tim Bauer & Stan Herd.

LP Don Washington (Bebo), Kevin Willmott (Huddie), Nadine Griffith (Carrie Mae), Byron Myrick (Love), Isaac Hayes (Tippytoe), Queen Key (Mama Butler), Kaycce Moore (Pop-Bottle Ruby), Martin Sheen (Father Frank).

Writer-director Willmott took seven years to bring his story to the screen. It deals with growing up in Junction City, Missouri, a once booming "Jump City" that had fallen on hard times by 1968, the period of the film. There is a steady stream of army recruits from nearby Fort Reilly who take advantage of the black-owned juke joints, pool halls and streetwalkers of the area. It's an episodic memory piece.

2143. Nixon (1995, Hollywood Pictures–Buena Vista, 190m, c). D Oliver Stone, P Clayton Townsend, Stone & Andrew G. Vajna, W Stephen J. Rivele†, Christopher Wilkinson† & Stone†, PH Robert Richardson, ED Brian Berdan & Hank Corwin, M John Williams†, PD Victor Kempster, AD Donald Woodruff, Richard Mays & Margery Zweizig, SD Merideth Boswell.

LP Anthony Hopkins† (Richard M. Nixon), Joan Allen† (Pat Nixon), Powers Boothe (Alexander Haig), Ed Harris (E. Howard Hunt), Bob Hoskins (J. Edgar Hoover), E.G. Marshall (John Mitchell), David Paymer (Ron Ziegler), David Hyde Pierce (John Dean), Paul Sorvino (Henry Kissinger), Mary Steenburgen (Hannah Nixon), J.T. Walsh (John Ehrlichman), James Woods (H.R. Haldeman), Annabeth Gish (Julie Nixon).

There are some excellent performances in this film depicting recent history, particularly by Hopkins as "Tricky Dick" and Allen as long-suffering Pat. The other actors seemed to be chosen on the basis of how closely, aided by makeup, they can resemble the person they are playing. Those who lived through Nixon's presidency and watched with shock the unfolding of Watergate and his political downfall will not be surprised nor learn anything new from the movie. The examination of Nixon's earlier life may have meant to explain his makeup and character, but it doesn't do so. Once again Stone gives his particular twist on history and, as with *JFK*, it's not completely satisfying, although it is entertaining.

2144. No Escape (1994, Savoy Pictures, 118m, c). D Martin Campbell, P Gale Anne Hurd, W Michael Gaylin & Joel Gross (based on the novel *The Penal Colony* by Richard Herley), PH Phil Meheux, ED Terry Rawlings & Amy Pawlowski, M Graeme Revell, PD Allan Cameron, AD Ian Gracie, SD Lesley Crawford.

LP Ray Liotta (Robbins), Lance Henriksen (The Father), Stuart Wilson (Marek), Kevin Dillon (Casey), Kevin J. O'Connor (Stephano), Don Henderson (Killian), Ian McNeice (King), Jack Shepherd (Dysart).

In the year 2022, decorated soldier Liotta is sent to prison for shooting his commanding officer. The prison is on an island. There are no walls and no guards. The prisoners are left to kill each other. Eventually, Liotta finds a group of prisoners, called the "Insiders," who are relatively more civilized than the mangy bunch of killers known as the "Outsiders." War will have to be declared between the two groups.

2145.　*No Looking Back* (1998, Gramercy/ 20th Century–Fox, 96m, c). D & W Edward Burns, P Ted Hope, Michael Nozik & Burns, PH Frank Prinzi, ED Susan Graef, M Joe Delia, PD Therese DePrez, SD Diane Lederman.

LP Lauren Holly (Claudia), Edward Burns (Charlie), Jon Bon Jovi (Michael), Blythe Danner (Claudia's Mom), Connie Britton (Kelly), Jennifer Esposito (Teresa).

Burns returns to his hometown with the sole intention of winning back his girlfriend Holly whom he abandoned three years earlier. He finds that she is practically engaged to Bon Jovi, Burns' best friend since first grade. That about sums it up.

2146.　*No Place to Hide* (1993, Cannon Pictures, 95m, c). D & W Richard Danus, P Alan Amiel, PH Roberto D'Ettore Piazzoli, ED Alain Jakubowicz, M Robert O. Ragland, PD Richard Sherman, SD Gene Serdena.

LP Kris Kristofferson (Joe Garvey), Drew Barrymore (Tinsel Hanley), Martin Landau (Frank McCay), O.J. Simpson (Allie Wheeler), Dey Young (Karen), Zeev Revach (Gloved Hand), Bruce Weitz (Captain Nelson Silva), Lydie Denier (Pamela Hanley).

Dancer Denier insists that her sister Barrymore hide a videotape. Shortly thereafter Denier is stabbed to death by a heavily cloaked figure during a ballet performance. Barrymore, now in danger, is hidden in a nunnery by burned-out cop Kristofferson. She won't be safe until the vigilante leader who is caught on the videotape is brought to justice.

2147.　*Nobody's Fool* (1994, Paramount, 112m, c). D Robert Benton, P Scott Rubin, W Benton† (based on the novel by Richard Russo), PH John Bailey, ED John Bloom, M Howard Shore, PD David Gropman, AD Dan Davis, SD Gretchen Rau.

LP Paul Newman† (Donald "Sully" Sullivan), Jessica Tandy (Miss Beryl), Bruce Willis (Carl Roebuck), Melanie Griffith (Toby Roebuck), Dylan Walsh (Peter), Pruitt Taylor Vince (Rub Squeers), Gene Saks (Wirf), Josef Sommer (Clive Peoples, Jr.).

Newman proves that despite pushing seventy, he can still steal a movie and play a romantic role. Newman plays a younger man, a 60-year-old construction worker who, during a holiday season, discovers how to play the role of father and grandfather despite his reluctance to be either. He's a perfectly ordinary man — well, as much as Newman can ever be perfectly ordinary. Let's just say his character is a flawed man who has some good points, which viewers are allowed to discover at the same time his friends and family take note of them.

2148.　*Nobody's Perfect* (1990, Panorama–Moviestore, 89m, c). D Robert Kaylor, P Benni Korzen, W Annie Korzen & Joel Block, PH Claus Loof, ED Robert Gordon, M Robert Randles.

LP Chad Lowe (Stephen/Stephanie), Gail O'Grady (Shelly), Patrick Breen (Andy), Kim Flowers (Jackie), Todd Schaefer (Brad), Robert Vaughn (Dr. Duncan).

To be near his dream girl O'Grady, Lowe masquerades as a female so he can join the girl's tennis team. Well, no film is an ace, especially not this one.

2149.　*Noises Off* (1992, Touchstone–Buena Vista, 104m, c). D Peter Bogdanovich, P Frank Marshall, W Marty Kaplan (based on the play by Michael Frayn), PH Tim Suhrstedt, ED Lisa Day, M Phil Marshall, PD Norman Newberry, AD Daniel E. Maltese, SD Jim Duffy.

LP Carol Burnett (Dotty Otley/Mrs. Clackett), Michael Caine (Lloyd Fellowes), Denholm Elliott (Selsdon Mowbray/The Burglar), Julie Hagerty (Poppy Taylor), Marilu Henner (Belinda Blair/Flavia Brent), Mark Linn-Baker (Tim Allgood), Christopher Reeve (Frederick Dallas/ Philip Brent), John Ritter (Garry Lejeune/Roger Tramplemain), Nicollette Sheridan (Brooke Ashton/Vicki).

This comedy exploits the assorted romances

of director Caine and the performers in a play. The farcical play, a sex-comedy, isn't as much fun as what's happening behind the scenery. While somewhat enjoyable, it must have been better on the stage.

2150. *Normal Life* (1996, Fire Line, 102m, c). D John McNaughton, P Richard Maynard, W Peg Haller & Bob Schneider, PH Jean De-Segonzac, ED Elena Maganini, M Robert Mc-Naughton & Ken Hale, PD Rick Paul, SD Nancy Fallace.

LP Ashley Judd (Pam Anderson), Luke Perry (Chris Anderson), Bruce Young (Agent Parker), Jim True (Mike Anderson), Dawn Maxey (Eva), Tom Towles (Frank Anderson), Penelope Mil-ford (Adele Anderson).

Rookie cop Perry falls for sexy biker chick Judd and the two marry. Two years pass and irresponsible Judd has really messed up their lives. Perry, now a security guard, is forced to pull some bank heists to pay for the things she demands. It's based on a true story of a couple who went on a bank robbing spree in 1991.

2151. *North* (1994, Castle Rock–Columbia, 88m, c). D & P Rob Reiner, W Alan Zweibel & Andrew Scheinman (based on the novel by Zweibel), PH Adam Greenberg, ED Robert Leighton, M Marc Shaiman, PD J. Michael Riva, AD David Klassen & Bob Shaw, SD Michael Taylor, Darrell L. Wight, Dawn Snyder, Virginia Randolf, Rob Woodruff & George DeTitta.

LP Elijah Wood (North), Bruce Willis (Narrator), Jason Alexander (North's Dad), Julia Louis-Dreyfus (North's Mom), Matthew Mc-Curley (Winchell), Jon Lovitz (Arthur Belt), Alan Arkin (Judge Buckle), Dan Aykroyd (Pa Tex), Reba McEntire (Ma Tex).

In this not completely satisfying fantasy, Wood is the perfect son of imperfect parents Alexander and Louis-Dreyfus. He decides to leave them and seek out a more compatible family. Willis, appearing in a pink bunny suit, acts as Wood's guardian bunny and helps him discover what's really important.

2152. *Nostradamus* (1994, U.K./Germany, Orion Classics, 118m, c). D Roger Christian, P Edward Simons & Harold Reichebner, W Knut Boeser & Piers Ashworth (based on a story by Boeser, Ashworth & Christian), PH Denis Crossan, ED Alan Strachan, M Bar-rington Pheloung, PD Peter J. Hampton, AD Christian Nicul, SD Michael D. Ford.

LP Tcheky Karyo (Michel de Nostra-damus), F. Murray Abraham (Dr. Scalinger), Rutger Hauer (Mystic Monk), Amanda Plummer (Catherine de Medici), Julia Ormond (Marie), Assumpta Serna (Anne).

This story of the legendary medieval physician and seer is one long bore. Nostradamus' prophecies may still be of interest but this story of his life is not.

2153. *The Nostradamus Kid* (1995, Australia, LIVE Ent., 120m, c). D & W Bob Ellis, P Terry Jennings, PH Geoff Burton, ED Henry Dangar, M Chris Neal, PD Roger Ford, AD Laurie Faen.

LP Noah Taylor (Ken Elkin), Miranda Otto (Jennie O'Brien), Jack Campbell (McAllister), Erick Mitsak (Wayland), Alice Garner (Esther), Lucy Bell (Sarai), Arthur Dignam (Pastor Anderson).

In this funny story, Taylor, a religious Australian youth, is convinced the world is coming to an end. He hates to see this happen while he's still a virgin, so he sets out to do something about it — and he does, and does, and does…

2154. *Not Like Us* (1996, Concord-New Horizons, 86m, c). D David Payne, P Mike Elliott, W Daniella Purcell, PH Michael Mickens, ED Brian Katkin, M Tyler Bates, PD Nava, AD Kevin Mentzer.

LP Joanna Pacula (Anita Clark), Peter Onorati (Sam Clark), Rainer Grant (Janet Jones), Morgan Englund (John Jones), Billy Brunette (Jody), Annabelle Gurwitch (Vicki).

Roger Corman has never lost money by underestimating the taste of his audiences — but this one is pretty awful. It's about aliens who skin human beings in order to move around the earth without being noticed. Sure, most people have loose skin.

2155. *Not of This Earth* (1996, Concorde–New Horizons, 88m, c). D Terence H. Winkless, P Mike Elliott, W Charles Philip Moore (based on a screenplay by Charles B. Griffith & Mark Hanna), PH Philip Holahan, ED James Stellar, Jr., M Jeff Winkless, PD Nava, AD Aaron Mays.

LP Michael York (Paul Johnson), Parker Stevenson (Jack Sherbourne), Richard Belzer

(Jeremy Pallin), Elizabeth Barondes (Amanda Sayles), Ted Davis (Rodman Felder), Mason Adams (Dr. Rochelle).

By all appearances a human, York is actually an alien from a distant planet, sent to earth in search of a cure for a rare blood disease threatening the inhabitants of his world. Human blood seems to work.

2156. Not Without My Daughter (1991, MGM-Pathé, 114m, c). D Brian Gilbert, P Harry J. Ufland & Mary Jane Ufland, W David W. Rintels (based on the novel by Betty Mahmoody & William Hoffer), PH Peter Hannan, ED Terry Rawlings, M Jerry Goldsmith, PD Anthony Pratt, AD Desmond Crowe & Avi Avivi, SD Shlomo Zafir & Joe Litsch.

LP Sally Field (Betty Mahmoody), Alfred Molina (Moody), Sheila Rosenthal (Mahtob), Roshan Seth (Houssein), Sarah Badel (Nicole), Mony Rey (Ameh Bozorg), Georges Corraface (Mohsen).

This film is based on the true story of a Michigan housewife, played by Field, who travels with her Iranian husband Molina to his homeland for a visit. She finds he plans to relocate there, and makes her and her daughter virtual prisoners. She struggles to escape with her daughter back to the USA.

2157. Nothing But Trouble (1991, Warner Bros., 94m, c). D & W Dan Aykroyd (based on the story by Peter Aykroyd), P Robert K. Weiss, PH Dean Cundey, ED James Symons & Malcolm Campbell, M Michael Kamen, PD William Sandell, AD James Tocci, SD Michael Taylor.

LP Chevy Chase (Chris Thorne), Dan Aykroyd (J.P./Bobo), John Candy (Dennis/Eldona), Demi Moore (Diane Lightston), Taylor Negron (Fausto), Bertila Damas (Renalda).

Here is a weird comedy in which Chase, Moore and others are arrested in a remote area and are taken to a strange court with an even stranger judge, Aykroyd. His notion of justice and punishment is pretty extreme. There's a lot of comedic talent in the picture, but very little comedy.

2158. Nothing Personal (AKA: *All Our Fault*) (1995, Ireland/U.K., Trimark, 85m, c). D Thaddeus O'Sullivan, P Jonathan Cavendish & Tracey Seaward, W Daniel Mornin (based on his novel *All Our Fault*), PH Dick

Pope, ED Michael Parker, M Philip Appleby, PD Mark Geraghty, AD Fiona Daly.

LP John Lynch (Liam), Ian Hart (Ginger), James Frain (Kenny), Michael Gambon (Leonard), Maria Doyle Kennedy (Ann), Gary Lydon (Eddie), Ruaidhri Conroy (Tommy), Jeni Courtney (Katherine).

This film examines the human suffering in Belfast when a bombing escalates the hostility between terrorist factions.

2159. Nothing to Lose (1997, Touchstone-Buena Vista, 97m, c). D & W Steve Oedekerk, P Martin Bregman, Michael Bregman & Dan Jinks, PH Donald E. Thorin, ED Malcolm Campbell, M Robert Folk, PD Maria Caso, AD James J. Murakami & Kevin Constant, SD Cloudia.

LP Martin Lawrence (T. Paul), Tim Robbins (Nick Beam), John C. McGinley (Davis "Rig" Lanlow), Giancarlo Esposito (Charlie Dunt), Kelly Preston (Ann Beam), Michael McKean (Philip Barrow).

When ad exec Robbins comes home unexpectedly to find his wife Preston in the throes of passion with a lover, he goes into shock. He drives away. At a stop sign Lawrence jumps into the car intent on robbery. But he's picked the wrong guy on the wrong day. Robbins doesn't care if he lives or dies, and so begins a road comedy which should have been a lot funnier considering the talent of Lawrence and Robbins.

2160. Notting Hill (1999, U.K., Polygram/Universal, 123m, c). D Roger Michell, P Duncan Kenworthy, W Richard Curtis, PH Michael Coulter, ED Nick Moore, M Trevor Jones, PD Stuart Craig, AD Andrew Ackland-Snow & David Allday.

LP Julie Roberts (Anna Scott), Hugh Grant (William Thacker), Hugh Bonneville (Bernie), Emma Chambers (Honey), James Dreyfus (Martin), Rhys Ifans (Spike), Tim McInnerny (Max), Gina McKee (Bella).

In this delightful romantic comedy, Roberts is a world famous movie star. She is a prime target of the paparazzi because of her great looks, her legendary affairs with bad boyfriends and various facts and fictions about her love life, past and present. Grant is a low keyed London bookstore owner who has the good fortune to find himself bedding and loving the famous beauty — but then discovering he's not able to handle her fame and his new notoriety. In this modern fairytale Roberts appears at Grant's bookstore and dismisses her fame by telling him that she is just a girl standing before a boy asking him to love her. At that point one yearns for Grant to sweep her into his arms. The two stars are ably supported by a fine ensemble cast, with Ifans particularly noteworthy as Grant's peabrained flat mate.

2161.   The November Conspiracy   (1997, Miracon Pictures, 102m, c). D Conrad Janis, P Maria Janis, John Michaels & Tim Cooney, W Maria Grimm, PH Francis Mohajerin & Monty Rowan, ED John Orland, M Tony Humecke, PD W. Brooke Wheeler, AD Hayley Tolkin, SD Carrie Malandrino.

LP Paige Turco (Jenny Barron), Dirk Benedict (John Mackie), George Segal (Sen. Beau Ashton), Elliott Gould (Sen. George H. Kahn), Conrad Janis (Frank Donaldson), Bo Hopkins (Capt. Brogan), Lois Nettleton (Pigeon).

In this inept political thriller, reporter Turco seeks an interview with presidential contender Segal. At a rally Segal and his running mate Gould escape assassination at the hands of a gunman. Something doesn't quite ring true and our gal is going to straighten things out on her own.

2162.   November Men   (1994, Jaguar; Sun Lion Films, 100m, c). D Paul Williams, P Williams & Rodney Bryon Ellis, W James Andronica, PH Susan Emerson, ED Chip Brooks, M Scott Thomas Smith.

LP Paul Williams (Arthur Gwendolyn), Leslie Bevis (Elizabeth), James Andronica (Duggo), Beau Starr (Chief Agent Granger), Robert Davi (Himself), Coralissa Gines (Laura).

The film is a spoof of assassination and conspiracy theories, in this case involving a conspiracy to assassinate a Republican president.

2163.   Now and Then   (1995, New Line, 96m, c). D Lesli Linda Glatter, P Suzanne Todd & Demi Moore, W I. Marlene King, PH Ueli Steiger, ED Jacqueline Cambas, M Cliff Eidelman, AD Gershon Ginsburg, SD Anne Kuljian.

LP Demi Moore (Samantha Albertson), Melanie Griffith (Tina Tercell), Rosie O'Donnell (Roberta Martin), Rita Wilson (Christina Dewitt), Christina Ricci (Young Roberta), Thora Birch (Young Teeny), Gaby Hoffmann

(Young Samantha), Ashleigh Aston (Young Chrissy).

Four women gather for a reunion 25 years after their most eventful childhood summer to relive the good old days. The best part of the film is when we go back to that summer and experience it with the youngsters.

2164.   Nowhere   (1997, Fine Line, 85m, c). D & W Gregg Araki, P Araki & Andrea Sperling, PH Arturo Smith, ED Araki, PD Patti Podesta.

LP James Duval (Dark), Rachel True (Mel), Nathan Bexton (Montgomery), Chiara Mastroianni (Kriss), Debi Mazar (Kozy), Kathleen Robertson (Lucifer), Christina Applegate (Dingbat), Sarah Lassez (Egg).

To enjoy a film of Araki one needs a rather bizarre sense of humor. The film's main character, Duval, sums up things in the opening line: "L.A. is like nowhere — everybody who lives there is lost." Then for 85 minutes Araki shows how lost.

2165.   Nowhere to Run   (1993, Columbia, 94m, c). D Robert Harmon, P Craig Baumgarten & Gary Adelson, W Joe Eszterhas, Leslie Bohem & Randy Feldman (based on a story by Eszterhas & Richard Marquand), PH David Gribble, Douglas Milsome & Michael A. Benson, ED Zach Staenberg & Mark Helfrich, M Mark Isham, PD Dennis Washington, AD Joseph P. Lucky, SD Anne McCulley & Richard McKenzie.

LP Jean-Claude Van Damme (Sam), Roseanna Arquette (Clydie), Kieran Culkin (Mookie), Ted Levine (Mr. Dunston), Joss Ackland (Franklin Hale), Tiffany Taubman (Bree), Edward Blatchford (Lennie).

Lonely and lovely widow Arquette is about to lose her farm to the bank. To the rescue comes escaped con Van Damme, who kicks some sense into the bankers.

2166.   Nuns on the Run   (1990, G.B., Handmade–20th Century–Fox, 90m, c). D & W Jonathan Lynn, P Michael White, Ph Michael Garfath, ED David Martin, M Yello & Hidden Faces, PD Simon Holland, AD Clinton Cavers, SD Michael Seirton.

LP Eric Idle (Brian Hope), Robbie Coltrane (Charlie McManus), Camille Coduri (Faith), Janet Suzman (Sister Superior), Doris Hare (Sister Mary of the Sacred Heart), Lila Kaye

(Sister Many of the Annunciation), Robert Patterson ("Case" Casey).

It's a Monty Python–like farce, with Idle and Coltrane as two members of a robbery gang who double-cross their vicious boss Patterson. To escape his wrath they disguise themselves as nuns at a Catholic school for girls — rather mature girls, as it turns out. It's a one- joke slapstick, but the two leads make the most of it.

2167. *The Nutcracker Prince* (1990, Canada, Warner Bros., 75m, c). D Paul Schibli, P Kevin Gillis, W Patricia Watson & E.T.A. Hoffman, AD Peter Moehrle.

LP Voices: Peter O'Toole (Pantaloon), Kiefer Sutherland (Nutcracker/Hans), Megan Follows (Clara), Michael MacDonald (Mouseking), Noam Zylberman (Fritz), Peter Boretski (Uncle Drosselmeier).

It's a feature-length animation film of the classical Christmas tale.

2168. *The Nutty Professor* (1996, Universal, 95m, c). D Tom Shadyac, P Brian Grazer & Russell Simmons, W David Sheffield, Barry W. Blaustein, Shadyac & Steve Oedekerk (based on the film written by Jerry Lewis & Bill Richmond), PH Julio Macat, ED Don Zimmerman, M David Newman, PD William Elliott, AD Greg Papalia, SD Kathryn Peters.

LP Eddie Murphy (Sherman Klump/Buddy Love/Lance Perkins/Papa Klump/Mama Klump/ Grandma Klump/Ernie Klump), Jada Pinkett (Carla Purty), James Coburn (Harlan Hartley), Larry Miller (Dean Richmond), Dave Chappelle (Reggie Warrington), John Ales (Jason).

In this remake of Jerry Lewis' 1963 comedy, Murphy portrays an obese, bright and sensitive professor who meets Pinkett, the woman of his dreams. He sees nothing coming of it because of his weight. He slugs down his own secret potion that transforms him into a slim and cocky Murphy, which we all know — and some love. Those who thought Lewis was masterful in the original won't care for the remake and those who never cared much for Lewis will see no need for a remake — unless they find appealing the notion of a family of hefty slobs, all played by Murphy, competing in breaking wind.

2169. *The Object of Beauty* (1991, Avenue Ent., 101m, c). D & W Michael Lindsay-

Hogg, P Jon S. Denny, PH David Watkin, ED Ruth Foster, M Tom Bahler, PD Derek Dodd.

LP John Malkovich (Jake), Andie MacDowell (Tina), Lolita Davidovich (Joan), Rudi Davies (Jenny), Joss Ackland (Mr. Mercer), Bill Paterson (Victor Swayle), Ricci Harnett (Steve), Peter Riegert (Larry).

Low on money in London, Jet-setters Malkovich and MacDowell decide to sell their prize possession, a tiny Henry Moore sculpture. When it disappears, so does their relationship. It's an inconsistent comedy, which perhaps might have been better handled by different leads.

2170. *The Object of My Affection* (1998, 20th Century–Fox, 112m, c). D Nicholas Hytner, P Laurence Mark, W Wendy Wasserstein (based on the novel by Stephen McCauley), PH Oliver Stapleton, ED Tariq Anwar, M George Fenton, PD Jane Musky, AD Patricia Woodbridge, SD Susan Bode.

LP Jennifer Aniston (Nina Borowski), Paul Rudd (George Hanson), Alan Alda (Sidney Miller), Nigel Hawthorne (Rodney Fraser), John Pankow (Vince McBride), Tim Daly (Dr. Robert Joely), Allison Janney (Constance Miller).

Aniston is none too happy with her relationship with boyfriend Pankow. She offers solace and a room in her Brooklyn walk-up to gay Rudd when he is dumped by his lover Daly. The two sort of fall in love.

2171. *Occasional Coarse Language* (1998, Australia, Village Roadshow–Flickering Films, 81m, c). D & W Brad Hayward, P Trish Piper, PH John Biggins, ED Simon Martin, PD Rebecca Barry, AD Madeleine Hetherton.

LP Sara Browne (Min), Astrid Grant (Jaz), Nicholas Bishop (David), Michael Walker (Stanley), Lisa Denmeade (Claire), Michelle Fillery (Alex), Belinda Hoare (Soph).

This dramatic comedy has barely enough plot to make much of the lifestyles of two 21-year-old women living in the suburbs of Sydney. Browne's life is a mess when Grant suggests they share a room and help each other get over unhappy relationships.

2172. *October Sky* (1999, Universal, 108m, c). D Joe Johnston, P Charles Gordon & Larry Franco, W Lewis Colick (based on the book *Rocket Boys* by Homer H. Hickam, Jr.),

PH Fred Murphy, ED Robert Dalva, M Mark Isham, PD Barry Robison, AD Tony Fanning.

LP Jake Gyllenhaal (Homer Hickam), Chris Cooper (John Hickam), Laura Dern (Miss Riley), Chris Owen (Quentin), William Lee Scott (Roy Lee), Chad Lindberg (O'Dell).

This is the story of Homer Hickam, Jr., who grew up to become a NASA engineer. As a youth in 1957, the announcement of the launching of Sputnik had quite an effect on Hickam, played by Gyllenhaal, and his buddies. He began to read everything he could get his hands on about rockets. Encouraged by helpful teacher Dern, and despite the opposition of his coal miner father Cooper, Gyllenhaal and a few buddies experiment with producing rockets of their own, becoming the "rocket boys." Those who recall with amazement the launch of Sputnik and the promise it seemed to offer the world can identify with these lads. Others who came later will discover that this taut, well-acted film is a winner.

2173. The Odd Couple II (AKA: *Neil Simon's the Odd Couple II*) (1998, Paramount, 96m, c). D Howard Deutch, P Neil Simon, Robert W. Cort & David Madden, W Simon, PH Jamie Anderson, ED Seth Flaum, M Alan Silvestri, PD Dan Bishop.

LP Jack Lemmon (Felix Unger), Walter Matthau (Oscar Madison), Christine Baranski (Thelma), Barnard Hughes (Beaumont), Jonathan Silverman (Brucey Madison), Jean Smart (Holly), Lisa Waltz (Hannah Unger).

Right from their first film together Lemmon and Matthau just seemed to click. Thus the fact that this film is such a dud must be laid at the feet of Simon, who may have demonstrated once again the wisdom that "you can't go home again." Thirty years have passed in the lives of Felix and Oscar, but it hasn't changed their personalities much. They find themselves on the road together when their children Waltz and Silverman decide to marry each other. The "grumpy old men" need more to work with than what Simon gives them.

2174. Of Mice and Men (1992, MGM, 110m, c). D Gary Sinise, P Russ Smith, W Horton Foote (based on the novel by John Steinbeck), PH Kenneth MacMillan, ED Robert L. Sinise, M Mark Isham, PD David Gropman, AD Dan Davis, SD Karen Schulz & Anne Gilstrap.

LP John Malkovich (Lennie), Gary Sinise (George), Ray Walston (Candy), Casey Siemaszko (Curley), Sherilyn Fenn (Curley's Wife), John Terry (Slim), Richard Riehle (Carlson), Joe Morton (Crooks), Noble Willingham (The Boss).

This version of John Steinbeck's story is a quite decent remake of the classic 1939 version starring Burgess Meredith as George and Lon Chaney, Jr., as Lennie. Malkovich is a lumbering man, strong of body, weak of mind. His companion Sinise does his best to watch after him. But when the big simpleton accidentally kills Fenn, the wife of the boss' son, he's forced to treat his friend like a poor old dog whose life is over.

2175. Office Killer (1997, Strand Releasing, 81m, c). D Cindy Sherman, P Christine Vachon & Pamela Koffler, W Elise MacAdam & Tom Kalin (based on a story by Sherman & MacAdam), PH Russell Fine, ED Merril Stern, M Evan Lurie, PD Kevin Thompson, AD Ford Wheeler, SD Amy Silver.

LP Carol Kane (Dorine Douglas), Molly Ringwald (Kim Poole), Jeanne Tripplehorn (Norah Reed), Barbara Sukowa (Virginia Wingate), Michael Imperioli (Daniel Birch), David Thornton (Gary Michaels), Mike Hodge (Mr. Landau).

After accidentally killing her boss, mousy misfit Kane begins collecting bodies, killing anyone from her office who crosses her. This first film directed by photographer Cindy Sherman has some startling visual effects. Kane, in her way, is funny and appealing, as well as dangerous, but the story just doesn't work.

2176. Office Space (1999, 20th Century-Fox, 89m, c). D & W Mike Judge, P Michael Rotenberg & Daniel Rappaport, PH Tim Suhrstedt, ED David Rennie, M John Frizzell, PD Edward McAvoy, AD Adele Plauche.

LP Ron Livingston (Peter Gibbons), Jennifer Aniston (Joanne), David Herman (Michael Bolton), Ajay Naidu (Samir), Diedrich Bader (Lawrence).

Computer programmer Livingston hates everything about his job. He seeks help from an "occupational hypnotherapist," who helps change Livingston's attitude towards the rat race. The hypnotist dies before he can revive his patient from an attitude adjusting trance.

The young man ceases to concern himself with his job, doing just about anything he pleases. Among his allies in his new way of looking at things is waitress Aniston, who has her own problems with work.

2177. *Oh, What a Night* (1992, Canada, Comfort Creek Prods., 93m, c). D Eric Till, P Peter R. Simpson, W Richard Nielsen, PH Brian Hebb, ED Susan Shipton, M Ian Thomas, AD David Moe.

LP Corey Haim (Eric), Robbie Coltrane (Todd), Barbara Williams (Vera), Keir Dullea (Thorvald), Genevieve Bujold (Eva), Andrew Miller (Donald).

Still trying to cope with the death of his mother, 17-year-old Haim moves with his father and stepmother to a chicken farm in Ontario in 1955. He falls in love with Williams, an older married woman with two kids. It's a bittersweet tale of coming of age.

2178. *Old Explorers* (1991, Taurus Ent., 91m, c). D William M. Pohlad, P & W David P. Herbert & Pohlad (based on the play by James Cada & Mark Keller), PH Jeffrey Laszlo, ED Miroslav Janek, M Billy Barber, PD Peter Stolz, SD Lisa Duckler.

LP Jose Ferrer (Warner Watney), James Whitmore (Leinen Roth), Jeffrey Gadbois (Alex Watney), Caroline Kaiser (Leslie Watney), William Warfield (Tugboat Captain).

Ferrer and Whitmore may be old, but they don't allow that to keep them from a full, exciting life. They regularly get together to set out on dangerous, imaginary adventures. After one suffers a stroke, they set out on a real-life adventure on a tugboat cruising down the Mississippi River.

2179. *Oleanna* (1994, U.S./U.K., Samuel Goldwyn Co., 90m, c). D & W David Mamet (based on his play), P Patricia Wolf & Sarah Green, PH Andrzej Sekula, ED Barbara Tulliver, M Rebecca Pidgeon, PD David Wasco & Sandy Reynolds Wasco, SD Kate Conklin.

LP William H. Macy (John), Debra Eisenstadt (Carol).

We could never figure out exactly how Macy was harassing Eisenstadt — unless it be by talking her to death. Mamet's two-person play is about a professor whose life is already in an uproar of uncertainty when a female student with problems of her own accuses him of sexual harassment. The accusation couldn't come at a worse time; he's being considered for tenure and trying to buy a house. It distracts from the story to find that Macy, a non-tenured assistant professor, not only has a mammoth private office with built-in book cases but also an adjoining conference room. We don't know any professor with such a sweet deal, tenured or not, full professor or otherwise.

2180. *On Deadly Ground* (1994, Warner Bros., 108m, c). D Steven Seagal, P Seagal, Julius R. Nasso & A. Kitman Ho, W Ed Horowitz & Robin U. Russin, PH Ric Waite, Ed Robert A. Ferretti & Don Brochu, M Basil Poledouris, PD William Ladd Skinner, AD Lou Montejeno, SD John Anderson & Ronald R. Reiss.

LP Steven Seagal (Forrest Taft), Michael Caine (Michael Jennings), Joan Chen (Masu), John C. McGinley (MacGruder), R. Lee Ermey (Stone), Shari Shattuck (Liles), Billy Bob Thornton (Homer Carlton).

Seagal brings all of his self-righteous machismo to kicking the hell out of the plans of oil tycoon Caine, preventing him from raping the interior of Alaska and unleashing an ecological disaster.

2181. *On the Block* (1991, Vidmark Ent., 95m, c). D Steve Yeager, P Yeager & Manuel Cabrera-Santos, W Yeager & Linda Chambers, PH Erich Roland, ED Yeager, M Charlie Barnett, AD Barbara Talbot.

LP Howard E. Rollins, Jr. (Clay Beasley), Blaze Starr (Herself), Marilyn Jones (Libby), Jerry Whiddon (Lt. Tom Rucci), Michael Gabel (Hugo), Erika Bogren (Mimi).

The "workers" in some Baltimore strip joints find their livelihood threatened by a greedy land developer.

2182. *Once Around* (1991, Universal, 115m, c). D Lasse Hallstrom, P Griffin Dunne & Amy Robinson, W Malia Scotch Marmo & Hallstrom, PH Theo Van De Sande, ED Andrew Mondshein, M James Horner, PD David Gropman, AD Dan Davis, Michael Foxworthy & Gretchen Rau.

LP Richard Dreyfuss (Sam Sharpe), Holly Hunter (Renata Bella), Danny Aiello (Joe Bella), Laura San Giacomo (Jan Bella), Gena Rowlands (Marilyn Bella), Roxanne Hart (Gail Bella), Danton Stone (Tony Bella).

Hunter is a loser in the sea of love until she meets cocky salesman Dreyfuss, who sweeps her off her feet. He tries hard, way too hard, to ingratiate himself with her close-knit Italian family. The film should have been better than it is, considering the cast, but despite some hilarious moments, it disappoints.

2183. *Once Upon a Crime* (1992, MGM, 100m, c). D Eugene Levy, P Dino De Laurentiis, W Charles Shyer, Nancy Meyers, Steve Kluger, Rodolfo Sonego, Giorgio Arlorio, Stefano Strucchi & Vincenzoni (based on Sonego's story), PH Giuseppe Rotunno, ED Patrick Kennedy, M Richard Gibbs, PD Pier Luigi Basile, SD Gianfranco Fumagalli.

LP John Candy (Augie Morosco), James Belushi (Neil Schwary), Cybill Shepherd (Marilyn Schwary), Sean Young (Phoebe), Richard Lewis (Julian Peters), Ornella Muti (Elena Morosco), Giancarlo Giannini (Inspector Bonnard), George Hamilton (Alfonso de la Pena).

In this mishmash masquerading as an all-star comedy, a bunch of strangers traveling through Europe become involved with a murder and a stray dachshund. Everyone in the cast is over-the-top and seems to believe being as loud as possible will pass for humor. No way!

2184. *Once Upon a Forest* (1993, Hanna-Barbera Prods.–20th Century–Fox, 72m, c). D Charles Grosvenor, P David Kirschner & Jerry Mills, W Mark Young & Kelly Ward, M James Horner, AD Carol Holman Grosvenor, ANIM Dave Michener.

LP Voices: Michael Crawford (Cornelius the Badger), Ben Vereen (Phineas), Ellen Blain (Abigail), Ben Gregory (Edgar), Paige Gosney Russell), Elisabeth Moss (Michelle).

It's an animated story of three woodland friends who desperately seek a cure for a friend who has become ill from breathing fumes at a chemical spill. It has a message of environmental awareness but it may be just too gloomy for family entertainment.

2185. *Once Upon a Time ... When We Were Colored* (1996, IRS Releasing, 113m, c). D Tim Reid, P Reid & Michael Bennett, W Paul W. Cooper (based on the book by Clinton Taulbert), PH John Simmons, ED David Pincus, M Steve Tyrell, PD Michael

Clausen, AD Geoffrey S. Grimsman, SD Kristen McGary.

LP Al Freeman, Jr. (Poppa), Phylicia Rashad (Ma Ponk), Leon Robinson (Uncle Melvin), Paula Kelly (Mama Pearl), Salli Richardson (Miss Alice), Anna Maria Horsford (Miss Annie), Bernie Casey (Mr. Walter), Isaac Hayes (Preacher Hurn), Richard Roundtree (Cleve), Polly Bergin (Miss Maybry).

This very fine film is based on the memories of writer Taulbert of his Mississippi childhood in the years between WWII and the start of the Civil Rights movement. It's perhaps a bit schmaltzy, but it's good family fare with outstanding performances from the large cast.

2186. *Once Were Warriors* (1995, New Zealand, Fine Line, 99m, c). D Lee Tamahori, P Robin Scholes, W Riwia Brown (based on the novel by Alan Duff), PH Stuart Dryburgh, ED Michael Horton, M Murray Grindlay & Murray McNabb, PD Michael Kane, AD Shayne Radford.

LP Rena Owen (Beth Heke), Temuera Morrison (Jake Heke), Mamaengaroa Kerr-Bell (Grace Heke), Julian Arahanga (Nig Heke), Taungaroa Emile (Boogie Heke), Rachel Morris, Jr. (Polly Heke), Joseph Kairau (Huata Heke).

A poor urbanized Maroi family is held together only due to the strength of feisty mother Owen. She comes to the realization that she can no longer endure the psychological and physical abuse of her out-of-work, boozing husband. It is a powerful story with fine performances all around, but most especially that of Owen.

2187. *One Crazy Night* (1993, Australia, Trimark, 92m, c). D & P Michael Pattison, W Jan Sardi, PH David Connell, ED Peter Carrodus, M David Dobbyn.

LP Noah Taylor (Randolph), Beth Champion (Emily), Danni Minogue (Didi), Malcolm Kennard (Danny), Willa O'Neill (Vicki).

When five Melbourne teenagers crash a hotel where the Beatles are staying they become trapped in the basement. There they spend the time swapping secrets.

2188. *187* (AKA: *One Eight Seven*) (1997, Warner Bros., 116m, c). D Kevin Reynolds, P Bruce Davey & Stephen McEveety, W Scott Yagemann, PH Ericson Core, ED Stephen

Semel, PD Stephen Storer, AD Mark Zuelzke, SD Marcia Calosio.

LP Samuel L. Jackson (Trevor Garfield), John Heard (Dave Childress), Kelly Rowan (Ellen Henry), Clifton Gonzalez Gonzalez (Cesar), Tony Plana (Garcia), Karina Arroyave (Rita), Jonah Rooney (Steve Middleton).

The number 187 is the police codeword for homicide. Bedford- Stuyvesant science teacher Jackson finds "187" scrawled with a marker on page after page of his textbook. He knows he's in trouble. A thuggish student stabs but does not kill him. After a period of physical recovery, Jackson is now a substitute teacher in the barrio of East L.A., where the students are no less dangerous. The film gives graphic evidence of how much more dangerous it is for teachers to try to do their jobs than it was in *The Blackboard Jungle* of 1955.

2189. *One False Move* (1992, IRA Media, 105m, c). D Carl Franklin, P Jesse Beaton & Ben Myron, W Billy Bob Thornton & Tom Epperson, PH James L. Carter, ED Carole Kravitz, M Peter Haycock & Derek Holt, PD Gary T. New, AD Dana Torrey, SD Troy Mycrs.

LP Cynda Williams (Fantasia/Lila), Bill Paxton (Dale "Hurricane" Dixon), Billy Bob Thornton (Ray Malcolm), Jim Metzler (Dud Cole), Michael Beach (Pluto), Earl Billings (McFeely).

Thornton, Beach and Williams are poor-trash, low-level drug dealers in L.A. When things get too hot for them, they take off for Dirt Road, Arkansas. There they must cope with the local sheriff and two L.A. cops sent after them.

2190. *One Fine Day* (1996, 20th Century–Fox, 108m, c). D Michael Hoffman, P Lynda Obst, W Terrel Seltzer & Ellen Simon, PH Oliver Stapleton, ED Garth Craven, M James Newman Howard, PD David Gropman, AD John Warnke, SD Anne Kuljian.

LP Michelle Pfeiffer (Melanie Parker), George Clooney (Jack Taylor), Mae Whitman (Maggie), Alex D. Linz (Sammy), Charles Durning (Lew), Holland Taylor (Rita), Jon Robin Baitz (Yates, Jr.), Ellen Greene (Elaine Lieberman), Joe Grifasi (Manny Feinstein).

Single parents Pfeiffer and Clooney are thrown together during a hectic work day for both. Of necessity they must watch over each other's kids at different times during the day. Sure, they fall in love. What did you expect?

2191. *One Good Cop* (1991, Hollywood–Buena Vista, 107m, c). D & W Heywood Gould, P Laurence Mark, PH Ralf Bode, ED Richard Marks, M William Ross, PD Sandy Veneziano, AD Daniel E. Maltese, SD John H. Anderson.

LP Michael Keaton (Artie Lewis), Rene Russo (Rita Lewis), Anthony LaPaglia (Stevie Diroma), Kevin Conway (Lt. Danny Quinn), Rachel Ticotin (Grace), Tony Plana (Beniamino).

When his partner is killed in a shoot-out with a drug-crazed killer, young officer Keaton and his wife Russo adopt the deceased's three young daughters. Keaton gets the opportunity to enact some revenge.

2192. *One Good Turn* (1996, First Look Pictures, 90m, c). D Tony Randel, P Zane W. Levitt & Mark Yellen, W Jim Piddock, PH Jacques Haitkin, ED Kevin Tent, M Joel Goldsmith, PD Carol Strober, SD Traci Kirshbaum.

LP James Remar (Simon), Suzy Amis (Laura), Lenny Von Dohlen (Matt), John Savage (Santapietro), Richard Minchenberg (John), Audie England (Kristen).

Van Dohlen allows Remar, a man who had saved his life twelve years earlier, to stay in his home. He doesn't realize that Remar has been carrying a grudge all this time and is about to do something about it.

2193. *100 Proof* (1997, Mammoth Pictures, 94m, c). D & W Jeremy Horton, P George Maranville, PH Harold Jarboe, ED Maranville, M Michael Mosier, PD Patrick McNeese, AD Mike Brower.

LP Pamela Holden Stewart (Rae), Tara Bellando (Carla), Jack Stubblefield (Arco), Minnie Bates (Sissy), Larry Brown (Eddie), Kevin Hardesty (Roger), Jim Varney (Rae's Father).

In this extremely low budget film, Stewart and Bellando steal some money from the elderly man they care for in order to buy liquor and drugs. Thus begins their hellish adventure as female outlaws.

2194. *101 Dalmatians* (1996, Walt Disney–Buena Vista, 103m, c). D Stephen Herek,

P John Hughes & Ricardo Mestres, W Hughes (based on the novel by Dodie Smith), PH Adrian Biddle, ED Trudy Ship, M Michael Kamen, PD Assheton Gorton, AD Alan Tompkins & John Ralph, SD Joanne Woollard.

LP Glenn Close (Cruella DeVil), Jeff Daniels (Roger), Joely Richardson (Anita), Joan Plowright (Nanny), Hugh Laurie (Jasper), Mark Williams (Horace), John Shrapnel (Skinner).

If it weren't for Close's over-the-top performance, this remake of the Disney animated film of 1961 would be totally redundant. In fact, even with her ranting and raving it's hard to make a case that another version of the story of a ruthless woman who wants the pelts of a bunch of poor dogs for her fur fashion house is needed.

2195. *One Last Run* (1992, Prism Ent., 82m, c). D, P & W Peter Winograd & Glenn Gebhard, PH Thomasy Callaway, ED Tim Huntley, PD Virginia Lee.

LP Tracy Scoggins (Cindy), Nels Van Patten (Charlie), Ashley Laurence Jane), Craig Branham (Tom), Jimmy Aleck (Joe), Franz Weber (Franz), Chuck Conners (Buddy).

This film is only for skiing enthusiasts — and only those among them who do not insist on story and character development. A group of people deal with their troubles through some risky skiing stunts.

2196. *One Man's Hero* (1999, MGM–Orion Pictures, 121m, c). D Lance Hool, P Hool & William J. Macdonald, W Milton S. Gelman, PH Joao Fernandez, ED Mark Conte, M Ernest Troost, PD Peter Wooley, AD Hector Romero, SD Enrique Estevez.

LP Tom Berenger (John Riley), Joaquim De Almeida (Cortina), Daniela Romo (Marta), Mark Moses (Col. Benton Lacey), Stuart Graham (Cpl. Kennedy), James Gammon (Gen. Zachary Taylor), Stephen Tobolowsky (Capt. Gaine), Carlos Carrasco (Dominguez), Patrick Bergin (Gen. Winfield Scott).

Irish recruits, who have left Ireland to escape the potato famine, are punished for exercising their religious convictions by anti–Catholic officers. Army lifer Berenger finally intervenes when his men are to be unfairly punished, and leads them into Mexico to fight on the side of the Mexican army during the 1840s.

2197. *One Man's Justice* (1996, LIVE Ent., 100m, c). D Kurt Wimmer, P William Webb, W Steven Selling, PH Jurgen Baum & John Huneck, ED Michael Thibault, M Anthony Marinelli, PD Terri Schaetzle, AD Lece Edwards-Bonilla, SD Courtney Jackson.

LP Brian Bosworth (John North), Bruce Payne (Karl Savak), Jeff Kober (Marcus), Dejuan Guy (Mickey), M.C. Hammer (Dexter Kane).

Former pro football player Bosworth is an army drill sergeant who heads for Venice, California, to take revenge for the death of his wife and daughter, killed by a scummy drug dealer.

2198. *One Night Stand* (1997, New Line, 103m, c). D & W Mike Figgis, P Figgis, Annie Stewart & Ben Myron, PH Declan Quinn, ED John Smith, M Figgis, PD Waldemar Kalinowski, AD Barry Kingston, SD Florence Fellman.

LP Wesley Snipes (Max Carlyle), Natassja Kinski (Karen), Robert Downey, Jr. (Charlie), Ming-Na Wen (Mimi Carlyle), Kyle MacLachlan (Vernon), Glenn Plummer (George), Amanda Donohoe (Margaux).

While in New York City to visit his HIV-positive friend Downey, commercial director Snipes finds himself trapped in the city. There he has a one night stand with Kinski. Back home in L.A. his wife Ming-Na Wen, who is into wild, rough sex, suspects him of infidelity. About a year later Snipes is back in New York to be with Downey, who is now near death. After Downey's death, Snipes pursues Kinski, who just happens to be Downey's sister-in-law. When they sneak away to have sex, who should they find doing the same thing but his wife and Natassja's husband MacLachlan. What does it all mean? Your guess is as good as ours.

2199. *One Tough Cop* (1998, Patriot Pictures, 90m, c). D Bruno Barreto, P Michael Bregman & Martin Bregman, W Jeremy Iacone (based on the novel by Bo Dietl), PH Ron Fortunato, ED Ray Hubley, M Bruce Broughton, PD Perri Gorrara, SD Megan Less & Lisa Nilsson.

LP Stephen Baldwin (Bo Dietl), Chris Penn (Duke Finnerty), Mike McGlone (Richie La Cassa), Gina Gershon (Joey O'Hara), Paul Guilfoyle (Frankie "Hot" Salvano), Amy Irving (FBI Agent Jean Devlin).

New York policeman Baldwin is a take-no-prisoners type of cop. Similar behavior forced the real Dietl to retire at 35. In the film, he and his hard-drinking, hot-headed partner Penn investigate the rape and mutilation of a nun near her Harlem convent school.

2200. *One True Thing* (1998, Universal, 127m, c). D Carl Franklin, P Harry Ufland & Jesse Beaton, W Karen Croner (based on the novel by Anna Quindlen), PH Declan Quinn, ED Carole Kravetz, M Cliff Eidelman, PD Paul Peters, AD Jefferson Sage, SD Leslie A. Pope & Elaine O'Donnell.

LP Meryl Streep† (Kate Gulden), Renee Zellweger (Ellen Gulden), William Hurt (George Gulden), Tom Everett Scott (Brian Gulden), Lauren Graham (Jules), Nicky Katt (Jordan Belzer).

In 1987–88, recent Harvard grad Zellweger is trying to make a name for herself with a major investigative story for *New York* magazine. She hears from her father Hurt that her mother Streep must undergo cancer surgery, and Zellweger is needed back home to care for her mother. She reluctantly agrees but insists she will continue to work on her article. The problem is that Streep and Zellweger have never gotten along, and the former's illness hasn't changed the situation. In what would seem to be the family's last holidays together, Zellweger begins to see things in a different light. Despite the subject, the film is not morbid. Streep and Zellweger really sell the story.

2201. *Onegin* (1999, U.K., Seven Arts Intl., 106m, c). D Martha Fiennes, P Ileen Maisel & Simon Bosanquet, W Peter Ettedgui & Michael Ignatieff (based on the verse novel by Aleksandr Pushkin), PH Remi Adefarasin, ED Jim Clark, M Magnus Fiennes, PD Jim Clay, AD Chris Seagers & Vera Zeliskaya.

LP Ralph Fiennes (Evgeny Onegin), Liv Tyler (Tatyana Larin), Toby Stephens (Vladimir Lensky), Lena Headey (Olga Larin), Martin Donovan (Prince Nikitin), Alum Armstrong (Zaretsky), Harriet Walter (Mme. Larina), Irene Worth (Princess Alina).

First of all, this is a pretty picture and cinematographer Adefarasin should be asked to take a bow. Martha Fiennes does a very credible job directing older brother Ralph as a bored and weary 1820s St. Petersburg socialite. When he inherits a country estate, he makes the acquaintance of his neighbors and is intrigued by the lovely Tyler. She is more than smitten with him, finding him a breath of fresh air and sophistication come into her life. Shall they ride off in a troika into a winter sunset and be eternally happy? Of course not, this is a Russian story. Expect disastrous results due to the fact that Fiennes is late coming to the realization that he loves Tyler.

2202. *Only the Brave* (1995, Australia, First Run Features, 62m, c). D Ana Kokkinos, P Fiona Eagger, W Kokkinos & Mira Robertson, PH James Grant, ED Mark Atkin, M Philip Brophy, AD Georgina Campbell.

LP Elena Mandalis (Alex), Dora Kaskanis (Vicki), Maude Davey (Kate Groves), Helen Athanasiadis (Maria), Tina Zerella (Sylvie), Bob Bright (Reg).

Teenage working class girls Mandalis and Kaskanis live in the shadow of an Australian oil refinery. They spend most of their time hanging out, smoking dope and getting in trouble. And, oh yes, Mandalis comes to realize that her feelings for Kaskanis are sexual.

2203. *Only the Lonely* (1991, 20th Century-Fox, 105m, c). D & W Chris Columbus, P John Hughes & Hunt Lowry, PH Julio Macat, ED Raja Gosnell & Peter Teschner, M Maurice Jarre, PD John Muto, AD Dan Webster, SD Rosemary Brandenburg.

LP John Candy (Danny Muldoon), Maureen O'Hara (Rose Muldoon), Ally Sheedy (Theresa Luna), Kevin Dunn (Patrick), Milo O'Shea (Doyle), Bert Remsen (Spats), Anthony Quinn (Nick), James Belushi (Sal), Joe V. Greco (Johnny Luna), Marvin J. McIntyre (Father Strapovic).

The best thing about this story of Chicago cop Candy is the return to the screen of O'Hara, looking just as beautiful as ever. Candy is so under the thumb of his domineering mother that he can't make any progress in his romance with mortician's beautician Sheedy. As mom, O'Hara considers herself candid, but she is often merely cruel. Another old timer, Quinn, offers her his love but she's not too interested. He seems to thrive on her indifference and verbal abuse.

2204. *The Only Thrill* (1998, Galley Motion Pictures–Moonstone Ent., 103m, c). D Peter Masterson, P Yael Stroh, James Holt &

Gabriel Grunfeld, W Larry Ketron (based on his play *The Hitching Post*), PH Don E. Fauntleroy, ED Jeff Freeman, M Peter Rodgers Melnick, PD John Frick.

LP Diane Keaton (Carol Fitzsimmons), Sam Shepard (Reece McHenry), Diane Lane (Katherine Fitzsimmons), Robert Patrick (Tom McHenry), Sharon Lawrence (Joleen Quillet), Stacey Travis (Lola Jennings), Tate Donovan (Eddie).

When widow Keaton arrives in a 1966 Texas town, she is hired by Shepard, who runs a used clothes store. They begin an affair, but since his wife lies in a coma from which she can never recover, he feels he can't make a commitment. Years later, Keaton's daughter Lane falls in love with Shepard's son Patrick. Still, little has changed in the relationship of Keaton and Shepard. Finally, Keaton decides to move to Canada to be with her terminally ill sister. Shepard is stunned but doesn't try to stop her. They will meet again in 1990, and once more in 1996. Will they ever get together permanently? No.

2205.   Only You   (1994, TriStar, 108m, c). D Norman Jewison, P Jewison, Cary Woods, Robert N. Freid & Charles Mulvehill, W Diane Drake, PH Sven Nykvist, ED Stephen Rivkin, M Rachel Portman, PD Luciana Arrighi, AD Stephano Ortolani, Maria Teresa Barbasso & Gary Kosko, SD Ian Whittaker, Alessandra Querzola & Diana Stoughton.

LP Marisa Tomei (Faith), Robert Downey, Jr. (Peter), Bonnie Hunt (Kate), Joaquim de Almeida (Giovanni), Fisher Stevens (Larry), Billy Zane (The False Damon Bradley), Adam LeFevre (Damon Bradley).

As a child, Tomei's character learned from a Ouija board that she was destined to marry a man named Damon Bradley. Twenty years later she still hasn't come across Bradley. Just when she's about to marry boring podiatrist Stevens, one of his old friends calls to say he can't attend the wedding because he must fly to Venice. His name — Damon Bradley. Tomei is off like a flash for Venice, and finds her man has left for Rome. She follows, and when she loses a shoe, it is retrieved by Downey who, upon hearing of her quest, announces that he is Bradley. A fine romance between the two seems in the offing, but then he must reveal that he's not really Bradley. He offers to help Tomei find the elusive man of her dreams who

is reported to have gone to Positano. Sure enough, there he is, in the person of Zane, as handsome as she had hoped. But before long she discovers he's a real bore and a lout. Looks like Downey may not be Mr. Bradley, but he *is* Mr. Right.

2206.   Operation Dumbo Drop   (1995, Walt Disney–Buena Vista, 108m, c). D Simon Wincer, P David Madden & Diane Nabatoff, W Jim Kouf, Graham Yost & Gene Quintano (based on a story by Jim Morris), PH Russell Boyd, ED O. Nicholas Brown, M David Newman, PD Paul Peters, AD Lisette Thomas & Steve Spence, SD Jim Erickson.

LP Danny Glover (Captain Sam Cahill), Ray Liotta (Captain T.C. Doyle), Denis Leary (David Poole), Doug E. Doug (Harvey "H.A." Ashford), Corin Nemec (Lawrence Farley), Dinh Thien Le (Linh), Tcheky Karyo (Goddard).

When Liotta takes over a group of commandos from Glover, an elephant vital to the economy of a Vietnamese village is killed. The two Green Berets promise a replacement. Keeping their promise is a major task, and the two learn much more about elephants than they ever wanted to know.

2207.   Opportunity Knocks   (1990, Universal, 105m, c). D Donald Petrie, P Mark R. Gordon & Christopher Meledandri, W Mitchel Katlin & Nat Bernstein, PH Steven Poster, ED Marion Rothman, M Miles Goodman, PD Tim Sexton, AD Leslie A. Pope, SD Derek Hill.

LP Dana Carvey (Eddie Farrell), Robert Loggia (Milt Malkin), Todd Graff (Lou Pasquino), Julia Campbell (Annie Malkin), Milo O'Shea (Max), James Tolkan (Sal Nichols), Doris Belack (Mona).

While hiding from a vengeful gangster, con man Carvey convinces a rich suburban family to take him in. He wins the love of the daughter. It's Carvey's first film and could have been funnier, but it's not too bad.

2208.   The Opposite of Sex   (1998, Sony Pictures Classics, 105m, c). D & W Don Roos, P David Kirkpatrick, PH Hubert Taczanowski, ED David Codron, M Mason Daring, PD Michael Clausen, SD Kristin V. Peterson.

LP Christina Ricci (Dedee Truitt), Martin Donovan (Bill Truitt), Lisa Kudrow (Lucia),

Lyle Lovett (Sheriff Carl Tippett), Johnny Galecki (Jason), Ivan Sergei (Matt Mateo).

After burying her stepfather, 16-year-old Louisiana tramp Ricci travels to Indiana and, unannounced, barges in on her straitlaced gay half-brother Donovan. The latter's longtime mate died of AIDS, and he's trying to find a new life with Sergei. Little sis has her own plans about who will sleep with whom.

2209. *The Opposite Sex and How to Live with Them* (1993, Miramax, 87m, c). D Matthew Meshekoff, P Stanley M. Brooks & Robert Newmyer, W Noah Stern, PH Jacek Laskus, ED Adam Weiss, M Ira Newborn, PD Alex Tavoularis.

LP Ayre Gross (David), Courteney Cox (Carrie), Kevin Pollak (Eli), Julie Brown (Zoe), Jack Carter (Rabbi), Frank Birney (Priest).

It's meant to be a sexual comedy, but not the way this cast does it.

2210. *Original Gangstas* (1996, Orion, 99m, c). D Larry Cohen, P Fred Williamson, W Aubrey Rattan, PH Carlos Gonzalez, ED David Kern & Peter B. Ellis, M Valdimir Horunzhy, PD Elayne Barbara Ceder.

LP Fred Williamson (John Bookman), Jim Brown (Jake Trevor), Pam Grier (Laurie Thompson), Paul Winfield (Reverend Dorsey), Isabel Sanford (Gracie Bookman), Oscar Brown, Jr. (Marvin Bookman), Richard Roundtree (Slick), Ron O'Neal (Bubba).

It's a reunion of the big stars of the black exploitation films. After his father is brutally murdered, Williamson returns home to Gary, Indiana, to deal with the gang leader responsible. He enlists the help of childhood friends Brown, Roundtree and O'Neal to take back the streets from the young thugs now controlling the gang.

2211. *Orlando* (1993, U.K./Netherlands/ Italy/France, Sony Pictures, 92m, c). D & W Sally Potter (based on the novel by Virginia Woolf), P Christopher Sheppard, PH Alexei Rodionov, ED Herve Schneid, SD Jan Roeles† & Ben Van Os†, AD Michael Buchanan, Michael Howells, Stanislav Romanovsky & Igor Gulyenko, SD Christopher Hobbs.

LP Tilda Swinton (Orlando), Billy Zane (Shelmerdine), Lothaire Bluteau (The Khan), John Wood (Archduke Harry), Charlotte Valandrey (Sasha), Heathcote Williams (Nick

Greene/Publisher), Quentin Crisp (Queen Elizabeth I), Peter Eyre (Mr. Pope).

It's a beautifully filmed version of Virginia Woolf's 1928 novel. It covers 400 years in the life of an English nobleman who, during the period, changes his sex. Swinton first appears as a nobleman in the court of Elizabeth I, played by Crisp. Things keep happening to her, and about 1750 she becomes a woman. It's not until the 20th century that she's allowed romantic fulfillment.

2212. *Oscar* (1991, Touchstone–Buena Vista, 109m, c). D John Landis, P Leslie Belzberg, W Michael Barrie & Jim Mulholland (based on the play by Claude Magnier), PH Mac Ahlberg, ED Dale Beldin, M Elmer Bernstein, PD Bill Kenney, AD William Ladd Skinner, SD Rick T. Gentz.

LP Sylvester Stallone (Angelo "Snaps" Provolone), Ornella Muti (Sofia Provolone), Peter Riegert (Arlo), Vincent Spano (Anthony Rossano), Marisa Tomei (Lisa Provolone), Elizabeth Barondes (Theresa), Kirk Douglas (Snaps' Father), Ken Howard (Kirkwood), Chazz Palminteri (Connie), Tim Curry (Dr. Poole), Don Ameche (Father Clemente).

In this farce, crime boss Stallone swears to his dying father Douglas to go straight, but finds it extremely difficult to keep his word. It's nothing to get excited about.

2213. *Oscar and Lucinda* (1997, Australia, Fox Searchlight, 120m, c). D Gillian Armstrong, P Robin Dalton & Timothy White, W Laura Jones (based on the novel by Peter Carey), PH Geoffrey Simpson, ED Nicholas Beauman, M Thomas Newman, PD Luciana Arrighi, AD John Ralph & Paul Ghiradani.

LP Ralph Fiennes (Oscar Hopkins), Cate Blanchett (Lucinda Leplastrier), Ciaran Hinds (Reverend Dennis Hasset), Tom Wilkinson (Hugh Stratton), Clive Russell (Theophilus), Richard Roxburgh (Mr. Jeffris).

In the mid-nineteenth century, Anglican priest Fiennes and Australian heiress Blanchett form an unusual friendship after they discover they share the same passion for gambling. It's a superbly crafted film with top rate performances from the entire cast, particularly the leads.

2214. *Othello* (1995, U.K., Castle Rock–Columbia, 124m, c). D & W Oliver Parker (based on the play by William Shakespeare), P Luc Roeg & David Barron, PH David Johnson, ED Tony Lawson, M Charlie Mole, PD Tim Harvey, AD Desmond Crowe & Livia Borgognoni.

LP Laurence Fishburne (Othello), Irene Jacob (Desdemona), Kenneth Branagh (Iago), Nathaniel Parker (Cassio), Michael Maloney (Roderigo), Anna Patrick (Emilia), Nicholas Farrell (Montano).

The performances by Fishburne as the tragic Moor, Branagh as the scheming Iago, and Jacob as the sinned against Desdemona make this version of Shakespeare's play workable. Purists may be put off a bit by the rearrangment of and additions to the Bard's scenes and dialogue.

2215. Other People's Money (1991, Warner Bros., 101m, c). D Norman Jewison, P Jewison & Ric Kidney, W Alvin Sargent (based on the play by Jerry Sterner), PH Haskell Wexler, ED Lou Lombardo, M David Newman, PD Philip Rosenberg, AD Nathan Haas & Robert Guerra, SD Tom Roysden.

LP Danny DeVito (Lawrence Garfield), Gregory Peck (Andrew "Jorgy" Jorgenson), Penelope Ann Miller (Kate Sullivan), Piper Laurie (Bea Sullivan), Dean Jones (William J. Coles).

Corporate raider DeVito sets his sights on a family-owned cable business. His adversary in the unfriendly take-over is Miller, the lawyer daughter of the company's owner, Peck. DeVito comes to love Miller almost as much as he loves doughnuts.

2216. The Other Sister (1999, Touchstone–Buena Vista, 129m, c). D Garry Marshall, P Mario Iscovich & Alexandra Rose, W Marshall & Bob Brunner (based on a story by Rose, Blair Richwood, Marshall & Brunner), PH Dante Spinotti, ED Bruce Green, M Rachel Portman, PD Stephen J. Lineweaver, AD Clayton R. Hartley, SD Jay Hart.

LP Juliette Lewis (Carla), Diane Keaton (Elizabeth), Tom Skerritt (Radley), Giovanni Ribisi (Danny), Poppy Montgomery (Caroline), Sarah Paulson (Heather), Juliet Mills (Winnie), Hector Elizondo (Ernie).

As the trailer for the movie explains, Lewis has had a lifelong handicap — her mother Keaton. Lewis portrays a mentally challenged young woman who is overly protected by her mother. As she tells her doctor, she'd like to get her parents off her back. Lewis meets Ribisi, likewise mentally challenged, and the two fall in love. Can these two take care of each other as husband and wife? Everyone in the audience is bound to root for these two special and appealing people.

2217. Other Voices, Other Rooms (1997, U.S./U.K., RSO Films, 98m, c). D David Rocksavage, P Peter Wentworth & Rocksavage, W Sara Flanigan & Rocksavage (based on the novel by Truman Capote), PH Paul Ryan, ED Cynthia Scheider, M Chris Hajian, PD Amy McGary.

LP Lothaire Bluteau (Randolph Skully), Anna Thomson (Amy Skully), David Speck (Joel Sansom), April Turner (Zoo), Frank Taylor (Ed), Aubrey Dollar (Idabell), Bob Kingdom (Narration).

The story is based on Capote's first novel. Speck, a lonely 13-year-old boy moves to Louisiana to stay with his father after his mother's death. The father is nowhere to be found. Instead, he moves in with cousins Thomson and Bluteau, who assure him he will see his father when the latter recovers from an illness. The film moves on at a leisurely pace, not really going anywhere, but it is a pleasant ride because of the cinematography, editing and direction.

2218. The Other Woman (1992, Axis Films Int., 99m, c). D Jag Mundhra, P Andrew Garroni & Alexander Gregory Hippolyte, W Georges Des Esseintes, PH James Michaels, ED Ron Resnick, M Joseph Smith, PD Blair Martin.

LP Adrian Zmed (Greg Mathews), Lee Anne Beaman (Jessica Mathews), Jenna Persaud (Tracy Collins), Daniel Moriarty (Carl), Craig Stepp (Paul), Melissa Moore (Elysse).

Investigative reporter Beaman believes her husband is having an affair with a hooker. She then finds herself sexually attracted to the "other" woman.

2219. Out for Justice (1991, Warner Bros., 91m, c). D John Flynn, P Arnold Kopelson & Steven Seagal, W David Lee Henry & Seagal, PH Ric Waite, ED Robert A. Ferretti & Don Brochu, M David Michael Frank, PD Gene Rudolf, AD Pat Woodbridge, SD Elaine O'-Donnell.

LP Steven Seagal (Gino Felino), William Forsythe (Richie Madano), Jerry Orbach (Det. Ronnie Donziger), Jo Champa (Vicky Felino), Sal Richards (Frankie).

When Brooklyn hood Forsythe goes on a killing spree, one time homeboy turned cop Seagal must stop him. There's violence aplenty for those looking for that kind of thing.

2220. Out of Sight (1998, Universal, 122m, c). D Steven Soderbergh, P Danny De-Vito, Michael Shamberg & Stacy Sher, W Scott Frank† (based on the novel by Elmore Leonard), PH Elliot Davis, ED Anne V. Coates†, M David Holmes, PD Gary Frutkoff, AD Phil Messina, SD Maggie Martin.

LP George Clooney (Jack Foley), Jennifer Lopez (Karen Sisco), Ving Rhames (Buddy Bragg), Don Cheadle (Maurice "Snoopy" Miller), Dennis Farina (Marshall Sisco), Albert Brooks (Richard Ripley).

During a prison break, thief Clooney kidnaps federal marshal Lopez. After he lets her go, she becomes obsessed with recapturing him. Their paths cross again as he prepares to pull a big score — stealing some diamonds from the home of crooked stockbroker Brooks. The playful crime drama is sexy and filled with a number of offbeat characters. The dialogue is bright and witty but not quite on a par with *Get Shorty*, another work of novelist Leonard.

2221. Out of the Cold (1999, U.S./Estonia/Russia, Old Town Pictures, 116m, c). D Sasha Buravsky, P Roee Sharon & Leonid Zagalsky, W Alex Kustanovich & Buravsky, PH Vladimir Klimov, ED Roger Bondelli, M Maxim Dunaevsky, PD Leslie Mcdonald, AD Ann Lumiste & Harry Lepp, SD Malle Jurgenson, Krista Lepland & Tea Tammelaan.

LP Keith Carradine (Dan Scott), Mia Kirschner (Deborah Berkowitz), Brian Dennehy (David Bards), Judd Hirsch (Leon Axelrod), Mercedes Ruehl (Tina), Bronson Pinchot (Max Kaplan), Kim Hunter (Elsa Lindepu).

Carradine is a song-and-dance man stranded behind the Iron Curtain in the late 1950s. Desperate to get to the U.S. Embassy in Moscow, he throws himself across the limousine of Ambassador Dennehy. Given temporary protection, Carradine explains in a series of flashbacks how he came to be in such a situation.

2222. Out on a Limb (1992, Universal, 82m, c). D Francis Veber, P Michael Hertzberg, W Daniel Goldin & Joshua Goldin, PH Donald E. Thorin, ED Glenn Farr, M Van Dyke Parks, PD Stephen Marsh, SD Peg Cummings.

LP Matthew Broderick (Bill Campbell), Jeffrey Jones (Matt Stearns/ Mayor Peter Van Der Haven), Heidi Kling (Sally), John C. Reilly (Jim Jr.), Marian Mercer (Ann Van Der Haven).

Corporate executive Broderick has a miserable journey from the big city to his rural home. He's robbed and abandoned by a woman hitchhiker and hounded by two moronic brothers. There are a lot of frantic chase scenes but too few laughs.

2223. Out to Sea (1997, 20th Century–Fox, 105m, c). D Martha Coolidge, P John Davis & David T. Friendly, W Robert Nelson Jacobs, PH Lajos Koltai, ED Anne V. Coates, M David Newman, PD James Spencer, AD William F. Matthews, SD Anne D. McCulley.

LP Jack Lemmon (Herb), Walter Matthau (Charlie), Dyan Cannon (Liz), Gloria DeHaven (Vivian), Brent Spiner (Gil Godwyn), Elaine Stritch (Mavis), Hal Linden (Mac), Donald O'Connor (Jonathan), Edward Mulhare (Carswell), Rue McClanahan (Mrs. Carruthers).

Think grumpy old men as dance instructors on a cruise filled with older women looking for a little exercise, fun and romance. The boys would be better served to return to the north and ice fishing. Matthau's love interest is Cannon, who, with her mother Stritch (who has the film's best lines), is conspiring to find a wealthy husband for Dyan. The latter's body still looks great, but her face looks like its been through several face lifts. As for Lemmon, he's a widower who hasn't got over the loss of his wife. He finds new love in the person of widow DeHaven. The movie is filled with so many older entertainers you'd think it was an episode of *Love Boat*.

2224. Outbreak (1995, Warner Bros., 128m, c). D Wolfgang Petersen, P Arnold Kopelson, Petersen & Gail Katz, W Lawrence Dworet & Robert Roy Poole, PH Michael Ballhaus, ED Stephen Rivkin, M James Newton Howard, PD William Sandell, AD Nancy Patton & Francis J. Pezza, SD Rosemary Brandenburg.

LP Dustin Hoffman (Colonel Sam Daniels), Rene Russo (Dr. Roberta "Robby" Keough), Morgan Freeman (General Billy Ford), Cuba Gooding, Jr. (Major Salt), Kevin Spacey (Major Casey Schuler), Patrick Dempsey (Jimbo Scott), Donald Sutherland (General Donald McClintock).

When a smuggled African monkey spits on a person (who proceeds to kiss someone else, who then sneezes on a third party, and so on), a highly contagious and mysterious disease spreads out in widening circles. Hoffman leads a team of scientists seeking a serum to combat the disease. It's suspenseful but not one of the best of the subgenre.

2225.　The Outfitters　(1999, Porchlight Ent., 106m, c). D & W Reverge Anselmo, P Anselmo & Penny Fearson, PH Joey Forsyte, ED Garth Craven & Sam Craven, PD Debbie Lee Cohen, SD Kristan Andrews.

LP Danny Nucci (P.D. Mitjans), Del Zamora (A.J. Mitjans), Sarah Lassez (Connie Binoculars), Dana Delany (Cat Bonfaim), Jerry Haynes (Father John).

In this broad Western comedy, two long-separated brothers, Nucci and Zamora, try to turn the family's run-down New Mexico ranch into a going operation.

2226.　The Out-of-Towners　(1999, Paramount, 92m, c). D Sam Weisman, P Robert Evans, W Marc Lawrence (based on the Neil Simon screenplay), PH John Bailey, ED Kent Beyda, M Marc Shaiman, PD Ken Adam, AD William F. O'Brien & Charley Beal, SD Kathryn Peters, Marvin March & George DeTitta.

LP Steve Martin (Henry Clark), Goldie Hawn (Nancy Clark), Mark McKinney (Greg), John Cleese (Mr. Mersault), Oliver Hudson (Allan Clark).

One can't fault this light comedy remake of the 1970 film starring Jack Lemmon and Sandy Dennis. Martin and Hawn are quite at home as the couple whose trip to New York for his job interview is a hellish experience. This can be traced to the indifference, insensitivity and injustice with which most people address the problems of others, particularly strangers. Most of the gags from the first film are repeated in the remake. Cleese, as an officious cross-dressing hotel manager, is a nice plus. The only real objection to the movie is that all of its best scenes are shown in its preview trailer.

2227.　Outside Ozona　(1998, TriStar Pictures–Sony Pictures, 100m, c). D & W J.S. Cardone, P Carol Kottenbrook & Scott Einbeinder, PH Irek Hartowicz, ED Amanda Kirpaul, M Taj Mahal & Johnny Lee Schell, PD Martina Buckley, Ad Hector Velez, SD Ivana Letica.

LP Robert Forster (Odell Parks), Kevin Pollak (Wit Roy), Sherilyn Fenn (Marcy Duggan), David Paymer (Alan Defaux), Penelope Ann Miller (Earlene Demers), Swoosie Kurtz (Rosalee), Taj Mahal (Dix Mayal), Meat Loaf (Floyd Bibbs).

This psychological thriller takes place one long night somewhere on the road between New Mexico and Texas. The various travelers are on a collision course with disaster–and not just because there's a serial killer in the vicinity. The cast makes the fairly routine story intriguing.

2228.　Outside Providence　(1999, Miramax, 103m, c). D Michael Corrente, P Corrente, Peter Farrelly, Bobby Farrelly & Randy Finch, W Peter Farrelly, Corrente & Bobby Farrelly (based on the novel by P. Farrelly), PH Richard Crudo, ED Kate Sanford, M Sheldon Mirowitz, PD Chad Detwiller, AD Tom Walden, SD Karen Weber.

LP Shawn Hatosy (Timothy Dunphy), Jon Abrahams (Drugs Delaney), Tommy Bone (Jackie Dunphy), Jonathan Brandis (Mousy), Jack Ferver (Irving Waltham), Kristen Shorten (Bunny Cote), Amy Smart (Jane Weston), Alec Baldwin (Old Man Dunphy).

You know you're a loser when your old man calls you "Dildo." You know you're a loser when your dog has only three legs. You know you're a loser when your mother disappeared years ago under suspicious circumstances and your brother is wheelchair-bound. You know you're a loser when you get in trouble with the Pawtucket cops. Then all of a sudden you are whisked off to a private school for a year, where your snooty classmates make sure you know that you are a loser and one who doesn't belong at their school. Fortunately, the only girl who seems to be on the campus thinks you're not such a loser.

2229.　Over Exposed　(1990, Concorde, 80m, c). D Larry Brand, P Roger Corman, W Brand & Rebecca Reynolds, PH David Sperling, ED Patrick Rand, M Mark Governor, PD Robert Franklin.

LP Catherine Oxenberg (Kristen), David Naughton (Phillip), Jennifer Edwards (Helen), John Patrick Reger (Terrance), William Bumiller (Hank), Larry Brand (Morrison), Karen Black (Mrs. Trowbridge).

Oxenberg is a soap star, beloved by all the wackos in creation. One of her admirers is a killer. Guess which one.

2230. Over the Hill (1993, Australia, Village Roadshow Pictures, 102m, c). D George Miller, P Bernard Terry & Robert Caswell, W Caswell (based on the book *Alone in the Australian Wilderness* by Gladys Taylor), PH David Connell, ED Henry Dangar, M David McHugh, PD Graham "Grace" Walker, AD Stewart Way.

LP Olympia Dukakis (Alma Harris), Sigrid Thornton (Elizabeth), Derek Fowlds (Dutch), Bill Kerr (Maurio), Steve Bisley (Benedict), Martin Jacobs (Alan Forbes).

After burying her husband of many years, Dukakis feels at loose ends. She arrives unannounced at the Sydney home of her daughter Thornton and her husband Jacobs. When this doesn't work out, she buys a souped-up 1959 Chevy Bel-Air and sets off across the wilderness of Eastern Australia for Melbourne. She has a number of adventures with an assortment of people along the way.

2231. Overkill (1995, Trimark, 92m, c). D Dean Ferrandini, P Carrie Chambers & Andy Howard, W Ron Swanson, Ferrandini & Jerry Lazarus, PH John Stephens, ED David Kern, M Jim Ervin, PD Howard Smith, AD Deanne Lomma, SD Melissa Levander.

LP Aaron Norris (Jack Hazard), Michael Nouri (Lloyd Wheeler), Kenny Moskow (Gary Steiner), Pamela Dickerson (Catherine Howard), David Rowe (Joseph Douglas), Enrique Munroz (Colonel).

Here's one more rip-off of *The Most Dangerous Game*. Vigilante cop Norris is ordered to take a vacation in Costa Rica by his superiors. There he becomes the prey of land developer Nouri.

2232. Pacific Heights (1990, Morgan Creek–20th Century–Fox, 107m, c). D John Schlesinger, P Scott Rudin & William Sackheim, W Daniel Pyne, PH Amir Mokri, ED Mark Warner, M Hans Zimmer, PD Neil

Spisak, AD Gershon Ginsberg & Sharon Seymour, SD Clay A. Griffith & Debra Shutt.

LP Melanie Griffith (Patty Palmer), Matthew Modine (Drake Goodman), Michael Keaton (Carter Hayes), Mako (Toshio Watanabe), Nobu McCarthy (Mira Watanabe), Laurie Metcalf (Stephanie MacDonald), Tippi Hedren (Florence Peters).

2233. The P.A.C.K. (1997, Spectrum Films, 88m, c). D Bryan Todd, P Michael W. Evans, Jr., & Todd, W David A. Prior & Evans, Jr., PH Rick Johnson, ED James E. Nownes, M Alan Pasqua, PD Kristin Bicksler, AD Arlo Strine.

LP Sandahl Bergman (Rachael), Ted Prior (T-7043), Red West (Sheriff Charlie Stone), Dave Scott (Hopper), Earl Jarrett (McCall), Jim Petulla (Bennett), Brian Donnellan (P.A.C.K./Deputy #3).

"P.A.C.K." stands for "Prefabricated Animalistic Cybernetic Killer." It refers to Donnellan who, when his space capsule crashes near Mobile, Alabama, goes on a killing spree. He is pursued by Prior, an alien tracker, assisted by Bergman, the only survivor of one of Donnellan's attacks.

Yuppie couple Griffith and Modine pool their resources to purchase and renovate a large Victorian home in an upscale San Francisco neighborhood. They rent a unit in the house to sociopath Keaton, a tenant from hell. He knows how to drive his landlords crazy without being evicted.

2234. The Pagemaster (1994, 20th Century–Fox, 75m, c). D Joe Johnston, P David Kirschner, Paul Gertz & Michael R. Joyce, W David Casci, Kirschner & Ernie Contreras, M James Horner, PD Gay Lawrence, AD Pixote, ANIM Maurice Hunt.

LP Macaulay Culkin (Richard Tyler), Ed Begley, Jr. (Alan Tyler), Mel Harris (Claire Tyler), Christopher Lloyd (Mr. Dewey/The Pagemaster), Patrick Stewart (Adventure), Whoopi Goldberg (Fantasy).

In this animation–live action feature, timid young Culkin takes refuge in a library after getting caught in a rainstorm. He sustains a knock on the head and is transformed into a cartoon character who meets Lloyd, the Pagemaster. The latter will help Culkin find his way out of his predicament as he passes through several well-known novels and talking books.

2235. *Paint It Black* (1990, Vestron, 102m, c). D Tim Hunter, P Anne Kimmel & Mark Forstater, W Tim Harris & Herschel Weingrod, PH Mark Irwin, ED Curtiss Clayton, M Jurgen Knieper, PD Steven Legler, SD Steven Karatzas.

LP Rick Rossovich (Jonathan Dunbar), Doug Savant (Eric Kinsley), Julie Carmen (Gina Hayworth), Sally Kirkland (Marion Easton), Peter Frechette (Gregory Paul).

Struggling artist Rossovich is in commercial and sexual bondage to gallery owner Kirkland, who keeps him in her power by promising him a one-man show. Rossovich meets psychotic art collector Savant, who is crazy for Rossovich's work and does him the favor of killing Kirkland. Since he has no motive for the crime and Rossovich does, the latter is the number one suspect.

2236. *Painted Hero* (1996, Cabin Fever Ent., 105m, c). D Terry Benedict, P Benedict, Peter Greene, Jeff Waxman & Richard Weinman, W Benedict & Stan Bertheaud, PH David Bridges, ED Gary McLaughlin, M Rick Marotta, PD Elayne Barbara Ceder, SD Cindy Downes.

LP Dwight Yoakam (Virgil Kidder), Michelle Joyner (Katelin), Kiersten Warren (Teresa), Cindy Pickett (Sadie), John Getz (Sheriff Acuff), Bo Hopkins (Brownie), Walton Goggins (Roddy).

Country music star Yoakam portrays a rodeo clown/bullrider. He must confront his past and the people he left when he reluctantly reenters big-time rodeo shows.

2237. *The Pallbearer* (1996, Miramax, 104m, c). D Matt Reeves, P Jeffrey Abrams & Paul Webster, W Jason Katims & Reeves, PH Robert Elswit, ED Stan Salfas, M Stewart Copeland, PD Robin Standefer, AD Stephen Alesch, SD Kate Yatsko.

LP David Schwimmer (Tom Thompson), Gwyneth Paltrow (Julie DeMarco), Michael Rapaport (Brad), Toni Collette (Cynthia), Carol Kane (Tom's Mother), Bitty Schram (Lauren), Barbara Hershey (Ruth Abernathy).

College graduate Schwimmer can't seem to get his life and career as an architect on track. He agrees to attend the funeral of a "best friend" he doesn't remember. The film has some amusing bits, and the lovely Paltrow is his love interest.

2238. *Palmetto* (1998, Columbia–Sony Pictures, 114m, c). D Volker Schlondorff, P Matthias Wendlandt, W E. Max Frye (based on the novel *Just Another Sucker* by James Hadley Chase), PH Thomas Kloss, ED Peter Przygodda, M Klaus Doldinger, PD Claire Jenora Bond.

LP Woody Harrelson (Harry Barber), Elisabeth Shue (Rhea Malroux), Gina Gershon (Nina), Rolf Hoppe (Felix Malroux), Michael Rapaport (Donnelly), Chloe Sevigny (Odette), Tom Wright (John Renick).

Bitter after spending two years in prison framed for a crime, former newsman Harrelson reluctantly returns to his old stomping ground Palmetto, Florida, with his girlfriend Gershon. He meets Shue and lets her talk him into a pretend abduction of the former's stepdaughter Sevigny. They plan to bilk her old man, Hoppe, out of enough money to hide out until she turns 18. Smell like another frame? You betcha!

2239. *Palookaville* (1996, Samuel Goldwyn Co.–Orion, 92m, c). D Alan Taylor, P Uberto Pasolini, W David Epstein, PH John Thomas, ED David Leonard, M Rachel Portman, PD Anne Stuhler, AD Roswell Hamrick.

LP Adam Trese (Jerry), Vincent Gallo (Russ), William Forsythe (Sid), Gareth Williams (Ed), Lisa Gay Hamilton (Betty), Bridgit Ryan (Enid), Kim Dickens (Laurie), Frances McDormand (June).

Three incompetent crooks can't seem to make a go of a criminal career despite all their plotting. They attempt to break into a jewelry store and break into the bakery next door instead.

2240. *Panther* (1995, Gramercy, 125m, c). D Mario Van Peebles, P Preston Holmes, Mario Van Peebles, Melvin Van Peebles, W Melvin Van Peebles, PH Eddie Pei, ED Earl Watson, M Larry Robinson, PD Richard Hoover, AD Bruce Hill, SD Robert Kensinger.

LP Kadeem Hardison (Judge), Bokeem Woodbine (Tyrone), Joe Dan Baker (Brimmer), Courtney B. Vance (Bobby Seale), Tyrin Turner (Cy), Marcus Chong (Huey Newton), Anthony Griffith (Eldridge Cleaver), Bobby Brown (Rose), Nefertiti (Alma), James Russo (Rodgers), Jenifer Lewis (Rita), Richard Dysart (J. Edgar Hoover).

In a cliché-filled whitewash that even real-life

Panther Bobby Seale denounced, the filmmakers provide only a superficial examination of the organization and actions of the Black Panthers. The leads come across less as dedicated revolutionaries than just one more street gang put upon by the FBI and the mob.

2241. *The Paper* (1994, Universal, 112m, c). D Ron Howard, P Brian Glazer & Frederick Zollo, W David Koepp & Stephen Koepp, PH John Seale, ED Daniel Hanley & Michael Hill, M Randy Newman, PD Todd Hallowell, AD Maher Ahmad, SD Debra Schutt.

LP Michael Keaton (Henry Hackett), Robert Duvall (Bernie White), Glenn Close (Alicia Clark), Marisa Tomei (Martha Hackett), Randy Quaid (McDougal), Jason Robards (Graham Keighley), Jason Alexander (Marion Sandusky), Spalding Gray (Paul Bladden).

Keaton, the city editor of a New York daily newspaper, is caught in a moral dilemma when managing editor Close wants to publish a story that declares two black youths are guilty of a murder, even though the issue is still in doubt. It's a battle of ethics versus the bottom line of selling newspapers and advertising space in this interesting but less-than-thrilling comedy-drama.

2242. *Paper Mask* (1991, U.K., Castle Hill Prods., 105m, c). D & P Christopher Morahan, W John Collee (from his novel), PH Nat Crosby, ED Peter Coulson, M Richard Harvey, PD Caroline Hanania, AD Andrew Rothschild.

LP Paul McCann (Matthew Harris), Amanda Donohoe (Christine Taylor), Frederick Treves (Dr. Mumford), Tom Wilkinson (Dr. Thorn), Barbara Leigh-Hunt (Celia Mumford), Jimmy Yuill (Alec Moran).

McCann, posing as an emergency room doctor, is responsible for the death of Leigh-Hunt. Will nurse Donohoe expose him or cover for him?

2243. *Paperback Hero* (1999, Australia, Polygram, 96m, c). D & W Anthony J. Bowman, P Lance W. Reynolds & John Winter, PH David Burr, ED Veronika Jenet, M Berkhard Dallwitz, PD John Dowding, AD Adam Head.

LP Claudia Karvan (Ruby Vale), Hugh Jackman (Jack Willis), Angie Milliken (Ziggy Keane), Andrew S. Gilbert (Hamish).

Meant to be a screwball comedy, this film is merely screwy. Hunk Jackman writes a best-selling Gothic novel using the name of his buddy Karvan. The publishers want to meet her, so Karvan must pretend to be the author of a book she hasn't read. Consider the comedy possibilities. Too bad director-writer Bowman found so few.

2244. *Paperback Romance* (AKA: *Lucky Break*) (1994, Australia, Samuel Goldwyn Company, 90m, c). D & W Ben Lewin, P Bob Weis, PH Vincent Monton, ED Peter Carrodus, M Phil Grabowsky, PD Peta Lawson, AD Victoria Hobday.

LP Gia Carides (Sophie), Anthony LaPaglia (Eddie), Rebecca Gibney (Gloria), Robyn Nevin (Anne-Marie LePine), Marshall Napier (George LePine), Jacek Koman (Yuri).

Carides, a writer of erotic fiction, is unable to walk due to childhood polio. She meets LaPaglia, who deals in selling stolen jewels. She falls and breaks her leg, giving her a fine excuse for not being able to walk. While having sex, LaPaglia cuts his tongue on her cast, affecting his speech for a sizable portion of the movie. The film is a romantic comedy about the consequences of withholding important information when entering into a love affair.

2245. *The Paperboy* (1994, Canada, Republic Pictures, 94m, c). D Douglas Jackson, P Tom Berry & Franco Battista, W David Peckinpah, PH Rodney Gibbons, ED Kaja Fehr & Jeffrey Patch, M Milan Kymlicka, PD Perri Gorrara, Ad Patricia Christie, SD Ann Smart.

LP Marc Marut (Johnny), Alexandra Paul (Melissa Thorpe), Brigid Tierney (Cammie), William Katt (Brian), Frances Bay (Mrs. Rosemont), Krista Errickson (Diana).

Deranged teen Marut's fascination with a neighbor sets him on a murderous rampage.

2246. *Paradise* (1991, Touchstone–Buena Vista, 110m, c). D & W Mary Agnes Donoghue (based on the short story "Le Grand Chemin" by Jean-Loup Hubert), PH Jerzy Zielinski, ED Eva Gardos & Debra McDermott, M David Newman, PD Evelyn Sakash & Marcia Hinds, SD Donna J. Hattin.

LP Melanie Griffith (Lily Reed), Don Johnson (Ben Reed), Elijah Wood (Willard Young), Thora Birch (Billie Pike), Sheila McCarthy

(Sally Pike), Eve Gordon (Rosemary), Louise Latham (Catherine Reston Lee).

Griffith and Johnson are a troubled rural couple trying to cope with the death of their baby. They take care of Wood, the son of friends, for the summer. He befriends tomboy Birch, who helps him come out of his shell. Wood, in turn, helps Griffith and Johnson deal with their tragic loss.

2247. *Paradise Road* (1997, U.S./Australia, Fox Searchlight, 122m, c). D Bruce Beresford, P Sue Milliken & Greg Coote, W David Giles, Martin Meader, Alfred Uhry & Beresford, PH Peter James, ED Timothy Wellburn, M Ross Edwards, PD Herbert Pinter, AD Ian Gracie, SD Brian Edmonds.

LP Glenn Close (Adrienne Pargiter), Pauline Collins (Margaret "Daisy" Drummond), Julianna Margulies (Topsy Merritt), Frances McDormand (Dr. Verstak), Cate Blanchett (Susan Macarthy), Jennifer Ehle (Rosemary Leighton-Jones), Elizabeth Spriggs (Mrs. Roberts), Joanna Ter Steege (Sister Wilhelmina).

The film is the true story of a group of women from various Allied nations who are caught behind enemy lines in Sumatra during WWII. The women are roughed up, herded together and forced to make a long march across the countryside to an internment center. There they endure beatings and humiliations. Some die of malaria and fatigue; others are killed by the Japanese for minor infractions of camp rules. The women, of so many different backgrounds, nationalities, cultures, languages and classes, do not get along. It is reminiscent of the excellent TV film *Playing for Time*. Close and Collins form a vocal orchestra that performs great works of classical music by singing notes instead of playing them. This outlet helps lift their spirits. Unfortunately, the film doesn't do quite as good a job of allowing audiences to get to know these women and learn of their individual means of coping in order to survive.

2248. *Parallel Sons* (1996, Black Brook Films–Eureka Films, 93m, c). D & W John G. Young, P James Spione & Nancy Larsen, PH Matthew M. Howe, ED Young & Spione, SD Emile Menasche, PD Cindi Sfinas, AD Joanne Berman, SD Chris Schiavo.

LP Gabriel Mann (Seth Carlson), Laurence Mason (Knowledge Johnson), Murphy Guyer (Sheriff Mott), Graham Alex Johnson (Peter Carlson), Heather Gottlieb (Kristen Mott), Josh Hopkins (Marty).

Mann, who would like to leave his little New York village for the Big Apple so he may study art, forms an unlikely friendship with escaped convict Mason when the latter, bleeding from a wound, tries to rob the diner where Mann works. The friendship is so close that when the sheriff comes for Mason, Mann shoots and kills him. Then the odd couple flee for the Canadian border.

2249. *The Parent Trap* (1998, Walt Disney–Buena Vista, 124m, c). D Nancy Meyers, P Charles Shyer, W David Swift, Meyers & Shyer (based on the book *Das Doppelte Lottchen* by Erich Kastner), PH Dean A. Cundey, ED Stephen A. Rotter, M Alan Silvestri, PD Dean Tavoularis, AD Alex Tavoularis & John Fenner, SD Dianne Wager, James Bayliss & Kelly Hannafin.

LP Lindsay Lohan (Hallie Parker/Annie James), Dennis Quaid (Nick Parker), Natasha Richardson (Elizabeth James), Elaine Hendrix (Meredith Blake), Lisa Ann Walker (Chessy), Simon Kunz (Martin).

In this updated version of Disney's 1961 comedy, Lohan plays twins separated as babies when their parents Quaid and Richardson divorced. In one of those coincidences found so often in movies, the girls discover each other when they are both sent to the same summer camp. They hatch a plot to reunite their parents. Why do kids think they know what's best for grown-ups?

2250. *Party Girl* (1995, First Look, 98m, c). D Daisy von Scherler Mayer, P Harry Brickmayer & Stephanie Koules, W von Scherler Mayer & Brickmayer (based on a story by von Scherler Mayer, Brickmayer & Sheila Gaffney), PH Michael Slovis, ED Cara Silverman, M Anton Sanko, PD Kevin Thompson, SD Jennifer Baime.

LP Parker Posey (Mary), Guillermo Diaz (Leo), Omar Townsend (Mustafa), Sasha von Scherler (Judy Lindendorf), Anthony DeSando (Derrick), Donna Mitchell (Rene), Liev Schreiber (Nigel).

Party girl Posey comes to the realization that she can't just attend wild parties all her life. Despite a lack of training, she becomes a librarian with the New York Public Library. The Old Lady will never be the same again.

2251. *Passed Away* (1992, Hollywood–Buena Vista, 96m, c). D & W Charlie Peters, P Larry Brezner & Timothy Marx, PH Arthur Albert ED Harry Keramidas, M Richard Gibbs, PD Catherine Hardwicke, AD Gilbert Mercier, SD Gene Serdena.

LP Bob Hoskins (Johnny Scanlan), Blair Brown (Amy Scanlan), Tim Curry (Boyd Pinter), Frances McDormand (Nora Scanlan), William Petersen (Frank Scanlan), Pamela Reed (Terry Scanlan), Peter Riegert (Peter Syracusa), Maureen Stapleton (Mary Scanlan), Nancy Travis (Cassie Slocombe), Jack Warden (Jack Scanlan).

In this black comedy, Warden's family must cope with his sudden death. They also need to deal with the arrival at his funeral of his apparent young mistress, whom they suspect of being after their inheritance.

2252. *Passenger 57* (1992, Warner Bros., 90m, c). D Kevin Hooks, P Dan Paulson, Lee Rich & Dylan Sellers, W David Loughery & Dan Gordon (based on a story by Gordon & Stewart Raffill), PH Mark Irwin, ED Richard Nord, M Stanley Clarke, PD Jaymes Hinkle, AD Alan Muraoka, SD Don K. Ivey.

LP Wesley Snipes (John Cutter), Bruce Payne (Charles Rane), Tom Sizemore (Sly Delvecchio), Alex Datcher (Marti Slayton), Bruce Greenwood (Stuart Ramsey), Robert Hooks (Dwight Henderson), Elizabeth Hurley (Sabrina Ritchie).

When arch-criminal Payne and his gang hijack a plane, they are unaware that crack anti-terrorist Snipes is aboard. It's an enjoyable but predictable action piece.

2253. *Passion* (1999, Australia-U.S., REP Release, 98m, c). D Peter Duncan, P Matt Carroll, W Don Watson (based on the play *Percy & Rose* by Rob George and an original screenplay by George and Peter Goldsworthy), PH Martin McGrath, ED Simon Martin, PD Murray Picknett, AD Karen Land.

LP Barbara Hershey (Rose), Richard Roxburgh (Percy), Emily Wolf (Karen Holten), Claudia Karvan (Alfhild de Luce), Simon Burke (Herman Sandby).

This film explores the rumored sadomasochistic and incestuous relationship between colorful and outlandish Australian-born pianist and composer Percy Grainger and his mother Rose.

2254. *Passion Fish* (1992, Miramax, 136m, c). D John Sayles, P Sarah Green & Maggie Renzi, W Sayles†, PH Roger Deakins, ED Sayles, M Mason Daring, PD Dan Bishop & Dianna Freas.

LP Mary McDonnell† (Mary-Alice Culhane), Alfre Woodard (Chantelle), David Strathairn (Rennie), Vondie Curtis-Hall (Sugar LeDoux), Angela Bassett (Dawn/Rhonda), Lenore Banks (Nurse Quick), William Mahoney (Max).

Paraplegic McDonnell, a former famous soap opera star, was crippled by a New York taxi. She returns to her home town on the Louisiana bayou to drink and wallow in self-pity. She has a rapid turnover in house nurses because of the way she abuses them, but finally meets her match in Woodard.

2255. *The Passion of Darkly Noon* (1996, U.K./Germany/Belgium, Fugitive Films, 101m, c). D & W Philip Ridley, P Dominic Anciano, Frank Henschke & Alan Keytsman, PH John de Borman, ED Leslie Healey, M Nick Bicat, PD Hubert Pouille, AD Willem Klewais & Vern Dobroschke.

LP Brendan Fraser (Darkly Noon), Ashley Judd (Callie), Viggo Mortensen (Clay), Loren Dean (Jude), Grace Zabriskie (Roxie), Lou Meyers (Quincey), Kate Harper (Ma), Mel Cobb (Pa).

Fraser, the only survivor of a religious community, is taken in by free-spirited Judd, who lives in a secluded forest house. He sexually pines for her and just about goes mad when her lover, Mortensen, returns.

2256. *A Passion to Kill* (1994, A-Pix Ent., 93m, c). D Rick King, P Bruce Cohn Curtis, W William Delligan, PH Paul Ryan, ED David F. Lloyd, M Robert Sprayberry, PD Ivo Cristante, SD Tim Colohan.

LP Scott Bakula (Dr. David Lawson), Chelsea Field (Diane Chamberlain), Sheila Kelly (Beth), John Getz (Jerry Chamberlain), Rex Smith (Ted), France Nuyen (Lou Mazaud).

Psychiatrist Bakula has a secret affair with Field, his best friend's wife. When husband Getz is killed, he suspects that Field may be responsible.

2257. Past Tense (1994, Republic Pictures, 95m, c). D Graeme Clifford, P Stephen Brown & Nana Greenwald, W Scott Frost & Miguel Tejada-Flores, PH Chuck Minsky, ED Paul Rubell, M Stephen Graziano, PD Toby Corbett.

LP Scott Glenn (Gene Ralston), Anthony LaPaglia (Larry), Lara Flynn Boyle (Tory Bass), David Ogden Stiers (Frank).

In a film in which it's not quite clear what is reality and what is imagination, police detective and mystery writer Glenn has a series of fantasies, all involving neighbor Boyle. Expect many surprises.

2258. Pastime (AKA: *One Cup of Coffee*) (1991, Miramax, 94m, c). D Robin B. Armstrong, P Eric Tynan Young & Armstrong, W David M. Eyre, Jr., PH Tom Richmond, ED Mark S. Westmore, M Lee Holdridge, PD David W. Ford, SD Ellen Totleben.

LP William Russ (Roy Dean Bream), Scott Plank (Randy Keever), Reed Rudy (Spicer), Ricky Paull Goldin (Hahn), Peter Murnik (Simmons), John Jones (Colbeck), Glenn Plummer (Tyrone Debray), Jeffrey Tambor (Peter Laporte).

Aging minor-league pitcher Russ once had a brief stint in the major leagues. He is the butt of his teammates' jokes because he still hopes to return to the "show," despite his apparent lack of talent. He befriends Plummer, a shy young black pitcher who may just have what it takes to make it to the big time.

2259. Patch Adams (1998, Universal, 115m, c). D Tom Shadyac, P Barry Kemp, Mike Farrell, Marvin Minoff & Charles Newirth, W Steve Oedekerk (based on the book *Gesundheit: Good Health Is a Laughing Matter* by Hunter Doherty Adams & Maureen Mylander), PH Phedon Papamichael, ED Don Zimmerman, M Marc Shaiman†, PD Linda DeScenna, AD Jim Nedza.

LP Robin Williams (Patch Adams), Daniel London (Truman), Monica Potter (Carin), Philip Seymour Hoffman (Mitch), Bob Gunton (Dean Walcott), Josef Sommer (Dr. Eaton), Irma P. Hall (Joletta), Frances Lee McCain (Judy), Harve Presnell (Dean Anderson), Harold Gould (Arthur Mendelson), Richard Kiley (Dr. Titan).

This film shamelessly plays on the viewers' heartstrings, but they may not mind. Williams appears as a real-life physician who strongly believes in the value of laughter in the treatment of patients. His approach is viewed as disgraceful by humorless Dean Gunton, but the film demonstrates that there is something to his touchy-feely relationship with his patients. When a troubled patient kills London, who Williams loves, he just about loses his chance to graduate for treating patients without a medical license. He gives a stirring defense at his hearing and is allowed to graduate. Williams is a talented actor who can be very funny, and there are several hilarious scenes in the movie, but the overall diagnosis of the film is not encouraging. Williams' character is just too perfect to be true.

2260. Patriot Games (1992, Paramount, 113m, c). D Phillip Noyce, P Mace Neufeld & Robert Rehme, W W. Peter Iliff & Donald Stewart (based on the novel by Tom Clancy), PH Donald M. McAlpine, ED Neil Travis & William Hoy, M James Horner, PD Joseph Nemec, III, AD Joseph P. Lucky, SD John M. Dwyer.

LP Harrison Ford (Jack Ryan), Anne Archer (Dr. Cathy Ryan), Patrick Bergin (Kevin O'-Donnell), Sean Bean (Sean Miller), Thora Birch (Sally Ryan), James Fox (Lord Holmes), Samuel L. Jackson (Robby Jackson), Polly Walker (Annette), James Earl Jones (Admiral James Greer), Richard Harris (Paddy O'Neil).

In thwarting an assassination attempt on a member of the Royal Family, Ford kills one of the terrorists. This makes him and his family a target of Bean, the dead man's brother. The excitement peters out about midway through the film, and the ending is a disappointment.

2261. Paulie (1998, DreamWorks Pictures, 91m, c). D John Roberts, P Mark Gordon, Gary Levinsohn & Allison Lyon Segan, W Laurie Craig, PH Tony Pierce-Roberts, ED Bruce Cannon, M John Debney, PD Dennis Washington, AD Tom Taylor, SD John Berger.

LP Gena Rowlands (Ivy), Tony Shalhoub (Misha), Cheech Marin (Ignacio), Bruce Davison (Dr. Reingold), Jay Mohr (Voice of Paulie/Benny), Trini Alvardo (Adult Marie), Buddy Hackett (Artie).

No, this isn't a Paulie Shore movie. The Paulie of this film is an intelligent parrot who has many owners. If you are not in the 5- to

11-year-old range, the movie and the parrot will do little for you.

2262. Payback (1995, Trimark, 89m, c). D Anthony Hickox, P Sam Bernard & Natan Zahavi, W Bernard, PH David Bridges, ED Anita Brandt-Burgoyne, M Anthony Marinelli, PD Stuart Blatt.

LP C. Thomas Howell (Oscar Bonsetter), Joan Severance (Rose Gullerman), Marshall Bell (Tom "Gully" Gullerman), Richard Burgi (Al Keegan), John Toles-Bey (Marcus Jackson), R.G. Armstrong (Old Mac).

In exchange for revealing the location of some buried loot, prisoner Howell promises Armstrong, a dying old con, to take revenge on Bell, the guard who beat him. Howell isn't able to keep his end of the bargain immediately, but years later he hasn't forgotten his promise.

2263. Payback (1999, Paramount, 110m, c). D Brian Helgeland, P Bruce Davey, W Helgeland & Terry Hayes (Based on the novel *The Hunter* by Richard Stark), PH Ericson Core, ED Kevin Stitt, M Chris Boardman, PD Troy Sizemore, SD Sandy Struth.

LP Mel Gibson (Porter), Gregg Henry (Val), Maria Bello (Rosie), Deborah Kara Unger (Lynn), David Paymer (Stegman), Bill Duke (Detective Hicks), William Devane (Carter), Kris Kristofferson (Bronson).

Shot and left for dead by his druggie wife Unger and partner Henry after the trio pull off a brazen heist, Gibson is really p.o.'d. This adaptation of the novel *The Hunter* is quite a bit like the movie *Point Blank* (1967), starring Lee Marvin, which was adapted from the same source. Intent on retribution, Gibson repeatedly risks his life taking on the "Outfit" to get his cut of the loot, which is a modest $70,000. The film is extremely violent, but this is somewhat offset by some funny one-liners. Charming Gibson is not so charming in this role, but he's still more likeable than others in the cast.

2264. PCU (1994, 20th Century–Fox, 79m, c). D Hart Bochner, P Paul Schiff, W Adam Leff & Zak Penn, PH Reynaldo Villalobos, ED Nicholas C. Smith, M Steve Vai, PD Steven Jordan, AD David M. Davis, SD Enrico Campana.

LP Jeremy Piven (Droz), Chris Young (Tom Lawrence), Megan Ward (Katy), Jon Favreau (Gutter), Sarah Trigger (Samantha), David Spade (Rand McPherson), Alex Desert (Mullaney), Jessica Walter (President Garcia-Thompson).

This film's attempt to combine *Animal House* with a satire on political correctness is PU. It's a sophomoric comedy populated by a lot of forgettable characters and likely forgettable young actors.

2265. The Peacekeeper (1997, Film Line Inc.–Nu Image, 98m, c). D Frederic Forestier, P Nicolas Clermont, W James H. Stewart & Robert Geoffrion, PH John Berrie, ED Yves Langlois, M Francois Forestier, PD John Meighen, AD David Blanchard, SD Josiane Noreau.

LP Dolph Lundgren (Major Cross), Michael Sarrazin (Murphy), Roy Scheider (President), Montel Williams (Lt. Colonel Northrop), Monika Schnarre (Jane), Christopher Heyerdahl (Hettinger).

Given the job as the keeper of the "Black Bag," a briefcase that contains the launch codes of America's thermonuclear deterrents, by President Scheider, Lundgren loses the dang thing to terrorists on his first day on the job. Guess he'll have to get it back.

2266. Peacemaker (1990, Fries, 90m, c). D & W Kevin S. Tenney, P Wayne Crawford & Andrew Lane, PH Thomas Jewett, ED Dan Duncin, PD Rob Sissman, AD Tucker Johnston.

LP Robert Forster (Yates), Lance Edwards (Townsend), Hilary Shepard (Dori Caison), Robert Davi (Sgt. Frank Ramos), Bert Remsen (Doc).

An interplanetary serial killer is tracked down on Earth by a policeman from his home planet. However, it's not made exactly clear which is which.

2267. The Peacemaker (1997, DreamWorks SKG, 122m, c). D Mimi Leder, P Walter Parkes & Branko Lustig, W Michael Schiffer (based on an article by Leslie and Andrew Cockburn), PH Dietrich Lohmann, ED David Rosenbloom, M Hans Zimmer, PD Leslie Dilley, SD Rosemary Brandenburg.

LP George Clooney (Lt. Col. Thomas Devoe), Nicole Kidman (Dr. Julia Kelly), Armin Mueller-Stahl (Dimitri Vertikoff), Marcel Iures (Dusan Gavrich), Alexander

Baluev (Gen. Alexsander Kodoroff), Rene Medvesek (Vlado Mirich).

With a little help from nuclear scientist Kidman, Army Intelligence officer Clooney throws away the book while tracking down Russian terrorists, led by renegade general Baluev. The bad guys have stolen nuclear warheads and are willing to sell them to the highest bidder.

2268.   *The Pebble and the Penguin* (1995, MGM/UA, 74m, c). D Don Bluth, P Russell Boland, W Rachel Koretsky & Steve Whitestone, ED Thomas V. Moss, M Barry Manilow, PD David Goetz, ANIM John Pomeroy, Richard Bazley, Ralf Palmer, Len Simon, Sylvia Hoefnagels, John Hill & John Power.

LP Voices: Shani Wallis (Narrator), Martin Short (Hubie), James Belushi (Rocko), Tim Curry (Drake), Annie Golden (Marina), Scott Bullock (Chubby/Gentoo).

Shy penguin Hubie falls for girl penguin Marina, but he must deal with evil penguin Drake. The latter vanquishes Hubie and the rest of the film deals with our hero's efforts to get back to his love, with the help of penguin friend Rocko. All penguins look alike.

2269.   *Pecker*   (1998, Fine Line, 87m, c). D & W John Waters, P John Fiedler & Mark Tarlov, PH Robert Stevens, ED Janice Hampton, M Stewart Copeland, PD Vincent Peranio.

LP Edward Furlong (Pecker), Christina Ricci (Shelley), Mary Kay Place (Joyce), Martha Plimpton (Tina), Brendan Sexton III (Matt), Mark Joy (Jimmy), Mink Stole (Precinct Captain), Lili Taylor (Rorey).

The reason that Furlong is nicknamed "Pecker" is that as a child he "pecked" at his food. Despite himself, working class teen Furlong becomes a superstar photographer when his shots of family and friends are discovered by New York art dealer Taylor. Furlong learns that there is a price to be paid for his overnight celebrity status.

2270.   *The Pelican Brief*   (1993, Warner Bros., 140m, c). D & W Alan J. Pakula (based on the novel by John Grisham), P Pakula & Pieter Jan Brugge, PH Stephen Goldblatt, ED Tom Rolf & Trudy Ship, M James Horner, PD Philip Rosenberg, AD Robert Guerra, SD Lisa Fischer, Rick Simpson, Sarah Stollman & Monroe Kelly.

LP Julia Roberts (Darby Shaw), Denzel Washington (Gray Grantham), Sam Shepard (Thomas Callahan), John Heard (Gavin Verheek), Tony Goldwyn (Fletcher Coal), James B. Sikking (FBI Director F. Denton Voyles), William Atherton (Bob Gminski), Robert Culp (President of the U.S.).

Law student Roberts uncovers the plot behind the assassination of two Supreme Court justices. Journalist Washington comes to Roberts' aid, helping her survive when her detective work gets too close to exposing the culprits. As is the case in most Grisham novels and films based on his work, the wrapup doesn't live up to the promise of the beginning.

2271.   *Pentathlon*   (1995, LIVE Ent., 101m, c). D Bruce Malmuth, P Martin Caan & Dolph Lundgren, W William Stadiem, Gary MacDonald & Gary Devore (based on a story by Stadiem & Malmuth), PH Misha Suslov, ED Richard Nord, M David Spear, PD James Hynkle, AD David W. Ford.

LP Dolph Lundgren (Eric Brogar), Renee Coleman (Julie), Roger E. Mosley (Creese), David Soul (Mueller), Evan James (Offerman), Daniel Riordan (Rhinehardt).

East German athlete Lundgren defects to the United States. Years later his ex-coach does what he can to ruin Lundgren's comeback.

2272.   *The People Under the Stairs*   (1991, Alive Films–Universal, 101m, c). D & W Wes Craven, P Marianne Maddalena & Stuart M. Besser, PH Sandi Sissel, ED James Coblentz, M Don Peake, PD Bryan Jones, AD Steve Lloyd Shroyer, SD Molly Flanegin.

LP Brandon Adams (Fool), Everett McGill (Man), Wendy Robie (Woman), A.J. Langer (Alice), Ving Rhames (LeRoy), Sean Whalen (Roach), Bill Cobbs (Grandpa Booker), Kelly Jo Minter (Ruby).

Hoping to steal some money to help his cancer-stricken mother, 13-year-old Adams breaks into the house of bizarre couple McGill and Robie. These two keep a group of young boys imprisoned in their basement.

2273.   *The People vs. Larry Flynt*   (1996, Columbia, 130m, c). D Milos Forman†, P Oliver Stone, Janet Yang & Michael Hausman, W Scott Alexander & Larry Karaszewski, PH Philippe Rousselot, ED Christopher Tellefsen, M Thomas Newman, PD Patrizia

Von Brandenstein, AD James Nezda & Shawn Hausman, SD Maria A. Nay.

LP Woody Harrelson† (Larry Flynt), Courtney Love (Althea Leasure), Edward Norton (Isaacman), Brett Harrelson (Jimmy Flynt), Miles Chapin (Miles), Donna Hanover (Ruth Carter Stapleton), James Cromwell (Charles Keating), Crispin Glover (Arlo), Vincent Schiavelli (Chester), James Carville (Simon Leis), Richard Paul (Jerry Falwell).

Several critics argued that this film was making a case for protection of the Bill of Rights–assured freedom of speech. Maybe, but Flynt, as portrayed by Harrelson, doesn't come off exactly as a patriot. He's a sleaze king married to a bisexual, drug-addicted HIV-positive stripper, played by Love. And although he and his "readers" have the right to view the trash he publishes, most people would rather not see it or attempt to equate it with great ideas, great art or even great sex.

2274. *The Perez Family* (1995, Samuel Goldwyn Co., 91m, c). D Mira Nair, P Michael Nozik & Lydia Dean Pilcher, W Robin Swicord (based on the novel by Christine Bell), PH Stuart Dryburgh, ED Bob Estrin, M Alan Silvestri, PD Mark Friedberg, AD Ken Hardy, SD Stephanie Carroll.

LP Marisa Tomei (Dottie Perez), Anjelica Huston (Carmela Perez), Alfred Molina (Juan Raul Perez), Chazz Palminteri (Lt. John Pirelli), Trini Alvarado (Teresa Perez), Celia Cruz (Luz Paz).

Set against the backdrop of the 1980 Mariel boatlift of Cuban refugees, this film focuses on Molina, who has spent twenty years as a political prisoner in Castro's jail. He hopes to find his wife Huston in Miami. Instead, floozy Tomei sees him as her ticket out of the detention camp. Meanwhile, Huston, despairing of ever seeing her husband again, finds love with Palminteri.

2275. *A Perfect Murder* (1998, Warner Bros., 105m, c). D Andrew Davis, P Arnold Kopelson, Anne Kopelson, Christopher Mankiewicz & Peter Macgregor-Scott, W Patrick Smith Kelly (based upon the play *Dial M for Murder* by Frederick Knott), PH Dariusz Wolski, ED Dennis Virkler & Dov Hoenig, M James Newton Howard, PD Philip Rosenberg, AD Patricia Woodbridge, SD Debra Schutt.

LP Michael Douglas (Steven Taylor), Gwyneth Paltrow (Emily Bradford), Viggo Mortensen (David Shaw), David Suchet (Det. Mohammed Karaman), Constance Towers (Sandra Bradford).

Let's count the reasons why this remake of Alfred Hitchcock's thriller *Dial M for Murder* fails to thrill. Douglas is not as charming as Ray Milland. Paltrow is not as appealing as Grace Kelly. Mortensen can't stack up to Robert Cummings and Anthony Dawson, whose two roles he's forced to merge into one. Suchet isn't as insightful as John Williams. Davis is no Hitchcock. The latter was a master of style; the former is a formula-driven director with a tired old formula. Well, at least it wasn't a scene-by-scene remake. For the record, Paltrow is having an affair with Mortensen. Her husband Douglas knows about it, but because she has the money, he can't just split. He talks Mortensen into murdering his lover for profit. But things go wrong when the intruder who is supposed to kill Paltrow is killed by her instead.

2276. *The Perfect Weapon* (1991, Paramount, 90m, c). D Mark DiSalle, P DiSalle & Pierre David, W David Campbell Wilson, PH Russell Carpenter, ED Wayne Wahrman, M Gary Chang, PD Curtis A. Schnell, AD Colin D. Irwin, SD Archie D'Amico.

LP Jeff Speakman (Jeff Sanders), John Dye (Adam), Dante Basco (Jimmy Ho), Toru Tanaka (Tanaka), Mako (Kim), Seth Sakai (Master Lo).

It's a routine martial arts film with Speakman out for revenge for the killing of an old family friend.

2277. *A Perfect World* (1993, Warner Bros., 130m, c). D Clint Eastwood, P Mark Johnson & David Valdes, W John Lee Hancock, PH Jack N. Green, ED Joel Cox & Ron Spang, M Lennie Niehaus, PD Henry Bumstead, AD Jack Taylor, Jr., SD Alan Hicks, Charlie Vassar & Antoinette Gordon.

LP Kevin Costner (Butch Haynes), Clint Eastwood (Red Garnett), Laura Dern (Sally Gerber), T.J. Lowther (Phillip Perry), Keith Szarabajka (Terry Pugh), Leo Burmester (Tom Adler), Paul Hewitt (Dick Scuttle).

Playing against type, Costner is an escaped convict who takes a young boy hostage. Texas Ranger Eastwood is hot on their trail. Costner still can't act, but at least in this film he's in his element and his lack of talent isn't as noticeable.

2278. *Perfectly Normal* (1991, Canada, Four Seasons Ent., 104m, c). D Yves Simoneau, P Michael Burns, W Eugene Lipinski & Paul Quarrington, PH Alain Dostie, ED Ronald Sanders, M Richard Gregoire, PD Anne Pritchard, SD Gordon Sim.

LP Robbie Coltrane (Alonzo Turner), Michael Riley (Renzo Parachi), Deborah Duchene (Denise), Eugene Lipinski (Karl Hoblisch), Jack Nichols (Duane Bickle), Elizabeth Harpur (Gloria).

Mysterious stranger Coltrane enlivens the life of a brewery worker. It's an offbeat comedy, not for everyone.

2279. *Permanent Midnight* (1998, Artisan Ent., 85m, c). D & W David Veloz (based on the book by Jerry Stahl), P Jane Hamsher & Don Murphy, PH Robert Yeoman, ED Steven Weisberg & Cara Silverman, M Daniel Light, PD Jerry Fleming.

LP Ben Stiller (Jerry Stahl), Elizabeth Hurley (Sandra), Maria Bello (Kitty), Owen Wilson (Nicky), Lourdes Benedicto (Viola), Peter Greene (Gus), Cheryl Ladd (Pamela Verlaine).

This film is based on the true story of Jerry Stahl, played by Stiller, and his attempts to juggle his successful writing for TV with his serious drug problem.

2280. *Persuasion* (1995, U.K., Sony Pictures Classics, 103m, c). D Roger Michell, P Fiona Finlay, W Nick Dear (based on the novel by Jane Austen), PH Margot Hayhoe, PH John Daly, ED Kate Evans, M Jeremy Sams, PD William Dudley & Brian Sykes, AD Linda Ward.

LP Amanda Root (Anne Elliot), Ciaran Hinds (Captain Wentworth), Susan Fleetwood (Lady Russell), Corin Redgrave (Sir Walter Elliot), Fiona Shaw (Mrs. Croft), John Woodvine (Admiral Croft), Phoebe Nicholls (Elizabeth Elliot), Samuel West (Mr. Elliot), Sophie Thompson (Mary Musgrove), Simon Russell Beale (Charles Musgrove), Emma Roberts (Louisa Musgrove).

In this film version of Jane Austen's last novel, Root is still in love with Hinds, the man she spurned years earlier. Now she must endure seeing him court her brother-in-law's younger sister. Good show!

2281. *The Pest* (1997, Columbia TriStar, 82m, c). D Paul Miller, P Sid Sheinberg, Bill Sheinberg & Jon Sheinberg, W David Bar Katz (based on a story by Katz & John Leguizamo), PH Roy H. Wagner, ED Ross Albert & David Rawlins, M Kevin Kiner, PD Roger E. Maus, AD Suzette Ervin, SD Jim Duffy.

LP John Leguizamo (Pestario "Pest" Vargas), Jeffrey Irons (Gustav Shank), Edoardo Ballerini (Himmel Shank), Freddy Rodriguez (Ninja), Aries Spears (Chubby), Tammy Townsend (Xantha Kent).

Street scam artist Leguizamo agrees to become the human prey for wealthy hunters. The story is merely a setting for a series of scatological jokes, raunchy dialogue and disgusting sight gags that should offend just about everyone.

2282. *Pet Sematary II* (1992, Paramount, 100m, c). D Mary Lambert, P Ralph S. Singleton, W Richard Outten, PH Russell Carpenter, ED Tom Finan, PD Michelle Minch, AD Karen Steward, SD Susan Benjamin.

LP Anthony Edwards (Chase Matthews), Edward Furlong (Geoff Matthews), Clancy Brown (Gus), Jason McGuire (Drew), Jared Rushton (Clyde), Jim Peck (Dr. Yolander), Lisa Waltz (Amanda), Darlanne Fluegel (Renee Matthews).

Despite having seen his best friend's dog and stepfather revived as savage killers, Furlong hopes to bring his mother back to life.

2283. *Peter's Friends* (1992, U.K./U.S., Samuel Goldwyn Co., 100m, c). D & P Kenneth Branagh, W Rita Rudner & Martin Bergman, PH Roger Lanser, ED Andrew Marcus, M Jacques Offenbach, PD Tim Harvey.

LP Hugh Laurie (Roger), Imelda Staunton (Mary), Stephen Fry (Peter), Emma Thompson (Maggie), Kenneth Branagh (Andrew), Alphonsia Emmanuel (Sarah), Rita Rudner (Carol), Phyllida Law (Vera), Alex Lowe (Paul), Tony Slattery (Brian).

A group of British theatrical types gather together at Fry's manor. There are two outsiders: Branagh's American wife Rudner and Emmanuel's married lover, Slattery. Thompson is looking for love — any kind of love. She appears nude at Fry's door; and while he's touched by the offer, he's gay. There are some good moments, but Rudner's script isn't as crisp as the performers.

2284. *Phantasm III: Lord of the Dead* (1994, Starway International, 91m, c). D, P & W Don Coscarelli, PH Chris Chomyn, ED Norman Buckley, M Frederic Myrow & Christopher L. Stone, PD Ken Aichele.

LP Angus Scrimm (The Tall Man), Reggie Bannister (Reggie), A. Michael Baldwin (Mike Pearson), Bill Thornbury (Jody Pearson), Gloria Lynne Henry (Rocky), Cindy Ambuehl (Edna).

Once again The Tall Man is back, and the weird horror series repeats itself. But if you wish to be scared, this just may do the trick.

2285. *The Phantom* (1996, Paramount, 96m, c). D Simon Wincer, P Robert Evans & Alan Ladd, Jr., W Jeffrey Boam (based on the Phantom characters created by Lee Falk), PH David Burr, ED O. Nicholas Brown & Bryan H. Carroll, M David Newman, PD Paul Peters, AD Lisette Thomas, SD Amy Wells.

LP Billy Zane (Phantom/Kit Walker), Kristy Swanson (Diana Palmer), Treat Williams (Xander Drax), Catherine Zeta Jones (Sala), James Remar (Quill), Cary-Hiroyuki Tagawa (Kabai Sengh), Bill Smitrovich (Uncle Dave), Casey Siemaszko (Morgan), Patrick McGoohan (Phantom's Dad).

Zane appears as the latest version of "The Ghost Who Walks." He's not a superhero with super powers; merely a masked purple avenger who outsmarts and foils power-mad villain Williams.

2286. *Phantom of the Ritz* (1992, Prism Ent., 89m, c). D Allen Plone, P Carol Marcus-Plone, W Allen Plone & Tom Dempsey (based on the novel *The Phantom of the Opera* by Gaston Leroux), PH Ron Diamond, M John Madara, Dave White & Wendy Frazier, SD Anthony Ricardi.

LP Peter Bergman (Ed Blake), Deborah Van Valkenburg (Nancy), Cindy Vincino (Sally), Joshua Sussman (The Phantom), Russell Curry (Marcus), Steve Geng (Detective Lassarde), Frank Tranchina (Dutch).

A drag race in 1952 ends in tragedy. Thirty years later Bergman plans to reopen the infamous Ritz Theater. He soon realizes that there is an evil presence in the theater. It's not quite *The Phantom of the Opera*, but the music by the Coasters helps.

2287. *Phantoms* (1998, Miramax, 91m, c). D Joe Chappelle, P Joel Soisson, Michael Leahy, Robert Pringle & Steve Lane, W Dean Koontz (based on his novel), PH Richard Clabaugh, ED Randolph K. Bricker, M David Williams, PD Deborah Raymond & Dorian Vernacchio, AD Daniel Bradford & Ken Larson, SD Jack Bishop.

LP Peter O'Toole (Timothy Flyte), Rose McGowan (Lisa Pailey), Joanna Going (Jenny Pailey), Liev Schreiber (Deputy Stu Wargle), Ben Affleck (Sheriff Bryce Hammond), Nicky Katt (Deputy Steve Shanning).

When sisters McGowan and Going arrive for a skiing vacation in a small Colorado community, they find it teeming with gruesome corpses. The culprit seems to be something called "The Ancient Enemy," a supernatural power responsible for mass human disappearances for millennia. Most discredit the thing's existence, except eccentric professor O'Toole, who has made it his life study.

2288. *Pharaoh's Army* (1996, Cinepix Film Props., 90m, c). D & W Robby Henson, P Henson & Doug Lodato, PH Doron Schlair, ED Henson, M Vince Emmett, Charles Ellis, Michael Stamper & Robert Friedman, PD Jana Rosenblatt.

LP Chris Cooper (Captain John Hull Ashton), Patricia Clarkson (Sarah Anders), Kris Kristofferson (Preacher), Richard Tyson (Rodie), Robert Joy (Chicago), Frank Clem (Neely), Huckleberry Fox (Newt).

In this anti-war story, stoical Kentucky woman Clarkson tries to protect her run-down farm and son from the Yankees during the Civil War. She slowly builds an understanding with Yankee officer Cooper. It's a quiet and slow-moving — but meaningful — story.

2289. *Phat Beach* (1996, LIVE Ent.–Orion, 99m, c). D Doug Ellin, P Cleveland O'Neal, W Brian E. O'Neal, Ben Morris & Ellin, PH Jim Lebovitz & Jurgen Baum, ED Richard Nord, PD Terri Schaetzle & Colleen Devine, AD Le'ce Edwards-Bonilla & Susan Muszynskio.

LP Jermaine "Huggy" Hopkins (Benny King), Brian Hooks (Durrel Jackson), Coolio (Himself), Tiny Lister, Jr. (Tiny), Greg D. Vance (Mikey Z.), Claudia Kaleem (Candace Williams), Sabrina De Pina (Tanya Watkins).

Looking to take off for the beach for a summer vacation, and having no money, a pair of friends "borrow" the Mercedes of the father of one and take off for trouble.

2290. *Phenomenon* (1996, Touchstone Pictures–Buena Vista, 117m, c). D Jon Turteltaub, P Barbara Boyle & Michael Taylor, W Gerald DiPego, PH Phedon Papamichael, ED Bruce Green, M Thomas Newman, PD Gareth Stover, AD Bruce Alan Miller, SD Jay Hart.

LP John Travolta (George Malley), Kyra Sedgwick (Lace Pennamin), Forest Whitaker (Nate Pope), Robert Duvall (Doc), David Gallagher (Al), Ashley Buccille (Glory), Tony Genaro (Tito), Jeffrey DeMunn (Professor Ringold), Richard Kiley (Dr. Wellin).

On his 37th birthday, sweet natured Travolta sees a blinding light that heightens his awareness of everything around him. He is able to learn new things with extraordinary speed. As amazed as he is by what has happened to him, it frightens others. Ultimately, it is also his undoing when some scientists want to use him as a living laboratory. His romance with Sedgwick is remarkably beautiful, and she is most appealing — as is Travolta in a marvelous performance.

2291. *Philadelphia* (1993, Tri-Star, 119m, c). D Jonathan Demme, P Edward Saxon & Demme, W Ron Nyswaner†, PH Tak Fujimoto, ED Craig McKay, M Howard Shore, PD Kristi Zea, AD Tim Galvin, SD Karen O'Hara.

LP Tom Hanks* (Andrew Beckett), Denzel Washington (Joe Miller), Antonio Banderas (Miguel Alvarez), Ron Vawter (Bob Seidman), Joanne Woodward (Sarah Beckett), Jason Robards (Charles Wheeler), Robert Ridgely (Walter Kenton), Paul Lazar (Dr. Klenstein).

Hanks won his first Oscar for his role as a gay attorney who believes that his law firm turned against him when he developed AIDS. He recruits homophobic lawyer Washington to help him fight for his rights. There is much to admire in this film; Hanks' performance merely heads the list. The ignorance about AIDS is given a fair hearing, as is the discrimination, which is doubled when one is both gay and dying of the horrible disease.

2292. *The Philadelphia Experiment 2* (1993, Trimark Pictures, 100m, c). D Stephen Cornwell, P Mark Levinson & Doug Curtis, W Kevin Rock & Nick Paine, PH Ronn Schmidt, ED Nina Gilberti, M Gerald Gouriet, PD Armin Ganz.

LP Brad Johnson (David Herdeg), Marjean Holden (Jess), Gerrit Graham (Mailer/Mahler), Cyril O'Reilly (Decker), James Greene (Professor Longstreet).

In this engaging time-travel flick, Johnson's modern-day stealth bomber makes an unexpected landing in Nazi Germany during WWII.

2293. *Phoenix* (1998, Lakeshore Ent., 104m, c). D Danny Cannon, P Victoria Nevinny & Tracie Graham, W Eddie Richey, PH James L. Carter, ED Zack Staenberg, M Graeme Revell, PD Charles Breen.

LP Ray Liotta (Harry Collins), Anthony LaPaglia (Mike Henshaw), Anjelica Huston (Leila), Daniel Baldwin (James Nutter), Jeremy Piven (Fred Shuster), Tom Noonan (Chicago).

Phoenix police detective Liotta is in way over his head with debts to loan sharks. He and three fellow officers hit a crime czar's club to get the cash to pay his debt.

2294. *Photographing Fairies* (1997, U.K., Starry Night Film Company, 104m, c). D Nick Willing, P Michele Camarda, W Willing & Chris Harrald (based on the novel by Steve Szilagyi), PH John de Borman, ED Sean Barton, M Simon Boswell, PD Laurence Dorman.

LP Toby Stephens (Charles Castle), Emily Wood (Linda), Ben Kingsley (Reverend Templeton), Philip Davis (Roy), Frances Barber (Beatrice Templeton), Hannah Bould (Clara Templeton), Edward Hardwicke (Sir Arthur Conan Doyle).

This is the second of two films that deal with the 1917 "Cottingley fairies" hoax, pulled off by two English girls who produced photos that they claimed proved the existence of fairies. The other film is *Fairy Tale: A True Story*. The girls even had Sir Arthur Conan Doyle convinced of the authenticity of the photographs and the existence of fairies.

2295. *PI* (1998, LIVE Ent., 85m, b&w). D & W Darren Aronofsky, P Eric Watson, PH Matthew Libatique, ED Oren Sarch, M Clint Mansell, PD Matthew Maraffi.

LP Sean Gullette (Max Cohen), Mark Margolis (Sol Robeson), Ben Shenkman (Lenny

Meyer), Pamela Hart (Marcy Dawson), Stephen Pearlman (Rabbi Cohen), Samia Shoaib (Devi).

Gullette, a mathematical genius, hunts for a pattern in the random numbers of the stock market. He believes anything can be understood in terms of numbers. (So did the ancient Greeks.) When it appears that he may be having some success, a Wall Street firm and a breakaway Hasidic sect try to force him to share his findings with them. While not for everyone, the film and its star provide just about enough tension to maintain the interest of curious audience members.

2296.   The Piano†   (1993, New Zealand, Miramax, 120m, c). D Jane Campion†, P Jan Chapman†, W Campion*, PH Stuart Dryburgh†, ED Veronika Jenet†, M Michael Nyman, PD Andrew McAlpine.

LP Holly Hunter* (Ada McGrath), Sam Neill (Stewart), Harvey Keitel (George Baines), Anna Paquin* (Fiona McGrath), Kerry Walker (Aunt Morag), Genevieve Lemon (Nessie).

This film is director Campion's masterpiece. Hunter, a mute by choice, travels to the untamed jungles of nineteenth century New Zealand with her daughter Paquin and her beloved piano to marry Neill, whom she has never met. Neill isn't much interested in the piano and leaves it on the beach. Neighbor Keitel rescues the instrument and offers to allow Hunter to play it in his home in exchange for sexual favors. Neill doesn't take it well when he discovers he is being cuckolded. The four main performers are truly outstanding. In particular, Hunter and Paquin's Oscar-winning work is memorable. A great sensuous scene: Keitel toys with the skin of Hunter's leg through a small tear in her stocking.

2297.   The Pickle   (1993, Columbia, 103m, c). D, P & W Paul Mazursky, PH Fred Murphy & David Stump, ED Stuart Pappe, M Michel Legrand, PD James Bissell, AD Christopher Burian-Mohr, John Berger & James Hegedus.

LP Danny Aiello (Harry Stone), Dyan Cannon (Ellen Stone), Clotilde Courau (Francoise), Shelley Winters (Yetta), Barry Miller (Ronnie Liebowitz), Jerry Stiller (Phil Hirsch), Christopher Penn (Gregory Stone), Little Richard (President).

Aiello is a self-involved director who hasn't

had a hit in a long, long time, and things don't appear to be getting any better. His latest epic is a sci-fi film about an overgrown pickle. Now Aiello the actor is in need of a hit after appearing in this pickle relish.

2298.   Picture Bride   (1995, Miramax, 90m, c). D Kayo Hatta, P Lisa Onodera & Diane Mei Lin Mark, W Kayo Hatta & Mari Hatta (based on their story with Mark), PH Claudio Rocha, ED Lynzee Klingman & Mallori Gottlieb, PD Paul Guncheon.

LP Youki Kudoh (Riyo), Akira Takayama (Matsuji), Tamlyn Tomita (Kana), Cary-Hiroyuki Tagawa (Kanzaki), Toshiro Mifune (The Benshi), Yoki Sugi (Aunt Sode).

A young Japanese woman with a troubled past travels to Hawaii as a "picture bride" in the early 1900s. She finds her new married life a great deal different than what she imagined and hoped it would be.

2299.   Picture Perfect   (1997, 20th Century–Fox, 102m, c). D Glenn Gordon Caron, P Erwin Stoff, W Arleen Sorkin, Paul Slansky & Gordon Caron (based on a story by Sorkin, Slansky & May Quigley), PH Paul Sarossy, ED Robert Reitano, M Carter Burwell, PD Larry Fulton, AD John Wright Stevens, SD Debra Schutt.

LP Jennifer Aniston (Kate Mosley), Jay Mohr (Nick), Olympia Dukakis (Rita Mosley), Illena Douglas (Darcy O'Neal), Kevin Dunn (Mr. Alan Mercer), Kevin Bacon (Sam), Anne Twomey (Sela), Faith Prince (Mrs. Mercer).

Aniston is a talented and ambitious ad agency employee who is informed that her career will remain stalled unless she gets some personal commitments — like, say, a husband and kids in her life. She creates a fictitious relationship with Mohr to win her promotion. She also attracts the attention of Bacon, who is only interested in supposedly unavailable women. Everyone, including her boss, insists on meeting her fiancé, so she has to look up Mohr and get his cooperation. Sound familiar? Indeed it is, but it just about works because of Aniston's charm and comedic talent.

2300.   The Pillow Book   (1996, U.K./Netherlands/France, CFP Distribution, 126m, c). D & W Peter Greenaway, P Kees Kasander, PH Sacha Vierny, ED Chris Wyatt & Greenaway, PD Wilbert van Dorp, Andree Putman

& Emi Wada, AD Koichi Hamamura & Vincent De Pater.

LP Vivian Wu (Nagiko Kiohara), Yoshi Oida (The Publisher), Ken Ogata (The Father), Ewan McGregor (Jerome), Hideko Yoshida (Sei Shonagon/The Aunt/The Maid), Judy Ongg (The Mother).

In Hong Kong, young Japanese fashion model Wu is sexually excited by having calligraphy drawn on her nude body. She discovers Englishman McGregor, who allows her to write on his body. Then they transcribe the writing to a Pillow Book, a Japanese diary. This story of exotic sex turns gruesome.

2301. *Pinocchio's Revenge* (1996, Vidmark, 94m, c). D & W Kevin S. Tenney, P Jeff Geoffray & Walter Josten, PH Eric Anderson, ED Daniel Duncan, M Dennis Michael Tenney, PD Candi Gutteres.

LP Rosalind Allen (Jennifer Garrick), Brittany Alyse Smith (Zoe Garrick), Todd Allen (David Kaminsky), Aaron Lustig (Dr. Edwards), Candace McKenzie (Sophia), Lewis Van Bergen (Vincent Gotto).

This is no Walt Disney story about a puppet who dreams of being a real boy. The Pinocchio puppet in this thriller doesn't just have a dream, he has a mission: becoming a vicious murderer.

2302. *The Pit and the Pendulum* (1991, Paramount, 95m, c). D Stuart Gordon, P Albert Band, W Dennis Paoli (based on the short story by Edgar Allan Poe), PH Adolfo Bartoli, ED Andy Horvitch, M Richard Band, AD Giovanni Natalucci.

LP Lance Henriksen (Torquemada), Rona DeRicci (Maria), Jonathan Fuller (Antonio), Frances Bay (Esmeralda), Jeffery Combs (Francisco), Tom Towles (Don Carlos).

Poe wouldn't recognize this story as anything he wrote. When DeRicci tries to prevent the beating of a small boy by the guards of the Spanish Inquisition, she's thrown into a dungeon and tortured. Of course, her clothes must be torn from her body.

2303. *Pizza Man* (1991, Megalomania Prods., 90m, c). D, W & ED J.D. Athens, P Jonathan F. Lawton, PH Fred Samina, M Daniel May, PD Theodore Charles Smudde, AD Francisco Gutierrez, Susan Lee & Tim Bradley, SD Jane Van Tamelen.

LP Bill Maher (Elmo Bunn), Annabelle Gurwitch (The Dame), David McKnight (Vince), Andy Roano (The Hood), Bob Delegall (Mayor Tom Bradley), Bryan Clark (Ronald Reagan).

In this political satire, Maher is a pizza delivery man who gets involved in a worldwide conspiracy.

2304. *Plan B* (1997, Curb Ent., 102m, c). D & W Gary Leva, P Lulu Baskins-Leva, Nancy Joslin & Gary Leva, PH Yoram Astrakhan, ED Kelly Knutzen, M Andrew Rose, PD Carol Strober.

LP Jon Cryer (Stuart Winer), Lisa Darr (Clare Sadler), Lance Guest (Jack Sadler), Mark Mathieson (Ricky Stone), Sara Mornell (Gina Ferris).

This film examines the activities of a group of L.A. friends, all approaching thirty. They note that their lives are not working out according to plan. Thus, they have to develop a plan B.

2305. *Play It to the Bone* (1999, Buena Vista–Touchstone Pictures, 124m, c). D & W Ron Shelton, P Stephen Chin, PH Mark Vargy, ED Paul Seydor & Patrick Flannery, M Alex Wurman, PD Claire Jenora Meredith, AD Mary Finn, SD Danielle Berman.

LP Antonio Banderas (Cesar Dominguez), Woody Harrelson (Vince Boudreau), Lolita Davidovich (Grace Pasic), Tom Sizemore (Joe Domino), Lucy Liu (Lia), Robert Wagner (Hank Goody), Richard Masur (Artie).

When two promising young boxers are killed in an automobile accident, promoter Sizemore is desperate to find combatants to fill the opening card of a Mike Tyson fight in a Las Vegas luxury hotel. He's so desperate that he meets the demands of two over-the-hill middleweights and best friends, Banderas and Harrelson. However, the two must get to Vegas from L.A. in time for the fight. There are some nice parts of this weird comedy. Davidovich is particularly appealing and convincing.

2306. *The Playboys* (1992, U.S./Ireland, Samuel Goldwyn Co., 110m, c). D Gillies MacKinnon, P William P. Cartlidge & Simon Perry, W Shane Connaughton & Kerry Crabbe, PH Jack Conroy, ED Humphrey Dixon, M Jean-Claude Petit, PD Andy Harris, AD Arden Gantly.

LP Albert Finney (Constable Hegarty), Aidan Quinn (Tom Casey), Robin Wright (Tara Maguire), Milo O'Shea (Freddie), Alan Devlin (Malone), Niamh Cusack (Brigid), Ian McElhinney (Cassidy), Stella McCusker (Rachel).

Wright scandalizes her provincial Irish village in the 1950s by having a child, although she's not married and refuses to name the father. Things become even more stirred up with the arrival of a travelling troupe of actors. She is rescued from the wrath of the locals by flamboyant actor Quinn.

2307. *The Player* (1992, Fine Line Ent., 123m, c). D Robert Altman†, P David Brown, Michael Tolkin & Nick Wechsler, W Tolkin† (based on his novel), PH Jean Lepine, ED Geraldine Peroni† & Maysie Hoy, M Thomas Newman, PD Stephen Altman, AD Jerry Fleming, SD Susan Emshwiller.

LP Tim Robbins (Griffin Mill), Greta Scacchi (June Gudmundsdottir), Fred Ward (Walter Stuckel), Whoopi Goldberg (Detective Avery), Peter Gallagher (Larry Levy), Brion James (Joel Levison), Cynthia Stevenson (Bonnie Sherow), Vincent D'Onofrio (David Kahane), Dean Stockwell (Andy Civella), Richard E. Grant (Tom Oakley).

In this dark comedy, director Altman savages the film industry in telling the story of Robbins, a young movie executive who is threatened by a disgruntled screenwriter. Robbins chooses to take the law into his own hands. There are a score of cameos by an assortment of actors and actresses and many inside jokes that will tickle the movie buff.

2308. *The Players Club* (1998, New Line Cinema, 104m, c). D & W Ice Cube, P Patricia Charbonnet, PH Malik Sayeed, M Hidden Faces, PD Dina Lipton, AD Keith Neely.

LP Lisa Raye (Diana Armstrong/Diamond), Bernie Mae (Dollar Bill), Monica Calhoun (Ebony), A.J. Johnson (Li'l Man), Ice Cube (Reggie), Alex Thomas (Clyde), Jamie Foxx (Blue).

To pay her college tuition, beautiful single mother Raye takes a job as a stripper at the Players Club. Despite taking off her clothes and doing some occasional table dancing, she resists becoming a whore. Well, good for her. This comedy drama is just one further step in the transformation of Ice Cube from a rapper to a multidimensional filmmaker.

2309. *Playing by Heart* (1998, U.S./ U.K., Miramax, 121m, c). D & W Willard Carroll, P Carroll, Meg Liberman & Tom Wilhite, PH Vilmos Zsigmond, ED Pietro Scalia, M John Barry, PD Melissa Stewart, AD Charlie Daboub, SD Patte Strong & Mark Poll, SD Cindy Carr.

LP Gillian Anderson (Meredith), Angelina Jolie (Joan), Madeleine Stowe (Gracie), Anthony Edwards (Roger), Ryan Phillippe (Keenan), Gena Rowlands (Hannah), Sean Connery (Paul), Dennis Quaid (Hugh), Ellen Burstyn (Mildred).

In this talky drama, an ensemble cast explores relationships between men and women. The results in the painfully slow film are very definitely mixed. The search for love and intimacy in the late '90s is terribly artificial. The filmmakers try to throw in every kind of love they can think of, and the dialogue sounds like something someone would write but not say. Trying to keep all the balls in the air and tying together every loose string seems too much for writer-director Carroll.

2310. *Playing God* (1997, Touchstone–Buena Vista, 93m, c). D Andy Wilson, P Marc Abraham & Laura Bickford, W Mark Haskell Smith, PH Anthony B. Richmond, ED Louise Rubacky, M Richard Harley, PD Naomi Shohan, AD Troy Sizemore, SD Evette Frances Knight.

LP David Duchovny (Dr. Eugene Sands), Timothy Hutton (Raymond Blossom), Angelina Jolie (Claire), Michael Massee (Gage), Peter Stormare (Valdimir).

Duchovny, an unlicensed L.A. surgeon, becomes the personal physician for sleazy smuggler Hutton. The Doc falls in love with the hoodlum's girlfriend, Jolie. The latter, an informer for the FBI, hopes to get the goods on Hutton. To save her life, Duchovny fakes Jolie's death and takes her to his family's empty summer house, where he sweats out his drug addiction. Hutton stumbles onto the truth and soon is on their trail.

2311. *Playmaker* (1994, Odyssey Ent., 91m, c). D Yuri Zeltser, P Thomas Baer, Marc Samuelson & Peter Samuelson, W Zeltser & Michael Schroeder (based on a story by Kathryn Block & Darren Block), PH Ross Berryman, ED John Rosenberg, M Mark Snow, PD Phillip Vasels & Diane Hughes.

LP Colin Firth (Ross), Jennifer Rubin (Jamie), John Getz (Eddie), Jeff Perry (Allen), Arthur Taxier (Det. Chossman), Dean Norris (Det. Marconi), Belinda Waymouth (Angie).

The plot twists of this would-be exotic thriller only make the film more pretentious than most members of the audience will be able to stomach. Plenty of nudity, profanity and violence for those who find these things enjoyable can make even the worst script palpable.

2312. Pleasantville (1998, New Line Cinema, 123m, c/b&w). D & W Gary Ross, P Jon Kilik, Robert J. Degus, Steven Soderbergh & Ross, PH John Lindley, ED William Goldenberg, M Randy Newman†, PD Jeannine Oppewall†, AD Dianne Wager, SD Jay Hart†.

LP Tobey Maguire (David/Bud), Jeff Daniels (Mr. Johnson), Joan Allen (Betty), William H. Macy (George), J.T. Walsh (Bog Bob), Reese Witherspoon (Jennifer/Mary Sue), Don Knotts (TV Repairman), Paul Walker (Skip), Marley Shelton (Margaret).

If you ever wondered what it would be like if two '90s teenagers suddenly found themselves characters in a black-and-white '50s TV family show like *Father Knows Best*, this film has all the answers. While struggling with a TV remote, siblings Maguire and Witherspoon break it and, with the help of sinister TV repairman Knotts, are thrown into the cast of the show *Pleasantville*. Before long their '90s knowhow begins to change all of the show's characters, adding color to the scenes. Maguire is a very appealing young performer, and Witherspoon is as cute as a button.

2313. Plump Fiction (1998, Legacy/Rhino Films, 82m, c). D & W Rob Koherr, P Gary Binkow, PH Rex Nicholson, ED Neil Kirk, PD Jacques Herbert, AD Robert La Liberte, SD Nicole Lee.

LP Tommy Davidson (Julius), Julie Brown (Mimi), Paul Dinello (Jimmy), Sandra Bernhard (Bunny Roberts), Dan Castellaneta (Bumpkin), Colleen Camp (Viv).

This spoof of Quentin Tartantino's *Pulp Fiction* is too predictable to even rate a description.

2314. Plunkett & Macleane (1999, U.K., Polygram-Gramercy, 100m, c). D Jake Scott,

P Tim Bevan, Eric Fellner & Rupert Harvey, W Robert Wade, Neil Purvis & Charles McKeown (based on an original screenplay by Selwyn Roberts), PH John Mathieson, ED Oral Norrie Ottey, M Craig Armstrong, PD Norris Spencer, AD Petr Kunc & Jindrich Koci.

LP Robert Carlyle (Will Plunkett), Jonny Lee Miller (Capt. James Macleane), Liv Tyler (Lady Rebecca), Kent Stott (Chance), Michael Gambon (Lord Chief Justice Gibson), Alan Cumming (Lord Rochester).

There is not much to the story or the direction of this costume romp. It's about the exploits of Carlyle and Miller, two 18th century highwaymen who gain a reputation for the courtesy with which they treat their victims. Carlyle and Miller do play well together, but Tyler needs more practice on her accent to convince audiences that she's a well-bred English girl.

2315. Pocahontas (1995, Walt Disney–Buena Vista, 87m, c). D Mike Gabriel & Eric Goldberg, P James Pentecost, W Carl Binder, Susannah Grant & Philip LaZebnik (based on a story by Glen Keane, Joe Grant, Ralph Zondag, Burny Mattinson, Ed Gombert, Kaan Kaylon, Francis Glebas, Robert Gibbs, Bruce Morris, Todd Kurosawa, Duncan Majoribanks & Chris Buck), ED H. Lee Peterson, M Alan Menken* & Stephen Schwartz*, AD Michael Giaimo, ANIM Glen Keane, John Pomeroy, Majoribanks, Ruben Aquino, Nik Ranieri, Dave Prulksma, Buck & Ken Duncan.

LP Voices: Irene Bedard (Pocahontas, Speaking Voice), Judy Kuhn (Pocahontas, Singing Voice), Mel Gibson (Captain John Smith), Russell Means (Chief Powhatan), David Ogden Stiers (John Ratcliffe), Linda Hunt (Grandma Willow).

While not quite on a par with other recent Disney animated features, this historically inaccurate fantasy about a fair Indian maid and an Englishman is enjoyable, and the songs are decent.

2316. Poetic Justice (1993, Columbia, 110m, c). D & W John Singleton, P Steve Nicolaides & Singleton, PH Peter Lyons Collister, ED Bruce Cannon, M Stanley Clarke, PD Keith Brian Burns, AD Kirk M. Petrucelli, SD Dan May & Darrell Wright.

LP Janet Jackson (Justice), Tupac Shakur (Lucky), Tyra Ferrell (Jessie), Regina King

(Iesha), Joe Torry (Chicago), Roger Guenveur Smith (Heywood), Lori Petty (Penelope), Billy Zane (Brad).

Jackson makes her film debut as a would-be poet who falls in love with troubled young Shakur. While Jackson and Shakur should have stuck with their singing careers, at least Jackson had Maya Angelou writing her poetry.

2317. *Point Break* (1991, 20th Century–Fox, 123m, c). D Kathryn Bigelow, P Peter Abrams & Robert L. Levy, W W. Peter Iliff (based on a story by Iliff & Rick King), PH Donald Peterman, ED Howard Smith, M Mark Isham, PD Peter Jamison, AD Pamela Marcotte, SD Leslie Spheeris.

LP Patrick Swayze (Bodhi), Keanu Reeves (Johnny Utah), Gary Busey (Pappas), Lori Petty (Tyler), Bojesse Christopher (Grommet), Julian Reyes (Alvarez).

FBI agents Reeves and Busey investigate a series of bank robberies that may have been masterminded by surfer Swayze. Unfortunately, the wave of excitement the film is riding at the start breaks up by the end.

2318. *Point of No Return* (1993, Warner Bros., 109m, c). D John Badham, P Art Linson, W Robert Getchell & Alexandra Seros (based on the screenplay *La Femme Nikita* by Luc Besson), PH Michael Watkins & Michael Ferris, ED Frank Morriss, M Hans Zimmer, PD Philip Harrison, AD Sydney Z. Litwack, SD Julia Laughlin, Eric W. Orbom, James Bayliss, Sally Thornton & Roger C. Fortune.

LP Bridget Fonda (Maggie), Gabriel Byrne (Bob), Dermot Mulroney (J.P.), Miguel Ferrer (Kaufman), Anne Bancroft (Amanda), Olivia D'Abo (Angela), Richard Romanus (Fahd Bahkitar), Harvey Keitel (Victor the Cleaner).

In this U.S. remake of the exceptional *La Femme Nikita*, Fonda is saved from execution by government official Byrne, who recruits her to become a super-duper assassin. Even though this film is faithful to the original and Fonda gives a decent performance, it doesn't compare favorably to the French effort. It's sort of like anyone who can read can cook; but having a recipe doesn't make one a top chef.

2319. *Poison* (1991, Zeitgeist Films, 85m, c). D & W Todd Haynes (based on the novels *Our Lady of the Flowers, Miracle of the Roses* & *Thief's Journal* by Jean Genet), PH Maryse Alberti & Barry Ellsworth, ED James Lyons, M James Bennett, PD Sarah Stollman & John Hansen, AD Chas Plummer.

LP Edith Meeks (Felicia Beacon), Millie White (Millie Sklar), Buck Smith (Gregory Lazar), Anne Giotta (Evelyn McAlpert), Lydia Lafleur (Sylvia Manning), Ian Nemser (Sean White), Rob LaBelle (Jay Wete), Larry Maxwell (Dr. Graves), Susan Norman (Nancy), Scott Renderer (John Broom), James Lyons (Jack Bolton).

This low-budget independent effort won the Grand Jury Prize at the Sundance Film Festival. It interweaves three seemingly unconnected stories, each with its own independent film style. In one story a seven-year-old kills his father; another features a mad scientist transformed into a leper; and the final offers a sadistic homosexual relationship in prison.

2320. *Poison Ivy* (1992, New Line Cinema, 100m, c). D Katt Shea Ruben, P Katt Shea Ruben & Andy Ruben, W The Rubens (based on a story by Melissa Goddard & Peter Morgan), PH Phedon Papamichael, ED Gina Mittleman, M Aaron Davies, PD Virginia Lee, AD Hayden Yates, SD Michelle Munoz.

LP Sara Gilbert (Sylvie Cooper), Drew Barrymore (Ivy), Tom Skerritt (Darryl Cooper), Cheryl Ladd (Georgie Cooper), Alan Stock (Bob), Jeanne Sakata (Isabelle), E.J. Moore (Kid).

Barrymore is a sleazy teen seducer who insinuates herself into the home life of her awkward classmate Gilbert. Barrymore sets her sights on seducing Gilbert's father, Skerritt, whose wife Ladd is dying of emphysema. You can't blame the girl for wanting a family of her own, can you?

2321. *Poison Ivy: The New Seduction* (1997, New Line, 94m, c). D Kurt Voss, P Catalaine Knell, W Karen Kelly, PH Feliks Parnell, ED John Rosenberg, M Reg Powell, PD Elizabeth A. Scott, SD Mina Javid.

LP Megan Edwards (Joy Greer), Jaime Pressley (Violet), Michael Des Barnes (Ivan Greer), Greg Vaughan (Michael), Susan Tyrrell (Mrs. B), Gregory Vignolle (Alvaro), Michael McLafferty (Scott), Merete Van Kamp (Catherine).

This film has very little to do with *Poison Ivy*. Twenty-year-old Pressley shows up at the home of childhood friend Edwards and is invited to stay. She then uses sexual tactics, some learned while working as a dominatrix, to seduce Edwards' fiancé Vaughan and father Des Barnes. It seems Pressley wishes to take revenge on the family because her mother once had an affair with Des Barnes that ended badly. Pressley not only displays her fine body in passionless poses, she kills anyone who interferes with her plans.

2322. *Polish Wedding* (1998, Fox Searchlight, 107m, c). D & W Theresa Connelly, P Tom Rosenberg, Julia Chasman & Geoff Stier, PH Guy Dufaux, ED Curtiss Clayton & Suzanne Fenn, M Luis Bacalov, PD Kara Lindstrom.

LP Lena Olin (Jadzia Pzoniak), Gabriel Byrne (Bolek Pzoniak), Claire Danes (Hala Pzoniak), Adam Trese (Russell Schuster), Mili Avital (Sofie Pzoniak).

Burdened with a cliché-riddled script, Olin, Byrne and Danes nevertheless bring some class to this old-fashioned family comedy. It chronicles the sexual explorations of strong-willed and independent adolescent Danes with Trese, the cop on the beat in her Detroit working-class neighborhood. When she finds herself pregnant, Dane's mother Olin, who runs the family with an iron fist, decides a wedding is in order.

2323. *The Pompatus of Love* (1996, BMG Independents, 99m, c). D Richard Schenkman, P D.J. Paul & Jon Resnik, W Jon Cryer, Adam Oliensis & Richard Schenkman, PH Russell Lee Fine, ED Dan Rosen, M John Hill, PD Michael Krantz.

LP Jon Cryer (Mark), Adrian Pasdar (Josh), Tim Guinee (Runyon), Adam Oliensis (Phil), Mia Sara (Cynthia), Kristin Scott Thomas (Caroline), Arabella Field (Lori).

Four young men explore their feelings about life and love in a talky but entertaining film.

2324. *Pontiac Moon* (1994, Paramount, 108m, c). D Peter Medak, P Youssef Vahabzadeh & Robert Schaffel, W Finn Taylor & Jeffrey Brown (based on an idea by Taylor), PH Thomas Kloss, ED Anne V. Coates, M Randy Edelman, PD Jeffrey Beecroft, AD William Ladd Skinner, SD Robert J. Franco.

LP Ted Danson (Washington Bellamy), Mary Steenburgen (Katherine Bellamy), Ryan Todd (Andy Bellamy), Eric Schweig (Ernest

Ironplume), Cathy Moriarty (Lorraine), Max Gail (Jerome Bellamy), Lisa Jane Persky (Alicia Frook).

The Apollo XI astronauts inspire eccentric Danson to hit the road with his sheltered son Todd. Nothing much is accomplished or resolved.

2325. *Popcorn* (1991, U.S./Jamaica, Century Films, 93m, c). D Mark Herrier, P Torben Johnke, Gary Goch & Ashok Amritraj, W Alan Ormsby (based on the story by Mitchell Smith), PH Ronnie Taylor, ED Stan Cole, M Paul J. Zaza, PD Peter Murton, AD John Myhre.

LP Jill Schoelen (Maggie), Tom Villard (Toby), Dee Wallace Stone (Suzanne), Derek Rydall (Mark), Malcolm Danare (Bud), Elliott Hurst (Leon).

The audience of a horror film festival believes that a killer stalking victims is just part of the performance.

2326. *The Pope Must Diet!* (GB: *The Pope Must Die!*) (1992, U.K., Miramax, 97m, c). D Peter Richardson, P Stephen Woolley, W Richardson & Pete Richens, PH Frank Gell, ED Katherine Wenning, M Jeff Beck & Anne Dudley, PD John Ebden.

LP Robbie Coltrane (Pope), Beverly D'Angelo (Veronica Dante), Herbert Lom (Vittorio Corelli), Alex Rocco (Cardinal Rocco), Paul Bartel (Monsignor Vitchie), Balthazar Getty (Joe Don Dante).

On the verge of being defrocked, priest Coltrane is accidentally made Pope due to a misspelling made by a near-deaf dictation clerk. Devout Catholics won't be the only ones who won't find the idea funny.

2327. *The Portrait of a Lady* (1996, New Zealand/U.K./U.S., Gramercy, 144m, c). D Jane Campion, P Monty Montgomery & Steve Golin, W Laura Jones (based on the novel by Henry James), PH Stuart Dryburgh, ED Veronika Jenet, M Wojiech Kilar, PD Janet Patterson, AD Martin Childs, SD Jill Quertier.

LP Nicole Kidman (Isabel Archer), John Malkovich (Gilbert Osmond), Barbara Hershey† (Madame Serena Merle), Mary-Louise Parker (Henrietta Stackpole), Martin Donovan (Ralph Touchett), Shelley Winters (Mrs. Touchett), Richard E. Grant (Lord Warburton), Shelley Duvall (Countess Gemini),

Christian Bale (Edward Rosier), Viggo Mortensen (Caspar Goodwood), Valentina Cervi (Pansy Osmond), John Gielgud (Mr. Touchett).

As is usual in a Henry James–based story, independent minded American Kidman innocently faces the corruption of Europeans. She has turned down two promising proposals of marriage while living with her wealthy aunt and uncle in England. She finds her inspiration in the person of worldly and mysterious widow Hershey. When her uncle dies she is left an inheritance. She travels to Italy, where she meets American expatriate Malkovich who, prompted by Hershey, seduces Nicole. He's a cad, only interested in himself, don't you know. With whom is she to find happiness? See the fine film to find out.

2328. Portraits of a Killer (1996, U.S./Canada, LIVE Ent., 93m, c). D Bill Corcoran, P Bruce Harvey & Shauna Shapiro-Jackson, W Harvey, Nancy Laing & Scott McPherson, PH Curtis Petersen, ED Doug Forbes, M Graeme Coleman, PD Michael Nemirsky, SD Melodi McGill.

LP Jennifer Grey (Elaine Taylor), Costas Mandylor (George Kendell), Patricia Charbonneau (Carolyn Price), M. Emmet Walsh (Raymond Garrison), Michael Ironside (Sgt. Ernie Hansen), Roxanne Kraemer (Sandy).

Mandylor is wooden as a professional photographer who publishes a portfolio of young prostitutes, all of whom he has bedded. Unfortunately, four of his subjects are now dead. Prosecutor Charbonneau wants to pin the crimes on Mandylor, and Grey signs on for the defense. True to his ways, Mandylor beds Grey.

2329. Posse (1993, Gramercy Pictures, 112m, c). D Mario Van Peebles, P Jim Steele & Preston Holmes, W Dario Scardapane, PH Peter Menzies, ED Mark Conte, M Michel Colombier, PD Catherine Hardwicke, AD Kim Hix, SD Tessa Posnansky, Mark Worthington & John Westfal.

LP Mario Van Peebles (Jessie Lee), Stephen Baldwin (Little J.), Charles Lane (Weezie), Tiny Lister (Obobo), Big Daddy Kane (Father Time), Billy Zane (Colonel Graham), Blair Underwood (Sheriff Carver), Melvin Van Peebles (Papa Joe), Pam Grier (Phoebe).

Mysterious black drifter Van Peebles leads a posse of Army deserters in a search for stolen gold.

2330. Possums (1998, HSX Films, 97m, c). D & W J. Max Burnett, P Leanna Creel, PH Christopher Duskin, ED Karen Lee Smith, M Justin Caine Burnett, PD Chuck Price.

LP Mac Davis (Will Clark), Cynthia Sikes (Elizabeth Clark), Gregory Coolidge (Jake Malloy), Andrew Prine (Charles Lawton), Dennis Burkley (Orville Moss), Monica Lacy (Sarah Jacobs).

In this family drama, Davis portrays a small-town sports announcer. Despite their poor performances, he keeps the local high school football team, the Possums, alive.

2331. Postcards from America (1995, U.K., Strand Releasing, 89m, c). D & W Steve McLean (based on the books *Close to the Knives* and *Memories That Smell Like Gasoline* by David Wojnarowicz), P Christine Vachon & Craig Paull, PH Ellen Kuras, ED Elizabeth Gazzara M Stephen Endelman, PD Therese Duprez, AD Scott Pask.

LP James Lyons (David Wojnarowicz), Michael Tighe (Teenage David), Olmo Tighe (Young David), Michael Imperioli (The Hustler), Michael Ringer (Father), Maggie Low (Mother).

This film is a drama based on the tortured life of gay artist and AIDS activist David Wojnarowicz, who died in 1992. It is divided into three segments: the first dealing with his life as an abused child; then his late teens when he was a Times Square hustler, and finally his brief adult life.

2332. Postcards from the Edge (1990, Columbia, 101m, c). D Mike Nichols, P Nichols & John Calley, W Carrie Fisher (based on her novel), PH Michael Ballhaus, ED Sam O'Steen, M Carly Simon, PD Patrizia Von Brandenstein, AD Kandy Stern, SD Chris A. Butler.

LP Meryl Streep† (Suzanne Vale), Shirley MacLaine (Doris Mann), Dennis Quaid (Jack Falkner), Gene Hackman (Lowell), Richard Dreyfuss (Dr. Frankenthal), Rob Reiner (Joe Pierce), Mary Wickes (Grandma), Conrad Bain (Grandpa), Annette Bening (Evelyn Ames), Simon Callow (Simon Asquith).

This film is based on actress-screenwriter Carrie Fisher's real-life battle with alcohol and drug abuse. She is represented by Streep, with MacLaine as an aging star, á la mama Debbie Reynolds.

2333.   The Postman   (1997, Warner Bros., 170m, c). D Kevin Costner, P Jim Wilson, Steve Tisch & Costner, W Eric Roth & Brian Helgeland (based on the novel by David Brin), PH Stephen Windon, ED Peter Boyle, M James Newton Howard, PD Ida Random, SD Ron Reiss.

LP Kevin Costner (The Postman), Will Patton (General Bethlehem), Larcnz Tate (Ford Lincoln Mercury), Olivia Williams (Abby), James Russo (Idaho), Daniel Van Bargen (Sheriff Briscoe).

Costner's film is a heavy favorite in the race for the worst film of the year. It is the pretentious and ridiculous story of a post-apocalyptic time. Drifter Costner exchanges his rags for the clothes of a dead postman so he can bluff himself into a walled city, claiming to be a mail carrier sent by the newly restored government. Patton, the sociopathic leader of an army of brigands, wants no government to interfere with his gang's plundering; so Costner and all who help him become targets. There are so many things wrong with this film that it would take much too long to list them. But among the most obvious are Costner's acting and the length of the film. There's not enough story for nearly three hours.

2334.   Powder   (1995, Hollywood Pictures–Buena Vista, 111m, c). D & W Victor Salva, P Roger Birnbaum & Daniel Grodnik, PH Jerzy Zielinski, ED Dennis M. Hill, M Jerry Goldsmith, PD Waldemar Kalinowski, AD Barry Kingston, SD Florence Fellman.

LP Mary Steenburgen (Jessie Caldwell), Sean Patrick Flanery (Powder), Lance Henriksen (Sheriff Barnum), Jeff Goldblum (Donald Ripley), Brandon Smith (Duncan), Bradford Tatum (John Box), Susan Tyrrell (Maxine), Missy Crider (Lindsey).

Flanery, nicknamed "Powder," is a teen afflicted with an unusually severe albinotic disorder. He endures the pain of ostracism and physical abuse. But it becomes clear that he has some very special qualities.

2335.   Power 98   (1997, Λ-Vision, 89m, c). D & W Jaime Hellman, P Carole Curb Nemoy, Dana Lustig & Ram Bergman, PH Kent Wakeford, ED Duane Hartzell, M Jeff Beal, PD Nanci B. Roberts.

LP Eric Roberts (Karlin Pickett), Jason Gedrick (Jon Price), Jennie Garth (Sharon Penn), Stephen Tobolowsky (Rick Harris), James Pickens, Jr. (Detective Wilkison).

Shock jock Roberts and his on-the-air partner Gedrick become the prime suspects when a caller confesses to the murder of a woman with whom Gedrick had a brief fling.

2336.   The Power of One   (1992, U.S./Germany/France, Warner Bros., 111m, c). D John G. Avildsen, P Arnon Milchan, W Robert Mark Kamen (based on the novel by Bryce Courtenay), PH Dean Semler, ED Avildsen, M Hans Zimmer, PD Roger Hall, AD Martin Hitchcock & Kevin Phipps, SD Karen Brookes.

LP Stephen Dorff (PK, Age 18), Armin Mueller-Stahl (Doc), Morgan Freeman (Geel Piet), John Gielgud (Headmaster St. John), Fay Masterson (Maria Marais), Simon Fenton (PK, Age 12), Guy Witcher (PK, Age 7), Daniel Craig (Sgt. Jaapie Botha).

Set in the 1930s and '40s in South Africa, the story tells of an English boy who survives being tormented by youthful Afrikaners. He is aided by two men, one white (Mueller-Stahl), one black (Freeman). The boy battles racial injustice with native music and boxing.

2337.   Practical Magic   (1998, Warner Bros., 105m, c). D Griffin Dunne, P Denise Di Novi, W Robin Swicord, Akiva Goldsman & Adam Brooks (based on the novel by Alice Hoffman), PH Andrew Dunn, ED Elizabeth Kling & Craig McKay, M Alan Silvestri, PD Robin Standefer, AD Keith P. Cummingham & Stephen Alesch, SD Claire Jenora Bowen.

LP Sandra Bullock (Sally Owens), Nicole Kidman (Gillian Owens), Dianne Wiest (Aunt Jet), Stockard Channing (Aunt Frances), Aidan Quinn (Gary Hallet), Goran Visnjic (Jimmy).

Bullock and Kidman are such lovely witches that it's too bad the story doesn't provide any magic for them. Timid Bullock had about given up any expectation of finding her soul-mate, resigning herself to a mundane life with her psychic aunts, Wiest and Channing. Kidman is much more aggressive in using her supernatural powers to sexually control men. They will have to team up to use their "white magic" to deal with a nasty guy who just won't stay dead.

2338. *Prayer of the Rollerboys* (1992, U.S./Japan, Academy Ent., 94m, c). D Rick King, P Robert Mickelson, W W. Peter Iliff, PH Phedon Papamichael, ED Daniel Lowenthal, M Stacy Widelitz, PD Thomas A. Walsh, AD Jay Klein, SD Natalie K. Pope.

LP Corey Haim (Chris Griffin), Patricia Arquette (Casey), Christopher Collet (Gary Lee), J.C. Quinn (Jaworski), Julius Harris (Speedbagger).

In the near future, a group of drug-running teen fascists terrorize L.A. They zip around the city on rollerblades, thus their name.

2339. *The Preacher's Wife* (1996, Samuel Goldwyn–Buena Vista, 124m, c). D Penny Marshall, P Samuel Goldwyn, Jr., W Nat Mauldin & Allan Scott (based on the 1947 screenplay *The Bishop's Wife* by Robert E. Sherwood & Leonardo Bercovici, and the novel by Robert Nathan), PH Miroslav Ondricek, ED Stephen A. Rotter & George Bowers, M Hans Zimmer†, PD Bill Groom, AD Dennis Bradford, SD George Detitta.

LP Denzel Washington (Dudley), Whitney Houston (Julia Biggs), Courtney B. Vance (Henry Biggs), Gregory Hines (Joe Hamilton), Jenifer Lewis (Marguerite Coleman), Loretta Devine (Beverly), Justin Pierre Edmund (Jeremiah Biggs), Lionel Richie (Britsloe).

It's a remake of 1947's *The Bishop's Wife* with a black cast. In the role authored earlier by David Niven, Vance is a clergyman who is having problems both with his career and his wife Houston (standing in for Loretta Young). He prays for help and it arrives in the person of Washington (this year's Cary Grant), a too-handsome angel who's, just too, too attentive to Houston for Vance's taste. Houston is taken with Washington, and it appears he has some un-angel thoughts about her. Everything works out heavenly in the end.

2340. *Precious Find* (1996, Initial Ent. Group, 90m, c). D Philippe Mora, P Brian Rix, Jane Ubell & John Remark, W Lenny Britton, PH Walter Bal, ED Ross Guidici, M Ron Hay & Craig Stuart Garfinkle, PD W. Brooke Wheeler, AD Charles R. Dutrow II, SD David A. Koneff.

LP Harold Pruett (Ben), Brion James (Sam Horton), Rutger Hauer (Armond Crile), Joan Chen (Camilla Jones), Morgan Hunter (Saloman), Don Stroud (Loo Seki).

Taking some ideas from *The Treasure of the Sierra Madre*, this film is about gold prospectors looking for the precious stuff on an asteroid. Because of their greed and mistrust, the results are calamitous.

2341. *Predator 2* (1990, 20th Century-Fox, 108m, c). D Stephen Hopkins, P Lawrence Gordon, Joel Silver & John A. Davis, W James E. Thomas & John C. Thomas, PH Peter Levy, ED Mark Goldblatt & Bert Lovitt, M Alan Silvestri, PD Lawrence G. Paull, AD Geoff Hubbard, SD Alan Manzer, Richard Mays, Louis Mann & Sally Thornton.

LP Danny Glover (Mike Harrigan), Gary Busey (Peter Keyes), Ruben Blades (Danny Archuletta), Maria Conchita Alonso (Leona Cantrell), Bill Paxton (Jerry Lambert), Robert Davi (Heinemann), Adam Baldwin (Garber), Kent McCord (Captain Pilgrim), Martin Downey, Jr. (Pope), Calvin Lockhart (King Willie).

L.A. police officer Glover must take time from his fight with drug-traffickers to deal with an extraterrestial who arrives in the city and goes on a destructive rage.

2342. *Prefontaine* (1997, Hollywood Pictures–Buena Vista, 106m, c). D Steve James, P Irby Smith, Jon Lutz, Mark Doonan & Peter Gilbert, W James, Eugene Corr & Tom Jordan, PH Gilbert, ED Peter Frank & Susanne Suffredin, M Mason Daring, PD Carol Winstead Wood, AD Gregory A. Weimerskirch, SD Nina Bradford.

LP Jared Leto (Steve Prefontaine), Amy Locane (Nancy Alleman), Lindsay Crouse (Elfriede Prefontaine), Peter Anthony Jacobs (Ray Prefontaine), R. Lee Ermey (Coach Bill Bowerman), Ed O'Neill (Bill Dellinger).

This film, in documentary style, examines the life of 1970s track star Steve Prefontaine. The athlete from Coos Bay, Oregon, makes it to the Munich Olympics. While the performances are good, the pace wins no medals.

2343. *Prelude to a Kiss* (1992, 20th Century-Fox, 110m, c). D Norman Rene, P Michael Gruskoff & Michael I. Levy, W Craig Lucas (based on his play), PH Stefan Czapsky, ED Stephen A. Rotter, M Howard Shore, PD Andrew Jackness, AD W. Steven Graham, SD Cindy Carr.

LP Alec Baldwin (Peter Hoskins), Meg Ryan

(Rita Boyle), Kathy Bates (Leah Blier), Ned Beatty (Dr. Boyle), Patty Duke (Mrs. Boyle), Richard Riehle (Jerry Blier), Stanley Tucci (Taylor), Sydney Walker (Julius, The Old Man).

Boy, what a dumb movie. Baldwin and Ryan meet, fall in love and plan to marry. Unfortunately, on their wedding day the soul of the young bride and seventy-year-old stranger Walker are transposed. Ryan, up until that point a healthy, vital young woman, develops fatigue and illness. How to get her back to her old self? Yes, we know it's an AIDS allegory, but it just doesn't work for us.

2344. *Presumed Innocent* (1990, Mirage–Warner Bros., 127m, c). D Alan J. Pakula, P Sydney Pollack & Mark Rosenberg, W Frank Pierson & Pakula (based on the novel by Scott Turow), PH Gordon Willis, ED Evan Lottman, W John Williams, PD George Jenkins, AD Bob Guerra, SD Carol Joffe.

LP Harrison Ford (Rusty Sabich), Brian Dennehy (Raymond Horgan), Raul Julia (Sandy Stern), Bonnie Bedelia (Barbara Sabich), Paul Winfield (Judge Larren Lyttle), Greta Scacchi (Carolyn Polhemus), John Spencer (Detective Lipranzer), Joe Grifasi (Tommy Molto), Tom Mardirosian (Nico Della Guardia).

For the greatest part of this movie, the story is exciting and plausible. Veteran prosecutor Ford finds his life shattered when he is accused of the rape and brutal murder of associate Scacchi, with whom he has had an affair. This latter sin is no big thing, everyone has had a turn with Greta as the young lawyer slept her way to success. The problem is that the resolution of the story is just too pat and rests on a series of fortunate coincidences. Still, the work of Ford, Bedelia as his wife, Julia as his lawyer, and Scacchi as the good-time had by all is engaging.

2345. *Pretty Woman* (1990, Touchstone/Buena Vista, 119m, c). D Garry Marshall, P Arnon Milchan & Steven Reuther, W J.F. Lawton, PH Charles Minsky, ED Priscilla Nedd, M James Newton Howard, PD Albert Brenner, AD David M. Haber, SD Garrett Lewis.

LP Richard Gere (Edward Lewis), Julia Roberts† (Vivian Ward), Ralph Bellamy (James Morse), Jason Alexander (Philip Stuckey),

Laura San Giacomo (Kit De Luca), Alex Hyde-White (David Morse), Amy Yasbeck (Elizabeth Stuckey), Elinor Donahue (Bridget), Hector Elizondo (Hotel Manager).

Roberts became a big bankable star with her role as a streetwalking whore picked up by businessman Gere. He hires her to be his "plaything" while he's in town making some more millions. She cleans up very nicely in this delightful romantic comedy. Gere is something of a stiff, whom Roberts never quite can loosen up, but then it's her film and she really delivers. Good work is also offered by Alexander, San Giacomo and especially Elizondo.

2346. *A Price Above Rubies* (1998, Miramax, 117m, c), D & W Boaz Yakin, P Lawrence Bender & John Penotti, PH Adam Holender, ED Arthur Coburn, M Lesley Barber, PD Dan Leigh, SD Leslie E. Rollins.

LP Renee Zellweger (Sonia), Christopher Eccleston (Sender), Glenn Fitzgerald (Mendel), Allen Payne (Ramon), Julianna Marguiles (Rachel), Kim Hunter (Rebbitzn), John Randolph (Rebbe).

This film is set in Brooklyn's Orthodox Jewish community. Housewife Zellweger finds it difficult to adjust to her traditional marriage to Fitzgerald. She is sexually unfulfilled until her husband's older brother Eccleston forces himself on her. He also offers her the opportunity to go into the family jewelry business, where she proves to be quite successful. Zellweger gives an outstanding performance, and the scenes of Hasidic life are interesting.

2347. *Priest* (1995, U.K., Miramax, 97m, c). D Antonia Bird, P George Faber & Josephine Ward, W Jimmy McGovern, PH Fred Tammes, ED Susan Spivey, M Andy Roberts, PD Raymond Langhorn, AD Sue Pow.

LP Linus Roache (Father Greg Pilkington), Tom Wilkinson (Father Matthew Thomas), Cathy Tyson (Maria Kerrigan), Robert Carlyle (Graham) James Ellis (Father Ellerton), Lesley Sharp (Mrs. Unsworth), Robert Pugh (Mr. Unsworth).

Conservative young priest Roache has a crisis of faith as he tries to control his own carnal nature while serving his Liverpool working-class parishioners.

2348. *Primal Fear* (1996, Paramount, 130m, c). D Gregory Hoblit, P Gary Lucchesi,

W Steve Shagan & Ann Biderman (based on the novel by William Diehl), PH Michael Chapman, ED David Rosenbloom, M James Newton Howard, PD Jeannie Oppewall, AD William Arnold, SD Cindy Carr.

LP Richard Gere (Martin Vail), Laura Linney (Janet Venable), John Mahoney (Shaughnessy), Alfre Woodard (Shoat), Frances McDormand (Molly), Edward Norton† (Aaron/Roy), Terry O'Quinn (Yancy), Andre Braugher (Goodman).

Arrogant criminal lawyer Gere becomes Norton's counselor when the young man is accused of the murder of a Cardinal, who had some secrets of his own. Norton may have been the murderer, but the instigator seems to have been some controlling other nature. The film is filled with twists, turns and red herrings, and the outcome is always in doubt until the shocking ending.

2349.   Primary Colors (1998, Universal, 143m, c). D & P Mike Nichols, W Elaine May† (based on the novel by Anonymous [Joe Klein]), PH Michael Ballhaus, ED Arthur Schmidt, M Ry Cooder, PD Bo Welch, AD Tom Duffield, SD Sean Haworth, SD Cheryl Carasik.

LP John Travolta (Gov. Jack Stanton), Emma Thompson (Susan Stanton), Billy Bob Thornton (Richard Jemmons), Kathy Bates† (Libby Holden), Adrian Lester (Henry Burton), Maura Tierney (Daisy), Larry Hagman (Gov. Fred Picker), Diane Ladd (Mamma Stanton), Paul Guilfoyle (Howard Ferguson).

In this frequently funny *film à clef*, a beefed-up Travolta plays a politician who behaves very much like Bill Clinton — roving eyes, hands and all. Thompson is his long-suffering wife. Some will get a certain sense of satisfaction when she slugs Travolta for his behavior. The film examines the 1992 presidential campaign and shows the candidate with all his warts. What it fails to show is why this character and the guy it's based upon thinks he can behave the way he does and exist in the high-profile role of a politician and president.

2350.   Primary Target (1990, MGM-UA, 85m, c). D & W Clark Henderson, P Isabel Sumayao, PH Austin McKinney, ED Marc Tarnate & Joseph Zucchero, M Jeff Mar, AD Ricky Yu, SD Mar De Guzman.

LP John Calvin (Cromwell), Miki Kim (Pao), Joey Aresco (Frank Rosi), Chip Lucia (Jack Sturges), John Ericson (Phil Karlson), Colleen Casey (Mrs. Karlson).

A mercenary gathers together his former Vietnam guerilla force to rescue a diplomat's wife in the Laotian jungles.

2351.   The Prince of Egypt (1998, DreamWorks, 97m, c). D Brenda Chapman, Steve Hickner & Simon Wells, P Penney Finkelman Cox & Sandra Rabins, W Philip LaZebnik, ED Nick Fletcher, M Hans Zimmer† & Stephen Schwartz†, PD Derek Gogol, AD Kathy Altieri & Richard Chavez.

LP Voices: Val Kilmer (Moses, God), Ralph Fiennes (Rameses), Michelle Pfeiffer (Tzipporah), Sandra Bullock (Miriam), Jeff Goldblum (Aaron), Danny Glover (Jethro), Patrick Stewart (Pharaoh Seti), Helen Mirren (The Queen), Steve Martin (Hotep), Martin Short (Huy).

There is much to like and admire about this handsome animated production of the Moses saga. Fortunately, DreamWorks has resisted the Disney impulse to lighten up the story with cute little creatures to provide comedy relief. Just for the record, as in the big hit (and long-winded) *The Ten Commandments* (1956), a princess of Egypt finds a baby whom she names Moses. The child is raised along with Rameses, the boy who will become pharaoh. When the adult Moses discovers he is really a Hebrew slave, he returns to his people, is banished and later returns to lead his people on an exodus to the Promised Land.

2352.   Prince of Tides† (1991, Columbia, 132m, c). D Barbra Streisand, P Streisand† & Andrew Karsch†, W Becky Johnston† & Pat Conroy† (based on his novel), PH Stephen Goldblatt, ED Don Zimmerman, M James Newton Howard†, PD Paul Sylbert†, AD Steven Graham, SD Caryl Heller†, Arthur Howe, Jr., & Leslie Ann Pope.

LP Nick Nolte† (Tom Wingo), Barbra Streisand (Dr. Susan Lowenstein), Blythe Danner (Sally Wingo), Kate Nelligan† (Lila Wingo Newbury), Jeroen Krabbé (Herbert Woodruff), Melinda Dillon (Savannah Wingo), George Carlin (Eddie Detreville), Jason Gould (Bernard Woodruff), Brad Sullivan (Henry Wingo).

Married high school football coach Nolte travels from his southern home to New York when his sister Dillon is admitted to a psychiatric hospital. He meets her doctor, Streisand, and the two have a brief affair. She helps him to confront his horrific childhood experience that so adversely affected everyone in his family. Nelligan is terrific as his mother. The film garnished seven Oscar nominations, but Streisand was snubbed as director and star.

2353. *Princes in Exile* (1991, Canada, Fries Ent., 104m, c). D Giles Walker, P John Dunning, Marrin Canell & Irene Litinsky, W Joe Wiesenfeld (based on the novel by Mark Schreiber), PH Savas Kalogeras, ED Richard Todd, M Normand Corbeil, PD Charles Dunlop, SD Donna Noon.

LP Zachary Ansley (Ryan Rafferty), Nicholas Shields (Robert), Stacie Mistysyn (Holly), Andrea Roth (Marlene Lancaster), Alexander Chapman (Gabriel).

The cast of unknowns handle themselves most effectively, portraying a group of cancer stricken teenagers at a wooded Canadian summer retreat. Ansley has two goals before he dies: to publish his journal and to lose his virginity. He and his fellow cancer campers are princes in exile waiting to enter the castle of life.

2354. *Princess Caraboo* (1994, U.K./U.S., Tri-Star, 97m, c). D Michael Austin, P Andrew Karsch & Simon Bosanquet, W Austin & John Wells, PH Freddie Francis, ED George Akers, M Richard Hartley, PD Michael Howells, AD Sam Riley, SD Sasha Schwerdt.

LP Jim Broadbent (Mr. Worrall), Phoebe Cates (Princess Caraboo), Wendy Hughes (Mrs. Worrall), Kevin Kline (Frixos), John Lithgow (Professor Wilkinson), Stephen Rea (Gutch).

Cates is found wandering the English countryside in a strange costume, speaking a language no one understands. She is taken in by social-climbing couple Broadbent and Hughes, who assume her to be foreign royalty.

2355. *Prisoners of the Sun* (1991, Australia, Village Roadshow Pictures, 109m, c). D Stephen Wallace, P Charles Waterstreet, Brian A. Williams & Denis Whitburn, W Whitburn & Williams, PH Russell Boyd, ED Nicholas Beauman, M David McHugh, PD Bernard Hicks.

LP Bryan Brown (Captain Robert Cooper), George Takei (Vice Admiral Baron Takahashi), Terry O'Quinn (Major Tom Beckett), John Bach (Major Frank Roberts), Toshi Shioya (Lieutenant Hideo Tanaka), John Clarke (Mike Sheedy), Deborah Unger (Sister Carol Littell), Russell Crowe (Lieutenant Jack Corbett), Tetsu Watanabe (Captain Wadami Ikeuchi), John Polson (Private Jimmy Fenton).

During WWII, 1,100 Australians were interred in a Japanese prison camp on the island of Ambon, Indonesia. After the war only 300 survivors returned home. The remaining flyers, never incarcerated as prisoners of war, were killed in mass executions. Military lawyer Brown eagerly wishes to prosecute those responsible, but because of bureaucracy, politics and differing cultures, only Shioya, the second-in-command, is offered up as a scapegoat, allowing the camp commander Takei to go unpunished for ordering the executions.

2356. *Private Parts* (1997, Paramount, 110m, c). D Betty Thomas, P Ivan Reitman, W Len Blum (based on the book by Howard Stern), PH Walt Lloyd, ED Peter Teschner, M Van Dyke Parks, PD Charles Rosen, AD Rick Butler, SD Beth Kushnick.

LP Howard Stern (Himself), Mary McCormack (Alison), Robin Quivers (Herself), Fred Norris (Himself), Jackie Martling (Himself), Gary Dell'Abate (Himself), Richard Portnow (Ben Stern), Kelly Bishop (Ray Stern).

If you aren't a fan of Howard Stern and his outrageous radio and TV shows, this film about his life and career will offend you. Not everyone is interested in Stern's "private parts."

2357. *Problem Child* (1990, Universal, 81m, c). D Dennis Dugan, P Robert Simonds, W Scott Alexander & Larry Karaszewski, PH Peter Lyons Collister, ED Daniel Hanley & Michael Hill, M Miles Goodman, PD George Costello, AD Michael Bingham, SD Denise Pizzini.

LP John Ritter (Ben Healy), Jack Warden (Big Ben Healey, Sr.), Michael Oliver (Junior), Gilbert Gottfried (Mr. Igor Peabody), Amy Yasbeck (Flo Healy), Michael Richards (Marvin Beck).

Always-arguing yuppie couple Ritter and Yasbeck adopt a child so they can get invited to upscale children's birthday parties. The kid, Oliver, is a foul-mouthed destructive demon.

2358. *Problem Child 2* (1991, Universal, 91m, c). D Brian Levant, P Robert Simonds, W Scott Alexander & Larry Karaszewski, PH Peter Smokler, ED Lois Freeman-Fox, M David Kitay, PD Maria Caso, AD Allen Terry, SD Damon Medlen.

LP John Ritter (Ben Healy), Michael Oliver (Junior Healey), Jack Warden ("Big" Ben Healy), Laraine Newman (LaWanda Dumore), Amy Yasbeck (Annie Young).

The family is back again with more of the same vulgarity and scatological humor. Save your money and buy a dog instead of the video featuring this brat.

2359. *The Professional* (1994, France/U.S., Gaumont–Columbia, 106m, c). D & W Luc Besson, P Luc Besson & Claude Besson, PH Thierry Arbogast, ED Sylvie Landra, M Eric Serra, PD Dan Weil, AD Carol Nast & Gerard Drolon, SD Carolyn Cartwright & Francoise Benoit-Fresco.

LP Jean Reno (Leon), Gary Oldman (Stansfield), Natalie Portman (Mathilda), Danny Aiello (Tony), Peter Appel (Malky), Michael Badalucco (Mathilda's Father), Ellen Green (Mathilda's Mother), Elizabeth Regen (Mathilda's Sister).

Hitman Reno befriends Portman when pill-popping psycho cop Oldman wipes out her family. Reno and Portman are both appealing, but Oldman really chews up the sets with his out-of-control emoting.

2360. *The Program* (1993, Samuel Goldwyn Co.–Buena Vista, 114m, c). D David S. Ward, P Samuel Goldwyn, Jr., W Ward & Aaron Latham, PH Victor Hammer & Charles Cohen, ED Paul Seydor & Kimberly Ray, PD Albert Brenner, AD Carol Winstead Wood, SD Kathe Klopp & Howard Fuhrman.

LP James Caan (Coach Sam Winters), Halle Berry (Autumn), Omar Epps (Darnell Jefferson), Craig Sheffer (Joe Kane), Kristy Swanson (Camille), Abraham Benrubi (Bid-Lite), Duane Davis (Alvin Mack).

Sheffer is the troubled quarterback of a college football team. He finds the pressure of performing and continually excelling more than he can handle.

2361. *Project: Shadowchaser* (1992, U.K./Canada, Prism Ent., 97m, c). D John E. Eyres, P Eyres & Geoff Griffiths, W Steven Lister, PH Alan M. Trow, ED Delhak Wreen, M Gary Pinder, PD Mark Harris, AD Simon Lamont.

LP Martin Kove (Michael DaSilva), Meg Foster (Sarah), Frank Zagarino (Romulus), Paul Koslo (Trevanian), Joss Ackland ("Kinderman").

Kove is trapped in a high-rise hospital that has been taken over by terrorists. Sounds like *Die Hard* did you say?

2362. *Proof* (1992, Australia, Fine Line Features, 86m, c). D & W Jocelyn Moorhouse, P Lynda House, PH Martin McGrath, ED Ken Sallows, M Not Drowning Waving, PD Patrick Reardon.

LP Hugo Weaving (Martin), Genevieve Picot (Celia), Russell Crowe (Andy), Heather Mitchell (Martin's Mother), Jeffrey Walker (Young Martin), Daniel Pollock (Gary — The Punk).

Blind since birth, Weaving is convinced that his mother hated him for his affliction. He hopes to find someone to describe for him the countless photographs he takes — and give him proof of his long-dead mother's love.

2363. *The Prophecy* (AKA: *God's Army*) (1995, First Look Pictures, 96m, c). D & W Gregory Widen, P Joel Soisson, W.K. Border & Michael Leary, PH Bruce D. Johnson & Richard Clabaugh, ED Sonny Baskin, M David C. Williams, PD Clark Hunter, SD Michele Spadaro.

LP Christopher Walken (Angel Gabriel), Elias Koteas (Thomas Dagget), Eric Stoltz (Angel Simon), Virginia Madsen (Katherine), Moriah Shining Dove Snyder (Mary), Adam Goldberg (Jerry), Amanda Plummer (Rachael).

This highly original horror story about a second battle of heavenly angels makes quite a statement about good and evil.

2364. *The Proposition* (1998, Polygram Films, 110m, c). D Lesli Linka Glatter, P Ted Field, Diane Nabatoff & Scott Kroopf, W Rick Ramage, PH Peter Sova, ED Jacqueline Cambas, M Stephen Endelman, PD David Brisbin, AD Kenneth A. Hardy, SD Tracey Doyle.

LP Kenneth Branagh (Father Michael McKinnon), Madeleine Stowe (Eleanor Barret), William Hurt (Arthur Barret), Neil Patrick Harris (Roger Martin), Robert Loggia (Hannibal

Thurman), Josef Sommer (Father Dryer), Blythe Danner (Syril Danning).

In a hopelessly confused story, wealthy 1930s couple Stowe and Hurt want to have a baby. Problem is, Hurt is sterile. Unwilling to adopt because Stowe wishes to experience pregnancy, they arrange for young Harris to be the surrogate parent. By the time he impregnates her he's in love with Stowe, and the couple have a heck of a time getting rid of him. Meanwhile, priest Branagh shows up to announce that he is Hurt's nephew, the son of a Nazi-leaning, British-based businessman. Harris is killed, Stowe loses her baby and the search for a new surrogate is on. It's much too complex to make any real sense.

2365. *Prospero's Books* (1991, U.K./ Netherlands/France/Italy, Miramax, 120m, c). D & W Peter Greenaway (based on the play *The Tempest* by William Shakespeare), PH Sacha Vierny, ED Marina Bodbyl, M Michael Nyman, PD Ben Van Os & Jan Roelfs.

LP John Gielgud (Prospero), Michael Clark (Caliban), Michel Blanc (Alonso), Erland Josephson (Gonzalo), Isabelle Pasco (Miranda), Tom Bell (Antonio), Kenneth Cranham (Sebastian).

Director and writer Greenaway's visually fascinating version of Shakespeare's *The Tempest* will not please everyone. The screen is splattered with nudity and shocking graphic exactness. Gielgud gives voice to every character in the film.

2366. *Proteus* (1996, U.K., Vidmark, 97m, c). D Bob Keen, P Paul Brooks, W John Brosnan (based on the novel *Slimer* by Harry Adam Knight [aka Brosnan]), PH Adam Rogers, ED Liz Webber, M David A. Hughes & John Murphy, PD Mike Grant, AD James Ridpath.

LP Craig Fairbass (Alex), Toni Barry (Linda), William Marsh (Mark), Jennifer Calvert (Rachel), Robert Firth (Paul), Margot Steinberg (Christina), Doug Bradley (Leonard Brimstone).

When their boat sinks, six survivors take refuge on an abandoned oil rig — but it's not really abandoned.

2367. *Psycho* (1998, Universal, 109m, c). D Gus Van Sant, P Brian Grazer & Van Sant, W Joseph Stefano (based on a novel by Robert Bloch), PH Christopher Doyle, ED Amy Duddleston, M Bernard Hermann, PD Tom Foden, AD Carlos Barbosa.

LP Vince Vaughn (Norman Bates), Anne Heche (Marion Crane), Julianne Moore (Lila Crane), Viggo Mortensen (Sam Loomis), William H. Macy (Milton Arbogast), Robert Forster (Dr. Simon), Philip Baker Hall (Sheriff Chambers), Chad Everett (Tom Cassidy).

Why was this film made? We can't conceive of any reason. One reason we have heard given is that young people won't look at the 1960 Hitchcock classic because it's in black and white. What nonsense! Those who would refuse to view a film as outstanding as the earlier version probably only attend action films with chases, crashes and large body counts. They'd have no interest in a suspenseful thriller, which, of course, this version is not. Van Sant claimed he made the film shot for shot like the Hitchcock movie so he could see how it would feel to be the Master of Suspense. That seems a very weak, self-serving and impossible reason for making a movie. In case you have forgotten, Heche, unhappy the way her affair with Mortensen is going, steals money from her boss ($400,000, up from the $40,000 stolen by Janet Leigh — inflation, you know) and hits the road. She ends up at the Bates Motel, where she meets Vaughn and where her shower is deadly.

2368. *Public Access* (1996, Triboro, 89m, c). D Bryan Singer, P Kenneth Kokin, W Christopher McQuarrie, Singer & Michael Feit Dugan, PH Bruce Douglas Johnson, ED John Ottman, M John Ottman, PD Jan Sessler, AD Bruce Sulzberg, SD Martin Dammaschk.

LP Ron Marquette (Whiley Pritcher), Burt Williams (Bob Hodges), Leigh Hunt (Intersect Host), John Renshaw (Jock Talk Host), Dina Brooks (Rachel), Charles Kavanagh (Mayor Breyer).

Newcomer Marquette sets up a local call-in program to discuss what's wrong with the community. His show just about tears the town apart.

2369. *Public Enemies* (1996, Vidmark, 95m, c). D Mark Lester, P Lester & Dana Dubovsky, W Courtney Joyner, PH Misha Suslov, ED David Berlatsky, M Christopher Franke, PD Trae King, AD Brian Massey, SD Troy Myers.

LP Theresa Russell (Ma Barker), Alyssa Milano (Amaryllis), Eric Roberts (Arthur Dunlop), Leah Best (Young Kate Clarke), Chip Heller (Mr. Clarke), Richard Eden (George Barker), Frank Stallone (Melvin Purvis).

Russell and her four sadistic sons terrorize the Midwest during the Depression.

2370. *The Public Eye* (1992, Universal, 98m, c). D & W Howard Franklin, P Sue Baden-Powell, PH Evan Lottman, M Mark Isham, PD Marcia Hinds-Johnson, AD Bo Johnson & Dina Lipton, SD Jan K. Berstrom.

LP Joe Pesci (Leonard "The Great Bernzini" Bernstein), Barbara Hershey (Kay Levitz), Richard Riehle (Officer O'Brien), David Gianopoulos (Portofino), Stanley Tucci (Sal).

It's the story of a 1940s tabloid photographer who specializes in dead bodies and major criminal types.

2371. *Pulp Fiction†* (1994, Miramax, 149m, c). D Quentin Tarantino†, P Lawrence Bender†, W Tarantino* & Roger Avary* (based on stories by Tarantino & Avary), PH Andrzej Sekula, ED Sally Menke†, PD David Wasco, AD Charles Collum, SD Sandy Reynolds-Wasco.

LP John Travolta† (Vincent Vega), Samuel L. Jackson† (Jules Winnfield), Uma Thurman† (Mia Wallace), Harvey Keitel (The Wolf), Tim Roth (Pumpkin), Amanda Plummer (Honey Bunny), Maria de Medeiros (Fabienne), Ving Rhames (Marsellus Wallace), Eric Stoltz (Lance), Rosanna Arquette (Jody), Christopher Walken (Captain Koons), Bruce Willis (Butch Coolidge), Quentin Tarantino (Jimmie), Steve Buscemi (Surly Buddy Holly Waiter).

Some viewers got terribly concerned while watching this movie when Travolta reappeared in scenes after ones in which he was killed. They weren't the only ones confused by Tarantino's marvelously campy and excitingly violent film. It restarted Travolta's career and didn't do any harm to the many other performers who were allowed the opportunity of creating memorable characters. It's a classic and would be one of a kind if other moviemakers didn't try to imitate it and its success. For the record, Travolta and Jackson are mobster Rhames' hitmen. Willis is a boxer who double-crosses Rhames. Thurman is Rhames girlfriend, who almost overdoses. Keitel is in charge of cleaning up mistakes made by Rhames' mobsters. Roth and Plummer try to stick up the diner where Travolta and Jackson are having a quiet meal.

2372. *Pump Up the Volume* (1990, Canada/U.S., New Line, 105m, c). D & W Allan Moyle, P Rupert Harvey & Sandy Stern, PH Walt Lloyd, ED Wendy Bricmont, Ric Keeley & Kurt Hathaway, PD Bruce Bolander.

LP Christian Slater (Mark Hunter), Samantha Mathis (Nora), Ellen Greene (Jan Emerson), Scott Paulin (Keith Hunter), Cheryl Pollak (Paige), Andy Romano (Murdock), Mimi Kennedy (Martha Hunter).

New to his high school, loner Slater creates an alter ego with a pirate radio station. He "talks hard," and what he has to say seems right on target to both the hip and misfit kids who listen to him.

2373. *Pure Country* (1992, Warner Bros., 108m, c). D Christopher Cain, P Jerry Weintraub, W Rex McGee, PH Richard Bowen, ED Jack Hofstra, M Steve Dorff, PD Jeffrey Howard, SD Derek R. Hill.

LP George Strait (Dusty Wyatt Chandler), Lesley Ann Warren (Lula Rogers), Isabel Glasser (Harley Tucker), Kyle Chandler (Buddy Jackson), John Doe (Earl Blackstock), Rory Calhoun (Ernest Tucker), Molly McClure (Grandma Ivy Chandler).

Country singer Strait is, what else, a personable country singer. If you like his songs, the simple story will suit you just fine.

2374. *Pure Luck* (1991, Universal, 96m, c). D Nadia Tass, P Sean Daniel & Lance Hool, W Herschel Weingrod & Timothy Harris, PH David Parker, ED Billy Weber, M Jonathan Sheffer, PD Peter Wooley, AD Hector Romero, Jr.

LP Martin Short (Eugene Proctor), Danny Glover (Raymond Campanella), Sheila Kelley (Valerie Highsmith), Sam Wanamaker (Mr. Highsmith), Scott Wilson (Grimes), Harry Shearer (Monosoff).

Ineffective detective Glover must team with bumbling accountant Short to locate the world's most accident-prone heiress.

2375. *Pushed to the Limit* (1992, Imperial Ent. Corp., 96m, c). D Michael Mileham, P & W Mimi Lesseos, PH Bodo Holst, ED Peter Cohen, M Miriam Cutler.

LP Mimi Lesseos (Mimi), Verrel Lester Reed, Jr. (Vern), Henry Hayshi (Harry Lee), Greg Ostrin (John Cordon), Michael Foley (Nick).

Wrestling queen Lesseos takes on Hayshi, a ruthless Asian drug dealer who killed her brother Ostrin.

2376. Pushing Tin (1999, 20th Century–Fox, 124m, c). D Mike Newell, P Art Linson, W Glen Charles & Les Charles (based on the article "Something's Got to Give" by Darcy Frey), PH Otto Nemenz & Gale Tattersall, ED Jon Gregory, M Anne Dudley, PD Bruno Rubeo, AD John Dondertman, SD Ellis Lam & Gordon White.

LP John Cusack (Nick Falzone), Billy Bob Thornton (Russell Bell), Cate Blanchett (Connie Falzone), Angelina Jolie (Mary Bell), Vicki Lewis (Tina Leary), Jake Weber (Barry Plotkin).

The comedy-drama examines the stress-filled world of air traffic controllers. It compares the one-upmanship between Cusack, who seemingly can take any pressure involved with guiding 7,000 planes a day, and supercool Thornton. The story pulls in their wives as well. Cusack's spouse Blanchett is loving and supportive. Thornton's young wife Jolie dresses and acts like a tramp, and drinks to excess. Don't try some of these guys' stunts at your local airport, kids.

2377. Pyrates (1991, Mixedbreed Films, 98m, c). D & W Noah Stern, P Jonathan Furie, PH Janusz Kaminski, ED Gib Jaffe, M Peter Himmelman, PD Sherman Williams, SD Robert Eberz.

LP Kevin Bacon (Sam), Kyra Sedgwick (Ari), Bruce Martin Payne (Liam), Kristin Dattilo (Pia).

Whenever photographer Bacon and cellist Sedgwick meet, they make love so hot that they literally start fires.

2378. A Pyromaniac's Love Story (1995, Hollywood Pictures–Buena Vista, 96m, c). D Joshua Brand, P Mark Gordon, W Morgan Ward, PH John Schwartzman, ED David Rosenbloom, M Rachel Portman, PD Dan Davis, AD Peter Grundy, SD Elena Kenney.

LP William Baldwin (Garet), John Leguizamo (Sergio), Sadie Frost (Hattie), Erika Eleniak (Stephanie), Michael Lerner (Perry), Joan Plowright (Mrs. Linzer), Armin Mueller-Stahl (Mr. Linzer), Richard Crenna (Businessman).

After a bakery fire, just about everyone claims responsibility except the arsonist.

2379. Q & A (1990, Tri-Star, 134m, c). D & W Sidney Lumet (based on the book by Edwin Torres), P Arnon Milchan & Burtt Harris, PH Andrzej Bartkowiak, ED Richard Cirincione, M Ruben Blades, PD Philip Rosenberg, AD Beth Kahn, SD Gary Brink.

LP Nick Nolte (Lt. Mike Brennan), Timothy Hutton (Al Reilly), Armand Assante (Bobby Texador), Patrick O'Neal (Kevin Quinn), Lee Richardson (Leo Bloomenfeld), Luis Guzman (Det. Luis Valentin), Charles Dutton (Det. Sam Chapman), Jenny Lumet (Nancy Bosch).

Inexperienced Assistant D.A. Hutton is given the assignment of investigating the murder of a druggie by racist, homophobic cop Nolte. Hutton uncovers departmental corruption. Assante portrays a gangster involved in the dirty dealings.

2380. The Quarrel (1992, Canada, American Playhouse Theatrical Films, 88m, c). D Eli Cohen, P Kim Todd & David Brandes, W Brandes (based on the play by Joseph Telushkin, and the story "My Quarrel with Hersh Rasseyner" by Chaim Grade), PH John Berrie, ED Havelock Gradidge, M William Goldstein, PD & AD Michael Joy.

LP Saul Rubinek (Hersh Rasseyner), R.H. Thomson (Chaim Kovler).

Holocaust survivors Rubinek and Thomson exchange ideas about their faith. The performances of the duo are outstanding.

2381. Queens Logic (1991, Seven Arts Pictures, 153m, c). D Steve Rash, P Stuart Oken & Russ Smith, W Tony Spiridakis (based on a story by Joseph Savino), PH Amir Mokri, ED Patrick Kennedy, M Joe Jackson, PD Edward Pisoni, AD Okowita, SD Marcie Dale.

LP Kevin Bacon (Dennis), Linda Fiorentino (Carla), John Malkovich (Eliot), Joe Mantegna (Al), Ken Olin (Ray), Tony Spiridakis (Vinny), Chloe Webb (Patricia), Tom Waits (Monte), Jamie Lee Curtis (Grace).

A group of thirtysomething friends return to their old neighborhood for a wedding, preceded by a fateful bachelor party. It's a bit of *The Big Chill* mixed with *Diner*.

2382. *The Quest* (1996, Universal, 95m, c). D Jean-Claude Van Damme, P Moshe Diamant, W Steven Klein & Paul Mones (based on a story by Frank Dux & Van Damme), PH David Gribble, ED John F. Link & William J. Meshover, M Randy Edelman, PD Steve Spence, AD Chaiyan "Lek" Chunsuttiwat, SD Kuladee "Gai" Suchatanont.

LP Jean-Claude Van Damme (Chris Dubois), Roger Moore (Dobbs), James Remar (Maxie), Janet Gunn (Carrie), Jack McGee (Harry), Aki Aleong (Khao), Abdel Qissi (Khan).

Van-Damme makes his directorial debut in this mishmash story of the activities of a young New York gang, kidnapping by pirates, and an international martial arts championship in the Himalayas.

2383. *Quest for Camelot* (1998, Warner Bros., 85m, c). D Frederick Du Chan, P Dalisa Cooper Cohen, W Kirk De Micco, William Schifrin, Jacqueline Feather & David Seidler (based on the novel *The King's Damsel* by Vera Chapman), PH Stanford C. Allen, M Patrick Doyle, PD Steve Pilcher, AD Carol Kieffer Police & J. Michael Spooner.

LP Voices: Jessalyn Gilsig (Kayley speaking), Andrea Corr (Kayley singing), Cary Elwes (Garrett speaking), Bryan White (Garrett singing), Gary Oldman (Ruber), Eric Idle (Devon), Don Rickles (Cornwall), Jane Seymour (Juliana), Pierce Brosnan (King Arthur speaking), Steve Perry (King Arthur singing).

When her brave father is killed by would-be usurper Ruber, plucky Kayley is left with the task of finding Arthur's sword Excalibur before Ruber and his forces can overrun Camelot. The animation is not uniformly excellent, but the film is a likeable fantasy.

2384. *The Quick and the Dead* (1995, TriStar, 103m, c). D Sam Raimi, P Joshua Donen, Allen Shapiro & Patrick Markey, W Simon Moore, PH Dante Spinotti, ED Pietro Scalia, M Alan Silvestri, PD Patrizia von Brandenstein, AD Steve Saklad, SD Hilton Rosemarin.

LP Sharon Stone (Ellen), Gene Hackman (Herod), Russell Crowe (Cort), Leonardo DiCaprio (Kid), Tobin Bell (Dog Kelly), Roberts Blossom (Doc Wallace), Kevin Conway (Eugene Dred), Lance Henriksen (Ace Hanlon).

What a dumb story. What a waste of talent.

Female gunslinger Stone seeks revenge against Hackman for killing her father. She enters a quick-draw competition so she can get to him. It's a winner-take-all contest with only one survivor.

2385. *Quick Change* (1990, Warner Bros., 88m, c). D Howard Franklin & Bill Murray, P Robert Greenhut & Murray, W Franklin (based on the book by Jay Cronley), PH Michael Chapman, ED Alan Heim, M Randy Edelman & Howard Shore, AD Speed Hopkins, SD Dave Weinman & Susan Bode.

LP Bill Murray (Grimm), Geena Davis (Phyllis), Randy Quaid (Loomis), Jason Robards, Jr. (Chief Rotzinger).

Murray, Davis and Quaid pull off a perfect bank robbery. Their problem is making their getaway from New York City with cop Robards on their trail.

2386. *The Quiet Room* (1996, Australia/ Italy, Fine Line, 91m, c). D & W Rolf de Heer, P Domenico Procacci & de Heer, PH Tony Clark, ED Tania Nehme, M Graham Tardif, PD Fiona Paterson, AD Beverley Freeman.

LP Celine O'Leary (Mother), Paul Blackwell (Father), Chloe Ferguson (Girl, Age seven), Phoebe Ferguson (Girl, Age three).

Through her thoughts we learn why seven-year-old Ferguson at age three was driven into silence by her incompatible parents' constant arguing.

2387. *Quigley Down Under* (1990, Pathé/ MGM-UA, 120m, c). D Simon Wincer, P Stanley O'Toole & Alexandra Rose, W John Hill, PH David Eggby, ED Adrian Carr, M Basil Poledouris, PD Ross Major, AD Ian Gracie.

LP Tom Selleck (Matthew Quigley), Laura San Giacomo (Crazy Cora), Alan Rickman (Elliott Marston), Chris Haywood (Maj. Pitts), Ron Haddrick (Grimmelman).

American cowboy Selleck travels to mid-nineteenth century Australia to work for ruthless rancher Rickman. When Tom refuses to become an assassin, he is left for dead in the Outback but survives and sets out to settle matters with Rickman.

2388. *Quiz Show†* (1994, Hollywood Pictures–Buena Vista, 120m, c). D Robert Redford†, P Redford†, Michael Jacobs†, Julian

Krainin† & Michael Nozik†, W Paul Attanasio† (based on the book *Remembering America: A Voice for the Sixties* by Richard N. Goodwin), PH Michael Ballhaus, ED Stu Linder, M Mark Isham, PD Jon Hutman, AD Tim Galvin, SD Samara Schaffer.

LP John Turturro (Herb Stempel), Rob Morrow (Richard Goodwin), Ralph Fiennes (Charles Van Doren), Paul Scofield† (Mark Van Doren), David Paymer (Dan Enright), Hank Azaria (Albert Freedman), Christopher McDonald (Jack Barry), Johann Carlo (Toby Stempel), Elizabeth Wilson (Dorothy Van Doren), Allan Rich (Robert Kintner), Mira Sorvino (Sandra Goodwin), Martin Scorsese (Sponsor).

In a film filled with appealing performances, Fiennes portrays Charles Van Doren, a University instructor and member of the literary Van Doren family. He is picked by the producers of the television quiz show *Twenty-one* to be their new champion, replacing long-running champ Turturro, who isn't considered as appealing. Turturro is forced to take a "dive," missing a very simple question. At first Fiennes doesn't suspect anything, but soon he finds that he is being fed the questions ahead of time. Congressional investigator Morrow looks into the matter and, despite finding that he really likes Fiennes and his family, is convinced that the show, its producers and Fiennes are crooked. The movie once again demonstrates what a marvelous actor is Scofield, who portrays Fiennes' father; but the work of Paymer is also outstanding.

2389. *Race the Sun* (1996, TriStar, 105m, c). D Charles T. Kanganis, P Richard Heus & Barry Morrow, W Morrow, PH David Burr, ED Wendy Greene Bricmont, M Graeme Revell, PD Owen Paterson, AD Richard Hobbs & Michelle McGahey, SD Lea Worth.

LP Halle Berry (Sandra Beecher), James Belushi (Frank Machi), Bill Hunter (Commissioner Hawkes), Casey Affleck (Daniel Webster), Eliza Dushku (Cindy Johnson), Kevin Tighe (Jack Fryman).

In the tradition of *Breaking Away* and other such films, a group of young underachievers travel to Australia from Hawaii to compete for the prize in a solar car competition. The scenery is beautiful but the story is ho-hum.

2390. *Radio Flyer* (1992, Columbia, 120m, c). D Richard Donner, P Lauren Shuler-Donner, W David Mickey Evans, PH Laszlo Kovacs, ED Stuart Baird & Dallas Puett, M Hans Zimmer, PD J. Michael Riva, AD David Frederick Klassen, SD Michael Taylor.

LP Lorraine Bracco (Mary), John Heard (Daugherty), Adam Baldwin (The King), Elijah Wood (Mike), Joseph Mazzello (Bobby), Ben Johnson (Geronimo Bill), Sean Baca (Fisher), Robert Munic (Older Fisher), Tom Hanks (Narrator).

Bracco and her two boys, Wood and Mazzello, move to Northern California where mom marries drunken mechanic and child abuser Baldwin. The boys plan to turn their wagon into a flying machine. When Baldwin kills their dog, Mazzello takes off in the radio flyer, apparently with tragic results.

2391. *Radioland Murders* (1994, Universal, 112m, c). D Mel Smith, P Rick McCallum & Fred Roos, W Willard Huyck, Gloria Katz, Jeff Reno & Ron Osborne (based on a story by George Lucas), PH David Tattersall, ED Paul Trejo, M Joel McNeely, PD Gavin Bocquet, AD Peter Russell, SD Jim Ferrell.

LP Brian Benban (Roger), Mary Stuart Masterson (Penny Henderson), Ned Beatty (General Whalen), George Burns (Milt Lackey), Scott Michael Campbell (Billy), Brion James (Bernie King), Michael Lerner (Lt. Cross), Stephen Tobolowsky (Max Applewhite).

Benban should have stuck with his successful cable TV series *Dream On*. In this period comedy piece a group of stock characters are featured as victims and suspects when a series of killings take place on the air at a 1939 Chicago radio station.

2392. *The Rage* (1998, Canada, Norstar Ent., 95m, c). D Sidney J. Furie, P Robert Snukal & Dan Grodnik, W Gregg Mellott, PH Donald Morgan, ED Nick Rotundo, M Paul Zara, PD Dan Lomino, AD Timothy Kirkpatrick.

LP Lorenzo Lamas (Nick Travis), Roy Scheider (Taggart), Gary Busey Gacy), Kristen Cloke (Kelly McCord), David Carradine (Lucas).

When mutilated corpses of tourists begin piling up in the Pacific Northwest, FBI chief Scheider reluctantly teams FBI agent Lamas with profiler Cloke to investigate the case. Things have not been right between Lamas and Scheider every since the latter interfered in a standoff with gunmen, resulting in an unnecessary massacre.

2393. The Rage: Carrie 2 (1999, MGM/UA, 101m, c). D Katt Shea, P Paul Monash, W Rafael Moreu (based on characters created by Stephen King), PH Donald M. Morgan, ED Richard Nord, M Danny P. Harvey, PD Peter Jamison, AD Geoffrey S. Grimsman, SD Linda Spheeris.

LP Emily Bergi (Rachel Lang), Jason London (Jesse Ryan), Dylan Bruno (Mark), J. Smith-Cameron (Barbara Lang), Amy Irving (Sue Snell), Zachary Ty Brown (Eric).

In this sequel to Brian De Palma's 1976 horror classic starring Sissy Spacek, Bergi is a high school student who has inherited lethal telekinetic powers. She unleashes them after her best friend jumps off a building, just one of a group of virgins driven to suicide by a bunch of jocks.

2394. A Rage in Harlem (1991, U.K., Miramax, 115m, c). D Bill Duke, P Stephen Woolley & Kerry Boyle, W John Toles-Bey & Bobby Crawford (based on the novel by Chester Himes), PH Toyomichi Kurita, ED Curtiss Clayton, M Elmer Bernstein, PD Steven Legler.

LP Forest Whitaker (Jackson), Gregory Hines (Goldy), Robin Givens (Imabelle), Zakes Mokae (Big Kathy), Danny Glover (Easy-Money), Badja Djola (Slim), John Toles-Bey (Jodie).

Classy operator Givens arrives in Harlem with a load of gold sought by an assortment of crooks. Nice guy and mama's boy Whitaker sees himself as her protector. The film offers an expected blend of humor and violence.

2395. The Raggedy Rawney (1990, U.K., Handmade/Island, 102m, c). D Bob Hoskins, P Bob Weis, W Hoskins & Nicole De Wilde, PH Frank Tidy, ED Alan Jones, M Michael Kamen, PD Jiri Matolin.

LP Bob Hoskins (Darky), Dexter Fletcher (Tom), Zoe Nathenson (Jessie), David Hill (Lamb), Ian Dury (Weasel), Zoe Wanamaker (Elle), J.G. Devlin (Jake), Perry Fenwick (Victor).

Hoskins is the writer, director and star of this tale of an army deserter who dons women's clothes and hides out with a band of gypsies. It has appeal for a very limited audience.

2396. The Rain Killer (1991, Concorde, 93m, c). D Ken Stein, P Jonathan Winfrey, W Ray Cunneff, PH Janusz Kaminski, ED Patrick Rand, M Terry Plumeri, AD John LeTenoux, SD Colin DeRouin & Michele Munroz.

LP Ray Sharkey (Vince Capra), David Beecroft (Wesley Dalton), Tania Coleridge (Adele), Michael Chiklis (Reese), Bill LaVallee (Hacket), Woody Brown (Rosewall).

A big city cop and a government agent team up to seek a serial killer who murders women during precipitation.

2397. Rain Without Thunder (1993, Orion Classics, 99m, c). D & W Gary Bennett, P Nanette Sorenson & Gary Sorenson, PH Karl Kases, ED Mallory Gottlieb & Suzanne Pillsbury, M Randall Lynch & Allen Lynch, PD Ina Mayhew.

LP Ali Thomas (Alison Goldring), Betty Buckley (Beverly Goldring), Carolyn McCormick (Reporter), Iona Morris (Andrea Murdoch), Jeff Daniels (Jonathan Garson), Frederic Forrest (Walker Point Warden), Linda Hunt (Atwood Society Director).

It's a fake documentary about a time in the future when abortion is illegal. The very one-sided presentation of the question of "choice versus fetal rights" follows the story of a mother and daughter jailed for trying to flee to Sweden so the younger woman can get an abortion.

2398. Raining Stones (1994, U.K., Norther Arts Ent., 90m, c). D Kenneth Loach, P Sally Hibbin, W Jim Allen, PH Barry Ackroyd, ED Jonathan Morris, M Stewart Copeland, PD Martin Johnson, AD Fergus Clegg.

LP Bruce Jones (Bob), Julie Brown (Anne), Gemma Phoenix (Coleen), Ricky Tomlinson (Tommy), Tom Hickey (Father Barry), Mike Fallon (Jimmy), Jonathan James (Tansey).

Desperate to get the money to purchase a costly first communion dress for his daughter, Jones engages in numerous misadventures to raise the funds.

2399. Raising Cain (1992, Universal, 95m, c). D & W Brian De Palma, P Gale Anne Hurd, PH Stephen H. Burum, ED Paul Hirsch, Bonnie Koehler & Robert Dalva, M Pino Donaggio, PD Doug Kraner, AD Mark Billerman, SD Barbara Munch.

LP John Lithgow (Dr. Carter Nix/Cain/Josh/Margo), Lolita Davidovich (Jenny), Steven Bauer (Jack Dante), Frances Sternhagen (Dr. Waldheim), Gregg Henry (Lt. Terri), Tom Bower (Sgt. Cully).

Lithgow has four roles in this thriller. His Norwegian father arrives in the States needing his psychiatrist son's help in stealing babies for a child development experiment. Lithgow's murderous alter-ego is only too glad to help, especially when he discovers his wife with another man.

2400. *Rambling Rose* (1991, Seven Arts, 112m, c). D Martha Coolidge, P Renny Harlin, W Calder Willingham (based on his novel), PH Johnny Jensen, ED Steven Cohen, M Elmer Bernstein, PD John Vallone, AD Christian Wagener, SD Bob Gould.

LP Laura Dern† (Rose), Robert Duvall (Daddy Hillyer), Diane Ladd† (Mother Hillyer), Lukas Haas (Buddy Hillyer), John Heard (Willcox "Buddy" Hillyer), Kevin Conway (Doctor Martinson), Robert Burke (Police Chief Dave Wilkie), Lisa Jakub (Doll Hillyer).

The entire cast in this delightful period piece is very precious. Dern is a free-spirited and sexually-yearning young woman taken into Duvall's Southern family in 1935. She has quite an effect on Duvall and his son Haas. The latter is an adolescent filled with curiosity about sex and lust for Dern. She, on the other hand, would be more than willing to offer herself to Duvall. The matriarch of the family, Ladd, is most understanding and sympathetic to the feelings of Dern, wishing to shake off the restraints placed on women of the time. There is a scene in the film, years after the story being told, when Haas has grown to be Heard and Duvall is an old man. Watching Duvall become this old man, with an old man's shuffle and other movements, is to be reminded of what a superb actor the man is.

2401. *Rampage* (1992, DeLaurentiis Ent. Group, 97m, c). D & W William Friedkin (based on the novel by William P. Wood), P David Salven, PH Robert D. Yeoman, ED Jere Huggins, M Ennio Morricone, PD Buddy Cone, AD Carol Clements, SD Nancy Nye.

LP Michael Biehn (Anthony Fraser), Alex McArthur (Charles Reece), Nicholas Campbell (Albert Morse), Deborah Van Valkenburgh (Kate Fraser), John Harkins (Dr. Keddie), Art Lafleur (Mel Sanderson), Royce D. Applegate (Gene Tippetts), Billy Greenbush (Judge McKinsey), Grace Zabriskie (Naomi Reece).

This film, made in 1987, wasn't released until 1992 due to financial difficulties with the production company. Liberal D.A. Biehn argues against the insanity plea of McArthur, who had gone on a murdering spree, mutilating the bodies of his victims.

2402. *Random Hearts* (1999, Sony Pictures–Columbia Pictures, 133m, c). D Sydney Pollack, P Pollack & Marykay Powell, W Kurt Luedtke, adapted by Darryl Ponicsan (based on the novel by Warren Adler), PH Philippe Rousselot, ED William Steinkamp, M Dave Grusin, PD Barbara Ling, AD Chris Shriver, SD Scott Murphy & Susan Bode.

LP Harrison Ford (Dutch Van Den Broeck), Kristin Scott Thomas (Kay Chandler), Charles S. Dutton (Alcee), Bonnie Hunt (Wendy Judd), Dennis Haysbert (Detective George Beaufort), Sydney Pollack (Carl Broman), Richard Jenkins (Truman Trainor), Paul Guilfoyle (Dick Montoya), Susanna Thompson (Peyton Van Den Broeck), Peter Coyote (Cullen Chandler).

Considering the talent involved in this movie, it's surprising that it is so ordinary. Ford is a police sergeant whose wife Thompson is killed in a plane crash along with her lover Coyote, husband of congresswoman Scott Thomas. Ford and Scott Thomas meet, and slowly their grief and anger turn to love. The story is soapy and bland; and besides, Ford should get a new hair style.

2403. *Ransom* (1996, Touchstone Pictures–Buena Vista, 121m, c). D Ron Howard, P Scott Rudin, Brian Grazer & B. Kipling Hagopian, W Richard Price & Alexander Ignon (based on a story by Cyril Hume & Richard Maibaum), PH Piotr Sobocinski, ED Dan Hanley & Mike Hill, M James Horner, PD Michael Corenblith, AD John Kasarda, SD Susan Bode.

LP Mel Gibson (Tom Mullen), Gary Sinise (Jimmy Shaker), Rene Russo (Kate Mullen), Delroy Lindo (Lonnie Hawkins), Lili Taylor (Maris Connor), Brawley Nolte (Sean Mullen), Liev Schreiber (Clark Barnes), Donnie Wahlberg (Cubby Barnes).

This film is a remake of the 1956 Glenn Ford

movie of the same name. In both cases, a wealthy father decides to turn the tables on his son's kidnapper by refusing to pay the ransom, instead offering the money as a bounty on the kidnapper's head. Neither Russo in this film nor Donna Reed in the earlier version do much except fall apart and accuse their husbands of playing games with their child's life.

2404. Rapa Nui (1994, Warner Bros., 107m, c). D Kevin Reynolds, P Jim Wilson & Kevin Costner, W Tim Rose Price & Reynolds, PH Stephen F. Windon, ED Peter Boyle, M Stewart Copeland, PD George Liddle, AD Ian Allen.

LP Jason Scott Lee (Noro), Esai Morales (Make), Sandrine Holt (Ramana), Emilio Tuki Hito (Messenger), Gordon Hatfield (Riro), Faenza Reuben (Heke).

Rapa Nui is the Polynesian name for Easter Island, where this story is set during the 17th century. The film shows the customs of the people who constructed the giant stone statues for which the island is so famous. Basically, it's a love triangle with Lee, Morales and Holt as the vertices.

2405. Rapid Fire (1992, 20th Century–Fox, 96m, c). D Dwight H. Little, P Robert Lawrence, W Alan B. McElroy, Cindy Cirile & Paul Attanasio (based on a story by McElroy & Cirile), PH Ric Waite, ED Gib Jaffe, M Christopher Young, PD Ron Foreman, AD Charles Butcher, SD Leslie Frankenheimer.

LP Brandon Lee (Jake Lo), Powers Boothe (Mace Ryan), Nick Mancuso (Antonio Serrano), Raymond J. Barry (Agent Stuart), Kate Hodge (Karla Withers), Tzi Ma (Kinman Tau).

L.A. art student Lee gets caught up in a three-way vendetta involving competing drug lords, Mancuso and Tzi Ma, and tough Chicago cop Boothe.

2406. The Rapture (1991, New Line Cinema–Fine Line Features, 102m, c). D & W Michael Tolkin, P Nick Wechsler, Nancy Tenenbaum & Karen Koch, PH Bojan Bazelli, ED Suzanne Fenn, M Thomas Newman, PD Robin Standefer, AD Kathleen M. McKernin, SD Susan Benjamin.

LP Mimi Rogers (Sharon), David Duchovny (Randy), Patrick Bauchau (Vic), Kimberly Cullum (Mary), Will Patton (Sheriff Foster), Terri Hanauer (Paula), James LeGros (Tommy).

Rogers is trapped in a dead end job as a telephone service operator. To add a little excitement to her life, she and her boyfriend Bauchau regularly participate in group sex with strangers. Rogers takes up with Duchovny, who confesses he once killed a man. Confused about her feelings and her life, she takes a drive with no destination in mind, picks up hitchhiker LeGros and goes to a hotel with him. Feeling disgusted with herself, she reads the Gideon bible and returns to her job where she announces she has found God. She marries Duchovny, has a baby, and six years later Duchovny is murdered. In a moment of religious rapture she accedes to her young daughter's wish to be in heaven with her father by shooting and killing the child, but she is unable to turn the gun on herself to reunite the entire family.

2407. Ratcatcher (1999, U.K., Pathé/BBC Films, 93m, c). D & W Lynne Ramsay, P Gavin Emerson, PH Alwin Kuchler, ED Lucia Zucchetti, M Rachel Portman, PD Jane Morton, AD Robina Nicholson.

LP William Eadie (James), Tommy Flanagan (Da), Mandy Matthews (Ma), Michelle Stewart (Ellen), Lynne Ramsay, Jr. (Anne Marie), Leanne Muller (Margaret Anne).

This film examines the grim life of a working-class Glasgow family, made all the more squalid due to a prolonged garbage collector's strike and an accumulation of rat-infested trash. Twelve-year-old Eadie has a fight with another lad on the banks of a canal, which results in the other boy's drowning death. Eadie says nothing of the incident, but his guilt haunts him.

2408. Ravenous (1999, 20th Century–Fox, 100m, c). D Antonia Bird, P Adam Fields, W Ted Griffin, PH Anthony B. Richmond, ED Neil Farrell, M Michael Nyman & Damon Albarn, PD Bryce Perrin.

LP Guy Pearce (Capt. John Boyd), Robert Carlyle (Colqhoun/Ives), Jeremy Davies (Toffler), Jeffrey Jones (Hart), John Spencer (General Slauson).

Very loosely based on the infamous Donner party incident, Carlyle portrays a mountain man who turns to cannibalism in the Sierra Nevadas, circa 1847.

2409. *Raw Justice* (1994, Republic Pictures, 92m, c). D & W David Prior, P David Winters, PH Don Fauntleroy & Carlos Gonzalez, AD Linda Lewis.

LP David Keith (Mace), Robert Hays (Mitch), Pamela Anderson (Sarah), Charles Napier (Mayor Stiles), Stacy Keach (Bob Jenkins), Leo Rossi (Detective Atkins), Bernard Hocke (Bernie).

Bounty hunter Keith enlists the reluctant help of call girl Anderson to track down his primary suspect in the murder of the daughter of a powerful Southern mayor. The threesome must band together to prevent their own murders.

2410. *Raw Nerve* (1991, AIP, 93m, c). D David A. Prior, P Ruta K. Aras, W Prior & Lawrence L. Simeone, PH Andrew Parke, ED Tony Malanowski, M Greg Turner, AD Betty "BJ" Cline.

LP Glenn Ford (Captain Gavin), Jan-Michael Vincent (Lt. Bruce Ellis), Sandahl Bergman (Gloria Freeman), Randall "Tex" Cobb (Blake Garrett), Ted Prior (Jimmy Clayton), Traci Lords (Gina Clayton).

A race car driver has visions of a serial killer. When he reports them to the police he becomes their number one suspect.

2411. *Ready to Wear* (AKA: *Pret-a-Porter*) (1994, Miramax, 133m, c). D & P Robert Altman, W Altman & Barbara Shulgasser, PH Pierre Mignot & Jean Lepine, ED Geraldine Peroni & Suzy Elmiger, M Michel Legrand, PD Stephen Altman, AD William Abello, SD Jean Canovas & Francoise Dupertuis.

LP Julia Roberts (Anne Eisenhower), Tim Robbins (Joe Flynn), Stephen Rea (Milo O'Brannagan), Lauren Bacall (Slim Chrysler), Marcello Mastroianni (Sergei), Sophia Loren (Isabella de la Fontaine), Anouk Aimee (Simone Lowenthal), Lili Taylor (Fiona Ulrich), Kim Basinger (Kitty Potter), Sally Kellerman (Sissy Wanamaker), Tracey Ullman (Nina Scant), Linda Hunt (Regina Krumm), Rupert Everett (Jack Lowenthal), Forest Whitaker (Cy Bianco).

Robert Altman takes audiences behind the scenes and on the runways of the fashion industry. His ensemble cast and numerous cameo appearances make his satire an interesting if not very important film. The plots and subplots revolve around a series of stereotypes, and (as in real life) not all dangling strings of the stories are tied off.

2412. *The Real Blonde* (1998, Paramount, 105m, c). D & W Tom DiCillo, P Marcus Viscidi & Tom Rosenberg, PH Frank Prinzi, ED Camilla Toniolo & Keiko Deguchi, M Jim Farmer, PD Christopher Nowak, AD Paul Austerberry, SD Gordon Sim & Marlene Rain.

LP Matthew Modine (Joe), Catherine Keener (Mary), Daryl Hannah (Kelly), Maxwell Caulfield (Bob), Elizabeth Berkley (Tina), Marlo Thomas (Blair), Bridgette Wilson (Sahara), Buck Henry (Dr. Leuter), Christopher Lloyd (Ernst), Kathleen Turner (Dee Dee Taylor).

This slice-of-life story is about several young people trying to find love and success in the glamour industries. Most of the characters have nothing to recommend them, with only their faults shown, thus making them one-dimensional and the film uninteresting.

2413. *The Real Howard Spitz* (1998, U.K./Canada, Metrodome/Imagex–Telefilm Canada, 102m, c). D Vadim Jean, P Paul Brooks & Christopher Zimmer, W Jurgen Wolff, PH Glen MacPherson, ED Pia di Ciaula, M David A. Hughes & John Young, PD Chris Townsend, AD Anglea Murphy.

LP Kelsey Grammer (Howard Spitz), Amanda Donohoe (Laura Kershaw), Genevieve Tessier (Samantha Kershaw), Joseph Rutten (Lou), Patrick McKenna ("Howard Spitz"), Kay Tremblay (Theodora Winkle).

Grammer is good at what he does on his hit TV show, so it seems a waste to appear in nothing movies such as this. He portrays a writer of seedy, hard-boiled detective novels who has lost his touch. When he switches to kiddie fiction he becomes a winner.

2414. *The Real McCoy* (1993, Universal, 104m, c). D Russell Mulcahy, P Michael Scott Bregman, Willi Baer & Martin Bregman, W Sally Robinson & Wesley Strick, PH Denis Crossan, ED Peter Honess, PD Kim Colefax, AD Paul Huggins, SD Richard Charles Greenbaum & Jonathan Short.

LP Kim Basinger (Karen McCoy), Val Kilmer (J.T. Barker), Terence Stamp (Jack Schmidt), Gailard Sartain (Gary Buckner), Zach English (Patrick).

Just out of prison, Basinger wants to go straight and raise her son. But her former associates kidnap her child and force her to return to her bank-robbing ways. It's a dumb movie, not even worth a look on free TV.

2415. *The Real Thing* (AKA: *Livers Ain't Cheap*) (1996, Windy City International, 89m, c). D & W James Merendino, P Kurt Mac-Carley, PH Gregg Littlewood, ED Esther Russell, M Peter Leinheiser, PD Charlotte Malmlof, AD Sandy Grass, SD Segolen Koschu.

LP James Russo (Rupert), Jeremy Piven (John), Fabrizio Bentivoglio (Alfredo), Robert LaSardo (Eric), Ashley Lawrence (Carla).

Ex-con Russo leads a team that plans to rob a popular nightclub on New Year's Eve. Problems arise when another gang gets the same idea.

2416. *Reality Bites* (1994, Universal, 99m, c). D Ben Stiller, P Danny DeVito & Michael Shamberg, W Helen Childress, PH Emmanuel Lubezki, ED Lisa Churgin & John Spence, M Karl Wallinger, PD Sharon Seymour, AD Jeff Knipp, SD Michael Armani & Maggie Martin.

LP Winona Ryder (Lelaina Pierce), Ethan Hawke (Troy Dyer), Janeane Garofalo (Vicki Miner), Steve Zahn (Sammy Gray), Ben Stiller (Michael Grates), Swoosie Kurtz (Charlane McGregor), Harry O'Reilly (Wes McGregor).

It is a Generation X film about four recent college graduates working at growing up or resisting growing up in Houston. If you are not a devotee of MTV you may not find much in the movie to admire.

2417. *A Reason to Believe* (1995, Castle Hill, 109m, c). D & W Douglas Tirola, P Tirola & Gail Dickersin, PH Sarah Cawley, ED Sabine Hoffman, PD Carol O'Neil, AD Constance Lemasson, SD Tracy Keegan.

LP Allison Smith (Charlotte Byrne), Jay Underwood (Jim Current), Danny Quinn (Wesley Grant), Georgia Emelin (Linda Berryman), Kim Walker (Judith), Keith Coogan (Potto), Lisa Lawrence (Alison).

This film looks at the problem of date rape on college campuses. Smith goes to her boyfriend's frat party even though he's not going to be there and has asked her to stay away. She drinks a lot, flirts with Underwood, passes out and is raped. But Underwood claims she was

a quite willing participant. The problem deserves a better treatment than this superficial film.

2418. *Rebecca's Secret* (1997, Maverick Ent., 82m, c). D & W Ellyn Michaels, P Charles Moon, PH Al Carbon, ED Nick Cahuenga, M Greg Poree, AD Nick Papadakis, SD Beatrice Barto.

LP Amy Rochelle (Rebecca Hensley), Michael Baci (Jonathan), Lauren Hays (Gwen Parker), Brenda Stone (Elaine Mathews), Christopher Bennett (Max).

In this rip-off of *Diabolique* (1955), Rochelle is the owner of the world's largest lingerie company. Husband Baci amuses himself by bedding the models used in their catalogue. Not only does this upset Rochelle but his mistress Hays as well. The two women push his car over a cliff with him in it. He's dead — isn't he?

2419. *Reckless* (1995, Samuel Goldwyn Company, 90m, c). D Norman Rene, P Amy J. Kaufman, W Craig Lucas (based on his play), PH Frederick Elmes, ED Michael Berenbaum, M Stephen Endelman, PD Andrew Jackness, AD Philip Messina, SD Daniel Boxer.

LP Mia Farrow (Rachel), Mary-Louise Parker (Pooty), Scott Glenn (Lloyd), Tony Goldwyn (Tom), Eileen Brennan (Sister Margaret), Giancarlo Esposito (Tim Timko), Stephen Dorff (Tom, Jr.).

On Christmas Eve, happily married Farrow (she thinks) discovers that her husband Goldwyn has hired a hitman to kill her. He changes his mind and sends her on the run. Lost in a snowstorm, she is rescued by Glenn and his apparently deaf wife Parker. Farrow moves in with the couple and is relatively happy — until the time of the next Christmas when Goldwyn shows up and wants Farrow back. But their adventures have just begun.

2420. *Reckless Kelly* (1994, Australia, Warner Bros., 94m, c). D Yahoo Serious, P Serious & Warwick Ross, W Serious, Ross, Lulu Serious & David Roach, PH Kevin Hayward, ED Roach, Anthony Gray & Robert Gibson, M Tommy Tycho & Anthony Marinelli, PD Grace Walker, AD Ian Gracie.

LP Yahoo Serious (Reckless Kelly), Melora Hardin (Robin Banks), Alexei Sayle (Major

Wimp), Hugo Weaving (Sir John), Kathleen Freeman (Mrs. Delance), John Pinette (Sam Delance).

Australian comedian Serious appears in a spoof of the notorious Australian outlaw Ned Kelly. It's not as funny as you would hope it to be.

2421. Red Corner (1997, MGM, 119m, c). D Jon Avnet, P Avnet, Jordan Kerner, Charles B. Mulvehill & Rosalie Swedlin, W Robert King, PH Karl Walter Lindenlaub, ED Peter E. Berger, M Thomas Newman, PD Richard Sylbert, AD Virginia Randolph-Weaver, SD William Kemper Wright.

LP Richard Gere (Jack Moore), Bai Ling (Shen Yuelin), Bradley Whitford (Bob Ghery), Byron Mann (Lin Dan), Tsai Chin (Chairman Xu), James Hong (Lin Shou), Roger Yuan (Huan Minglu), Robert Stanton (Ed Pratt), Jessey Meng (Hong Ling).

Lawyer Gere, is in Beijing to negotiate a deal with the Chinese government on behalf of his client, an American entertainment concern. While out on the town he encounters fashion model Meng. The two end up in his bed. The next morning he awakens to find her dead. He is arrested and then finds that Chinese courts operate a lot differently than American ones. He is considered guilty until he can prove himself innocent. He is not allowed a non–Chinese attorney and is advised that an innocent plea will be held against him. He ultimately is able to convince his court-appointed lawyer Bai Ling that he was framed. Now the only problem is to prove it.

2422. Red Rock West (1994, Propaganda Films, 98m, c). D John Dahl, P Sigurjon Sighvatsson & Steve Golin, W John Dahl & Rick Dahl, PH Marc Reshovsky, ED Scott Chestnut, M William Olvis, PD Robert Pearson, AD Don Diers, SD Kate Sullivan.

LP Nicolas Cage (Michael Williams), Dennis Hopper (Lyle), Lara Flynn Boyle (Suzanne Brown), J.T. Walsh (Wayne Brown), Craig Reary (Jim), Vance Johnson (Mr. Johnson).

Perennial loser Cage lands in the little town of Red Rock where he is mistaken for the hitman crooked sheriff Walsh has hired to do away with his wife Boyle. She offers Cage more than her husband to turn the tables on the lawman; and then Hopper, the real hitman, shows up.

2423. Red Scorpion 2 (1996, MCA Universal, 94m, c). D Michael Kennedy, P Robert MacLean, W Troy Bolotnick & Barry Victor (based on characters created by Arne Olsen), PH Curtis Petersen, ED Gary Zubeck, M George Blondheim, PD Brent Thomas, AD Randy Chodak, SD Lesley Beale.

LP Matt McColm (Nick Stone), John Savage (Andrew Kendrick), Jennifer Rubin (Sam Guiness), Michael Ironside (Colonel West), Paul Ben-Victor (Vince d'Angelo), Michael Covert (Billy Ryan).

This film is just another version of *The Dirty Dozen*. A team of good-bad guys are formed to go after a neo-fascist businessman who employs skinheads to cause havoc in minority communities.

2424. Red Sun Rising (1995, Imperial Ent., 100m, c). D Francis Megahy, P Paul Maslak & Neva Friedenn, W David S. Green (based on a story by Green, Friedenn & Maslak), PH John Newby, ED John Weidner, M John Coda, PD Wendy Guidery, AD Roz Johanna Gross.

LP Don "The Dragon" Wilson (Thomas Hoshino), Terry Farrell (Karen Ryder), Soon-Teck Oh (Yamata), James Lew (Jaho), Mako (Buntoro Iga).

Detective Wilson drops into the middle of a turf war between the Japanese mafia and L.A. street gangs.

2425. Red Surf (1990, Arrowhead, 105m, c). D H. Gordon Boos, P Richard C. Weinman, W Vincent Robert (based on a story by Brian Gamble, Jason Hoffs & Vincent Robert, and additional material by Boos), PH John Schwartzman, ED Dennis Dolan, M Sasha Matson, PD Lynda Burbank.

LP George Clooney (Mark Remar), Doug Savant (Attila), Dedee Pfeiffer (Rebecca), Gene Simmons (Doc), Philip McKeon (True Blue), Rick Najera (Calavera).

Surfers Clooney and Savant become involved with drug gangs. There is nothing much of interest here for most people, unless one is into surfing or drugs.

2426. The Red Violin (1998, Canada, Universal, 131m, c). D Francois Girard, P Niv Fichman, W Don McKellar & Girard, PH Alain Dostie, ED Gaetan Huot, M John Corigliano*, PD Francois Seguin.

LP Carlo Cecchi (Nicolo Bussotti), Irene Grazioli (Anna Bussotti), Jean-Luc Bideau (Georges Poussin), Christoph Koncz (Kaspar Weiss), Greta Scacchi (Victoria Byrd), Jason Flemyng (Frederick Pope), Sylvia Chang (Xiang Pei), Liu Zifeng (Chou Yuan), Samuel L. Jackson (Charles Morritz), Colm Feore (Auctioneer).

In present day Montreal, a famous Bussotti violin, known as "the red violin," is being auctioned. During the auction the scene flashes back to the creation of the violin in 17th century Italy. The film follows the violin as it moves from owner to owner, from country to country, from century to century, until it arrives in Montreal and at the auction.

2427. Redball (1999, Australia, Palace Films, 88m, c.) D & W Jon Hewitt, P Meredith King & Phillip Parslow, PH Mark Pugh, ED Alan Woodruff & Cindy Clarkson, M Neil McGrath, PD Vanessa Cerene.

LP Belinda McClory (Jane JJ Wilson), John Brumpton (Robbie Walsh), Frank Magree (Chris Hill), Peter Docker (James Fry), Anthea Davis (Toni Johnston).

Detectives McClory and Brumpton are assigned the case of a series of brutal child murders. The cops dub the serial killer Mr. Creep, but evidence points to one of their own.

2428. The Ref (AKA: *Hostile Hostages*) (1994, Touchstone–Buena Vista, 92m, c). D Ted Demme, P Ron Bozman, Richard LaGravenese & Jeff Weiss, W Marie Weiss & LaGravenese (based on a story by Marie Weiss), PH Adam Kimmel, ED Jeffrey Wolf, M David A. Stewart, PD Dan Davis, AD Dennis Davenport, SD Jaro Dick.

LP Denis Leary (Gus), Judy Davis (Caroline), Kevin Spacey (Lloyd), Robert J. Steinmiller, Jr. (Jesse), Glynis Johns (Rose), Raymond J. Barry (Huff), Richard Bright (Murray), Christine Baranski (Connie).

Jewel thief Leary has plenty to be sorry for when he takes bickering married couple Davis and Spacey hostage in their ritzy home. He plots his escape while posing as the couple's marriage counselor, staying with them during the Christmas holidays.

2429. The Reflecting Skin (1991, U.K./Canada, Prestige Films, 95m, c). D & W Philip Ridley, P Dominic Anciano & Ray Burdis, PH Dick Pope, ED Scott Thomas, M Nick Bicat, AD Rick Roberts, SD Andrea French.

LP Viggo Mortensen (Cameron Dove), Lindsay Duncan (Dolphin Blue), Jeremy Cooper (Seth Dove), Sheila Moore (Ruth Dove), Duncan Fraser (Luke Dove), David Longworth (Joshua), Robert Koons (Sheriff Ticker).

In a 1950s prairie town young Cooper observes the strange and bizarre characters of his community. This leads him to fantasize that Duncan, the young widow who lives next door, is a vampire. His older brother Mortensen, who falls in love with Duncan, becomes increasingly pale and begins to lose weight and his hair. Several friends of Cooper are found sodomized and dead. The film is a challenge for audiences to watch because of the grotesqueness it shows.

2430. Reflections in the Dark (AKA: *Reflections on a Crime*; *Regina*) (1995, New Horizons, 84m, c). D & W Jon Purdy, P Gwen Field, Barbara Klein, Carol Dunn Trussell & Alida Camp, PH Teresa Medina, ED Norman Buckley, M Parmer Fuller, PD Arlan Jay Vetter, AD Roger Belk.

LP Mimi Rogers (Regina), Billy Zane (Colin), John Terry (James), Kurt Fuller (Howard), Lee Garlington (Tina), Nancy Fish (Ellen).

On the eve of her execution for the murder of her overbearing husband, beautiful condemned prisoner Rogers relates her story to guard Zane. Flashbacks show different means of disposing of her husband.

2431. Regarding Henry (1991, Paramount, 107m, c). D Mike Nichols, P Scott Rudin & Nichols, W Jeffrey Abrams, PH Giuseppe Rotunno, ED Sam O'Steen, M Hans Zimmer, PD Tony Walton, AD Dan Davis & William Elliott, SD Susan Bode, Amy Marshall & Cindy Carr.

LP Harrison Ford (Henry Turner), Annette Bening (Sarah Turner), Bill Nunn (Bradley), Mikki Allen (Rachel), Donald Moffat (Charlie), Nancy Marchand (Mrs. O'Brien), Elizabeth Wilson (Jessica), Robin Bartlett (Phyllis), John Leguizamo (Gunman).

Successful, self-centered attorney Ford loses his memory when he is shot in the head by a robber at a convenience store. He is changed into a childlike man who is much more appealing to his wife and child than before. He even is shocked by the unethical behavior of members of his law firm. Now *that* is a transformation.

2432. The Regenerated Man (1994, Arrow Releasing, 89m, c). D Ted A. Bohus, P Bohus & Danny Provenzano, W Bohus & Jack Smith (based on a story by Bohus), PH John R. Rosnell, ED Joe Morelli, Will Kelly, Randy J. Popkave & Bohus, M Ariel Shallit, AD Rena D'Angela.

LP Arthur Lundquist (Dr. Robert Clarke), Cheryl Hendricks (Kathryn), Andrew Fetherolf (Tony "Oni" Agar), Greg Sullivan (Det. Winter), Eric Marshall (Hobo Ronald).

Forced to drink his own formula for regenerating flesh, Lundquist becomes a monster.

2433. Regeneration (1998, U.K./Canada, BBC Films–Alliance Releasing, 113m, c). D Gillies MacKinnon, P Allan Scott & Peter R. Simpson, W Scott (based on the novel by Pat Barker), PH Glen MacPherson, ED Pia Di Ciaula, M Mychael Danna, PD Andy Harris, AD John Frankish.

LP Jonathan Pryce (Dr. William Rivers), James Wilby (Siegfried Sassoon), Jonny Lee Miller (Billy Prior), Stuart Bunce (Wilfred Owen), Tanya Allen (Sarah), John Neville (Dr. Yealland).

In this talky film, Wilby, a poet and decorated WWI hero, is declared mentally unstable and sent to a hospital in the Scottish countryside after publishing a denouncement of the war. He is treated by Pryce, who finds his patient sane but is pressured to get the young man to renounce his own denouncement.

2434. Relax ... It's Just Sex (1998, Atlas Ent., 110m, c). D & W P.J. Castellaneta, P Steven J. Wolfe, Megan O'Neill & Harold Warren, PH Lon Magdich, ED Tom Seid, M Lori Eschler Frystak, PD Timm Bergen.

LP Jennifer Tilly (Tara Ricoto), Mitchell Anderson (Vincey Sauris), Cynda Williams (Sabrina Classer), Lori Petty (Robin Moon), Serena Scott Thomas (Megan Pillsbury).

This romantic comedy deals with the affairs, love and otherwise, of a group of friends composed of gays, lesbians and straights. Tilly acts as the group's good-natured mother hen.

2435. The Relic (1997, Paramount, 110m, c). D Peter Hyams, P Gale Anne Hurd & Sam

Mercer, W Amy Holden Jones, John Raffo, Rick Jaffa & Amanda Silver (based on the novel *Relic* by Douglas Preston and Lincoln Child), PH Hyams, ED Steven Kemper, M John Debney, PD Philip Harrison, AD Eric Orbom & James J. Murakami, SD John Anderson.

LP Penelope Ann Miller (Dr. Margo Green), Tom Sizemore (Lt. Vincent D'Agosta), Linda Hunt (Dr. Ann Cuthbert), James Whitmore (Dr. Albert Frock), Clayton Rohner (Detective Hollingsworth), Chi Muoi Lo (Greg Lee).

Evolutionary biologist Miller receives a shipment of crates from Brazil that contain nothing but leaves with a strange fungus attached. The crew of the ship that brought the crates are found decapitated. Then a guard at the museum is also found decapitated. It takes a bit too long for Miller and others to make the connection between the killings and the leaves. Finally, a monstrous mutant known to the Brazilian tribes makes his appearance and goes on a rampage at a gala party being held at the museum.

2436. The Remains of the Day† (1993, Columbia, 134m, c). D James Ivory†, P Mike Nichols†, John Calley† & Ismail Merchant†, W Ruth Prawer Jhabvala† (based on the novel by Kazuo Ishiguro), PH Tony Pierce-Roberts, Ed Andrew Marcus, M Richard Robbins†, PD Luciana Arrighi†, AD John Ralph, SD Ian Whittaker†.

LP Anthony Hopkins† (Stevens), Emma Thompson† (Miss Kenton), James Fox (Lord Darlington), Christopher Reeve (Lewis), Peter Vaughan (Father), Hugh Grant (Cardinal), Michael Lonsdale (Dupont D'Ivry), Tim Pigot-Smith (Benn).

Hopkins, the perfect English butler, suppresses all emotion or self-fulfillment in his dedication to his craft. He misses his one opportunity for love with housekeeper Thompson because he knows no way to acknowledge his feelings for her or to express them. His loyalty to his unworthy master Fox doesn't allow him to have any life of his own. Hopkins and Thompson are magnificent.

2437. Renaissance Man (1994, Touchstone–Buena Vista, 125m, c). D Penny Marshall, P Sara Colleton, Elliot Abbot & Robert Greenhut, W Jim Burnstein, PH Adam Greenberg, ED George Bowers & Battle Davis, M

Hans Zimmer, PD Geoffrey Kirkland, AD Richard Johnson, SD Robert Fechtman, Jennifer Williams & John Arnone.

LP Danny DeVito (Bill Rago), Gregory Hines (Sergeant Cass), Cliff Robertson (Colonel James), James Remar (Captain Murdoch), Lillo Brancato, Jr. (Donnie Benitez), Stacey Dash (Miranda Meyers), Kadeem Hardison (Jamaal Montgomery).

Unemployed ad executive DeVito is hired to teach Shakespeare to a group of bonehead army recruits. It's not as funny as it should be, nor as heartwarming as filmmakers intended it to be.

2438. *Rent-A-Kid* (1995, Canada, Viacom, 90m, c). D Fred Gerber, P Dan Howard, W Paul Bernbaum, PH Rene Ohashi, ED George Ralston, M Ron Famin, PD Jeff Gunn.

LP Leslie Nielsen (Harry), Christopher Lloyd (Lawrence), Matt McCoy (Russ), Sherry Miller (Val), Tabitha Lupien (Molly), Amos Crawley (Brandon), Cody Jones (Kyle), Tony Rosato (Cliff Haber).

Businessman Nielsen minds an orphanage for his son for a week. When approached by a young couple who aren't sure about having a family, Nielsen offers them three kids for rent so they can see how they like it.

2439. *The Replacement Killers* (1998, Columbia Pictures–Sony Pictures, 86m, c). D Antoine Fugua, P Brad Grey & Bernie Brillstein, W Ken Sanzel, PH Peter Lyons Collister, ED Jay Cassidy, M Harry Gregson-Williams, PD Naomi Shohan, AD David Lazan, SD Evette Knight.

LP Chow Yun-Fat (John Lee), Mira Sorvino (Meg Coburn), Michael Rooker (Stan [Zeedo] Zedkov), Jurgen Prochnow (Michael Kogan), Kenneth Tsang (Terence Wei).

Asian action hero Chow Yun-Fat, famous for his guns-in-both-hands diving-in-all-directions style, makes his American film debut here. He's a hired gun with a contract to murder the seven-year-old son of cop Rooker, but he can't do it. He finds himself the target of the same assassins, as is master forger Sorvino.

2440. *Repossessed* (1990, New Line, 84m, c). D & W Bob Logan, P Steven Wizan, PH Michael Margulies, ED Jeff Freeman, M Charles Fox, PD Shay Austin, AD Gae Buckley, SD Lee Cunningham.

LP Linda Blair (Nancy Alger), Ned Beatty (Ernest Weller), Leslie Nielsen (Fr. Mayii), Anthony Starke (Fr. Brophy), Melissa Moore (Bimbo).

Once more Blair is possessed by a demon in this spoof of the demonic possession subgenre. A number of actors show up in brief comedy sequences, lampooning current celebrities.

2441. *The Rescuers Down Under* (1990, Walt Disney/Buena Vista, 109m, c). D Hendel Butoy & Michael Gabriel, P Thomas C. Schumacher, W Jim Cox, Karey Kirkpatrick, Byron Simpson & Joe Ranft, ED Michael Kelly, M Bruce Broughton, AD Maurice Hunt, ANIM Glen Keane, Mark Henn, Russ Edmonds, David Cutler, Ruben A. Aquino, Nik Ranieri, Ed Gombert, Anthony DeRosa, Kathy Zielinski, Duncan Majoribanks & Lisa Keene.

LP Voices: Bob Newhart (Bernard), Eva Gabor (Miss Bianca), John Candy (Wilbur), Tristan Rogers (Jake), Adam Ryen (Cody), Wayne Robson (Frank), George C. Scott (McLeach), Douglas Seale (Krebbs).

Heroic mice Bernard and Miss Bianca protect a young boy and a rare golden eagle from poachers. It's not top quality Disney stuff.

2442. *Reservoir Dogs* (1992, Miramax, 99m, c). D & W Quentin Tarantino, P Lawrence Bender, PH Andrzej Sekula, ED Sally Menke, M Karyn Rachtman, PD David Wasco.

LP Harvey Keitel (Mr. White/Larry), Tim Roth (Mr. Orange/Freddy), Michael Madsen (Mr. Blonde/Nic), Christopher Penn (Nice Guy/Eddie), Steve Buscemi (Mr. Pink), Lawrence Tierney (Joe Cabot), Randy Brooks (Holdaway), Kirk Baltz (Marvin Nash).

If one can bear to sit through the great amount of horrific violence in the film, this is a very fine heist story. Six professional criminals, using color code names to protect their identities, are recruited by Tierney to pull off a diamond robbery.

2443. *Restoration* (1995, Miramax, 113m, c). D Michael Hoffman, P Cary Brokaw, Andy Patterson & Sarah Ryan Black, W Rupert Walters (based on the novel by Rose Tremain), PH Oliver Stapleton, ED Garth Craven, M James Newton Howard, PD Eugenio Zanetti*, AD Alan Cassie, Lucy Richardson & Jonathan Lee, SD Zanetti.

LP Robert Downey, Jr. (Merivel), Sam Neill (King Charles II), David Thewlis (Pearce), Polly Walker (Celia), Meg Ryan (Katherine), Ian McKellen (Will Gates), Hugh Grant (Finn), Ian McDiarmid (Ambrose).

Set in 1660s England, the story takes place just as the Puritanical rule is replaced by a monarchy and a court interested in the arts, the sciences and hedonistic living. It's a lush costume piece with a modestly interesting story of the times, as seen through the eyes of heroic young physician Downey.

2444. *Retroactive* (1998, Orion, 91m, c). D Louis Morneau, P Brad Krevoy, Steve Stabler, David Bixler & Michael Nadeau, W Michael Hamilton-Wright, Robert Strauss & Philip Badger, PH George Mooradian, ED Glenn Garland, M Tim Truman, PD Philip Duffin, SD Kelly Potter.

LP James Belushi (Frank), Kylie Travis (Karen), Shannon Whirry (Rayanne), Frank Whaley (Brian), Jesse Borrego (Jesse), M. Emmet Walsh (Sam).

Government scientist Whaley has discovered how to reverse time for brief periods. Police psychiatrist Travis is on the road after quitting her job when a hostage situation she was involved in turned into a massacre. When her car breaks down, she is picked up by small-time crook Belushi and his wife Whirry. At a truckstop Belushi learns Whirry has been seeing another man. He shoots and kills her, but before he can kill Travis she escapes and runs into one of Whaley's experiments, which sends her back in time some 20 minutes. Can she defuse the situation with Belushi and generate a different outcome?

2445. *The Return of Superfly* (1990, Vidmark, 95m, c). D Sig Shore, P Shore & Anthony Wisdom, W Wisdom, PH Anghel Decca, ED John Mullen, M Curtis Mayfield, AD Jeremie Frank, SD Charlotte Snyder.

LP Nathan Purdee (Superfly), Margaret Avery (Francine), Sam Jackson (Nate Cabot), Leonard Thomas (Joey), Kirk Taylor (Renaldo), Carlos Carrasco (Hector), Tico Wells (Willy Green), Luis Ramos (Manuel).

Purdee replaces Ron O'Neal as an ex-pusher who returns to Harlem from a new life in Paris and once again finds himself in the middle of the drug scene.

2446. *Return of the Living Dead III* (1993, Trimark Pictures, 96m, c). D Brian Yuzna, P Yuzna & Gary Schmoeller, W Jon Penney, PH Gerry Lively, ED Chris Roth, PD Antony Tremblay, AD Aram Allen, SD Greg Bartkus.

LP Mindy Clarke (Julie), J. Trevor Edmond (Curt Reynolds), Basil Wallace (Riverman), Kent McCord (Colonel Reynolds).

Army brat Edmond tries to revive his thrill-seeking girlfriend Clarke with an experimental nerve gas. It turns her into a brain-sucking monster.

2447. *Return to Paradise* (1998, Polygram Films, 109m, c). D Joseph Ruben, P Alain Bernheim & Steve Golin, W Wesley Strick & Bruce Robinson (based on the film *Force Majeure* written by Pierre Jolivet & Oliver Schatzky, directed by Jolivet), PH Reynaldo Villalobos, ED Andrew Mondshein & Craig McKay, M Mark Mancina, PD Bill Groom, AD Dennis Bradford, SD Betsy Klompus.

LP Vince Vaughn (Sheriff), Anne Heche (Beth), Joaquin Phoenix (Lewis), David Conrad (Tony), Vera Farmiga (Kerrie), Nick Sandow (Ravitch), Jada Pinkett Smith (M.J. Major).

Irresponsible Vaughn, Phoenix and Conrad roam around Asia chasing "rum, girls and good cheap Hash." Vaughn and Conrad return to the U.S., but Pheonix is arrested and is to be executed for his drug deals unless the other two agree to return and accept their punishment. The film shows how the two deal with their moral dilemma.

2448. *Return to the Blue Lagoon* (1991, Columbia, 98m, c). D William A. Graham, P Frank Price, W Leslie Stevens & Doug Day Stewart (based on the novel *The Garden of God* by Henry DeVere Stacpoole), PH Robert Steadman, ED Ronald J. Fagan, M Basil Poledouris, PD Jon Dowding, AD Paul Ammitzboll.

LP Milla Jovovich (Lilli), Brian Krause (Richard), Lisa Pelikan (Sarah Hargrave), Courtney Phillips (Young Lilli), Garette Patrick Ratliff (Young Richard).

Two youngsters are stranded on a deserted island. When they become adolescents they discover sex. That's about it. It's all been seen before.

2449. ***Return to Two Moon Junction***
(1994, Trimark Pictures, 96m, c). D Farhad
Mann, P Melvin Pearl, W Dyanne Asimow,
ED Dianne M. Ryder.

LP Louise Fletcher (Grandma Belle), Mindy
Clarke (Savannah), John Clayton Schafer (Jake),
Montrose Higgins (Ruth), Yorgo Constantine
(Robert).

Fletcher is upset when her granddaughter
Clarke shows interest in Schafer, the grandson
of a family with whom she has been feuding
for years. Eventually, Fletcher and Clarke find
the means to bond.

2450. ***Revenge*** (1990, Columbia–New
World, 124m, c). D Tony Scott, P Hunt Lowry
& Stanley Rubin, W Jim Harrison & Jeffrey
Fiskin (based on the novel by Harrison), PH
Jeffrey Kimball, ED Chris Lebenzon, M Jack
Nitzsche, PD Michael Seymour & Benjamin
Fernandez, AD Tom Sanders & Jorge Sainz,
SD Crispian Sallis & Fernando Solorio.

LP Kevin Costner (Cochran), Anthony
Quinn (Tiburon "Tibey" Mendes), Madeleine
Stowe (Miryea Mendes), Tomas Milian (Cesar),
Joaquin Martinez (Mauro), James Gammon
(Texan), Jesse Corti (Madero), Sally Kirkland
(Rock Star).

Former pilot Costner has an affair with
Stowe, the beautiful, bored wife of millionaire
gangster Quinn, in Mexico. The latter gets
wind of it and has the two nearly beaten to
death. Then it's their turn to seek revenge.

2451. ***The Revengers' Comedies*** (1998,
U.K./France, J&M Ent.–BBC Films, 82m, c).
D & W Malcolm Mowbray (based on the
plays by Alan Ayckbourn), P Simon Bosan-
quet, PH Romain Winding, ED Barrie Vince,
M Alexandre Desplat, PD Stuart Walker.

LP Sam Neill (Henry Bell), Helena Bonham
Carter (Karen Knightly), Kristin Scott Tho-
mas (Imogen Staxton-Billing), Rupert Graves
(Oliver Knightly), Martin Clunes (Anthony
Staxton-Billing), Steve Coogan (Bruce Tick).

Both depressed businessman Neill and orphaned aristocrat Bonham Carter plan to jump
from London's Tower Bridge. Instead, they
save each other's lives. They hatch a plot of revenge worthy of *Strangers on a Train*. She will
punish Coogan, who stole Neill's job from
him, and he will destroy Scott Thomas, who
drove her husband Clunes into Bonham Carter's
arms only to win him back again.

2452. ***Reversal of Fortune*** (1990, Warner
Bros., 120m, c). D Barbet Schroeder†, P Ed-
ward R. Pressman & Oliver Stone, W Nicholas
Kazan† (based on the book by Alan Dersho-
witz), PH Luciano Tovoli, ED Lee Percy, M
Mark Isham, PD Mel Bourne.

LP Jeremy Irons* (Claus von Bulow), Glenn
Close (Sunny von Bulow), Ron Silver (Alan
Dershowitz), Anabella Sciorra (Carol), Uta
Hagen (Maria), Fisher Stevens (David Mar-
riott), Christine Baranski (Andrea Reynolds).

Irons won an Oscar for his performance as
the unlikeable Claus von Bulow. He may or
may not be responsible for his wife Close
falling into a coma, which she hasn't, come out
of yet. Silver is the high powered lawyer who
wins Irons acquittal. It was the O.J. Simpson
case of its era, and about as many people believe that von Bulow got away with attempted
murder.

2453. ***Rhythm Thief*** (1995, Film Four
Intl., 88m, B&W). D Matthew Harrison, P
Jonathan Starch, W Christopher Grimm &
Harrison, PH Howard Cooke, ED Harrison,
M Danny Brenner, Hugh O'Donovan, John L.
Horn & Kevin Okurland, AD Daniel Fisher.

LP Jason Andrews (Simon), Eddie Daniels
(Marty), Kevin Corrigan (Fuller), Kimberly
Flynn (Cyd), Sean Hagerty (Shayme), Mark
Alfred (Mr. Bunch).

Hustler Andrews makes ends meet by selling pirated tapes of underground bands. One
of the ripped-off bands is out to get him. It's
a character study of a character hardly worth
studying.

2454. ***Rich Girl*** (1991, Study Three Film
Corp., 96m, c). D Joel Bender, P Michael B.
London, W Robert Elliot, PH Levie Isaacks,
ED Mark Helfrich, Richard Candib & Jackie
Reisman-Wernett, M Jay Chattaway, PD
Richard McGuire, SD Charlie Doane.

LP Jill Schoelen (Courtney Wells), Don
Michael Paul (Rick), Sean Kanan (Jeffrey),
Ron Karabatsos (Rocco), Paul Gleason (Mar-
vin Wells), Cherrie Currie (Michelle), Bentley
Mitchum (Scott).

Wealthy Schoelen wants to see how the
other half lives. She takes a job as a waitress in
a rock 'n' roll club and meets and falls for Paul,
a guy from the wrong side of the tracks. Naturally, they are a perfect match — well, almost
perfect.

2455. *Rich in Love* (1993, MGM, 105m, c). D Bruce Beresford, P Richard D. Zanuck & Lili Fini Zanuck, W Alfred Uhry (based on the novel by Josephine Humphreys), PH Peter James, ED Mark Warner, M Georges Delerue, PD John Stoddart, SD John Anderson & Carl Copeland.

LP Albert Finney (Warren Odom), Jill Clayburgh (Helen Odom), Kathryn Erbe (Lucille Odom), Kyle MacLachlan (Billy McQueen), Piper Laurie (Vera Delmage), Ethan Hawke (Wayne Frobiness), Suzy Amis (Rae Odom), Alfre Woodard (Rhody Poole).

Arriving home from school, Erbe finds a note from her mother Clayburgh to her father Finney announcing she has left to seek a new life. The film deals with the fallout experienced by the family left behind.

2456. *The Rich Man's Wife* (1996, Caravan Pictures–Buena Vista, 95m, c). D & W Amy Holden Jones, P Roger Birnbaum & Julie Bergman Sender, PH Haskell Wexler, Ed Wendy Greene Bricmont, M John Frizzell, PD Jeannine Oppewall, AD William Arnold, SD Cindy Carr.

LP Halle Berry (Josie Potenza), Christopher McDonald (Tony Potenza), Clive Owen (Jake Golden), Peter Greene (Cole), Charles Hallahan (Dan Fredericks), Frankie Faison (Ron Lewis), Clea Lewis (Nora Golden).

When she becomes the number one suspect in the murder of her cheating, alcoholic husband, Berry tells her story to a couple of investigating cops. It's a pretty sad tale of sex and violence.

2457. *Richard III* (1995, U.K./U.S., MGM/UA, 104m, c). D Richard Loncraine, P Lisa Katselas Pare & Stephen Bayly, W Ian McKellen & Loncraine (based on the stage production by Richard Eyre, and the play by William Shakespeare), PH Peter Biziou, ED Paul Green, M Trevor Jones, PD Tony Burrough†, AD Choi Ho Man & Richard Bridgland.

LP Ian McKellen (Richard III), Annette Bening (Queen Elizabeth), Maggie Smith (The Duchess of York), Nigel Hawthorne (Clarence), John Wood (King Edward IV), Robert Downey, Jr. (Earl Rivers), Kristin Scott Thomas (Lady Anne), Jim Broadbent (Buckingham), Jim Carter (Lord Hastings), Bill Patterson (Richard Ratcliffe), Adrian Dunbar (Corporal James Tyrell).

McKellen is magnificent portraying one of literature's great villains. He wipes out just about everyone, family or friend, who stands between him and the throne of England. Although the language of Shakespeare is maintained, the setting has been shifted centuries forward, to what appears to be the time between the World Wars, with McKellen and his followers reminiscent of the Hitler gang.

2458. *Richie Rich* (1994, Warner Bros., 94m, c). D Donald Petrie, P John Davis & Joel Silver, W Tom S. Parker & Jim Jennewein (based on a story by Neil Tolkin and the Harvey Comics characters), PH Don Burgess, ED Malcolm Campbell, M Alan Silvestri, PD James Spencer, AD William Matthews, SD John Anderson.

LP Macaulay Culkin (Richie Rich), John Larroquette (Lawrence Van Dough), Edward Herrmann (Richard Rich), Christine Ebersole (Regina Rich), Jonathan Hyde (Herbert Cadbury), Michael McShane (Professor Keenbean), Stephi Lineburg (Gloria).

Culkin's charm is running a bit thin by this film. In it he is the world's richest kid. He must foil villain Larroquette, who has stolen the family fortune from Culkin's father Herrmann. Hollywood appears to be hard pressed to find story lines, reaching even to one of the least amusing comic strips. Too bad all those great screenwriters of the studio system are dead and gone.

2459. *Ricochet* (1991, Warner Bros., 105m, c). D Russell Mulcahy, P Joel Silver & Michael Levy, W Steven E. DeSouza (based on the story by Fred Dekker & Menno Meyjes), PH Peter Levy, ED Peter Honess, M Alan Silvestri, PD Jimmy Jay Hinkle, AD Christian Wagener, SD Richard Goddard, Sam Gross & Eric Orbom.

LP Denzel Washington (Nick Styles), John Lithgow (Earl Talbot Blake), Ice-T (Odessa), Kevin Pollak (Larry), Lindsay Wagner (Priscilla Brimleigh), Victoria Dillard (Alice).

Insane serial killer Lithgow seeks revenge against Washington, the politically ambitious cop who sent him to prison.

2460. *Ride* (1998, Dimension Films, 83m, c). D & W Millicent Shelton, P Warren Hudlin, PH Frank Byers, ED Earl Watson, M Dunn Pearson, Jr., PD Bryan Jones, AD Vera Mills.

LP Malik Yoba (Poppa), Melissa De Sousa (Leta), Sticky Fingaz (Brotha X), Kellie Williams (Tuesday), Julia Garrison (Blacke), Idalis de Leon (Charity), Fredro Starr (Geromino), Downtown Julie Brown (Bleau Kelly).

Just out of film school, aspiring director De Sousa is hired as an assistant to music video director Brown. She is sent to Harlem for the first time in her life to round up some young street singers for an upcoming video. There she encounters inner-city activist Yoba, who introduces her to some of the local talent. She sets off with the musicians for Miami and the video shoot, but they have some predictable troubles along the way.

2461. *The Ride* (1998, World Wide Pictures, 101m, c). D & W Michael O. Sajbel (based on a screenplay by David Bowen), P Laurie Leinonen, PH Michael T. Balog, ED Michael Fallavollita, M James Covell, PD Jo-Ann Chorney.

LP Michael Biehn (Smokey Banks), Brock Pierce (Danny O'Neil), Jennifer Blanc (Linnette Stillwell), Chris Owen (Steve), Jennifer O'Neill (Ellen Stillwell).

It's routine contemporary Western drama about a former rodeo bull-rider and boozer in trouble with some bad guys who want what he owes them or his hide.

2462. *Ride with the Devil* (1999, USA Films–Universal, 138m, c). D Ang Lee, P Ted Hope, Robert Colesberry & James Schamus, W Schamus (based on the novel *Woe to Live On* by Daniel Woodrell), PH Frederick Elmes, M Mychael Danna, ED Tim Squyres, PD Mark Friedberg, AD Steve Arnold, SD Jonathan Scott & Steve Lauberth.

LP Skeet Ulrich (Jack Bull Chiles), Tobey Maguire (Jake Roedel), Jewel (Sue Lee Shelley), Jeffrey Wright (Daniel Holt), Simon Baker (George Clyde), Jonathan Rhys Meyeres (Pitt Mackerson).

Ang Lee's film examines the conflicts between families and neighbors, divided by the Civil War, along the Missouri-Kansas border. He doesn't offer easy identification of the good and bad guys, but shows how both Southern Bushwhackers and Union Jayhawkers believed that their cause was just.

2463. *Riff-Raff* (1993, U.K., Fine Line Features, 94m, c). D Kenneth Loach, P Sally Hibbin, W Bill Jesse, PH Barry Ackroyd, ED Jonathan Morris, M Stewart Copeland, PD Martin Johnson.

LP Robert Carlyle (Stevie), Emer McCourt (Susan), Jimmy Coleman (Shem), George Moss (Mo), Ricky Tomlinson (Larry), David Finch (Kevin).

It's a realistic, documentary-style story of drifter Carlyle who is hired to work at a London construction site. He meets and has a tender love affair with Irish beauty McCourt, but their cultural differences are too deep to prolong the relationship.

2464. *Ring of Fire* (1991, Imperial Ent. Corp., 91m, c). D Richard W. Munchkin, P Charla Driver, Richard Pepin & Joseph Merhi, W Munchkin & Jake Jacobs, ED Geraint Bell & John Weidner, M John Gonzalez.

LP Don "The Dragon" Wilson (Johnny), Steven Vincent Leigh (Terry), Eric Lee (Kwong), Dale Edmond Jacoby (Brad), Maria Ford (Julie).

Rival gangs of white surfers and Asians from nearby Chinatown hang out at Venice Beach in Southern California. They take their feud to underground, no-holds-barred kickboxing matches. When Ford meets Wilson, the trouble between the two groups really gets bad.

2465. *Ringmaster* (1998, Artisan Ent.– MPCA, 90m, c). D Neil Abramson, P Jerry Springer, Gina Rugolo-Judd, Brad Jenkel, Steve Stabler & Gary W. Goldstein, W Jon Bernstein, PH Russell Lyster, ED Suzanne Hines, M Kennard Ramsey, PD Dorian Vernacchio & Deborah Raymond, SD Jodi Ginnever.

LP Jerry Springer (Jerry Farrelly), Jaime Pressley (Angel Zorzak), Molly Hogan (Connie Zorzak), Michael Dudikoff (Rusty), Ashley Holbrook (Willie), Wendy Raquel Robinson (Starletta).

Trash talkshow host Springer portrays a host of a national talkshow known for its extremely bad taste. Boy, what an acting stretch! We doubt that Springer's real-life audience will get down from their couches in sufficient numbers to make this piece of junk a winner. Springer sure likes to test the depths of American bad taste and constantly finds he can go lower.

2466. *Ripe* (1997, Trimark, 93m, c). D & W Mo Ogrodnik, P Suzy Landa & Tom Razzano, PH Wolfgang Held, ED Sarah Durham,

M Anton Sanko, PD Sally Petersen, AD Hannah Moseley.

LP Monica Keena (Violet), Daisy Eagan (Rosie), Gordon Currie (Pete), Ron Brice (Ken), Vincent Laresca (Jimmy), Karen Lynn Gorney (Janet Wyman), Scott Sowers (Colonel Wyman).

After their parents are killed in a car crash, 14-year-old fraternal twins Keena and Eagan hitch a ride aboard a military supply truck driven by Currie. They convince him to let them live with him on the base, passed off as his nieces. Their sexual awakenings lead to tragedy.

2467. *Rising Sun* (1993, 20th Century–Fox, 129m, c). D & W Philip Kaufman (based on the novel by Michael Crichton), P Peter Kaufman, PH Michael Chapman, ED Stephen A. Rotter & William S. Scharf, M Toru Takemitsu, PD Dean Tavoularis, AD Angelo Graham, SD Gary Fettis, Peter Kelly & Robert Goldstein.

LP Sean Connery (John Connor), Wesley Snipes (Web Smith), Harvey Keitel (Tom Graham), Cary-Hiroyuki Tagawa (Eddie Sakamura), Kevin Anderson (Bob Richmond), Mako (Yoshida-San), Ray Wise (Senator John Morton), Tia Carrere (Jingo Asakuma), Tatjana Patitz (Cheryl Lynn Austin).

In this Japanese-bashing film, wise old hand Connery advises his partner, loose cannon Snipes, as the two LAPD liaison officers investigate a murder in the boardroom of a major Japanese corporation. Their investigation embroils them in the U.S.-Japanese trade war. The Japanese are portrayed as sneaky and as lacking in fair play as those responsible for the attack on Pearl Harbor. Nah, they are just businessmen.

2468. *Risk* (1994, Seventh Art, 85m, c). D & W Deirdre Fishel, P Gordon McLennan, PH Peter Pearce, ED Fishel & McLennan, M John Paul Jones, PD Flavio Galuppo.

LP Karen Sillas (Maya), David Ilku (Joe), Molly Price (Nicki), Jack Gwaltney (Karl), Christie MacFadyen (Alice), Barry Snider (Phil).

Struggling artist Sillas encounters Ilku on a bus. They hit it off and he spends the night. Both have some personality problems. His includes criminal tendencies. When he steals a car, she accompanies him to visit his sister in Connecticut, where things don't go well.

2469. *Rites of Passage* (1999, World Intl., 92m, c). D & W Victor Salva, P J. Todd Harris & Pierre David, PH Don E. Fauntleroy, ED Ed Marx, M Bennett Salvay, PD William J. Peretti.

LP Dean Stockwell (Del Farraday), Jason Behr (Campbell Faraday), Robert Keith (D.J. Faraday), Jamiz Wolvett (Red), James Remar (Frank).

Stockwell and his two sons Behr and Keith arrive at the family's mountain cabin to clear the air about their relationships. Two escaped cons, Wolvett and Remar, show up to add to the volatility.

2470. *River of Death* (1990, Cannon, 103m, c). D Steve Carver, P Harry Alan Towers & Avi Lerner, W Edward Simpson & Andrew Deutsch (based on the novel by Alistair MacLean), PH Avi Karpick, ED Ken Bornstein, M Sasha Matson, AD John Rosewarne, SD Dankert Guillaume.

LP Michael Dudikoff (John), Robert Vaughn (Wolfgang Manteuifil), Donald Pleasence (Heinrich Spaatz), Herbert Lom (Col. Diaz), Cynthia Erland (Maria), Sarah Maur Thorp (Anna), L.Q. Jones (Hiller).

While in an Amazon jungle seeking his fortune, Dudikoff encounters Nazi scientists and war criminals. If the film only attempted to be a standard action film it might have been OK for a limited audience, but it has pretensions of being much more — and it is much less.

2471. *River Red* (1998, Miller Ent. Group, 104m, c). D & W Eric Drilling (based on his play), P Drilling, Stephen Schlueter & Avram Ludwig, PH Paul Streicher, M Johnny Hickman, PD Roshelle Berliner, AD Josh Outerbridge.

LP Tom Everett Scott (Dave Holden), David Moscow (Tom Holden), Cara Buono (Rachel), David Lowery (Billy), Denis O'Hare (Daniel Holden), Michael Kelly (Frankie).

Set in rural New England, Scott fatally stabs his alcoholic and abusive father in order to protect younger brother Moscow. The latter takes the rap and is sent to a juvenile detention center. Scott discovers that his father has left nothing but debts, and before long the young man turns to robbery.

2472. *A River Runs Through It* (1992, Columbia, 123m, c). D Robert Redford, P

Patrick Markey & Redford, W Richard Friedenberg† (based on the novella by Norman MacLean), PH Philippe Rousselot*, ED Lynzee Klingman & Robert Estrin, M Mark Isham†, PD Jon Hutman, AD Walter Martishius, SD Gretchen Rau.

LP Craig Sheffer (Norman MacLean), Brad Pitt (Paul MacLean), Tom Skeritt (Reverend MacLean), Brenda Blethyn (Mrs. MacLean), Emily Lloyd (Jesse Burns), Edie McClurg (Mrs. Burns), Stephen Shellen (Neal Burns), Joseph Gordon-Levitt (Young Norman), Vann Gravage (Young Paul), Nicole Burdette (Mabel), Susan Traylor (Rawhide).

This film is almost enough to make city folks yearn to travel to Montana for some fly-fishing. The story deals with the bond between two sons, Sheffer and Pitt, and their minister father Skerritt, for whom fishing is much more than a sport; it is sacred. The older brother, Sheffer, is responsible and a bit dull. The younger, Pitt, is rebellious, reckless and hellbent for doom.

2473.   *The River Wild* (1994, Universal, 108m, c). D Curtis Hanson, P David Foster & Lawrence Turman, W Denis O'Neill, PH Robert Elswit, ED Joe Hutshing & David Brenner, M Jerry Goldsmith, PD Bill Kenney, AD Mark Mansbridge, SD William Hiney & Rick T. Gentz.

LP Meryl Streep (Gail Hartman), Joseph Mazzello (Roarke Hartman), David Strathairn (Tom Hartman), Kevin Bacon (Wade), John C. Reilly (Terry), William Lucking (Frank).

Streep, a white-river rafting expert, is experiencing marital troubles as she and husband Strathairn and son Mazzello travel downstream. Bigger problems appear in the person of escaped criminal Bacon and his companions, who terrorize the family as they attempt to make their escape.

2474.   *The Road to Wellville* (1994, Columbia, 120m, c). D & W Alan Parker (based on the novel by T. Coraghessan Boyle), P Robert F. Colesberry, Parker & Armyan Bernstein, PH Peter Biziou, ED Gerry Hambling, M Rachel Portman, PD Brian Morris, AD John Willett & Richard Earl, SD Claudette Didul.

LP Anthony Hopkins (Dr. John Harvey Kellogg), Bridget Fonda (Eleanor Lightbody), Matthew Broderick (Will Lightbody), John Cusack (Charles Ossining), Dana Carvey (George Kellogg), Michael Lerner (Goodloe Bender), Colm Meaney (Dr. Lionel Badger), John Neville (Endymion Hart-Jones), Lara Flynn Boyle (Ida Muntz), Traci Lind (Nurse Irene Graves).

Hopkins portrays the eccentric scientist who made cereal a breakfast staple. At the time of the film, he's more than a bit wacky as he runs a spa/hospital in Battle Creek, Michigan, where the guests and patients are denied meat and sex (although some get plenty of the latter) and are constantly having their bowels cleansed with enemas of various kinds. The cast is appealing and make the most of the bathroom humor. Besides Hopkins, Broderick scores as a husband who submits himself to the indignities of the place for the sake of his marriage to true believer Fonda. Carvey is quite convincing as Hopkins' adopted idiot son.

2475.   *Roadside Prophets* (1992, Fine Line Features, 96m, c). D & W Abbe Wool (based on an idea of David Swinson), P Peter McCarthy & Swinson, PH Tom Richmond, ED Nancy Richardson, M Pray For Rain, PD J. Rae Fox.

LP John Doe (Joe Mosely), Adam Horovitz (Sam), Timothy Leary (Salvadore), Arlo Guthrie (Harvey), David Carradine (Othello Jones), John Cusack (Caspar), David Anthony Marshall (Dave Coleman).

After Marshall, a fellow worker, is electrocuted playing a video game at a bar, factory worker Doe sets off on his beloved motorcycle from L.A. seeking the "legendary" city of El Dorado in Nevada. He intends to spread Marshall's ashes at the site.

2476.   *Rob Roy* (1995, United Artists, 134m, c). D Michael Caton-Jones, P Peter Broughton & Richard Jackson, W Alan Sharp, PH Karl Walter Lindenlaub, ED Peter Honess, M Carter Burwell, PD Assheton Gorton, Ad John Ralph & Alan Tomkins, SD Ann Mollo.

LP Liam Neeson (Rob Roy), Jessica Lange (Mary), John Hurt (Montrose), Tim Roth† (Cunningham), Eric Stoltz (McDonald), Andrew Keir (Argyll), Brian Cox (Killearn), Brian McCardie (Alasdair), Gilbert Martin (Guthrie).

The British are beasts in this story of peaceloving family man Neeson. He reluctantly becomes the leader of the MacGregor clan when the local representative of the English crown,

Hurt, and his murdering dandy henchman Roth abuse the local Scots and rape Neeson's wife Lange.

2477. Robert A. Heinlein's the Puppet Masters (AKA: *The Puppet Masters*) D Stuart Orme, P Ralph Winter, W David Goyer, Ted Elliot & Terry Rossio (based on the novel by Robert A. Heinlein), PH Clive Tickner, ED William Goldenberg, M Colin Towns, PD Daniel A. Lomino, AD James Hegedus, SD Cloudia Rebar.

LP Donald Sutherland (Andrew Nivens), Eric Thal (Sam), Julie Warner (Mary), Yaphet Kotto (Ressler), Keith David (Holland), Will Patton (Dr. Lawrence Riggs), Richard Belzer (Jarvis), Tom Mason (President Douglas).

In a Cold War parable, a parasite latches onto the spinal cord of victims and bores into the brain, taking control of its host and stripping the poor soul of his free will.

2478. Roberta (1999, Moving Parts Production, 86m, c). D & W Eric Mandelbaum, P David Kashkooli & Mandelbaum, PH Kevin Murphy, ED Sam Adelman, PD Katherine M. Szilagyi, AD Lisa Padovani.

LP Kevin Corrigan (Jonathan), Daisy Rojas (Roberta), Amy Ryan (Judy), Bill Sage (Philip), Brian Tarantina (Donald), Johnny Tran (Sam), Ed Vassallo (Alex).

Young computer consultant Corrigan encounters Rojas, a prostitute whom he believes is a girl he knew when they were both children in Queens. He is intrigued with her, begins to follow her and becomes obsessed with helping her.

2479. Robin Hood: Men in Tights (1993, 20th Century–Fox, 102m, c). D & P Mel Brooks, W Brooks & J. David Shapiro (based on a story by Shapiro & Evan Chandler), PH Michael O'Shea, Ed Stephen E. Rivkin, M Hummie Mann, PD Roy Forge Smith, AD Stephen Myles Berger, SD Ronald R. Reiss, Bruce Robert Hill & Gary A. Lee.

LP Cary Elwes (Robin Hood), Richard Lewis (Prince John), Roger Rees (Sheriff of Rottingham), Amy Yasbeck (Maid Marian), Mark Blankfield (Blinkin), David Chappelle (Ahchoo), Issac Hayes (Asneeze), Patrick Stewart (King Richard).

Mel Brooks takes on Robin Hood and his band of merry men. Robin Hood and audiences are the losers. It's the familiar story, filled with one-liners, sight gags and mugging performers, with most of the spoof missing the target.

2480. Robin Hood: Prince of Thieves (1991, Warner Bros., 143m, c). D Kevin Reynolds, P Richard B. Lewis, Pen Densham & John Watson, W Densham & Watson (based on a story by Densham), PH Doug Milsome, ED Peter Boyle, M Michael Kamen, PD John Graysmark, AD Alan Tomkins, Fred Carter & John Ralph, SD Peter Young.

LP Kevin Costner (Robin of Locksley/Robin Hood), Morgan Freeman (Azeem), Mary Elizabeth Mastrantonio (Maid Marian), Christian Slater (Will Scarlett), Alan Rickman (Sheriff of Nottingham), Geraldine McEwan (Mortianna), Michael McShane (Friar Tuck), Brian Blessed (Lord Locksley), Michael Wincott (Guy of Gisborne), Nick Brimble (Little John), Soo Drouet (Fanny), Daniel Newman (Wulf), Sean Connery (King Richard).

This new Robin Hood story is less a fantasy than the 1939 version which starred Errol Flynn. Costner doesn't have the charm of the dashing Flynn. In this version of the myth, young nobleman Costner returns from the crusades. He becomes a bandit of Sherwood Forest to counter the ambitions of Rickman, the Sheriff of Nottingham, who has his eyes on the British throne while King Richard is away on the Crusades. Rickman is such a lovely villain that he makes the stiff performance of Costner almost bearable.

2481. Robocop 2 (1990, Orion, 118m, c). D Irvin Kershner, P Jon Davison, W Frank Miller & Walon Green (based on a story by Miller, and characters created by Edward Neumeier & Michael Miner), PH Mark Irwin, ED William Anderson, M Leonard Rosenman, PD Peter Jamison, AD Pam Marcotte, SD Colin Irwin.

LP John Glover (Magnavolt Salesman), Mario Machado (Casey Wong), Leeza Gibbons (Jess Perkins), Belinda Bauer (Juliette Foxx), Peter Weller (Robotcop), Daniel O'Herlihy (Old Man), Nancy Allen (Lewis).

It's a violent follow-up to the story of a Detroit police officer who is brutally murdered in the line of duty. His brains and bits of his body are salvaged and merged with machinery to form a law enforcement robot. The special effects and the mayhem will satisfy those for whom a new story line is not necessary.

2482. Robocop 3 (1993, Orion Pictures, 105m, c). D Fred Dekker, P Patrick Crowley, W Frank Miller & Dekker (based on a story by Miller, and characters created by Edward Neumeier & Michael Miner), PH Gary B. Kibbe & Frank M. Holgate, ED Bert Lovitt, M Basil Poledouris, PD Hilda Stark, AD Cate Bangs & Rebecca Marie, SD Robert J. Franco.

LP Robert Burke (Robocop/Alex J. Murphy), Nancy Allen (Anne Lewis), Rip Torn (Merritt W. Morton), John Castle (McDaggett), Jill Hennessy (Dr. Marie Lazarus), CCH Pounder (Bertha), Mako (Kanemitsu).

He's back! Well, actually Peter Weller isn't back. He's been replaced by Robert Burke, but the action, violence and story haven't changed much. There's still a tiny spark of humanity in Robocop, which gets in the way of his duty.

2483. The Rock (1996, Hollywood Pictures–Buena Vista, 136m, c). D Michael Bay, P Don Simpson & Jerry Bruckheimer, W David Weisberg, Mark Rosner & Douglas S. Cook (based on a story by Weisberg & Cook), PH John Schwartzman, ED Richard Francis-Bruce, M Nick Glennie-Smith & Hans Zimmer, PD Michael White, AD Mark Mansbridge & Ed McAvoy, SD Rosemary Brandenburg, Sound Kevin O'Connell†, Greg P. Russell† & Keith A. Wester†.

LP Sean Connery (John Patrick Mason), Nicolas Cage (Stanley Goodspeed), Ed Harris (General Francis X. Hummel), John Spencer (FBI Director Womack), David Morse (Major Tom Baxter), William Forsythe (Ernest Paxton), Michael Biehn (Commander Anderson), Vanessa Marcil (Carla Pestalozzi).

A crack team of marines headed by Harris takes over Alcatraz island and threatens to launch chemical warheads into San Francisco unless the government coughs up $100 million and, more importantly, proper military honors for comrades who had needlessly died in a secret operation. FBI scientist Cage and former Alcatraz con Connery join a special task force to break into the prison to take out the renegades. It's a suspenseful thriller, very violent and quite unbelievable — but it's an enjoyable two-plus hours.

2484. Rock-A-Doodle (1992, Samuel Goldwyn Co., 74m, c). D Don Bluth, P Bluth,

Gary Goldman & John Pomeroy, W David N. Weiss, ED Bernie Caputo, Fiona Trayler & Lisa Dorney, M Robert Folk, PD David Goetz, AD Don Moore, ANIM Tom Higgins, Tamara Anderson, Paul Kelly & Jan Haylor.

LP Voices: Glen Campbell (Chanticleer), Eddie Deezen (Snipes), Sandy Duncan (Peepers), Charles Nelson Reilly (Hunch), Ellen Green (Goldie), Phil Harris (Patou), Christopher Plummer (The Duke), Toby Scott Granger (Edmond).

Combining real-life action with animation, farm boy Granger is sucked into an animated world where he encounters Plummer plotting to extinguish the sun. It's a bit like *The Wizard of Oz*.

2485. Rock 'n' Roll High School Forever (1991, Concorde, 93m, c). D Deborah Brock, P Jed Horovitz & Bruce Stubblefield, W Deborah Brock (based on the characters created by Allan Akush & Joe Dante), PH Jim Mathers, ED Kevin Tent, M Alain Moschulksi & Natasha Schneider, PD Virginia Lee, AD Paul Burge, SD Michele Munroz.

LP Corey Feldman (Jesse Davis), Mary Woronov (Dr. Vadar), Mojo Nixon (The Spirit of Rock 'n' Roll), Evan Richards (Mag Sludge), Michael Cerveris (Eigelbauer), Liane Curtis (Stella).

Forget this lame sequel and rent the video of *Rock 'n' Roll High School* instead. Feldman wants to rock 'n' roll all the time, but the principal of his high school doesn't share his passion. Isn't it a shame how educators think schools are meant to be places where young people learn the many things they don't know, rather than a place where those who believe they already know all they need to know hang out.

2486. The Rocketeer (1991, Walt Disney–Buena Vista, 108m, c). D Joe Johnston, P Lawrence Gordon, Charles Gordon & Lloyd Levin, W Danny Bilson & Paul DeMeo (based on the story by Bilson, DeMeo and William Deer, based on the graphic novel by Dave Stevens), PH Hiro Narita, ED Arthur Schmidt, M James Horner, PD Jim Bissell, AD Christopher Burian-Mohr, SD Linda DeScenna.

LP Bill Campbell (Cliff), Jennifer Connelly (Jenny), Alan Arkin (Peevy), Timothy Dalton (Neville Sinclair), Paul Sorvino (Eddie Valentine), Terry O'Quinn (Howard Hughes), Ed Lauter (Fitch), James Handy (Wooly).

With this film, one very much gets the feeling of watching a comic strip. In it test pilot Campbell accidentally acquires an octane rocket pack that allows him to fly about and frustrate the plans of Nazis in 1930s Hollywood. This film never really gets off the ground.

2487. *Rocketman* (1997, Walt Disney Pictures–Buena Vista, 93m, c). D Stuart Gillard, P Roger Birnbaum, W Craig Mazin & Greg Erb (based on a story by Oren Aviv, Mazin & Erb), PH Steven Poster, ED William D. Gordean, M Michael Tavera, PD Roy Forge Smith, AD Michael Rizzo & Joseph Hodges, SD Brenda Meyers-Ballard.

LP Harland Williams (Fred Z. Randall), Jessica Lundy (Mission Specialist Julie Ford), William Sadler (Cmdr. "Wild Bill" Overbeck), Jeffrey DeMunn (Chief Flight Director Paul Wick), James Pickens, Jr. (Ben Stevens), Beau Bridges (Bud Nesbitt).

Disney launches its version of the first manned mission to mars, but they should have scrubbed it before takeoff. Williams, as the computer genius with a hyperactive imagination, is much too clumsy to ever be seriously considered for a member of the mission team.

2488. *Rocky V* (1990, MGM-UA, 104m, c). D John G. Avildsen, P Irwin Winkler & Robert Chartoff, W Sylvester Stallone, PH Steven Poster & Victor Hammer, ED Avildsen & Michael N. Knue, M Bill Conti, PD William J. Cassidy, AD William Durrell, Jr., SD John Dwyer.

LP Sylvester Stallone (Rocky Balboa), Talia Shire (Adrian Balboa), Burt Young (Paulie), Sage Stallone (Rocky Balboa, Jr.), Burgess Meredith (Mickey), Tommy "Duke" Morrison (Tommy Gunn), Richard Gant (George Washington Duke), Tony Burton (Tony).

Now punch-drunk and broke, Stallone is pitted against a former protégé whom he trained. Sly should have hung up the gloves for good at the end of IV.

2489. *Rogue Trader* (1999, U.K., Pathé–Granada, 101m, c). D & W James Dearden (Based on the book *Rogue Trader: How I Brought Down Barings Bank and Shook the Financial World* by Nicholas Leeson & Edward Whitley), P Dearden, Paul Raphael & Janette Day, PH Jean-Francois Robin, ED Catherine

Creed, M Richard Hartley, PD Alan Macdonald, AD Christina Moore.

LP Ewan McGregor (Nick Leeson), Anna Friel (Lisa Leeson), Yves Beneyton (Pierre Bonnefoy), Betsy Brantley (Brenda Granger), Caroline Langrishe (Ash Lewis), Nigel Lindsay (Ron Baker).

This film is the unsatisfying account of how in 1955 Singapore-based futures trader Nick Leeson managed to bankrupt the United Kingdom's most venerable merchant bank, Baring Brothers.

2490. *Romeo Is Bleeding* (1994, Gramercy Pictures, 108m, c). D Peter Medak, P Paul Webster & Hilary Henkin, W Henkin, PH Dariusz Wolski, ED Walter Murch, M Mark Isham, PD Stuart Wurtzel, AD Wray Steven Graham, SD Beth Rubino.

LP Gary Oldman (Jack Grimaldi), Lena Olin (Mona Demarkov), Annabella Sciorra (Natalie Grimaldi), Juliette Lewis (Sheri), Michael Wincott (Sal), Roy Scheider (Don Falcone), Ron Perlman (U.S. Attorney), Dennis Farina (Nick Gazzara).

Police detective Oldman augments his pay by informing mob boss Scheider of the location and identities of those in the witness protection program. He meets his match in the person of kinky hitwoman Olin, who enjoys violence. To round out the female cast, Sciorra is a nothing as Oldman's wife, and Lewis is his annoying mistress.

2491. *Romper Stomper* (1993, Australia, Academy Ent., 107m, c). D & W Geoffrey Wright, P Ian Pringle & Daniel Scharf, PH Ron Hagen, ED Bill Murphy, M John Clifford White, PD Steve Jones-Evans.

LP Russell Crowe (Hando), Daniel Pollock (Davey), Jacqueline McKenzie (Gabe), Alex Scott (Martin), Leigh Russell (Sonny Jim).

Crowe leads a gang of white supremacist Melbourne skinheads who lash out at Asians in their neighborhood. The film is reminiscent of *A Clockwork Orange*.

2492. *Romy and Michele's High School Reunion* (1997, Touchstone–Buena Vista, 91m, c). D David Mirkin, P Laurence Mark, W Robin Schiff, PH Reynaldo Villalobos, ED David Finfer, M Steve Bartek, PD Mayne Berke, SD Jackie Carr.

LP Mira Sorvino (Romy), Lisa Kudrow

(Michele), Janeane Garofalo (Heather), Alan Cumming (Sandy Frank), Julia Campbell (Christie), Mia Cottet (Cheryl), Kristin Bauer (Kelly), Elaine Hendrix (Lisa), Vincent Ventresca (Billy), Camryn Manheim (Toby), Justin Theroux (Cowboy).

In high school in Tucson, Arizona, Sorvino and Kudrow were not members of the A-group. Sorvino had a crush on Ventresca, the school stud; but she didn't stand a chance with him, mainly because of head cheerleader Christie, the acknowledged queen of the campus. Nerdish Cumming yearned for Kudrow, who couldn't see him, as he couldn't see foul-mouthed rebel Garofalo, who adored him. Ten years later, Sorvino and Kudrow plan to attend their reunion, but come to the realization that they haven't been very successful in the interim — no love interests, no decent jobs. They decide to pretend they are successful. Audiences see two versions of their return to Tucson, one in a dream and one in reality. In neither case are they able to carry off their deception, but as soon as they revert to being themselves — outlandishly dressed, cheap-looking, but appealing — they have their revenge on those who treated them so shabbily. Most members of the audience can in some way identify with the girls, because so few belonged to a high school's in-crowd — or should want to, for that matter.

2493. Ronin (1998, MGM/U.A., 118m, c). D John Frankenheimer, P Frank Mancuso, W J.D. Zeik & Robert Weisz (based on a story by Zeik), PH Robert Fraisse, ED Tony Gibbs, M Elia Cmiral, PD Michael Z. Hanan, AD Gerard Viard, SD Robert Le Corre.

LP Robert De Niro (Sam), Jean Reno (Vincent), Natascha McElhone (Deirdre), Stellan Skarsgard (Gregor), Sean Bean (Spence), Skipp Sudduth (Larry), Michael Lonsdale (Jean-Pierre), Jonathan Pryce (Seamus), Katarina Witt (Natacha Kirilova).

In an old fashion action thriller, an international gang is put together by Irish ringleader McElhone to take part in an ambush in order to retrieve a mysterious briefcase from some criminals. The fast-paced film is filled with exciting shootouts, betrayals and chases, but yet one finds the results uninspiring.

2494. The Rookie (1990, Warner Bros., 121m, c). D Clint Eastwood, P David Valdes,

Howard Kazanjian & Steven Siebert, W Boaz Yakin & Scott Spiegel, PH Jack N. Green, ED Joel Cox, M Lennie Niehaus, PD Judy Cammer, AD Ed Verreaux, SD John Berger & Dawn Snyder.

LP Clint Eastwood (Nick Pulovski), Charlie Sheen (David Ackerman), Raul Julia (Strom), Sonia Braga (Liesel), Tom Skerritt (Eugene Ackerman), Lara-Flynn Boyle (Sarah), Pepe Serna (Lt. Ray Garcia), Marco Rodriquez (Loco).

You know the story — older, tired and disillusioned cop Eastwood teamed with young, ambitious and clueless Sheen join up to crack a stolen car ring.

2495. Rookie of the Year (1993, 20th Century-Fox, 105m, c). D Daniel Stern, P Robert Harper, W Sam Harper, PH Jack N. Green, ED Donn Cambern & Raja Gosnell, M Bill Conti, PD Steven Jordan, AD William Arnold, SD Les Bloom.

LP Thomas Ian Nicholas (Henry Rowengartner), Gary Busey (Chet Steadman), Albert Hall (Martinella), Amy Morton (Mary Rowengartner), Dan Hedaya (Larry "Fish" Fisher), Bruce Altman (Jack Bradfield), Eddie Bracken (Bob Carson), Daniel Stern (Brickman).

Twelve-year-old Nicholas dreams of becoming a major league baseball player. When he falls and breaks his arm it heals in a funny way. He finds himself the proud possessor of a spectacular pitching arm; so spectacular that he is immediately signed by the Chicago Cubs, whom he leads to the World Series. Each year lifetime Cub fans pray it will be the one in which the team finally finds its way to its first World Series since 1945. This is just a fantasy, but hey, maybe this year loyal Cubbie fans will be rewarded.

2496. Roommates (1995, PolyGram Buena Vista, 108m, c). D Peter Yates, P Ted Field, Scott Kroopf & Robert W. Cort, W Max Apple & Stephen Metcalfe (based on the novel by Apple), PH Mike Southon, ED John Tintori, M Elmer Bernstein, PD Dan Bishop, AD Jefferson Sage, SD Dianna Freas.

LP Peter Falk (Rocky), D.B. Sweeney (Michael Holeczak), Julianne Moore (Beth), Ellen Burstyn (Judith), Jan Rubes (Bolek Krupa), Joyce Rheeling (Barbara), Ernie Sabella (Stash), Noah Fleiss (Michael, Age five), Lisa Davis (Betty).

Orphaned at five, Fleiss is taken in by his cantankerous 75-year-old grandfather Falk. They share their lives for some 30 years, with Fleiss growing into Sweeney. The two bicker all the time, but Sweeney comes to realize that his 100-year-old-plus gramps is filled with wisdom which he freely shares.

2497. Rosencrantz and Guildenstern Are Dead (1991, U.K., Cinecom Int., 118m, c). D & W Tom Stoppard (based on his play), P Michael Brandman & Emanuel Azenberg, PH Peter Bizou, ED Nicolas Gaster, M Stanley Meyers, PD Vaughan Edwards, AD Ivo Husnjak.

LP Gary Oldman (Rosencrantz), Tim Roth (Guildenstern), Richard Dreyfuss (Player King), Joanna Roth (Ophelia), Iain Glen (Hamlet), Donald Sumpter (Claudius), Joanna Miles (Gertrude), Ljubo Zecevic (Osric), Ian Richardson (Polonius).

Oldman and Roth are marvelous as two minor characters in Shakespeare's play *Hamlet*. In Stoppard's play and film, the audience only sees and understands that part of the story of *Hamlet* that these two see and understand. As they are rather dim, that isn't a whole lot. We loved the sequence in which the duo flipped a coin, hundreds of times, always coming up the same way. Somehow this doesn't quite seem reasonable to them, but they aren't bright enough to figure out why.

2498. Rosewood (1997, Warner Bros., 141m, c). D John Singleton, P Jon Peters, W Gregory Poirier, PH Johnny E. Jensen, ED Bruce Cannon, M John Williams, PD Paul Sylbert, AD Chris Gorak, SD Mark Garner.

LP Jon Voight (John Wright), Ving Rhames (Mann), Don Cheadle (Sylvester Carrier), Bruce McGill (Duke), Loren Dean (James Taylor), Esther Rolle (Sarah Carrier), Elise Neal (Scrappie), Catherine Kellner (Fannie Taylor), Michael Rooker (Sheriff Walker), Robert Patrick (Fannie's Lover).

This film is based on a true story of the massacre and destruction of a black Florida town in 1923. The spark is set off when promiscuous white woman Kellner is beaten by her lover Patrick and claims she was attacked by a black man. Her husband Dean and his white-trash neighbors use this as an excuse to mount a massive lynching party against the citizens of Rosewood. Voight portrays a local shopkeeper

who helps mysterious black stranger Rhames rescue some of the town's women and children. But before this happens, the mob kill many of Rosewood's men and completely burn down the town's houses. Director and screenwriter Poirier is preaching here, and the use of saintly blacks and stereotyped racist, cruel and cowardly whites lessens both the message and the drama, but perhaps it is understandable.

2499. Rough Magic (1995, U.K., Goldwyn/MEG, 104m, c). D Clare Peploe, P Laurie Parker & Declan Baldwin, W Robert Mundy, William Brookfield & Peploe (based on the novel *Miss Shumway Waves a Wand* by James Hadley Chase), PH John J. Campbell, ED Suzanne Fenn, M Richard Hartley, PD Waldemar Kalinowski, AD Barry M. Kingston & Britte Broch, SD Florence Fellman & Andre Krassoievitch.

LP Bridget Fonda (Myra Shumway), Russell Crowe (Alex Ross), Jim Broadbent (Doc Ansell), D.W. Moffett (Cliff Wyatt), Kenneth Mars (Magician), Paul Rodriguez (Diego).

In 1952, magician's assistant Fonda flees to Mexico after her fiancé Wyatt murders her boss. Reporter Crowe is sent to find her, and when he does, he falls in love with her. The film seems to be trying to blend too many subgenres. Is it film noir? A romantic comedy? A fantasy film?

2500. Round Trip to Heaven (1992, Prism Ent., 97m, c). D Alan Roberts, P Ronnie Hadar, W Shuki Levy & Winston Richards, PH Jim Mathers, ED Greg Sanders, M Noam Kaniel & Levy, PD Robert Benedict, AD & SD Heather Ross.

LP Corey Feldman (Larry), Ray Sharkey (Stoneface), Zach Galligan (Steve), Julie McCullough (Lucille), Rowanne Brewer (April), Lloyd Battista (Mike).

Feldman and his friends "borrow" a Rolls Royce to travel to Feldman's date with super model Brewer, the prize of a contest. They are unaware that the trunk is loaded with stolen money. His felon uncle, Sharkey, who planted the loot there, doesn't care what he has to do to get it back.

2501. Rounders (1998, Miramax, 120m, c). D John Diehl, P Joel Stillman & Ted Demme, W David Levien & Brian Koppelman, PH Jean Yves Escoffier, ED Scott Chestnut, M

Christopher Young, PD Rob Pearson, AD Rick Butler, SD Beth Kushnick.

LP Matt Damon (Mike McDermott), Edward Norton (Worm), John Turturro (Joey Knish), Gretchen Mol (Jo), Famke Janssen (Petra), John Malkovich (Teddy KGB), Martin Landau (Abe Peterovsky).

Law student and reformed cardsharp Damon disappoints his faithful girlfriend Moll when he allows his paroled pal Norton to induce him to return to the world of high-stakes poker to pay off his debts. In a *Hustler*-like story, Damon is the charming youngster being taught about character by the crusty old pro, Malkovich. The film holds few good cards, so it should fold its hand.

2502. *Rover Dangerfield* (1992, Warner Bros., 74m, c). D James George & Robert Seeley, P Thomas L. Wilhite & Willard Carroll, W Rodney Dangerfield (based on the story by Dangerfield & Harold Ramis), ED Tony Mizgalski, M David Newman, PD Fred Cline.

LP Voices: Rodney Dangerfield (Rover), Susan Boyd (Daisy), Dana Hill (Danny), Sal Landi (Rocky), Ned Luke (Raffles), Ronnie Schell (Eddie), Shawn Southwic (Connie).

Dangerfield is the voice of a loveable hound who never gets any respect. If you are a Dangerfield fan you'll find this to be a howl.

2503. *Rubin & Ed* (1992, U.K., IRS Releasing, 82m, c). D & W Trent Harris, P Paul Webster, PH Bryan Duggan, ED Brent Schoenfield, M Fredric Myrow, PD Clark Hunter, SD Michelle Spaddro.

LP Crispin Glover (Rubin Farr), Howard Hesseman (Ed Tuttle), Karen Black (Rula), Michael Greene (Mr. Busta), Brittney Lewis (Poster Girl).

Studying to be a salesman, Hesseman must bring someone — anyone — to the success seminar he's attending. His choice is really weird '60s dude Glover. The latter takes Hesseman along on a search for the perfect graveside for his long-dead cat. The two become stranded in Death Valley and have some fun hallucinations.

2504. *Ruby* (1992, Triumph Releasing, 110m, c). D John MacKenzie, P Sigurjon Sighvatsson & Steve Golin, W Stephen Davis (based on his play *Love Field*), PH Phil Meheux, ED Richard Trevor, M John Scott, PD

David Brisbin, AD Kenneth A. Hardy, SD Lauri Gaffin.

LP Danny Aiello (Jack Ruby), Sherilyn Fenn (Candy Cane), Frank Orsatti (Action Jackson), Jeffrey Nordling (Hank), Willie Garson (Lee Harvey Oswald), Marc Lawrence (Santos Alicante), Arliss Howard (Maxwell), Tobin Bell (David Ferrie).

Aiello portrays the man who shot and killed Lee Harvey Oswald, the supposed assassin of John F. Kennedy in Dallas. If you can't get enough of conspiracy theories, this one's for you.

2505. *Ruby in Paradise* (1993, October Films, 115m, c). D & W Victor Nunez, P Keith Crofford & Sam Gowan, PH Alex Vlacos, ED Nunez, M Charles Engstrom, PD John Iacovelli, AD Burton Rencher.

LP Ashley Judd (Ruby Lee Gissing), Todd Field (Mike McCaslin), Bentley Mitchum (Ricky Chambers), Allison Dean (Rochelle Bridges), Dorothy Lyman (Mildred Chambers).

Judd makes an impressive film debut as a woman who escapes her dead-end life with her husband in Tennessee to travel to Florida, hoping for a better life. There she is pursued by two quite different men, but she seems more interested in exploring her own identity.

2506. *Rude* (1996, Canada, Alliance Intl., 88m, c). D & W Clement Virgo, P Damon D'Oliveira & Karen A. King, PH Barry Stone, ED Susan Maggi, M Aaron Davis, PD Bill Fleming.

LP Maurice Dean Witt (General), Rachael Crawford (Maxine), Clark Johnson (Reece), Richard Chevolleau (Jordan), Sharon M. Lewis (Rude), Melanie Nicholls-King (Jessica).

This film mingles the stories of a woman getting over a failed relationship, a confused athlete and an ex-con who would like to go straight but finds it isn't easy.

2507. *Rudolph the Red-Nosed Reindeer: The Movie* (1998, Legacy, 83m, c). D & P Bill Kowalchuk, W Michael Aschner (based on the song "Rudolph the Red-Nosed Reindeer" by Johnny Marks, and a story by Robert L. May), ED Tom Hok, M Michael Lloyd & Al Kasha.

LP Voices: John Goodman (Santa Claus), Eric Idle (Slyly the Fox), Bob Newhart

(Leonard the Polar Bear), Debbie Reynolds (Mrs. Santa Claus), Richard Simmons (Boone), Whoopi Goldberg (Stormella), Eric Popisil (Young Rudolph), Kathleen Barr (Grown-up Rudolph).

A film based on a 60-year-old classic Christmas song is almost impossible to criticize. It will find its audience.

2508.   Rudy   (1993, TriStar, 112m, c). D David Anspaugh, P Cary Woods & Robert N. Fried, W Angelo Pizzo, PH Oliver Wood, Ed David Rosenbloom, M Jerry Goldsmith, PD Robb Wilson King, SD Martin Price.

LP Sean Astin (Rudy Ruettiger), Jon Favreau (D-Bob), Ned Beatty (Daniel), Greta Lind (Mary), Scott Benjaminson (Frank), Christopher Reed (Pete), Jason Miller (Ara Parseghian), Robert Prosky (Father Cavanaugh).

This film is based on the real-life experiences of an undersized and undertalented youngster who dreams of playing football for the University of Notre Dame. As Astin portrays the young man, if he lacks talent for the job, he certainly has determination. Our hero finally achieves his dream in one brief moment of glory. It's bathos, but it is hard not to cheer the ending.

2509.   Rudyard Kipling's the Second Jungle Book: Mowgli and Baloo   (AKA: *Jungle Book Two*) (1997, Columbia TriStar, 88m, c). D Duncan McLachlan, P Raju Patel, W Bayard Johnson & Matthew Horton (based on the work of Rudyard Kipling), PH Adolfo Bartoli, ED Marcus Manton, M John Scott, PD Errol Kelly, AD Paul Takis & Sunil Wijeratne.

LP Jamie Williams (Mowgli), Bill Campbell (Harrison), Roddy McDowall (King Murphy), David Paul Francis (Chuchundra), Gulshan Grover (Buldeo), Dyrk Ashton (Karait).

This retelling of Kipling's tale about the boy "born of man, raised by animals" is entertaining but can't compete on the same level as the 1967 animated *The Jungle Book.*

2510.   The Rugrats Movie   (1998, Nickelodeon–Paramount, 79m, c). D Norton Virgien & Igor Kovalyov, P Arlene Klasky & Gabor Csupo, W David N. Weiss & J. David Stem, ED John Bryant, M Mark Mothersbaugh, AD Dima Malanitchev.

LP Voices: E.G. Daly (Tommy Pickles),

Christine Cavanaugh (Chuckie Finster), Kath Soucie (Phil and Lil De Ville), Cheryl Case (Angelica Pickles), Tara Charendoff (Dil Pickles), Melanie Chartoff (Didi Pickles), Jack Riley (Stu Pickles).

Like the long-running Nickelodeon TV series, this film details the misadventures of a group of precocious toddlers, ranging in age from one to three. Somehow the kiddies become stranded in a spook forest, where they must show their grit. The fantasy film with its juvenile puns and malapropisms, like the TV show, will appeal to older kids — say from four to six — and their parents who don't find *South Park* entertaining.

2511.   Rule #3   (1994, Seven Star Prods., 93m, c). D & W Mitchell Cox, P Lynda Cox Ferrick & Phillip J. Roth, PH Joseph Grabowski, PD Heather Ross.

LP Mitchell Cox (Travis West), Marcia Swayze (Jennifer), Jerry Rector (Bob Skylar/ Steve), Dena Ridgley (Danielle Reese), Brandon Miller (David Compton), Kathy Lambert (Becky Skylar).

Filled with double and triple crosses, this *Sting*-wannabe stars Cox as a con man trying to pull off two scams at the same time.

2512.   Rumble in the Streets   (1997, Concorde–New Horizons, 75m, c). D & P Bret McCormick, W McCormick, Andy Ruben & Katt Shea Ruben, PH R. Scott Wilson, ED Haley Richter, M Ray Machado, AD Barbara Connon.

LP David Courtemarche (Sy), Kimberly Rowe (Tori), Patrick DeFazio (Lumley), Tom Young (Bagley), Sean Cordobes (Allen).

This thriller about homeless kids being stalked by a psycho cop is of extremely low quality.

2513.   Rumpelstiltskin   (1996, Trimark–Vidmark, 91m, c). D Mark Jones, P Joe Ruby, Ken Spears & Michael Prescott, W Jones & Ruby (based on the fairy tale by the Brothers Grimm), PH Doug Milsome, ED Christopher Holmes, M Charles Bernstein, PD Ivo Cristante, AD Ken Larson, SD Tim Colohan.

LP Kim Johnson Ulrich (Shelly Stewart), Tommy Blaze (Max Bergman), Allyce Beasley (Hildy), Max Grodenchik (Rumpelstiltskin), Vera Lockwood (Matilda), Jay Pickett (Russell Stewart).

The story book character Rumpelstiltskin, played by Grodenchik, is loose in modern day L.A. and is still steamed about losing out on the princess baby. The devilish dwarf has plans of getting Ulrich's baby from her.

2514. Run (1991, Buena Vista, 89m, c). D Geoff Burrowes, P Raymond Wagner, W Dennis Shryack & Michael Blodgett, PH Bruce Surtees & Brenton Spencer, ED Jack Hofstra & Stephen E. Rivkin, M Phil Marshall, PD John Willett, AD Willie Heslup, SD Elizabeth Wilcox.

LP Patrick Dempsey (Charlie Farrow), Kelly Preston (Karen Landers), Ken Pogue (Matt Halloran), Alan C. Peterson (Denny Halloran), James Kidnie (Sammy), Sean McCann (Marv), Michael Macrae (O'Rourke).

Wrongly accused of the murder of the son of a mob boss, law student Dempsey must contend with both the family of the dead man and corrupt police.

2515. The Run of the Country (1995, U.S./U.K., Castle Rock–Columbia, 109m, c). D Peter Yates, P Yates & Ruth Boswell, W Shane Connaughton (based on his book), PH Mike Southon, ED Paul Hodgson, M Cynthia Millar, AD Dave Wilson, SD Mark Geraghty.

LP Albert Finney (Father), Matt Keeslar (Danny), Victoria Smurfit (Annagh), Anthony Brophy (Prunty), David Kelly (Father Gaynor), Dearbhla Molloy (Mother), Carole Nimmons (Mrs. Prunty).

It's the grand story of the coming of age of Keeslar in a small Irish town and his relationship with his bullying pa Finney. Things really begin to fall apart with the death of his mum.

2516. Runaway Bride (1999, Paramount, 116m, c). D Garry Marshall, P Ted Field, Tom Rosenberg, Scott Kroopf & Robert Cort, W Josann McGibbon & Sara Parriott, PH Stuart Dryburgh, ED Bruce Green, M James Newton Howard, PD Mark Friedberg, AD Wray Steven Graham, SD Thomas Minton & Charles McCarry, SD Stephanie Carroll.

LP Julia Roberts (Maggie Carpenter), Richard Gere (Ike Graham), Joan Cusack (Peggy Flemming), Hector Elizondo (Fisher), Rita Wilson (Ellie), Paul Dooley (Walter), Christopher Meloni (Coach Bob), Donal Logue (Priest Bob).

Those hoping for some more romantic fun from the trio that brought us the 1990 hit *Pretty Woman* will not be disappointed. Director Marshall shepherds Roberts and Gere through their paces in a film with a bit of the charm of *It Happened One Night*. Gere is a columnist fired for his article on runaway bride Roberts, who can't seem to get past the "I do" part of the wedding ceremony. She's left three different bridegrooms wondering what happened. Gere sees a way to regroup with a freelance magazine piece that tells the real story of Roberts as she heads for a fourth trip to the altar. It will surprise no one that the prolonged proximity of Roberts and Gere will move from hostility to more tender feelings. Roberts is lovely, and the chemistry between her and the usually wooden Gere feels just about right.

2517. The Runestone (1992, Hyperion Ent., 107m, c). D & W Willard Carroll (based on the novella by Mark E. Rogers), P Thomas L. Wilhite & Harry E. Gould, Jr., PH Misha Suslov, ED Lynne Southerland, M David Newman, PD Jon Gary Steele, AD Stella Wang, SD Nancy Arnold.

LP Alexander Godunov (The Clockmaker), Peter Riegert (Fanducol), Joan Severance (Marla Stewart), William Hickey (Lars Hagstron), Tim Ryan (Sam Stewart), Mitchell Laurance (Martin Almquist), Lawrence Tierney (Chief Richardson).

An ancient Norse relic is discovered in a Pennsylvania mine. It has a profound effect on archaeologist Laurence, who keeps the discovery to himself. His meddling with the stone unleashes a wolf-beast that terrorizes New York City.

2518. Running Free (1994, Trimark Pictures, 90m, c). D Steve Kroschel, P Cynthia Gamble & Kroschel, W Kroschel & Mary Beth Smith (based on a story by Kroschel), Ph Kroschel & Mark Dionne, ED Gamble, M Bob Jenkins & Dave Reynolds, SD Dionne & Ron Brodigan.

LP Jesse Montgomery Smith (Garrett), Jamie Lee Misfeldt (Carrie), Michael Pena (Burk), Michael Hood (Carl Meekin), Neil O'Leary (Trapper).

Smith, an unhappy youngster, travels with Misfeldt, his naturalist mother, to the Alaskan wilderness where he befriends — or, perhaps more correctly, is befriended by — a wolverine cub.

2519. Rush (1991, MGM-Pathé, 120m, c). D Lili Fini Zanuck, P Richard D. Zanuck, W Pete Dexter (based on the novel by Kim Wozencraft), Ph Kenneth MacMillan, Ed Mark Warner, M Eric Clapton, PD Paul Sylbert, SD Phillip Leonard.

LP Jason Patric (Jim Raynor), Jennifer Jason Leigh (Kristen Cates), Sam Elliott (Larry Dodd), Max Perlich (Walker), Gregg Allman (Will Gaines), Tony Frank (Chief Donald Nettle).

Rookie cop Leigh goes undercover with experienced partner Patric to nab a major drug dealer, Allman. She falls in love with Patric, but the two find themselves being drawn further and further into the drug world.

2520. Rush Hour (1998, New Line Cinema, 98m, c). D Brett Ratner, P Roger Brinbaum & Arthur Sarkissian, W Jim Kouf & Ross LaManna (based on a story by LaManna), PH Adam Greenberg, ED Mark Helfrich, M Lalo Schifrin, PD Robb Wilson King, AD Thomas Fichter.

LP Jackie Chan (Det. Inspector Lee), Chris Tucker (Det. James Carter), Tom Wilkinson (Thomas Griffin), Elizabeth Pena (Tania Johnson), Philip Baker Hall (Capt. Diel), Tzi Ma (Consul Han).

Chan is an entertaining and amusing action star. In this one, the Asian superstar joins forces with equally funny Tucker as an odd couple of cops who seek the kidnapped daughter of a Chinese consul.

2521. Rushmore (1998, Touchstone–Buena Vista, 89m, c). D Wes Anderson, P Barry Mendel & Paul Schiff, W Anderson & Owen Wilson, PH Robert Yeoman, ED David Moritz, M Mark Mothersbaugh, PD David Wasco, AD Andrew Laws, SD Alexandra Reynolds.

LP Jason Schwartzman (Max Fischer), Bill Murray (Herman Blume), Olivia Williams (Rosemary Cross), Seymour Cassel (Bert Fischer), Brian Cox (Dr. Guggenheim), Mason Gamble (Dirk Calloway).

Schwartzman is a 15-year-old misfit at Rushmore, a private school for bratty and offensive boys. While not very brilliant in the classroom, he is a marvel at extracurricular activities, many of which he forms just for himself. His passion, however, is for Williams, a lovely English widow and teacher at Rushmore. He finds himself in competition for her attention with Murray, the father of two of the most obnoxious boys at the school. Murray is wonderful in a restrained performance, allowing amazing Schwartzman to carry the show. The youngster is the son of Talia Shire and thus a member of the talented Coppola family.

2522. The Russia House (1990, Pathé/MGM-UA, 123m, c). D Dred Schepisi, P Schepisi & Paul Maslansky, W Tom Stoppard (based on the novel by John le Carre), PH Ian Baker, ED Peter Honess, M Jerry Goldsmith, PD Richard MacDonald, SD Simon Wakefield.

LP Sean Connery (Barley Blair), Michelle Pfeiffer (Katya), Roy Scheider (Russell), James Fox (Ned), John Mahoney (Brady), Klaus Maria Brandauer (Dante), Ken Russell (Walter), J.T. Walsh (Quinn).

Russian scientist Brandauer has written an exposé of Soviet claims of military supremacy and attempts to pass it along to British editor Connery by way of his ex-lover Pfeiffer. It's not as suspenseful or thrilling as was the novel.

2523. Sabrina (1995, Paramount, 127m, c). D Sydney Pollack, P Scott Rudin & Pollack, W Barbara Benedek & David Rayfiel (based on the 1954 screenplay by Billy Wilder, Samuel Taylor & Ernest Lehman, and the play *Sabrina Fair* by Taylor), PH Giuseppe Rotunno, ED Frederic Steinkamp, M John Williams†, PD Brian Morris, AD John Kasarda, SD George DeTitta, Jr.

LP Harrison Ford (Linus Larrabee), Julia Ormond (Sabrina Fairchild), Greg Kinnear (David Larrabee), Nancy Marchand (Maude Larrabee), John Wood (Fairchild), Richard Crenna (Patrick Tyson), Angie Dickinson (Ingrid Tyson), Lauren Holly (Elizabeth Tyson).

This remake of the 1954 film of the same name disappoints for the same reason as did the original. Harrison Ford is too old for Julia Ormond, and there is no electricity between them. This was the case with Humphrey Bogart and Audrey Hepburn. Ormond is the daughter of the chauffeur of a wealthy family, consisting of Nancy Marchand and her two sons, Ford and Greg Kinnear. Ormond believes she has always loved playboy Kinnear, but when she comes back from school in France, looking all grown up and glamorous, Ford has to step in and romance her to keep her from snagging Kinnear, who is being used as marriage bait in a business merger.

2524. Sacred Cargo (1995, Arrow Releasing, 97m, c). D Alexander Buravsky, P Peter Yuval & Oleg Kapanets, W Buravsky & Alexander Cary, PH Misha Suslov, ED Annamaria Szanto, M Vladimir Horunzhy, AD Ludvik Siroky.

LP Chris Penn (Vince Kanevsky), J.T. Walsh (Father Stanislav), Martin Sheen (Father Andrew Kanevsky), Anna Karin (Sasha Romanov), Louisa Mosendz (Marina), Alexander Yatsko (Oleg).

Brothers Penn and Sheen are in Russia to help a group of Franciscan priests, led by Walsh, smuggle out relics, valued at $200 million, to the U.S.

2525. Safe (1995, Sony Pictures Classics, 123m, c). D & W Todd Haynes, P Christine Vachon & Lauren Zalaznick, PH Alex Nepomniaschy, ED James Lyons, M Ed Tomney, PD David Bomba, AD Anthony Stabley, SD Mary E. Gullickson.

LP Julianne Moore (Carol White), Peter Friedman (Peter), Xander Berkeley (Greg White), Susan Norman (Linda), Kate McGregory Stewart (Claire), Mary Carver (Nell), Steven Gilborn (Dr. Hubbard).

When California housewife Moore finds her body slowly ravaged by allergic reactions to everyday chemicals, fragrances and fumes, the medical profession can find nothing physically wrong with her. She sets off for New Mexico, and a New Age spa and resort, for a cure.

2526. Safe Men (1998, Andell Ent., 94m, c). D & W John Hamburg, P Andrew Hauptman, Ellen Bronfman, Jeffrey Clifford & Jonathan Cohen, PH Michael Barrett, ED Suzanne Pillsbury, M Theodore Shapiro, PD Anthony Gasparro, AD Ondine Karady, SD Cat Thomas.

LP Sam Rockwell (Sam), Steve Zahn (Eddie), Paul Giamatti (Veal Chop), Michael Schmidt (Bernie Jr.), Michael Lerner (Big Fat Bernie Gayle), Mark Ruffalo (Frank), Christina Kirk (Hannah), Harvey Fierstein (Leo).

In this comedy, set in Providence, Rhode Islan,; Rockwell and Zahn are two singers of little talent. They are mistakenly believed by the city's underworld, in the persons of Lerner and his number one rival, Fierstein, to be the best safecrackers around. They are left little choice but to live up to their billing.

2527. Safe Passage (1995, New Line, 98m, c). D Robert Allan Ackerman, P Gale Anne Hurd, W Deena Goldstone (based on the novel by Ellyn Bache), PH Ralf Bode, ED Rick Shaine, M Mark Isham, PD Dan Bishop, AD Jefferson Sage, SD Dianna Freas.

LP Susan Sarandon (Mag Singer), Sam Shepard (Patrick Singer), Robert Sean Leonard (Alfred Singer), Sean Astin (Izzy Singer), Marcia Gay Harden (Cynthia), Nick Stahl (Simon Singer), Jason London (Gideon Singer), Matt Keeslar (Percival Singer), Philip Arthur Ross (Merle Singer), Steven Robert Ross (Darren Singer), Philip Bosco (Mort).

Sarandon probably deserved an Oscar nomination for her performance as the mother of seven sons. She rallies the family as they wait to learn if one of the boys, a Marine, survived a barracks bombing in the Middle East. The story and its presentation aren't memorable, but Sarandon's performance is once again worthy of praise.

2528. The Saint (1997, Paramount, 114m, c). D Phillip Noyce, P David Brown, Robert Evans, William J. MacDonald & Mace Neufeld, W Jonathan Hensleigh & Wesley Strick (based on a story by Hensleigh, and the character created by Leslie Charteris), PH Phil Meheux, ED Terry Rawlings, M Graeme Revell, PD Joseph Nemec III, AD Alan Cassie & Leslie W. Tomkins, SD Peter Young.

LP Val Kilmer (Simon Templar), Elisabeth Shue (Dr. Emma Russell), Rade Serbedzija (Ivan Tretiak), Valery Nikolaev (Ilya Tretiak), Henry Goodman (Dr. Lev Botvin), Alun Armstrong (Chief Inspector Teal), Michael Byrne (Vereshagin), Evgeny Lazarev (President Karpov).

Books, movies and TV series featuring Leslie Charteris' creation, Simon Templar — (better known as "The Saint"), have been very entertaining — until now. This story has Kilmer agreeing to steal a fusion formula for a Russian general. He falls in love with Shue, the scientist who came up with the equations. The movie is dumb from the beginning and gets dumber as it moves along. Kilmer has none of the charm of previous actors, such as Louis Hayward, George Sanders and Roger Moore, who have appeared as the roguish adventurer.

2529. The Saint of Fort Washington (1993, Warner Bros., 108m, c). D Tim Hunter, P David V. Picker & Nessa Hyams, W Lyle Kessler, PH Frederick Elmes, ED Howard Smith, M James Newton Howard, PD Stuart Wurtzel, AD Steve Saklad, SD Debra Schutt.

LP Danny Glover (Jerry), Matt Dillon (Matthew), Rick Aviles (Rosario), Nina Siesmaszko (Tamsen), Ving Rhames (Little Leroy), Joe Seneca (Spits), Harry Ellington (Arthur).

At a prison-like shelter called Fort Washington, newly homeless and schizophrenic photographer Dillon is befriended by homeless Vietnam veteran Glover. Both actors give strong performances in this disturbing examination of a growing social problem — the homeless.

2530. Sally Marshall Is Not an Alien (1999, Australia/Canada, UIP Pictures–Cinar, 97m, c). D Mario Andreacchio, P Terry J. Charatsis & Micheline Charest, W Robert Geoffrion & Amanda McKay (based on the novel by McKay), PH Tony Clark, ED Jean-Marie Drog, M Christopher Dedrick, PD Rita Zanchetta.

LP Helen Neville (Pip Lawson), Natalie Vansier (Sally Marshall), Thea Gumbert (Rhonnie Bronston), Glenn McMillan (Ben Handelman), Danielle de Grossi (Melinda), Mignon Kent (Kylie).

This film, which teaches the timeless message of the importance of welcoming strangers into one's community, is aimed at prepubescent females. When Vansier moves into Neville's neighborhood, her behavior and accent is decidedly different from that of the other kids in the Adelaide suburb. Bullying Gumbert, who runs the 12-year-olds, asserts that Vansier and her family are aliens from outer space. Neville intends to prove her wrong.

2531. Sam and Sarah (1991, Full Circle Films, 90m, c). D John Strysik, P Wanda Rohm & Robert Rothman, W Rothman & Strysik, PH & ED Michael K. Goi, M Craig Snider & Elliott Delman, PD Thomas B. Mitchell.

LP Robert Rothman (Sam), Kathleen Sykora (Sarah), Michael Bacarella (Astro), Carolyn Kodes (Terry Quinn), Charles Gerace (T.J.).

Rothman is a severely traumatized homeless Vietnam veteran who likes to burst into Hamlet's soliloquy "To be or not to be." He comes to the rescue of shy Sykora when she is attacked by a gang. He is badly beaten. Because he fought so bravely for her, Sykora takes him to her cubbyhole in a deserted building. The story is an effective examination of a human relationship.

2532. Samantha (1993, Academy Ent., 101m, c). D Stephen LaRocque, P Donald P. Borchers, W LaRocque & John Golden, PH Lisa Churgin, M Joel McNeely, PD Dorian Vernacchio & Deborah Raymond.

LP Martha Plimpton (Samantha Stigg), Dermot Mulroney (Henry), Hector Elizondo (Walter), Mary Kay Place (Marilyn), Ione Skye (Elaine), Marvin Silbersher (Milos).

In this desperate comedy, 21-year-old Plimpton discovers her parents aren't her parents. She was left on their doorstep when a baby. She's determined to learn her true identity.

2533. Sand Trap (1998, PM Ent., 100m, c). D Harris Done, P Erik Done, Harris Done & Jerry Rapp, W Harris Done & Rapp, PH Roy Unger & Mark W. Gray, ED Michael Mayhew, M Bennet Salvay, PD Naython Vane, AD Daniel Harrison Bornstein.

LP David John James (Nelson Yeagher), Brad Keopenick (Jack), Elizabeth Morehead (Margo Yeagher), Bob Thompson (Sheriff), Kirk Woller (Carl).

A masked invader nearly kills James. The next day he, his wife Morehead and his lawyer Keopenick drive out into the desert to look at an investment property. Keopenick pushes James over a cliff. It seems the attorney and Morehead had been lovers for a long time and wish to kill James to collect his insurance. The killers bring sheriff Thompson to the scene of the "accident," but James' body isn't where they left it. He survived but is now lost, wandering in the desert. Keopenick and Morehead must find and kill James before the sheriff gets to him.

2534. The Sandlot (1993, 20th Century–Fox, 109m, c). D David Mickey Evans, P Dale De La Torre & William S. Gilmore, W Evans & Robert Gunter, PH Anthony B. Richmond & Michael Ferris, ED Michael A. Stevenson, M David Newman, PD Chester Kaczenski, AD Marc Dabe, SD Judi Sandin.

LP Tom Guiry (Scotty Smalls), Mike Vitar (Benjamin Franklin Rodriguez), Patrick Renna

(Hamilton "Ham" Porter), Chauncey Leopardi (Michael "Squints" Palledorous), Marty York (Alan "Yeah-Yeah" McClennan), Karen Allen (Mom), James Earl Jones (Mr. Mertle).

A group of 1960s fifth graders enjoy the summer playing baseball. Everything is wonderful until the prized possession of the father of one of the boys, a ball autographed by Babe Ruth, gets knocked into a junkyard guarded by the legendary "The Beast," a ferocious dog who loves to take bites out of kids.

2535. Sandman (1992, Third Coast, 93m, c). D & W Eric Woster (based on a story by Woster & Frank Rhodes), P Rhodes, PH Rick Lamb, ED Raymond Ferris & James Boyd, M Don Peake, AD Michael Gaglio.

LP Eric Woster (Nick Hanson), Frank Rhodes (Alex Stockwell), Ramon Sheen (Jake), Dedee Pfeiffer (Lana Hawkins), Tiffany Ballenger (Amy), Gailard Sartain (Dave), Robert Wuhl (Victor Giles), Stuart Whitman (Isaac Tensor).

Director, writer and star Woster died just as the film neared completion. It is the story of a house that has a door leading to its past.

2536. The Santa Clause (1994, Walt Disney–Buena Vista, 95m, c). D John Pasquin, P Brian Reilly, Jeffrey Silver & Robert Newmyer, W Steve Rudnick & Leo Benvenuti, PH Walt Lloyd, ED Larry Bock, M Michael Convertino, PD Carol Spier, AD James McAteer, SD Elinor Galbraith.

LP Tim Allen (Scott Calvin), Judge Reinhold (Neal), Wendy Crewson (Laura), Eric Lloyd (Charlie), David Krumholtz (Bernard), Larry Brandenburg (Detective Nunzio), Mary Gross (Mrs. Daniels), Paige Tamada (Elf—Judy), Peter Boyle (Mr. Whittle).

One Christmas Eve, divorced dad Allen accidentally kills Santa Claus. He slips on the Santa suit and is able to perform the seasonal duties of the merry old elf; but then he discovers he's to have the job permanently. When his young son, Krumholtz, brags about his dad's new position in life, mom Crewson and her new husband Reinhold hurriedly call in the psychiatrists and the police. Allen grows into the job, but the film isn't likely to become a Christmas classic.

2537. Santa Claws (1996, New Age Pictures, 83m, c). D & W John A. Russo, P Bob

Michelucci & Jack Smith, PH Bill Hinzman, ED Tara Alexander, M Paul McCullough, PD Michelucci.

LP Debbie Rochon (Raven Quinn), Grant Kramer (Wayne), John Mowod (Eric Quinn), Karl Hardman (Bruce Brunswick), Marilyn Eastman (Mrs. Quinn).

In a terribly ordinary horror film, demented Kramer dresses as Santa Claus and kills people.

2538. Santa with Muscles (1996, Legacy Releasing, 98m, c). D John Murlowski, P Brian Shuster, W Jonathan Bond, Fred Mata & Dorrie Krum Raymond, PH Michael Gfelner, ED William D. Marrinson & Stephen Myers, M James Covell, PD Chuck Conner, Ad Chase Harlan.

LP Hulk Hogan (Blake Thorn), Ed Begley, Jr. (Ebner Frost), Don Stack (Lenny), Robin Curtis (Leslie Morgan), Kevin West (Blight).

When selfish health-food tycoon Hogan is knocked unconscious, he loses his memory. Hustler Stack convinces Hogan that he is the real Santa Claus. For reasons of which he's not quite sure, Hogan foils evil Begley and his henchmen, who are after money meant for an orphanage.

2539. Sarafina! (1992, U.S./U.K./France/So. Africa, Miramax–Buena Vista, 96m, c). D Darrell James Roodt, P Anant Singh & David M. Thompson, W William Nicholson & Mbongeni Ngema (based on his play), PH Mark Vicente, ED Peter Hollywood, Sarah Thomas & David Heitner, M Stanley Myers, PD David Barkham.

LP Leleti Khumalo (Sarafina), Whoopi Goldberg (Mary Masembuko), Miriam Makeba (Angelina), John Kani (School Principal), Dumisani Dlamini (Crocodile), Mbongeni Ngema (Sabela), Sipho Kunene (Guitar), Tertius Meintjes (Lt. Bloem), Robert Whitehead (Interrogator).

Goldberg stars in this powerful musical play about the struggle for freedom of South Africa's black school children. Khumalo is excellent as a teenage girl who dreams of portraying Nelson Mandela in a school play. Instead, she finds herself in trouble with the white oppressors. Call this an interesting but disappointing attempt to deal with the South Africa of not so many years ago.

2540. *Saturn* (1999, Sibling Ent.–Plantain Films, 94m, c). D & W Rob Schmidt, P Palmer West, PH Matthew Libatique, ED Gabriel Wrye, M Ryeland Allison, PD James Chinlund, AD Leanne Tosca.

LP Scott Caan (Drew), Leo Burmester (Dad), Mia Kirshner (Sara), Anthony Ruivivar (Arturo).

Trying to find time to pursue his dream of becoming an engineer while caring for his Alzheimer's-afflicted father Burmester, Caan is lured into a drug deal by old buddy Ruivivar and Kirshner, a wild girl for whom he procures drugs.

2541. *Savage Beach* (1990, RCA–Columbia, 95m, c). D, P & W Andy Sidaris, PH Howard Wexler, ED Michael Haight, M Gary Stockdale, PD Jimmy Hadder.

LP Hope Marie Carlton (Taryn), Dona Speir (Donna Hamilton), John Aprea (Capt. John Andreas), Bruce Pehhall (Bruce Christian), Rodrigo Obegron (Rodrigo Martinez), Al Leone (Fu).

Ex-*Playboy* Playmates Carlton and Speir are Drug Enforcement agents who uncover a plot to retrieve gold lost during WWII.

2542. *Saving Private Ryan†* (1998, DreamWorks Pictures–Paramount, 169m, c). D Steven Spielberg*, P Spielberg, Ian Bryce, Mark Gordon & Gary Livingston, W Robert Rodat†, PH Janusz Kaminski*, ED Michael Kahn*, M John Williams†, PD Tom Sanders†, AD Daniel T. Dorrance, Ricky Eyres, Tom Brown, Chris Seagers & Alan Tompkins, SD Lisa Dean Kavanaugh†.

LP Tom Hanks† (Capt. John Miller), Edward Burns (Pvt. Reiben), Tom Sizemore (Sgt. Horvath), Jeremy Davies (Cpl. Upham), Vin Diesel (Pvt. Caparzo), Adam Goldberg (Pvt. Mellish), Barry Pepper (Pvt. Jackson), Giovanni Ribisi (T/4 Medic Wade), Matt Damon (Pvt. James Ryan), Ted Danson (Captain Hamill).

This World War II drama opens with the most horrific reminder of how terrible war is. As troops hit the beach on D-Day, they are slaughtered by German fire. Whether one reaches the land or not is a matter of pure chance. Those that do must walk over the bodies of their fallen comrades and through water turned red with blood. Among those surviving this onslaught is Hanks and his squad of men. They are given the assignment of locating a certain private who parachuted into France. The reason for the special attention is that three of his brothers have recently been killed in combat, and government policy dictates that as the last surviving son he should be sent home to his family. Hanks and his men eventually find the soldier, played by Damon, and give him the opportunity to live to a ripe old age, but one by one it costs each of their lives. The absurdity of war has never been more clearly shown in a movie.

2543. *Savior* (1998, U.K., First Independent, 103m, c). D Peter Antonijevic, P Oliver Stone & Janet Yang, W Robert Orr, PH Ian Wilson, ED Ian Crafford & Gabriellea Cristiani, M David Robbins, PD Vladislav Lasic.

LP Dennis Quaid (Joshua Rose/Guy), Natassja Kinski (Maria), Stellan Skarsgard (Peter), Natasa Ninkovic (Vera), Sergej Trifunovic (Goran), Nebojsa Glogovac (Vera's Brother).

Mercenary soldier Quaid exorcises his personal demons by rescuing a baby during the war in Bosnia.

2544. *Sawbones* (1996, Concorde‡ New Horizons, 86m, c). D Catherine Cyran, P Mike Elliott, W Sam Montgomery, PH Christopher Baffa, ED Norman Buckley, M Don Preston, PD Michael Pearce, AD Danielle Berman, SD Dan Sherrill & Kelly Eddleman.

LP Adam Baldwin (Burt Miller), Nina Siemaszko (Jennie Sloan), Barbara Carrera (Rita Baldwin), Don Stroud (Capt. Mowbray), Don Harvey (Willy Knapp), Nicholas Sadler (Brad Fraser).

Siemaszko seeks to solve medical-related serial killings. It's about what you would expect from films of this nature.

2545. *Scanner Cop* (1994, Republic Pictures, 94m, c). D & P Pierre David, W George Saunders & John Bryant Hedberg (based on a story by David, based on characters created by David Cronenberg), PH Jacques Haitkin, ED Julian Semilian, M Louis Febre, PD Deborah Raymond & Dorian Vernacchio.

LP Daniel Quinn (Sam Staziak), Darlanne Fluegel (Dr. Joan Alden), Richard Lynch (Dr. Carl Glock), Hilary Shepard (Zena), Richard Grove (Sgt. Peter Harrigan), Mark Rolston (Lt. Harry Brown).

In this third sequel to the 1982 sci-fi classic,

rookie cop Quinn unleashes his scanner powers after several members of the police force are killed. The clues to the murders suggest someone with scanner abilities. This grisly comic book material is not for the squeamish.

2546. *Scanners II: The New Order* (1991, Canada, Allegro Films, 105m, c). D Christian Duguay, P Rene Malo, W B.J. Nelson (based on characters created by David Cronenberg), PH Rodney Gibbons, ED Yves Langlois, M Marty Simon, PD Richard Tasse.

LP David Hewlett (David Kellum), Deborah Raffin (Julie Vale), Yvon Ponton (Commander John Forrester), Isabelle Mejias (Alice Leonardo), Tom Butler (Dr. Morse), Raoul Trujillo (Drak).

In this first sequel to David Cronenberg's 1981 *Scanners*, there is a new breed of scanners roaming the streets, causing people to hemorrhage and explode. If splatter-shots are your cup of tea, this film won't disappoint.

2547. *Scanners III: The Takeover* (1992, U.S./Canada, Malofilm Group, 101m, c). D Christian Duguay, P Rene Malo, W B.J. Nelson, Malo, David Preston & Julie Richard (based on the characters created by David Cronenberg), PH Hughes DeHaeck, ED Yves Langlois, M Marty Simon, PD Michael Joy, AD Lynn Trout, SD Andre Chamberland.

LP Liliana Komorowska (Helena Monet), Valerie Valois (Joyce Stone), Steve Parrish (Alexa Monet), Collin Fox (Dr. Elton Monet), Daniel Pilon (Michael, the Lawyer), Michel Perron (Charlie), Harry Hill (Dr. Baumann), Peter Wright (Mark Dragon).

In this dull second sequel to *Scanners*, Parrish returns from self-imposed exile when his sister Komorowska is turned into a mind-bending megalomaniac by an experimental drug.

2548. *Scanners IV: The Showdown* (1995, Republic Pictures, 95m, c). D Steve Barnett, P Pierre David, W Mark Sevi (based on characters created by David Cronenberg), PH Thomas Jewett, ED Patrick Rand, M Richard Bowers, PD Terri Schaetzle.

LP Daniel Quinn (Sam Staziak), Patrick Kilpatrick (Karl Volkin), Khrystyne Haje (Carrie Goodart), Stephen Mendel (Jim Mullins), Robert Forster (Capt. Jack Bitters).

It's a scan or be scanned fight to the death between police detective Quinn and a serial killer.

2549. *The Scarlet Letter* (1995, Hollywood Pictures, 118m, c). D Roland Joffe, P Joffe & Andrew G. Vajna, W Douglas Day Stewart (based on the novel by Nathaniel Hawthorne), PH Alex Thomson, ED Thom Noble, M John Barry, PD Roy Walker, AD Tony Wollard, SD Rosalind Shingleton.

LP Demi Moore (Hester Prynne), Gary Oldman (Arthur Dimmesdale), Robert Duvall (Roger Prynne), Lisa Jolliff-Andoh (Mituba), Edward Hardwicke (John Bellingham), Robert Prosky (Horace Stonehall), Roy Dotrice (Thomas Cheever), Joan Plowright (Harriet Hibbons).

The filmmakers didn't think that Hawthorne's story had an ending that would play with today's young audience. But a happy ending to the tragic story is just the final insult to a classic that has been filmed with greater success in 1926, 1934 and 1973. Moore struts her stuff for the new minister Oldman in Puritanical New England. She's married to Duvall, but he's such a dour creature that a girl surely must have the right to a fling in the hay. She finds herself with child, deserted by Oldman, persecuted by her husband and the community, and winning herself a scarlet letter A, standing for adulteress, which she is compelled to wear on her ample chest. It's almost laughable, but the joke is on those who waste time viewing the film.

2550. *Scarred City* (1998, Nu Image Prod., 96m, c). D & W Ken Sanzel, P Avi Lerner & Elie Samaha, PH Michael Slovis, ED Troy T. Takaki, M Anthony Marinelli, PD Ann Stuhler, AD Roswell Hamrick, SD Jennifer Alex.

LP Stephen Baldwin (John Trace), Chazz Palminteri (Lt. Laine Devon), Tia Carrere (Candy), Gary Dourdan (Sgt. Dan Creedy), Michael Rispoli (Sam Bandusky).

When beat cop Baldwin gives chase to a crack dealer, he shoots him under the mistaken impression that the deceased was going for a gun. When the plainclothes officers arrive, they conveniently supply the dead man with a gun. Then they blackmail Baldwin into joining a covert unit that deals in vigilante action against undesirables like the dead drug dealer.

2551. *Scenes from a Mall* (1991, Touchstone–Buena Vista, 87m, c). D & P Paul Mazursky, W Mazursky & Roger L. Simon, PH Fred Murphy, ED Stuart Pappe, M Marc Shaiman, PD Pato Guzman, AD Steven J. Jordan, SD Les Bloom.

LP Bette Midler (Deborah), Woody Allen (Nick), Bill Irwin (Mime), Daren Firestone (Sam), Rebecca Nickels (Jennifer), Paul Mazursky (Dr. Hans Clava).

What a waste of comical talent. Midler and Allen are wife and husband. She's a high-powered psychologist (sure, sure) and he's a major promoter (sure, sure). They employ the Beverly Mall as a setting for their whining, fighting and boring behavior. Who wrote this crap? Oh, yeah. Well, at least it wasn't Allen.

2552. *Scent of a Woman†* (1992, Universal, 157m, c). D Mark Brest†, P Brest†, W Bo Goldman† (based on the characters created by Ruggero Maccari & Dino Risi from the novel *Il Buio e il Miele* by Giovanni Arpino), PH Donald E. Thorin, ED William Steinkamp, Michael Tronick & Harvey Rosenstock, M Thomas Newman, PD Angelo Graham, AD W. Steven Graham, SD George DeTitta, Jr.

LP Al Pacino* (Lt. Col. Frank Slade), Chris O'Donnell (Charlie Simms), James Rebhorn (Mr. Trask), Gabrielle Anwar (Donna), Philip S. Hoffman (George Willis, Jr.), Richard Venture (W.R. Slade), Bradley Whitford (Randy), Rochelle Oliver (Gretchen), Margaret Eginton (Gail).

Pacino finally wins an Oscar, portraying a pain-in-the-ass blind ex-military man. Prep school student O'Donnell is hired to watch Pacino over the Thanksgiving holiday. O'Donnell will have to face a major crisis in his life back at school after the holiday. Pacino wants a last hurrah before he ends it all. This includes further alienating his brother Venture and his family, drinking a large amount of John Daniels (he knows Jack Daniels so well he calls him John), insulting O'Donnell at every turn, having a final fling in New York City, driving an expensive automobile through deserted New York streets at high speeds, and tangoing with pretty Anwar at a posh hotel. O'Donnell prevents Pacino from wasting himself, and Pacino shows up at O'Donnell's school to save the day. It's as meaty a role as Pacino has had since *The Godfather*. It's even better than that of Michael Corleone because Pacino is able to go way over the top, chew up the scenery and still win audience applause. But he is a major pain in the ass.

2553. *Schindler's List** (1993, Universal, 185m, b&w/c). D Steven Spielberg*, P Spielberg*, Branko Lustig* & Gerald R. Molen*, W Steven Zallian* (based on the novel *Schindler's Ark* by Thomas Keneally), PH Janusz Kaminski*, ED Michael Kahn*, M John Williams*, PD Allan Starski*, AD Marciej Walczak, Ewa Tarnowska, Ryszard Melliwa & Grzegorz Piatkowski, SD Ewa Braun*.

LP Liam Neeson† (Oskar Schindler), Ben Kingsley (Itzhak Stern), Ralph Fiennes† (Amon Goeth), Caroline Goodall (Emilie Schindler), Jonathan Sagalle (Poldek Pfefferberg), Embeth Davidtz (Helen Hirsch), Andrzej Seweryn (Julian Scherner), Norbert Weisser (Albert Hujar).

Even the jealous types in Hollywood cannot refuse Steven Spielberg recognition for this masterful drama. A German industrialist, played beautifully by Neeson, saves the lives of hundreds of Jews through his collaboration with the Nazis and his deft manipulation of them. It's a powerful film, which will help us remember that which should never be forgotten or viewed as ancient history — the Holocaust and the bravery of a few who made some difference. In his first important role, Fiennes is perfectly beastly as the embodiment of the horrible Nazi exterminators. Ben Kingsley brings quiet dignity to his role as a Jewish accountant who assists Neeson in his role as savior. We trust young viewers won't miss this one because it's filmed in black and white.

2554. *Schizopolis* (1997, Northern Arts Ent., 96m, c). D, W & PH Steven Soderbergh, P John Hardy, ED Sarah Flack, M Cliff Martinez, Joseph Wilkins, Mark Mangini & Harry Garfield.

LP Steven Soderbergh (Fletcher Munson/ Dr. Jeffrey Korchek), Betsy Brantley (Mrs. Munson/Attractive Woman #2), David Jensen (Elmo Oxygen), Eddie Jemison (Nameless Numberheadman), Scott Allen (Right Hand Man), Mike Malone (T. Azimuth Schwitters).

Director and writer Soderbergh appears as a speechwriter for Malone, the leader of a Scientology-like cult. The film examines the unknowable nature of the modern world. It's an unusual film which some will consider a masterpiece and others a massive mistake.

2555. *School Ties* (1992, Paramount, 107m, c). D Robert Mandel, P Sherry Lansing & Stanley R. Jaffe, W Dick Wolf & Darryl Ponicsan (based on a story by Wolf), PH Freddie Francis, ED Jerry Greenberg & Jacqueline Cambas, M Maurice Jarre, AD Steven Wolff, SD Rosemary Brandenburg.

LP Brendan Fraser (David Greene), Matt Damon (Charlie Dillon), Chris O'Donnell (Chris Reece), Randall Batinkoff (Rip Van Kelt), Andrew Lowery (McGivern), Cole Hauser (Jack Connors), Ben Affleck (Chesty Smith), Anthony Rapp (McGoo), Amy Locane (Sally Wheeler), Peter Donat (Headmaster Dr. Bartram).

In the 1950s, lower-middle class Kid Fraser is a top notch athlete recruited by exclusive St. Matthews School to upgrade their football program. Trouble is he's Jewish and his classmates are anti–Semites who have learned their hatred from their parents all too well.

2556. *Scissors* (1991, DDM Film Corporation, 107m, c). D & W Frank DeFelitta (based on the story by Joyce Selznick), P Hal W. Polaire, Mel Pearl & Don Levin, PH Anthony B. Richmond, ED John Schreyer, M Alfi Kabiljo, PD Craig Stearns, AD Randy Moore, SD Kara Lindstrom.

LP Sharon Stone (Angie), Steven Railsback (Alex Morgan/Cole Morgan), Ronny Cox (Dr. Carter), Michelle Phillips (Ann), Vicki Frederick (Nancy).

Stone either is going insane or someone is trying to drive her insane. What's your guess? Here's a little clue: Scissors are the weapons used in the film's mayhem. This film is not of *Gaslight* quality. Pity!

2557. *Scorned* (1994, Prism Pictures, 100m, c). D Andrew Stevens, P Damian Lee, W Barry Avrich, PH Christian Sebaldt, ED David Mitchell, M Ronald J. Weiss, PD John Gillespie, AD Karen Liebrand, SD Kathleen Coates.

LP Andrew Stevens (Alex Weston), Shannon Tweed (Patricia Langley), Kim Morgan Greene (Marina Weston), Dan McVicar (Truman Langley), Michael D. Arenz (Robey Weston), Perla Walters (Belle).

When a businessman kills himself after a deal goes wrong, his wife Tweed seeks revenge against those responsible for the tragedy. She decides the guilty party is family man Stevens.

She insinuates herself into his life, poses as tutor for his son, and goes about the process of tearing his family apart.

2558. *Scorned 2* (1997, A-Pix Ent., 97m, c). D Rodney McDonald, P Andrew Stevens, W Sean McGinly, PH Gary Graver, ED Les Kaye, M Patrick Seymour, PD Steve Ralph.

LP Tane McClure (Amanda Foley), Andrew Stevens (Alex Weston), Myles O'Brien (Mark Foley), Wendy Schumacher (Cynthia Meadows), John McCook (Dr. Robert Greenfield).

McClure takes over from Shannon Tweed as the vengeance-seeking killer. Having lost her memory, McClure is happily married to her former therapist O'Brien. She is haunted by nightmares. Put under hypnosis by McCook, she recalls her past after the suicide of her first husband. When she discovers her present husband en flagrante with student Schumacher, McClure is ready to return to her nasty ways.

2559. *The Scout* (1994, 20th Century-Fox, 101m, c). D Michael Ritchie, P Albert S. Ruddy & Andre E. Morgan, W Andrew Bergman, Albert Brooks, Monica Johnson & Lloyd Fonvielle (based on material by Roger Angell), PH Laszlo Kovacs, ED Don Zimmerman & Pembroke Herring, M Bill Conti, PD Stephen Hendrickson, AD Okowita, SD Meredith Boswell.

LP Albert Brooks (Al Percolo), Brendan Fraser (Steve Nebraska), Dianne Wiest (Doctor Aaron), Anne Twomey (Jennifer), Lane Smith (Ron Wilson), Michael Rapaport (Tommy Lacy), Barry Shabaka Henley (McDermott).

Brooks is a scout for the New York Yankees. Fraser is the greatest pitcher since Cy Young. Brooks brings him back to the States from Mexico, but the kid is a mental case. Enter shrink Wiest. This will not compete for the title of best baseball picture.

2560. *Scream* (1996, Dimension Films, 100m, c). D Wes Craven, P Cary Woods & Cathy Konrad, W Kevin Williamson, PH Mark Irwin, ED Patrick Lussier, M Marco Beltrami, PD Bruce Alan Miller, AD David Lubin, SD Michele Poulik.

LP Drew Barrymore (Casey), Courteney Cox (Gale Weathers), David Arquette (Dewey), Roger Jackson (Phone Voice), Kevin Patrick Wells (Casey's Father), Carla Hatley (Casey's

Mother), Neve Campbell (Sidney), Skeet Ulrich (Billy).

Is this a spoof of slasher films or a horror-comedy story? Who cares? Some stalker dressed as Death butchers teens, "just to see what your insides look like." The kids in the film, a group of promising young performers (with the exception of Drew Barrymore, that is), demonstrate what not to do when a slasher is roaming the area.

2561.   Scream 2 (1997, Dimension Films, 120m, c). D Wes Craven, P Cathy Konrad & Marianne Maddalena, W Kevin Williamson, PH Peter Deming, ED Patrick Lussier, M Marco Beltrami & Danny Elfman, PD Bob Ziembicki, AD Ted Berner, SD Bob Keninger.

LP David Arquette (Dewey Riley), Neve Campbell (Sidney Prescott), Courteney Cox (Gale Weathers), Sarah Michelle Gellar (Cici), Jamie Kennedy (Randy Meeks), Laurie Metcalf (Debbie Salt), Elise Neal (Hallie), Jerry O'Connell (Derek), Jada Pinkett (Maureen), Liev Schreiber (Cotton Weary).

When tabloid TV reporter Cox interviews the survivors of the original massacre to promote a film based on the murders, someone gets the bright idea of donning a similar fright mask, leading to a new bloodbath.

2562.   Screamers (1996, Canada, Allegro Films, 107m, c). D Christian Duguay, P Tom Berry & Franco Battista, W Dan O'Bannon & Miguel Tejada-Flores (based on the short story "Second Variety" by Philip K. Dick), PH Rodney Gibbons, ED Yves Michael Devine, SD David Jaquest.

LP Peter Weller (Hendricksson), Roy Dupuis (Becker), Jennifer Rubin (Jessica), Andy Lauer (Ace), Charles Powell (Ross), Ron White (Elbarak).

The year is 2078. Weller commands a force attempting to survive after a war between corporate interests and workers on a mining planet.

2563.   The Sea Change (1998, U.K., Winchester Films, 88m, c). D Michael Bray, P Billy Hurman & Gary Smith, W Bray & Hurman, PH Joseph M. Civit, ED Bryan Oates, M Mark Thomas, PD Michael Grant.

LP Maryam D'Abo (Alison), Sean Chapman (Rupert), Ray Winstone (Charles), Andree Bernard (Sarah).

Workaholic merchant banker Chapman has little time for his girlfriend D'Abo, who, unbeknownst to him, is pregnant. This trifling film shows the humbling of this arrogant yuppie.

2564.   Search and Destroy (1995, October Films, 90m, c). D David Salle, P Ruth Charny, Dan Lupovitz & Ellie Cohn, W Michael Almereyda (based on the play by Howard Korder), PH Bobby Bukowski & Michael Spiller, ED Michelle Gorchow, M Elmer Bernstein, PD Robin Standefer, AD Stephen Alesch, SD Amy Tapper.

LP Griffin Dunne (Martin Mirkheim), Illena Douglas (Marie Davenport), Dennis Hopper (Dr. Waxling), Christopher Walken (Kim Ulander), John Turturro (Ron), Rosanna Arquette (Lauren Mirkheim), Ethan Hawke (Roger), Martin Scorsese (The Accountant).

A Florida film producer tries to buy off the IRS by making a film based on the lunatic writings of new-age Guru Hopper. The movie is financed by drug dealer Walken and his underworld buddies. We're not sure what message, if any, is intended here.

2565.   The Search for One-Eye Jimmy (1996, Orenda Films, 82m, c). D & W Sam Henry Kass, P Robert Nickson & Lisa Bruce, PH Chuck Levey & Lodge Kerrigan, ED Mark Juergens, M Bill Bloom, PD Ray Recht, AD & SD Mario R. Ventenilla.

LP Nick Turturro (Junior), Steve Buscemi (Ed Hoyt), Michael Baldalucco (Joe Head), Ray "Boom Boom" Mancini (Lefty), Holt McCallany (Les), Anne Meara (Holly Hoyt), John Turturro (Disco Bean), Samuel L. Jackson (Colonel Ron), Jennifer Beals (Ellen).

This film is set in a Brooklyn neighborhood overflowing with colorful characters. It's a funny film with a great ending, but no noticeable story or plot. Take it for what it is (or isn't), for its outrageousness is worth a look.

2566.   Searching for Bobby Fisher (1993, Paramount, 110m, c). D & W Steve Zaillian (based on the book by Fred Waitzkin), P Scott Rudin & William Horberg, PH Conrad L. Hall†, ED Wayne Wahrman, M James Horner, PD David Gropman, AD Gregory Keen.

LP Max Pomeranc (Josh Waitzkin), Joe Mantegna (Fred Waitzkin), Joan Allen (Bonnie Waitzkin), Ben Kingsley (Bruce Pandolfini),

Laurence Fishburne (Vinnie), Michael Nirenberg (Jonathan Poe), David Paymer (Kalev).

Seven-year-old Pomeranc is a chess whiz. His parents Mantegna and Allen want him to have some sort of normal life. Fishburne is a speed-playing chess hustler, and Kingsley is a demanding chess teacher who believes Pomeranc can be another Bobby Fischer.

2567. Second Best (1994, U.K., Warner Bros., 104m, c). D Chris Menges, P Sarah Radclyffe, W David Cook (based on his novel), PH Ashley Rowe, ED George Akers, M Simon Boswell, PD Michael Howells, AD Roger Thomas, SD Sam Riley.

LP William Hurt (Graham), Chris Cleary Miles (James), John Hurt (Uncle Turpin), Jane Horrocks (Debbie), Prunella Scales (Margery), Keith Allen (John), Alan Cumming (Bernard), Jodhi May (Alice).

Emotionally repressed and lonely Welsh postmaster William Hurt decides to adopt a son. His choice, Miles, is a 10-year-old fighting his own demons. The anticipated difficulties the two pose for each other give way to a mutual chance for happiness.

2568. Secret Agent Club (1997, Cabin Fever Ent., 90m, c). D John Murlowski, P David Silberg & James R. Rosenthal, W Rory Johnston, PH S. Douglas Smith, ED Leslie Rosenthal, M Jan Hammer, PD James Scanlon, AD Donovan Miller, SD Bill Reinert.

LP Terry "Hulk" Hogan (Ray Chase), Mathew McCurley (Jeremy Chase), Lesley-Anne Down (Eve), Maurice Woods (Sly), Danny McCue (Bart).

Hogan is a toy store owner by day and a secret agent by night. His son McCurley thinks his dad's a real klutz. He learns better when Hogan must take on international arms merchant Down and her gang of bad guys.

2569. Secret Friends (1992, Briar Patch Film Corp., 97m, c). D & W Dennis Potter (based on his novel Ticket to Ride), P Rosemarie Whitman, PH Sue Gibson, ED Clare Douglas, M Nicholas Russell-Pavier, PD Gary Williamson.

LP Alan Bates (John), Gina Bellman (Helen), Frances Barber (Angela), Tony Doyle (Martin), Joanna David (Kate), Colin Jeavons (Vicar), Rowena Cooper (Vicar's Wife).

Deeply disturbed, guilt-ridden and jealous artist Bates is obsessed with killing his young sexy wife Bellman. It's a muddled story at best.

2570. The Secret Garden (1993, American Zoetrope–Warner Bros., 101m, c). D Agnieszka Holland, P Fred Fuchs, Fred Roos & Tom Luddy, W Caroline Thompson (based on the novel by Frances Hodgson Burnett), PH Roger Deakins, ED Isabelle Lorente, PD Stuart Craig, AD Peter Russell, SD Stephanie McMillan.

LP Kate Maberly (Mary Lennox), Heydon Prowse (Colin Craven), Andrew Knott (Dickon), Maggie Smith (Mrs. Medlock), Laura Crossley (Martha), John Lynch (Lord Craven).

After the death of her parents, Maberly is sent to live with her uncle in England. She has grown up in India. She is selfish, lonely and unhappy until she discovers two secrets on her uncle's estate: a crippled cousin she didn't know she had and a neglected garden she is determined to bring back to life.

2571. The Secret Kingdom (1997, U.S./Romania, Full Moon, 82m, c). D David Schmoeller, P Vlad Paunescu & Christopher Landry, W Benjamin Carr, PH Gabriel Kosuth, ED Barry Taylor, M Carl Dante, PD Radu Corciova, AD Viorel Ghenea, SD Ica Varna.

LP Billy O'Sullivan [billed as Billy O'] Mark), Tricia Dickinson (Callie), Gerald S. O'Laughlin (Chartwell), Jamieson K. Price (Regent), Andrew Ducote (Zak).

New Orleans teen O'Sullivan discovers a tiny kingdom hidden beneath the kitchen sink. He and his sister Dickinson are drawn into a battle between rebels of the kingdom and tyrant Price.

2572. The Secret of Roan Inish (1995, First Look Prods., 102m, c). D & W John Sayles (based on the book The Secret of Ron Mor Skerry by Rosalie K. Fry), P Maggie Renzi & Sarah Green, PH Haskell Wexler, ED Sayles, M Mason Daring, PD Adrian Smith, AD Henry Harris, SD Tom Conroy.

LP Jeni Courtney (Fiona Coneelly), Mick Lally (Hugh Coneelly), Eileen Colgan (Tess Coneelly), Richard Sheridan (Eamon), John Lynch (Tadhg), Susan Lynch ("Selkie" Woman), Gerard Rooney (Liam).

This fantasy film is the story of 10-year-old Courtney sent to live with her grandparents in post WWI County Donegal. There she is enthralled by her grandfather's tales of the family's ancestral home on the island of Roan Inish and the loss of her baby brother, who was carried out to sea. When Courtney visits the island, she becomes convinced her sibling is alive and being cared for by a Selkie — a beautiful seawoman.

2573. *The Secret Rapture* (1994, U.K. Castle Hill, 96m, c). D Howard Davies, P Simon Relph, W David Hare (based on his play), PH Ian Wilson, ED George Akers, M Richard Hartley, PD Barbara Gosnold, AD Fiona McNeil.

LP Juliet Stevenson (Isobel Coleridge), Joanne Whalley-Kilmer (Katherine Coleridge), Penelope Wilton (Marion French), Neil Pearson (Patrick Steadman), Alan Howard (Tom French).

Sisters Stevenson and Wilton clash when brought together after their father's death. Stevenson grieves for her father, but scheming Wilton looks to take advantage of the situation to take over the family business. Both must deal with their young stepmother Whalley-Kilmer.

2574. *Secrets & Lies†* (1996, U.K., October Films, 142m, c). D Mike Leigh†, P Simon Channing-Williams†, W Mike Leigh†, PH Dick Pope, ED John Gregory, M Andrew Dickson, PD Alison Chitty & Georgina Lowe.

LP Timothy Spall (Maurice), Phyllis Logan (Monica), Brenda Blethyn† (Cynthia), Claire Rushbrook (Roxanne), Marianne Jean-Baptiste† (Hortense), Elizabeth Berrington (Jane), Michele Austin (Dionne).

After the death of her black stepparents, Jean-Baptiste decides to seek out her birth parents. She discovers her mother is white factory worker Blethyn, who lives with her daughter Rushbrook and photographer brother Spall. The film is a bit too long, but the performances in this story of family and identity are top-notch.

2575. *Secrets in the Attic* (1994, Vidmark, 89m, c). D Dianne Haak, P Bernard Wilets, Michael Wright & Haak, PH Tom Evans, M Firstcom.

LP Amanda Roese (Amy), Lindsay Jackson (Aunt Claire), Rebekah Baker (LouAnn), Lissa Reynolds (Mother), Bob Chaffee (Handyman), J.J. Reardon (Boyfriend).

While playing in her grandparents' attic, 12-year-old Roese comes across dolls representing her grandparents, which seem to identify the murderer in a long-ago killing.

2576. *Selena* (1997, Warner Bros., 127m, c). D & W Gregory Nava, P Moctesuma Esparza & Robert Katz, PH Edward Lachman, ED Nancy Richardson, M Dave Grusin, PD Cary White.

LP Jennifer Lopez (Selena), Edward James Olmos (Abraham Quintanilla, Jr.), Jon Seda (Chris Perez), Constance Marie (Marcela Quintanilla), Jacob Vargas (Abie Quintanilla), Lupe Ontiveros (Yolanda Saldivar).

This film purports to tell the story of the rise and fall of the *Tejano* singer whose life was tragically cut short at age 23 by Ontiveros, the embezzling manager of the singer's fashion boutique and president of the Selena fan club. Performances are mostly below par, although Lopez is able to carry off the sassy look of Selena.

2577. *Sense and Sensibility†* (1995, Mirage–Columbia, 135m, c). D Ang Lee, P Lindsay Doran†, W Emma Thompson* (based on the novel by Jane Austen), PH Michael Coulter†, ED Tim Squyres, M Patrick Doyle†, PD Luciana Arrighi, AD Philip Eton, SD Ian Whittaker.

LP Emma Thompson† (Elinor Dashwood), Kate Winslet† (Marianne Dashwood), Alan Rickman (Colonel Brandon), Hugh Grant (Edward Ferrars), Greg Wise (John Willoughby), Emilie Francois (Margaret Dashwood), Elizabeth Spriggs (Mrs. Jennings), Imogen Stubbs (Lucy Steele), Gemma Jones (Mrs. Dashwood), Harriet Walter (Fanny Dashwood), James Fleet (John Dashwood).

This film, scripted by Emma Thompson from Austen's first novel, is filled with marvelous characters portrayed by marvelous character actors. When her father dies, Thompson, her mother Jones and her two younger sisters, Winslet and Francois, are prevented from getting much of an inheritance because of the machinations of her greedy stepbrother Fleet and his wife Walter. Forced to move into a modest cottage on a country estate, Thompson and Winslet's romances do not run smoothly. Thompson's hopes for marriage lie with Grant, but he has other commitments. Winslet is pursued by both dashing Wise and middle-aged Rickman. Wise turns out to be a rotter and Rickman wins the day. There is also a happy ending for Thompson.

2578. Senseless (1998, Dimension Films, 93m, c). D Penelope Spheeris, P David Hoberman, W Greg Erb & Craig Mazin, PH Daryn Okada, ED Ross Albert, M Yello, PD Peter Jamison, AD Ann Harris, SD Linda Spheeris.

LP Marlon Wayans (Darryl Witherspoon), David Spade (Scott Thorpe), Matthew Lillard (Tim LaFlour), Brad Dourif (Dr. Wheedon), Tamara Taylor (Janice), Rip Torn (Randall Tyson), Richard McGonagle (Robert Bellweather).

Trying to win the annual analyst competition, man-of-many-jobs and college student Wayans faces several obstacles. One is blue-blooded twit Spade, his greatest competition. Also holding him back is the fact that he doesn't belong to a good fraternity or excel in sports. He tries to rectify the last two defects and is only modestly successful, but his determined attempts are funny.

2579. Separate Lives (1995, Trimark Pictures, 102m, c). D David Madden, P Diane Nabatoff & Guy Riedel, W Steven Pressfield, PH Kees Van Ostrum, ED Janice Hampton, M William Olvis, PD Bernt Capra, AD Walter Cahall, SD Karen L. McCaughey.

LP James Belushi (Tom Beckwith), Linda Hamilton (Lauren Porter/Lena), Vera Miles (Dr. Ruth Goldin), Elisabeth Moss (Ronnie Beckwith), Drew Snyder (Robert Porter), Mark Lindsay Chapman (Keno Sykes).

Hamilton has two personalities: a psychology professor and a sexy alter ego who may have killed someone. The professor seeks help from her student and ex-cop Belushi to sort things out.

2580. Sgt. Bilko (1996, Universal, 94m, c). D Jonathan Lynn, P Brian Grazer, W Andy Breckman (based on the TV series created by Nat Hiken), PH Peter Sova, ED Tony Lombardo, M Alan Silvestri, PD Lawrence G. Paull, AD Bruce Crone, SD Rick Simpson.

LP Steve Martin (Master Sgt. Ernest G. Bilko), Dan Aykroyd (Colonel Hall), Phil Hartman (Major Thorn), Glenne Headly (Rita Robbins), Daryl Mitchell (Wally Holbrook),

Max Casella (Dino Paparelli), Eric Edwards (Duane Doberman), Dan Ferro (Tony Morales).

Those who were around when Phil Silvers and his gang of GI misfits and con men entertained TV audiences with predictable, repetitive, but funny situations could have told moviemakers that there was no percentage in making a big-screen version. Martin and Aykroyd do not make us forget Silvers and Paul Ford, and they also don't make us yearn to rush to watch the reruns of the show either.

2581. Serial Mom (1994, Savoy Pictures, 93m, c). D & W John Waters, P John Fiedler & Mark Tarlov, PH Bobby Stevens, ED Janice Hampton & Erica Huggins, M Basil Poledouris, PD Vincent Peranio, AD David Bomba, SD Susan Kessel.

LP Kathleen Turner (Mom—Beverly Sutphin), Sam Waterston (Dad—Eugene Sutphin), Ricki Lake (Misty Sutphin), Matthew Lillard (Chip Sutphin), Scott Wesley (Detective Pike), Walt MacPherson (Detective Gracey), Justin Whalin (Scotty).

It's such a shame that Turner, who delighted audiences with her steamy roles and great looks, seems to have run out of steam and is limited to lousy roles, as in this film. When it comes to her kids, she'll help them get whatever they want, even if it requires her to commit mayhem and murder.

2582. Set It Off (1996, New Line, 126m, c). D F. Gary Gray, P Dale Pollock & Oren Koules, W Kate Lanier & Takashi Bufford (based on a story by Bufford), PH Marc Reshovsky, ED John Carter, M Christopher Young, PD Robb Wilson King, SD Lance Lombardo.

LP Jada Pinkett (Stony), Queen Latifah (Cleo), Vivica A. Fox (Frankie), Kimberly Elise (Tisean), John C. McGinley (Detective Strode), Blair Underwood (Keith).

Four African-American women turn to robbing banks and raising hell to supplement their earnings as poorly-paid janitors.

2583. Seven (1995, New Line, 107m, c). D David Fincher, P Arnold Kopelson & Phyllis Carlyle, W Andrew Kevin Walker, PH Darius Khondji, ED Richard Francis-Bruce, M Howard Shore, PD Arthur Max, AD Gary Wissner, SD Clay A. Griffith.

LP Brad Pitt (Detective David Mills), Morgan Freeman (Lt. William Somerset), Gwyneth Paltrow (Tracy), Richard Roundtree (Talbot), John C. McGinley (California), Kevin Spacey (John Doe).

Police detectives Pitt and Freeman are charged with the task of tracking down a serial killer whose modus operandi is inspired by the seven deadly sins: gluttony, greed, sloth, pride, envy and wrath. The murders are horribly grotesque, and the investigation is chilling.

2584. Seven Years in Tibet (1997, Columbia TriStar, 131m, c). D Jean-Jacques Annaud, P Annaud, Iain Smith & John H. Williams, W Becky Johnston (based on the book by Heinrich Harrer), PH Robert Fraisse, ED Noelle Boisson, M John Williams, PD Al Hoang, AD Pierre Queffelean & George Richardson, SD Jim Erickson.

LP Brad Pitt (Heinrich Harrer), David Thewlis (Peter Aufschnaiter), B.D. Wong (Ngawang Jigme), Mako (Kungo Tsarong), Danny Denzongpa (Regent), Jetsun Pema (Great Mother), Victor Wong (Chinese "Amban"), Jamyang Wang Chuck (Dalai Lama, Aged 14), Tenzin Wang Chuck (Dalai Lama, Aged 18).

Pitt, an Austrian mountaineer and former member of the Nazi party, is part of an Aryan team climbing a Himalayan peak in 1939. In Tibet he forges an unlikely friendship with the young Dalai Lama. The friendship provides Pitt with a spiritual cleansing. The film also features the Communist China decision to annex Tibet and supplant its spiritual and political leader. Pitt isn't a perfect match for the part, though he does try.

2585. The Seventh Coin (1993, Hemdale Releasing, 92m, c). D Dror Soref, P Lee Nelson & Omri Maron, W Soref & Michael Lewis, PH Avi Karpick, ED Jerry Shepard, M Misha Segal, PD Yoram Shier, SD Eyal Shalem.

LP Peter O'Toole (Emil Saber), Navin Chowdhry (Salim Zouabi), Alexandra Powers (Ronnie Segal), John Rhys-Davies (Captain Galil), Ally Walker (Lisa), Whitman Mayo (Julius Washington).

Coin collector O'Toole is obsessed with getting his hands on seven coins bearing the image of legendary King Herod. O'Toole is quite mad, believing himself the reincarnation

of Herod. He's located six of the coins, but the seventh has fallen into the hands of pickpocket Chowdhry, who doesn't realize what he has.

2586. Severed Ties (1992, Fangoria Films, 96m, c). D Damon Santostefano & Richard Roberts, P Christopher Webster, W John Nystrom & Henry Dominic (based on the story by Santostefano & David A. Casci), PH Geza Sinkovics, ED Richard Roberts, M Daniel Licht, PD Don Day.

LP Oliver Reed (Dr. Hans Vaughan), Elke Sommer (Helena Harrison), Garrett Morris (Stripes), Billy Morrisette (Harrison Harrison), Johnny Legrand (Preacher), Denise Wallace (Eve).

Genetic scientist Reed experiments with limb regeneration in hopes of regrowing his accidentally severed arm. Well, he's successful to some extent, but there are some problems with his new reptilian arm.

2587. The Sex Monster (1999, Trimark–Sun-Lite Pictures, 97m, c). D & W Mike Binder, P Binder & Scott Stephens, PH Keith Smith, ED Lee Grubin, PD Katie Lipsitt, SD Rosie Tupta.

LP Mariel Hemingway (Laura Barnes), Mike Binder (Marty Barnes), Renee Humphrey (Didi), Taylor Nichols (Billy), Missy Crider (Diva), Stephen Baldwin (Murphy).

L.A. building contractor Binder pesters his wife Hemingway to open up their marriage and increase their sexual pleasure by adding another body to their bed. She finally agrees and he lives to regret it. The film is a modest farce without any outrageous sex scenes.

2588. S.F.W. (1995, Gramercy Pictures, 92m, c). D Jeffery Levy, P Dale Pollock, W Levy & Danny Rubin (based on the novel by Andrew Wellman), PH Peter Deming, ED Lauren Zuckerman, M Graeme Revell, PD Eve Cauley, AD Philip Messina, SD Sandy Struth.

LP Stephen Dorff (Cliff Spab), Reese Witherspoon (Wendy Pfister), Jake Busey (Morrow Streeter), Joey Lauren Adams (Monica Dice), Pamela Gidley (Janet Streeter), David Barry Gray (Scott Spab).

Surly teen Dorff becomes a nationwide hero after being held hostage for thirty-six days by convenience store terrorists. The kid has a way of turning a phrase, and the media is anxious to report his every word to his peers, who adopt them as their generation's pearls of wisdom.

2589. *The Shadow* (1994, Universal, 112m, c). D Russell Mulcahy, P Martin Bregman, Willi Baer & Michael S. Bregman, W David Koepp (based on characters created by Walter B. Gibson), PH Stephen H. Burum, ED Peter Honess, M Jerry Goldsmith, PD Joseph Nemec III, AD Dan Olexiewicz, Steve Wolff & Jack Johnson, SD Garrett Lewis, William Law III, Carl Stensel & James Tucci.

LP Alec Baldwin (Lamont Cranston/The Shadow), John Lone (Shirwan Khan), Penelope Ann Miller (Margo Lane), Peter Boyle (Moe Shrevnitz), Ian McKellen (Reinhardt Lane), Tim Curry (Farley Claymore), Jonathan Winters (Wainwright Barth).

Here's another film version of an old radio superhero. "The Shadow," mysterious character who aids the forces of law and order, is really Lamont Cranston (Baldwin), a wealthy, young man-about-town. Several years ago in the Orient, Cranston learned a strange and mysterious secret ... the hypnotic power to cloud men's minds so they cannot see him. The "Lamont Cranston" character was the model for such celebrated crime-fighters as "Superman," "Batman," and "Captain Marvel." "Who knows what evil lurks in the hearts of men? The Shadow knows!... The weed of crime bears bitter fruit. Crime does not pay. The Shadow knows!" Unfortunately, the film isn't as enjoyable or memorable as the radio program. Perhaps it's because Baldwin doesn't measure up to Orson Welles, who once played Cranston. In fact, Baldwin doesn't measure up to Bret Morrison, who played the part for 12 years.

2590. *Shadow Conspiracy* (1997, Hollywood Pictures–Buena Vista, 103m, c). D George Pan Cosmatos, P Terry Collis, W Adi Hasak & Ric Gibbs, PH Buzz Feitshans IV, ED Robert A. Ferretti, M Bruce Broughton, PD Joe Alves, AD Bill Hiney, SD Anne D. McCulley.

LP Charlie Sheen (Bobby Bishop), Linda Hamilton (Amanda Givens), Stephen Lang (The Agent), Donald Sutherland (Jake Conrad), Ben Gazarra (Vice President Saxon), Sam Waterston (The President), Charles Cioffi (Gen-

eral Blackburn), Theodore Bikel (Professor Yuri Pochenko).

In this film noir wannabe, Bikel and the entire staff of his think tank are killed, execution style. Before his assassination, Bikel warned his young protégé Sheen of a plot to kill the president, Waterston. Unfortunately, he wasn't able to tell Sheen the name of the high official he believed to be behind the scheme.

2591. *Shadow of the Wolf* (1993, Canada/France, Triumph Releasing, 108m, c). D Jacques Dorfmann, P Claude Leger, W Rudy Wurlitzer & Evan Jones (based on the novel *Agaguk* by Yves Theriault), PH Billy Williams, ED Francoise Bonnot, PD Wolf Kroeger, AD Richard Holland, SD Jim Erickson.

LP Lou Diamond Phillips (Agaguk), Toshiro Mifune (Ramook), Jennifer Tilly (Iriook), Donald Sutherland (Henderson), Bernard-Pierre Donnadieu (Brown), Qalingo Tookalak (Tulugak).

Eskimo couple Phillips and Tilly battle overwhelming odds of nature and fate. They are alone in the harsh Arctic tundra after leaving their village when Phillips cannot accept the white man's intrusion.

2592. *Shadowlands* (1993, U.K., Savoy Pictures, 130m, c). D Richard Attenborough, P Attenborough & Brian Eastman, W William Nicholson† (based on his play), PH Roger Pratt, ED Lesley Walker, M George Fenton, PD Stuart Craig, AD Michael Lamont, SD Stephanie McMillan.

LP Anthony Hopkins (Jack Lewis), Debra Winger† (Joy Gresham), John Wood (Christopher Riley), Edward Hardwicke (Warnie Lewis), Robert Flemyng (Claude Bird), Joseph Mazzello (Douglas Gresham), Gerald Sim (Superintendent Registrar), Peter Firth (Dr. Craig), Julian Fellowes (Desmond Arding).

As excellent as this film is, we prefer the 1985 British version starring Joss Ackland as C.S. Lewis and Claire Bloom as Joy Gresham. In this version, Hopkins portrays the Oxford don and author of *The Lion, the Witch, and the Wardrobe.* He's a confirmed bachelor, but he begins a correspondence with American divorcée Winger. She arrives with her two young sons to visit him and his bachelor brother Hardwicke. Later Hopkins marries her so she can stay in England. Just about the time they discover that she is dying, he realizes that he loves her. Winger was nominated for an Oscar for her performance, but this merely shows how few good female roles were available in the year. Winger's reading of the character seems less convincing than that of Bloom's. Raising the decibels of one's speech is not the best way to display emotional power. Hopkins and Ackland were both superb.

2593. *Shadows and Fog* (1992, Orion, 83m, c). D & W Woody Allen, P Robert Greenhut, PH Carlo DiPalma, ED Susan E. Morse, M Kurt Weill, PD Santo Loquasto, AD Speed Hopkins, SD George DeTitta, Jr. & Amy Marshall.

LP Woody Allen (Kleinman), Kathy Bates (Prostitute), John Cusack (Student Jack), Mia Farrow (Irmy), Jodie Foster (Prostitute), Fred Gwynne (Hacker's Follower), Julie Kavner (Alma), Madonna (Marie), John Malkovich (Clown), Kenneth Mars (Magician), Kate Nelligan (Eve), Donald Pleasence (Doctor), Lily Tomlin (Prostitute), Philip Bosco (Mr. Paulson), Wallace Shawn (Simon Carr), David Ogden Stiers (Hacker).

Allen gathers together an ensemble cast in this Kafka-like story about a schnook, Allen, recruited by a vigilante group to help capture a stranger, who is terrorizing the city. The comical elements are slight.

2594. *Shadowzone* (1990, Paramount, 88m, c). D & W J.S. Cardone, P Carol Kottenbrook, PH Karen Grossman, ED Thomas Meshelski, M Richard Band, PD Don Day, SD Ginnie Durden.

LP David Beecroft (Capt. Hickock), Louise Fletcher (Dr. Erhardt), James Hong (Dr. Van Fleet), Frederick Flynn (Tommy Shivers), Lu Leonard (Mrs. Cutter).

Due to NASA experiments with dream travel, an interdimensional monster is unleashed into the real world to seek victims.

2595. *Shadrach* (1998, Millennium Films, 86m, c). D Susanna Styron, P Bridget Terry, W Styron & Terry (based on the short story by William Styron), PH Hiro Narita, ED Colleen Sharp, M Van Dyke Parks, PD Burton Rencher, SD Valerie Fann.

LP Harvey Keitel (Vernon), Andie MacDowell (Trixie), John Franklin Sawyer (Shadrach), Scott Terra (Paul), Daniel Treat (Little Mole).

Set in the South during the Great Depression, a poor family faces a moral dilemma. Ninety-nine-year-old former slave Sawyer appears out of the blue requesting to be buried on their land, which used to be the plantation where he was born into slavery.

2596. *Shakes the Clown* (1992, IRS Media, 86m, c). D & W Bobcat Goldthwait, P Paul Colichman & Ann Luly-Goldthwait, PH Elliot Davis & Bobby Bukowski, ED J. Kathleen Gibson, M Tom Scott, PD Pamela Woodbridge.

LP Bobcat Goldthwait (Shakes the Clown), Julie Brown (Judy), Bruce Baum (Ty the Rodeo Clown), Steve Bean (Beaten Mime in Park), Blake Clark (Stenchy the Clown), Paul Dooley (Owen Cheese), Robin Williams (Mime Jerry), Florence Henderson (The Unknown Woman).

In this zany film, alcoholic Goldthwait is an aspiring clown in the all-clown town of "Palukaville." He's framed for murder by the boss of his arch-rival and must take it on the lam with girlfriend Brown to clear himself.

2597. *Shakespeare in Love* (1998, Miramax/Universal, 122m, c). D John Madden†, P David Parfitt, Donna Gigliotti, Harvey Weinstein, Edward Zwick* & Marc Norman*, W Norman & Tom Stoppard, PH Richard Greatrex†, ED David Gamble†, M Stephen Warbeck*, PD Martin Childs*, AD Mark Raggett, SD Jill Quertier*.

LP Joseph Fiennes (Will Shakespeare), Gwyneth Paltrow* (Viola De Lesseps), Geoffrey Rush† (Philip Henslowe), Judi Dench* (Queen Elizabeth), Simon Callow (Tinley, Master of the Revels), Colin Firth (Lord Wessex), Imelda Staunton (Nurse), Ben Affleck (Ned Alleyn), Tom Wilkinson (Hugh Fennyman), Jim Carter (Ralph Bashford), Martin Clunes (Richard Burbage).

Fiennes, the Bard of Avon, is suffering from writer's block (it happens even to the best, apparently). He is pressured by debt-ridden theater owner Rush to produce a hit. Needing a muse to get his writing juices flowing again, Fiennes meets and falls in love with lovely Paltrow. She fans his passion so much that he is able to complete his play *Romeo and Ethel, the Pirate's Daughter*, which he wisely renames *Romeo and Juliet*. Unbeknownst to the rest of the cast, she poses as a lad and is given the role of Romeo, playing opposite a lad appearing as Juliet. The story and the film are delightful, and the large cast plays their roles with the gusto one would expect from a work of, say, Shakespeare. Particularly impressive is the work of Rush, Staunton, Wilkinson and Dench, the latter as an admirable, earthy Elizabeth I. Paltrow is lovely and gives her finest performance. Fiennes is dashing as Will and deserves more credit for the success of the production. If young people will attend the movie, they will see Shakespeare as a flesh and blood man of parts, not some legendary figure from English classes, whose plays are required readings.

2598. *Shaking the Tree* (1992, Castle Hill Prods., 98m, c). D Duane Clark, P Robert J. Wilson, W Clark & Steven Wilde, PH Ronn Schmidt, ED Martin L. Bernstein, M David E. Russo, PD Sean Mannion.

LP Ayre Gross (Barry), Gale Hansen (John "Sully" Sullivan), Doug Savant (Michael), Steven Wilde (Terry "Duke" Keegan), Courteney Cox (Kathleen), Christina Haag (Michelle).

Four former high school buddies still haven't found their niche ten years later. Will they ever develop any responsibility? Due to the lack of quality of the story and acting, it's difficult to care.

2599. *Shallow Grave* (1995, U.K., Gramercy, 94m, c). D Danny Boyle, P Andrew Macdonald, W John Hodge, PH Brian Tufano, ED Masahiro Hirakubo, M Simon Boswell, PD Kate Quinn, AD Zoe MacLeod.

LP Kerry Fox (Juliet Miller), Christopher Eccleston (David Stephens), Ewan McGregor (Alex Law), Ken Scott (Detective McCall), Keith Allen (Hugo), John Bett (Brian McKinley).

Three housemates are faced with a moral dilemma when their newest roomie overdoses on drugs, leaving behind a suitcase filled with cash. No, their problem isn't to determine whose money it is, but how best to dispose of the body and keep the loot for themselves.

2600. *Shame* (1994, Prism Ent., 120m, c). D Dan Lerner, P Joseph Plager & Michele MacLaren, W Rebecca Soladay (based on the screenplay of the 1987 film by Michael Brindley and Beverly Blankenship), PH Ron Orieux,

ED Victor Dubois, M David McHugh, PD Donald Higgins.

LP Amanda Donohoe (Diana Cadell), Fairuza Balk (Lizzie Curtis), Dean Stockwell (Tim Curtis), Shelley Owens (Lorna), Dan Gauthier (Danny), Wyatt Orr (Andrew Rudolph).

In a small logging town, women are being raped by high school hoods and are too intimidated to go to the police. When lawyer Donohoe is stranded in the town and learns what's been going on, she convinces one victim, Balk, to speak out about the crimes. This makes Donohoe the target for violence from both the rapists and the "good" people of the town who would like to hush up everything.

2601. *Shameless* (1996, U.K., Moviescreen Ent., 99m, c). D Henry Cole, P Peter Watson-Wood & Nigel Thomas, W Tim Sewell (based on a story by Cole), PH John Peters, ED Simon Hilton & Lionel Selwyn, M Barrie Guard, PD Tony Stringer, AD Sonja Klaus.

LP Elizabeth Hurley (Antonia Dyer), C. Thomas Howell (Mike Stone), Joss Ackland (Sam Stringer), Frederick Treves (Sir Harry Dyer), Andrew Connolly (Clive Nathan), Jeremy Brett (Tony Vernon-Smith), Claire Bloom (Liz Stringer), Louise Delamere (Sandy).

Rich young drug addict Hurley spends most of her time partying at the house of her drug supplier Brett. Veteran cop Ackland is shocked to learn that his stepdaughter, with whom he has been having an affair, is really his daughter. These two are on a collision course in this competent but ultimately disappointing thriller, filled with violence and nudity.

2602. *Shattered* (1991, U.S./Germany, MGM-Pathé, 98m, c). D & W Wolfgang Petersen (based on the novel *The Plastic Nightmare* by Richard Neely), P Petersen & John Davis, PH Laszlo Kovacs, ED Gregg Fonseca, AD Bruce Miller, SD Dorree Cooper.

LP Tom Berenger (Dan Merrick), Bob Hoskins (Gus Klein), Greta Scacchi (Judith Merrick), Joanne Whalley-Kilmer (Jenny Scott), Corbin Bernsen (Jeb Scott), Theodore Bikel (Dr. Berkus).

When Berenger wakes up in a hospital with a loss of memory, his faithful wife is there to console him, showing him pictures of their life together. Somehow he senses there are more problems here than his amnesia.

2603. *Shattered Image* (1998, Seven Arts Pictures, 102m, c). D Raul Ruiz, P Barbet Schroeder, Susan Hoffman & Lloyd A. Silverman, W Duane Poole, PH Robbie Muller, ED Michael Duthie, M Jorge Arriagada, PD Robert DeVico.

LP Anne Parillaud (Jessie), William Baldwin (Brian), Lisanne Falk (Paula/Laura), Graham Greene (Conrad/Mike), Billy Wilmot (Lamond).

Parillaud is a woman with a split personality. One personality is a brutal murderer. Her other side is softer and remembers what her other self has done only as nightmares.

2604. *The Shawshank Redemption†* (1994, Columbia, 142m, c). D Frank Darabont, P Niki Marvin†, W Darabont† (based on the short story "Rita Hayworth and Shawshank Redemption" by Stephen King), PH Roger Deakins†, ED Richard Francis-Bruce†, M Thomas Newman†, PD Terence Marsh, AD Peter Smith, SD Michael Seriton.

LP Tim Robbins (Andy Dufresne), Morgan Freeman† (Ellis Boyd "Red" Redding), Bob Gunton (Warden Norton), William Sadler (Heywood), Clancy Brown (Captain Hadley), Gil Bellows (Tommy), Mark Rolston (Bogs Diamond), James Whitmore (Brooks Hatlen).

No one believes Robbins' protests that he didn't murder his wife and her lover. He is convicted and sentenced to prison for life. There he is befriended by experienced con Freeman, abused by sadistic guard Brown, and hassled by warden Gunton. Despite this, Robbins refuses to compromise his particular moral code and is able to achieve some minor improvements in the lives of the other prisoners. The film moves along slowly, but there is much here to admire.

2605. *The Sheltering Sky* (1990, It./G.B., Warner Bros., 135m, c). D Bernardo Bertolucci, P Jeremy Thomas, W Bertolucci & Mark Peploe (based on the novel by Paul Bowles), PH Vittorio Storaro, ED Gabriella Cristiani, M Richard Horowitz & Ryuichi Sakamoto, PD Gianni Silvestri & Ferdinando Scarfiotti, AD Andrew Sanders.

LP John Malkovich (Port Moresby), Debra Winger (Kit Moresby), Campbell Scott (Turner), Eric Vu-An (Belqassim), Jill Bennett (Mrs. Lyle), Timothy Spall (Eric Lyle).

American couple Winger and Malkovich, accompanied by socialite Scott, travel to Africa for a trip to the Sahara desert, where they hope to revitalize their spirits and love life. Instead, Winger and Scott have an affair. The scenery is superior to the story.

2606. *She's All That* (1999, Miramax, 91m, c). D Robert Iscove, P Peter Abrams, Robert L. Levy & Richard N. Gladstein, W R. Lee Fleming, Jr., PH Francis Kenny, ED Casey O. Rohrs, M Stewart Copeland, PD Charles Breen, AD Gary Diamond.

LP Freddie Prinze, Jr. (Zack Siler), Rachael Leigh Cook (Laney Boggs), Matthew Lillard (Brock Hudson), Paul Walker (Dean Sampson), Jodi Lyn O'Keefe (Taylor Vaughan), Kevin Pollak (Wayne Boggs), Anna Paquin (Mackenzie Siler).

Returning from spring break, Prinze discovers that his high school girlfriend O'Keefe has dumped him for Lillard. With nothing better to do, Prinze accepts a bet from friend Walker that he can't woo the school's dorky ugly duckling Cook and make her into a beautiful princess by the time of the prom. Yeah, she was a fox all along.

2607. *She's So Lovely* (1997, Miramax, 96m, c). D Nick Cassavetes, P Rene Cleitman, W John Cassavetes, PH Thierry Arbogast, ED Petra Von Oelffen, M Joseph Vitarelli, PD David Wasco, AD Daniel Bradford, SD Sandy Reynolds-Wasco.

LP Sean Penn (Eddie Quinn), Robin Wright Penn (Maureen Quinn), John Travolta (Joey), Gena Rowlands (Miss Green), Harry Dean Stanton (Shorty), Debi Mazar (Georgie), James Gandolfini (Kiefer).

This film is based on a script written by John Cassavetes twenty years earlier. When her husband Penn pulls yet another of his disappearing acts, Wright Penn seeks solace with her neighbor Gandolfini. At the end of the evening he beats and rapes her. When she finally locates her husband, she tries to keep the incident from him. Penn finds out, is unsuccessful in killing Gandolfini, but does kill a department of mental health worker. He spends ten years in a mental hospital and is released, believing he's only been away three months. In the meantime, Wright Penn has married Travolta and has started a new family. Wright Penn has a choice to make between husbands and lives, as Penn and Travolta are both determined to keep her.

2608. ***She's the One*** (1996, Fox Searchlight, 96m, c). D & W Edward Burns, P Ted Hope, James Schamus & Burns, PH Frank Prinzi, ED Susan Graef, M Tom Petty, PD William Barclay, AD Caty Maxey, SD Harriet Zucker.

LP Jennifer Aniston (Renee), Maxine Bahns (Hope), Edward Burns (Mickey Fitzpatrick), Cameron Diaz (Heather Davis), John Mahoney (Mr. Fitzpatrick), Mike McGlone (Francis Fitzpatrick).

Burns takes another shot at his *Brothers McMullen* story, now with a much bigger budget. He is a shy cabby who hasn't yet recovered from the shock of discovering his ex-wife Diaz's affair. One thing he didn't discover was that her lover was his own brother. Mahoney, as the boys' father, steals the show with his great comic lines.

2609. ***Shiloh*** (1997, Legacy Releasing, 93m, c). D & W Dale Rosenbloom (based on the novel by Phyllis Reynolds Naylor), P Zane W. Levitt & Rosenbloom, PH Frank Byers, ED Mark Westmore, M Joel Goldsmith, PD Amy Ancona, SD Melissa Levander.

LP Michael Moriarty (Ray Preston), Scott Wilson (Judd Travers), Blake Heron (Marty Preston), Rod Steiger (Doc Wallace), Ann Dowd (Louise Preston), Bonnie Bartlett (Mrs. Wallace).

Shiloh is a sad, beaten and starved beagle, befriended by adolescent Heron. The dog's owner is cruel and sullen Wilson, who threatens to kill the dog if it runs away again. Heron makes a deal with Wilson to save the dog, but when the latter reneges, it's time for Heron's father Moriarty to confront Wilson. The story isn't enough for a feature film.

2610. ***Shine†*** (1996, Australia, Fine Line, 105m, c). D Scott Hicks†, P Jane Scott†, W Jan Sardi† (based on a story by Hicks†), PH Geoffrey Simpson, ED Pip Karmel†, M David Hirschfelder†, PD Vicki Niehus.

LP Geoffrey Rush* (David Helfgott as an adult), Armin Mueller-Stahl† (Peter), Lynn Redgrave (Gillian), Noah Taylor (David as a Young Man), John Gielgud (Cecil Parkes), Alex Rafalowicz (David as a Child), Googie Withers (Katharine Susannah Prichard), Sonia Todd (Sylvia), Nicholas Bell (Ben Rosen).

Seeing this film it is natural to be quite impressed with the three performances of Rafa-lowicz, Taylor and, finally, Rush. They portray a musical prodigy whose relationship with his chilling and cruel father, Mueller-Stahl, leads him to a mental breakdown just when he is on the verge of being recognized as an international pianist. As an adult, he is childlike and compulsive, speaking in a rush of words, some meaningful, some meaningless. He still has some ability to play the piano, if not enough to master the Rachmaninoff Concerto that has been his impossible dream. Rush is superb as the real-life Helfgott, but probably should share his Oscar with Rafalowicz and Taylor.

2611. ***Shining Through*** (1992, 20th Century–Fox, 127m, c). D & W David Seltzer (based on the novel by Susan Isaacs), P Howard Rosenman & Carol Baum, PH Jan De Bont, ED Craig McKay, M Michael Kamen, PD Anthony Pratt, AD Desmond Crowe & Kevin Phipps, SD Peter Howitt.

LP Michael Douglas (Ed Leland), Melanie Griffith (Linda Voss), Liam Neeson (Franze-Otto Dietrich), Joely Richardson (Margrete Von Eberstien), John Gielgud (Sunflower), Francis Guinan (Andrew Berringer).

In a real stinker, Griffith's baby-voice sounds particularly ill-suited to her role as a spy sent behind enemy lines in Germany by hero Douglas. Circumstances force him to go in and rescue her. The two send off no sparks as lovers, acting more like two people who would rather not even touch.

2612. ***Shock 'Em Dead*** (1991, Academy Ent., 93m, c). D Mark Freed, P Eric Louzil, W Freed, David Tedder & Andy Cross, PH Ron Chapman, ED Terry Blythe, M Robert Decker, PD Randy Lapin.

LP Traci Lords (Lindsay Roberts), Troy Donahue (Record Executive), Stephen Quadros (Angel/Martin), Tyger Sodipe (Voodoo Priestess), Aldo Ray (Tony), Tim Moffet (Greg).

Nerdish devil-worshipper Quadros trades his soul for a chance to become a rock and roll star and win sexy Lords.

2613. ***A Shock to the System*** (1990, Corsair, 91m, c). D Jan Egleson, P Patrick McCormick, W Andrew Klavan (based on the novel by Simon Brett), PH Paul Goldsmith, ED Peter C. Frank & William Anderson, M

Gary Chang, PD Howard Cummings, AD Robert K. Shaw, Jr., SD Robert J. Franco.

LP Michael Caine (Graham Marshall), Elizabeth McGovern (Stella Anderson), Peter Riegert (Robert Benham), Swoosie Kurtz (Leslie Marshall), Will Patton (Lt. Laker), Jenny Wright (Melanie O'Connor), John McMartin (George Brewster), Barbara Baxley (Lillian).

Passed over for promotion in favor of less experienced men, Caine discovers that murder is a sure way to climb the corporate ladder. Sounds a bit like a business executive Richard III.

2614. Shooting Fish (1997, U.K., Fox Searchlight, 93m, c). D Stefan Schwartz, P Richard Holmes & Glynis Murray, W Schwartz & Holmes. PH Henry Braham, ED Alan Strachan, M Stanislas Syrewicz, PD Max Gottlieb, AD Sue Ferguson.

LP Dan Futterman (Dylan), Stuart Townsend (Jez), Kate Beckinsale (Georgie), Nickolas Grace (Mr. Stratton-Luce), Claire Cox (Floss), Ralph Ineson (Mr. Ray).

Both con man Futterman, a smooth-talker with a talent for numbers, and his partner, electronics expert Townsend, are sweet on their scrappy assistant Beckinsale. When they become involved with a horse racing sting, they become some kind of urban Robin Hoods.

2615. Shopping (1996, U.K., Concorde, 86m, c). D & W Paul Anderson, P Jeremy Bolt, PH Tony Imi, ED David Stiven, M Barrington Pheloung, PD Max Gottlieb, AD Chris Townsend.

LP Sadie Frost (Jo), Jude Law (Billy), Sean Pertwee (Tommy), Fraser James (Be Bop), Sean Bean (Venning), Marianne Faithfull (Bev), Jonathan Pryce (Conway).

In a not too distant future, bored teens get their kicks by stealing cars and driving to malls, where they steal everything not nailed down.

2616. Short Cuts (1993, Fine Line Features, 189m, c). D Robert Altman†, P Altman & Scott Bushnell, W Altman & Frank Barhydt (based on short stories and a poem by Raymond Carver), PH Walt Lloyd, ED Geraldine Peroni, M Mark Isham, PD Stephen Altman, AD Jerry Fleming, SD Susan Emshwiller.

LP Tim Robbins (Gene Shepard), Tom Waits (Earl Piggot), Lily Tomlin (Doreen Piggot), Madeleine Stowe (Sherri Shepard), Peter Gallagher (Stormy Weathers), Anne Archer (Claire Kane), Fred Ward (Stuart Kane), Buck Henry (Gordon Johnson), Huey Lewis (Vern Miller), Bruce Davison (Howard Finnigan), Andie MacDowell (Ann Finnigan), Jack Lemmon (Paul Finnigan), Lori Singer (Zoe Trainer), Matthew Modine (Dr. Ralph Wyman), Robert Downey, Jr. (Bill Bush), Jennifer Jason Leigh (Lois Kaiser), Frances McDormand (Betty Weathers).

The superstar-filled cast in Altman's adaptation of Raymond Carver stories portrays a series of unhappy Southern Californians. The connections between the various lovers, couples, friends, etc. is minimal, which may turn off those who prefer nice linear story lines; but (as we are only briefly a part of the lives of most people we encounter) the quality of the work doesn't make it seem a great inconvenience.

2617. Short Time (1990, 20th Century-Fox, 97m, c). D Gregg Champion, P Todd Black, W John Blumenthal & Michael Berry, PH John Connor, ED Frank Morriss, M Ira Newborn, PD Michael Bolton, AD Eric Fraser, SD Gwendolyn Margetson.

LP Dabney Coleman (Burt Simpson), Matt Frewer (Ernie Dills), Teri Garr (Carolyn Simpson), Barry Corbin (Captain), Joe Pantoliano (Scalese), Xander Berkeley (Stark), Rob Roy (Dan Miller).

Soon-to-retire police officer Coleman is wrongly diagnosed as having a terminal disease. Since he has little else to leave his wife, he spends his last days on the force trying to get killed so she can collect his insurance.

2618. Shout (1991, Universal, 97m, c). D Jeffrey Hornaday, P Robert Simonds, W Joe Gayton (based on his story), PH Robert Brinkmann, ED Seth Flaum, M Randy Edelman, PD William F. Matthews, AD P. Michael Johnston, SD Jim Duffy.

LP John Travolta (Jack Cabe), James Walters (Jesse Tucker), Heather Graham (Sara Benedict), Richard Jordan (Eugene Benedict), Linda Fiorentino (Molly), Scott Coffey (Bradley).

This film was made before Travolta made his comeback. It will not be part of any film festival featuring his best work. He's a fugitive hired as a music teacher at a school for wayward kids in the 1950s. Travolta introduces the kids to the new music of rock and roll, and, Gee, it's swell.

2619. *A Show of Force* (1990, Paramount, 93m, c). D Bruno Barreto, P John Strong, W Evan Jones & Strong (based on the book *Murder Under Two Flags* by Anne Nelson), PH James Glennon, ED Henry Richardson, M Georges Delerue, PD William J. Cassidy.

LP Amy Irving (Kate Ryan de Melendez), Andy Garcia (Luis Angel Mora), Lou Diamond Phillips (Jesus Fuentes), Robert Duvall (Howard Baslin), Kevin Spacey (Frank Curtin).

Irving is a crusading TV reporter investigating a murder cover-up. Is it the work of terrorists, as the government claims, or is there some political hanky-panky behind the killings?

2620. *Showdown at Williams Creek* (1991, Canada, Crescent Prods., 97m, c). D Allan Kroeker, P Gary Payne, W John Gray, PH Ron Orieux, ED Lara Mazur, M Michael Conway Baker, PD Jill Scott, SD Gordon Clapp.

LP Tom Burlinson (John George "Kootenai" Brown), Donnelly Rhodes (McTooth/ Eben Campbell), Raymond Burr (Judge Webster), Stephen E. Miller (Sheriff), Michelle Thrush (Olivia D'Lonais).

In the Canadian Northwest Territory in 1870, Australian actor Burlinson appears as an Irishman, adopted by French-Indians, who marries one of their women, becoming what was known as a "squaw man." He is brought to trial for the murder of a charming rogue, Scotsman Rhodes. It's a story of racism, exploitation, greed and survival.

2621. *Showdown in Little Tokyo* (1991, Warner Bros., 78m, c). D Mark K. Lester, P Martin E. Caan & Lester, W Stephen Glantz & Caliope Brattlestreet, PH Mark Irwin, ED Steven Kemper & Robert A. Ferretti, M David Michael Frank, PD Craig Stevens, AD Bill Rea, SD Ellen Totleben.

LP Dolph Lundgren (Detective Chris Kenner), Brandon Lee (Johnny Murata), Carey-Hiroyuki Tagawa (Yoshida), Tia Carrere (Minako Okeya), Toshihiro Obata (Sato), Philip Tan (Tanaka).

Lundgren and Lee team up to kick some evil Japanese druglord butts.

2622. *The Showgirl Murders* (1996, Califilm, 85m, c). D Gene Hertel, P Darin Spillman, W Christopher Wooden, PH Harry Box, ED J.J. Jackson, M David Wurst & Eric Wurst, PD Nava, AD Louis Moulinet.

LP Maria Ford (Jessica), Matt Preston (Mitch), D.S. Case (Carolyn), Bob McFarland (Ridley), Kevin Alber (Joey).

In a story borrowed from *The Postman Always Rings Twice* and *Double Indemnity*, this semi-pornographic film features Ford as a sultry blonde who seduces bar owner Preston and plots with him to kill his wife Case. As for the ending, the filmmakers have lifted it directly from *Body Heat.*

2623. *Showgirls* (1995, MGM/United Artists, 131m, c). D Paul Verhoeven, P Alan Marshall & Charles Evans, W Joe Eszterhaus, PH Jost Vacano, ED Mark Goldblatt & Mark Helfrich, M David A. Stewart, PD Allan Cameron, AD William F. O'Brien, SD Richard C. Goddard.

LP Elizabeth Berkley (Nomi Malone), Kyle MacLachlan (Zack Carey), Gina Gershon (Cristal Connors), Glenn Plummer (James Smith), Robert Davi (Al Torres), Alan Rachins (Tony Moss), Gina Ravera (Molly Abrams), Lin Tucci (Henrietta Bazoom), William Shockley (Andrew Carver).

Here's a new take on the plot of *42nd Street.* Tough-talking Berkley has a body just meant for Las Vegas fleshpots. What she doesn't have is any acting talent. But the girl is so intensely eager that if one watches the film as some kind of high-camp exercise, its almost fun. Berkley is ready and willing to replace Gershon as Ms. Nude Showgirl, screw jerky MacLachlan to a fare-thee-well, and kick the crap out of Shockley when he leads a gang rape on Berkley's best friend Ravera. The film doesn't offer much of a story or acting talent, but if you're a voyeur (and you know if you are), there's enough nudity and shaking of fine young flesh to justify the cost of a ticket or a video rental.

2624. *The Shrimp on the Barbie* (1990, Unity, 86m, c). D Allen Smithee, P R. Ben Efraim, W Grant Morris, Ron House & Alan Shearman, ED Fred Chulack.

LP Cheech Marin (Carlos Munroz), Emma Samms (Alex Hobart), Vernon Wells (Bruce Woodley), Terence Cooper (Ian Hobart),

Jeanette Cronin (Maggie), Carole Davis (Dominique).

Samms' father turns thumbs down on her choice of husband material. So she hires lowlife Marin to pose as her new boyfriend to make anyone else look better.

2625. *Shrunken Heads* (1994, Full Moon Ent., 86m, c). D Richard Elfman, P Charles Band, W Matthew Bright, PH Stephen McNutt, ED Charles Simmons, M Richard Band & Danny Elfman, PD Milo, AD John Zachary, SD Nicki Roberts.

LP Aeryk Egan (Tommy Larson), Bo Sharon (Bill Turner), Darris Love (Freddy Thompson), Julius Harris (Mr. Sumatra), Becky Herbst (Sally), Meg Foster (Big Moe).

Three teens trying to clean up the mean streets on which they live are killed. Their heads are severed by voodoo priest Harris. He reanimates them and gives them special powers to track down their killers.

2626. *Siam Sunset* (1999, Australia, UIP, 91m, c). D John Polson, P Al Clark, W Max Dann & Andrew Knight, PH Brian Breheny, ED Nicholas Beauman, M Paul Grabowsky, PD Steven Jones-Evans, AD Richard Hobbs.

LP Linus Roche (Perry), Victoria Hill (Maree), Danielle Cormack (Grace), Ian Bliss (Martin), Roy Billing (Bill), Alan Brough (Stuart), Rebecca Hobbs (Jane).

In this frequently violent comedy, British design executive Roche is working on developing a shade of red to be called "Siam Sunset." He is happily married to attractive Hill, but tragedy strikes from the sky when a refrigerator falls from an airplane and flattens her. When he wins a contest whose prize is a trip to Australia, he decides it may help him with his bereavement. Instead, he finds the prize is a decidedly third-class bus trip in the Australian outback. There are plenty of laughs interspersed with more unexpected acts of violence.

2627. *Sibling Rivalry* (1990, Castle Rock/Columbia, 88m, c). D Carl Reiner, P David Lester, Don Miller & Liz Glotzer, W Martha Goldhirsh, PH Reynaldo Villalobos, ED Bud Molin, M Jack Elliott, PD Jeannine Claudia Oppewall, SD Lisa Fischer.

LP Kirstie Alley (Marjorie Turner), Jami Gertz (Jeanine), Bill Pullman (Nick), Carrie

Fisher (Iris), Scott Bakula (Harry Turner), Sam Elliott (Charles Turner), Ed O'Neill (Wilbur Meany), Frances Sternhagen (Mrs. Turner), John Randolph (Mr. Turner).

Doctor's wife Alley encounters a stranger, Elliott, and wears him out in bed. Well, it's a bit worse than that — he has a heart attack and dies. Later Alley discovers that Elliott is her long-lost brother-in-law.

2628. *Side Out* (1990, Tri-Star, 100m, c). D Peter Israelson, P Gary Foster, W David Thoreau, PH Ron Garcia, ED Conrad Buff, M Jeff Lorber, PD Dan Lomino, AD Bruce Crone, SD Cloudia.

LP C. Thomas Howell (Monroe Clark), Peter Horton (Zack Barnes), Courtney Thorne-Smith (Samantha), Harley Jane Kozak (Kate Jacobs), Christopher Rydell (Wiley Hunter), Terry Kiser (Uncle Max), Randy Stoklos (Rollo Vincent).

Well, they finally did it, and it's about time. Moviemakers have tackled (or maybe that's spiked) volleyball. It's a fun game to play, and many of the fine young bodies who romp in the sun and sand are pleasant to watch, but it really doesn't have much dramatic impact.

2629. *Side Streets* (1998, Merchant Ivory Prods/CEO Films, 131m, c). D Tony Gerber, P Bruce Weiss, W Lynn Nottage & Gerber, PH Russell Lee Fine, ED Kate Williams, M Evan Lurie, PD Stephen McCabe, SD Paul Cheponis.

LP Valerie Golino (Sylvie Otti), Shashi Kapoor (Vikram Raj), Leon (Errol Boyce), Art Malik (Bipin Raj), Shabana Azmi (Chandra Raj).

This film offers five interconnecting stories set during a very hot summer day in each of the five boroughs of New York City.

2630. *Sidekicks* (1993, Triumph Releasing, 102m, c). D Aaron Norris, P Don Carmody, W Donald G. Thompson, Carmody & Louis Illar (based on his story), PH Joao Fernandes, ED David Rawlins & Bernard Weiser, M Alan Silvestri, PD Reuben Freed, SD Steven K. Barnett.

LP Chuck Norris (Himself), Jonathan Brandis (Barry Gabrewski), Beau Bridges (Jerry Gabrewski), Joe Piscopo (Stone), Danica McKellar (Lauren), Mako (Mr. Lee), Julia Nickson-Soul (Noreen Chen).

Asthmatic high school kid Brandis is bullied at school and gets no help at home from his parents. He has Walter Mitty–like fantasies — and then along comes his fairy-godfather Norris.

2631. *The Siege* (1998, 20th Century–Fox, 116m, c). D Edward Zwick, P Lynda Obst & Zwick, W Lawrence Wright, Menno Meyjes & Zwick (based on a story by Wright), PH Otto Nemenz & Roger Deakins, ED Steven Rosenblum, M Graeme Revell, PD Lilly Kilvert, AD Chris Shrivel, SD Gretchen Rau.

LP Denzel Washington (Anthony Hubbard), Annette Bening (Elsie Kraft/ Sharon Bridger), Bruce Willis (Gen. William Devereaux), Tony Shalhoub (Frank Haddad), Sami Bonajila (Samir Nazhde), David Proval (Danny Sussman).

Arab-American groups protested this film, supposedly without seeing it, because it is the tale of New York City under attack by Arab terrorists. The villains in the movie were drawn along the lines of those responsible for the World Trade Center bombing. The U.S. Army doesn't come off looking very good, but FBI agent Washington and undercover National Security Agency operative Bening keep their cool throughout the tense situation.

2632. *Silence of the Hams* (1995, Italy/U.S., October Films, 85m, c). D & W Ezio Greggio, P Greggio & Julie Corman, PH Jacques Haitkin, ED Robert Barrere & Andy Horvitch, M Parmer Fuller, PD Jim Newport, AD Russel Smith, SD Natalie Kendrick Pope.

LP Ezio Greggio (Antonio Motel), Dom DeLuise (Dr. Animal Cannibal Pizza), Billy Zane (Joe Dee Fostar), Joanna Pacula (Lily), Charlene Tilton (Jane), Martin Balsam (Detective Balsam), John Astin (Ranger) Bubba Smith (Olaf), Rip Taylor (Mr. Laurel), Shelley Winters (Mother).

It's an embarrassing knockdown of *Silence of the Lambs* and other films, and this stinker wasn't even produced and directed by Mel Brooks.

2633. *The Silence of the Lambs** (1991, Orion, 118m, c). D Jonathan Demme*, P Edward Saxon*, Kenneth Utt* & Ron Bozman*, W Ted Tally* (based on the novel by Thomas Harris), PH Tak Fujimoto, ED Craig McKay†,

M Howard Shore, PD Kristi Zea, AD Tim Galvin, SD Karen O'Hara.

LP Jodie Foster* (Clarice Starling), Anthony Hopkins* (Dr. Hannibal Lecter), Scott Glenn (Jack Crawford), Ted Levine (Jame Gumb), Anthony Heald (Dr. Frederick Chilton), Brooke Smith (Catherine Martin), Charles Napier (Sergeant Boyle), Diane Baker (Senator Ruth Martin), Kasi Lemmons (Ardelia Mapp).

Here's the real thing. Foster is an FBI agent-in-training, chosen by her boss Glenn to seek help from Hopkins, "Hannibal the Cannibal," to develop a profile of mass murderer "Buffalo Bill," who likes to skin his victims. It's not possible to offer too much praise for the twin performances of Hopkins and Foster. When the two are together, the film is at its best. Hopkins is a charming psycho-killer, and Foster is a true professional who wins the admiration, if that's really an achievement, of psychopath Hopkins. For her part, she treats the brilliant but deadly Hopkins with all the respect she might reserve for a favorite instructor. There are a lot of thrills and chills in this award-winning movie.

2634. *The Silencer* (1993, Academy Ent., 84m, c). D Amy Goldstein, P Brian J. Smith, W Goldstein & Scott Kraft, PH Daniel Berkowitz, ED Rick Blue, PD John Myhre.

LP Lynette Walden (Angelica), Chris Mulkey (George), Paul Ganus (Tony), Brook Parker (Didi).

Walden is a hitwoman for a top governmental agency. To relieve the tension of her work, she pulls guys in off the street and into her bed. She begins to suspect someone wants her taken out.

2635. *Silent Fall* (1994, Morgan Creek–Warner Bros., 100m, c). D Bruce Beresford, P James G. Robinson, W Akiva Goldsman, PH Peter James, ED Ian Crafford, M Stewart Copeland, PD John Stoddart, AD David Bomba, SD Patty Malone.

LP Richard Dreyfuss (Jake Rainer), Linda Hamilton (Karen Rainer), John Lithgow (Dr. Harlinger), J.T. Walsh (Sheriff Mitch Rivers), Ben Faulkner (Tim Warden), Liv Tyler (Sylvie Warden).

Reclusive physician Dreyfuss comes out of exile to help an autistic nine-year-old witness to a double murder.

2636. Silent Night, Deadly Night 5: The Toy Maker (1991, Silent Films, 90m, c). D Martin Kitrosser, P Brian Yuzna & Richard N. Gladstein, W Yuzna & Kitrosser, PH James Mathers, ED Norman Buckley, M Matthew Morse, PD W. Brooke Wheeler.

LP Mickey Rooney (Joe Petto), William Thorne (Derek Quinn), Brian Bremer (Pino), Tracy Frain (Noah), Jane Higginson (Sarah).

Apparently there is still milk in this old cow, even though the story of this film has little to do with others in the series. When young Thorne sees his father killed by a lethal plaything, he is so traumatized that he becomes a mute. Responsibility for planting the deadly toy spreads in various directions, including local toymaker Rooney and his son Bremer.

2637. Silent Tongue (1994, Trimark Pictures, 101m, c). D & W Sam Shepard, P Carolyn Pfeiffer & Ludi Boeken, PH Jack Conroy, ED Bill Yahraus, M Patrick O'Hearn, PD Cary White, AD John Frick & Michael Sullivan, SD Barbara Haberecht.

LP Richard Harris (Prescott Roe), Sheila Tousey (Awbonnie/Ghost), Alan Bates (Eamon McCree), River Phoenix (Talbot Roe), Dermot Mulroney (Reeves McCree), Jeri Arredondo (Velada McCree), Tantoo Cardinal (Silent Tongue).

A sideshow owner trades his Indian daughter Tousey to Richard Harris as a wife for his son Phoenix. Unfortunately, the woman dies in childbirth. Pheonix can't accept the death. He refuses to have her buried. This leads to her spirit returning for vengeance.

2638. The Silent Touch (1993, U.K./Poland/Denmark, Metronome Prods., 92m, c). D Krzystof Zanussi, P Mark Forstater, W Mark Wadlow & Peter Morgan (based on a story by Zanussi & Edward Zebrowski), PH Jaroslaw Zamojda, ED Marek Denys, M Wojciech Kilar, PD Ewa Braun.

LP Max Von Sydow (Henry Keszdy), Lothaire Bluteau (Stefan Bugajski), Sarah Miles (Helena), Peter Hesse Overgaard (Joseph), Lars Lunoe (Dr. Hans Jurgen), Sofie Grabol (Annette).

Von Sydow is a composer who believes his musical contributions all belong to the past. Along comes admirer Bluteau to show him he still has something to offer.

2639. Silk Degrees (1994, Imperial Ent., 90m, c). D Armand Garabidian, P Alan B. Bursteen, W Stuart Gibbs, Douglas J. Sloan & Robert Gottlieb, PH William Boatman, ED Jose Ponce, PD Michael Pearce, AD Gert Broekema.

LP Marc Singer (Baker), Deborah Shelton (Alex Ramsey), Mark Hamill (Johnson), Charles Napier (Schultz), Michael Des Barres (De Grillo), Katherine Armstrong (Nicole), Stephen Quadros (Willie).

Federal agents Singer and Hamill try to protect temperamental TV star Shelton, the only witness to a murder.

2640. Silk 'n' Sabotage (1994, Academy Ent., 73m, c). D & P Joe Cauley, W R.D. Robinson & Joe Cauley (based on a story by Deidra Bruder), PH Joe Broderick, M Francois Lapardaux.

Julie Skiru (Jamie), Stephanie Champlin (Lynn), Cherilyn Shea (Dagny), Darren Foreman (Michael), Marshall Hilliard (Robert).

The story of this erotic fantasy is easier to see through than the flimsy negligees modeled by its shapely young female cast members. But for the record, while Shea and Champlin earn their keep at endless negligee parties, their roommate Skiru has created a computer game which she believes will make her rich.

2641. Simon Birch (1998, Hollywood Pictures–Buena Vista, 113m, c). D & W Mark Steven Johnson (based on the novel *A Prayer for Owen Meaney* by John Irving), P Laurence Mark & Roger Birnbaum, PH Aaron E. Schneider, ED David Finfer, M Marc Shaiman, PD David Chapman, AD Dennis Davenport, SD Carolyn A. Loucks.

LP Ian Michael Smith (Simon Birch), Joseph Mazzello (Joe Wenteworth), Ashley Judd (Rebecca Wenteworth), Oliver Platt (Ben Goodrich), David Strathairn (Reverend Russell), Dana Ivey (Grandmother Wenteworth), Jim Carrey (Adult Joe Wenteworth).

John Irving sold the movie rights to his novel but wouldn't give the studio permission to use the book's title or character names. That's how Owen Meaney became Simon Birch. In the film, Carrey is the briefly seen narrator who leads the audience back to the early 1960s where, as Mazzello, his life is dramatically changed because of his friendship with Smith. In real life Smith suffers from

Morquio Syndrome. He lacks an enzyme that breaks down complex carbohydrates. As a result, his bones, ligaments and joints failed to develop normally. Both young Mr. Smith and the tragic character he portrays have an unbelievable spirit and zest for life.

2642. Simon Sez (1999, Independent Artists, 85m, c). D Kevin Elders, P Moshe Diamant & Ringo Lam, W Andrew Miller & Andrew Lowery, PH Avraham Karpick, ED Alain Jakubowicz, M Brian Tyler, PD Damien Lanfranchi.

LP Dennis Rodman (Simon), Dane Cook (Nick), Natalia Cigliuti (Claire), Filip Nicolic (Michael), John Pinette (Macro), Jerome Pradon (Ashton), Ricky Harris (Micro).

While he played basketball in the NBA, helping the Chicago Bulls to three championships, many people felt Rodman was a very bad actor with serious mental problems. Still others felt he was really quite a good actor, cashing in on a persona that he adopted which left no one neutral in their feelings about him. The truth is that this film would never have been made, never released to theaters and never reviewed if Rodman wasn't in it. So there! By the way, he portrays an ex–CIA agent now working as an Interpol agent. It's a spoof of spy stories, which has been done often and, God knows, much better.

2643. Simpatico (1999, Fine Line Features, 106m, c). D Matthew Warchus, P Dan Lupovitz, Timm Oberwelland & Jean-Francois Fonlupt, W Warchus & David Nicholls (based on the play by Sam Shepard), PH John Toll, ED Pasquale Buba, M Stewart Copeland, PD Amy Ancona, AD Andrew Laws, SD Ellen Brill.

LP Nick Nolte (Vinnie), Jeff Bridges (Carter), Sharon Stone (Rosie), Catherine Keener (Cecilia), Albert Finney (Simms), Shawn Hatosy (Young Vinnie), Liam Waite (Young Carter), Kimberly Williams (Young Rosie).

This somber comedy drama tells (in flashback) the story of three friends, Hatosy, Waite and Williams, who pull a scam at a racetrack that nets them big returns. Racing commissioner Finney gets wise to their scheme, and to silence him they concoct an ugly blackmail plot that costs Finney his career, family and dignity. In the present, the trio, now played, respectively, by Nolte, Bridges and Stone, share

guilty secrets that have haunted their lives and left them with some score-settling and soul-cleansing needs. The cast is terrific and the story, despite some obvious flaws, is first rate.

2644. Simple Men (1992, U.S./U.K., Fine Line Features, 105m, c). D & W Hal Hartley, PH Michael Spiller, ED Steve Hamilton & Hartley, M Hartley, PD Daniel Ouellette, AD Therese DePrez, SD Jeff Hartmann.

LP Robert Burke (Bill McCabe), William Sage (Dennis McCabe), Karen Sillas (Kate), Elina Lowensohn (Elina), Martin Donovan (Martin), Chris Cooke (Vic), Jeffrey Howard (Ned Rifle), John Alexander MacKay (Dad — William McCabe, Sr.).

Two strange brothers, Burke and Sage, set out to find MacKay, their fugitive father, a former Brooklyn Dodgers shortstop who became a bomb-throwing anarchist.

2645. A Simple Plan (1998, Paramount, 121m, c). D Sam Raimi, P James Jacks & Adam Schroeder, W Scott B. Smith† (based on his novel), PH Alar Kivilo, ED Arthur Coburn & Eric L. Beason, M Danny Elfman, PD Patrizia von Brandenstein, AD James F. Truesdale, SD Hilton Rosemarin.

LP Bill Paxton (Hank), Billy Bob Thornton† (Jacob), Brent Briscoe (Lou), Bridget Fonda (Sarah), Jack Walsh (Tom Butler), Chelcie Ross (Carl), Gary Cole (Baxter).

When brothers Paxton and Thornton come across the wreckage of a small plane and a decaying corpse in a deserted field, they decide to keep the $4 million they find in the rubble. Their simple plan gets them caught up in escalating mayhem when they can't keep their mouths shut.

2646. A Simple Twist of Fate (1994, Touchstone–Buena Vista, 106m, c). D Gillies MacKinnon, P Ric Kidney, W Steve Martin (based on the novel *Silas Marner* by George Eliot), PH Andrew Dunn, ED Humphrey Dixon, M Cliff Eidelman, PD Andy Harris, AD Tim Galvin, SD Maria Nay.

LP Steve Martin (Michael McMann), Gabriel Byrne (John Newland), Laura Linney (Nancy Newland), Catherine O'Hara (Mrs. Simon), Stephen Baldwin (Tanny Newland), Byron Jennings (Keating).

Martin stars in and wrote the screenplay for this modern *Silas Marner* story of a man who cuts himself out of his family's life when he discovers the child his wife is carrying isn't his.

2647. *A Simple Wish* (1997, Universal, 90m, c). D Michael Ritchie, P Sid Sheinberg, Bill Shienberg & Jon Sheinberg, W Jeff Rothberg, PH Ralf Bode, ED William Scharf, M Bruce Broughton, PD Stephen Hendrikson, AD Peter Grundy, SD Jaro Dick.

LP Martin Short (Murray), Kathleen Turner (Claudia), Mara Wilson (Anabel Greening), Robert Pastorelli (Oliver Greening), Francis Capra (Charlie Greening), Amanda Plummcr (Boots), Teri Garr (Rena), Ruby Dee (Hortense).

Wilson conjures up a novice "fairy godmother," Short, to help her beloved father achieve his goal of becoming an actor and singer on Broadway. Although Short is quite a comical talent, there isn't enough evidence of it in this film to save it from its terrible script.

2648. *Simply Irresistible* (1999, 20th Century–Fox, 95m, c). D Mark Tarlov, P John Fiedler, Jon Amiel & Joe Caracciolo, Jr., W Judith Roberts, PH Robert Stevens, ED Paul Karasick, M Gil Goldstein, PD John Kafarda & William Barclay, AD Beth Kuhn & Caty Maxey.

LP Sarah Michelle Gellar (Amanda Shelton), Sean Patrick Flanery (Tom Bartlett), Patricia Clarkson (Lois McNally), Dylan Baker (Jonathan Bendel), Christopher Durang (Gene O'Reilly).

This film borrows a bit from *Like Water for Chocolate* but is nowhere near as enjoyable as that film. TV's *Buffy the Vampire-Slayer* Gellar appears as a not very good cook who owns a small Manhattan restaurant. Fairy-godfather-like Durang magically gives her the ability to prepare not only tasteful meals but to spice her food with her emotions. Whatever she feels, those who eat her food feel as well. The one upon whom she most wishes to work her culinary spells is department store executive Flanery.

2649. *Single White Female* (1992, Columbia, 107m, c). D & P Barbet Schroeder, W Dan Roos (based on the novel *SWF Seeks Same* by Jon Lutz), PH Luciano Tovoli, ED Lee Percy, M Howard Shore, PD Milcna Canonero, AD P. Michael Johnston, SD Anne H. Ahrens.

LP Bridget Fonda (Alison Jones), Jennifer Jason Leigh (Hedra Carlson), Steven Weber (Sam Rawson), Peter Friedman (Graham Knox), Stephen Tobolowsky (Mitchell Meyerson), Francs Bay (Elderly Neighbor).

Fonda gets a roommate from hell in the person of Leigh, who wants so very much to be like Fonda. In fact, she plans to become Fonda and take over Fonda's life.

2650. *Singles* (1992, Warner Bros., 99m, c). D & W Cameron Crowe, P Richard Hashimoto & Crowe, PH Ueli Steiger, ED Richard Chew, M Paul Westerberg, PD Stephen J. Lineweaver, AD Mark Haack, SD Clay Griffith.

LP Bridget Fonda (Janet Livermore), Campbell Scott (Steve Dunne), Kyra Sedgwick (Linda Powell), Sheila Kelley (Debbie Hunt), Jim True (David Bailey), Matt Dillon (Cliff Poncier), Bill Pullman (Dr. Jamison), James LeGros (Andy).

A bunch of twentysomethings try to find romance and meaning in their lives in modern-day Seattle. For those who have no idea what is meant by "Generation X," this is the film to see for an explanation.

2651. *Sioux City* (1994, Rix-Ubell Prods., 100m, c). D Lou Diamond Phillips, P Brian Rix & Jane Ubell, W L. Virginia Browne, PH James W. Wrenn, ED Christopher Rouse & Mark Fitzgerald, M Christopher Lindsey, PD Randall Schmook, AD Vicki Roblan, SD Dawn Serry.

LP Lou Diamond Phillips (Jesse Rainfeather Goldman), Ralph Waite (Chief Drew McDermott), Melinda Dillon (Leah Goldman), Salli Richardson (Jolene Buckley), Lise Cutter (Allison).

Raised by Caucasian adoptive parents, Native-American medical student Phillips returns to his birthplace — a Lakota reservation — to investigate the murder of his biological mother. He uses tribal rites to solve the crime.

2652. *Sirens* (1994, Australia/U.K., Miramax, 94m, c). D & W John Duigan, P Sue Milliken, PH Geoff Burton, ED Humphrey Dixon, M Rachel Portman, PD Roger Ford, AD Laurie Faen, SD Kerrie Brown.

LP Hugh Grant (Anthony Campion), Tara Fitzgerald (Estella Campion), Sam Neill (Norman Lindsay), Elle MacPherson (Sheela), Portia De Rossi (Giddy), Kate Fischer (Pru),

Pamela Rabe (Rose Lindsay), Ben Mendelsohn (Lewis).

The time is the 1930s. The place is Australia. Straitlaced young minister Grant is sent to the secluded mountain estate of bohemian artist Neal to take him to task for submitting scandalous works combining religious subjects and sensuous nudes for public exhibitions. Grant and his somewhat sexually repressed wife Fitzgerald are all but seduced by Neill, his wife and his three freethinking models. There is plenty of nudity involving supermodel MacPherson, a woman meant to appear nude — but if you take the time to notice, you will agree that she does a nice acting job to boot.

2653. *Sister Act* (1992, Touchstone–Buena Vista, 96m, c). D Emile Ardolino, P Teri Schwartz, W Paul Rudnick, Eleanor Bergstein, Jim Cash, Jack Epps, Jr., Carrie Fisher, Robert Harling & Nancy Meyers, PH Adam Greenberg, ED Richard Halsey, M Marc Shaiman, PD Jackson DeGovia.

LP Whoopi Goldberg (Deloris), Maggie Smith (Mother Superior), Kathy Najimy (Mary Patrick), Wendy Makkena (Mary Robert), Mary Wickes (Mary Lazarus), Harvey Keitel (Vince LaRocca), Bill Nunn (Eddie Souther), Robert Miranda (Joey), Richard Portnow (Willy), Joseph Maher (Bishop O'Hara).

Lounge singer Goldberg witnesses her gangster boyfriend Keitel ordering a killing, which makes her a target for elimination. Wishing to put her on ice until she can testify against Keitel at his trial, cop Nunn arranges for her to pose as a new nun at a convent. She takes over as new choir director and, with the help of Najimy and Makkena, almost causes mother superior Smith to jump over the wall.

2654. *Sister Act 2: Back in the Habit* (1993, Touchstone–Buena Vista, 109m, c). D Bill Duke, P Dawn Steel & Scott Rudin, W James Orr, Jim Cruickshank & Judi Ann Mason (based on her musical *Knocking on Heaven's Door*), PH Oliver Wood, ED John Carter, Pembroke J. Herring & Stuart Pappe, M Miles Goodman, PD John DeCuir, Jr., AD Louis M. Mann, SD Bruce Gibeson, Lauren Cory & Sandy Getzler.

LP Whoopi Goldberg (Deloris Van Cartier/ Sister Mary Clarence), Kathy Najimy (Sister Mary Patrick), Barnard Hughes (Father Maurice), Mary Wickes (Sister Mary Lazarus), James Coburn (Mr. Crisp), Michael Jeter (Father Ignatius), Wendy Makkena (Sister Mary Robert).

The first film was so successful, a sequel was a no-brainer. Unfortunately, that's just about what it is. Goldberg gets back into the habit and, with the help of Najimy and Makkena, foils mean Coburn's plans to close the nun's decrepit school. Goldberg tutors inner-city kids for an all–State chorale competition. The spirituals almost make the slow-moving first half worthwhile.

2655. *Sister My Sister* (1995, U.K., Seventh Art Releasing, 89m, c). D Nancy Meckler, P Norma Heyman, W Wendy Kesselman (based on her play *My Sister in the House*), PH Ashley Rowe, ED David Stiven, M Stephen Warbeck, PD Caroline Amies, AD Frank Walsh.

LP Julie Walters (Madame Danzard), Joely Richardson (Christine), Jodhi May (Lea), Sophie Thursfield (Isabelle), Amelda Brown (Visitor), Lucita Pope (Visitor).

Based on a real-life crime case, which became the basis for Jean Genet's play *The Maids*, sisters May and Richardson are hired as maids by authoritarian Walters. She rules them and her daughter Thursfield with harsh discipline. It's an intriguing study of sexual repression and class struggle, with a violent climax.

2656. *Six Days, Seven Nights* (1998, Touchstone–Buena Vista, 101m, c). D Ivan Reitman, P Reitman, Wallis Nicita & Roger Birnbaum, W Michael Browning, PH Michael Chapman, ED Sheldon Kahn & Wendy Greene Bricmont, M Randy Edelman, PD J. Michael Riva, AD Richard F. Mays, SD Pamela Klamer & Patricia Klawonn, SD Lauri Gaffin.

LP Harrison Ford (Quinn Harris), Anne Heche (Robin Monroe), David Schwimmer (Frank Martin), Jacqueline Obradors (Angelica), Temuera Morrison (Jager), Allison Janney (Marjorie).

This romantic comedy stars Harrison as a South Pacific cargo pilot who becomes stranded on a desert island with Heche, a neurotic, high-powered New York Magazine editor. Naturally, the two can't stand each other at the beginning, but, according to formula, this will change. There are enough laughs and adventures to make this familiar story work.

2657. *Six Degrees of Separation* (1993, MGM, 102m, c). D Fred Schepisi, P Schepisi & Arnon Milchan, W John Guare (based on his play), PH Ian Baker, ED Peter Honess, M Jerry Goldsmith, PD Patrizia Von Brandenstein, AD Dennis Bradford, SD Gretchen Rau.

LP Stockard Channing† (Ouisa Kittredge), Will Smith (Paul), Donald Sutherland (Flan Kittredge), Ian McKellen (Geoffrey), Mary Beth Hurt (Kitty), Bruce Davison (Larkin), Richard Masur (Dr. Fine), Anthony Michael Hall (Trent Conway), Heather Graham (Elizabeth), Eric Thal (Rick).

Smith is a gay con man who ingratiates himself into the privileged world of gullible wealthy New Yorkers Channing and Sutherland by claiming to be Sidney Poitier's son. This satire turned tragedy is from Guare's acclaimed Broadway play, which was inspired by a true story. Smith gives a fascinating performance, and once again Channing demonstrates what a rare acting talent she possesses.

2658. *The Sixth Man* (1997, Touchstone–Buena Vista, 104m, c). D Randall Miller, P David Hoberman, W Christopher Reed & Cynthia Carle, PH Michael Ozier, ED Eric Sears, M Marcus Miller, PD Michael Bolton, AD Eric Fraser, SD Lin MacDonald.

LP Marlon Wayans (Kenny Tyler), Kadeem Hardison (Antoine Tyler), David Paymer (Coach Pederson), Kevin Dunn (Mikulski), Michael Michele (R.C. St. John), Chris Spencer (Jimmy Stubbs), Vladimir Cuk (Zigi Hrbacek), Travis Ford (Danny O'Grady).

In this sports comedy, Washington University basketball star Hardison suffers a heart attack and dies, leaving his brother Wayans to try to lead the team to the NCAA Final Four. Trouble is, Wayans had always played in the shadow of his older brother and is plagued with self-doubts about his talents. Feeling the pressure of forced leadership, Wayans prays to heaven for some help. He gets it — in the form of the ghost of his brother, whom only he can see.

2659. *The Sixth Sense†* (1999, Buena Vista–Hollywood Pictures, 107m, c). D M. Night Shyamalan, W Shyamalan†, P Frank Marshall†, Kathleen Kennedy† & Barry Mendel†, PH Tak Fujimoto, ED Andrew Mondshein†, M James Newton Howard, PD Larry Fulton, AD Philip Messina, SD Douglas Mowat.

LP Bruce Willis (Malcolm Crowe), Toni Collette† (Lynn Sear), Olivia Williams (Anna Crowe), Haley Joel Osment† (Cole Sear), Donnie Wahlberg (Vincent Gray), Glenn Fitzgerald (Sean).

This paranormal thriller plods along throughout most of the film but redeems itself in its last-minute story twist, requiring members of the audience to admit they didn't see it coming and to reevaluate what they have seen. Director and writer Shyamalan deserves praise for his finely crafted film. Willis is a child psychologist whose home is broken into by his former patient Wahlberg, blaming Willis for not helping him. Wahlberg shoots Willis and then turns the gun on himself. The next fall, a changed Willis is treating eight-year-old Osment, a very bright, troubled lad who finally shares his dreadful secret with Willis. He sees and hears the dead. Osment is a remarkable talent, giving an award-worthy performance that any seasoned actor would be proud of. Willis is excellent, completely under control in his performance, allowing Osment to be the focus of attention — something rare for Bruce, but most appreciated.

2660. *The Skateboard Kid* (1993, New Horizons Corp., 77m, c). D Larry Swerdlove, P Minard Hamilton, W Swerdlove & Gary Stuart Kaplan, PH Don E. Fauntleroy, ED Patrick Rand, M Adam Gorgoni, PD Amy Ancona, SD Michelle Munoz.

LP Timothy Busfield (Frank), Trevor Lissauer (Zack), Bess Armstrong (Maggie), Dom DeLuise (Voice of Rip).

In a predictable story, Lissauer is a skateboard whiz who moves with his father, Busfield, from the city to a small country town. There they meet Armstrong, the mother and wife they'd been missing. On the way they are forced to go to the mat with father and son bad guys.

2661. *Ski Patrol* (1990, Triumph, 91m, c). D Richard Correll, P Phillip B. Goldfine & Donald L. West, W Steven Long Mitchell & Craig W. Van Sickle (based on a story by Mitchell, Van Sickle & Wink Roberts), PH John Stephens, ED Scott Wallace, M Bruce Miller, PD Fred Weiler, AD Steven L. Nielsen, SD Steven A. Lee.

LP Roger Rose (Jerry), Yvette Nipar (Ellen), T.K. Carter (Iceman), Leslie Jordan (Murray),

Paul Feig (Stanley), Sean Gregory Sullivan (Suicide), Corky Timbrook (Lance), Ray Walston (Pops).

In what is billed as a comedy, a group of ski bums land jobs with a fancy resort. The film is filled with lame gags and old slapstick routines.

2662. Skinheads — The Second Coming of Hate (1990, Amazing Movies, 93m, c). D & P Greydon Clark, W Clark & David Reskin, PH Nicholas Von Sternberg, ED Travis Clark, M Dan Slider, AD Doug Abrahamson, SD Chris McCann.

LP Chuck Connors (Mr. Hutson), Barbara Bain (Martha), Jason Culp (Jeff), Brian Brophy (Damon), Elizabeth Sagal (Amy), Bill Kohne (Jeff), Lynna Hopwood (Liz), Gene Michael (Frank).

Some college friends encounter some neo–Nazi skinheads as they are backpacking. There is violence and nudity aplenty, meant to make up for a pitifully poor story and lackluster acting.

2663. Skyscraper (1996, PM Ent. Group, 96m, c). D Raymond Martino, P Richard Pepin & Joseph Merhi, W John Larrabee & William Applegate, Jr., PH Frank Harris, ED Kevin Mock, M Jim Halfpenny, AD Thomas Salvitti.

LP Anna Nicole Smith (Carrie Wink), Richard Steinmetz (Gordon Wink), Branko Cikatic (Zarkor), Charles Huber (Fairfax), Calvin Levels (Hakim), Jonathan Fuller (Jacques).

Smith is a gal who makes Dolly Parton look like Twiggy. But ogling her for 96 minutes is about as arousing as watching the skyscraper where mercenaries hold hostages. Helicopter pilot Smith to the rescue.

2664. Slappy and the Stinkers (1998, TriStar, 78m, c). D Barnet Kellman, P Sid, Bill & Jon Sheinberg, W Bob Wolterstorff & Mike Scott, PH Paul Maibaum, ED Jeff Wishengrad, M Craig Safan, PD Ivo Cristante, AD Ken Larson, SD Michael Claypool.

LP B.D. Wong (Morgan Brinway), Bronson Pinchot (Roy), Jennifer Coolidge (Harriet), Joseph Ashton (Sonny), Gary LeRoi Gray (Domino), Carl Michael Linder (Witz), Scarlett Pomers (Lucy), Travis Tedford (Loaf), Sam McMurray (Broccoli).

The Stinkers are five unruly second graders.

Slappy is an aquarium sea lion whom the kids decide to free while on a field trip. They smuggle the animal back to their school, where the slapstick action mostly takes place. To enjoy the film, one has to be very, very young and easily amused.

2665. Slaves to the Underworld (1997, First Look Pictures, 94m, c). D Kristine Peterson, P Peterson, Bill Cody & Raquel Caballes Maxwell, W Cody, PH Zoran Hochstatter, ED Eric Vizents, M Mike Martt, PD Michael Moran.

LP Molly Gross (Shelly), Marisa Ryan (Suzy), Jason Bortz (Jimmy), Bob Neuwirth (Big Phil), Natacha La Ferriere (Zoe), Claudia Rossi (Brenda), James Garver (Brian), Peter Szumlas (Dale).

Sulky twenty-year-old Gross, a guitar player with a Seattle girl's band, moves out on her male lover. She moves in with Ryan, the radical feminist and lesbian leader of the band. Besides playing their music, with its profane language, the group likes to attack newsstands that sell what they consider pornography against women. It doesn't sit well with Ryan when Gross once again starts seeing her male lover Bortz.

2666. SLC Punk (1999, Sony Pictures Classics, 97m, c). D & W James Merendino, P Sam Maydew & Peter Ward, PH Greg Littlewood, ED Esther P. Russell, M Melanie Miller, PD Charlotte Malmloff.

LP Matthew Lillard (Stevo), Michael Goorjian (Bob), Annabeth Gish (Trish), Jennifer Lien (Sandy), Christopher McDonald (Father), Devon Sawa (Sean).

Blue-haired Lillard and his Mohawk/spiked-haired buddy Goorjian share a trashed apartment and pick fights with "rednecks," hippies and a variety of other types. They get drunk and break things up. They believe they are rebelling against the System.

2667. Sleep with Me (1994, MGM, 86m, c). D Rory Kelly, P Michael Steinberg, Roger Hedden & Eric Stoltz, W Duane Dell'Amico, Hedden, Neal Jiminez, Joe Keenan, Kelly & Steinberg, PH Andrzej Sekula, ED David Moritz, M David Lawrence, PD Randy Eriksen, AD J. Michael Gorman, SD Adam Mead Faletti.

LP Meg Tilly (Sarah), Eric Stoltz (Joseph),

Craig Sheffer (Frank), Parker Posey (Athena), Adrienne Shelly (Pamela), Joey Lauren Adams (Lauren), Amaryllis Borrego (Amy), June Lockhart (Caroline).

Tilly and Stoltz are just about to march down the aisle to wedded bliss when his best friend, Sheffer, decides he wants Tilly for himself. He sets out to seduce her and screw his buddy. When Stoltz sees what's going on he's naturally miffed with Sheffer, but he also lays some blame on Tilly, reasoning that Sheffer wouldn't have made his move if she hadn't been giving him some encouragement. Stoltz also should point the finger of blame towards himself.

2668. Sleepers (1996, Warner Bros., 140m, c). D & W Barry Levinson (based on the novel by Lorenzo Carcaterra), P Steve Golin, PH Michael Ballhaus, ED Stu Linder, M John Williams†, PD Kristi Zea, AD Tim Galvin, SD Beth Rubino.

LP Jason Patric (Lorenzo/"Shakes"), Brad Pitt (Michael), Billy Crudup (Tommy), Ron Eldard (John), Robert De Niro (Father Bobby), Dustin Hoffman (Danny Snyder), Kevin Bacon (Sean Nokes), Vittorio Gassman (King Benny), Minnie Driver (Carol Martinez), Joe Perrino (Young "Shakes"), Brad Renfro (Young Michael), Jonathan Tucker (Young Tommy), Geoff Wigdor (Young John).

There's a lot of talent in this film; but the way the story is presented, it is hard to care about anyone involved, save Hoffman as a washed-up lawyer. Teens Perrino, Renfro, Tucker and Wigdor are sent to a reformatory when their senseless act of mischief results in a man's death. There the boys are brutally and sexually abused by sadistic guards, led by Bacon. Two of the boys grow up to be Crudup and Eldard, psychopathic criminals. They encounter Bacon in a bar and blow him away. The other two lads, now played by Pitt and Patric, try to save them from paying for their crime. They are assisted in one way or another by mobster Gassman and priest De Niro. Minnie Driver provides some pretty scenery but really has nothing much to contribute to the film. Hoffman does a nice job as the seedy but cagey defense lawyer.

2669. The Sleeping Car (1990, Vidmark/Triax, 87m, c). D & P Douglas Curtis, W Greg O'Neill, PH David Lewis, ED Allan Holzman & Betty Cohen, M Ray Colcord, PD Robert Benedict.

LP David Naughton (Jason), Judie Aronson (Kim), Kevin McCarthy (Vincent Tuttle), Jeff Conaway (Bud Sorenson), Dani Minnick (Joanne), John Carl Buechler (Mr. Erickson), Ernestine Mercer (Mrs. Erickson).

An old railroad sleeping car that has been converted into lodging for a group of people is haunted by an angry ghost.

2670. Sleeping with Strangers (1994, Canada, Skouras Pictures, 103m, c). D Richard Boden, P David Gordian, W Joan Carr-Wiggin, PH Les Erskine, ED Dan Rae, M Rick Friend & Robert Smart, PD Gary Myers, SD Eric McNab.

LP Adrienne Shelly (Jennifer Dole), Neil Duncan (Daniel), Kymberley Huffman (Teri), Shawn Alex Thompson (Mark), Scott McNeil (Tod Warren).

In this rowdy bedroom farce, promiscuous movie starlet Shelly arrives in a small village with her entourage and checks into one of the two inns, planting her boyfriend of the moment in another inn. There are mixed-up rooms, mistaken identities and the hovering media to turn things topsy-turvy.

2671. Sleeping with the Enemy (1991, 20th Century–Fox, 99m, c). D Joseph Ruben, P Leonard Goldberg, W Ronald Bass (based on the novel by Nancy Price), PH John W. Lindley, ED George Bowers, M Jerry Goldsmith, PD Doug Kraner, Ad Joseph P. Lucky, SD Lee Poll.

LP Julia Roberts (Laura Burney/Sara Waters), Patrick Bergin (Martin Burney), Kevin Anderson (Ben Woodward), Elizabeth Lawton (Chloe), Kyle Secor (Fleishman), Claudette Nevins (Dr. Rissner).

Beautiful wife Roberts just brings out the beast in her brutal husband Bergin. He knocks her around without much provocation. She decides she can't take it anymore and fakes her death by drowning so she can run away to seek a new life. She changes her name and even attracts the attention of a good man, Anderson, but Bergin belatedly catches on and is soon on her trail. He finds her.

2672. Sleepless in Seattle (1993, TriStar, 100m, c). D Nora Ephron, P Gary Foster, W Jeffrey Arch†, Ephron† & David S. Ward†,

PH Sven Nykvist, ED Robert Reitano, M March Shaiman, PD Jeffrey Townsend, AD Gershon Ginsberg & Charley Beal, SD Clay Griffith, Charles Daboub, Jr., Becky Weidner & Roberta Holinko.

LP Tom Hanks (Sam Baldwin), Meg Ryan (Annie Reed), Bill Pullman (Walter), Rosie O'Donnell (Becky), Rob Reiner (Jay), Rita Wilson (Suzy), Gaby Hoffman (Jessica), Carey Lowell (Maggie Baldwin), Ross Malinger (Jonah Baldwin).

One of the great feel-good films of the '90s, *Sleepless in Seattle* is the story of the trials of getting Hanks and Ryan, who would seem ideal for each other, together. Living in Seattle, lonely widower Hanks' son Malinger calls in to a national talk show and gets dad to speak about his wife. Ryan, who is engaged to nice but not very romantic Pullman, falls for Hanks' voice and dumps Pullman so she can pursue Hanks, whom she is sure is meant to be her soul-mate. The film and the stars take some direction from the 1957 romantic weeper *An Affair to Remember*. Will they or will they not be able to meet at the top of the Empire State Building? What do you think? What makes the film even more special is the score and the songs, sung so winningly by Jimmy Durante.

2673. *Sleepover* (1997, Artistic License Films, 88m, c). D & W John Sullivan, P Jim McNally, PH Joaquin Baca-Asay, ED McNally, M Elliott Goldkind, PD Roshelle Berliner.

LP Karl Giant (Sean), Michael Albanese (Mark), Ken Miles (Ken), Heather Casey (Brooke), Megan Shand (Megan), Shannon Barry (Anne).

This film looks at one day and night in the life of several bored Connecticut teenagers. The characters and the story are clichés.

2674. *Sleepy Hollow* (1999, Paramount, 105m, c). D Tim Burton, P Scott Rudin & Adam Schroeder, W Andrew Kevin Walker, screen story by Kevin Yagher & Walker (based on *The Legend of Sleepy Hollow* by Washington Irving), PH Emmanuel Lubeszki†, ED Chris Lebenzon, M Danny Elfman, PD Rick Heinrichs*, AD Les Tomkins, John Dexter, Ken Court & Andrew Nicholson, SD Peter Young*.

LP Johnny Depp (Ichabod Crane), Christina Ricci (Katrina Van Tassel), Miranda Richardson (Lady Van Tassel/Crone), Michael Gambon (Baltus Van Tassel), Casper Van Dien (Brom Van Brunt), Jeffrey Jones (Rev. Steenwyck), Christopher Lee (Burgomaster), Richard Griffiths (Magistrate Philipse), Ian McDiarmid (Doctor Lancaster), Michael Gough (Notary Hardenbrook), Christopher Walken (Hessian Horseman).

Those who can remember the 1949 Disney film *The Adventures of Ichabod and Mr. Toad* in which Bing Crosby narrated the tale of the Headless Horseman, will certainly find this revision of the Washington Irving story quite a shock. That's not meant as a criticism. This is a deliciously moody and bloody nightmare that will please audiences as it terrorizes them. Depp, as Ichabod Crane, is not a supercilious schoolmaster but rather a New York constable sent to Sleepy Hollow (actually constructed and filmed in England) to investigate a series of beheadings in a Dutch community with a violent past. Everyone insists that the one responsible for the grisly murders is a German mercenary who killed many settlers during the Revolutionary War before being killed himself. Depp, not quite as brave as a tracker of modern-day serial killers should be, relies on "scientific" crime-solving methods and notices that the victims are not quite as random as the townsfolk claim. Depp doesn't believe that some ghost is responsible until he is given firsthand evidence to the contrary. The entire cast are excellent in their performances, complementing a fine bit of work by Depp. Ricci, as audiences have come to expect, grows in stature with each of her films. Some people will be put off by all the gore and rolling heads.

2675. *Sliding Doors* (1999, U.K./U.S., Miramax, 105m, c). D & W Peter Howitt, P William Horberg, Philippa Braithwaite & Sydney Pollack, PH Remi Adefarasin, ED John Smith, M David Hirschfelder, PD Maria Djurkovic, AD John Martyn.

LP Gwyneth Paltrow (Helen), John Hannah (James), John Lynch (Gerry), Jeanne Tripplehorn (Lydia), Zara Turner (Anna), Douglas McFerran (Russell).

Paltrow has the unusual experience of both catching and missing a London subway at the very same moment, allowing her to have two separate experiences. It's an interesting premise, but Paltrow and first-time director Howitt don't make the most of it.

2676. Sling Blade (1996, Miramax, 135m, c). D Billy Bob Thornton, P Brandon Rosser & David L. Bushell, W Billy Bob Thornton† (based on his screenplay *Some Folks Call It a Sling Blade*), PH Barry Markowitz, ED Hughes Winborne, M Daniel Lanois, PD Clark Hunter, SD Traci Kirschbaum.

LP Billy Bob Thornton† (Karl Childers), Dwight Yoakam (Doyle Hargraves), J.T. Walsh (Charles Bushman), John Ritter (Vaughan Cunningham), Lucas Black (Frank Wheatley), Natalie Canerday (Linda Wheatley), James Hampton (Jerry Woolridge), Robert Duvall (Karl's Father).

As a child, Thornton killed his mother and her lover when he caught them going at it. He has spent the ensuing twenty-five years in an asylum. The simpleminded killer is released and returns to his home town, where he is befriended by young Black. Thornton seems to have special skills fixing things and finds a job with a garage. Both Thornton and Black rightly note that Black's mother's (Canerday) latest boyfriend (Yoakam) is a rotter. More tragedy is lurking just around the corner. Besides Thornton, with his appealing demeanor and unusual speaking voice, Ritter gives a fine performance as Canerday's gay employer.

2677. A Slipping Down Life (1999, DVC/ Raddon, 111m, c). D & W Toni Kalem (based on the novel by Anne Tyler), P Richard Raddon, PH Michael Barrow, ED Hughes Winborne, M Peter Himmelman, PD Russ Smith, AD John Frick, SD Sally Nicolaou.

LP Lili Taylor (Evie Decker), Guy Pearce (Drumstrings Casey), John Hawkes (David Elliot), Sara Rue (Violet), Irma P. Hall (Clotelia).

Painfully shy 17-year-old Taylor falls for sullen 19-year-old rock musician Pearce. Her attraction for him soon becomes obsession, and at one performance Taylor carves his name on her forehead. Boy, does that impress Pearce.

2678. Slipstream (1990, M.C.E.G./Virgin, 92m, c). D Steven Lisberger, P Gary Kurtz, W Tony Kayden, Charles Pogue & Lisberger (based on a story by Bill Bauer), PH Frank Tidy, ED Terry Rawlings, M Elmer Bernstein, PD Andrew McAlpine, AD Malcolm Stone.

LP Mark Hamill (Tasker), Kitty Aldridge (Belitski), Bill Paxton (Matt Owen), Tony Allen (Bartender), Susan Leong (Abigail), Rita Wolf (Maya), Bob Peck (Byron), F. Murray Abraham (Cornelius), Ben Kingsley (Avatar).

Hamill, a futuristic cop, tracks Paxton, a bounty hunter gone mad, to a damaged Earthscape. There the inhabitants seek to escape from a dangerous river of wind, a slipstream.

2679. Sliver (1993, Paramount, 106m, c). D Phillip Noyce, P Robert Evans, W Joe Eszterhas (based on the novel by Ira Levin), PH Vilmos Zsigmond, Michael A. Benson & Laszlo Kovacs, ED Richard Francis-Bruce & William Hoy, M Howard Shore, PD Paul Sylbert, AD Peter Lansdown Smith & Christopher Nowak, SD Lisa Fischer, Walter P. Martishius, Antoinette Gordon, K.C. Fox, Leslie Pope & Marion Kolsby.

LP Sharon Stone (Carly Norris), William Baldwin (Zeke Hawkins), Tom Berenger (Jack Lansford), Polly Walker (Vida), Colleen Camp (Judy), Amanda Foreman (Samantha), Martin Landau (Alex), CCH Pounder (Lt. Victoria Hendrix), Nina Foch (Mrs. McEvoy).

Who is going to believe that a sharp chick like Stone is going to find a personality-minus lump like Baldwin appealing? Would she really honor his request that she slip off the panties he has sent her and place them on the plate in front of her at a busy and expensive restaurant? Well, that aside, who's going to take seriously a story about Baldwin as the owner of a thin Manhattan apartment building (the sliver of the title), which he has designed so that he can indulge his voyeuristic urges by watching a bank of television screens, each one giving him a view of a room of one of his tenants? Did we mention that someone in the building is a murderer?

2680. Slums of Beverly Hills (1998, Fox Searchlight, 90m, c). D & W Tamara Jenkins, P Michael Nozik & Stan Wlodkowski, PH Tom Richmond, ED Pamela Martin, M Rolfe Kent, PD Dena Roth, AD Scott Plauche, SD Robert Greenfield.

LP Natasha Lyonne (Vivian), Alan Arkin (Murray), Marisa Tomei (Rita), Kevin Corrigan (Eliot), Eli Marienthal (Rickey), David Krumholtz (Ben), Jessica Walter (Doris), Carl Reiner (Mickey), Rita Moreno (Belle).

Set in 1976, the film is a bawdy situation comedy about a neurotic Jewish family. The story is narrated by newcomer Lyonne, and mostly deals with her coming of age at a time when her divorced father Arkin is willing to sacrifice anything to ensure that his three children can continue attending school in the Beverly Hills school district. The details of Lyonne's sexual awakening is raunchy and at times gross.

2681. Small Faces (1996, U.K., October Films, 109m, c). D Gillies MacKinnon, P Billy MacKinnon & Steve Clark-Hall, W G & B MacKinnon, PH John de Borman, ED Scott Thomas, M John Zeane, PD Zack MacLeod, AD Pat Campbell.

LP Iain Robertson (Lex MacLean), Joseph McFadden (Alan MacLean), J.S. Duffy (Bobby MacLean), Laura Fraser (Joanne MacGowan), Garry Sweeney (Charlie Sloan), Claire Higgins (Lorna MacLean).

In 1968, three Glasgow youths become embroiled in the war between teen gangs. The story might be more interesting if one could make out what was being said with those thick Scottish accents.

2682. Small Kill (1993, Rayfield Co. II, 87m, c). D Rob Fresco, P Tom Foster & Fred Carpenter, W Carpenter & James McTernan, PH Gerard Hughes, ED Suzanne Pillsbury, M Mark Leggett, AD Jack Parente.

LP Gary Burghoff (Fleck/Lady Esmeralda), Jason Miller (Mikie), Fred Carpenter (Armand Conti), Donni Kehr (Mary Bannon), Rebecca Ferratti (Dianna Conti).

For those wondering whatever happened to *M*A*S*H*'s "Radar," here he is playing a psycho who kidnaps children and sells them back to their parents.

2683. Small Soldiers (1998, Universal–DreamWorks SKG, 105m, c). D Joe Dante, P Michael Finnell & Colin Wilson, W Gavin Scott, Adam Rifkin, Ted Elliott & Terry Rossio, PH Jamie Anderson, ED Marshall Harvey, M Jerry Goldsmith, PD William Sandell, AD Mark W. Mansbridge & Bradford Ricker, SD Rosemary Brandenburg, ANIM David Andrews & Stefen Fangmeier.

LP Denis Leary (Gil Mars), Kirsten Dunst (Christy Fimple), Gregory Smith (Alan Abernathy), Ann Magnuson (Irene Abernathy), Phil Hartman (Phil Fimple).

Voices: Tommy Lee Jones (Chip Hazard), Frank Langella (Archer), Ernest Borgnine (Kip Killagin), Jim Brown (Butch Meathook), Bruce Dern (Link Static), George Kennedy (Brick Bazooka), Clint Walker (Nick Nitro), Sarah Michelle Geller (Gwendy Doll), Christina Ricci (Gwendy Doll).

In a story similar to Dante's *Gremlins*, a group of destructive little invaders are brought to life by computer chips intended for military applications. The "Commandos," led by Chip Hazard (voice of Tommy Lee Jones), are programmed to seek out and destroy the "Gorgonites," led by the gentle Langella. Teen Smith must find a way to stop the brutal small soldiers from completely devastating his suburban neighborhood. The behavior of these little grunts is probably too violent for small kids.

2684. Small Time (1991, Panorama Ent. Corp., 88m, c). D, P & W Norman Loftis, PH Michael C. Miller, ED Victor Kanefsky & March Cohen, M Arnold Bieber, PD Nancy Evangelista.

LP Richard Barboza (Vince Williams), Carolyn Kinebrew (Vicki), Scott Ferguson (Mike), Keith Allen (Peppy), Robert F. Amico (Lt. Gallaway).

Barboza knows nothing but abuse and indifference in his Harlem neighborhood. This and peer pressure lead him to a criminal life as a thief, and eventually to a fatal crime.

2685. A Smile Like Yours (1997, Paramount, 99m, c). D Keith Samples, P David Kirkpatrick & Tony Amatullo, W Kevin Meyer & Samples, PH Richard Bowen, ED Wayne Wahrman, M William Ross, PD Gareth Stover, AD Chris Cornwell, SD Larry Dias.

LP Greg Kinnear (Danny Robertson), Lauren Holly (Jennifer Robertson), Joan Cusack (Nancy Tellen), Jay Thomas (Steve Harris), Jill Hennessy (Lindsay Hamilton), Christopher McDonald (Richard Halstrom), Donald Moffatt (Dr. Felber), France Nuyen (Dr. Chin).

Thanks to an aphrodisiac she has developed, Holly and Kinnear's sex life is excellent. But the young couple are having trouble conceiving a baby. Friend Cusack offers Holly a series of conception tricks, which we supposed were meant to be comical, but the gags seem trite.

2686. Smoke (1995, Miramax–Smoke Prods, 112m, b&w/c). D Wayne Wang, P Greg Johnson, Peter Newman, Hisami Kuriowa & Kenzo Horikoshi, W Paul Auster (based on his story "Auggie Wren's Christmas Story"), PH Adam Holender, ED Maisie Hoy, M Rachel Portman PD Kalina Ivanov, AD Jeff McDonald, SD Karin Wiesel.

LP Harvey Keitel (Auggie Wren), William Hurt (Paul Benjamin), Harold Perrineau, Jr. (Thomas "Rashid" Cole), Forest Whitaker (Cyrus Cole), Stockard Channing (Ruby McNutt), Victor Argo (Vinnie), Erica Gimpel (Doreen Cole), Clarice Taylor (Ethel), Ashley Judd (Felicity), Michelle Hurst (Aunt Em).

Not everyone will warm to this slice-of-life story of a Brooklyn smoke shop, its manager Keitel and an odd assortment of people from the neighborhood and beyond who drop in at the store from time to time. Yet for some, it offers further proof (if further proof is needed), of what a rare talent is Keitel. Be prepared to be moved, perhaps to tears, by the Christmas story Keitel tells writer Hurt at the end of the film. Under no circumstances should you miss the final credits of the movie.

2687. Smoke Signals (1998, Miramax, 89m, c). D Chris Eyre, P Larry Estes & Scott Rosenfelt, W Sherman Alexie (based on stories from his book *The Lone Ranger and Tonto Fistfight in Heaven*), PH Brian Capener, ED Brian Berdan, M B.C. Smith, PD Charles Armstrong, AD Jonathan Saturen, SD Dawn Ferry.

LP Adam Beach (Victor Joseph), Evan Adams (Thomas Builds-the-Fire), Gary Farmer (Arnold Joseph), Tantoo Cardinal (Arlene Joseph), Irene Bedard (Suzy Song), Cody Lightning (Young Victor Joseph), Simon Baker (Young Builds-the-Fire).

When news arrives at his Idaho reservation that his father Farmer, who abandoned his family years earlier, has died, Beach and his friend Adams decide to travel to Arizona to get the dead man's ashes. Along the way, the two talk a great deal and come to some sort of understanding about life and each other.

2688. Snake Eyes (1998, Paramount, 91m, c). D & P Brian De Palma, W David Koepp & De Palma, PH Stephen H. Burum, ED Bill Pankow, M Ryuichi Sakamoto, PD Anne Pritchard, AD James Fox, Isabelle Guay & Real Proulx, SD Daniel Carpenter.

LP Nicolas Cage (Rick Santoro), Gary Sinise (Kevin Dunne), Carla Gugino (Julia Costello), Kevin Dunn (Lou Logan), Joel Fabiani (Charles

Kirkland), Luis Guzman (Cyrus), John Heard (Gilbert Powell).

Corrupt Atlantic City detective Cage is on hand to help with security at an internationally televised boxing match where the U.S. Secretary of Defense is gunned down. Cage smells a conspiracy, and the rest of the film deals with how he goes about investigating it. Cage once again gives an over-the-top performance, but the film is likeable.

2689. The Snapper (1993, U.K., Miramax, 94m, c). D Stephen Frears, P Lynda Myles, W Roddy Doyle (based on his novel), PH Oliver Stapleton, ED Mick Audsley, PD Mark Geraghty.

LP Tina Kellegher (Sharon), Colm Meaney (Dessie), Ruth McCabe (Kay), Colin O'Byrne (Darren), Eanna Macliam (Craig), Ciara Duffy (Kimberley), Joanne Gerrard (Lisa), Peter Rowen (Sonny), Fionnula Murphy (Jackie), Pat Laffan (George Burgess).

Twenty-year-old Dublin miss Kellegher finds herself pregnant and refuses to name the father. Her family and friends rally until they discover the man's identity. The acting honors go to Meaney, who portrays Kellegher's father. He looks forward to becoming a Grandad, even though he's not too keen on being a dad.

2690. Sneakers (1992, Universal, 125m, c). D Phil Alden Robinson, P Walter F. Parkes & Lawrence Lasker, W Robinson, Lasker & Parkes, PH John Lindley, ED Tom Rolf, M James Horner & Branford Marsalis, PD Patrizia Von Brandenstein, AD Diane Wager, SD Samara Schaffer.

LP Robert Redford (Martin Bishop), Sidney Poitier (Crease), Dan Aykroyd (Mother), David Strathairn (Whistler), River Phoenix (Carl Arbogast), Mary McDonnell (Liz), Timothy Busfield (Dick Gordon), Ben Kingsley (Cosmo), Stephen Tobolowsky (Dr. Werner), Eddie Jones (Buddy Wallace), Donal Logue (Dr. Gunter Janek).

In a film where nothing is as it seems, a team of computer hackers, led by security expert Redford, is forced by government agents to steal a "black box" containing vital security secrets from one of his former clients. The film is quite suspenseful and moves along sharply.

2691. Sniper (1993, TriStar, 99m, c). D Luis Llosa, P Robert L. Rosen, W Michael

Frost Beckner & Crash Leyland, PH Bill Butler, ED Scott Smith, M Gary Chang, PD Herbert Pinter, AD Nicholas McCallum, SD Leanne Cornish & Angus Tattle.

LP Tom Berenger (Thomas Beckett), Billy Zane (Richard Miller), J.T. Walsh (Chester Van Damme), Aden Young (Doug Papich), Ken Radley (El Cirujano).

Berenger is a paid assassin who enjoys his work but operates by a code of honor; no innocents are to be hurt. He is teamed with neophyte killer Zane. They are sent to a Panamanian jungle to eliminate Radley, a politician planning a coup.

2692. Snow Days (1999, Marcus Bros. Prod., 90m, c). D Adam Marcus, P & W Kipp Marcus, PH Ben Weinstein, ED Joe Klotz, M Sean McCourt, PD Melissa Schrock.

LP Kipp Marcus (James Ellis), Alice Dylan (Sarah Milson), Bernadette Peters (Elise Ellis), Henry Simmons (Mitch Jennings), Miriam Shor (Beth).

After his parents split up, Marcus' mother, Peters, goes through a succession of suitors (which he calls the International House of Boyfriends). Marcus meets Dylan one magical snowy day and their lives will be forever intertwined.

2693. Snow Falling on Cedars (1999, Universal, 126m, c). D Scott Hicks, P Kathleen Kennedy, Frank Marshall, Ufland Bass, Carol Baum & Lloyd A. Silverman, W Ron Bass & Hicks (based on the novel by David Guterson), PH Robert Richardson†, ED Hank Corwin, M James Newton Howard, PD Jeannine Oppewall, AD Bill Arnold.

LP Ethan Hawke (Ishmael Chambers), James Cromwell (Judge Fielding), Richard Jenkins (Sheriff Art Moran), James Rebhorn (Alvin Hooks), Sam Shepard (Arthur Chambers), Eric Thal (Carl Heine, Jr.), Max von Sydow (Nels Gudmundsson).

Set in the Pacific Northwest of the 1950s, the film tells the story of small-town newspaperman Hawke, who looks into the case of a young Japanese-American accused of murdering a local fisherman. The film brings the audience up to speed through a series of flashbacks, as it examines the themes of prejudice and racial inequity shortly after WWII. For all its good intentions, the film is ultimately rather dull. The photography is the star of the show.

2694. Snowboard Academy (1997, Columbia, 89m, c). D John Shepphird, P Rudy Rupak, W Rupak & James Salisko, PH Bruno Philip, ED Richard Comeau, M Ross Vanelli, PD Patrice Vermette.

LP Corey Haim (Chris Barry), Jim Varney (Rudy James), Brigitte Nielsen (Mimi), Joe Flaherty (Mr. Barry), Andreas Apergis (Red Eagle), Daniela Akerblom (Jessica).

This film has a cast of actors as one-dimensional as their characters. It's the downhill drama of what happens when a bunch of snowboarding punks takes to the ski slopes and endanger the regular customers.

2695. So I Married an Axe Murderer (1993, TriStar, 110m, c). D Thomas Schlamme, P Robert K. Fried & Cary Woods, W Robbie Fox, Mike Myers & Neil Mullarkey (based on the story by Fox), PH Julio Macat, ED Richard Halsey & Colleen Halsey, M Bruce Broughton, PD John Graysmark, AD Michael Rizzo, SD Jim Poynter, Peg Cummings & Barbara Mesney.

LP Mike Myers (Charlie Mackenzie/Stuart Mackenzie), Nancy Travis (Harriet Michaels), Anthony LaPaglia (Tony Giardino), Amanda Plummer (Rose Michaels), Brenda Fricker (Mary Mackenzie), Matt Doherty (Heed).

Hip bookstore owner and beat poet Myers falls for and marries butcher's assistant Travis. He comes to believe that she's a serial killer, with her beloved husband as her next intended victim. The film has some laughs for those who are amused by Myers and his various impersonations.

2696. Soapdish (1991, Paramount, 100m, c). D Michael Hoffman, P Alan Greisman & Aaron Spelling, W Robert Harling & Andrew Bergman (based on a story by Harling), PH Ueli Steiger, ED Garth Craven, M Alan Silvestri, PD Eugenio Zanetti, AD Jim Dultz, SD Lee Poll.

LP Sally Field (Celeste Talbert), Cathy Moriarty (Montana Moorehead), Teri Hatcher (Ariel Maloney), Robert Downey, Jr. (David Barnes), Paul Johansson (Bolt Brennan), Elisabeth Shue (Lori Craven), Whoopi Goldberg (Rose Schwartz), Kevin Kline (Jeffrey Anderson), Kathy Najimy (Tawny Miller), Carrie Fisher (Betsy Faye), Garry Marshall (Edmund Edwards).

Field is the longtime star of a long-running

TV soap opera. Others in the cast, most notably Moriarty, would like to see Field have a final tragedy (real or imaginary) and be bounced from the show. Sex-crazed producer Downey tries to do what he can to help Moriarty have her way by hiring both Field's former lover Kline as her new co-star and her daughter Shue, of whom Kline may be the father, to vie for airtime with Field. The film is too disjointed to be really fun, but it has its moments.

2697. *Sodbusters* (1994, Canada, Atlantis Films, 98m, c). D Eugene Levy, P Brian Parker, W Levy & John Hemphill, PH Ray Brounstein, ED Bill Goddard, M Lou Natale, AD Tim Bider, SD Ian Grieg.

LP Kris Kristofferson (Destiny), John Vernon (Slade Cantrell), Fred Willard (Clarence Gentry), Wendel Meldrum (Lilac Gentry), Steve Landesberg (Gunther Schteuppin), Max Gail (Tom Partridge), Cody Jones (Joe Gentry, Jr.).

What would you think about making a parody of the movie *Shane*, say, with Kristofferson as a maimed gunfighter who rides into a small Colorado community and sides with the farmers against a greedy railroad tycoon? Don't think much of it, eh? Better hurry and Tell Eugene Levy before he makes it.

2698. *The Soft Kill* (1994, Triboro Ent. Group, 92m, c). D Eli Cohen, P Ehud Bleiberg, Yitzhak Ginsberg & Larry Ratner, W Alex Kustanovich & Michele Noble (based on a story by Ginsberg & Kustanovich), PH Nancy Schreiber, ED Barry Zetlin, M William Goldstein, PD Elisabeth Scott.

LP Michael Harris (Jack Ramsey), Brion James (Ben McCarthy), Carrie-Anne Moss (Jane Turner), Matt McCoy (Vinnie Lupino), Corbin Bernsen (Martin Lewis), Kim Morgan Greene (Kimberly Lewis).

Shortly after private eye Harris beds Greene, the wife of district attorney Bernsen, she is found strangled to death — and Harris finds himself the number one suspect.

2699. *Soldier* (1998, U.S./U.K., Warner Bros., 96m, c). D Paul Anderson, P Jerry Weintraub, W David Webb Peoples, PH David Tattersall, ED Martin Hunter, PD David L. Snyder, AD Tom Valentine, SD Kate Sullivan.

LP Kurt Russell (Sgt. Todd), Jason Scott Lee (Caine 607), Connie Nielsen (Sandra), Gary Busey (Captain Church), Michael Chiklis (Jimmy Pig), Jason Isaacs (Col. Mekum).

In 2036, old-fashioned soldier Russell is pitted against genetically engineered Lee, who is bigger, faster and stronger. It's a piece of cake for Russell when he returns from exile as a guerila fighter.

2700. *A Soldier's Daughter Never Cries* (1998, October Films, 120m, c). D James Ivory, P Ismail Merchant, W Ivory & Ruth Prawer Jhabvala (based on the novel by Kaylie Jones), PH Jean-Marc Fabre, ED Noelle Boisson, M Richard Robbins, PD Jacques Bufnoir & Pat Garner.

LP Kris Kristofferson (Bill Willis), Barbara Hershey (Marcella Willis), Leelee Sobieski (Channe Willis), Jesse Bradford (Billy Willis), Jane Birkin (Mrs. Fortescue), Dominique Blanc (Candida), Luisa Conlon (Young Channe), Anthony Roth Costanzo (Francis Fortescue), Samuel Gruen (Benoit/Young Billy).

Based on the novel by Kaylie Jones, the daughter of James Jones (the author of *From Here to Eternity*), this is the story of a functioning family. Kristofferson and his wife Hershey adopt a six-year-old French boy, Gruen, who doesn't get along with Conlon, the couple's birth child. Later the two children grow into Bradford and Sobieski, respectively. When they move from France back to the U.S., both children have difficulty adjusting. Bradford is teased for his accent and withdraws into himself. Sobieski experiments with several different sexual partners. It's a sensitive coming of age film, with Kristofferson giving his best performance.

2701. *A Soldier's Sweetheart* (1998, Paramount, 112m, c). D & W Thomas Michael Donnelly (based on the short story "Sweetheart of the Song Tra Bong" by Tim O'Brien), P William S. Gilmore, PH Jacek Laskus, ED Anthony Sherin, M Gary Chang, PD Doug Kraner, AD Ralph Davies.

LP Kiefer Sutherland (Rat), Georgina Cates (Marianne), Skeet Ulrich (Fossie), Daniel London (Eddie), Louis Vanaria (Boobie D).

Set on a hillside in Vietnam, this film has army medic Ulrich putting the black market in motion to hire a hooker to service himself and his buddies. Surprise! Surprise! Who should show up but innocent teenager Cates, who just happens to be Ulrich's hometown girlfriend. Her presence at the blood-spattered field hospital changes her and the men around her.

2702. A Soldier's Tale (1992, New Zealand, Mirage Ent., 99m, c). D & P Larry Parr, W Parr & Grant Hinden Miller (based on the novel by M.K. Joseph), PH Alun Bollinger, ED Michael Horton, M John Charles, PD Ivan Maussion, AD Reston Griffiths.

LP Gabriel Byrne (Saul Scourby), Marianne Basler (Belle), Paul Wyett (Charlie), Judge Reinhold (The Yank).

During WWII British soldier Byrne has an affair with French woman Basler, who is accused by the French Resistance of collaborating with the Germans.

2703. Solitaire for Two (1996, U.K., Dove Intl./Cavalier Features, 105m, c). D & W Gary Sinyor, P Sinyor & Richard Holmes, PH Henry Braham, ED Ewa J. Ling, M David A. Hughes, PD Carmel Collins, AD Tim Ellis, SD John Hand.

LP Mark Frankel (Daniel Becker), Amanda Pays (Katie Burrill), Roshan Seth (Sandip Tamar), Jason Isaacs (Harry), Maryam d'Abo (Caroline).

Philandering professor Frankel falls for paleontologist Pays. Trouble is, she is able to read minds. Her unsolicited pronouncements about what Frankel and his friends are thinking aren't appreciated.

2704. Solo (1996, U.S./Mexico, Triumph Releasing, 93m, c). D Norberto Barba, P John Flock & Joseph Newton Cohen, W David Corley (based on the novel *Weapon* by Robert Mason), PH Christopher Walling, ED Scott Conrad, M Christopher Franke, PD Markus Canter, AD Jose Luis Aguilar, SD Jorge Lara Sanchez.

LP Mario Van Peebles (Solo), Barry Corbin (General Clyde Haynes), William Sadler (Colonel Madden), Jaime Gomez (Lorenzo), Damian Bechir (Rio), Seidy Lopez (Agela).

African American android Van Peebles is just what the government ordered — until he develops feelings. No problem, a little adjustment to his microchips and he'll be as right as rain. But he doesn't want to change, so he flees to South America and becomes a hero to the local peasants who are being harassed by armed rebels.

2705. Some Mother's Son (1996, Ireland/ U.S./U.K., Castle Rock–Columbia, 112m, c). D Terry George, P Jim Sheridan, Arthur Lappin & Ed Burke, W George & Sheridan, PH Geoffrey Simpson, ED Craig McKay, M Bill Whelan, PD David Wilson, AD Conor Devlin, SD Carolyn Scott.

LP Helen Mirren (Kathleen Quigley), Aidan Gillen (Gerald Quigley), Fionnula Flanagan (Annie Higgins), David O'Hara (Frank Higgins), John Lynch (Bobby Sands), Tim Woodward (Harrington).

Set during the 217-day hunger strike by 10 imprisoned IRA members, including leader Bobby Sands, this film examines the human drama and tragedy from the viewpoint of two mothers. Both Mirren and Flanagan's sons join the hunger strike, refuse to wear prison uniforms and prepare to die for their convictions. As the two men get closer to death, will their mothers allow them to die or save them against their wishes?

2706. Someone to Love (1994, October Films, 103m, c). D Alexandre Rockwell, P Lila Cazes, W Sergei Bodrov & Rockwell, PH Robert Yeoman, ED Elena Maganini, M Mader & Tito Larriva, PD J. Rae Fox, AD Eric Polczwartek, SD Michelle Munroz.

LP Rosie Perez (Mercedes), Michael DeLorenzo (Ernesto), Harvey Keitel (Harry), Anthony Quinn (Emilio), Steve Buscemi (Mickey), Stanley Tucci (George).

Taxi dancer Perez has her heart set on becoming a Hollywood star. Young laborer DeLorenzo falls for her and will do anything for her. She is already the mistress of ex–movie actor Keitel. When she needs money to go to New York to further her ambitions, DeLorenzo becomes a hitman for crime boss Quinn to get her the dough. It costs him his life.

2707. Something to Believe In (1998, U.K./Germany, Warner Bros., 112m, c). D & P John Hough, W John Goldsmith, PH Tony Pierce Roberts, ED Peter Tanner, M Lalo Schifrin, PD Nello Giorgetti.

LP William McNamara (Mike), Maria Pitillo (Maggie), Tom Conti (Monsignore Calogero), Maria Schneider (Maria), Ian Bannen (Don Pozzi), Robert Wagner (Brad).

Las Vegas croupier Pitillo travels to Italy hoping that a weeping statue of the Madonna will save her from lymphoma and a life expectancy of only a few weeks. Young American pianist and composer McNamara picks up hitchhiking Pitillo and takes her to Trevino, where the claims about the statue are being investigated by Conti, a representative from the Vatican. It's an old-fashioned tearjerker.

2708. _Something to Talk About_ (1995, Warner Bros., 106m, c). D Lasse Hallstrom, P Anthea Sylbert & Paula Weinstein, W Callie Khouri, PH Sven Nykvist, ED Mia Goldman, M Hans Zimmer & Graham Preskett, PD Mel Bourne, SD Roberta Holinko.

LP Julia Roberts (Grace), Dennis Quaid (Eddie), Robert Duvall (Wyly King), Gena Rowlands (Georgia King), Kyra Sedgwick (Emma Rae), Brett Cullen (Jamie Johnson), Haley Aull (Caroline), Muse Watson (Hank Corrigan).

When Roberts learns that her charming husband Quaid has been finding love in all the wrong places, she packs up their daughter and goes home to her overbearing father Duvall and long-suffering mother Rowlands. Quaid is determined to win back his family. It's an all-too-familiar story, but the leads handle it rather well.

2709. _Somewhere in the City_ (1998, Artistic License Films, 93m, c). D Ramin Niami, P Niami & Karen Robson, W Patricia Dillon & Niami, PH Igor Sunara, ED Elizabeth Gazzara & Niami, M John Cole, PD Lisa Albin.

LP Sandra Bernhard (Betty), Ornella Muti (Marta), Robert John Burke (Frankie), Peter Stormare (Graham), Bai Ling (Lu Lu), Paul Anthony Stewart (Che), Bulle Ogier (Brigitte).

This comedy-romance is a mixed bag. It examines the lives of a number of tenants of a building in New York's Lower East Side. The best work is done by Bernhard as a bitter therapist and Stormare as a frustrated acting teacher.

2710. _Sommersby_ (1993, Warner Bros., 112m, c). D Jon Amiel, P Arnon Milchan & Steve Reuther, W Nicholas Meyer & Sarah Kernochan (based on the story by Meyer & Anthony Shaffer, and the screenplay for _Le Retour de Martin Guerre_ by Daniel Vigne & Jean-Claude Carriere), PH Philippe Rousselot, ED Peter Boyle, M Danny Elfman, PD Bruno Rubeo, AD P. Michael Johnston, SD Michael Seirton & Marco Rubeo.

LP Richard Gere (Jack), Jodie Foster (Laurel), Lanny Flaherty (Buck), Wendell Wellman (Travis), Bill Pullman (Orin), Brett Kelley (Little Rob), William Windom (Reverend Powell), Clarice Taylor (Esther), James Earl Jones (Judge Issacs).

The French film _The Return of Martin Guerre_ is transformed from 16th century France to the post–Civil War South. Gere portrays a returning soldier who is welcomed home and into the bed of his wife Foster. But is he the same man who went away to war? No, we mean is he the same man? Whomever he is, he's in a no-win situation. After leading his village to agriculture and economic recovery he is accused of having murdered a man, who may be his true identity.

2711. _Son-In-Law_ (1993, Hollywood Pictures–Buena Vista, 95m, c). D Steve Rash, P Michael Rotenberg & Peter M. Lenkov, W Patrick J. Clifton, Susan McMartin, Shawn Schepps, Kathy Cohen, Neil Cohen, Fox Bahr & Adam Small (based on a story by McMartin & Peter M. Lenkov), PH Peter Deming & Michael Sajbel, ED Dennis M. Hill, M Richard Gibbs PD Joseph T. Garrity, AD Pat Tagliaferro, SD Barry Chusid & Dena Roth.

LP Pauly Shore (Crawl), Carla Gugino (Rebecca), Lane Smith (Walter Warner), Cindy Pickett (Connie Warner), Mason Adams (Walter, Sr.), Patrick Renna (Zack), Dennis Burkley (Theo).

Hoping to derail the plans of a local beau to pop the question, college cutie Gugino springs campus goof-off Shore on her conservative parents during the Thanksgiving holiday, passing him off as her intended. It's typical Shore stuff but not quite up to the standards of the humor on TV's _Hee Haw_.

2712. _Sonny Boy_ (1990, Trans World/Triumph, 98m, c). D Robert Martin Carroll, P Ovidio G. Assonitis & Peter Shepherd, W Graham Whiffler, PH Roberto D'Ettore Piazzoli, ED Claudio Cutry, M Claudio Mario Cordio, PD Mario Molli.

LP David Carradine (Pearl), Paul L. Smith (Slue), Brad Dourif (Weasel), Conrad Janis (Dr. Bender), Sydney Lassick (Charlie), Savina Gersak (Sandy), Alexandra Powers (Rose), Michael Griffin (Sonny Boy).

Carradine appears in drag throughout this movie. No good trying to hide yourself,

David, we recognize you anyway. Even your dad John, who seemed, late in his career, to accept any stupid role in any rotten film, would have passed on this mess. For the record, Carradine is the mother of a horrid and horrible family that terrorizes a small desert town. He-she and her husband Dourif kidnap Griffin to raise as their own little monster.

2713. Soul Food (1997, 20th Century–Fox, 114m, c). D & W George Tillman, Jr., P Tracey E. Edmonds & Robert Teitel, PH Paul Elliott, ED John Carter, M Wendy Melvoin & Lisa Coleman, PD Maxine Shepard, AD Cydney Harris, SD Joe Bristol.

LP Vanessa Williams (Teri Joseph), Vivica A. Fox (Maxine Joseph), Nia Long (Bird Joseph), Michael Beach (Miles), Mekhi Phifer (Lem), Jeffrey D. Sams (Kenneth — "Kenny"), Irma P. Hall (Mother Joe), Carl Wright (Reverend Williams), Gina Ravera (Faith).

The only thing keeping her family together are the Sunday dinners Hall prepares. When her leg amputation leads to a stroke, her three daughters, Williams, Fox and Long, feud more than usual. The film has plenty of food and plenty of family values, both appetizingly presented.

2714. The Sound of One Hand Clapping (1998, Australia, Palace Films, 93m, c). D & W Richard Flanagan (based on his novel), P Rolf De Heer, PH Martin McGrath, ED John Scott & Tania Nehme, M Cezary Skubiszewski, PD Bryce Perrin, AD John Wrigglesworth.

LP Kerry Fox (Sonja Buloh), Rosie Flanagan (Sonja, age eight), Kristof Kaczmarek (Bojan Buloh), Evelyn Krape (Jenja), Melita Jurisic (Maria Buloh).

This film is a somber drama about the difficulties faced by Central European refugees in Australia.

2715. Sour Grapes (1998, Castle Rock–Sony Pictures, 91m, c). D & W Larry David, P Laurie Lennard, PH Victor Hammer, ED Priscilla Nedd-Friendly, PD Charles Rosen, AD Chas. Butler, SD Anne D. McCulley.

LP Steven Weber (Evan Maxwell), Craig Bierko (Richie Maxwell), Matt Keeslar (Danny Pepper), Karen Sillas (Joan), Robyn Peterman (Roberta), Viola Harris (Selma Maxwell).

Down to their last coins in the gambling casinos of Atlantic City, Bierko gets two coins from his cousin Weber for one last pull on the slot machine. He hits a jackpot of $400,000. Weber believes he deserves to share the fortune since it was his coins with which it was won. Bierko doesn't quite see it that way.

2716. South Beach (1993, Prism Ent., 93m, c). D Fred Williamson, P Krishna Shah & Williamson, W Michael Montgomery, PH Carlos Gonzalez, ED Doug Bryan, PD Charlie Jason.

LP Fred Williamson (Mack Derringer), Gary Busey (Lenny), Peter Fonda (Jake), Robert Forster (Detective Ted Coleman), Vanity (Jennifer), Sam J. Jones (Billy), Henry Silva (Santiago).

Has-been football players and wannabee private eyes Williamson and Busey accept an assignment from the gorgeous Vanity. The film shows some of the seamier sites in Miami, but not much happens.

2717. South Central (1992, Warner Bros., 99m, c). D & W Steve Anderson (based on the novel *Crips* by Donald Bakeer), P Janet Yang & William B. Steakley, PH Charlie Lieberman, ED Steve Nevius, M Tim Truman, PD David Brian Miller & Marina Kieser, AD Andrew D. Brothers, SD Caroline Stover.

LP Glenn Plummer (Bobby Johnson), Carl Lumbly (Ali), Byron Keith Minns (Ray Ray), Lexie D. Bigham (Bear), Vincent Craig Dupree (Loco), LaRita Shelby (Carole), Kevin Best (Genie Lamp).

Former gang leader Plummer has spent ten years in prison for murder. He returns home to find his wife is a drug addict and his son moving into the same kind of life that he had once chosen. Plummer tries to re-establish a relationship with his son to prevent him from making the same mistakes he had made.

2718. South Park: Bigger, Longer & Uncut (1999, Paramount/Warner Bros.–Comedy Central, 80m, c). D Trey Parker, P Parker & Matt Stone, W Parker, Stone & Pam Brady, ED John H. Venzon, M Parker & Marc Shaiman, ANIM Eric Stough.

LP Voices: Trey Parker (Stan Marsh, Eric Cartman, Mr. Garrison, Mr. Hat, Officer Barbrady), Matt Stone (Kyle Broflovski, Kenny McCormick), Mary Kaye Bergman (Mrs. Cartman, Sheila Broflovksi, Sharon Manson,

Mrs. McCormick, Wendy Testaburger), Isaac Hayes (Chef).

The objectionable little tykes of TV's *South Park* are despicable. The story line is tasteless, gross and, at least to many, hilarious. The big-screen version merely magnifies all these characteristics. Fans who can't get enough of the TV series will flock to the theaters to see this R-rated adaptation. Some will wander in out of curiosity. The remainder will never understand or even care to understand the appeal of this parody starring pint-size third-graders with potty mouths.

2719. *Southie* (1998, American World Pictures, 95m, c). D John Shea, P Bill McCutchen & Hugh Wilson, W Shea, James Cummings & Dave McLaughlin, PH Allen Baker, ED Tracy Granger, M Wayne Sharp, PD G.W. Mercier.

LP Donnie Wahlberg (Danny Quinn), Rose McGowan (Kathy Quinn), Anne Meara (Mrs. Quinn), James Cummings (Joey Ward), Amanda Peet (Marianne).

In another *Mean Streets* knockoff, Wahlberg is a troubled South Boston lad who returns from New York to his home to tie up some loose ends.

2720. *Space Jam* (1996, Warner Bros., 87m, c). D Joe Pytka, P Ivan Reitman, Joe Medjuck & Daniel Goldberg, W Leo Benvenuti, Steve Rudnick, Timothy Harris & Herschel Weingrod (based on characters created by Chuck Jones, Tex Avery & Friz Freleng), PH Michael Chapman, ED Sheldon Kahn, M James Newton Howard, PD Geoffrey Kirkland, AD David Klassen, ANIM Bruce Smith, Tony Cervone, Ron Tippe & Bill Perkins.

LP Michael Jordan (Himself), Theresa Randle (Juanita Jordan), Danny DeVito (Voice of Swackhammer), Billy West (Voices of Bugs Bunny & Elmer Fudd), Wayne Knight (Stan Podolak), Bradley Baker (Voice of Daffy Duck), Bill Murray (Himself).

Michael Jordan is the greatest basketball player ever to lace up sneakers. He is among the most recognized and admired personalties in the world. He makes money hand over fist. In this partially animated film, he is recruited to play in a basketball game with cartoon teammates against aliens who have stolen the abilities of several prominent NBA players.

They must save the toons from destruction. The film made Air Jordan money. But it certainly won't be one of the factors in those wanting to "Be like Mike."

2721. *Spaced Invaders* (1990, Touchstone–Buena Vista, 102m, c). D Patrick Read Johnson, P Luigi Congolani, W Johnson & Scott Alexander, PH James L. Carter, ED Seth Gaven & Daniel Gross, M David Russo, PD Tony Tremblay, AD Scott Alexander, SD Chava Danielson.

LP Douglas Barr (Sheriff Sam Hardy), Royal Dano (Old Man Wrenchmuller), Arianna Richards (Kathy Hoxly), J.J. Anderson (Brian "Duck"), Gregg Berger (Steve W. Klembecker), Wayne Alexander (Vern).

Sometimes one wonders if potential filmmakers don't turn to those with money and propose making a really dumb movie with nothing to recommend it just to see how gullible moviegoers really are. If this is the case, this movie about aliens landing in a Midwestern town on Halloween and being mistaken for "Trick-or-Treaters" might have been the story being pitched.

2722. *The Spanish Prisoner* (1998, Sony Pictures Classics, 112m, c). D & W David Mamet, P Jean Doumanian, PH Gabriel Beristain, ED Barbara Tulliver, M Carter Burwell, PD Tim Galvin, AD Kathleen Rosen, SD Jessica Lanier.

LP Campbell Scott (Joe Ross), Rebecca Pidgeon (Susan Ricci), Steve Martin (Jimmy Dell), Ben Gazzara (Mr. Klein), Ricky Jay (George Lang), Felicity Huffman (Pat McCune).

Inventor Scott falls in with the wrong crowd while trying to raise money to support his development of a secret "process." As in Hitchcock movies, the nature of the process is of importance only to the characters, not the audience.

2723. *Spank* (1999, Australia, Palace, 89m, c). D Ernie Clark, P David Lightfoot, W Lightfoot & David Farrell, PH David Foreman, ED Edward McQueen-Mason, M Sean Timms, PD Aphrodite Kondos, AD Phil McPherson.

LP Robert Mammone (Paulie), Vince Poletto (Rocky), Victoria Dixon-Whittle (Jo), Mario Gamma (Nick), Lucia Mastrantone (Tina), Checc Musolino (Vinny).

This film explores the various relationships of a bunch of Italo-Australians involved in the café society of Adelaide.

2724. Spanking the Monkey (1994, Fine Line, 110m, c). D & W David O. Russell, P Dean Silvers, PH Michael Mayers, ED Pamela Martin, M Mark Sandman, PD Susan Block.

LP Jeremy Davies (Raymond Aibelli), Alberta Watson (Susan Aibelli), Benjamin Hendrickson (Tom Aibelli), Carla Gallo (Toni Peck), Matthew Puckett (Nicky).

In this black comedy, Davies must give up his plans to take care of his attractive, controlling and bedridden mother Watson. His family is dysfunctional, to say the least. Prepare yourself for issues of sexual politics, masturbation and incest. The film is a worthy effort, dealing with sensitive subjects, by first-time director and screenwriter Russell.

2725. Spawn (1997, New Line, 96m, c). D Mark A.Z. Dippe, P Clint Goldman, W Dippe & Alan McElroy (based on the comic book created by Todd McFarlane), PH Guillermo Navarro, ED Michael N. Knue & Todd Busch, M Graeme Revell), PD Philip Harrison, AD Eric W. Orbom, SD Dena Roth.

LP Michael Jai White (Al Simmons/Spawn), John Leguizamo (Clown), Martin Sheen (Agent James Wynn), Theresa Randle (Wanda Simmons), Nicol Williamson (Cogliostro), Melinda Clarke (Jessica Priest), D.B. Sweeney (Terry Fitzgerald).

"Spawn" is short for "Hellspawn," the hero of a comic book series that has become very popular with young males. When government assassin White wants out, he is set on fire by his boss Sheen and literally blown to hell, where he spends the next five years. In exchange for agreeing to lead the armies of Hell against Heaven, White, now known as "Spawn," is allowed to see his wife Randle and avenge his own murder.

2726. Speak Like a Child (1999, U.K., BFI Prods., 80m, c). D John Akomfrah, P Fiona Morham & Lazell Daley, W Danny Padmore, PH Jonathan Collinson, ED Annabel Ware, M Adrian Thomas, PD Paul Cheerham, AD Patrick Bill.

LP Cal Macaninch (Billy, age 30), Daniel Newman (Billy, age 14), Richard Mylan (Sammy, age 30), Fraser Ayres (Sammy, age 14), Rachel Fielding (Ruby, age 30), Alison Mac (Ruby, age 14).

Three childhood friends, Macaninch, Mylan and Fielding, meet for a tense reunion at an abandoned home on the edge of a rocky coastline. Flashbacks reveal their times together as 14-year-olds at some home for children. Fielding and Macaninch are married, but pregnant Fielding makes it clear that she wouldn't be opposed to a bit of action with Mylan.

2727. The Specialist (1994, Warner Bros., 109m, c). D Luis Llosa, P Jerry Weintraub, W Alexandra Seros, PH Jeffrey L. Kimball, ED Jack E. Muraoka, SD Scott Jacobson.

LP Sylvester Stallone (Ray Quick), Sharon Stone (May Munro), James Woods (Ned Trent), Rod Steiger (Joe Leon), Eric Roberts (Tomas Leon), Mario Ernesto Sanchez (Charlie).

Stone's parents were killed by the Cuban gangster family of Steiger and his son Roberts. She wants an eye for an eye. Stone seeks out ex–CIA bomb specialist Stallone to help get her revenge. He's willing to help out because his screw-loose ex-partner Woods now works for Steiger. There are a lot of explosions for those who get a kick out of that sort of thing.

2728. Species (1995, MGM/United Artists, 111m, c). D Roger Donaldson, P Frank Mancuso, Jr. & Dennis Feldman, W Feldman, PH Andrzej Bartkowiak, ED Conrad Buff, M Christopher Young, PD John Muto, AD Dan Webster, SD Jackie Carr.

LP Ben Kingsley (Fitch), Michael Madsen (Press), Alfred Molina (Arden), Forest Whitaker (Dan), Marg Helgenberger (Laura), Natasha Henstridge (Sil), Michelle Williams (Young Sil).

When a galactic message reaches earth with instructions on how to combine alien DNA with human DNA, scientist Kingsley and his team "create" half-alien, half-human Williams. She will grow into supermodel Helgenberger, who in turn becomes a procreating and killing machine. Expect scenes to make you gag or, for the more sensitive, lose your lunch.

2729. Species II (1998, MGM, 93m, c). D Peter Medak, P Frank Mancuso, Jr., W Chris Brancato (based on characters created by Dennis Feldman), PH Matthew F. Leonetti, ED Richard Nord, M Edward Shearmur, PD Miljen Kreka Kljakovic, AD Mark Zuelzke, SD Suzette Sheets.

LP Michael Madsen (Press Lennox), Natasha Henstridge (Eve), Marg Helgenberger (Dr. Laura Baker), Mykelti Williamson (Dennis Gamble), George Dzundza (Col. Carter Burges, Jr.), James Cromwell (Sen. Ross).

This film is a rehash of the 1995 sci-fi shock hit. The first man on Mars returns to earth as a tentacle-sprouting creature intent on bedding all earth women. Then he runs afoul of a half-human, half-alien clone named Eve.

2730. *Specimen* (1997, Canada, A-Pix Ent., 85m, c). D John Bradshaw, P Damian Lee, W Sheldon Inkol & Lauren McLaughlin (based on a story by Bradshaw & Lee), PH Gerald R. Goozee, ED Paul G. Day, M Terence Gowan, PD Tim Boyd, AD Jim Lambie, SD Glenn Atkinson.

LP Mark Paul Gosselaar (Mike Hillary), Doug O'Keefe (Eleven), Ingrid Kalevaars (Jessica), David Herman (Sheriff Masterson), Andrew Jackson (Sixty-Six), Michelle Johnson (Sarah).

Minor league ballplayer Gosselaar attempts to discover the identity of his father, of whom his mother never talked. Turns out the old man was an alien.

2731. *Speechless* (1994, MGM, 98m, c). D Ron Underwood, P Renny Harlin & Geena Davis, W Robert King, PH Don Peterman, ED Richard Francis-Bruce, M Marc Shaiman, PD Dennis Washington, AD Thomas T. Targownik, SD Marvin March.

LP Michael Keaton (Kevin Vallick), Geena Davis (Julia Mann), Christopher Reeve (Bob Freed), Bonnie Bedelia (Annette), Ernie Hudson (Ventura), Charles Martin Smith (Kratz).

Keaton and Davis are speechwriters for opposing senatorial clients. They fall in love, but that doesn't stop them from using each other to make their guy look better. Frankly, neither of the candidates seem worthy of a senatorial post — but perhaps that's one of the points the movie is making. The film has some funny moments, but it's not funny enough to qualify as a screwball comedy, like those of the '30s, for which it may have been aiming. Their day may be gone forever.

2732. *Speed* (1994, 20th Century–Fox, 115m, c). D Jan De Bont, P Mark Gordon, W Graham Yost, PH Andrzej Bartkowiak, ED John Wright†, M Mark Mancina, PD Jack

DeGovia, AD John R. Jensen, SD K.C. Fox, Louis Mann, Peter Romero & Stan Tropp.

LP Keanu Reeves (Jack Traven), Dennis Hopper (Howard Payne), Sandra Bullock (Annie), Joe Morton (Captain MacMahon), Jeff Daniels (Harry), Alan Ruck (Stephens).

Reeves is an L.A. SWAT team cop who must do battle with mad bomber Hopper. It's an old film device; what makes it new and exciting is that Hopper has planted a bomb on a bus which will go bang-bang if its speed drops below 50 miles per hour. To complicate things, the bus driver is shot and Bullock has to take over. Reeves manages to get on the bus and must find a way to defuse things while Bullock watches the speedometer and weaves her way through heavy traffic. Naturally, they have time to fall in love, or something like that.

2733. *Speed 2: Cruise Control* (1997, 20th Century–Fox, 125m, c). D Jan De Bont, P Steve Perry, Michael Peyser & De Bont, W Randall McCormick & Jeff Nathanson (based on a story by De Bont and McCormick and characters created by Graham Yost), PH Jack N. Green, ED Alan Cody, M Mark Mancina, PD Joseph Nemec III & Phil Kenney, AD Daniel Ross, Daniel Olexiewicz & Bill Skinner, SD Cindy Carr.

LP Sandra Bullock (Annie Porter), Jason Patric (Alex Shaw), Willem Dafoe (John Geiger), Temuera Morrison (Juliano), Brian McCardie (Merced), Christine Firkins (Drew), Michael G. Hagerty (Harvey), Colleen Camp (Debbie), Lois Chiles (Celeste).

Bullock really made *Speed* a hit. But she didn't have it in her to push this big-budget disaster to a box office smash. Perhaps, she should have gotten back on the bus rather than a cruise ship. Her Caribbean vacation with her boyfriend Patric is just about ruined when disgruntled employee Dafoe takes control of the ship and fixes its computers to head on a suicide trip towards the rocks off the island of St. Martin. Well, it's up to Bullock and Patric to prevent that from happening. All the money the filmmakers threw at this film didn't make it exciting, suspenseful or fun.

2734. *Sphere* (1998, Warner Bros., 133m, c). D Barry Levinson, P Levinson, Michael Crichton & Andrew Wald, W Stephen Hauser, Paul Attanasio & Kurt Wimmer (based on the novel by Crichton), PH Adam Greenberg, ED

Stu Linder, M Elliot Goldenthal, PD Norman Reynolds, AD Mark Mansbridge & Jonathan McKinstry, SD Anne Kuljian.

LP Dustin Hoffman (Dr. Norman Goodman), Sharon Stone (Beth Halperin), Samuel L. Jackson (Harry Adams), Peter Coyote (Barnes), Liev Schreiber (Ted Fielding), Queen Latifah (Fletcher), Marga Gomez (Jane Edmunds).

This science-fiction feature is a three-dimensional zero and a waste of valuable talent. Hoffman, Stone, Jackson and others are more threatened by their own fears than by aliens.

2735. *Spice World* (1997, U.K., Polygram/ Sony, 92m, c). D Bob Spiers, P Uri Fruchtman & Barnaby Thompson, W Kim Fuller (based on an idea by the Spice Girls & Fuller), PH Clive Tickner, ED Andrea MacArthur, M Paul Hardcastle, PD Grenville Horner, AD David Walley & Colin Blaymires.

LP Mel B., Emma, Mel C., Geri, Victoria (The Spice Girls), Richard E. Grant (Clifford), Alan Cumming (Piers), George Wendt (Film Producer), Claire Rushbrook (Deborah), Mark McKinney (Graydon), Richard O'Brien (Damien), Roger Moore (Chief).

This film takes a fantasy look at the days leading up to a concert at Albert Hall by the Spice Girls. Grant plays their manager. If you don't fancy their music, there's nothing here.

2736. *Spider & Rose* (1996, Australia, Southern Star, 94m, c). D & W Bill Bennett, P Lyn McCarthy & Graeme Tubbenhauer, PH Andrew Lesnie, ED Henry Dangar, M Cruel Sea, PD Ross Major.

LP Simon Bossell (Spider McCall), Ruth Cracknell (Rose Dougherty), Max Cullen (Jack), Henry Bennett (Miles), Nallie Bennett (Sarah), Tina Bursill (Sister Abbott).

The story line of two vastly different people overcoming their initial dislike for each other and finally coming to respect one another has been filmed more times than can be counted. But this one, featuring Cracknell as a 70-year-old woman and Bossell as a 21-year-old punk given the job of driving her from the hospital to her son's home (a six-hour drive), is one that works very well.

2737. *Spirit Lost* (1997, LIVE Ent., 90m, c). D Neema Barnette, P Tim Reid, W Joyce Renee Lee (based on the book by Nancy

Thayer), PH Yuri Neyman, ED Quinnie Martin, Jr. & John Lafferty, M Lionel Cole, PD Edward Burbridge, SD Penny Barrett.

LP Regina Taylor (Willy), Leon Robinson, billed as Leon (John), Cynda Williams (Arabella), Juanita Jennings (Vera), Tamara Tunie (Anne), Reed McGants (Mark).

Robinson quits his job and moves with his wife Taylor to a remote seaside house where he can pursue a career as a painter. After discovering she is pregnant, Taylor begins to see apparitions of Williams, a 200-year-old spirit. The latter entices Robinson into a sexual relationship and seeks to get rid of Taylor.

2738. *The Spirit of '76* (1991, Commercial Pictures, 82m, c). D & W Lucas Reiner (based on the story by Reiner & Roman Coppola), P Susie Landau, PH Stephen Lighthill, ED Glen Scantlebury, M David Nichtern, PD Daniel Talpers, AD Isabelle Kirkland, SD Thomas Weigand.

LP David Cassidy (Adam-11), Olivia D'Abo (Chanel-6), Geoff Hoyle (Heinz-57), Leif Garrett (Eddie Trojan), Jeff McDonald (Chris), Steve McDonald (Tommy).

This film is an unsuccessful rip-off of *Bill and Ted's Excellent Adventure*. Time-travellers Cassidy, D'Abo and Hoyle, from ozone-less America of 2176, are sent back to 1776 to recover the U.S. Constitution because the U.S.'s entire historical memory bank has been wiped out due to a gigantic magnetic storm. Instead, they land in bicentennial America in 1976.

2739. *Spirits* (1992, Vidmark Ent., 88m, c). D Fred Olen Ray, P T.K. Lankford, W Jeff Falls & R.U. King, PH Gary Graver, ED Chris Ross, M Tim Landers, AD Ted Tunny.

LP Erik Estrada (Father Anthony Vicci), Carol Lynley (Sister Jillian), Robert Quarry (Dr. Richard Wicks), Brinke Stevens (Amy Goldwyn), Kathrin Lautner (Beth), Oliver Darrow (Harry).

Priest Estrada joins a group of psychic researchers investigating a house supposedly haunted because of a series of murders that took place there ten years earlier. Plagued by lust-filled dreams, the padre sins with a woman who turns out to be a murderer.

2740. *The Spitfire Grill* (1996, Columbia, 90m, c). D & W Lee David Zlotoff, P Forest Murray, PH Rob Draper, ED Margie

Goodspeed, M James Horner, PD Howard Cummings, AD Peter Brock, SD Larry Dias.

LP Alison Elliott (Percy Talbott), Ellen Burstyn (Hannah Ferguson), Marcia Gay Harden (Shelby Goddard), Will Patton (Nahum Goddard), Kieran Mulroney (Joe Sperling), Gailard Sartain (Sheriff Gary Walsh).

Female bonding in a small Maine town involves Burstyn, the owner of the popular Spitfire Grill; Elliott, recently released from a prison, her criminal past a mystery; and Harden, a meek and abused wife. It's a competent effort, but it will have limited appeal because very little happens.

2741. Splendor (1999, Summit Ent.–Newmarket Capital Group, 93m, c). D, W & ED Gregg Araki, P Damian Jones, Graham Broadbent & Araki, PH Jim Fealy, ED Tatiana S. Riegel, M Daniel Licht, PD Patti Podesta.

LP Kathleen Robertson (Veronica), Jonathan Schaech (Abel), Matt Keeslar (Zed), Kelly Macdonald (Mike), Eric Mabius (Ernest).

In this screwball, erotically surrealistic comedy, Robertson addresses the camera and narrates her amorous escapades with simultaneous lovers Schaech and Keeslar, and her inability to commit to just one.

2742. Split Second (1992, U.K., InterStar Releasing, 90m, c). D Tony Maylam, P Laura Gregory, W Gary Scott Thompson, PH Clive Tickner, ED Dan Rae, M Francis Haines & Stephen Parsons, PD Chris Edwards, AD Humphrey Bangham & Ian Baille.

LP Rutger Hauer (Harley Stone), Kim Cattrall (Michelle), Neil Duncan (Dick Durkin), Michael J. Pollard (The Rat Catcher), Pete Postlethwaite (Paulsen), Ian Dury (Jay Jay), Roberta Eaton (Robin).

In London in 2008, Hauer is a grizzled and grizzly cop who, with the assistance of his over-educated new partner Duncan, seeks a serial killer. It's a mix of sci-fi and old-cop/new-cop story, and it's not very well-told or well-acted.

2743. Splitting Heirs (1993, U.K., Universal, 100m, c). D Robert Young, P Simon Bosanquet & Redmond Morris, W Eric Idle, PH Tony Pierce-Roberts, ED John Jympson, M Michael Kamen, PD John Beard, AD Rod McLean & Lucy Richardson, SD Joanne Woollard.

LP Rick Moranis (Henry), Eric Idle (Tommy), Barbara Hershey (Duchess Lucinda), Catherine Zeta-Jones (Kitty), John Cleese (Shadgrind), Sadie Frost (Angela), Stratford Johns (Butler), Brenda Bruce (Mrs. Bullock).

As a child Idle was accidentally abandoned by his wealthy parents and was raised by poor Pakistanis. His real mother reclaimed the wrong abandoned baby. He discovers that he is the legitimate heir to a dukedom. He makes plans to kill the unknowing imposter, dumb as grass Moranis. The shenanigans of would-be assassin and victim and others, including Cleese as a shyster lawyer, isn't as funny as was intended. In fact, laughs are at about the level of the double-meaning title.

2744. Sprung (1997, Trimark, 105m, c). D Rusty Cundieff, P Darin Scott, W Cundieff & Scott, PH Joao Fernandes, ED Lisa Bromwell, M Stanley Clarke, PD Terrence Foster, AD Jim Moores, SD Melanie Paizis.

LP Tisha Campbell (Brandy), Joe Torry (Clyde), Paula Jai Parker (Adina), Rusty Cundieff (Montel), John Witherspoon (Detective), Jennifer Lee (Veronica), Clarence Williams III (Grand Daddy).

After their respective best friends, Torry and Parker, break up the romance of Cundieff and Campbell, they turn around and do what they can to get them together again. This war-of-the-sexes comedy in the African-American community, like a number of TV series, shows blacks as one-dimensional folks with only sex on their mind.

2745. Spy Hard (1996, Hollywood Pictures–Buena Vista, 81m, c). D Rick Friedberg, P Freidberg, Doug Draizin & Jeffrey Konvitz, W Dick Chudnow, R. Friedberg, Jason Friedberg & Aaron Seltzer, PH John R. Leonard, ED Eric Sears, M Bill Conti, PD William Creber, AD William J. Durrell, Jr., SD Ernie Bishop.

LP Leslie Nielsen (Dick Steele—Agent WD-40), Nicollette Sheridan (Veronique Ukrinsky—Agent 3.14), Charles Durning (The Director), Marcia Gay Harden (Miss Cheevus), Barry Bostwick (Norman Coleman), John Ales (Kabul), Andy Griffith (General Rancor), Elya Baskin (Professor Ukrinsky).

Warning: This farce, which spoofs any number of action films, is only for hard-core

Nielsen fans who found his work in *Naked Gun* films the height of comical genius. For those who care, Nielsen comes out of retirement to take on madman and would-be world conqueror Griffith, who has the habit of losing portions of his body. But he's a game guy who perseveres in his maniacal quest.

2746. *The Spy Within* (1995, Concorde-New Horizons, 92m, c). D Steve Railsback, P Mike Elliott, W Lewis Green, PH Anghel Decca, ED Roderick Davis, M David Wurst & Eric Wurst, PD Robert De Vico, AD Kenny Minster, SD Jordan Steinberg.

LP Scott Glenn (Will Rickman), Theresa Russell (Alex Canis), Lane Smith (Stephen Hahn), Terence Knox (Jonathan "J.B." Brandeis), Katherine Helmond (Dr. Pamela Schilling).

Spy Russell works undercover as a call girl. Glenn is an explosives expert on the run. Their lives cross as they find themselves the targets of a covert organization, which for some obscure reason wants them dead.

2747. *Squanto: A Warrior's Tale* (1994, Buena Vista, 101m, c). D Xavier Koller, P Kathryn Galan, W Darlene Craviotto & Bob Dolman, PH Robbie Greenberg, ED Lisa Day, PD Gemma Jackson, AD Claude Pare, SD Anthony Greco.

LP Adam Beach (Squanto), Eric Schweig (Epenow), Michael Gambon (Sir George), Nathaniel Parker (Thomas Dermer), Mandy Patinkin (Brother Daniel), Alex Norton (Harding).

Native American Indian Beach is captured by English traders and taken to England to be shown off as an example of the new world's "savages." Somehow he escapes and stows away on a ship headed for the Massachusetts colonies. There he is instrumental in bringing about peace between the Pilgrims and a neighboring tribe. This leads to the first Thanksgiving, as celebrated each year by grade school kids learning about brotherhood.

2748. *Squeeze* (1997, Miramax, 95m, c). D & W Robert Patton-Spruill (based on stories from Emmett Folgert), P Ari Newman, Garen Topalian, Stephanie Danan & Patricia Moreno, PH & ED Richard Moos, M Bruce Flowers, PD Maximillian Cutler, AD Ben Dulong.

LP Tyrone Burton (Tyson—"Ty"), Eddie Cutanda (Hector), Phuong Duong (Bao), Geoffrey Rhue (JJ), Russell G. Jones (Tommy), Leigh Williams (Marcus).

Three Boston buddies in their early teens find that the only source of walking-around money in the neighborhood is earned working for the local drug dealer.

2749. *Stanley and Iris* (1990, MGM-UA, 104m, c). D Martin Ritt, P Arlene Sellers & Alex Winitsky, W Harriet Frank, Jr. & Irving Ravetch, PH Donald McAlpine, ED Sidney Levin, M John Williams, PD Joel Schiller, AD Alicia Keywan & Eric Orbom, SD Steve Shewchuk & Les Bloom.

LP Jane Fonda (Iris King), Robert De Niro (Stanley Everett Cox), Swoosie Kurtz (Sharon), Martha Plimpton (Kelly King), Harley Cross (Richard King), Jamey Sheridan (Joe), Feodor Chaliapin, Jr. (Leonides Cox), Zohra Lampert (Elaine).

Fortunately for this film, De Niro and Fonda are excellent actors, because the story of an illiterate blue collar worker who falls in love with a recent widow is slow-moving and not particularly interesting.

2750. *Star Kid* (1998, Trimark, 101m, c). D & W Manny Coto, P Jennie Lew Tugend, PH Ronn Schmidt, ED Bob Ducsay, M Nicholas Pike, PD C.J. Strawn, AD Michael D. Welch, SD Irina Rivera.

LP Joseph Mazzello (Spencer Griffith), Joey Simmrin (Turbo Bruntley), Alex Daniels (Cyborsuit), Arthur Burghardt (Cyborsuit Voice), Brian Simpson (Bloodwarrior).

Introverted seventh-grader Mazzello finds a "cyborsuit" (superpowered alien armor), which he uses to get the courage to deal with a bully and speak to a pretty girl. But the cyborsuit has its own problems, and the two must join forces to fight giant, evil alien warrior Simpson, who arrives to destroy cyborsuit.

2751. *Star Maps* (1997, Fox Searchlight, 86m, c). D & W Miguel Arteta (based on a story by Matthew Greenfield & Arteta), P Greenfield, PH Chuy Chavez, ED Jeff Betancourt, Tom McArdle & Tony Selzer, PD Carol Strober, AD Karen Numme, SD Nathalie Cohen.

LP Douglas Spain (Carlos), Efrain Figueroa (Pepe), Kandeyce Jorden (Jennifer), Martha

Velez (Teresa), Lysa Flores (Maria), Annette Murphy (Letti), Robin Thomas (Martin), Vincent Chandler (Juancito).

Eighteen-year-old Latino Spain has aspirations of becoming an actor. To escape his dysfunctional family he turns to prostitution as a first step towards his goal.

2752. *Star Quest: Beyond the Rising Moon* (AKA: *Beyond the Rising Moon*; *Space 2074*) (1990, Pentan–VidAmerica, 85m, c). D, W, PH & ED Philip Cook, P & AD John Ellis, M David Bartley, PD John Poreda, SD Dale Alan Hoyt.

LP Tracy Davis (Pentan), Hans Bachmann (Harold Brickman), Michael Mack (John Moseby), Ron Ikejiri (Takashi Kuriyama), Rick Foucheux (Robert Thornton), James Hild (Kyle).

It's a woman's rights film in which Davis, the woman in question, has been genetically engineered. She fights to win her freedom from the corporate bad guys who created her.

2753. *Star Trek: First Contact* (1996, Paramount, 105m, c). D Jonathan Frakes, P Rick Berman, W Berman, Brannon Braga & Ronald D. Moore, PH Matthew Leonetti, ED John W. Wheeler, M Jerry Goldsmith, PD Herman Zimmerman, AD Ron Wilkinson, SD John M. Dwyer.

LP Patrick Stewart (Captain Jean-Luc Picard), Jonathan Frakes (Cmdr. William Riker), Brent Spiner (Lt. Cmdr. Data), LeVar Burton (Lt. Cmdr. Geordi La Forge), Michael Dorn (Lt. Cmdr. Worf), Gates McFadden (Dr. Beverly Crusher), Marina Sirtis (Counselor Deanna Troi), Alfre Woodard (Lily Sloane).

The eighth film in the *Star Trek* series is the first one without any cast members of the original TV series. Stewart and the crew of his new starship must travel to the 21st century to fight the Borg, a race of cyborgs, and prevent them from annihilating existing humanity.

2754. *Star Trek: Generations* (1994, Paramount, 118m, c). D David Carson, P Rick Berman, W Brannon Braga & Ronald D. Moore (based on a story by Braga, Moore & Berman, and the characters created by Gene Roddenberry), PH John A. Alonzo, ED Peter E. Berger, M Dennis McCarthy, PD Herman Zimmerman, AD Sandy Venziano, SD John

M. Dwyer, Robert Fetchman, Ron Wilkinson & Dianne Wager.

LP Patrick Stewart (Captain Jean-Luc Picard), Jonathan Frakes (Cmdr. William T. Riker), Brent Spiner (Lt. Cmdr. Data), LeVar Burton (Lt. Cmdr. Geordi La Forge), Michael Dorn (Lt. Worf), Malcolm McDowell (Soren), James Doohan (Scotty), Walter Koenig (Chekhov), William Shatner (Captain James T. Kirk), Whoopi Goldberg (uncredited cameo appearance).

This film brings together Shatner and Stewart, the captain of the new starship, when the former is blown into the future by an accident aboard the Enterprise. The two heroes team up to save the galaxy from would-be world-beater McDowell and assorted renegade Klingons. The show is a great deal of fun, pumping some new life into the story of the dangers and adventures found in deep space.

2755. *Star Trek: Insurrection* (1998, Paramount, 100m, c). D Jonathan Frakes, P Rick Berman, W Michael Piller (based on the story by Piller, and *Star Trek* created by Gene Roddenberry), PH Matthew F. Leonetti, ED Peter E. Berger, M Jerry Goldsmith, PD Herman Zimmerman, AD Ron Wilkinson, SD John Dwyer.

LP Patrick Stewart (Capt. Jean-Luc Picard), Jonathan Frakes (Cmdr. William Riker), Brent Spiner (Lt. Cmdr. Data), LeVar Burton (Lt. Cmdr. Geordi La Forge), Michael Dorn (Lt. Cmdr. Worf), Gates McFadden (Dr. Beverly C. Crusher), Martina Sirtis (Lt. Cmdr. Deanna Troi), F. Murray Abraham (Ru'afro).

In the ninth installment of the *Star Trek* saga, Stewart and the Enterprise crew take on Abraham, the leader of a dying civilization. He plans to displace the people of Ba'ku, where the 600-odd inhabitants live for hundreds and hundreds of years.

2756. *Star Trek VI: The Undiscovered Country* (1991, Paramount, 110m, c). D Nicholas Meyer, P Ralph Winter & Steven-Charles Jaffe, W Meyer & Denny Martin Flinn (based on the story by Leonard Nimoy, Lawrence Konner & Mark Rosenthal, and the characters created by Gene Roddenberry), PH Hiro Narita, ED William Hoy & Ronald Roose, M Cliff Eidelman, PD Herman Zimmerman, AD Nilo Rodis-Jamero, SD Mickey S. Michaels.

LP William Shatner (Admiral James T. Kirk), Leonard Nimoy (Captain Spock), DeForest Kelley (Doctor Leonard "Bones" McCoy), James Doohan (Montgomery "Scotty" Scott), Walter Koenig (Pavel Chekhov), Nichelle Nichols (Nytoba Uhuru), George Takei (Hikaru Sulu), Kim Cattrall (Lt. Valeris), Mark Leonard (Sarek), Grace Lee Whitney ("Excelsior" Communications Officer), Brock Peters (Admiral Cartwright), Christopher Plummer (General Chang), David Warner (Chancellor Gorkon), Iman (Martia).

In the final chapter of the long-running series, peace between the Federation and the Klingon Empire seems at hand. But when a Klingon ship is attacked, Shatner, his crew and his ship Enterprise are blamed. To clear themselves they must find the real culprits.

2757. Star Wars: Episode I — the Phantom Menace (1999, 20th Century–Fox, 133m, c). D & W George Lucas, P Rick McCallum, PH David Tattersall, ED Paul Martin Smith, M John Williams, PD Gavin Bocquet, AD Peter Russell, SD Peter Walpole.

LP Liam Neeson (Qui-Gon Jinn), Ewan McGregor (Obi-Wan Kenobi), Natalie Portman (Queen Amidala), Jake Lloyd (Anakin Skywalker), Pernilla August (Shmi Skywalker), Frank Oz (Yoda), Ian McDiarmid (Senator Palpatine), Oliver Ford Davies (Sio Bubble), Ray Park (Darth Maul), Peter Serafinowicz (Voice of Darth Maul).

The film, not the story of the film, is the center of attention in this prequel to the 1977 blockbuster. Few movies have had so much hype prior to release, or generated so much frenzied anticipation by would-be moviegoers. Why? Well, it may be as simple as the fact that moviegoers are starving for entertainment — entertainment with old-fashioned values, where there are good guys and bad guys and it's easy to tell the difference. Then there are the splendid special effects expected by one and all. Add to this a cast consisting of some interesting people, and one has the basis for a hit — a very big hit. The fact that many will be of necessity disappointed in the film, finding it not quite the greatest thing ever to hit the screen, is inevitable. When Star Wars burst onto the screen, everything about it seemed new, fresh and fascinating. It's very difficult to expect even George Lucas to make it possible to reexperience the wonder felt when viewing

his earlier, magical film. This one may become one of the greatest box office hits of all time but certainly will not rival any of the greatest films. Some critics have described the film as a rapid-fire videogame. Perhaps that's a bit harsh, but not overly so. For those who won't have made it to the theater or rented a video of the film by the time this book is in print, the plot is as follows. Neeson is a fearless Jedi warrior, and McGregor is his young apprentice. The two heroes take on the Trade Federation, which has galaxy domination in mind. The boys become the protector of the planet Naboo, ruled by Portman. They take her with them to Tatooine where they encounter young Lloyd, who is the chosen one who will ultimately bring balance to the Force and beget Luke Skywalker.

2758. Stargate (1994, U.S./France, Carolco–MGM, 119m, c). D Roland Emmerich, P Joel B. Michaels, Oliver Eberle & Dean Devlin, W Emmerich & Devlin, PH Karl Walter Lindenlaub, ED Michael J. Duthie & Derek Brechin, M David Arnold, PD Holger Gross, AD Peter Murton, Frank Bollinger & Mark Zuelzke, SD Jim Erickson.

LP Kurt Russell (Col. Jonathan "Jack" O'Neil), James Spader (Dr. Daniel Jackson), Jaye Davidson (Ra), Viveca Lindfors (Catherine), Alexis Cruz (Skaara), Mili Avital (Sha'uri).

A Military contingent, headed by burnt-out Russell, recruits scholar Spader, an expert on hieroglyphics, to decipher markings on an ancient stone gateway. It turns out to be the entrance to another galactic universe, where peace-loving desert tribes are mercilessly ruled by evil alien Davidson. He will always be remembered for The Crying Game, but nothing in this film demonstrates that he has acting ability.

2759. The Stars Fell on Henrietta (1995, Warner Bros., 110m, c). D James Keach, P Clint Eastwood & David Valdes, W Philip Railsback, PH Bruce Surtees, ED Joel Cox, M David Benoit, PD Henry Bumstead, AD Jack Taylor, Jr., SD Alan Hicks.

LP Robert Duvall (Mr. Cox), Aidan Quinn (Don Day), Frances Fisher (Cora Day), Brian Dennehy (Big Dave), Lexi Randall (Beatrice Day), Katylyn Knowles (Pauline Day), Francesca Ruth Eastwood (Mary Day).

During the Depression, prospector Duvall

discovers oil on the land of dirt-poor farmers Quinn and Fisher. Duvall convinces them to drill for oil, but he must steal the money to pay for the project from wealthy oil man Dennehy. It's the kind of film role that Duvall almost exclusively owns.

2760. *Starship Troopers* (1997, Columbia TriStar, 129m, c). D Paul Verhoeven, P Alan Marshall & Jon Davison, W Ed Neumeier (based on the novel by Robert A. Heinlein), PH Jost Vacano, ED Mark Goldblatt & Caroline Ross, M Basil Poledouris, PD Allan Cameron.

LP Casper Van Dien (Johnny Rico), Dina Meyer (Dizzy Flores), Denise Richards (Carmen Ibanez), Jake Busey (Ace Levy), Neil Patrick Harris (Carl Jenkins), Clancy Brown (Sergeant Zim), Seth Gilliam (Sugar Watkins), Patrick Muldoon (Zander Barcalow), Michael Ironside (Jean Rasczak).

Sometime in the distant future four young people are caught up in the war between Earth's World Federation and an alien insectoid race, the "Bugs," which has attacked Earth by hurling asteroids at its cities.

2761. *Starving Artists* (1999, Panorama Ent., 98m, c). P, D, W & ED Allan Piper, PH Robert Ballo, M Claire Harding, AD Christie Allan-Piper.

LP Allan Piper (Zach), Bess Wohl (Joy), Joe Smith (Jay), Sandi Carroll (Doris), John De-Vore (Bob).

In this whimsical comedy, Piper is a struggling playwright who tries to woo aspiring graphic artist Wohl. They live in the same apartment building, as do Wohl's friends, a would-be director and a cinematographer (Smith and Carroll, respectively), who are busy shooting an independent film while trying to resist becoming involved romantically. Piper's roommate DeVore thinks the noises being made upstairs by the film crew are criminal in nature, and he plays detective — with disastrous results.

2762. *State of Grace* (1990, Orion, 134m, c). D Phil Joanou, P Ned Dowd, Randy Ostrow & Ron Rotholz, W Dennis McIntyre & David Rabe (uncredited), PH Jordan Cronenweth, ED Claire Simpson, M Ennio Morricone, PD Patrizia Von Brandenstein & Doug Kraner, AD Shawn Hausman & Timothy Galvin, SD George DeTitta.

LP Sean Penn (Terry Noonan), Ed Harris (Tommy Flannery), Gary Oldman (Jackie Flannery), Robin Wright (Kathleen Flannery), John Turturro (Nick), John C. Reilly (Stevie), R.D. Call (Nicholson), Joe Viterelli (Borelli), Burgess Meredith (Finn), Deirdre O'Connell (Irene).

Think *Mean Streets* with the Italian hoods replaced by Irish hoods. Penn and Oldman belong to a Hell's Kitchen gang of thugs who are particularly brutal and savage in their dealings with anyone who gets in their way.

2763. *Stay Tuned* (1992, Morgan Creek–Warner Bros., 89m, c). D Peter Hyams, W Tom S. Parker & Jim Jennewein (based on the story by Parker, Jennewein & Richard Siegel), PH Hyams, ED Peter E. Berger, M Bruce Broughton, PD Philip Harrison, AD Richard Hudolin, SD Rose Marie McSherry.

LP John Ritter (Roy Knable), Pam Dawber (Helen Knable), Jeffrey Jones (Spike), Eugene Levy (Crowley), David Tom (Darryl Knable), Heather McComb (Diane Knable).

It's a dumb movie with a stupid plot, and it's not worth getting into a car to drive to the multiplex for. But if it is shown on cable or satellite, you could find worse ways to waste an hour and a half. Video nut Ritter is offered access to 666 channels of the ultimate in interactive TV by Jones, one of Satan's helpers. Ritter and wife Dawber are sucked into their television satellite and thrown from one familiar former TV series to another. But the shows of this "Old Nick at Night" are more dangerous than nostalgic.

2764. *Steal Big, Steal Small* (1995, Savoy Pictures, 130m, c). D Andrew Davis, P Davis & Fred Caruso, W Davis, Lee Blessing, Jeanne Blake & Terry Kahn, PH Frank Tidy, ED Don Brochu & Tina Hirsch, M William Olvis, PD Michael Haller, AD Mark E. Zuelzke, SD Gene Serdena.

LP Andy Garcia (Ruben Partida Martinez/Robert Martin), Alan Arkin (Lou Perilli), Rachel Ticotin (Laura Martinez), Joe Pantoliano (Eddie Agopian), Holland Taylor (Mona Rowland-Downey), Ally Walker (Bonnie Martin), David Ogden Stiers (Judge Winton Myers).

Garcia plays twins — one is a good guy who wants to help migrant workers with his inheritance; the other is a bad guy who wants to turn the California ranch left to his bro into a string of expensive condos. Doesn't sound very interesting? It isn't.

2765. *Stealing Beauty* (1996, Italy/U.K./France, Fox Searchlight, 119m, c). D Bernardo Bertolucci, P Jeremy Thomas, W Susan Minot (based on a story by Bertolucci), PH Darius Khondji, ED Pietro Scalia, M Richard Hartley, PD Gianni Silvestri, AD Domenico Sica, SD Cinzia Sleiter.

LP Liv Tyler (Lucy Harmon), Jeremy Irons (Alex Parrish), Sinead Cusack (Diana Grayson), Carlo Cecchi (Carlo Lisca), Jean Marais (M. Guillaume), Donal McCann (Ian Grayson).

Tyler burst on the movie scene here as a toothsome young American innocent who, following her mother's suicide, spends the summer with family friends in Tuscany. There she poses for a portrait by McCann while eagerly awaiting the return of a boy with whom she shared a kiss during an earlier visit. She reads her mother's diaries, looking for a clue to the identity of her biological father. Tyler shows an interest in losing her virginity, and terminally ill playwright Irons would like to do what he can to oblige her.

2766. *Steel* (1997, Warner Bros., 96m, c). D & W Kenneth Johnson (based on characters published by DC Comics, created by Louise Simonson & Jon Bogdanove), P Quincy Jones, David Salzman & Joel Simon, PH Mark Irwin, ED John F. Link, M Mervyn Warren, PD Gary Wissner & Adam Scher, AD Gershon Ginsburg, SD Don Kraft.

LP Shaquille O'Neal (John Henry Irons/Steel), Annabeth Gish (Lt. Sparks), Richard Roundtree (Uncle Joe), Judd Nelson (Nathaniel Burke), Irma P. Hall (Grandma Odessa), Ray J. (Martin Irons), Charles Napier (Colonel David).

O'Neal makes many NBA players look like pygmies. Just imagine how normal-sized actors would seem next to him. O'Neal's character, a comic book hero, is an idealistic army weapons engineer who battles old associate Nelson. The latter is selling a lethal weapon they designed to criminals.

2767. *Steele's Law* (1992, Academy Ent., 96m, c). D & P Fred Williamson, W Charles Johnson, PH David Blood, ED Doug Bryan, M Mike Logan.

LP Fred Williamson (John Steele), Bo Svenson (Sheriff Barnes), Doran Inghram (Joe Keno), Phyllis Cicero (Rose Holly).

It's another routine Williamson action flic. He's a cop who has to bend and break the law to track down an insane assassin.

2768. *Stella* (1990, Touchstone–Buena Vista, 106m, c). D John Erman, P Samuel Goldwyn, Jr., W Robert Getchell (based on the novel *Stella Dallas* by Olive Higgins Prouty), PH Billy Williams, ED Jerrold L. Ludwig, M John Morris, PD James Hulsey, AD Jeffrey Ginn, SD Steve Shewchuk.

LP Bette Midler (Stella Claire), John Goodman (Ed Munn), Trini Alvarado (Jenny Claire), Stephen Collins (Dr. Stephen Dallas), Marsha Mason (Janice Morrison), Eileen Brennan (Mrs. Wilkerson), Linda Hart (Debbie Whitman).

The 1937 film *Stella Dallas* received more praise than it deserved. But it did have Barbara Stanwyck convincingly and painfully portraying a low-class, no-class woman who becomes pregnant by a socialite, who marries her (remember, it was 1937). Shortly after the baby arrives he becomes her ex. Later, as the child grows into a young woman, Stanwyck, who always (if often misguidedly) tries to do what is best for her daughter, decides the girl will be better off with her father. She valiantly and heartbreakingly bows out of the girl's life. In this remake, Midler, as Stella, is an unwed mother who also eventually sees herself for what she is and sends daughter Alvarado to dear old dad Collins, who hadn't done much for either Midler or Alvardo up to that point. There was no reason to remake the weeper, which was an aging and hackneyed chestnut way back when.

2769. *Stephen King's Sleepwalkers* (1992, Columbia, 91m, c). D Mick Garris, P Mark Victor, Michael Grais & Nabeel Zahid, W Stephen King, PH Rodney Charters, ED O. Nicholas Brown, M Nicholas Pike, PD John DeCuir, Jr., AD Sig Tinglof, SD Bruce A. Gibeson.

LP Brian Krause (Charles Brady), Madchen Amick (Tanya Robertson), Alice Krige (Mary Brady), Jim Haynie (Ira), Cindy Pickett (Mrs. Robertson), Ron Perlman (Captain Soames).

After Krige and her son Krause move into a small Indiana town, a slew of virgins have the life force sucked out of them. It seems the new-comers are sleepwalkers, cat-like vampire creatures who can only survive by frequently dipping into virginal blood banks.

2770. Stepmom (1998, Columbia–Sony Pictures, 124m, c). D Chris Columbus, P Wendy Finerman, Chris Columbus, Mark Radcliffe & Michael Barnathan, W Gigi Levangie, Jessie Nelson, Steven Rogers, Karen Leigh Hopkins & Ron Bass (based on a story by Levangie), PH Donald M. McAlpine, ED Neil Travis, M John Williams, PD Stuart Wurtzel, AD Raymond Kluga, SD George De Titta, Jr.
LP Julia Roberts (Isabel), Susan Sarandon (Jackie), Ed Harris (Luke), Jena Malone (Anna), Liam Aiken (Ben), Lynn Whitfield (Dr. Sweikert).
In a nutshell, Sarandon is Harris' ex-wife. Roberts is his current live-in lover who isn't thrilled with the weekend visits of his kids. Even less thrilled about the situation is Sarandon. But about a third of the way into the film, Sarandon is diagnosed with cancer. The rest of the film deals with how the trio cope with the fact that Sarandon is going to die and her kids will be brought up by Roberts. It seems that when as many as five screenwriters are brought in for the story, the results are going to be mixed. In this case they are disappointing.

2771. Stepping Out (1991, Canada/U.S., Paramount, 106m, c). D & P Lewis Gilbert, W Richard Harris (based on his play), PH Alan Hume, ED Humphrey Dixon, M Peter Matz, PD Peter Mullins, AD Alicia Keywan, SD Steve Shewchuck.
LP Liza Minnelli (Mavis Turner), Julie Walters (Vera), Shelley Winters (Mrs. Fraser), Ellen Greene (Maxine), Bill Irwin (Geoffrey), Andrea Martin (Dorothy), Jane Krakowski (Lynne).
Aspiring Broadway dancer Minnelli gives tap dancing lessons to an assortment of characters in an old church. When given the opportunity to put on a show, her inept pupils pull it all together, and in the finale Minnelli gets the chance to show she can still strut her stuff.

2772. The Sterling Chase (1999, Weinberg Ent.; Indyssey Ent., 92m, c). D & W Tanya Fenmore (based on a story by Fenmore & Jeremy Dauber), P Fenmore, Katrina S. Pavlos & Cynthia Perez-Brown, PH David Bridges, ED David Codron & Edward R. Abroms, M Mark Adler, PD Norm Dodge, AD Peggy Hervas.
LP Andrea Ferrell (Melissa), John Livingston (Buns), Irene Ng (Cathy), Jack Noseworthy (Todd), Devon Odessa (Chris), Sean Patrick Thomas (Darren), Nicholle Tom (Alexis), Alanna Ubach (Jenna).
The story centers on three graduating seniors: Tom, a senator's daughter; Thomas, one of the few black students on campus; and Jenna, the school's most outspoken feminist. Each are nominees for Chadley College's prestigious award, which goes to the student who has exemplified "loyalty, integrity and strength." In the 48 hours leading up to graduation, each will need these qualities to deal with conflicts in their lives.

2773. Stigmata (1999, MGM–FGM Ent., 103m, c). D Rupert Wainwright, P Frank Mancuso, Jr., W Tom Lazarus & Rick Ramage (based on a story by Lazarus), PH Jeffrey L. Kimball, ED Michael R. Miller & Michael J. Duthie, M Billy Corgan & Elia Cmiral, PD Waldemar Kalinowski, AD Anthony Stabley, SD Florence Fellman.
LP Patricia Arquette (Frankie Paige), Gabriel Byrne (Father Andrew Kieran), Jonathan Pryce (Cardinal Daniel Houseman), Nia Long (Donna Chadway), Thomas Kopache (Father Durning), Rade Sherbedgia (Marion Petrocelli), Enrico Colantoni (Father Dario).
Soon after Pittsburgh hairdresser Arquette comes into possession of rosary beads that once belonged to a saintly priest in Brazil, she begins to display stigmata, marks resembling the wounds of Jesus on the cross. Byrne portrays a Catholic priest sent to investigate. He comes to believe that Arquette is indeed blessed; meanwhile, back at the Vatican, Cardinal Pryce does all he can do to have her declared a fraud.

2774. Still Breathing (1998, October Films, 109m, c). D & W James F. Robinson, P Robinson & Marshall Persinger, PH John Thomas, ED Sean Albertson, M Paul Mills, PD Denise Pizzini, AD Bob West, SD Lisa Lopez.
LP Brendan Fraser (Fletcher McBracken), Joanna Going (Roz Willoughby), Celeste Holm (Ida McBracken), Ann Magnuson (Elaine),

Toby Huss (Cameron), Angus MacFayden (Philip).

San Antonio street performer Fraser has a vision of his perfect woman. His vision didn't inform him that Going, the lady he finds who fits the bill, is a con woman who scams wealthy men and then scares them off by informing them that she is HIV positive. Will love conquer all — well, it wouldn't make much sense to produce this bit of hokum otherwise, would it?

2775. Still Crazy (1998, U.K., Columbia TriStar, 95m, c). D Brian Gibson, P Amanda Marmot, W Dick Clement & Ian La Fresnais, PH Ashley Rowe, ED Peter Boyle, M Clive Langer, PD Max Gottlieb, AD Sarah-Jane Cornish.

LP Stephen Rea (Tony Costello), Billy Connolly (Hughie), Jimmy Nail (Les Wickes), Timothy Spall (David [Beano] Baggot), Bill Nighy (Ray Simms), Juliet Aubrey (Karen Knowles), Helena Bergstrom (Astrid Simms).

Five middle-aged losers reassemble their rock band that broke up in the 1970s. British critics have likened the comedy to *This Is Spinal Tap* (1984). You don't have to be an aging rock fan to enjoy the humorous observations about the quintet's foibles.

2776. Still Life: The Fine Art of Murder (1993, Greycat Films, 85m, c). D Graeme Campbell, P Nicolas Stiliadis & Paco Alvarez, W Michael Taav, Dean Parisot & Campbell, PH Ludek Bogner, ED Marvin Lawrence, M Mychael Danna & Jeff Danna, PD Ian Brock.

LP Jason Gedrick (Peter Sherwood), Jessica Steen (Nellie Ambrose), Stephen Shellen (Teddy), Gary Farmer (Mugger), Sam Malkin (Mugger).

A serial killer, dubbed the "Art Killer," makes sculptures of his victims.

2777. Stir of Echoes (1999, Artisan Ent., 110m, c). D & W David Koepp (based on the novel by Richard Matheson), P Gavin Polone & Judy Hofflund, PH Fred Murphy, ED Jill Savitt, M James Newton Howard, PD Nelson Coates, AD David Krummel, SD Susan Goulder.

LP Kevin Bacon (Tom Witzky), Kathryn Eyre (Maggie Witzky), Illeana Douglas (Lisa), Liza Weil (Debbie Kozac), Kevin Dunn (Frank McCarthy), Conor O'Farrell (Harry Damon), Jennifer Morrison (Samantha), Zachary David Cope (Jake Witzky).

Like the supernatural hit *The Sixth Sense*, this thriller features Cope as another kid who talks with the dead. The real story, however, is what happens when Bacon is put into a trance by his sister-in-law Douglas, who implants the post-hypnotic suggestion that he be more "open" in his thinking. Douglas had one thing in mind, but Bacon begins to perceive spirits in his home.

2778. Stone Cold (1991, Columbia, 90m, c). D Craig R. Baxley, P Mace Neufeld & Yoram Ben Ami, W Walter Doniger, PH Alexander Gryszynski, ED Mark Helfrich, M Sylvester Levay, PD John Mansbridge & Richard Johnson.

LP Brian Bosworth (Joe Huff/John Stone), Lance Henriksen (Chains), William Forsythe (Ice), Arabella Holzbog (Nancy), Sam McMurray (Lance).

Dedicated cop Bosworth is angered at how criminals are treated with kid gloves. The FBI recruits him to go undercover to infiltrate a white supremacist biker gang. He does, using the name "John Stone." The film is not merely routine, it's stupid.

2779. The Stoned Age (1994, Trimark Pictures, 90m, c). D James Melkonian, P Neal Moritz & David Heyman, W Melkonian & Rich Wilkes, PH Paul Holahan, ED Peter Schink, M David Kitay, PD Teri Whittaker, AD Easton Smith, SD Susan A. Chooljian.

LP Michael Kopelow (Joe), Bradford Tatum (Hubbs), China Kantner (Jill), Clifton Gonzalez Gonzalez (Tack), Renee Ammann (Lanie).

It's the 1970s and three stoneheads are on the prowl for drugs, babes and parties. It's predictable, but the music of the time helps.

2780. Stop or My Mom Will Shoot (1992, Universal, 81m, c). D Roger Spottiswoode, P Ivan Reitman, Joe Medjuck & Michael C. Gross, W Blake Snyder, William Osborne & William Davies, PH Frank Tidy, ED Mark Conte & Lois Freeman-Fox, M Alan Silvestri, PD Charles Rosen, AD Diane Yates, SD Don Remacle.

LP Sylvester Stallone (Sgt. Joe Bomowksi), Estelle Getty (Tutti Bomowski), JoBeth Williams (Lt. Gwen Harper), Roger Rees (Parnell),

Martin Ferrero (Paulie), Gailard Sartain (Munroe), John Wesley (Tony).

Some people thought it would be a hilarious idea to team action hero Stallone in a comedy with Getty, the linchpin of TV's *The Golden Girls*. They would be mistaken. Sly is a tough cop visited by his mommy. When she witnesses a murder she insists that she aid in the investigation. And Stallone can't say no to mother.

2781. *The Story of a Bad Boy* (1999, Sweet Films, 85m, c). D & W Tom Donaghy, P Jean Doumanian, PH Garrett Fisher, ED Barbara Tulliver, M Angelo Badalamenti, PD Dina Goldman.

LP Jeremy Hollingworth (Pauly), Christian Camargo (Noel), Stephen Lang (Spyrgo), Julie Kavner (Elaine), Lauren Wood (Ludmilla).

Seventeen-year-old Hollingworth is in a very explorative sexual stage with both males and females. He is expelled from his Catholic school for kissing a nun. At the public school in which he enrolls he ardently yearns for handsome student teacher Camargo. It's a comedy-drama brimming with clichés.

2782. *The Story of Us* (1999, Universal-Castle Rock, 94m, c). D Rob Reiner, P Reiner, Alan Zweibel & Jessie Nelson, W Zweibel & Nelson, PH Michael Chapman, ED Robert Leighton & Alan Edward Bell, M Eric Clapton & Mark Shaiman, PD Lilly Kilvert, AD Chris Burian-Mohr, Jess Gonchor & Francesco Chianese, SD John Perry Goldsmith & Anthony D. Parrillo.

LP Bruce Willis (Ben Jordan), Michelle Pfeiffer (Katie Jordan), Tim Matheson (Marty), Rob Reiner (Stan), Rita Wilson (Rachel), Paul Reiser (Dave), Julie Hagerty (Liza), Jayne Meadows (Dot), Tom Poston (Harry), Betty White (Lillian), Red Buttons (Arnie).

Many in the audience can identify with the predicament of Willis and Pfeiffer. They have been married 15 years and have never worked very hard at finding out what would make the relationship last after the glow of their early romance wore off. Both husband and wife share the guilt in allowing a one-time happy relationship to wither on the vine due to lack of nourishment in the form of growing together, rather than apart. Less one suspect the film is a tearjerker, it's advertised as a romantic comedy; and yes, there is some romance, some

comedy and some tears. It's not a great film, nor is it among the best work of the leads or of director Reiner; but it strikes a familiar chord for any who have found a once-happy marriage going downhill.

2783. *Storyville* (1992, 20th Century–Fox, 110m, c). D Mark Frost, P David Roe & Edward R. Pressman, W Frost & Lee Reynolds (based on the book *Juryman* by Frank Galbally & Roger Macklin), PH Ron Garcia, ED B.J. Sears, M Carter Burwell, PD Richard Hoover, AD Kathleen M. McKernin, SD Brian Kasch.

LP James Spader (Cray Fowler), Joanne Whalley-Kilmer (Natalie Tate), Jason Robards (Clifford Fowler), Charlotte Lewis (Lee Tran), Michael Warren (Nathan LeFleur), Michael Parks (Michael Tevallian).

Feckless young lawyer Spader runs for the Senate position vacated by his father, who died after being indicted for some political misdealings. Spader is no knight in shining armor himself, and his unscrupulous uncle Robards doesn't help things. To add some luster to the campaign, married Spader is blackmailed for his involvement with a mysterious beauty who has been videotaping their lovemaking. Oh yes, he becomes involved in a murder investigation. Just another day in the life of a politician, you say? Well, there may be just a trifle too many complications to be credible.

2784. *Straight Out of Brooklyn* (1991, Samuel Goldwyn Company, 91m, c). D, P & W Matty Rich, PH John Rosnell, ED Jack Haigis, M Harold Wheeler.

LP George T. Odom (Ray Brown), Ann D. Sanders (Frankie Brown), Lawrence Gilliard, Jr. (Dennis Brown), Barbara Sanon (Carolyn Brown), Reana E. Drummond (Shirley), Matty Rich (Larry).

It's a raw look at the struggles of and means of survival employed by a black family in a Brooklyn housing project.

2785. *The Straight Story* (1999, U.S./France, Independent Film, 111m, c). D David Lynch, P Neil Edelstein, Alain Sarde & Mary Sweeney, W John Roach II & Sweeney, PH Freddie Francis, ED Sweeney, M Angelo Badalamenti, PD Jack Fisk, SD Barbara Haberecht.

LP Richard Farnsworth† (Alvin Straight), Sissy Spacek (Rose Straight), Harry Dean Stanton (Lyle Straight), Everett McGill (Tom the Dealer), John Farley (Thorvald Olsen), Kevin P. Farley (Harold Olsen).

Seventy-three-year-old Farnsworth takes a six week trip to mend his relationship with his older brother, who is sick. Because of his eyesight he's lost his driver's license, so he makes the trip on his riding lawn mower. The film is based on a real occurrence. The story was also presented in this year's *Abilene*, with Ernest Borgnine as the lawn mower rider.

2786. *Straight Talk* (1992, Hollywood–Buena Vista, 90m, c). D Barnet Kellman, P Robert Chartoff & Fred Berner, W Craig Bolotin & Patrick Resnick (based on the story by Bolotin), PH Peter Sova, ED Michael Tronick, M Brad Fiedel, PD Jeffrey Townsend, AD Michael T. Perry.

LP Dolly Parton (Shirlee Kenyon), James Woods (Jack Russell), Griffin Dunne (Alan), Michael Madsen (Steve), Deirdre O'Connell (Lily), John Sayles (Guy Girardi), Teri Hatcher (Janice), Spalding Gray (Dr. Erdman), Jerry Orbach (Milo Jacoby), Philip Bosco (Gene Perlman).

Hired as a receptionist for a Chicago radio station, Parton is mistaken for the new radio psychologist. By the time the mistake is discovered, she has become a huge success dishing out down-home advice from her well of Arkansas wisdom. It's amusing up to a point, but it's as obvious and contrived as Parton's generous chest.

2787. *Strange Days* (1995, 20th Century–Fox, 145m, c). D Kathryn Bigelow, P James Cameron & Steven-Charles Jaffe, W Cameron & Jay Cocks, PH Matthew F. Leonetti, ED Howard Smith, M Graeme Revell, PD Lilly Kilvert, AD John Warnke, SD Kara Lindstrom.

LP Ralph Fiennes (Lenny Nero), Angela Bassett (Lornette "Mace" Mason), Juliette Lewis (Faith Justin), Tom Sizemore (Max Peltier), Michael Wincott (Philo Gant), Vincent D'Onofrio (Burton Steckler), Glenn Plummer (Jeriko One).

A lot of moviegoers missed this film. If Fiennes doesn't strike you as the perfect actor to portray a small-time hustler who sells discs showing real-life sick experiences, this may explain its hasty exit from theaters. Still, Fiennes is such a fine actor that he makes you care about his lowlife character. Bassett sizzles as a security agent who comes to Fiennes' aid when he gets in over his head after a snuff video shows the murder of a hooker who had been his friend.

2788. *Strange Fits of Passion* (1999, Australia, Beyond Films, 83m, c). D & W Elise McCredie, P Lucy Maclaren, PH James Grant, ED Chris Branagan & Ken Sallows, M Cezary Skubiszewski, PD Macgregor Knox.

LP Michela Noonan (She), Mitchell Butel (Jimmy), Samuel Johnson (Josh), Steve Adams (Pablo), Anni Finsterer (Judy).

Noonan portrays an unnamed 20-year-old Melbourne woman who is testing her sexuality and trying to lose her virginity.

2789. *Strange Planet* (1999, Australia, New Vision, 95m, c). D Emma Katz-Croghan, P Stavros Kazantzidis & Anastasia Sideris, W Croghan & Kazantzidis (based on a story by Kazantzidis), PH Justin Brickle, ED Ken Sallows, PD Annie Beauchamp.

LP Claudia Karvan (Judy), Naomi Watts (Alice), Alice Garner (Sally), Tom Long (Ewan), Aaron Jeffrey (Joel), Felix Williamson (Neil), Hugo Weaving (Steven), Marshall Napier (Robert).

This picture begins and ends on successive New Year's Eves. The cast consists of three pretty girls and three best buddies who have never met but will be properly paired off by the fade-out.

2790. *A Stranger Among Us* (1992, Hollywood–Buena Vista, 111m, c). D Sidney Lumet, P Steve Golin, Sigurjon Sighvatsson & Howard Rosenman, W Robert J. Avrech, PH Andrzej Bartkowiak, ED Andrew Mondshein, M Jerry Bock, PD Philip Rosenberg, AD Steven Graham, SD Gary Brink.

LP Melanie Griffith (Emily Eden), Eric Thal (Ariel), John Pankow (Levine), Tracy Pollan (Mara), Lee Richardson (Rebbe), Mia Sara (Leah), James Sheridan (Nick Kemp), Jake Weber (Yaakov).

Every time we think Griffith has hit a new low in her film roles, something like this comes along. She's a tough police detective who moves in with a community of New York City Hasidic Jews when a jeweler is found dead and $1 million in diamonds are missing. Usually undercover cops are meant to blend in, but that's not Griffith's style. Instead she uses her baby voice and brassy attitude to win the love of Thal, one of the most devout members of the group.

2791. *Strangers in Good Company* (AKA: *The Company of Strangers*) (1991, Canada, First Run Features/Castle Hill Prods., 100m, c). D Cynthia Scott, P & ED David Wilson, W Gloria Demers, Scott, Wilson & Sally Bochner, PH David De Volpi, M Marie Bernard.

LP Alice Diablo (Alice), Constance Garneau (Constance), Winifred Holden (Winnie), Cissy Meddings (Cissy), Mary Meigs (Mary), Catherine Roche (Catherine), Michelle Sweeney (Michelle), Beth Webber (Beth).

A group of Canadian actresses portray themselves. The slow-moving but interesting story is about how they react and interact when the bus they are traveling on breaks down, stranding them in the Canadian wilderness.

2792. *Street Asylum* (1990, Magnum, 94m, c). D Gregory Brown, P Walter D. Gernert, W John Powers (based on a story by Brown), PH Paul Desatoff, ED Kert Vander Meulen, M Leonard Marcel, PD Robert Fox.

LP Wings Hauser (Sgt. Arliss Ryder), Alex Cord (Capt. Bill Quinton), Roberta Vasquez (Kristin), G. Gordon Liddy (Jim Miller), Marie Chambers (Dr. Weaver Cane).

Liddy, of Watergate infamy, is as bad an actor as those who broke into the Democratic headquarters were burglars. He comes up with a plan to clear the streets of scum by planting in cops a device that makes them kill anyone whose looks they don't like.

2793. *Street Fighter* (1994, U.S./Japan, Universal, 95m, c). D & W Steven E. de Souza, P Edward R. Pressman & Kenzo Tsujimoto, PH William A. Fraker, ED Dov Hoenig, M Graeme Revell, PD William J. Creber, AD Ian Gracie, SD Susan Mayberry & Lesley Crawford.

LP Jean-Claude Van Damme (Guile), Raul Julia (M. Bison), Ming Na Wen (Chun-Li), Damian Chapa (Ken), Kylie Minogue (Cammy), Simon Callow (A.N. Official), Roshan Seth (Dhalsim), Wes Studi (Sagat).

Based on the popular video game, this film stars Van Damme as the leader of a group of elite troops who are dispatched to the mythical nation of Shadaloo to ruin the plans of evil dictator Julia, intent on world domination.

Too bad Julia had to make his final film appearance in such an unworthy vehicle.

2794. *Street Knight* (1993, Cannon Pictures, 93m, c). D Albert Magnoli, P Mark DiSalle, W Richard Friedman & Jeff Schechter, PH Yasha Sklansky, ED Wayne Wahrman, M David Michael Frank, PD Curtis Schnell, AD Michael L. Fox, SD Archie D'Amico.

LP Jeff Speakman (Jake Barrett), Christopher Neame (Franklin), Lewis Van Bergen (Lt. Bill Crowe), Jennifer Gatti (Rebecca), Bernie Casey (Raymond), Richard Coca (Carlos), Stephen Liska (Santino).

Ex-cop Speakman finds himself in the middle when the truce between two street gangs is broken by mysterious murders of members of both groups.

2795. *Street Soldiers* (1991, Academy Ent., 98m, c). D Lee Harry, P Jun Chong, W Spencer Grendhal & Harry (based on the story by Chong), PH Dennis Peters, ED Harry, M David Bergeaud, PD Matthew Jacobs, AD David Koneff.

LP Jun Chong (Master Han), Jeff Rector (Priest), David Homb (Troy), Johnathan Gorman (Max), Joon Kim (Charles), Katherine Armstrong (Julie), Jason Hwang (Tok).

Martial arts experts attempt to take back the streets from punks and other undesirables.

2796. *Streets* (1990, Concorde, 83m, c). D & W Katt Shea Ruben, P & W Andy Ruben, PH Phedon Papamichael, ED Stephen Mark, M Aaron Davis, PD Virginia Lee, AD Johan Le Tenoux, SD Abigail Scheuer.

LP Christina Applegate (Dawn), David Mendenhall (Sy), Eb Lottimer (Lumley), Patrick Richwood (Bob), Kady Tran (Dawn's Blonde Roommate).

Applegate has had a lot of practice posing as an illiterate teen in her role on TV's *Married with Children*. This film looks at the problems of teen runaways who try to survive on the streets in Venice, California.

2797. *Strictly Ballroom* (1993, Australia, Miramax, 92m, c). D Baz Luhrmann, P Tristram Miall & Ted Albert, W Luhrmann & Craig Pearce, PH Steve Mason, ED Jill Bilcock, M David Hirshfelder, PD Catherine Martin.

LP Paul Mercurio (Scott Hastings), Tara

Morice (Fran), Bill Hunter (Barry Fife), Barry Otto (Doug Hastings), Pat Thompson (Shirley Hastings), Gia Carides (Liz Holt), Peter Whitford (Les Kendall), John Hannan (Ken Railings), Sonia Kruger-Taylor (Tina Sparkle).

What a jolly good film. It examines the world of ballroom dancing contests down under. The son of ballroom dancers, Mercurio has been in training to win the championship since he was barely old enough to tie his dance shoes. When his longtime partner deserts him, he chooses beginner Morice as his new partner. The two click together because, don't you see, she loves him. The duo has to overcome the dishonest tricks of a promoter and the prejudice of other competitors before — well, do you really expect they'd make a movie in which they lost?

2798. *Strictly Business* (1991, Warner Bros., 83m, c). D Kevin Hooks, P Andre Harrell & Pam Gibson, W Gibson & Nelson George, PH Zoltan David, ED Richard Nord, M Michel Colombier, PD Ruth Ammon, AD Rowena Rowling, SD Sonja Roth.

LP Tommy Davidson (Bobby Johnson), Joseph C. Phillips (Waymon Tinsdale III), Halle Berry (Natalie), David Marshall Grant (David), Anne Marie Johnson (Diedre), Jon Cypher (Drake).

Black broker Phillips learns that lovely Berry finds him square and boring, even though he's about to close a multi-million dollar deal for his firm. He turns for help to mail-room worker Davidson for advice on how to dress and behave.

2799. *Strike!* (1998, U.S./Canada, Miramax, 110m, c). D & W Sarah Kernochan, P Ira Deutchman & Peter Newman, PH Anthony Janelli, ED Peter C. Frank, M Graeme Revell, PD John Kasarda, AD Kim Karon.

LP Lynn Redgrave (Miss McVane), Gaby Hoffman (Odie), Kirsten Dunst (Verena), Monica Keena (Tinka), Merritt Wever (Momo), Heather Matarazzo (Tweety).

This comedy-drama is the story of the revolt that takes place in the early 1960s when an all-female boarding school is forced to go coeducational.

2800. *Strike It Rich* (AKA: *Loser Take All*) (1990, BBC–Ideal–Flamingo, 87m, c). D & W James Scott (based on the novel *Loser Takes All* by Graham Greene), P Christine Oestre-

icher & Graham Easton, PH Robert Paynter, ED Thomas Schwalm, PD & SD Christopher Hobbs, AD Mike Buchanan.

LP Molly Ringwald (Cary Porter), Robert Lindsay (Ian Bertram), John Gielgud (Herbert Dreuther), Max Wall (Bowles), Simon de la Brosse (Philippe).

After a whirlwind courtship, prudish British accountant Lindsay and his new wife Ringwald honeymoon in Monte Carlo. Running out of money to pay their way back home, they try their luck at the gambling tables. It seems he's a whiz with numbers and is sure that he can come up with a surefire system for winning at roulette. He does, but just about loses Ringwald in the process.

2801. *Striking Distance* (1993, Columbia, 101m, c). D Rowdy Herrington, P Arnon Milchan, Tony Thomopoulos & Hunt Lowry, W Herrington & Martin Kaplan, PH Mac Ahlberg & Tom Priestley, ED Pasquale Buba, Mark Helfrich & Harry B. Miller III, M Brad Fiedel, PD Gregg Fonseca, AD Bruce Miller & William Arnold, SD Jay Hart, Steve Arnold & Gina Granham.

LP Bruce Willis (Tom Hardy), Sarah Jessica Parker (Jo Christman), Dennis Farina (Nick Detillo), Tom Sizemore (Danny Detillo), Brion James (Detective Eddie Eiler), Robert Pastorelli (Jimmy Detillo), Timothy Busfield (Tony Sacco), John Mahoney (Vince Hardy).

Believing that his cop father Mahoney was killed by a serial killer who was also a cop, fifth-generation cop Willis is transferred to River patrol, with Parker as his partner. When the serial killer begins to choose women victims who have some connection to Willis, he has to find the perpetrator quickly before Parker is next.

2802. *Striptease* (1996, Castle Rock–Columbia, 115m, c). D & W Andrew Bergman (based on the novel by Carl Hiaasen), P Mike Lobell, PH Stephen Goldblatt, ED Anne V. Coates, M Howard Shore, PD Mel Bourne, AD Elizabeth Lapp, SD Leslie Bloom.

LP Demi Moore (Erin Grant), Armand Assante (Al Garcia), Ving Rhames (Shad), Burt Reynolds (Congressman David L. Dilbeck), Robert Patrick (Darrell Grant), Paul Guilfoyle (Malcolm Moldovsky), Jerry Grayson (Orly), Rumer Willis (Angela Grant), William Hill (Jerry Killian).

Moore, formerly a secretary with the FBI, loses her daughter in a bitter custody fight. Needing more money than she can earn as a secretary, Moore takes a job with a strip club. She soon becomes the favorite of club bouncer Rhames; loyal customer Hill, who is a social misfit; and congressman Reynolds, who can't control his dissipation. When Hill is found drowned, Miami cop Assante enters the picture. Moore shows about as much grace and seductiveness in her stripping as would a male longshoreman in drag at a bachelor party. Somehow the murder gets solved, the congressman gets his comeuppance and Moore gets back her daughter.

2803. Stuart Little (1999, Sony Pictures–Columbia Pictures, 92m, c). D Rob Minkoff, P Douglas Wick, W M. Night Shyamalan & Greg Brooker (based on the book by E.B. White), PH Guillermo Navarro, ED Tom Finan, M Alan Silvestri, PD Bill Brzeski, AD Philip Toolin, SD Clay A. Griffith.

LP Geena Davis (Mrs. Little), Hugh Laurie (Mr. Little), Jonathan Lipnicki (George Little), Brian Doyle-Murray (Cousin Edgar), Estelle Getty (Grandma Estelle), Julia Sweeney (Mrs. Keeper), Dabney Coleman (Dr. Beechwood). Voices: Michael J. Fox (Stuart Little), Nathan Lane (Snowbell), Chazz Palminteri (Smokey), Steve Zahn (Monty), Jim Doughan (Lucky), David Alan Grier (Red), Bruno Kirby (Mr. Stout), Jennifer Tilly (Mrs. Stout).

Lipnicki was expecting his parents Davis and Laurie to bring home a little brother to play with from the adoption agency. Instead, for some unexplained reason they arrive with a mouse named Stuart. And so, E.B. White's delightful character is introduced to the screen. Fox gives him a voice, and a fine voice it is. The little rodent is not welcomed by the family cat, voiced by Lane, who is told that Stuart is a member of the family and one does not eat members of the family. Not satisfied with sharing his home with a mouse, Lane and feline crime boss Palminteri, borrowing from the musical *Annie*, bring in a pair of mice, Kirby and Tilly, to pose as Stuart's long-lost real parents. All ends well, however.

2804. Stuart Saves His Family (1995, Paramount, 100m, c). D Harold Ramis, P Lorne Michaels & Trevor Albert, W Al Franken (based on his book), PH Lauro Es-corel, ED Pembroke Herring & Craig Herring, M Marc Shaiman, PD Joseph T. Garrity, AD Thomas P. Wilkins, SD Dena Roth.

LP Al Franken (Stuart Smalley), Laura San Giacomo (Julia), Vincent D'Onofrio (Donnie), Shirley Knight (Stuart's Mom), Harris Yulin (Stuart's Dad), Lesley Bone (Jodie), John Link Graney (Kyle).

Franklin recreates his *Saturday Night Live* character Stuart Smalley. After being fired from his Chicago public access station, the New Age advice guru attempts to help members of his dysfunctional family with their problems. If you enjoyed the characterization on SNL, you may enjoy this feature. If you don't watch SNL, you'll probably wish to pass.

2805. Stuff Stephanie in the Incinerator (1990, Troma/Allied, 97m, c). D & P Don Nardo, W Nardo & Peter Jones, PH Herb Fuller, ED James Napoli.

LP Catherine Dee (Stephanie/Casey), William Dame (Paul/Jared), M.R. Murphy (Roberta/Robert), Dennis Cunningham (Nick/Rory), Paul Nielsen (Henchman/Butler).

Well, the title about tells it all. Those of you who will race to a video store to rent this one know what it is you like about Troma films. Others are better off not looking into them any further.

2806. The Stupids (1996, New Line, 93m, c). D John Landis, P Ron Howard, Brian Grazer & Leslie Belzberg, W Brent Forrester (based on characters created by James Marshall & Harry Allard), PH Manfred Guthe, ED Dale Beldin, M Christopher Stone, PD Phil Dagort, AD Rocco Matteo, SD Carol Lavoie.

LP Tom Arnold (Stanley Stupid), Jessica Lundy (Joan Stupid), Bug Hall (Buster Stupid), Alex McKenna (Petunia Stupid), Christopher Lee (Evil Sender).

Comedian Arnold is still trying to find his niche in pictures. Keep looking, Tom. He's the head of a family that lives up to its surname as they blunder their way through a series of dangerous adventures.

2807. Sub Down (1998, Carousel Picture Co., 91m, c). D Alan Smithee, P Daniel Sladek, Silvio Muragila & Jeffrey White, W Howard Chelsey, PH Hiro Narita, ED Cary Short, M Stefano Mainetti, AD Peter Powis, SD Beck Taylor.

LP Stephen Baldwin (Rick Postley), Tom Conti (Harry Rheinhardt), Gabrielle Anwar (Laura Dyson), Chris Mulkey (Commander John Kirsch), Tony Plana (Lt. Cmdr. Meiges), Joe Dain (Sonar Chief).

When a director takes his name off a film and credits it to Alan Smithee, as does Greg Champion here, it usually means the film is really a dud. Surprisingly, this story of three scientists trying to come to the aid of a disabled nuclear submarine stuck below the arctic ice cap isn't half bad.

2808. *The Substance of Fire* (1996, Miramax, 101m, c). D Daniel Sullivan, P Jon Rubin Baitz, Randy Finch & Ron Kastner, W Baitz (based on his play), PH Robert Yeoman, ED Pamela Martin, M Joseph Vitarelli, PD John Lee Beatty, AD Mark Ricker, SD Shelley Barclay.

LP Benjamin Ungar (Young Isaac Geldhart), Ron Rifkin (Isaac Geldhart), Tony Goldwyn (Aaron Geldhart), Lee Grant (Cora Cahn), Gil Bellows (Val Chenard), Eric Bogosian (Gene Byck), Timothy Hutton (Martin Geldhart).

Rifkin, a childhood survivor of the Holocaust, runs a respectable but not profitable publishing firm. He would rather risk bankruptcy by publishing a four-volume history of Nazi medical experiments than any commercial project. He finds himself in constant conflict over publishing decisions with his son and partner Goldwyn, who enlists his siblings in an effort to wrest control of the company from their father. It's a good effort, dealing with some important ideas.

2809. *The Substitute* (1996, Orion, 114m, c). D Robert Mandel, P Morrie Eisenman & Jim Steele, W Roy Frumkes, Rocco Simonelli & Alan Ormsby, PH Bruce Surtees, ED Alex Mackie, M Gary Chang, PD Ron Foreman, AD Richard Fojo, SD Barbara Peterson.

LP Tom Berenger (Shale), Diane Venora (Jane Hetzko), Ernie Hudson (Rolle), Marc Anthony (Juan Lucas), Glenn Plummer (Mr. Sherman), Maria Celedonio (Lisa).

Vietnam veteran Berenger poses as a substitute teacher at the school where his girlfriend Venora teaches. She has been beaten up for interfering in drug activities at the school. Not only does he make the school drug free, he has some positive effects on his surly students.

2810. *The Substitute Wife* (1995, Vidmark Ent., 92m, c). D Peter Werner, P Michael O. Gallant, W Stan Daniels, PH Neil Roach, ED Martin Nicholson, M Mark Snow, PD Cary White, AD Michael Sullivan, SD Barbara Haberecht.

LP Farrah Fawcett (Pearl Hickson), Lea Thompson (Amy Hightower), Peter Weller (Martin Hightower), Karis Bryant (Jessica Hightower), Cory Lloyd (Nathan Hightower).

Dying frontier woman Thompson seeks a new wife for her husband Weller to help him on his isolated farm and raise their four children. The only woman willing to tackle the job is prostitute Fawcett, fed up with the life of a working girl.

2811. *Suburban Commando* (1991, New Line Cinema, 99m, c). D Burt Kennedy, P Howard Gottfried, W Frank Cappello, PH Bernd Heinl, ED Terry Stokes, M David Michael Frank, PD Ivo Cristante, AD Karen D. Kornbau & Antoine Bonsorte, SD Cliff Cunningham.

LP Hulk Hogan (Shep Ramsey), Christopher Lloyd (Charlie Wilcox), Shelley Duvall (Jenny Wilcox), Larry Miller (Adrian Beltz), William Ball (General Suitor), JoAnn Dearing (Margie Tanen), Jack Elam (Col. Dustin "Dusty" McHowell).

Pro wrestler Hogan is an alien bounty hunter vacationing on earth, trying to be inconspicuous. Besides dealing with his arch interstellar enemy, he teaches nebbish Lloyd how to deal with his overbearing boss.

2812. *The Suburbans* (1999, MPCA, 81m, c). D Donal Lardner Ward, P Michael Burns, Brad Krevoy, J.J. Abrams & Leanna Creel, W Ward & Tony Guma, ED Kathryn Himoff, M Robbie Kondor, PD Susan Bolles, SD Catherine Pierson.

LP Craig Bierko (Mitch), Amy Brenneman (Grace), Antonio Fargas (Magee), Will Ferrell (Gil), Tony Guma (Rory), Jennifer Love Hewitt (Kate), Robert Loggia (Jules), Ben Stiller (Jay Rose).

An '80s New Wave band, consisting of Bierko, Ward, Ferrell and Guma, that proved to be a one-hit wonder reunites in the '90s for one last stab at stardom.

2813. *Suburbia* (1997, Castle Rock, 121m, c). D Richard Linklater, P Anne Walker-McBay,

W Eric Bogosian (based on his play *subUrbia*), PH Lee Daniel, ED Sandra Adair, M Sonic Youth, PD Catherine Hardwicke, AD Seth Reed, SD Keith Fletcher.

LP Giovanni Ribisi (Jeff), Steve Zahn (Buff), Amie Carey (Sooze), John Cherico (Shopping Channel Host), Samia Shoaib (Pakessa), Ajay Naidu (Nazeer), Nicky Katt (Tim), Jayce Bartok (Pony), Parker Posey (Erica).

A group of twenty-year-olds congregate each night in a convenience store in the suburban town of Burnfield to kill time long into the night. Most are losers, trying to find something to do with their lives but not working very hard at it.

2814. Sudden Death (1995, Universal, 110m, c). D Peter Hyams, P Moshe Diamant & Howard Baldwin, W Gene Quintano (based on a story by Karen Baldwin), PH Peter Hyams, ED Steven Kemper, M John Debney, PD Philip Harrison, AD William Barclay, SD Caryl Heller.

LP Jean-Claude Van Damme (Darren), Powers Boothe (Joshua Foss), Raymond J. Barry (Vice President), Whittni Wright (Emily), Ross Malinger (Tyler), Dorian Harewood (Hallmark).

Terrorists grab the vice president of the U.S. and his daughter at the Stanley Cup Hockey finals held in the Pittsburgh arena. They threaten to blow up the place and everyone in it if their demands are not met. What they didn't reckon on is that troubled fireman Van Damme and his kids are in the building. It's a kind of *Die Hard* with Jean-Claude swinging over the boards to replace Bruce Willis.

2815. Sudden Manhattan (1997, Phaedra Cinema, 85m, c). D & W Adrienne Shelly, P Marcia Kirkley, PH Jim Denault, ED Jack Haigis, M Pat Irwin, PD Teresa Mastropierro, AD Tina Khayat, SD Christina Manaca.

LP Adrienne Shelly (Donna), Tim Guinee (Adam), Roger Rees (Murphy), Louise Lasser (Dominga), Hynden Walch (Georgie), Jon Sklaroff (Alex), Paul Cassell (Ian).

Twenty-year-old neurotic Shelly isn't happy due to her lack of a job, lack of a love life and lack of direction. Her life has no meaning. Will she find any in this amusing comedy? Perhaps.

2816. Sugar Hill (1994, 20th Century–Fox, 123m, c). D Leon Ichaso, P Rudy Langlais

& Gregory Brown, W Barry Michael Cooper, PH Bojan Bazelli, ED Gary Karr, M Terence Blanchard, PD Michael Helmy, AD J. Jergensen, SD Kathryn Peters.

LP Wesley Snipes (Roemello Skuggs), Khandi Alexander (Ella Skuggs), Clarence Williams III (A.R. Skuggs), Abe Vigoda (Gus Molino), Michael Wright (Raynathan Skuggs), Kimberly Russell (Chantal), Theresa Randle (Melisa).

Having watched both his parents destroyed by heroin, Harlem drug dealer Snipes has had enough and tries to get out of the business. This doesn't sit well with his hothead, druggie brother Wright.

2817. Sugar Town (1999, October Films–Film Four, 92m, c). D & W Allison Anders & Kurt Voss, P Dan Hassid, PH Kristien Bernier, ED Chris Figler, M Larry Klein, PD Alyssa Coppleman.

LP Jade Gordon (Gwen), Michael Des Barres (Nick), Ally Sheedy (Liz), Rosanna Arquette (Eva), John Taylor (Clive), Martin Kemp (Jonesy), Larry Klein (Burt), Beverly D'Angelo (Jane).

This film examines the midlife crises of aging rock musicians in the L.A. rock 'n' roll subculture. Asking "Who cares?" is not meant to be a flippant kiss-off of the film. We're wondering which segment of the moviegoing audience will find this interesting — and can't think of any.

2818. Suicide Kings (1998, LIVE Ent., 106m, c). D Peter O'Fallon, P Morrie Eisenman & Wayne Rice, W Rice, Josh McKinney & Gina Goldman (based on the short story "The Hostage" by Don Stanford), PH Christopher Baffa, ED Chris Peppe, M Graeme Revell, PD Clark Hunter, AD Max Biscoe, SD Traci Kirshbaum.

LP Christopher Walken (Charles Barrett/Carlo Bartolucci), Denis Leary (Lono Vecchio), Sean Patrick Flanery (Max Minot), Johnny Galecki (Ira Reder), Jay Mohr (Brett Campbell), Laura San Giacomo (Lydia), Henry Thomas (Avery Chasten), Jeremy Sisto (T.K.), Laura Harris (Elise "Lisa" Chasten).

When Harris is kidnapped and her parents are unable to come up with the ransom of $2 million, her brother Thomas and her boyfriend Flanery, along with Mohr and Sisto, kidnap Mafia capo Walken, hoping to make a trade. It's a dangerous game.

2819. *The Sum of Us* (1995, Australia, Samuel Goldwyn Co., 100m, c). D Kevin Dowling & Geoff Burton, P Hal McElroy, W David Stevens (based on his play), PH Burton, ED Frans Vandenburg, M Dave Faulkner, PD Graham "Grace" Walker, AD Ian Gracie, SD Kerrie Brown.

LP Jack Thompson (Harry Mitchell), Russell Crowe (Jeff Mitchell), John Polson (Greg), Deborah Kennedy (Joyce Johnson), Joss Morony (Young Jeff), Mitch Mathews (Gran).

In a charming and witty film, Thompson is a fun-loving, working-class widower who not only knows his son Crowe is gay but is enthusiastic about it, hoping the younger man will find his special person.

2820. *The Summer House* (1993, U.K., Samuel Goldwyn Co., 82m, c). D Waris Hussein, P Norma Heyman, W Martin Sherman (based on the novel *The Clothes in the Wardrobe* by Alice Thomas Ellis), PH Rex Maidment, ED Ken Pearce, M Stanley Myers, PD Stuart Walker.

LP Jeanne Moreau (Lili), Joan Plowright (Mrs. Monro), Julie Walters (Monica), David Threlfall (Syl), Maggie Steed (Mrs. Raffald), John Wood (Robert), Gwyneth Strong (Cynthia), Roger Lloyd Pack (Derek), Catherine Schell (Marie-Clair), Lena Headley (Margaret).

Moreau is not just getting older, she's getting better — at comedy, that is. She's the high-spirited girlhood chum of Walters. She comes to visit at the time of Walters' daughter Headley's wedding to boorish next-door neighbor Threlfall. That they are not right for each other should be obvious to all, but at least it is to Moreau. She teams with Plowright, the mother of the groom, to derail the wedding. Moreau once had an affair with Plowright's husband, and what better way to break things up than to take his son in the same summer house that she had his father.

2821. *Summer of Sam* (1999, Buena Vista–Touchstone, 142m, c). D Spike Lee, P Jon Kilik & Lee, W Victor Colicchio, PH Ellen Kuras, ED Barry Alexander, M Terence Blanchard, PD Therese DePrez, AD Nicholas Lundy, SD Denise Lunderman.

LP John Leguizamo (Vinny), Adrien Brody (Ritchie), Mira Sorvino (Dionna), Jennifer Esposito (Ruby), Anthony LaPaglia (Detective Lou Petrocelli), Patti LuPone (Helen), Ben Gazzara (Luigi), Joe Lisi (Tony Olives), Michael Badalucco (Son of Sam).

One may grow weary before this long film ends, despite the excitement of director Lee's examination of the effect of the murderous rampage of a monstrous killer, known as "the Son of Sam," in the Bronx in 1977. The story is not told from the point of view of the killer, but rather that of Italian Americans living in the neighborhood where he operates. Things come to a head during a blackout, which leads to riots.

2822. *Summer of the Monkeys* (1998, Canada, Edge Prods., 101m, c). D Michael Anderson, P David Doerksen, Ellen Freyer & Chris Harding, W Greg Taylor & Jim Smith (based on the book by Wilson Rawls), PH Michael Storey, ED Lenka Svab, M George Blondheim, PD Seamus Flannery, AD Bill Ives, SD Dan Conley.

LP Michael Ontkean (John Lee), Leslie Hope (Sara Lee), Wilford Brimley (Grandpa Sam Ferens), Corey Sevier (Jay Berry Lee), Katie Stuart (Daisy Lee), Don Francks (Bayliss Hatcher).

Set in some unspecified time in rural America, this family film preaches the same family values found in *The Waltons* and *Little House on the Prairie*. The story isn't of much importance.

2823. *Sunchaser* (1996, Warner Bros., 121m, c). D Michael Cimino, P Arnon Milchan, Cimino, Larry Spiegel, Judy Goldstein & Joseph M. Vecchio, W Charles Leavitt, PH Doug Milsome, ED Joe D'Augustine, M Maurice Jarre, PD Victoria Paul, AD Lee Mayman & Edward L. Rubin, SD Jackie Carr.

LP Woody Harrelson (Dr. Michael Reynolds), Jon Seda (Brandon "Blue" Monroe), Anne Bancroft (Dr. Renata Baumbauer), Alexandra Tydings (Victoria Reynolds), Matt Mulhern (Dr. Chip Byrnes), Talisa Soto (Navajo Woman).

In a farfetched adventure story, L.A. oncologist Harrelson is forced at gun point to drive 16-year-old convict Seda, suffering from abdominal cancer, to the Sacred Healing Mountain of the Navajos. Along the way the unlikely pair don't get along, as one would expect, but ultimately they begin to meet each other halfway, as moviegoers would expect.

2824. Sunday (1997, CFP Distribution, 93m, c). D Jonathan Nossiter, P Nossiter & Alix Madigan, W James Lasdun & Nossiter, PH Michael Barrow & John Foster, ED Madeleine Gavin, PD Dena Sidney, AD Stephen Beatrice, SD Anna Park.

LP David Suchet (Matthew/Oliver), Lisa Harrow (Madeleine Vesey), Jared Harris (Ray), Larry Pine (Ben Vesey), Joe Grifasi (Scotti Elster), Arnold Barkus (Andy).

This film concentrates on one dreary Sunday afternoon in the life of a group of aimless misfits living in a section of Queens. Suchet has just lost his job as an IBM accountant. He wanders into the life of washed-up acting beauty Harrow and allows her to believe that he is a famed art-film director. The film won Best Picture honors at the Sundance Film Festival. It's well worth a look.

2825. Sundown: The Vampire in Retreat (1991, Vestron, 104m, c). D Anthony Hickox, P Jefferson Richard, W Hickox & John Burgess, PH Levie Isaacks, ED Christopher Cibelli, M Richard Stone, PD David Miller, AD Fernando Altschul.

LP David Carradine (Count Mardulak), Deborah Foreman (Sandy), Jim Metzler (David Harrison), Morgan Brittany (Sarah), Maxwell Caulfield (Shane), M. Emmet Walsh (Milt), Bruce Campbell (Van Helsing), Dana Ashbrook (Jack), John Ireland (Jefferson).

In this vampire comedy, a family stumbles into a present day Western town inhabited by bloodsuckers trying unsuccessfully to kick the habit.

2826. Sunset Grill (1993, New Line Cinema, 103m, c). D Kevin Connor, P Faruque Ahmed, W Marcus Wright & Ahmed, PH Douglas Milsome, ED Barry Peters, M Ken Thorne, PD Yehuda Ako, SD Lisa Deutsch.

LP Peter Weller (Ryder Hart), Lori Singer (Loren Duquesne), Stacy Keach (Harrison Shelgrove), Michael Anderson, Jr. (Carruthers), Alexandra Paul (Anita), John Rhys-Davies (Stockton).

While investigating the murder of his wife, down-and-out private detective Weller is lured south of the border by singer Singer. She brings him to her boss, who is behind a series of grisly murders in a moneymaking scheme.

2827. Sunset Park (1996, TriStar, 100m, c). D Steve Gomer, P Danny DeVito, Michael Shamberg & Dan Paulson, W Seth Zvi Rosenfeld & Kathleen McGhee-Anderson, PH Robbie Greenberg, ED Arthur Coburn, M Miles Goodman & Kay Gee, PD Victoria Paul, AD Lee Mayman, SD Brian Kasch.

LP Rhea Perlman (Phyllis Saroka), Fredo Starr (Shorty), Carol Kane (Mona), Terrence DaShon Howard (Spaceman), Camille Saviola (Barbara), De'Aundre Bonds (Busy-Bee), James Harris (Butter).

Coaches trying to appear humble often express the sentiment that what makes a good coach are good players. Perlman is a Brooklyn P.E. teacher who finds herself the coach of a high school basketball team. Despite her complete lack of knowledge about the game, the team makes it to the city championship. She must have had the horses.

2828. The Super (1991, 20th Century–Fox, 84m, c). D Rod Daniel, P Charles Gordon, W Sam Simon, PH Bruce Surtees, ED Jack Hofstra, M Miles Goodman, PD Kristi Zea, AD Jeremy Conway, SD Leslie Pope.

LP Joe Pesci (Louie Kritski), Vincent Gardenia (Big Lou Kritski), Madolyn Smith Osborne (Naomi Bensinger), Ruben Blades (Marlon), Stacey Travis (Heather), Carole Shelley (Irene Kritski), Kenny Blank (Tito), Paul Benjamin (Gilliam).

Pesci and his father Gardenia are slumlords facing jail because of their neglect of their properties. Gardenia is able to shift the responsibility to Pesci. His punishment is to be forced to live in one of his rat holes until he provides reasonable living conditions to all his apartments. There are lessons to be learned, and he learns them.

2829. Super Mario Bros. (1993, Hollywood Pictures–Buena Vista, 104m, c). D Rocky Morton & Annabel Jankel, P Jake Eberts & Roland Joffe, W Ed Solomon, Terry Runte & Parker Bennett, PH Dean Semler, James Devis & Charles A. Schumann, ED Mark Goldblatt & Caroline Ross, M Alan Silvestri, PD David L. Snyder, AD Walter P. Martishius, SD Beth Rubino, John Kretschmer, Timothy Galvin, John P. Goldsmith, Geoffrey S. Grimsman, Clare Scarpulla, Kathleen Sullivan, Tim Eckel, Nancy Mickelberry & Bruton Jones.

LP Bob Hoskins (Mario Mario), John Leguizamo (Luigi Mario), Dennis Hopper (King

Koopa), Samantha Mathis (Daisy), Fisher Stevens (Iggy), Richard Edson (Spike), Fiona Shaw (Lena).

First the video game, now the movie! If you find it hard to believe that it is possible to make an entertaining film from a video about two toon-like characters attempting to rescue a princess who has been kidnapped, you would be correct.

2830. Superstar (1999, Paramount, 82m, c). D Bruce McCulloch, P Lorne Michaels, W Steven Wayne Koren (based on a character created by Molly Shannon), PH Walt Lloyd, ED Malcolm Campbell, M Michael Gore, PD Gregory Keen, AD Peter Grundy, SD Doug McCullough.

LP Molly Shannon (Mary Katherine Gallagher), Will Ferrell (Sky), Elaine Hendrix (Evian), Harlan Williams (Slater), Mark McKinney (Father Ritley), Glynis Johns (Grandma), Emmy Laybourne (Helen).

Members of the cast of TV's *Saturday Night Live* constantly attempt to blow up a routine that works for a brief time on the tube into a full length feature on the big screen. Rarely are the SNL alumni successful. So one shouldn't expect much from Shannon and her clumsy Catholic schoolgirl who desperately attempts to win the affection of BMOC Ferrell. Well, one wouldn't be wrong in having limited expectations, as the laughs are too few and too far between.

2831. Surrender Dorothy (1998, Rich Ent., 87m, b&w). D, W & ED Kevin DiNovis, P Richard Goldberg, PH Jonathan Kovel, M Christopher Matarazzo, PD Michael Doyle, AD Jessica Anne Gurani.

LP Peter Pryor (Trevor), Kevin DiNovis (Lanh/Dorothy), Jason Centeno (Denis), Elizabeth Casey (Vicky), Marcos Muniz (Angel), Keri Merboth (Nadia).

Heroin addict DiNovis takes shelter with Pryor after robbing a dealer. Using drugs as an inducement, Pryor turns DiNovis into his drag queen slave. The film is less about sex than power and control.

2832. Survival Quest (1990, MGM-UA, 90m, c). D, W & ED Don Coscarelli, P Roberto Quezada, PH Daryn Okada, M Fred Myrow & Christopher L. Stone, PD Andrew Siegal, SD Robb Bradshaw & Scott Bruza.

LP Lance Henriksen (Hank Chambers), Dermot Mulroney (Gray Atkinson), Traci Lin (Olivia), Mark Rolston (Jake Cannon), Ben Hammer (Hal), Catharine Keener (Cheryl), Steve Antin (Raider).

Enrolled in a survival course set in the Rocky Mountains, students find that their greatest challenge to survival is not the elements but a a gang of bloodthirsty mercenaries who arrive in the same area.

2833. Surviving Picasso (1996, Warner Bros., 100m, c). D James Ivory, P Ismail Merchant & David L. Wolper, W Ruth Prawer Jhabvala, PH Tony Pierce-Roberts, ED Andrew Marcus, M Richard Robbins, PD Luciana Arrighi.

LP Anthony Hopkins (Pablo Picasso), Natascha McElhone (Francoise), Julianne Moore (Dora Maar), Joss Ackland (Henri Matisse), Peter Eyre (Sabartes), Jane Lapotaire (Olga Picasso).

Life with the most famous painter of the 20th century, here played by Hopkins, is told from the point of view of his young mistress McElhone. During the years 1943–53, she gives birth to two of his children and finds him a difficult man to live with. Ultimately she makes the break with him to live her own life.

2834. Surviving the Game (1994, New Line, 96m, c). D Ernest Dickerson, P David Permut, W Eric Bernt, PH Bojan Bazelli, ED Sam Pollard, M Stewart Copeland, PD Christiaan Wagener, AD Madelyne Marcom, SD George Toomer, Jr.

LP Ice-T (Jack Mason), Rutger Hauer (Burns), Charles S. Dutton (Cole), Gary Busey (Hawkins), F. Murray Abraham (Wolfe, Sr.), John C. McGinley (Griffin), William McNamara (Wolfe, Jr.).

In a modern-day version of *The Most Dangerous Game*, a group of bored, wealthy hunters hire homeless Ice-T to help them set up a hunt at a secluded wooded area. It's only later that he learns he's to be their prey.

2835. Susan's Plan (1998, Kushner-Locke Prods., 89m, c). D & W Jim Landis, P Leslie Belzberg, Brad Wyman & Landis, PH Ken Kelsch, ED Nancy Morrison, M Peter Bernstein, PD Stuart Blatt, AD Kitty Doris Bates.

LP Nastassja Kinski (Susan Holland), Billy Zane (Sam), Michael Biehn (Bill), Rob

Schneider (Steve), Lara Flynn Boyle (Betty Johnson), Dan Aykroyd (Bob), Carl Balentine (Henry Byers), Adrian Paul (Paul Holland).

In this comedy thriller, Kinski, with the assistance of her insurance salesman lover Zane, plots to murder her ex-husband Paul and collect on his insurance policy. The couple hire Boyle to lure Paul to a place where the victim will meet his end at the hands of Biehn and Schneider. Things do not go according to plan.

2836.   The Swan Princess   (1994, New Line, 90m, c). D Richard Rich, P Rich & Jared F. Brown, W Brian Nissen (based on a story by Nissen & Rich), ED Armetta Jackson-Hamlett & James Koford, M Lex deAzevedo, AD Mike Hodgson & James Coleman, ANIM Stephen E. Gordon.

LP Voices: Jack Palance (Rothbart), Howard McGillin (Prince Derek), Michelle Nicastro (Princess Odette), Liz Callaway (Princess Odette's singing voice), John Cleese (Jean-Bob), Stephen Wright (Speed).

The story is loosely based on *Swan Lake*, with a modern twist. Princess Odette is turned off by the emphasis her intended Prince Derek places on her beauty and flees the kingdom. She is snagged by evil Rothbart, an enchanter who turns her into a swan. She must be rescued by Derek, who has developed a more agreeable appreciation of Odette.

2837.   The Sweeper   (1996, PM Ent. Group, 101m, c). D Joseph Merhi, P Merhi & Richard Pepin, W William Applegate, Jr. & Karen McCoy (based on a story by Jacobsen Hart), PH Ken Blakey, ED Paul G. Volk, M K. Alexander Wilkinson, PD Robert Cowan, AD David Sandefur.

LP C. Thomas Howell (Mark Goddard), Ed Lauter (Molls), Kristen Dalton (Rachel), Janet Gunn (Melissa), Felton Perry (Foster), Max Slade (Young Mark), Cynda Williams (Diane).

Felons don't look forward to being arrested by cop Howell. Soon after being taken into his custody they die. When he is recruited by a secret society intent on dealing out their own brand of justice, he discovers the reason for his problem and the truth about the murder of his policeman father.

2838.   Sweet and Lowdown   (1999, Sony Classics–Sweetland Films, 95m, c). D & W Woody Allen, P Jean Doumanian, PH Zhao Fei, ED Alisa Lepselter, M Dick Hyman, PD Santo Loquasto, AD Tom Warren.

LP Sean Penn† (Emmet Ray), Samantha Morton† (Hattie), Uma Thurman (Blanche), Brian Markinson (Bill Shields), Anthony LaPaglia (Al Torrio), Gretchen Mol (Ellie), Vincent Gusataferro (Sid Bishop).

Allen's annual film is a fictionalized biopic of Emmet Ray, portrayed by Penn, who supposedly is a legendary American Jazz guitarist of the 1930s. Actually, Ray is a fictional character, played by Penn as an explosive, self-centered extrovert with an ego greater than the legend he seeks. He's no one to admire, except when he's making music. Not interested in having anything other than quick flings with women, whom he treats like dirt, he is nevertheless quite taken with mute Morton. He lives with and cheats on her regularly, finally leaving her to marry sultry writer Thurman, who doesn't give up her liaison with gangster LaPaglia. Penn soon realizes what a mistake he's made by leaving Morton.

2839.   The Sweet Hereafter   (1997, Canada, Fine Line, 110m, c). D Atom Egoyan†, P Camelia Frieberg & Egoyan, W Egoyan† (based on the novel by Russell Banks), PH Paul Sarossy, ED Susan Shipton, M Mychael Danna, PD Phillip Barker, AD Kathleen Climie, SD Patricia Cuccia.

LP Ian Holm (Mitchell Stephens), Sarah Polley (Nicole Burnell), Bruce Greenwood (Billy Ansell), Tom McCamus (Sam Burnell), Gabrielle Rose (Dolores Driscoll), Arsinee Khanjian (Wanda Otto), Alberta Watson (Risa Walker), Maury Chaykin (Wendell Walker).

This film examines the effects on the community of Sam Dent, British Columbia, after a school bus accident wipes out many of its children. The story is told from the points of view of four characters: Rose, is the school bus driver; Ansel, a widower who lost two children; Holm, a big-city lawyer in town hired to file a negligence suit; and Polley, a teenager who survived the crash but lost the ability to walk.

2840.   Sweet Justice   (1993, Triboro Ent., 92m, c). D Allen Plone, P Carol Marcus Plone, W Allen Plone & Jim Tabilio.

LP Marc Singer (Steve Cotton), Finn Carter (Sunny Justice), Frank Gorshin (Rivas), Catherine Hickland (Chris), Marjean Holden (M.J.).

Carter heads up a team of female commandos who avenge the sadistic murder of a friend.

2841. *Sweet Murder* (1993, Vidmark Ent., 101m, c). D & W Percival Rubens, P Paul Raleigh, PH Chris Schutte, ED Bernie Buys, M Russell Stirling.

LP Russell Todd (Del), Helen Udy (Lisa), Embeth Davidtz (Laurie), Danny Keough (Laurie's Stepfather), Michael McCabe (Mr. Pearson).

In a rip-off of *Single White Female*, Udy takes Davidtz as a roommate. She sort of resembles an ax-murderer.

2842. *Sweet Nothing* (1996, Warner Bros., 90m, c). D Gary Winick, P Rick Bowman & Winick, W Lee Drysdale, PH Makoto Watanabe, ED Niels Mueller, M Steven M. Stern, PD Amy Tapper, AD Amy Silver, SD Chad Jacobson.

LP Michael Imperioli (Angel), Mira Sorvino (Monika), Paul Calderon (Raymond), Patrick Breen (Greg), Richard Bright (Jack the Cop), Billie Neal (Rio).

Wall Street executive Imperioli is one of his own best customers in a sideline business of selling crack. Sorvino plays his faithful wife. It's tough watching his life and family disintegrate.

2843. *Sweet Talker* (1990, Australia, New Visions Pictures, 89m, c). D Michael Jenkins, P Ben Gannon, W Tony Morphett (based on the story by Morphett & Bryan Brown), PH Russell Boyd, ED Sheldon Kahn & Neil Thumpston, M Richard Thompson & Peter Filleul, PD John Stoddart, AD John Wingrove.

LP Bryan Brown (Harry Reynolds), Karen Allen (Julie), Justin Rosniak (David), Chris Haywood (Bostock), Bill Kerr (Cec), Bruce Spence (Norman Foster).

Smooth-talking and amicable con man Brown plans to play on the greed of the inhabitants of a remote Australian coastal town, where legend has it a pirate galleon loaded with gold is buried beneath the sand dunes. Brown falls in love with Allen and begins to have second thoughts about cheating his marks.

2844. *Swept from the Sea* (1998, U.K./U.S., Tri-Star, 115m, c). D Beeban Kidron, P Polly Tapson, Charles Steel & Kidron, W Tim Willocks (based on the short story "Amy Foster" by Joseph Conrad), PH Dick Pope, ED Alex Mackie & Andrew Mondshein, M John Barry, PD Simon Holland, AD Clinton Cavers, SD Neesh Ruben.

LP Vincent Perez (Yanko Gooral), Rachel Weisz (Amy Foster), Ian McKellen (Dr. James Kennedy), Joss Ackland (Mr. Swaffer), Kathy Bates (Miss Swaffer), Tom Bell (Isaac Foster).

Perez is the only survivor of a shipwreck off the coast of Cornwall in the late 19th century. Coming from the Carpathian mountains, he cannot be understood by the locals, who are suspicious of anything or anyone different. He is kept as a virtual slave but still is able to find love with serving girl Weisz, also an outsider, because she was born out of wedlock.

2845. *Swimming with Sharks* (AKA: *The Buddy Factor*) (1995, Trimark Pictures, 93m, c). D & W George Huang, P Steve Alexander & Joanne Moore, PH Steven Finestone, ED Ed Marx, M Tom Heil, PD Veronica Merlin & Cecil Gentry, AD Karen Haase.

LP Kevin Spacey (Buddy Ackerman), Frank Whaley (Guy), Michelle Forbes (Dawn Lockard), Benicio Del Toro (Rex), T.E. Russell (Foster Kane), Roy Dotrice (Cyrus Miles).

Screenwriter Whaley is repeatedly insulted and abused by his movie producer boss Spacey. Unable to stand the treatment any longer he kidnaps Spacey and reciprocates.

2846. *Swing* (1999, U.K., Tapestry, 98m, c). D & W Nick Mead (based on a story by Mead & Su Lim), P Su Lim & Louise Rosner, PH Ian Wilson, ED Norman Buckley, PD Richard Bridgland, AD Niki Longmuir.

LP Hugo Speer (Martin), Lisa Stansfield (Joan), Paul Usher (Liam), Tom Bell (Sid), Rita Tushingham (Mags), Danny McCall (Andy), Alexei Sayle (Mighty Mac).

While in prison Speer learned how to play the saxophone. On his release he looks up his former girlfriend, singer Stansfield, even though she's married the police officer responsible for putting him away. By the end of this musical comedy Speer will have become a musical success.

2847. *Swing Kids* (1993, Hollywood Pictures–Buena Vista, 112m, c). D Thomas Carter, P Mark Gordon & John Bard Manulis, W Jonathan Marc Feldman, PH Jerzy Zielinski,

ED Michael R. Miller, M James Horner, PD Allan Cameron, AD Steve Spence, Tony Reading & Michel Krska, SD Rosiland Shingleton.

LP Robert Sean Leonard (Peter), Christian Bale (Thomas), Frank Whaley (Arvid), Barbara Hershey (Frau Muller), Kenneth Branagh (SS Official), Tushka Bergen (Evey), David Tom (Willi), Julia Stemberger (Frau Linge).

In Germany in 1939, a group of young people rebel against Nazi conformity by taking up "swing" music. The kids would rather "bop" than join the Hitler youth. The film ultimately fails because it seems undecided as to what it is trying to be or what it is trying to say.

2848. Swingers (1996, Miramax, 96m, c). D Doug Liman, P Victor Simpkins & Nicole Shay LaLoggia, W Jon Favreau, PH Liman, ED Stephen Mirrione, M Justin Reinhardt, PD Brad Halvorson, AD David Gould & Diana Pederson.

LP Jon Favreau (Mike), Vince Vaughn (Trent), Ron Livingston (Rob), Patrick Van Horn (Sue), Alex Desert (Charles), Heather Graham (Lorraine), Deena Martin (Christy), Katherine Kendall (Lisa).

Follow a group of males as they sample the swinging lounges of present day Los Angeles. The rules of today's dating game are likely to make those of an older generation happy they are no longer contestants.

2849. Switch (1991, Warner Bros., 104m, c). D & W Blake Edwards, P Tony Adams, PH Dick Bush, ED Robert Pergament, M Henry Mancini, PD Rodger Maus, AD Sandy Getzler, SD John Franco, Jr.

LP Ellen Barkin (Amanda Brooks), Jimmy Smits (Walter Stone), JoBeth Williams (Margo Brofman), Lorraine Bracco (Sheila Faxton), Tony Roberts (Arnold Friedkin), Perry King (Steve Brooks), Bruce Martyn Payne (The Devil), Lysette Anthony (Liz), Victoria Mahoney (Felicia).

The 1964 film *Goodbye Charlie* dealt with a heel who dies and as a heavenly joke is sent back to earth as Debbie Reynolds. This is a sort-of remake. King has it just too easy when it comes to women. Three of them band together to kill him. For some reason he must return to earth, but this time in the form of Barkin. He-she learns how it feels to be on the other side of the chase. Smits plays a nice guy who mostly stands around wondering what's going on.

2850. Switchback (1997, Paramount, 120m, c). D & W Jeb Stuart, P Gale Anne Hurd, PH Oliver Wood, ED Conrad Buff, M Basil Poledouris, PD Jeffrey Howard, AD Carl J. Parks, SD Dena Roth.

LP Dennis Quaid (Agent Frank LaCrosse), Jared Leto (Lane Dixon), Danny Glover (Bob Goodall), Ted Levine (Nate Booker), R. Lee Ermey (Sheriff Buck Olmstead), William Fichtner (Police Chief Jack McGinnis), Leo Burmester (Shorty).

After killing a babysitter, a serial killer kidnaps the son of FBI agent Quaid and the two disappear. The kidnapper-killer sends pictures of his victims to Quaid, accompanied by taunting notes. Will Quaid find the killer before his son becomes the next victim?

2851. Swoon (1992, Fine Line Features, 90m, c). D Tom Kalin, P Christine Vachon, W Kalin & Hilton Als, PH Ellen Kuras, ED Kalin, M James Bennett, PD Therese Deprez, SD Stacey Jones.

LP Daniel Schlachet (Richard Loeb), Craig Chester (Nathan Leopold), Ron Vawter (State's Attorney Crowe), Michael Kirby (Detective Savage), Michael Stumm (Doctor Bowman), Valda Z. Drabla (Germaine Reinhardt), Natalie Stanford (Susan Lurie).

This film takes a stab at telling the story of the infamous 1924 kidnapping and murder of Bobby Franks by two wealthy and self-proclaimed young geniuses, Leopold and Loeb. They were saved from execution by the defense provided them by famous lawyer Clarence Darrow. The case was earlier fictionalized in Hitchcock's *Rope* (1948) and a closer-to-the-truth version, *Compulsion*, in 1959. In this version the homosexual relationship between the two killers, only hinted at in the other films, is graphically explored.

2852. The Swordsman (1993, Republic Pictures, 98m, c). D & W Michael Kennedy, P Nicolas Stiliadis, PH Ludek Bogner, ED Nick Rotundo, M Domenic Troiano & Rotundo, PD Raymond Lorenz, AD Ingrid Jurek, SD Rob Hepburn.

LP Lorenzo Lamas (Andrew), Claire Stansfield (Julie), Michael Champion (Stratos), Nicholas Pasco (Nick), Raoul Trujillo (Jojo).

Detective Lamas has the task of returning the legendary sword of Alexander the Great to its rightful place in a museum. He will have to compete in illegal swordplay entertainments that use real blades instead of foils.

2853.   Sworn Enemies (1997, Canada, A-Pix Ent., 101m, c). D Shimon Dotan, P Netaya Anbar & Dotan, W Rod Hewitt, PH Sylvain Brault, ED Anbar, M Walter Christian Rothe & Richard Anthony Boast, PD & AD Charles Boulay, SD Ghislaine Grenon.

LP Michael Pare (Pershing Quinn), Macha Grenon (Seira), Peter Greene (Clifton Santier/Bosco), Michel Perron (Arnold), Ian MacDonald (Lester), Robert Morelli (Boot), Alan Fawcett (Jack).

Former friends and partners Pare and Greene become sworn enemies. Pare is the sheriff of a small town, and Greene, hungry for power in the gangs, begins killing his rivals.

2854.   Tail Lights Fade (1999, Canada, Cadence Ent., 87m, c). D Malcolm Ingram, P Christien Haebler, W Matt Gissing, PH Brian Pearson, ED Reginald Harkema, M Neil Weisensel, PD Douglas Hardwick.

LP Denise Richards (Wendy), Breckin Meyer (Cole), Jake Busey (Bruce), Tanya Allen (Angie), Elizabeth Berkley (Eve), Jaimz Wolvett (Ben), Lisa Marie (Kitty).

When Wolvett is busted on pot-possession charges in Vancouver, a group of young people take off from Toronto in a race to get to B.C. and take control of his indoor marijuana farm before the police discover it. Other than drooling over bimbo Richards, temptress Berkley and vixen Marie, there's little here to interest audiences.

2855.   The Takeover (1996, LIVE Ent., 91m, c). D Troy Cook, P Cheryl Cook, W Gene Mitchell, PH T. Alexander, ED Bruce Cook, M Jimmy Lifton, PD James Scanlon, AD Jamie McCrae.

LP Billy Drago (Danny Stein), John Savage (Greg), Nick Mancuso (Tony Vilachi), David Amos (Jonathan Fitzsimmons), Gene Mitchell (Micki Lane), Cali Timmins (Kathy), Anita Barone (Cindy Lane).

East Coast crime lord Drago tries to take over West Coast crime lord Mancuso's operation. Usual stuff.

2856.   Taking Care of Business (1990, Hollywood–Buena Vista, 108m, c). D Arthur Hiller, P Geoffrey Taylor, W Jill Mazursky &

Jeffrey Abrams, PH David M. Walsh, ED William Reynolds, M Stewart Copeland, PD Jon Hutman, SD Charles William Breen.

LP James Belushi (Jimmy Dworski), Charles Grodin (Spencer Barnes), Anne DeSalvo (Debbie), Loryn Locklin (Jewel), Stephen Elliott (Walter Bentley), Hector Elizondo (Warden), Veronica Hamel (Elizabeth Barnes), Mako (Sakamoto), Gates McFadden (Diane).

Small-town crook Belushi goes AWOL to see his beloved Chicago Cubs in the World Series (it's a fantasy, you see). He finds the filofax of high-powered businessman Grodin. Mistaken for Grodin, he has just enough time before being missed at the prison to straighten out Grodin's business and personal affairs, make love to beautiful Locklin and catch a foul ball at a world series game.

2857.   The Taking of Beverly Hills (1991, Columbia, 95m, c). D Sidney J. Furie, P Graham Henderson, W Rick Natkin, David Fuller & David J. Burke (based on the story by Natkin, Fuller & Furie), PH Frank Johnson, ED Antony Gibbs, M Jan Hammer, PD Peter Lamont, AD Neil Lamont, SD Michael Ford.

LP Ken Wahl (Terry "Boomer" Hayes), Harley Jane Kozak (Laura Sage), Matt Frewer (Ed Kelvin), Tony Ganios (EPA Man), Robert Davi (Robert "Bat" Masterson), Lee Ving Rhames (Oliver Varney).

Quarterback Wahl must thwart the scheme of the owner of L.A.'s pro football team to engineer a false toxic-waste dumping. It's part of a scheme to loot the homes of the rich and famous of Beverly Hills.

2858.   Talent for the Game (1991, Paramount, 91m, c). D Robert M. Young, P Martin Elfand, W David Himmelstein, Tom Donnelly & Larry Ferguson, PH Curtis Clark, ED Arthur Coburn, M David Newman, PD Jeffrey Howard, SD Thomas L. Roysden.

LP Edward James Olmos (Virgil Sweet), Lorraine Bracco (Bobbie Henderson), Jamey Sheridan (Tim Weaver), Terry Kinney (Gil Lawrence), Jeff Corbett (Sammy Bodeen), Tom Bower (Rev. Bodeen), Janet Carroll (Rachel Bodeen).

Olmos is a scout for the California Angels baseball team. He discovers pitching "phenom" Corbett and then must protect the kid from the exploitation plans of Kinney, the slimy owner of the team.

2859.   The Talented Mr. Ripley   (1999, Paramount, 139m, c). D Anthony Minghella, W Minghella† (based on the novel by Patricia Highsmith), P William Horberg & Tom Sternberg, PH John Seale, ED Walter Murch, M Gabriel Yared†, PD Roy Walker†, AD Stefano Ortolani, SD Bruno Cesari†.

LP Matt Damon (Tom Ripley), Gwyneth Paltrow (Marge Sherwood), Jude Law† (Dickie Greenleaf), Cate Blanchett (Meredith Logue), Philip Seymour Hoffman (Freddie Miles), Jack Davenport (Peter Smith-Kingsley), James Rebhorn (Herbert Greenleaf), Philip Baker Hall (Alvin MacCarron), Sergio Rubini (Inspector Roverini), Lisa Eichhorn (Emily Greenleaf).

In this enjoyable film, Damon says "I always thought it would be better to be a fake somebody than a real nobody." He lives up to this ideal by reinventing himself to be someone better than he really is. His opportunity comes when he is hired to travel to Italy to convince Law to leave his life with girlfriend Paltrow and return to his family. Damon likes what he sees — Italy, the lifestyle, and especially Paltrow. He thinks he'll have some of that — no matter what it takes, even if this involves murder and extreme deception. His ability to think quickly saves him many times, but just how long can he get away with it before what he really is and what he has done to maintain his new life is discovered?

2860.   Tales from the Crypt: Demon Knight   (AKA: *Demon Knight*) (1995, Universal, 92m, c). D Ernest Dickinson, P Gilbert Adler, W Ethan Riff, Cyrus Voris, Mark Bishop, PH Rick Bota, ED Stephen Lovejoy, M Ed Shearmur & Danny Elfman, PD Christiaan Wagener, AD Colin Irwin, SD George Toomer.

LP John Kassir (Voice of the Crypt Keeper), Billy Zane (The Collector), William Sadler (Brayker), Jada Pinkett (Jeryline), Brenda Bakke (Cordelia), CCH Pounder (Irene), Dick Miller (Uncle Willy).

Demon Zane pursues Sadler who possesses a key that has been passed down for centuries in an effort to keep it from Zane who can use it to unleash Hell on Earth.

2861.   Tales from the Crypt Presents Bordello of Blood   (1996, Universal, 87m, c). D & P Gilbert Adler, W Al Katz & Adler (based on a story by Bob Gale & Robert Zemeckis,

and the *Tales from the Crypt* comic books originally published by William M. Gaines), PH Tom Priestley, ED Stephen Lovejoy, M Chris Boardman & Danny Elfman, PD Gregory Melton, AD Sheila Haley, SD Rose Marie McSherry & Annemarie Corbett.

LP John Kassir (Voice of the Crypt Keeper), Dennis Miller (Rafe Guttman), Erika Eleniak (Katherine Verdoux), Angie Everhart (Lilith), Chris Sarandon (Reverend Current), Corey Feldman (Caleb Verdoux), Aubrey Morris (McCutcheon), Phil Fondacaro (Vincent Prather).

Private eye Miller searches for Feldman, the missing brother of Eleniak, who works for televangelist Sarandon. The latter controls her with an ancient talisman. He uses her to dispose of sinners while he sells their personal belongings to line his pockets. Miller's investigation takes him to a brothel staffed by half-naked undead bimbos.

2862.   Tales from the Darkside: The Movie   (1990, Paramount, 93m, c). D John Harrison, P Richard P. Rubinstein & Mitchell Galin, W Michael McDowell & George Romero (based on stories by Arthur Conan Doyle, Stephen King & Michael McDowell), PH Robert Draper, ED Harry B. Miller III, M Harrison, Rubinstein, Jim Manzie & Chaz Jankel, PD Ruth Ammon.

LP Deborah Harry (Betty), Christian Slater (Andy Smith), David Johansen (Halston), William Hickey (Drogan), Rae Dawn Chong (Carola), Matthew Lawrence (Timmy), Robert Sedgwick (Lee), Steve Buscemi (Edward Bellingham), Julianne Moore (Susan), Robert Klein (Wyatt).

This film provides good fun in frightening audiences with scares provided by evil housewives, gargoyles, mummies and a black cat.

2863.   Tales from the Hood   (1995, Savoy Pictures, 97m, c). D Rusty Cundieff, P Darin Scott, W Cundieff & Scott, PH Anthony B. Richmond, ED Charles Bornstein, M Christopher Young, PD Stuart Blatt.

LP Clarence Williams III (Mr. Simms), Joe Torry (Stack), Wings Hauser (Strom), Tom Wright (Martin Moorehouse), David Alan Grier (Carl), Brandon Hammond (Walter), Corbin Bernsen (Duke Metger), Roger Smith (Rhodie), Rosalind Cash (Dr. Cushing).

In this horror anthology, creepy funeral

parlor director Williams entertains three drug-dealing youths with scary tales of the realities of life in the '90s. These deal with drug abuse, domestic violence, gang warfare, black-on-black crime, dishonest cops and racism. It's a bit preachy, but a couple of the tales are worth the price of admission.

2864. Talk of Angels (1998, Miramax, 97m, c). D Nick Hamm, P Patrick Cassavetti, W Ann Guedes & Frank McGuinness (based on the novel *Mary Lavelle* by Kate O'Brien), PH Alexei Rodionov, ED Gerry Hambling, M Trevor Jones, PD Michael Howells, AD Eduardo Hidalgo, SD Totty Whatley.

LP Polly Walker (Mary Lavelle), Vincent Perez (Francisco Areavaga), Franco Nero (Dr. Vicente Areavaga), Frances McDormand (Conlon), Ruth McCabe (O'Toole), Francisco Rabal (Don Jorge).

Set in 1936 Spain at the time of the civil war between the Loyalists and Franco's Rightists, the film is the story of Irish governess Walker. She falls in love with Perez, her wealthy employer Nero's married son. It's a very ordinary romantic drama.

2865. Talkin' Dirty After Dark (1991, New Line Cinema, 86m, c). D & W Topper Carew, P Patricia A. Stallone, PH Misha Suslov, ED Claudia Finkle, PD Naomi Shohan, AD Bruton Jones & Dan Whifler.

LP Martin Lawrence (Terry), John Witherspoon (Dukie Sinclair), Jedda Jones (Rubie Lin), "Tiny" Lister, Jr. (Bigg), Phyllis Yvonne Stickney (Aretha), Renee Jones (Kimmie), Martin Wright-Bey (Jackie).

Comedian Lawrence will go to any end to win a late-night stint at a comedy club. Too bad he couldn't be funnier.

2866. Talking About Sex (1996, Pegasus Prods.–Leo, 87m, c). D Aaron Speiser, P Gary M. Bettman, W Speiser & Carl Nelson, PH Thomas Jewett, ED Wayne Schmidt, M Tim Landers, AD Lauree S. James.

LP Kim Wayans (Andie White), Daniel Beer (Doug Penn), Daria Lynn (Joan Morgan), Randy Powell (Carl Morgan), Kerry Ruff (Michael Columbus), Marcy Walker (Rachel Parsons).

And talk about sex is just about all that happens in this tale of a group of Californians attending a party to hype a sex therapist's new self-help book. The guests seem all-too-anxious to reveal a great deal of a sexual nature about themselves to each other.

2867. The Tall Guy (1990, GB, LWT-Virgin Vision-A Working Title, 92m, c). D Mel Smith, P Tim Bevan, W Richard Curtis, PH Adrian Biddle, ED Dan Rae, M Peter Brewis, PD Grant Hicks.

LP Jeff Goldblum (Dexter King), Emma Thompson (Kate Lemon), Rowan Atkinson (Ron Anderson), Geraldine James (Carmen), Emil Wolk (Cyprus Charlie), Kim Thompson (Cheryl), Harold Innocent (Timothy), Anna Massey (Mary).

Because of his height, an expatriate American actor is only cast as bumbling fools in London stage productions. Then he is cast as the lead in *The Elephant Man* and becomes an overnight success.

2868. Tall Tale: The Unbelievable Adventures of Pecos Bill (1995, Walt Disney Co.–Buena Vista, 98m, c). D Jeremiah Chechik, P Joe Roth & Roger Birnbaum, W Steven L. Bloom & Robert Rodat, PH Janusz Kaminski, ED Richard Chew, M Randy Edelman, PD Eugenio Zanetti, AD Rick Heinrichs & Jim R. Dultz, SD Jerie Kelter.

LP Patrick Swayze (Pecos Bill), Oliver Platt (Paul Bunyan), Roger Aaron Brown (John Henry), Nick Stahl (Daniel Hackett), Scott Glenn (J.P. Stiles), Stephen Lang (Jonas Hackett), Jared Harris (Head Thug Pug), Catherine O'Hara (Calamity Jane), Moria Harris (Sarah Hackett).

When evil industrialist Glenn threatens to steal Lang's land, the latter's son Stahl is able to call on legendary Pecos Bill, Paul Bunyan and John Henry for help. Watch it but don't listen to it.

2869. Talons of the Eagle (1992, Canada, Film One Prods., 96m, c). D Michael Kennedy, P Jalal Mehri, W J. Stephen Maunder, PH Curtis Petersen, ED Reid Dennison, M VaRouje, AD Jasna Stefanovich, SD Rob Hepburn.

LP Billy Blanks (Tyler Wilson), Jalal Mehri (Michael Reed), James Hong (Mr. Li), Priscilla Barnes (Cassandra).

In a very ordinary crime and martial arts picture, DEA agent Blanks is transferred to

Toronto to help local officer Mehri bust up the drug ring of Hong.

2870. Tammy and the T-Rex (1994, Imperial Ent., 82m, c). D Stewart Raffill, P Diane Raffill, W Stewart Raffill & Gary Brockette, PH Roger Olkowski, ED Terry Kelley, M Jack Conrad & Tony Riparetti, SD E. Colleen Saro.

LP Denise Richards (Tammy), Paul Walker (Michael Brock), Terry Kiser (Dr. Wachenstein), Theo Forsett (Byron Black), George Pilgrim (Billy).

While seeking a date with beautiful Richards, Walker has his brain transplanted into a mechanical three-ton dinosaur by mad scientist Kiser.

2871. Tank Girl (1995, United Artists, 103m, c). D Rachel Talalay, P Pen Densham, John Watson & Richard B. Lewis, W Tedi Sarafian (based on the comic book by James Hewlett & Alan Martin), PH Gale Tattersall, ED James R. Symons, M Graeme Revell, PD Catherine Hardwicke, AD Phillip Toolin, Charles D. Lee, Richard Yanez-Toyon & Jim Dultz, SD Cindy Carr.

LP Lori Petty (Rebecca Buck — Tank Girl), Ice-T (T-Saint — The Rippers), Naomi Watts (Jet Girl), Don Harvey (Sgt. Small), Jeff Kober (Booga — The Rippers), Reg E. Cathey (Deetee — The Rippers), Scott Coffey (Donner — The Rippers), Malcolm McDowell (Kesslee).

In the post-apocalyptic future, comic-book heroine Petty and her mutant friends take on evil McDowell for control of the world's water supply.

2872. Tar (AKA: *Skulls and Bones*) (1997, Mongrel Movies, 90m, c). D Goetz Grossman, P Abigail Hunt, W Grossman, James A. Pearson & Gilbert Giles, PH Lloyd Handwerker, ED Sabine Krayenbuhl, M John Hill, PD Pavel Salek, AD Kate Moxham.

LP Kevin Thigpen (Curtis), Nicole Prescott (Tracy), Seth Gilliam (Tyrone), Ron Brice (Jamal), Chris McKinney (Silver), Frank Minucci (Hank), Traci Jade (Soledad).

Harlem youth Thigpen is recruited by urban terrorist Brice. He kidnaps billionaires and distributes the ransom money to the people. But when asked to demonstrate his loyalty to Brice by tarring and feathering the latest victim, Thigpen refuses — just as the police raid the hideout.

2873. Tarantella (1998, BWE, 84m, c). D Helen De Michiel, P George La Voo, De Michiel & Richard Hoblock, PH Teodoro Maniaci, ED Richard Gordon, M Norman Noll, PD Diane Lederman, AD Tina Khayat, SD Ondine Karady & Orna Yaary.

LP Mira Sorvino (Diana Di Sorella), Rose Gregorio (Pina De Nora), Matthew Lillard (Matt), Frank Pellegrino (Lou), Stephen Spinella (Frank), Antonia Rey (Grandmother).

The only reason this 1994 movie was released to a limited number of theaters in 1998 was that Sorvino had just been nominated for an Academy Award, which she won for her delightful performance in *Mighty Aphrodite*. In this drama, Sorvino has distanced herself from her family and her Italian heritage. After her mother's death she returns home to sell the house. With the help of Gregorio, her mother's best friend, she learns to understand and appreciate her heritage.

2874. Tarzan (1999, Walt Disney–Buena Vista, 88m, c). D Kevin Lima & Chris Buck, P Bonnie Arnold, W Tab Murphy, Bob Tzudiker & Noni White (based on the story *Tarzan of the Apes* by Edgar Rice Burroughs), ED Gregory Perler, M Mark Mancina, AD Daniel St. Pierre.

LP Voices: Brian Blessed (Clayton), Glenn Close (Kala), Minnie Driver (Jane), Tony Goldwyn (Tarzan), Nigel Hawthorne (Professor Porter), Lance Henriksen (Kerchak), Wayne Knight (Tantor), Alex D. Linz (Young Tarzan), Rosie O'Donnell (Terk).

While this film doesn't make one forget Johnny Weissmuller and Maureen O'Sullivan, the animated tale of a youngster, orphaned and left in a jungle to be raised by loving gorillas, is decent entertainment. The songs are used to background the story, and the technique is effective. The animation is excellent and contributes greatly to the story of Tarzan meeting his Jane and championing his jungle companions against uncivilized invaders from civilization.

2875. Tarzan and the Lost City (1998, Warner Bros., 84m, c). D Carl Schenkel, P Stanley Carter, Dieter Geissler and Michael Lake, W Bayard Johnson & J. Anderson Black (based on the stories by Edgar Rice Burroughs), PH Paul Gilpin, ED Harry Hitner, M Christopher Franke, PD Herbert Pinter, AD Emilia Roux & Anna Lennox.

LP Casper Van Dien (Tarzan), Jane March (Jane), Steven Waddington (Nigel Ravens), Winston Ntshona (Mugambi), Rapulana Seiphemo (Kaya), Ian Roberts (Capt. Dooley).

If filmmakers believed that this movie might reawaken an interest in the exploits of the Lord of the Apes, they were mistaken.

2876. Taxi Dancers (1993, American New Wave Films, 92m, c). D Norman Thaddeus Vane, P Reinhard Schreiner, PH Richard Jones, ED Peter Ransohoff, PD David Blass, AD Heather Palmund.

LP Brittany McCrena (Billie), Sonny Landham (Diamond Jim), Robert Miano (Miguelito), Tina Fite (Star), Mirage Micheaux (Mercedes), Michelle Hess (Candy).

McCrena arrives in Hollywood with dreams of being discovered. Instead she is forced to "dance" at a club; there she becomes involved with Landham, a gambler deeply in debt to some very mean people.

2877. Tea with Mussolini (1999, U.K./Italy, UIP/MGM, 116m, c). D Franco Zeffirelli, P Ricardo Tozzi, Giovannella Zannoni & Clive Parsons, W John Mortimer & Zeffirelli (based on *The Autobiography of Franco Zeffirelli*), PH David Watkin, ED Tariq Anwar, M Alessio Vlad & Stefano Arnaldi, AD Carol Centolavigna & Gioia Fiorella Mariani.

LP Cher (Elsa), Judi Dench (Arabella), Joan Plowright (Mary), Maggie Smith (Hester), Lily Tomlin (Georgie), Baird Wallace (Luca as a teen), Charlie Lucas (Luca as a child), Claudio Spadaro (Mussolini).

A fine cast wins older audiences' approval in this story of a group of English and American women eccentrics in northern Italy during the days of Fascism and WWII. Smith cannot believe that her old friend Mussolini would allow her to live in the squalor of a detention camp. Plowright is the loving mother hen of the group. Dench is a slightly demented artist and art protector. Cher is a glamorous American movie star who puts her faith in the wrong Italian lover (a lawyer—she should have known better). Tomlin is the wisecracking lesbian realist who should have known enough to leave Europe before war was declared between Italy and the U.S. Wallace is a fine looking teen who cares for the ladies, and Lucas is charming as the lad as a child. It's a soap opera, but with actresses such as these it is exemplary soap opera.

2878. Teaching Mrs. Tingle (1999, Dimension Films, 96m, c). D & W Kevin Williamson, P Cathy Konrad, PH Jerry Zielinski, ED Debra Neil-Fisher, M John Frizzell, PD Naomi Shohan, AD David Lazan, SD Lauren Cory & Scott P. Murphy.

LP Helen Mirren (Mrs. Tingle), Katie Holmes (Leigh Ann Watson), Jeffrey Tambor (Coach Wenchell), Barry Watson (Luke Churner), Marisa Coughlan (Jo Lynn Jordan), Liz Stauber (Trudie Tucker), Michael McKean (Principal Potter), Molly Ringwald (Miss Banks), Vivica A. Fox (Miss Gold).

In yet another teen-centered film, the adults are so mean and so stupid that young people feel they have every right to be equally mean and stupid. Mirren, a fine actress, may have made a poor career move in agreeing to star in this film. She portrays the nastiest history teacher of all time. She takes delight in crushing her students. A trio of them decide to take drastic measures. As a hint to these measures, the film's title, before recent high school slaughters, was *Killing Mrs. Tingle*.

2879. Ted (1999, Chronic Filmworks, 84m, b&w/c). D & W Gary Ellenberg, P A.J. Peralta, PH "Stops" Langensteiner, ED John Wolfenden, M Evan Eder, AD Erick Rogers.

LP Daniel Passer (Ted), Edie McClurg (Mother), Richard Fancy (Father), Jeff Corey (Professor), Paul Provenza (Brother), Andy Dick (Sheriff), Megan Cavanaugh (Girl Next Door).

This is a comic mockumentary on the life story of Unabomber Ted Kaczynsky. Some may feel that the story of this socially hapless and deadly wacko isn't funny.

2880. Ted & Venus (1991, Double Helix Films, 100m, c). D Bud Cort, P Randolf Turrow & William Talmadge, W Paul Ciotti & Cort (based on the story by Ciotti), PH Dietrich Lohmann, ED Peter Zinner & Katina Zinner, M David Robbins, PD Lynn Christopher, AD Robert Stover, SD Gene Serdena.

LP Bud Cort (Ted Whitley), James Brolin (Max Waters), Kim Adams (Linda Turner), Carol Kane (Colette/Colette's Twin Sister), Pamella D'Pella (Gloria), Brian Thompson (Herb), Rhea Perlman (Grace), Woody Harrelson (Homeless Vietnam Veteran).

The more Adams rejects him the more oddball poet Cort becomes infatuated with the beach beauty. He is given a lot of useless advice for winning her by his equally odd friends.

2881. ***Teenage Mutant Ninja Turtles*** (1990, New Line, 93m, c). D Steve Barron, P Kim Dawson, Simon Fields & David Chan, W Todd W. Langen & Bobby Herbeck (based on a story by Herbeck and characters created by Kevin Eastman & Peter Laird), PH Mike Brewster, M John Du Prez, AD Gary Wissner, SD Jerry Hall.

LP Judith Hoag (April O'Neil), Elias Koteas (Casey Jones), Josh Pais (Raphael/Passenger in Cap/Voice of Raphael), Michelan Sisti (Michelangelo/Pizza Man), Leif Tilden (Donatello/Foot Messenger), David Forman (Leonardo/Gang Member), James Saito (The Shredder), Kevin Clash (Voice of Splinter), Robbie Rist (Voice of Michelangelo), Brian Tochi (Voice of Leonardo), Corey Feldman (Voice of Donatello).

Four sewer-dwelling turtles have been turned into mutant Ninja warriors through radiation exposure. Assisted by their master, Splinter the rat, and TV reporter Hoag they banish an evil warlord and his gang. One dose of the popular comic book heroes is fun, but the two sequels must be considered mock turtles.

2882. ***Teenage Mutant Ninja Turtles II: The Secret of the Ooze*** (1991, New Line, 88m, c). D Michael Pressman, P Thomas K. Gray, Kim Dawson & David Chan, W Todd W. Langen (based on characters created by Kevin Eastman & Peter Laird), PH Shelly Johnson, ED John Wright & Steve Mirkovich, M John Du Prez.

LP Paige Turco (April O'Neil), David Warner (Prof. Jordan Perry), Michelan Sisti (Michelangelo/Soho Man), Leif Tilden (Donatello), Kenn Troum (Raphael), Mark Caso (Leonardo), Kevin Clash (Splinter), Ernie Reyes, Jr. (Keno).

The pizza-devouring turtles search for the toxic waste that made them what they are.

2883. ***Teenage Mutant Ninja Turtles III*** (1993, New Line Cinema, 95m, c). D & W Stuart Gillard (based on characters created by Kevin Eastman and Peter Laird), PH Richard Metz, ED William Gordean & James Symons, PD Roy Forge Smith, AD Mayne Schulyer Berke, SD Ronald R. Reiss.

LP Elias Koteas (Casey Jones/Whit Whitley), Paige Turco (April O'Neil), Stuart Wilson (Capt. Dirk Walker), Sab Shimono (Lord Norinaga), Vivian Wu (Mitsu), Mark Caso (Leonardo), Matt Hill (Raphael), Jim Raposa (Donatello), David Fraser (Michelangelo), James Murray (Splinter).

Enough already! The boys return to 17th century Japan to rescue their reporter friend Turco from Shimono, an evil lord, and English pirates.

2884. ***Telling Lies in America*** (1997, Banner Pictures, 101m, c). D Guy Ferland, P Ben Myron, Fran Rubel Kuzui & Joe Eszterhas, W Eszterhas, PH Reynaldo Villalobos, ED Jill Savitt, M Nicholas Pike, PD James Gelarden, SD Sarah Young.

LP Kevin Bacon (Billy Magic), Brad Renfro (Karchy Jonas), Maximillian Schell (Mr. Jonas), Calista Flockhart (Diney), Paul Dooley (Father Norton).

Because of his accent and harsh ways, Hungarian immigrant Renfro doesn't fit in at the exclusive Cleveland private school where his hard-working father Schell sends him in 1962. Renfro has a crush on Flockhart, some years older than he. Somehow Renfro is able to land a job as an assistant to his hero DJ, Bacon. Renfro finds that his admiration for Bacon is misplaced, as Kevin is grabbing all the payola money he is offered to push certain recordings.

2885. ***Telling You*** (1998, Miramax, 94m, c). D Robert DeFranco, P David Dupuy, W DeFranco & Marc Palmieri (based on a story by Palmieri & Denis Flood), PH Mark Doering-Powell, ED Louis Cioffi, M Russ Landau, PD Sandy Espinet.

LP Peter Facinelli (Phil Fazzulo), Dash Mihok (Dennis Nolan), Jennifer Love Hewitt (Deb Friedman, Frank Medrano (Sal Lombardo), Richard Libertini (Mr. P).

This comedy-drama tells of two New Jersey high school hotshots who, after college, lose their heat and end up working at a pizza parlor in their old neighborhood. They'd like to get back on track but haven't a clue how to do so.

2886. ***The Temp*** (1993, Paramount, 110m, c). D Tom Holland, P David Permut & Tom Engelman, W Kevin Falls (based on a story by Falls & Engelman), PH Steve Yaconelli,

Michael O'Shea & David Butler, ED Scott Conrad, M Frederic Talgorn, PD Joel Schiller, AD Gordon W. Clark, SD Kim MacKenzie Orlando & Siobhan Roome.

LP Timothy Hutton (Peter Derns), Lara Flynn Boyle (Kris Bolin), Dwight Schultz (Roger Jasser), Oliver Platt (Jack Hartsell), Steven Weber (Brad Montroe), Colleen Flynn (Sara Meinhold), Faye Dunaway (Charlene Towne).

Needing a bit of help in his job with a baked goods company, junior executive Hutton hires temp Boyle. At first she seems a gem, having unbelievable organizational talents. But she has a deadly ambition to climb the corporate ladder of success, with anyone in the way of her goal ending up as crushed rungs.

2887. *Ten Little Indians* (AKA: *Agatha Christie's Ten Little Indians*) (1990, Cannon, 98m, c). D Alan Birkinshaw, P Harry Alan Towers, W Jackson Hunsicker & Gerry O'Hara (based on the play by Agatha Christie), PH Arthur Lavis, ED Penelope Shaw, M George S. Clinton, PD Roger Orpen, AD George Cancs, SD Anita Fraser.

LP Donald Pleasence (Justice Wargrave), Frank Stallone (Capt. Philip Lombard), Sarah Maur Thorp (Vera Claythorne), Herbert Lom (Gen. Romensky), Brenda Vaccaro (Marion Marshall), Warren Berlinger (Detective Blore), Yehuda Efroni (Dr. Hans Werner), Paul L. Smith (Elmo Rodgers), Moira Lister (Ethel Rodgers), Neil McCarthy (Anthony Marston).

Here is another version of Agatha Christie's suspenseful story of a group of individuals lured to an almost inaccessible location, on the pretense of a pleasant weekend, by a host unknown to any of them. Instead they have been called to justice for past crimes, and each is to be killed by means described in the poem "Ten Little Indians." The definitive filming of the story was done in 1945, with the movie titled *And Then There Were None*. None of the various versions since, including this one, has improved on that film, which starred the likes of Barry Fitzgerald, Walter Huston, Louis Hayward, Roland Young, Judith Anderson, June Duprez and Mischa Auer.

2888. *Ten Things I Hate About You* (1999, Touchstone–Buena Vista, 97m, c). D Gil Junger, P Andrew Lazar, W Karen McCullah Lutz & Kristen Smith, PH Mark Irwin,

ED O. Nicholas Brown, M Richard Gibbs, PD Carol Winstead Wood, AD Gilbert Wong, SD Charles M. Graffeo.

LP Heath Ledger (Patrick Verona), Julia Stiles (Katarina Stratford), Joseph Gordon-Leavitt (Cameron James), Larisa Oleynik (Bianca Stratford), David Krumholtz (Michael Eckman), Andrew Keegan (Joey Donner), Larry Miller (Walter Stratford).

This teenage film is a modern version of Shakespeare's *The Taming of the Shrew* and is loads of fun. Both Ledger, as the shrew-slayer, and Stiles, as the shrew, are delightful. The story, which parallel's the Bard's play, is of two sisters. Oleynik, a sweet young thing, would like to begin the dating ritual. Her older sister Stiles, despite her perky beauty, has the guys running for the hills to get out of her way and away from her mean mouth. It seems the girls' father Miller won't let the younger one date until the older one does. Would-be boyfriends of Oleynik seek out someone to take on the task of asking Stiles out, and settle on mysterious new kid in town Ledger.

2889. *Tender Flesh* (1997, U.S./Spain, One Shot Prods., 92m, c). D & W Jess Franco, P Kevin Collins, Hugh Gallagher & Peter Blumenstock, PH Benjamin L. Gordon, ED Rosa Maria Almirall, M Daniel J. White, Franco & Sexy Sadies.

LP Amber Newman (Paula), Lina Romay (Gorgona), Monique Parent (Irina Kalman), Aldo Sambrell (Peter Kalman), Mikel Kronen (Carlos).

Dancer Newman's sexy striptease at a slimy club gains her an invitation to a remote island for a private performance for wealthy Sambrell and his wife Parent. There she is drugged and whipped as everyone engages in a series of bizarre sex acts.

2890. *Tequila Body Shots* (1999, Heartland Releasing/Showtown Films, 95m, c). D & W Tony Shyu, P Tony Shyu & Jong Shyu, PH Lawrence Schweich, ED Pamela Raymer, M Shayne Fair & Larry Herbstritt, PD Peter Kanter.

LP Joey Lawrence (Johnny Orpheus), Dru Mouser (Tamlyn), Nathan Anderson (Paul), Josh Marchette (Al), Robert Patrick Benedict (Ted), Jennifer Lyons (Angela), Senta Moses (Linda).

Trying to cash in on the popularity of

Scream, Shyu offers up pop star Lawrence as a film student who, with some pals, attends a Day of the Dead Party at Mexico's Rosaferno Beach. In Mexico he picks up a potion from a medicine man guaranteed to get him the woman of his dreams. Lots of familiar stuff here — but only worth a look late at night if one can't find something better to do.

2891. ***Teresa's Tattoo*** (1995, Vidmark Ent., 95m, c). D Julie Cypher, P Lisa Hansen & Phil McKeon, W Georgie Huntington, PH Sven Kirsten, ED Christopher Rouse, M Andrew Keresztes, PD Rando Schmook, AD Lisa Deutsch.

LP Adrienne Shelly (Teresa/Gloria), C. Thomas Howell (Carl), Nancy McKeon (Sara), Lou Diamond Phillips (Wheeler), Casey Siemaszko (Michael), Jonathan Silverman (Rick), Joe Pantoliano (Bruno).

In this dark comedy, the hostage of three incompetent kidnappers is killed in an accident. As the dead girl was the sister of a mean gangster, they have to find a replacement. Young college girl Shelley fits the bill, but she needs a tattoo to pull off the impersonation.

2892. ***Terminal Bliss*** (1992, Cannon Pictures, 91m, c). D & W Jordan Alan, P Brian Cox, PH Gregory Smith, ED Bruce Sinfosky, M Frank W. Becker, PD Catherine Tirr, AD David Poses.

LP Luke Perry (John Hunter), Timothy Owen (Alex Golden), Estee Chandler (Stevie Bradley), Sonia Curtis (Kirsten Davis), Micah Grant (Bucky O'Connor), Alexis Arquette (Craig Murphy).

A group of wealthy teenagers abuse drugs and life. It's all rather depressing and makes you want to go out and find some decent kids to assure yourself that the next generation isn't really represented by the likes of these.

2893. ***Terminal Impact*** (1996, Nu World, 94m, c). D Yossi Wein, P Danny Lerner, W Jeff Albert & Dennis Dimster Denk, PH Rod Stewart, ED Mac Errington, M Sam Sklair, PD Leith Ridley, AD Ray Wilson, SD Lisa Hart.

LP Frank Zagarino (Saint), Bryan Genesse (Max), Jennifer Miller (Evelyn), Ian Roberts (Sheen), Justin Illusion (Adam), Michael Brunner (Dr. Phelps).

Bounty hunters Zagarino and Genesse must go up against cyborgs who have been genetically engineered and computer enhanced so that, like cockroaches, they can survive atomic fallout.

2894. ***Terminal Justice*** (AKA: *Terminal Justice: Cybertech P.D.*) (1996, Skyvision Ent., 95m, c). D Rick King, P David Lancaster, W Wynne McLaughlin & Frederick Bailey, PH Chris Holmes, Jr., ED Jeff Bessner, M Michael Hoenig, PD Tim Bider, AD Benno Tutter, SD Terry Roberts.

LP Lorenzo Lamas (Chase), Chris Sarandon (Reggie Matthews), Peter Coyote (Dr. Vivyan), Kari Wuhrer, billed as Kari Salin (Pamela Travis), Barry Flatman (Phillips), Tod Thawley (Hiroshi).

Loner cop Lamas takes on criminal scientists Sarandon and Coyote. They use cloning to develop disposable love slaves who don't care how badly they are misused. Lamas protects porn star Wuhrer when Sarandon sends his goons to steal her DNA.

2895. ***Terminal Velocity*** (1994, Hollywood Pictures–Buena Vista, 102m, c). D Deran Sarafian, P Scott Kroopf & Tom Engelman, W David Twohy, PH Oliver Wood, ED Frank J. Urioste, M Joel McNeely, PD David L. Snyder, AD Sarah Knowles, SD Beth Rubino.

LP Charlie Sheen (Ditch Brodie), Nastassja Kinski (Chris Morrow), James Gandolfini (Ben Pinkwater), Christopher MacDonald (Kerr), Gary Bullock (Lex), Hans R. Howes (Sam), Melvin Van Peebles (Noble).

High-flying sky-diver Sheen is lured by beautiful Russian spy Kinski into helping her frustrate the plans of the vicious Russian Mafia. The film will please those who believe the best dialogue is gunfire and explosions.

2896. ***Terminator 2: Judgment Day*** (1991, TriStar, 135m, c). D & P James Cameron, W Cameron & William Wisher, PH Adam Greenberg, ED Conrad Buff†, Mark Goldblatt† & Richard A. Harris†, M Brad Fiedel, PD Joseph Nemec III, AD Joseph P. Lucky, SD John M. Dwyer.

LP Arnold Schwarzenegger (The Terminator), Linda Hamilton (Sarah Connor), Robert Patrick (T-1000), Edward Furlong (John Connor), Earl Boen (Dr. Silberman), Joe Morton (Miles Dyson), E. Epatha Merkerson (Tarissa Dyson).

Director Cameron likes to spend a lot of money on movies. This sequel to his hugely successful *The Terminator* (1984) cost $100 million. But, as we know now, that is almost chicken feed compared to his costs for *Titanic*. In the year 1997, evil cyborgs have sent the new, improved terminator unit (Patrick) back through time to eliminate teen Furlong who, if he lives, will become the future leader of the human reistance to the world domination by the cyborgs. Schwarzenegger, who had a similar assignment in the original film, has been reprogrammed to protect the youth and his mother Hamilton. She looks very sexy smeared with dirt and grease.

2897. Termini Station (1991, Canada, Northern Arts Entertainment, 105m, c). D & P Allan King, W Colleen Murphy (based on her play *All Other Destinations Are Cancelled*), PH Brian R.R. Hebb, ED Gordon McClellan, M Mychael Danna, PD Lillian Sarafinchan, SD Jaro Dick.

LP Colleen Dewhurst (Molly Dushane), Megan Fellows (Micheline Dushane), Gordon Clapp (Harvey Dushane), Debra McGrath (Liz Dushane), Leon Powell (Charles Marshall), Elliott Smith (Delaney).

Dewhurst gives a powerful performance as the alcoholic matriarch of a small-town Canadian family. She dreams of traveling to Italy. Her children dream of leaving her and finding a better life.

2898. Terror in Beverly Hills (1991, AIP Studios, 88m, c). D & W John Myhers (based on the story by Simon Bibiyan), P Ron Lavery & Pierre Mzadeh, PH Peter Wold, ED Richard L. Marks, M Alan Dermarderosian.

LP Frank Stallone (Hack Stone), Behrouz Vossughi (Abdul), Cameron Mitchell (Captain Stills), William Smith (President), Lysa Hayland (Margaret).

When the president's daughter is kidnapped, ex-marine Stallone is given the task of getting her back. His adversary is Vossughi, an old enemy who blames Stallone for the death of his wife and children.

2899. The Terror Within 2 (1991, Concorde, 89m, c). D & W Andrew Stevens (based on the characters created by Thomas M. Cleaver), P Michael Elliot, PH Janusz Kaminski, ED Brent Schoenfeld, M Terry Plumieri, PD Johan LeTenoux, AD Nicholas Thielker, SD Cherie Ledwith.

LP Andrew Stevens (David Pennington), Stella Stevens (Kara), Chick Vennera (Kyle), R. Lee Ermey (Von Demming), Burton Gilliam (Dewitt) Clare Hoak (Ariel).

The world has just been about destroyed by biological warfare. Warrior Andrew Stevens and Hoak travel through the badlands occupied by hideous mutants. She is raped by one of the monsters and within weeks delivers a horrible mutation.

2900. Texas Chainsaw Massacre: The Next Generation (AKA: *Return of the Texas Chainsaw Massacre*) (1996, Return Prods., 102m, c). D Kim Henkel, P Robert Kuhn, W Ken Henkel, PH Levie Isaacks, ED Sandra Adair, PD Debbie Pastor.

LP Renee Zellweger (Jenny), Matthew McConaughey (Vilmer), Robert Jacks (Leatherface), Tony Perenski (Darla), Joe Stevens (W.E.), Lisa Newmeyer (Heather).

Leatherface is back, but not many people saw him in the brief theatrical release of this independent film before it went to video. It's notable only for the appearance of Zellweger and McConaughey, who, despite appearing in this less than slick horror story, went on to better things.

2901. Texasville (1990, Columbia, 123m, c). D & W Peter Bogdanovich (Based on the novel by Larry McMurtry), P Barry Spikings & Bogdanovich, PH Nicholas von Sternberg, ED Richard Fields, PD Phedon Papamichael, SD Daniel Boxer.

LP Jeff Bridges (Duane Jackson), Cybill Shepherd (Jacy Farrow), Annie Potts (Karla Jackson), Timothy Bottoms (Sonny Crawford), Cloris Leachman (Ruth Popper), Randy Quaid (Lester Marlow), Eileen Brennan (Genevieve), William McNamara (Dickie Jackson), Angie Bolling (Marylou Marlow).

The Last Picture Show (1971) made audiences care about cocky Bridges, sensitive Bottoms, stuck-up beauty Shepherd and mousy adulteress Leachman. Seeing what they have become thirty years later left many indifferent. Bridges is now married to Potts, who worries a bit when it is learned that Shepherd is coming back for a visit. Bottoms is a shell of himself. Why, isn't clear. Leachman lurks around in the background with little to contribute.

The film misses Ben Johnson as Sam the Lion and sexy mamma Ellen Burstyn.

2902.   *That Darn Cat* (1997, Walt Disney Pictures–Buena Vista, 89m, c). D Bob Spiers, P Robert Simonds, W Scott Alexander & Larry Karaszewski (based on the novel *Undercover Cat* by Gordon & Mildred Gordon, and the screenplay by Bill Walsh), PH Jerzy Zielinski, ED Roger Barton, M Richard Kendall Gibbs, PD Jonathan Carlson, AD Jeremy A. Cassells, SD Susan Lee Degus.

LP Christina Ricci (Patti Randall), Doug E. Doug (Zeke Kelso), Dyan Cannon (Mrs. Flint), Dean Jones (Mr. Flint), George Dzundza (Boetticher), Peter Boyle (Pa), Michael McKean (Peter Randall), Bess Armstrong (Judy Randall).

This remake of Disney's 1965 comedy succeeds because of the work of Ricci. She is the owner of a cat who helps the FBI crack a kidnapping case. Doug E. Doug is an eager but inept FBI agent.

2903.   *That Old Feeling* (1997, Universal, 105m, c). D Carl Reiner, P Leslie Dixon & Bonnie Bruckheimer, W Dixon, PH Steve Mason, ED Richard Halsey, PD Sandy Veneziano, AD Alicia Keywan, SD Steve Shewchuk.

LP Bette Midler (Lilly Leonard), Dennis Farina (Dan DeMaura), Paula Marshall (Molly), Gail O'Grady (Rowena), David Rasche (Alan), Jamie Denton (Keith), Danny Nucci (Joey "The Cockroach" Danna).

Marshall fears that her wedding to conservative politician Denton will be marred by her divorced parents Midler and Farina. They can't seem to be in the same room two minutes without brawling. It seems the two also still haven't gotten over their yen for each other, despite marriages to therapist Rasche and voluptuous O'Grady. Somehow it fails to be the laugh riot the makers had in mind.

2904.   *That Thing You Do!* (1996, 20th Century–Fox, 110m, c). D & W Tom Hanks, P Gary Goetzman, Jonathan Demme & Edward Saxon, PH Tak Fujimoto, ED Richard Chew, M Howard Shore, PD Victor Kempster, AD Dan Webster, SD Merideth Boswell.

LP Tom Everett Scott (Guy Patterson), Liv Tyler (Faye Dolan), Jonathan Schaech (Jimmy Mattingly), Steve Zahn (Lenny), Ethan Embry (The Bass Player), Tom Hanks (Mr. White),

Charlize Theron (Tina), Bill Cobbs (Del Paxton).

Director and Writer Hanks offers a look at the lives and careers of a one-song, one-hit rock 'n' roll group. While one does get weary of hearing the title song over and over again, the story is right on target and the young cast is splendid. Best of the bunch is Scott as the drummer who gives the group its beat and sex appeal. Tyler looks fetching as the mistreated girlfriend of self-absorbed lead guitarist and songwriter Schaech. His demands lead to the loss of their record contract and the breakup of the group.

2905.   *Thelma & Louise* (1991, MGM-Pathé, 128m, c). D Ridley Scott†, P Scott & Mimi Polk, W Callie Khouri*, PH Adrian Biddle†, ED Thom Noble†, M Hans Zimmer, PD Norris Spencer, AD Lisa Dean, SD Mary Margaret Robinson, Anne Ahrens & Craig Graham.

LP Geena Davis† (Thelma), Susan Sarandon† (Louise), Harvey Keitel (Hal), Michael Madsen (Jimmy), Christopher McDonald (Darryl), Stephen Tobolowsky (Max), Brad Pitt (J.D.), Timothy Carhart (Harlan).

Thelma & Louise is a buddy picture. *Thelma & Louise* is a road picture. *Thelma & Louise* is a feminist picture. More Importantly, *Thelma & Louise* is a very entertaining picture with great work by its stars Davis and Sarandon, and with a little help from charming con artist Pitt and police detective Keitel. The latter is the only man in the film to come off looking good. Davis and Sarandon set off on a vacation. Stopping at a roadhouse, they put away quite a few drinks while Davis dances with a lanky cowboy who takes her outside and attempts to rape her. Sarandon interrupts and is forced to shoot and kill the lunk, forcing the women to become fugitives. Their dead-end trip to disaster is stylish and witty as they break away from male-dominated society and discover their own identities.

2906.   *Theodore Rex* (1996, New Line, 92m, c). D & W Jonathan Betuel, P Richard Abramson & Sue Baden-Powell, PH David Tattersall, ED Rick Shaine & Steve Mirkovich, M Robert Folk, PD Walter Martishius, AD Bo Johnson.

LP Whoopi Goldberg (Katie Coltrane), Armin Mueller-Stahl (Dr. Edgar Kane), Juliet

Landau (Dr. Shade), Bud Cort (Spinner), Stephen McHattie (Edge), Richard Roundtree (Commissioner Lynch), George Newborn (Voice of Theodore Rex), Carol Kane (Voice of Molly Rex).

In a future time, dinosaurs live among humans. When one is found murdered, police officer Goldberg is teamed with a Tyrannosaurus Rex to find the killer.

2907. *Theory of Flight* (1998, U.K., Fine Line Features, 99m, c). D Paul Greengrass, P Helena Spring, Ruth Caleb, David M. Thompson & Anant Singh, W Richard Hawkins, PH Ivan Strasburg, ED Mark Day, M Rolfe Kent, PD Melanie Allen.

LP Helena Bonham Carter (Jane Hatchard), Kenneth Branagh (Richard), Gemma Jones (Anne), Holly Aird (Julie), Ray Stevenson (Gigolo).

Confined to a wheelchair, Bonham Carter is dying of motor neuron disease. Branagh tries one flying stunt too many and is sentenced to 120 hours of community service: caring for Bonham Carter. She is delighted with his latest obsession, a rickety WWI biplane he's building. What she really wants, however, is to get laid before it's too late. Branagh declines to become her partner but takes her to London to find someone to do the deed. They settle on handsome gigolo Stevenson.

2908. *There Goes the Neighborhood* (1993, Paramount, 88m, c). D & W Bill Phillips, P Stephen Friedman, PH Walt Lloyd, ED Sharyn L. Ross, M David Bell, PD Dean Tschetter, AD Randy Moore, SD Michelle Starbuck.

LP Jeff Daniels (Willis Embry), Rhea Perlman (Lydia), Dabney Coleman (Jeffrey), Catherine O'Hara (Jessie), Hector Elizondo (Norman), Judith Ivey (Peedi), Harris Yulin (Boyd), Chazz Palminteri (Lyle).

In this comedy, prison psychiatrist Daniels learns that $8.5 million of Mafia loot is buried in the suburbs below a house in which highstrung O'Hara lives. She's in the middle of a divorce. Daniels wins her trust, and she helps him with the digging.

2909. *There's Nothing Out There* (1992, Valkhn Films, 90m, c). D & W Rolfe Kanefsky, P & ED Victor Kanefsky, M Christopher Thomas.

LP Craig Peck (Mike), Wendy Bednarz (Doreen), Mark Collver (Jim), Bonnie Bowers (Stacy), John Carhart III (Nick), Claudia Flores (Janet), Jeff Dachis (David), Lisa Grant (Sally).

It's a humorous entry into the sub-subgenre of teenagers lost in the middle of nowhere being preyed upon by an alien creature.

2910. *There's Something About Mary* (1998, 20th Century–Fox, 118m, c). D Peter Farrelly & Bobby Farrelly, P Frank Beddor, Michael Steinberg, Charles B. Wessler & Bradley Thomas, W Ed Decter, John J. Strauss, Peter & Bobby Farrelly (based on a story by Decter & Strauss), PH Mark Irwin, ED Christopher Greenbury, M Jonathan Richman, AD Arlan Jay Vetter.

LP Cameron Diaz (Mary Jenson), Matt Dillon (Pat Healy), Ben Stiller (Ted Stroehmann), Lee Evans (Tucker), Chris Elliott (Dom), Lin Shaye (Magda), Jeffrey Tambor (Sully), Markie Post (Mary's Mom), Keith David (Mary's Stepfather), W. Earl Brown (Warren).

This romantic comedy was the laugh hit of the year. Of course, audiences might feel a bit ashamed about what they are laughing at. The film allows audiences to ignore political correctness and laugh at the retarded, cruelty to animals, stalking, masturbation, homosexuality, serial murder, sexism, ageism and physical handicaps. All this happens when Stiller can't get beautiful Diaz out of his mind. The last time he saw her was on their disastrous but hilarious prom date. Ben hires Dillon to look up Diaz for him. Dillon does and falls hard for the naive beauty. Dillon's report to Stiller is meant to make him forget his dream girl, but it doesn't work. Stiller decides to see for himself and finds Diaz as wonderful as ever. The comical romantic triangle is more a quadrangle, as Evans, on crutches and wearing braces, also does his bit to win the lovely lady. There definitely is something about Cameron.

2911. *Thick as Thieves* (1999, October Films, 94m, c). D & W Scott Sanders, P Donald Zuckerman, Glenn Zoller & Jon Steingart, PH Christopher Walling, ED John Pace, M Chris Beck, PD Denise Griggs.

LP Alec Baldwin (Mackin), Andre Braugher (Dink), Ricky Harris (Rodney), Michael Jai White (Pointy), David Byrd (Sal Capetti).

Lifelong thief Baldwin does his jobs smoothly

and then retreats into his privacy to listen to his collection of old jazz records. White is also a thief, but more of an organization man. The two find themselves going to war against each other without really wanting to or quite understanding why they are doing so.

2912. Thicker Than Water (1999, Palm Pictures, 91m, c). D Richard Cummings, Jr., P Darryl Taja & Andrew Shack, W Ernest Nyle Brown, PH Robert Benavides, ED Danny Rafic, M QDIII, PD Skip Weaver.

LP Mack 10 (DJ), Fat Joe (Lonzo), Ice Cube (Slink), MC Eiht (Lil' Ant), CJ Mac (Gator), Big Pun (Tyree), Tom'ya Bowden (Leyla).

Rapper Mack 10 stars as an aspiring music producer. He leads a cast of rap stars in this boys-in-the-hood film. It will have a limited audience in theaters but probably a bigger one when it goes to video.

2913. A Thin Line Between Love and Hate (1996, Savoy Pictures–New Line, 107m, c). D Martin Lawrence, P Douglas McHenry & George Jackson, W Lawrence, Bentley Kyle Evans, Kenny Buford & Kim Bass (based on a story by Lawrence), PH Francis Kenny, ED John Carter, M Roger Troutman, PD Simon Dobbin, AD David Lazan, SD Tessa Posansky.

LP Martin Lawrence (Darnell), Lynn Whitfield (Brandi), Regina King (Mia), Bobby Brown (Tee), Della Reese (Ma Wright), Malinda Williams (Erica), Daryl Mitchell (Earl), Roger E. Mosley (Smitty).

Womanizer Lawrence has a rule: "Never say 'I love you' to a woman, no matter what." When he breaks his rule he finds himself in a comical *Fatal Attraction* situation.

2914. The Thin Red Line† (1998, 20th Century–Fox, 170m, c). D Terrence Malick†, W Malick† (based on the novel by James Jones), P Robert Michael Geisler, Jean Roberdeau & Grant Hill, PH John Toll†, ED Billy Weber†, Leslie Jones† & Saar Klein†, M Hans Zimmer†, PD Jack Fisk, AD Ian Gracie, SD Richard Hobbs & Suza Maybury.

LP Sean Penn (First Sgt. Edward Walsh), Adrien Brody (Cpl. Fife), Jim Caviezel (Pvt. Witt), Ben Chaplin (Pvt. Bell), George Clooney (Capt. Charles Bosche), John Cusack (Capt. John Gaff), Woody Harrelson (Sgt. Keck), Elias Koteas (Capt. James "Bugger" Staros),

Jared Leto (Second Lt. Whyte), Dash Mihok (PFC Doll), Nick Nolte (Lt. Col. Gordon Tall), John Savage (Sgt. McCron), John Travolta (Brig. Gen. Qintard).

Director-writer Malick hasn't made a film in twenty years; but he proves with this impressive anti-war statement that he hasn't lost the knack. Malick's adaptation of the 1962 Jones novel is set in the Pacific. It follows an Army rifle company attacking a Japanese-held hill on Guadalcanal. Unlike Steven Spielberg's *Saving Private Ryan*, which came out earlier in the year, Malick seems less interested in telling a single story of the men or allowing the audience to identify with them and hate their enemy. He and award-winning cinematographer Toll contrast scenes of tremendous violence with those of great beauty. The dialogue is sparse but the key roles are forcefully presented. Not so much a tale of the good guys versus the bad guys, Malick's picture offers visions of war that will never be forgotten. It is unnecessary to compare Malick's film to *Ryan*. They are both extraordinary WWII films.

2915. The Thing Called Love (1993, Paramount, 116m, c). D Peter Bogdanovich, P John A. Davis, W Carol Heikkinen, PH Peter James, ED Terry Stokes, PD Michael Seymour, AD Tom Wilkins, SD Claudia Rebar.

LP River Phoenix (James Wright), Samantha Mathis (Miranda Presley), Dermot Mulroney (Kyle Davidson), Sandra Bullock (Linda Lue Linden).

Several country singer-songwriters, hoping to make it big in Nashville, share experiences.

2916. Things to Do in Denver When You're Dead (1995, Miramax, 114m, c). D Gary Fleder, P Cary Woods, W Scott Rosenberg, PH Elliot Davis, ED Richard Marks, M Michael Convertino, PD Nelson Coates, AD Burton Rencher, SD Anne D. McCulley.

LP Andy Garcia (Jimmy "The Saint" Tosnia), Christopher Lloyd (Pieces), William Forsythe (Franchise), Bill Nunn (Easy Wind), Treat Williams (Critical Bill), Jack Warden (Joe Heff), Steve Buscemi (Mister Shhh), Fairuza Balk (Lucinda), Gabrielle Anwar (Dagney), Christopher Walken (The Man with a Plan).

When his former boss, wheelchair-confined Walken, asks ex-mobster Garcia to do one last easy money job, he reluctantly agrees. Garcia rounds up his old gang, which includes hair-trigger psycho Williams and porn movie projectionist Lloyd. The gang blows the assignment and find themselves the targets of hitman Buscemi.

2917.   *The Third Miracle* (1999, Sony Pictures Classics, 119m, c). D Agnieszka Holland, P Fred Fuchs, Steven Haft & Elie Samaha, W John Romano & Richard Vetere (based on a novel by Vetere), PH Jerzy Zielinski, ED David J. Siegel, M Jan A.P. Kaczmarek, PD Robert De Vico, AD Andrew M. Stearn.

LP Ed Harris (Frank Shore), Anne Heche (Roxanne), Armin Mueller-Stahl (Archbishop Werner), Charles Haid (Bishop Cahill), Michael Rispoli (John Leone), James Gallanders (Brother Gregory), Jean-Louis Roux (Cardinal Sarrazin), Ken James (Father Paul Panak), Caterina Scorsone (Maria Witkowski), Barbara Sukowa (Helen).

Harris portrays an American priest who investigates miracle claims. His work has left him with a dwindling faith. It will be tested further by Heche, the daughter of an Austrian-born immigrant, said to have performed miracles, leading her cult to call for her sainthood. It is reported that her statue weeps blood. The best part of the film is the struggle between Harris and Mueller-Stahl at a church tribunal called to debate the woman's qualifications for sainthood.

2918.   *The Thirteenth Floor* (1999, Columbia, 120m, c). D Josef Rusnak, P Roland Emmerich, Ute Emmerich & Marco Weber, W Rusnak & Ravel Centeno-Rodriguez, PH Wedigo von Schultzendorf, ED Henry Richardson, M Harald Kloser, PD Kirk M. Petrucelli, AD Barry Chusid, SD Evelyne Barbier & Leslie Thomas.

LP Craig Bierko (Douglas Hall), Armin Mueller-Stahl (Hannon Fuller), Gretchen Mol (Jane Fuller), Vincent D'Onofrio (Whitney/Ashton), Dennis Haysbert (Det. Larry McBain).

A supercomputer is designed to provide the user with simulated time travel. When the designer is murdered, Haysbert has a number of suspects and sends himself back to a simulated 1937 L.A. to get the low-down. Ho-hum.

2919.   *The Thirteenth Warrior* (1999, Buena Vista–Touchstone, 103m, c). D John McTiernan, P McTiernan, Michael Crichton & Ned Dowd, W William Wisher & Warren Lewis (based on the novel *Eaters of the Dead* by Crichton), PH Peter Menzies, Jr., ED John Wright, M Jerry Goldsmith, PD Wolf Kroeger, AD Helen V. Jarvis, Richard St. John Harrison & William Heslup, SD Rose Marie McSherry.

LP Antonio Banderas (Ahmed Ibn Fahdian), Diane Venora (Queen Hrothgar), Dennis Storhoi (Herger the Joyous), Vladimir Kulich (Buliwyf), Omar Sharif (Melchisdek), Anders T. Andersen (Wigliff, King Hrothgar's Son).

Produced in 1997, this Viking picture should cause fans of such movies to hurry to the stores to rent 1958's *The Vikings* with Kirk Douglas, Tony Curtis and Ernest Borgnine. Banderas portrays a poet from Bagdad who becomes the required thirteenth warrior of a group of twelve Norsemen fighting off raiders of their lands.

2920.   *30 Days* (1999, Arielle Tepper/Araca Group, 87m, c). D & W Aaron Harnick, P Matthew Rego, Michael Rego & Arielle Tepper, PH David Tumblety, ED Sean J. Campbell, M Andrew Sherman & Stephen J. Walsh, PD Michael Fagin, AD Kristin Costa.

LP Ben Shenkman (Jordan Trainer), Arija Bareikis (Sarah Meyers), Alexander Chaplin (Mike Charles), Bradley White (Tad Star), Thomas McCarthy (Brad Drazin), Catherine Kellner (Lauren).

Shenkman, afraid of commitment, nevertheless impetuously asks Bareikis to marry him. But the scene shifts to a month later. Now Shenkman announces his engagement to Kellner, Bareikis' best friend. From here on the film turns into a buddython.

2921.   *Thirty-Two Short Films About Glenn Gould* (1994, Canada, Samuel Goldwyn, 94m, c). D Francois Girard, P Niv Fichman, W Girard & Don McKellar, PH Alain Dostie, ED Gaetan Huot, M Assorted Classical Composers, AD John Rubino, SD Alexa Anthony.

LP Colm Feore (Glenn Gould), Derek Keurvorst (Gould's Father), Katya Lada (Gould's Mother), Devon Anderson (Glenn Gould, Age 3), Joshua Greenblatt (Glenn Gould, Age 8), Sean Ryan (Glenn Gould, Age 13).

The title of this film, about the life and career of reclusive concert pianist and recording artist Glenn Gould, echoes Beethoven's *Thirty Two Variations in C Minor*. As the title suggests, this is a fragmented and incomplete biography.

2922. **This Boy's Life** (1993, Warner Bros., 115m, c). D Michael Caton-Jones, P Art Linson, W Robert Getchell (based on the autobiography by Tobias Wolff), PH David Watkin, ED Jim Clark, M Carter Burwell, PD Stephen J. Lineweaver, AD Sandy Cochrane, SD Jim Erickson.

LP Robert De Niro (Dwight), Ellen Barkin (Caroline), Leonardo DiCaprio (Toby), Jonah Blechman (Arthur Gayle), Eliza Dushku (Pearl), Chris Cooper (Roy), Carla Gugino (Norma), Zack Ansley (Skipper).

In an acting triumph for the three leads, troubled teen DiCaprio hopes for a better life when his mother Barkin marries De Niro. They move to a small town in Washington where De Niro browbeats and physically thrashes the lad. This intriguing character study is a true story based on writer Tobias Wolff's autobiography.

2923. **This Is My Father** (1998, Filmline, 120m, c). D & W Paul Quinn, P Nicolas Clermont & Philip King, PH Declan Quinn, ED Glenn Berman, M Donal Lunny, PD Frank Conway, AD Claude Pare.

LP Aidan Quinn (Kieran O'Day), James Caan (Kieran Johnson), Stephen Rea (Father Quinn), John Cusack (Eddie Sharp), Moya Farrelly (Fiona Flynn), Jacob Tierney (Jack), Colm Meaney (Seamus Kearney).

Aged schoolteacher Caan comes across a set of photographs from his mother's past. They indicate that his father may have been an Irish farmer and not a Frenchman who died in the war, as he was led to believe.

2924. **This Is My Life** (1992, 20th Century–Fox, 105m, c). D Nora Ephron, P Lynda Obst, W Nora Ephron & Delia Ephron (based on the novel *This Is Your Life* by Meg Wolitzer), PH Bobby Byrne, ED Robert Reitano, M Carly Simon, PD David Chapman, AD Barbra Matis, SD Hilton Rosemarin & Jaro Dick.

LP Julie Kavner (Dottie Ingels), Samantha Mathis (Erica Ingels), Gaby Hoffman (Opal Ingels), Carrie Fisher (Claudia Curtis), Dan Aykroyd (Arnold Moss), Bob Nelson (Ed), Marita Geraghty (Mia Jablon).

Single mom Kavner aggressively pursues her dream of becoming a stand-up comedian. When her career takes off, her kids find themselves being neglected.

2925. **This Space Between Us** (1999, TSBU/LLC Prod., 110m, c). D & ED Matthew Leutwyler, P Scott Leutwyler & Matthew Leutwyler, W M. Leutwyler & Peter Rudy, PH Dave Scardino, ED Peter Schink, M Johannes Luley, PD Nathalie Dierickx, SD Patrick Sterling Ludden.

LP Jeremy Sisto (Alex Harty), Vanessa Marcil (Maggie Harty), Poppy Montgomery (Arden), Clara Bellar (Zoe Goddard), Erik Palladino (Jesse), Alex Kingston (Paternelle).

In this comedy drama, novice filmmaker Sisto loses both his wife and his career within one year of moving to the Hollywood scene.

2926. **This World, Then the Fireworks** (1997, Orion Classics, 100m, c). D Michael Oblowitz, P Chris Hanley, Brad Wyman & Larry Gross, W Gross (based on the novella by Jim Thompson), PH Tom Priestley, Jr., ED Emma E. Hickox, M Pete Rugolo, PD Maia Javan.

LP Billy Zane (Marty Lakewood), Gina Gershon (Carol Lakewood), Sheryl Lee (Patrolwoman Lois Archer), Rue McClanahan (Mom Lakewood), Seymour Cassel (Police Detective Harris), Will Patton (Police Lt. Morgan).

Thirty years earlier Zane and his sister Gershon witnessed their father killing the husband of a woman with whom he was having an affair. Now Zane is a reporter and Gershon, with whom he has had an incestuous relationship, is a prostitute. Zane looks to con Lee out of her beachfront home. Zane and his sister are not good guys. He kills a detective he finds trailing his sister, and she gives their mother an overdose of her medicine. Gershon dies of a botched abortion and Zane kills a man who breaks in on him and Lee. The former turns out to be her husband.

2927. **This Year's Love** (1999, U.K., Ent. Film Distributors, 108m, c). D & W David Kane, P Michele Camarada, PH Rob Alazraki, ED Sean Barton, M Simon Boswell, PD Sarah Greenwood, AD Philip Robinson.

LP Kathy Burke (Mary), Jennifer Ehle (Sophie), Ian Hart (Liam), Douglas Henshall (Danny), Catherine McCormack (Hannah), Dougray Scott (Cameron), Sophie Okenedo (Denise).

An ensemble cast give smart performances in this comedy about a sort of sexual musical chairs that begins within an hour of the marriage of Henshall and McCormack.

2928.   The Thomas Crown Affair (1999, MGM, 111m, c). D John McTiernan, P Pierce Brosnan & Beau St. Clair, W Leslie Dixon & Kurt Wimmer (based on a story by Alan R. Trustman), PH Tom Priestley, ED John Wright, M Bill Conti, PD Bruno Rubero, AD Dennis Bradford, SD Leslie Rollins.

LP Pierce Brosnan (Thomas Crown), Rene Russo (Catherine Banning), Denis Leary (Det. Michael McCann), Ben Gazarra (Andrew Wallace), Frankie Faison (Det. Paretti), Fritz Weaver (John Reynolds), Charles Keating (Golchan), Mark Margolis (Knutzhorn), Faye Dunaway (The Psychiatrist).

Those who found the teaming of Steve McQueen and Faye Dunaway an ideal pairing of a strong macho man with a seductive, lovely woman can only approach this remake with suspicion. Brosnan and Russo are attractive people, but can they compare to McQueen and Dunaway — or better yet, why should the movie even have been made? Well, with these negative thoughts in place, the film proves to be entertaining if not spectacular. Brosnan is a rich playboy who can't be true to one woman. He filches a $100 million Monet from New York's Metropolitan Museum of Art. Both police detective Leary and insurance investigator Russo are convinced Brosnan is the culprit. Russo always gets her man, even if it sometimes means bedding him. In the case of Brosnan, this seems more a pleasurable assignment than work. Who will get whom is the question in this cat-and-mouse romantic caper film.

2929.   A Thousand Acres (1997, Touchstone–Buena Vista, 104m, c). D Jocelyn Moorhouse, P Marc Abraham, Steve Golin, Lynn Arost, Kate Guinzberg & Sigurjon Sighvatsson, W Laura Jones (based on the novel by Jane Smiley), PH Tak Fujimoto, ED Maryann Brandon, M Richard Hartley, PD Dan Davis, AD James F. Truesdale, SD Andrea Fenton.

LP Jessica Lange (Ginny Cook Smith), Michelle Pfeiffer (Rose Cook Lewis), Jennifer Jason Leigh (Caroline Cook), Jason Robards, Jr. (Larry Cook), Colin Firth (Jess Clark), Keith Carradine (Ty Smith), Keith Anderson (Peter Lewis), Pat Hingle (Harold Clark).

In a modern-day *King Lear*, wealthy but bitter Robards plans to bequeath his large farm to his three daughters, Lange, Pfeiffer and Leigh. The latter is soon banned from the family, and Lange and Pfeiffer take over the property. Robards soon has reason to regret his decision when the two women try to curb his autonomy. Leigh, a lawyer, reenters the picture, offering to represent her father in a court fight with the other two sisters for the land.

2930.   Thousand Pieces of Gold (1991, Film Four Intl.-Greycat Films, 105m, c). D Nancy Kelly, P Kenji Yamamoto & Kelly, W Anne Makepeace (based on the novel by Ruthanne Lum McCunn), PH Bobby Bukowski, ED Yamamoto, M Gary Remal Malkin, PD Dan Bishop, SD Dianna Treas.

LP Rosalind Chao (Lalu Nathoy/Polly Bemis), Chris Cooper (Charlie), Michael Paul Chan (Hong King), Dennis Dun (Jim/Li Po), Jimmie F. Skaggs (Jonas), Will Oldham (Miles).

In this film, based on a true story, Chao portrays a young Chinese woman sold by her famine-stricken father into virtual slavery. She is eventually brought to San Francisco where she is bought at an auction by a horrible saloon keeper and taken to his dismal Idaho town. Resisting being forced into the life of a prostitute, she faces insurmountable odds in trying to preserve her dignity and win her freedom.

2931.   Three Kings (1999, Warner Bros., 115m, c). D & W David O. Russell (based on a story by John Ridley), P Charles Roven, Paul Junger Witt & Edward L. McDonnell, PH Newton Thomas Sigel, ED Robert K. Lambert, M Carter Burwell, PD Catherine Hardwicke, AD Derek R Hill & Jann Engel, SD Gene Serdena.

LP George Clooney (Archie Gates), Mark Wahlberg (Troy Barlow), Ice Cube (Chief Elgin), Spike Jonze (Conrad Vig), Nora Dunn (Adriana Cruz), Jamie Kennedy (Walter Wogaman), Mykelti Williamson (Col. Horn), Cliff Curtis (Amir Abdulah).

This film has some aspects of *Kelly's Heroes*,

in that four G.I.s plan to steal a fortune in hidden gold bullion stolen by the Iraqi soldiers from Kuwait during the Gulf War. On the other hand, director Russell has some political points to make about American foreign policy in this intriguing black comedy-drama. Ultimately, Clooney and company have crises of conscience and decide to do the right thing. It's a good story, well-directed; the acting is strong and the photography appealing.

2932. Three Men and a Little Lady (1990, Touchstone/Buena Vista, 100m, c). D Emile Ardolino, P Robert W. Cort & Ted Field, W Charlie Peters, PH Adam Greenberg, ED Michael A. Stevenson, M James Newton Howard, PD Stuart Wurtzel, AD David M. Haber, SD Antoinette Gordon.

LP Tom Selleck (Peter Mitchell), Steve Guttenberg (Michael Kellam), Ted Danson (Jack Holden), Nancy Travis (Sylvia), Robin Weissman (Mary Bennington), Christopher Cazenove (Edward), Sheila Hancock (Vera), Fiona Shaw (Miss Lomax).

In this pleasant if lightweight comic sequel to *Three Men and a Baby* (1987), a trio of bachelors, Selleck, Gutenberg and Danson, may lose their ward Weissman when her mother Travis decides to marry. Fortunately, her intended is something of a bounder, so Selleck steps forward and does the right thing by mother and daughter.

2933. The Three Musketeers (1993, Touchstone Pictures–Buena Vista, 105m, c). D Stephen Herek, P Joe Roth & Roger Birnham, W David Loughery (based on the novel by Alexandre Dumas), PH Dean Semler, ED John F. Link, M Michael Kamen, PD Wolf Kroeger, AD Herta Hareiter-Pischinger & Neil Lamont, SD Bruno Cesari.

LP Charlie Sheen (Aramis), Kiefer Sutherland (Athos), Chris O'Donnell (D'Artagnan), Oliver Platt (Porthos), Tim Curry (Cardinal Richelieu), Rebecca DeMornay (Milady De Winter), Gabrielle Anwar (Queen Anne), Michael Wincott (Count de Rochefort), Paul McGann (Girard/Jussac), Julie Delpy (Constance), Hugh O'Connor (King Louis).

Who got the bright idea that another version of the Dumas classic was needed, especially one so maddingly miscast? The filmmakers tried for camp and got crap. Sheen, Sutherland, O'Donnell and Platt are about as

believable in the parts as if the roles had been handed to the Teenage Mutant Ninja Turtles. Curry's take of Richelieu seems inspired by his work in *The Rocky Horror Picture Show.*

2934. 3 Ninjas (1992, U.S./South Korea, Buena Vista, 87m, c). D Jon Turteltaub, P Martha Chang, W Edward E. Manuel (based on the story by Kenny Kim), PH Richard Michalak, ED David Rennie, M Rick Marvin, PD Kirk Petruccelli, AD Ken Kirchener & Greg Grande, SD Carol Pressman.

LP Victor Wong (Grandpa), Michael Treanor (Rocky), Max Elliott Slade (Colt), Chad Power (Tum Tum), Rand Kingsley (Snyder), Alan McRae (Sam Douglas), Margarita Franco (Jessica Douglas).

Three kid ninjas help their mentor-grandfather take on a gang of evil ninjas.

2935. 3 Ninjas: High Noon on Mega Mountain (1998, TriStar–Sony Pictures, 93m, c). D Sean McNamara, P James Kang & Yoram Ben-Ami, W McNamara & Jeff Phillips, PH Blake T. Evans, ED Annamaria Szanto, M John Coda, PD Chuck Connor, AD Chase Harlan.

LP Hulk Hogan (Dave Dragon), Loni Anderson (Medusa), Jim Varney (Lothar Zogg), Mathew Botuchis (Rocky), Michael J. O'Laskey II (Colt), Victor Wong (Grandpa Mori).

Plot? A Ninja movie starring Hogan doesn't need to have any stinking plot. Listen, those who enjoy kung-fu action films aren't interested in a story. Just give them plenty of kick-ass action and some gratuitous flesh.

2936. Three of Hearts (1993, New Line Cinema, 102m, c). D Yurek Bogayevicz, P Joel Michaels & Matthew Irmas, W Adam Greenman & Mitch Glazer (based on a story by Greenman), PH Andrzej Sekula, ED Dennis M. Hill & Suzanne Hines, M Joe Jackson, PD Nelson Coates, AD Douglas Hall, SD Linda Lee Sutton & Guido DeCurtis.

LP William Baldwin (Joe Casella), Kelly Lynch (Connie), Sherilyn Fenn (Ellen), Joe Pantoliano (Mickey), Gail Strickland (Yvonne), Cec Verrell (Allison), Claire Callaway (Isabella).

Lesbian Lynch hires male escort Baldwin to woo, win and dump her ex-lover Fenn, hoping to win her back on the rebound. Unfortunately for her, Baldwin falls for Fenn.

2937. *Three to Tango* (1999, Warner Bros., 98m, c). D Damon Santostefano, P Bobby Newmyer, Jeffrey Silver & Bettina Sofia Viviano, W Rodney Vaccaro & Aline Brosh McKenna, PH Walt Lloyd, ED Stephen Semel, M Graeme Revell, PD David Nichols, AD Vlasta Svoboda, SD Enrico A. Campana.

LP Matthew Perry (Oscar Novak), Neve Campbell (Amy Post), Dylan McDermott (Charles Newman), Oliver Platt (Peter Steinberg), Cylk Cozart (Kevin Cartwright), John C. McGinley (Strauss).

Chicago architects Perry and Platt try to win a multi-million dollar job from tycoon McDermott. Somehow the latter gets the idea that Perry is gay and thus would be just the man to keep his mistress Campbell from taking up with other men. Silly McDermott. Silly Perry. Silly Campbell. It's Platt who's gay.

2938. *Three Wishes* (1995, Savoy Pictures, 105m, c). D Martha Coolidge, P Gary Lucchesi, Clifford Green & Ellen Green, W Elizabeth Anderson (based on a story by the Greens), PH Johnny E. Jensen, ED Steven Cohen, M Cynthia Millar, PD John Vallone, AD Gae Buckley, SD Robert Gould.

LP Patrick Swayze (Jack), Mary Elizabeth Mastrantonio (Jeanne), Joseph Mazzello (Tom), Seth Mumy (Gunny), David Marshall Grant (Phil), Jay O. Sanders (Coach Schramka), Michael O'Keefe (Adult Tom).

Mastrantonio's life, as well as those of her kids Mazzello and Mumy, is dramatically changed when the 1950s suburban widow takes home nonconformist Swayze after she hits him with her car. Besides scandalizing the neighborhood with nude sunbathing among other things, the mystical stranger teaches them all to listen to their heart. Whether audiences can endure listening to the entire muddle is another matter.

2939. *Threesome* (1994, Tri-Star, 93m, c). D & W Andrew Fleming, P Brad Krevoy & Steve Stabler, PH Alexander Gruszynski, ED William C. Carruth, M Thomas Newman, PD Ivo Cristante, AD Ken Larson, SD Tim Colohan.

LP Lara Flynn Boyle (Alex), Stephen Baldwin (Stuart), Josh Charles (Eddie), Alexis Arquette (Dick), Martha Gehman (Renay), Mark Arnold (Larry), Michelle Matheson (Kristen).

See how cute this is. Boyle's name is Alex.

Somehow the college cutie is assigned to share a dorm suite with male roommates Baldwin and Charles. Believe us, this is not a new version of the titillating but innocent TV series *Three's Company.* Sexual situations abound for those who care.

2940. *Thunderheart* (1992, TriStar Pictures, 118m, c). D Michael Apted, P Robert De Niro, Jane Rosenthal & John Fusco, W Fusco, PH Roger Deakins, ED Ian Crafford, M James Horner, PD Dan Bishop, AD Bill Ballou, SD Dianna Freas.

LP Val Kilmer (Ray Levoi), Sam Shepard (Frank Coutelle), Graham Greene (Walter Crow Horse), Fred Dalton Thompson (William Dawes), Fred Ward (Jack Milton), Sheila Tousey (Maggie Eagle Bear), John Trudell (Jimmy Looks Twice).

Cocky young FBI agent Kilmer has suppressed his Indian heritage. But since he is a token Indian, for political reasons his superior Thompson assigns him to investigate a possibly political murder on a reservation in South Dakota. Shepard, the local agent, seems to have the case all but wrapped up when Kilmer arrives. But no, there's more here than Kilmer was led to believe. The government is playing fast and loose with its obligations to the Indians. Some of the tribal elders "recognize" Kilmer as Thunderheart, an Indian hero slain at the Wounded Knee massacre. As the reincarnation of Thunderheart, Kilmer is expected to deliver the tribe from its current problems.

2941. *Thursday* (1998, Gramercy Pictures, 85m, c). D & W Skip Woods, P Alan Poul, PH Denis Lenoir, ED Paul Trejo & Peter Schink, M Luna, PD Chris Anthony Miller.

LP Thomas Jane (Casey Wells), Aaron Eckhart (Nick), Paulina Porizkova (Dallas), James Le Gros (Billy Hilly), Paula Marshall (Christine).

Jane tries to forge a new life for himself and his wife Marshall in Houston. His past life as an L.A. drug dealer comes back to haunt him with the arrival of his former partner Eckhart.

2942. *The Tic Code* (1999, Jazz Films, 91m, c). D Gary Winick, P Polly Draper & Karen Tangorra, W Draper, PH Wolfgang Held, ED Bill Pankow, M Michael Wolff, PD Rick Butler, SD Catherine Pierson.

LP Gregory Hines (Tyrone), Polly Draper

(Laura), Christopher Marquette (Miles), Desmond Robertson (Todd), James McCaffrey (Michael), Carol Kane (Miss Gimpole), Bill Nunn (Kingston).

Saxophone great Hines and budding ten-year-old jazz pianist Marquette share Tourette's syndrome. It's a rare, non–life-threatening disturbance that causes a person to wear his emotions on his sleeve. Hines likes the youngster and his loving seamstress mother Draper. The family drama, set in New York City's jazz world, is well-acted and should prove an enjoyable 90 minutes for jazz fans.

2943. *The Tichborne Claimant* (1998, U.K., Bigger Picture Co., 98m, c). D David Yates, P Tom McCabe, W Joe Fisher, PH Peter Thwaites, ED Jamie Trevill, M Nicholas Hooper, PD Brian Sykes.

LP John Kani (Andrew Bogle), Robert Pugh (The Claimant), Stephen Fry (Hawkins), Robert Hardy (Rivers), John Gielgud (Cockburn), Rachael Dowling (Mary-Anne), Paola Dionisotti (Dowager), Charles Gray (Arundell), Perry Fenwick (John Holmes).

Based on a true story, this film stars Kani as a black servant of the wealthy Tichborne family. In the mid–1970s he is sent to Australia to track down the family's scion and missing heir. Many claim to be the missing man, but Kani enters into a pact with Pugh to support his claim. Kani has to tutor Pugh in aristocratic manners and family background. Dionisotti accepts Pugh as the rightful heir, but when she dies, the rest of the family denounce him as an imposter. Kani hires hungry young lawyer Fenwick to carry Pugh's claim to the courts. The film is an old-fashioned delight.

2944. *Ticks* (AKA: *Infested*) (1994, Republic Pictures, 83m, c). D Tony Randel, P Jack F. Murphy, W Brent V. Friedman, PH Steve Grass, ED Leslie Rosenthal, M Christopher L. Stone, PD Tony Tremblay, AD Aram Allan, SD Greg Bartkus.

LP Peter Scolari (Charles Danson), Rosalind Allen (Holly Lambert), Ami Dolenz (Dee Dee Davenport), Alfonso Ribiero ("Panic" Lumley), Ray Oriel (Rome Hernandez).

When loads of steroids are dumped into the water supply, a species of woodticks beef up. They then terrorize a group of teenage campers in Northern California. Adding to the fun is a dandy forest fire.

2945. *The Tie That Binds* (1995, Hollywood Pictures–Buena Vista, 98m, c). D Wesley Strick, P David Madden, Patrick Markey, Susan Zachary & John Morrissey, W Michael Auerbach, PH Bobby Bukowski, ED Michael Knue, M Graeme Revell, PD Marcia Hinds-Johnson, AD Bo Johnson, SD Don Diers.

LP Daryl Hannah (Leann Netherwood), Keith Carradine (John Netherwood), Moira Kelly (Dana Clifton), Vincent Spano (Russell Clifton), Julia Devin (Janie), Ray Reinhardt (Sam Bennett), Barbara Tarbuck (Jean Bennett).

Sickos Hannah and Carradine are fugitive parents intent on reclaiming their daughter, who was adopted by Kelly and Spano after the child was taken from her parents' custody. Made by the producers of *The Hand That Rocks the Cradle* (1992), the film gives audiences two psychos for the price of one, but that only makes it twice as insipid.

2946. *'Til There Was You* (1997, Paramount, 114m, c). D Scott Winant, P Penney Finkelman Cox, Tom Rosenberg & Alan Poul, W Winnie Holzman, PH Bobby Bukowski, ED Richard Marks & Joanna Cappucilli, M Miles Goodman & Terence Blanchard, PD Craig Stevens, AD Randy Moore, SD Ellen Totleben.

LP Jeanne Tripplehorn (Gwen Moss), Dylan McDermott (Nick Dawkan), Sarah Jessica Parker (Francesca Lansfield), Jennifer Aniston (Debbie), Craig Bierko (Jon Hass), Ken Olin (Gregory), Nina Foch (Sophia Monroe).

While the lives of lonely Tripplehorn and McDermott are intertwined, they don't actually meet until the end of the movie, by which time audiences may have lost interest in their destinies. This is no *Sleepless in Seattle*.

2947. *Till There Was You* (1992, Australia, Ayer Productions, 94m, c). D John Seale, P Jim McElroy & Hal McElroy, W Michael Thomas, PH Geoffrey Simpson, ED Jill Bilcock, M Graeme Revell, PD George Liddle, AD Ian Allen.

LP Mark Harmon (Frank Flynn), Jeroen Krabbe (Robert "Viv" Vivaldi), Deborah Unger (Anna), Shane Briant (Rex), Ritchie Singer (Robbo).

We can only suppose that this movie was made to capitalize on the bungee jumping craze. Harmon travels to a faraway tropical island to solve the death of his brother. Pretty scenery, though.

2948. ***Tim Burton's the Nightmare Before Christmas*** (1993, Touchstone-Buena Vista, 75m, c). D Henry Selick, P Denise DiNovi & Tim Burton, W Caroline Thompson (based on a story and characters by Burton), PH Pete Kozachik, ED Stan Webb, M Danny Elfman, AD Deane Taylor, SD Gregg Olsson.

LP Danny Elfman (Singing Voice of Jack Skellington/Voice of Barrel/Clown with the Tear Away Face), Chris Sarandon (Voice of Jack Skellington), Catherine O'Hara (Voice of Sally/Shock), William Hickey (Voice of Evil Scientist), Paul Reubens (Voice of Lock).

In an imaginative and always entertaining animation feature, Jack Skellington, the Pumpkin King, has grown weary of Halloween and turns his attention to the holiday of Christmas. His efforts to redefine Christmas aren't eagerly embraced.

2949. ***Time Bomb*** (1991, MGM-Pathé, 96m, c). D & W Avi Nesher, P Raffaella DeLaurentiis, PH Anthony B. Richmond, ED Isaac Sehayek, M Patrick Leonard, PD Gregory Pruss & Curtis A. Schnell, AD Robert E. Lee.

LP Michael Biehn (Eddie Kay), Patsy Kensit (Dr. Anna Nolmar), Billy Blanks (Mr. Brown), Richard Jordan (Colonel Taylor), Tracy Scoggins (Ms. Blue), Raymond St. Jacques (Det. Sanchez), Ray "Boom Boom" Mancini (Mr. Black).

Amnesiac Biehn, finding himself a target for assassination, kidnaps psychiatrist Kensit to help him discover who he is and why his life is in peril.

2950. ***The Time Guardian*** (1990, Australia, Hemdale-Nelson, 89m, c). D Brian Hannant, P Norman Wilkinson & Robert Lagettie, W John Baxter & Hannant, PH Geoff Burton, ED Andrew J. Prowse, M Allan Zavod, PD George Liddle, AD Tony Raes & Andrew Blaxland, SD Christopher Webster & Vicki Niehus.

LP Tom Burlinson (Ballard), Nikki Coghill (Annie Lassiter), Carrie Fisher (Petra), Dean Stockwell (Boss), Damon Sanders (Smith), Tim Robertson (Ernie McCarthy), Wan Thye Liew (Dr. Sun-Wah).

Time travellers arrive in the Australian desert in 1988 to warn the inhabitants of the imminent arrival of killer cyborgs from the 40th century.

2951. ***A Time to Die*** (1991, PM Entertainment, 95m, c). D & W Charles Kanganis, P Joseph Merhi, Richard Pepin & Charla Driver, PH Ken Blakey, ED Paul Volk, M Louis Febre, PD Greg Martin.

LP Traci Lords (Jackie Swanson), Jeff Conaway (Frank), Robert Miano (Eddie Martin), Jesse Thomas (Kevin), Nitchie Barrett (Sheila), Richard Roundtree (Capt. Ralph Phipps), Bradford Bancroft (Sam).

Police photographer Lords' photos capture a cop in the act of murder. Now she's in trouble.

2952. ***A Time to Kill*** (1996, Warner Bros., 128m, c). D Joel Schumacher, P Arnon Milchan, Michael Nathanson, Hunt Lowry & John Grisham, W Akiva Goldsman (based on the novel by Grisham), PH Peter Menzies, Jr., ED William Steinkamp, M Elliott Goldenthal, PD Larry Fulton, AD Richard Toyon, SD Dorree Cooper.

LP Matthew McConaughey (Jake Brigance), Sandra Bullock (Ellen Roark), Samuel L. Jackson (Carl Lee Hailey), Kevin Spacey (Rufus Buckley), Oliver Platt (Harry Rex Vonner), Charles S. Dutton (Sheriff Ozzie Walls), Brenda Fricker (Ethel Twitty), Donald Sutherland (Lucien Wilbanks), Kiefer Sutherland (Freddie Cobb), Patrick McGoohan (Judge Omar Noose), Ashley Judd (Carla Brigance), Tonea Stewart (Gwen Hailey), Rae'ven Larrymore Kelly (Tonya Hailey), Nicky Katt (Billy Ray Cobb), Doug Hutchinson (Pete Willard).

When his preteen daughter is raped, beaten and nearly hanged by a couple of rednecks, Jackson kills them. It is up to idealistic young lawyer McConaughey to defend him. Everyone remotely associated with the case has their own agenda. Prosecutor Spacey has political ambitions. The Klu Klux Klan and relatives of the slain men want this black man to get what they believe he has coming to him. Black groups are willing to make Jackson a martyr. Grisham certainly can set up a good story, but his endings, as is the case with this movie, are disappointing.

2953. ***Timecop*** (1994, Universal, 98m, c). D & PH Peter Hyams, P Moshe Diamant,

Robert Tapert & Sam Raimi, W Mark Ver-heiden (based on his and Mark Richardson's story and their comic series), ED Steven Kemper & Brandon Willenber, M Mark Isham, PD Philip Harrison, AD Richard Hudolin, SD Rose Marie McSherry, AnnMarie Corbett & Peter Mills.

LP Jean-Claude Van Damme (Max Walker), Mia Sara (Melissa), Ron Silver (McComb), Bruce McGill (Matuzak), Gloria Reuben (Fielding), Scott Bellis (Ricky), Jason Schomburg (Atwood).

Van Damme is a cop in the year 2004. He must travel back in time to prevent a corrupt politician from altering history. Lots of action, little acting.

2954. Tin Cup (1996, Warner Bros., 133m, c). D Ron Shelton, P Gary Foster & David Lester, W Shelton & John Norville, PH Russell Boyd, ED Paul Seydor & Kimberly Ray, M William Ross, PD James Bissell, AD Gae Buckley & Chris Burian-Mohr, SD Ric McElvin.

LP Kevin Costner (Roy "Tin Cup" McAvoy), Rene Russo (Dr. Molly Griswold), Cheech Marin (Romeo Posar), Don Johnson (David Simms), Linda Hart (Doreen), Dennis Buckley (Earl), Lou Myers (Clint).

This is the kind of film Costner can handle easily. He should stay away from his message pictures. He's a West Texas golf hustler who has all the ability to be a top pro but not the discipline and/or ambition. He has a chance to qualify for the U.S. Open and turns to lovely psychologist Russo to help him pull himself together to make the effort. Naturally, he not only makes the tournament, but has a great chance of winning it. Just as naturally, he blows it — but how he blows it! The ending is rather farfetched, but all in all it's an extremely enjoyable sports movie.

2955. Titanic* (1997, 20th Century–Fox–Paramount, 194m, c). D James Cameron*, P James Cameron*, W James Cameron, PH Russell Carpenter*, ED Conrad Buff*, Cameron* & Richard A. Harris*, M James Horner*, PD Peter Lamont*, AD Charles Lee, SD Michael Ford*, SO Gary Rydstrom*, Tom Johnson*, Gary Summers* & Mark Ulano*.

LP Leonardo DiCaprio (Jack Dawson), Kate Winslet† (Rose DeWitt Bukater), Bill Paxton (Brock Lovett), Kathy Bates (Molly Brown), Suzy Amis (Lizzy Calvert), Gloria

Stuart† (Rose Calvert), David Warner (Spicer Lovejoy), Danny Nucci (Fabrizio DeRossi), Billy Zane (Cal Hockley), Frances Fisher (Ruth DeWitt Bukater), Bernard Hill (Captain E.J. Smith).

Everyone knows how expensive it was to make this movie and how it made dunces of know-it-alls by not only regaining all of the investment but being the top moneymaker of all time. Why? Well, it's not really due to the sinking of the unsinkable ship Titanic. That's been shown in several previous movies, including the excellent British *A Night to Remember* (1958) and the melodramatic but extremely watchable Hollywood version *Titanic* (1953). Yes, the special effects in this film are remarkable, but the success of the film can be directly traced to young fans falling for the romantic story of Leonardo DiCaprio and Kate Winslet. There is quite a spark between the two performers. The story is of a poor lad and a young woman, above his station, who, despite her outspokenness, is not free to choose her own life and man. Somehow they find, at a time of tragedy, an eternal love. Kudos to the kids!

2956. Titanic Town (1998, U.K., BBC Films, 100m, c). D Roger Michell, P George Faber & Charles Patterson, W Anne Devlin (based on the novel by Mary Costello), PH John Daly, ED Kate Evans, M Trevor Jones, PD Pat Campbell, AD Dave Arrowsmith.

LP Julie Walters (Bernie McPhelimy), Ciaran Hinds (Aidan McPhelimy), Nuala O'Neill (Annie McPhelimy), James Loughran (Thomas McPhelimy), Barry Loughran (Brendan McPhelimy), Elizabeth McMenamin (Sinead McPhelimy).

Walters and her family live in a Catholic neighborhood of a West Belfast town famous as the place where the Titanic was built. She's a feisty housewife who tries to become a peacemaker.

2957. Titus (1999, Fox Searchlight Pictures, 162m, c). D & W Julie Taymor (based on the play *Titus Andronicus* by William Shakespeare), P Jody Patton, Conchita Airoldi & Taymor, PH Luciano Tovoli, ED Francoise Bonnot, M Elliot Goldenthal, PD Dante Ferretti, AD Pier Luigi Basile, SD Carlo Gervasi.

LP Anthony Hopkins (Titus Andronicus), Jessica Lange (Tamora), Alan Cumming (Saturninus), Colm Feore (Marcus), James Frain

(Bassianus), Laura Fraser (Lavinia), Harry Lennix (Aaron), Angus Macfadyen (Lucius), Matthew Rhys (Demetrius).

Not even fans of Shakespeare's plays will appreciate this seldom performed story written by the Bard. Still, the acting is first rate and the direction is impressive. The story is a wild and savage tale of revenge in imperial Rome, with some very modern touches. Hopkins is a great Roman general returning from the wars with the Goths, accompanied by his prize prisoner, Lange, the Queen of the Goths. Hopkins enacts a religious ceremony by executing Lange's eldest son. She vows revenge. She gets her chance when she becomes the wife of the new emperor, Cumming. There are plenty of bloody killings, rapes and orgies to satisfy even the most hard-to-please fan of slasher movies.

2958. To Die For (1995, Columbia, 100m, c). D Gus Van Sant, P Laura Ziskin, W Buck Henry (based on the novel by Joyce Maynard), PH Eric Alan Edwards, ED Curtiss Clayton, M Danny Elfman, PD Missy Stewart, AD Vlasta Svoboda, SD Carol A. Lavoie.

LP Nicole Kidman (Suzanne Stone), Matt Dillon (Larry Maretto), Joaquin Phoenix (Jimmy Emmett), Casey Affleck (Russell Hines), Illeana Douglas (Janice Maretto), Allison Folland (Lydia Mertz), Dan Hedaya (Joe Maretto), Wayne Knight (Ed Grant), George Segal (Uncredited).

Gorgeous and ambitious Kidman is determined to make it as a television personality. She won't allow little things like no talent or disapproving husband Dillon get in her way. When the latter proves to be too much of a bother, she arranges to have three teen misfits, Phoenix, Affleck and Folland, kill him. It's a wonderful film. Kidman seems to be having a marvelous time. Douglas is excellent as Kidman's sister-in-law, never taken in by Nicole's act.

2959. To Die for 2: Son of Darkness (1991, Vidmark Ent., 95m, c). D David F. Price, P Richard Weinman, W Leslie King, PH Gerry Lively, ED Barry Zetlin, M Mark McKenzie, PD Stuart Blatt, AD James Vaughn, SD Robert Stover.

LP Rosalind Allen (Nina), Steve Bond (Tom), Scott Jacoby (Martin), Michael Praed (Max Schreck/Vlad Tepish), Jay Underwood (Danny), Amanda Wynn (Celia).

The 500-year-old bloodsuckers are back. Jacoby, who lost several friends in the 1989 original, rolls into town on a vampire hunting expedition. As far as films of this subgenre go, it has all the gore that fans could hope for.

2960. To Gillian on Her 37th Birthday (1996, Triumph, 93m, c). D Michael Pressman, P Marykay Powell & David E. Kelley, W Kelley (based on the play by Michael Brady), PH Tim Suhrstedt, ED William Scharf, M James Horner, PD & SD Linda Pearl, AD Michael Atwell.

LP Peter Gallagher (David Lewis), Michelle Pfeiffer (Gillian Lewis), Claire Danes (Rachel Lewis), Laurie Fortier (Cindy Bayles), Wendy Crewson (Kevin Dollof).

Widower Gallagher can't get over the loss of his wife Pfeiffer. He has little time for his daughter Danes, who is desperate for his attention.

2961. To Sleep with a Vampire (1993, Concorde, 76m, c). D Adam Friedman, P Mike Elliott, W Patricia Harrington, PH Michael Craine, ED Lorne Morris, M Nigel Holton, PD Stuart Blatt.

LP Scott Valentine (Jacob), Charlie Spradling (Nina), Richard Zobel, Ingrid Vold, Stephanie Hardy.

Bloodsucking vampire Valentine yearns for daylight. He nabs stripper Spradling, but before getting down to business pumps her about life in the sun. She sees her opportunity to save her life.

2962. To Sleep with Anger (1990, Samuel Goldwyn, 95m, c). D & W Charles Burnett, P Caldecot Chubb, Thomas S. Byrnes & Darin Scott, PH Walt Lloyd, ED Nancy Richardson, M Stephen James Taylor, PD Penny Barrett, AD Troy Myers.

LP Danny Glover (Harry Mention), Richard Brooks (Babe Brother), Paul Butler (Gideon), Mary Alice (Suzie), Carl Lumbly (Junior), Sheryl Lee Ralph (Linda), Vonetta McGee (Pat), Wonderful Smith (Preacher).

Charming Glover invades the life of a black middle-class family, entertaining them with sinister folktales told to him by his grandmother. He's a trickster — one who has come to steal souls — and he must be tricked to prevent it from happening.

2963. To Walk with Lions (1998, Canada/ U.K./Kenya, Kingsborough Pictures, 108m, c). D Carl Schultz, P Pieter Kroonenburg & Julie Allan, W Keith Ross Leckie, PH Jean Lepine, ED Angelo Corraro, M Alan Reeves, AD Michael Devine, SD Lulu Archer.

LP Richard Harris (George Adamson), John Michie (Tony Fitzjohn), Ian Bannen (Terence Adamson), Kerry Fox (Lucy Jackson), Hugh Quarshie (Maxwell), Honor Blackman (Joy Adamson), Geraldine Chaplin (Victoria Andrecelli).

This old-fashioned adventure yarn centers on cocky Michie who, when stranded in Kenya, takes a temporary job as a maintenance man at a rough compound run by Harris and his brother Bannen. These two have been working on the "rehabilitation" of lions, as were Elsa and her cubs in the film *Born Free* and its sequel. The time of this movie is much later. Blackman, as Joy Adamson, the heroine of her book and movie *Born Free*, shows up briefly after years of absence. It seems she never shared any profits from her book with husband Harris.

2964. To Wong Foo, Thanks for Everything: Julie Newmar (1995, Amblin Ent.– Universal, 108m, c). D Beeban L. Kidron, P G. Mac Brown, W Douglas Carter Beane, PH Steve Mason, ED Andrew Mondshein, M Rachel Portman, PD Wynn Thomas, AD Robert Guerra, SD Ted Glass.

LP Wesley Snipes (Noxeema Jackson), Patrick Swayze (Vida Boheme), John Leguizamo (Chi Chi Rodriguez), Stockard Channing (Carol Ann), Blythe Danner (Beatrice), Arliss Howard (Virgil), Jason London (Bobby Ray), Chris Penn (Sheriff Dollard), Melinda Dillon (Merna), Julie Newmar (Herself), RuPaul (Rachel Tensions).

Here's a U.S. version of *The Adventures of Priscilla, Queen of the Desert* (1994). Three drag queens, Swayze, Snipes and Leguizamo, motor to Hollywood in a 1967 Cadillac convertible. The car breaks down in Nebraska, where the trio is something never before seen nor imagined by the locals. Nevertheless, the "girls" win over the townsfolk with their charm. It's a fairy tale, don't you know!

2965. Tollbooth (1996, Roadkill Films, 108m, c). D & W Salome Breziner, P Stephen J. Wolfe, PH Henry Vargas, ED Peter Teschner, M Adam Gorgoni, PD Brenden Barry.

LP Fairuza Balk (Doris), Lenny Van Dohlen (Jack), Will Patton (Dash Pepper), Louise Fletcher (Lillian), Seymour Cassel (Larry Borders/Leon Borders), James Wilder (Vic).

Van Dohlen works at a tollbooth on a two-lane road in the Florida Keys. He dreams of becoming a Miami cop and marrying gas-station attendant Balk. She loves him also, but won't go away with him until her long-missing father Cassel returns. When he does, he's a drunken, knife-throwing creep. He's accidentally electrocuted by a bug zapper while trying to kill Van Dohlen. Rather than tell Balk about his part in her father's death, Van Dohlen and his friend Patton grinds Cassel's body into a "secret recipe" bait.

2966. Tom and Huck (1995, Walt Disney Pictures–Buena Vista, 93m, c). D Peter Hewitt, P Laurence Mark & John Baldecchi, W Stephen Sommers & David Loughery (based on the novel *The Adventures of Tom Sawyer* by Mark Twain), PH Bobby Bukowski, ED David Freeman, M Stephen Endelman, PD Gemma Jackson, AD Michael Rizzo, SD Ellen J. Brill.

LP Jonathan Taylor Thomas (Tom Sawyer), Brad Renfro (Huck Finn), Eric Schweig (Injun Joe), Charles Rocket (Judge Thatcher), Amy Wright (Aunt Polly), Michael McShane (Muff Potter), Marion Seldes (Widow Douglas), Rachael Leigh Cook (Becky Thatcher).

It's hard to keep track of all the film versions of the adventures of Mark Twain's two young heroes. One can't say that this one is a fine addition to the collection. Perhaps this one will be more appreciated by those new to the stories of Tom and Huck's misadventures near Hannibal, Missouri, and on the Mississippi River.

2967. Tom and Jerry — The Movie (1993, Miramax, 80m, c). D & P Phil Roman, W Dennis Marke, M Henry Mancini, AD Michael Peraza, ANIM Dale Baer & John Sparey.

LP Voices: Richard King (Tom), Dana Hill (Jerry), Andi Lynn McAfee (Robyn Starling), Charlotte Rae (Aunt Figg), Tony Jay (Lickboot), Henry Gibson (Applecheeks), Rip Taylor (Captain Kiddie).

Surely many will recall with pleasure various Tom and Jerry cartoons in which the playful mouse constantly gets the better of the hungry cat. In this full-length animated film there is a slight change, but not necessarily for the better. Both Tom and Jerry talk.

2968. *Tom & Viv* (1994, U.S./U.K., Miramax, 120m, c). D Brian Gilbert, P Marc Samuelson, Peter Samuelson & Harvey Kass, W Adrian Hodges & Michael Hastings (based on the play by Hastings), PH Martin Fuhrer, ED Tony Lawson, M Debbie Wiseman, PD Jamie Leonard, AD Mark Raggett, SD Jill Quertier.

LP Miranda Richardson† (Vivienne Haigh-Wood), Willem Dafoe (T.S. Eliot), Tim Dutton (Maurice), Nickolas Grace (Bertrand Russell), Clare Holman (Louise Purdon), Rosemary Harris† (Rose Haigh-Wood), Philip Locke (Charles Haigh-Wood), Joanna McCallum (Virginia Woolf).

This talky but curiously fascinating film shows celebrated poet T.S. Eliot in a rather bad light. At least he is in his treatment — or perhaps we should say *mis*treatment — of his wife.

2969. *Tombstone* (1993, Hollywood Pictures–Buena Vista, 128m, c). D George Pan Cosmatos, P James Jacks, Sean Daniel & Bob Misiorowski, W Kevin Jarre, PH William A. Fraker, ED Frank J. Urioste, Robert Silvi & Harvey Rosenstock, M Bruce Broughton, PD Catherine Hardwicke, AD Chris Gorak, Kim Hix & Mark Worthington, SD Gene Serdena, Tom Benson, Richard Prantis & Siobhan Roome.

LP Kurt Russell (Wyatt Earp), Val Kilmer (Doc Holliday), Michael Biehn (Johnny Ringo), Powers Boothe (Curly Bill Brocius), Robert Burke (Frank McLaury), Dana Delany (Josephine Earp), Sam Elliott (Virgil Earp), Stephen Lang (Ike Clanton), Terry O'Quinn (Mayor Clum), Joanna Pacula (Kate), Bill Paxton (Morgan Earp), Jason Priestley (Deputy Sheriff Billy Breakenridge).

This film is overly long. Usually the familiar Western saga of the Earp brothers and Doc Holiday ends shortly after the "Gunfight at the OK Corral" with the Clanton gang. This film goes on to examine the later life of the survivors, and it isn't their most interesting period.

2970. *Tommy Boy* (1995, Paramount, 96m, c). D Peter Segal, P Lorne Michaels, W Bonnie Turner, Terry Turner & Fred Wolf, PH Victor J. Kemper, ED William Kerr, M David Newman, PD Stephen Lineweaver, AD Alicia Keywan, SD Gordon Sim.

LP Chris Farley (Tommy Callahan), David Spade (Richard Hayden), Brian Dennehy (Big Tom Callahan), Bo Derek (Beverly), Dan Aykroyd (Zalinsky), Julie Warner (Michelle), Sean McCann (Rittenhauer), Rob Lowe (Paul).

The late Chris Farley had a certain clumsy comic appeal, especially when the fat man was teamed with slim Spade. Farley is a perpetual foul-up who sees his Dad die shortly after exchanging vows with Derek. It's up to the son and his friend Spade to save the old man's company from his scheming mother-in-law and her "dear friend" Lowe.

2971. *Tomorrow Never Dies* (1997, United Artists-MGM/UA, 119m, c). D Roger Spottiswoode, P Michael G. Wilson & Barbara Broccoli, W Bruce Fierstein, PH Robert Elswit, ED Dominique Fortin & Michel Arcand, M David Arnold, PD Allan Cameron, AD Jonathan Lee, Giles Masters, Tony Reading, Stephen Scott & Ken Court, SD Peter Young.

LP Pierce Brosnan (James Bond), Jonathan Pryce (Elliot Carver), Michelle Yeoh (Wai Lin), Teri Hatcher (Paris Carver), Judi Dench (M), Desmond Llewelyn (Q), Samantha Bond (Miss Moneypenny), Goetz Otto (Stamper), Joe Don Baker (Jack Wade), Ricky Jay (Henry Gupta).

Bronson is a delightful Bond, a bit more subtle in his dealings with the fair sex but every bit as successful in bedding beauties as were his predecessors. As for the villain Pryce, he is not a bit forgiving when his wife Hatcher falls into bed with Brosnan. With Teri out of the way, Brosnan teams up with Yeoh, who has all the moves necessary to kick the daylights out of Pryce's henchmen. Now what was it that Pryce was trying to do and the duo of Brosnan and Yeoh were trying to prevent? Oh yes, start WWIII.

2972. *Too Much Sun* (1991, CineTel Films, 100m, c). D Robert Downey, Sr., P Lisa M. Hansen, W Downey, Sr., Laura Ernst & Al Schwartz (based on his story), PH Robert Yeoman, ED Joseph D'Augustine, M David Robbins, PD Shawn Hausman.

LP Robert Downey, Jr. (Reed Richmond), Eric Idle (Sonny Rivers), Andrea Martin (Bitsy

Rivers), Jim Haynie (Father Seamus Kelly), Laura Ernst (Susan Connor), Leo Rossi (George Bianco), Ralph Macchio (Frank Della Rocca, Jr.), Howard Duff (O.M. Rivers).

In order to inherit their father's fortune, Idle and Martin must compete with each other to be the first to have a child. The farcical complication is that both are gay.

2973. *Top Dog* (1995, LIVE Ent., 87m, c). D Aaron Norris, P Andy Howard, W Ron Swanson (based on a story by Aaron Norris and Tim Grayem), PH Joao Fernandes, ED Peter Schink, PD Norm Baron, SD Bill Volland.

LP Chuck Norris (Jake Wilder), Peter Savard Moore (Karl Koller), Clyde Kusatsu (Captain Callahan), Michele Lamar Richards (Savannah Boyette), Timothy Bottoms (Nelson Houseman).

Loner cop Norris, known mostly for his boozing and karate kicks, is teamed with a canine named Reno. The pup's previous human partner was killed by a gang of neo–Nazis. The dog is in charge.

2974. *Topsy-Turvy* (1999, U.K., October Films–Pathé, 160m, c). D Mike Leigh, W Leigh†, P Simon Channing-Williams, PH Dick Pope, ED Robin Sales, M Carl Davis (based on operas by Arthur Sullivan), PD Eve Stewart†.

LP Jim Broadbent (W.S. Gilbert), Allan Corduner (Arthur Sullivan), Lesley Manville (Lucy Gilbert), Eleanor David (Fanny Ronalds), Ron Cook (Richard D'Oyly Carte), Timothy Spall (Richard Temple), Kevin McKidd (Lely), Martin Savage (Grossmith), Shirley Henderson (Leonora Braham), Jessie Bond (Dorothy Atkinson), Wendy Nottingham (Helen Lenoir), Lesley Manville (Lucy).

This film is an overly long biopic of the lives and careers of Gilbert and Sullivan. It's a loving salute to the genius of the two men, containing lavishly staged productions from several of their comic-operas. Not for everyone, it will nevertheless find an appreciative audience. Broadbent and Corduner are excellent as partners no longer on the best of terms. The actors who portrayed the performers in the Gilbert and Sullivan productions are uniformly delightful. Some critics rated it the best film of the year. That seems a stretch, even in a year with very few great movies.

2975. *Torn Apart* (1990, Castle Hill, 95m, c). D Jack Fisher, P Danny Fisher & Jerry Menkin, W Marc Kristal (based on the book *A Forbidden Love* by Chayym Zeldis), PH Barry Markowitz, ED Michael Garvey, M Peter Arnow.

LP Adrian Pasdar (Ben Arnon), Cecilia Peck (Laila Malek), Machram Huri (Mahmoud Malek), Arnon Zadok (Prof. Ibrahim Mansour), Margrit Polak (Ilana Arnon), Michael Morim (Moustapha).

It's a Romeo and Juliet story set in the Middle East. After spending six years in the U.S., Pasdar returns to Israeli for his military service and is reunited with Peck. She was a childhood friend who has grown into a lovely Arab woman. Expect the usual family and cultural problems for the young lovers.

2976. *Total Eclipse* (1995, Fine Line, 110m, c). D Agnieszka Holland, P Jean-Pierre Ramsey Levi, W Christopher Hampton, PH Yorgos Arvanitis, ED Isabel Lorente, M Jan A.P. Kaczmarek, PD Dan Weil.

LP Leonardo DiCaprio (Arthur Rimbaud), David Thewlis (Paul Verlaine), Romaine Bohringer (Mathilde Verlaine), Dominique Blanc (Isabelle Rimbaud), Felicie Pasotti Cabarbaye (Isabelle as a Child).

This film details the destructive sadomasochistic relationship between 19th century French poets Rimbaud and Verlaine, played by DiCaprio and Thewlis, respectfully. Based on fact, the movie just doesn't make it, perhaps because the central characters are so essentially unlikeable that it is difficult to care much about their problems.

2977. *Total Exposure* (1991, Republic Pictures, 97m, c). D John Quinn, P Steve Beswick & Jeff Prettyman, W Lynne Dahlgren & Quinn, PH Kent Wakeford, ED Kert Vander Muelen, M Sasha Matson, PD Gene Abel, AD Ann E. Job, SD Lauree Slattery.

LP Season Hubley (Andi Robinson), Michael Nouri (Dave Murphy), Bob Delegall (Detective Collins), Jeff Conaway (Keynes), Robert Prentiss (Zach).

When fashion photographer Hubley is charged with murdering her model, she turns to detective Nouri to clear her name. But he begins to suspect she may actually be guilty.

2978. *Total Recall* (1990, Tri-Star, 109m, c). D Paul Verhoeven, P Buzz Feitshans &

Ronald Shusett, W Shusett, Dan O'Bannon & Gary Goldman (based on a story by Shusett, O'Bannon & Jon Povill, from the short story "We Can Remember It for You Wholesale" by Phillip K. Dick), PH Jost Vacano, ED Frank J. Urioste, M Jerry Goldsmith, PD William Sandell, AD James Tocci & Jose Rodriguez Granada, SD Marco Trentini, Miguel Chang & Carlos Echeverria.

LP Arnold Schwarzenegger (Doug Quaid), Rachel Ticotin (Melina), Sharon Stone (Lori Quaid), Ronny Cox (Cohaagen), Michael Ironside (Richter), Marshall Bell (George/ Kuato), Mel Johnson, Jr. (Benny), Michael Champion (Helm), Roy Brocksmith (Dr. Edgemar), Ray Baker (McClane).

Sometime in the future, Schwarzenegger, married to Stone, has dreams, nightmares really, in which Ticotin appears. He discovers that his identity is fake, his marriage is fake — everything about him and his life is fake. He ventures to Mars to help fight a powerful madman. Then he discovers that his "real" identity and life is also a fake. There's lots of fantastic fantasy and action for lovers of both.

2979. **Touch** (1997, MGM/UA, 97m, c). D & W Paul Schrader (based on the novel by Elmore Leonard), P Lila Cazes & Fida Attieh, PH Ed Lachman, ED Cara Silverman, M David Grohl, PD David Wasco, AD Daniel Bradford, SD Sandy Reynolds Wasco.

LP Bridget Fonda (Lynn Faulkner), Christopher Walken (Bill Hill), Skeet Ulrich (Juvenal), Tom Arnold (August Murray), Gina Gershon (Debra Lusanne), Lolita Davidovich (Antoinette Baker), Paul Mazursky (Artie), Janeane Garofalo (Kathy Worthington).

One-time preacher Walken believes he's come across a surefire way to become rich. He encounters one-time Franciscan Ulrich, who seems to have performed a miracle in curing a woman's blindness with his touch.

2980. **Touch and Die** (1992, U.K./France/ Italy/Germany, Taurus Film, 108m, c). D Piernico Solinas, P Evelyne Madec, W John Howlett & Solinas.

LP Martin Sheen (Frank Magentz), Renee Estevez (Emma), David Birney (Senator John Scanzano), Franco Nero (Aquan), Veronique Jannot (Catherine), Horst Buchholz (Limey).

Sheen, the Rome bureau chief of an American newspaper, investigates the story of hand-less corpses turning up all over Europe. It has something to do with plutonium thieves.

2981. **Touch of a Stranger** (1991, RavenStar, 87m, c). D Brad Gilbert, P Hakon Gunderson & Andre Stone Guttfreund, W Joslyn Barnes & Gilbert, PH Michael Negrin, ED William Goldenberg, M Jack Ann Goga, PD Richard Sherman.

LP Shelley Winters (Lily), Anthony Nocerino (Jet), Danny Capri (Finny), Haley Taylor-Block (Grocery Girl).

When lonely recluse Winters opens her door to find young cop-killer Nocerino bleeding on her steps, she takes him in. The film is the story of an odd couple composed of two quite odd individuals. It's weird and wacky, with Winters giving a campy Norma Desmond–like performance and Nocerino bringing his special method-acting talent to his role as a violent, angry man.

2982. **Toy Soldiers** (1991, TriStar, 112m, c). D Daniel Petrie, Jr. P Doug Metzger, W Petrie & David Koepp (based on the novel by William P. Kennedy), PH Thomas Burstyn, ED Michael Kahn, M Robert Folk, PD Chester Kaczenski, AD Marc Dabe, SD Judi Sandin.

LP Sean Astin (Billy Tepper), Wil Wheaton (Joey Trotta), Keith Coogan (Snuffy Bradberry), Andrew Divoff (Luis Cali), R. Lee Ermey (General Kramer), Mason Adams (Deputy Director Brown), Denholm Elliott (Headmaster), Louis Gossett, Jr. (Dean Parker).

South American narco-terrorists seize an exclusive U.S. boys' school. Their hostages are a group of rich kids with talents for practical jokes, which they use to thwart their captors. The whole thing is pretty ludicrous.

2983. **Toy Story** (1995, Walt Disney Pictures–Buena Vista, 80m, c). D John Lasseter, P Ralph Guggenheim & Bonnie Arnold, W Joss Whedon†, Andrew Stanton†, Joel Cohen†, Alec Sokolow† (based on a story by Lasseter, Peter Docter, Stanton & Joe Ranft), ED Robert Gordon & Lee Unkrich, M Randy Newman†, AD Ralph Eggleston.

LP Voices: Tom Hanks (Woody), Tim Allen (Buzz Lightyear), Don Rickles (Mr. Potato Head), Jim Varney (Slinky Dog), Wallace Shawn (Rex), John Ratzenberger (Hamm), Annie Potts (Bo Peep).

This film is the first feature length, fully computer animated movie. The lives of a boy's toys are dramatically changed when a new toy arrives in the person of space ranger Buzz Lightyear. Woody the pull-string cowboy, the child's favorite till now, is more than a little jealous. The two toys soon find they must join forces to survive the threats of the world outside the toy box.

2984. *Toy Story 2* (1999, Walt Disney–Buena Vista, 92m, c). D John Lassetar, P Helene Plotkin & Karen Robert Jackson, W Andrew Stanton, Rita Hsiao, Doug Chamberlin, Chris Webb (from an original story by Lassetar, Pete Docter, Ash Brannon & Stanton), ED Edie Bleiman, David Ian Salter & Lee Unkrich, M Randy Newman, PD William Cone & Jim Pearson.

LP Voices: Tom Hanks (Woody), Tim Allen (Buzz Lightyear), Joan Cusack (Jessie), Kelsey Grammer (Slinky Pete the Prospector), Don Rickles (Mr. Potato Head), Jim Varney (Slinky Dog), Wallace Shawn (Rex), John Ratzenberger (Hamm), Annie Potts (Bo Peep), Wayne Knight (Al McWhiggin).

In yet another computer animation triumph, the team that brought us the 1995 smash hit is back with, if anything, a better product. When his arm is broken, Woody is left behind when his young master heads off to summer camp. He accidentally finds himself as an item in a yard sale and is snatched up by the owner of a local toy store. This baddy knows what Woody doesn't, that years ago he was a big TV star. Woody meets several new friends, but it is his old friends, led by Buzz Lightyear, who come to his rescue and save him from being shipped of to a Japanese museum.

2985. *Toys* (1992, 20th Century–Fox, 110m, c). D Barry Levinson, P Levinson & Mark Johnson, W Levinson & Valerie Curtin, PH Adam Greenberg, ED Stu Linder, M Hans Zimmer & Trevor Horn, PD Fernando Scarfioti†, AD Edward Richardson, SD Linda DeScenna†.

LP Robin Williams (Leslie Zevo), Michael Gambon (The General), Joan Cusack (Alsatia Zevo), Robin Wright (Gwen), L.L. Cool J. (Patrick), Donald O'Connor (Kenneth Zevo), Arthur Malet (Owens Owens), Jack Warden (Zevo, Sr.).

Williams is the son of toy manufacturer O'Connor. When the latter dies, the concern passes into the hands of Williams' uncle Gambon, a military man who wishes to convert the business to an armaments plant. The disappointing film is a huge waste of Williams' immense talent.

2986. *Traces of Red* (1992, Samuel Goldwyn Company, 105m, c). D Andy Wolk, P David V. Picker & Mark Gordon, W Jim Piddock, PH Timothy Suhrstedt, ED Trudy Ship, M Graeme Revell, PD Dan Bishop & Diana Freas.

LP James Belushi (Jack Dobson), Lorraine Bracco (Ellen Schofield), Tony Goldwyn (Steve Frayn), William Russ (Michael Dobson), Faye Grant (Beth Frayn), Michelle Joyner (Morgan Cassidy), Joe Lisi (Lt. J.C. Hooks).

When the women he takes to bed begin turning up dead, Palm Beach cop Belushi finds himself not only tracking down the killer but being tracked down himself.

2987. *Trading Mom* (1994, Trimark Pictures, 82m, c). D & W Tia Brelis, P Raffaella De Laurentiis, PH Buzz Feitshans, ED Isaac Sehayek, M David Kitay, PD Cynthia Charette, AD Troy Sizemore, SD Lisa Caperton.

LP Sissy Spacek (Mrs. Martin/Mom/Natasha), Anna Chlumsky (Elizabeth), Aaron Michael Metchik (Jeremy), Asher Metchik (Harry), Maureen Stapleton (Mrs. Cavour), Andre the Giant (Walrus).

Deciding that their Mom, Spacek, is no fun, three kids head to the "Mommy Market" for a replacement. This allows Sissy to play three additional roles before the kids realize that the Mommy they know is better than the Mommy they don't know.

2988. *Trained to Fight* (1992, Starlight Film, 95m, c). D Eric Sherman, P William Yuen & Theresa Woo, W Roxanne Reaver & Woo, PH Jurg Walther, ED Brian Varaday, M David Bergeaud.

LP Ken McLeod (James Caulfield), Matthew Ray Cohen (Craig Tanner), Mark Williams (Mark), Tang Tak Wing (Wing Chan), Kendra Tucker (Kimberly).

College Freshman McLeod must win $25,000 in a kung fu tournament to help underprivileged kids. Standing in his way is Cohen, the racist psycho leader of a street gang.

2989. *Trainspotting* (1996, U.K., Miramax, 93m, c). D Danny Boyle, P Andrew MacDonald, W John Hodge† (based on the novel by Irvine Welsh), PH Brian Tufano, ED Masahiro Hirakubo, PD Kave Quinn, AD Tracey Gallacher.

LP Ewan McGregor (Mark Renton), Ewen Bremner (Spud), Jonny Lee Miller (Sick Boy), Kevin McKidd (Tommy), Robert Carlyle (Begbie), Kelly Macdonald (Diane), Peter Mullan (Swanney).

Heroin-using McGregor would like to straighten out his life and be drug-free but realizes this means getting away from his friends. The film has received much deserved praise, but the life of junkies and their sick friends will not be to everyone's taste. Some scenes will be seen as downright nauseating.

2990. *Trapped in Paradise* (1994, 20th Century–Fox, 111m, c). D & W George Gallo, P Jon Davison & Gallo, PH Jack N. Green, ED Terry Rawlings, M Robert Folk, PD Bob Ziembicki, AD Gregory P. Keen.

LP Nicolas Cage (Bill Firpo), Dana Carvey (Alvin Firpo), Jon Lovitz (Dave Firpo), Madchen Amick (Sarah Collins), Vic Mazzucci (Vic Manni), Florence Stanley (Ma Firpo), Richard Jenkins (Shaddus Peyser), Donald Moffat (Clifford Anderson), Angela Paton (Hattie Anderson).

When his criminal brothers Carvey and Lovitz get out of jail, they force Cage to join them in a big robbery on Christmas Eve in the town of Paradise. The inhabitants of the town are just the nicest people in the world — the kind Norman Rockwell used to depict. The bungling crooks are no match for the innate goodness of the people of Paradise.

2991. *Traps* (1995, Australia, Filmopolis Pictures, 98m, c). D Pauline Chan, P Jim McElroy, W Chan & Robert Carter (based on the novel *Dreamhouse*, by Kate Grenville), PH Kevin Hayward, ED Nick Beauman, M Stephen Rae, PD Michael Phillips, AD Philip Drake.

LP Saskia Reeves (Louise Duffield), Robert Reynolds (Michael Duffield), Sami Frey (Daniel Renouard), Jacqueline McKenzie (Viola Renouard), Kiet Lam (Tuan), Hoa To (Tatie Chi).

In 1950 Australian journalist Reynolds and his English photographer wife Reeves arrive in French Indochina to write about and photograph the rubber plant managed by Frey. The plant is harassed by the increasingly militant Viet-Minh.

2992. *Trash* (1999, Dancing Babies Ent., 95m, c). D & W Mark Anthony Galluzzo, P Scott Tiano, Sean Entin & Todd Feldman, PH Thom Stukas, ED Adam P. Scott, M Michael Muhlfriedel, AD Jerry Ellar.

LP Jeremy Sisto (Sunny James), Eric Michael Cole (Anthony DeMarie), Jaime Pressly (C.J. Callum), Grace Zabriskie (Mrs. DeMarie), Jonathan Banks (Judge Callum).

Rural "white trash" Sisto and Cole both are marked for life by witnessing a pointless hunting death of a friend at the hands of a 10-year-old. Sisto figures life holds nothing for him so he might as well take whatever he can get. Cole, who once felt life had great promise for him, questions his options. In particular, he wonders if there is any chance of finding happiness with Pressly, a girl from the right side of the tracks.

2993. *Traveller* (1997, October Films, 100m, c). D & PH Jack N. Green, P Bill Paxton, Brian Swardstrom, Mickey Liddell & David Blocker, W Jim McGlynn, ED Michael Ruscio, M Andy Paley, PD Michael Helmy, SD Steve Davis.

LP Bill Paxton (Bokky), Mark Wahlberg (Pat), Julianna Margulies (Jean), James Gammon (Double D), Luke Askew (Boss Jack), Nikki Deloach (Kate), Danielle Wiener (Shane).

An enclave of gypsy con men are headquartered in a compound deep in the Southern backwoods. They fan out to surrounding communities to practice their illegal trade. Into this group comes Wahlberg whose recently deceased father was a member of the gang. He comes under the protection and tutelage of Paxton, who instructs the youngster in the ways of the scam.

2994. *Treasure Island* (1999, King Pictures, 83m, b&w). D, W & PH Scott King, P Adrienne Gruben, ED Dody Dorn, M Chris Anderson, PD Nathan Marsak, AD David Huffman.

LP Lance Baker (Frank), Nick Offerman (Samuel), Jonah Blechman (The Body), Pat Healy (Clark), Suzy Nakamura (Yo-Ji), Rachel Singer (Anna).

This movie focuses on two code specialists who, in the 1940s, are stationed at the naval base on Treasure Island in San Francisco Bay. Baker is a polygamist. He has a Japanese-American wife stashed in one apartment and an ailing second wife in another. Offerman has only one wife but can only have sex with her if another man is present during the act.

2995. Trees Lounge (1996, Orion Pictures, 94m, c). D & W Steve Buscemi, P Brad Wyman & Chris Hanley, PH Lisa Rinzler, ED Kate Williams, M Evan Lurie, PD Steve Rosenzweig, AD Jennifer Alex.

LP Steve Buscemi (Tommy Basilio), Mark Boone, Jr. (Mike), Chloe Sevigny (Debbie), Michael Buscemi (Raymond), Anthony La-Paglia (Rob) Elizabeth Bracco (Theresa), Daniel Baldwin (Jerry), Carol Kane (Connie).

Life is hell for boozer Steve Buscemi. His best friend and boss, LaPaglia, fires him and moves in with Bracco, Buscemi's pregnant ex-girlfriend. Buscemi takes a job driving an ice-cream truck and compounds his problems by becoming involved with Sevigny, a 17-year-old girl. Buscemi is one of the more intriguing character actors in films today.

2996. Tremors (1990, Universal, 96m, c). D Ron Underwood, P Brent Maddock & S.S. Wilson, W Wilson & Maddock (based on a story by Wilson, Maddock & Underwood), PH Alexander Gruszynski, ED O. Nicholas Brown, M Ernest Troost, PD Ivo Cristante, AD Donald Maskovich, SD Debra Combs.

LP Kevin Bacon (Valentine McKee), Fred Ward (Earl Basset), Finn Carter (Rhonda LeBeck), Michael Gross (Burt Gummer), Reba McEntire (Heather Gummer), Bobby Jacoby (Melvin Plug).

In this tongue-in-cheek horror movie, mysterious underground creatures invade a small, dusty Western town. Handymen Bacon and Ward face the difficult task of dealing harshly with the critters.

2997. The Trench (1999, U.K./Fr., Ent. Film Distributors, 98m, c). D & W William Boyd, P Steve Clark-Hall, PH Tony Pierce-Roberts, ED Jim Clark & Laurence Mery-Clark, M Evelyn Glennie & Greg Malcangi, PD Jim Clay, AD Phil Harvey.

LP Paul Nicholls (Billy Macfarlane), Daniel Craig (Telford Winter), Julian Rhind-Tutt

(Ellis Harte), Danny Dyer (Victor Dell), James D'Arcy (Colin Daventry), Tam Williams (Eddie Macfarlane).

This film focuses on a platoon of British soldiers as events move towards one of the bloodiest battles of WWI in the trenches of the Somme Valley in Northern France.

2998. Trespass (1992, Universal, 101m, c). D Walter Hill, P Neil Canton, W Robert Zemeckis & Bob Gale, PH Lloyd Ahern, ED Freeman Davies, M Ry Cooder, PD Jon Hutman, AD Charles Breen, SD Beth Rubino.

LP Bill Paxton (Vince), Ice-T (King James), William Sadler (Don), Ice Cube (Savon), Art Evans (Bradlee), De'Voreaux White (Lucky), Bruce A. Young (Raymond).

Redneck firemen Paxton and Sadler search for buried treasure in an abandoned building in East St. Louis. Their timing couldn't be worse, for they witness a gangland killing by druglords Ice-T and Ice-Cube. The film is a violent urban version of *The Treasure of the Sierra Madre*.

2999. The Trial (1992, U.K./Italy, Angelika Films, 118m, c). D David Jones, P Louis Marks, W Harold Pinter (based on the novel by Franz Kafka), PH Phil Meheux, ED John Stothart, M Carl Davis, PD Don Taylor, AD Jim Holloway & Jiri Matolin, SD John Bush.

LP Kyle MacLachlan (Josef K.), Anthony Hopkins (The Priest), Jason Robards (Dr. Huld), Jean Stapleton (Landlady), Juliet Stevenson (Fraulein Burstner), Polly Walker (Leni), Alfred Molina (Titorelli).

This picture is the second film adaptation of Kafka's 1925 novel. Orsen Welles' version was released in 1963. Set in some unnamed country in some past time, MacLachlan is a hapless clerk accused of an unspecified crime, set to go to trial some time yet unscheduled.

3000. Trial and Error (1997, New Line, 98m, c). D Jonathan Lynn, P Gary Ross & Lynn, W Sara Bernstein & Gregory Bernstein (based on a story by the Bernsteins & Cliff Gardner), PH Gabriel Beristain, ED Tony Lombardo, M Phil Marshall, PD Victoria Paul, AD Philip J. Messina, SD Kathe Klopp.

LP Michael Richards (Richard Rietti), Jeff Daniels (Charles Tuttle), Rip Torn (Benny Gibbs), Charlize Theron (Billie), Jessica Steen (Elizabeth Gardiner), Austin Pendelton (Judge

Graff), Alexandra Wentworth (Tiffany), Jennifer Coolidge (Jacqueline).

Because of his bachelor's party, lawyer Daniels is too drunk to appear in court in a trial vital to his career. His friend, actor Richards, agrees to impersonate him and ask for a continuance. There is no continuance and Richards has to wing it.

3001. *Trial by Jury* (1994, Morgan Creek–Warner Bros., 92m, c). D Heywood Gould, P James G. Robinson, Chris Meledandri & Mark Gordon, W Gould & Jordan Katz, PH Frederick Elmes, ED Joel Goodman, M Terence Blanchard, PD David Chapman, AD Barbra Matis, SD Steve Shewchuk.

LP Joanne Whalley-Kilmer (Valerie), Armand Assante (Pirone), Gabriel Byrne (Graham), William Hurt (Vesey), Kathleen Quinlan (Wanda), Margaret Whitton (Jane Lyle), Ed Lauter (John Boyle).

Whalley-Kilmer is a member of the jury in the trial of major mobster Assante. She is chosen as the jury's weak link. She and her son are threatened with death if she doesn't force the jury to find Assante innocent. The girl must wrestle with her moral dilemma.

3002. *Trick* (1999, Fine Line–Good Machine, 90m, c). D Jim Fall, P Eric d'Arbeloff, Fall & Ross Katz, W Jason Schafer, PH Terry Stacey, ED Brian A. Kates, M David Friedman, PD Jody Asnes.

LP Christian Campbell (Gabriel), John Paul Pitoe (Mark), Tori Spelling (Katherine), Steve Hayes (Perry), Kevin Chamberlin (Perry's Ex), Brad Beyer (Rich).

In this gay romantic comedy-drama, young, ambitious musical theater writer/composer Campbell finds that his love life leaves a great deal to be desired. When he finally meets Pitoe, the man of his dreams, a barrage of obstacles constantly prevent them from consummating their passion. You don't have to be gay to appreciate the frustration.

3003. *Tricks* (1998, Viacom, 96m, c). D Kenneth Fink, P Grazka Taylor & Barbara Gunning, W Deborah Amelon, PH John S. Bartley, ED Jay Friedkin, M Patrick Seymour, PD Michael Nemirsky, SD Andrea French.

LP Mimi Rogers (Jackie Simpson), Tyne Daly (Sarah), Ray Walston (Big Sam), Callum Keith Rennie (Adam), David Kaye (Joseph),

Ron Halder (Tommy), Kevin McNulty (Henry Rinaldi).

Former Las Vegas showgirl Rogers makes ends meet for herself and her sickly child working as a salesclerk and part-time call girl. The bell captain, Halder, who sets up her "dates" fixes her up with Reno powerbroker McNulty. He's a sickie who humiliates and beats Rogers. She seeks help in getting revenge, but none is available.

3004. *The Trigger Effect* (1996, Universal–Gramercy Pictures, 93m, c). D & W David Koepp (based on the BBC TV series *Connections*), P Michael Grillo, PH Newton Thomas, ED Jill Savitt, M James Newton Howard, PD Howard Cummings, AD Jeff Knipp, SD Larry Dias.

LP Kyle MacLachlan (Matthew), Elisabeth Shue (Annie), Dermot Mulroney (Joe), Richard T. Jones (Raymond), Bill Smitrovich (Steph), Michael Rooker (Gary).

A massive power failure knocks out all electric power, telephone and broadcast signals for hundreds of miles. A suburban neighborhood, teeming with yuppies, falls apart á la the boys in *Lord of the Flies*.

3005. *Trigger Fast* (1994, Vidmark, 96m, c). D David Lester, P Paul Matthews & Peter Edwards, W Matthews, ED Hugo Middleton.

LP Jurgen Prochnow (Jack Neumann), Martin Sheen (Jackson Baines Hardin), Corbin Bernsen (Brent Mallick), Christopher Atkins (Dusty Fog).

The President of the U.S. dispatches Confederate general Sheen to Mexico to pardon a group of Southern soldiers. There's plenty of violence in this low-budget film.

3006. *Trippin'* (1999, Rogue Pictures/Beacon Pictures, 94m, c). D David Raynr, P Marc Abraham & Catlin Scanlon, W Gary Hardwick, PH John Aronson, ED Earl Watson, M Michel Columbie, PD Aaron Osbourne, AD Eric Cocrain.

LP Deon Richmond (Gregory Reed), Donald Adeosun Faison (June), Maia Campbell (Cinny Hawkins), Guy Torry (Fish), Aloma Wright (Louise Reed), Harold Sylvester (Willie Reed).

High school student Richmond daydreams through his senior year rather than concentrating on what he will do with his life. In his fantasies he is surrounded by an assortment of nubile, bikini-clad, willing playmates. When not in his own private world, he discovers a real live beauty, studious Campbell. She lets him know she can't be bothered with him until he shows some seriousness about college and making something of himself.

3007. *Trojan Eddie* (1997, U.K./Ireland, Castle Hill, 103m, c). D Gillies MacKinnon, P Emma Burge, W Billy Roche, PH John De Borman, ED Scott Thomas, M John Keane, PD Frank Conway, AD John Paul Kelly.

LP Stephen Rea (Trojan Eddie), Richard Harris (John Power), Stuart Townsend (Dermot), Aislin McGuckin (Kathleen), Brendan Gleeson (Ginger), Sean McGinley (Raymie), Angeline Ball (Shirley).

Stephen Rea has a face that reveals so much, no matter what character he plays. In this film he's an Irish loser, a criminal with the gift of gab. He's abandoned by his wife and colleagues because he is so likeable. Harris, as Rea's criminal boss, is equally impressive.

3008. *Trojan War* (1997, Warner Bros., 100m, c). D George Huang, P Charles Gordon, W Andy Burg & Scott Myers, PH Dean Semler, ED Ed Marx, M George S. Clinton, PD Cecil Gentry, AD Shepherd Frankel, SD Regina O'Brien.

LP Will Freddie (Brad Kimble), Jennifer Love Hewitt (Lea), Marley Shelton (Brooke), Danny Masterson (Seth), Jason Mardsen (Josh), Eric Balfour (Kyle).

Virginal high school student Freddie can't see his longtime friend Hewitt as a romantic possibility because of his passion for dumb but beautiful cheerleader Shelton. He agrees to tutor the lame brain, and when she comes on to him, offering the heaven he has dreamed of, he must first come up with some "protection." The remainder of the film deals with his efforts to do so and satisfy his lust with his dream girl.

3009. *A Troll in Central Park* (1994, Warner Bros., 76m, c). D Don Bluth & Gary Goldman, P Bluth, Goldman & John Pomeroy, W Stu Krieger, ED Nicky Moss, M Robert Folk, PD Rowland Wilson, AD Barry Atkinson.

LP Voices: Dom DeLuise (Stanley), Cloris Leachman (Queen Gnorga), Phillip Glasser (Gus), Tawny Sunshine Glover (Rosie), Hayley Mills (Hilary), Jonathan Pryce (Alan), Charles Nelson Riley (King Llort).

Stanley is a sweet-natured troll who can grow anything, anywhere. His reward for being good (a no-no for trolls) is having evil Queen Gnorga banish him from her kingdom. He winds up in New York's Central Park. With the help of two kids who befriend him, he learns that "you can do anything if you really want to."

3010. *Tromeo and Juliet* (1997, Troma, 102m, c). D Lloyd Kaufman, P Michael Herz & Kaufman, W James Gunn & Kaufman (based on *Romeo and Juliet* by William Shakespeare), PH Brendan Flynt, ED Frank Reynolds, M Willie Wisely & Kaufman, PD Roshelle Berliner, AD Hannah Moseley.

LP Jane Jensen (Juliet Capulet), Will Keenan (Tromeo Que), Valentine Miele (Murray Martini), Maximillian Shaun (Cappy Capulet), Steve Gibbons (London Arbuckle), Sean Gunn (Sammy Capulet), Debbie Rochon (Ness), Stephen Blackehart (Benny Que), Flip Brown (Father Lawrence), Patrick Connor (Tyrone Capulet).

It's another reworking of the Romeo & Juliet story. Keenan lives in a rundown tenement with his father and operates a piercing salon. When he meets Jensen, fresh from a lesbian relationship, they instantly fall in love. Her father has already arranged a marriage for his daughter. Naturally the two families have had a long-standing feud. The story follows Shakespeare up to a point, but there is something of a weird happy ending.

3011. *Trouble Bound* (1993, ITC Ent. Group, 89m, c). D Jeff Reiner, P Tom Kuhn & Fred Weintraub, W Darrell Fetty & Francis Delia, PH Janusz Kaminski, ED Neil Grieve, M Vinnie Golia, PD Richard Sherman, SD Michael Warga.

LP Michael Madsen (Harry Talbot), Patricia Arquette (Kit Califano), Florence Stanley (Granny), Seymour Cassel (Santino), Sal Jenco (Danny), Billy Bob Thornton (Coldface).

In this slapstick black comedy, ex-con Madsen wins a Lincoln convertible in a card game and hits the road for Las Vegas to seek a new life. He should have checked the car's trunk. It holds a dead stiff. His troubles multiply when he picks up Arquette, a Mafia princess on the run from her family.

3012. True Colors (1991, Paramount, 111m, c). D Herbert Ross, P Laurence Mark & Ross, W Kevin Wade, PH Dante Spinotti, ED Robert Reitano & Stephen A. Rotter, M Trevor Jones, PD Edward Pisoni, AD William Barclay, SD Robert J. Franco.

LP John Cusack (Peter Burton), James Spader (Tim Garrity), Imogen Stubbs (Diana Stiles), Richard Widmark (Senator James B. Stiles), Dina Merrill (Joan Stiles), Philip Bosco (Senator Steubens), Paul Guilfoyle (John Lawry).

This film is the story of two law school roommates, Cusack and Spader, who take different career paths. Idealistic Spader joins the Justice Department, hoping to do good. Opportunistic Cusack hires on as a conniving senatorial aide, expecting to do well. When Cusack makes a run for Congress it tests more than the two's friendship.

3013. True Crime (1999, Warner Bros., 127m, c). D Clint Eastwood, P Eastwood, Richard D. Zanuck & Lili Fini Zanuck, W Larry Gross, Paul Brickman & Stephen Schiff (based on the novel by Andrew Klavan), PH Jack N. Green, ED Joel Cox, M Lennie Niehaus, PD Henry Bumstead, AD Jack G. Taylor, Jr., SD Richard Goddard.

LP Clint Eastwood (Steve Everett), Isaiah Washington (Frank Beachum), Denis Leary (Bob Findley), Lisa Gay Hamilton (Bonnie Beachum), James Woods (Alan Mann), Bernard Hill (Luther Plunkitt), Diane Venora (Barbara Everett), Michael McKean (Reverend Shillerman).

This film is confined to a 24-hour period prior to the planned execution of Washington for the murder of a pregnant convenience store clerk some six years earlier. Eastwood portrays a genial reprobate and married womanizer reporter who, at the eleventh hour, becomes convinced Washington is innocent. The film is constructed on parallel tracks so audiences can view the day through the eyes of both men and make comparisons. Will Eastwood get the evidence that will allow for a last-minute stay of execution? Well, see the movie.

3014. True Friends (1998, 2nd Generation Films, 103m, c). D James Quattrochi, P Danny Zavala, Darren Paskai & Joseph Paskai, W Quattrochi & Rodrigo Botero, PH Jeff Baustert, ED Barclay De Veau, M Charles Drayton, PD Robin Coburn, AD Jose Gonzales, SD Terry Miller.

LP James Quattrochi (Joey), Loreto Mauro (Louie), Rodrigo Botero (J.J.), Kyle Gibson (Joey as a child), Mario Renden (Louie as a child), Bryan Burke (J.J. as a child).

Set in New York's Spanish Harlem, the story is of the friendship of three kids over a generation. Their dream is to one day open a bar together. Unfortunately, drugs get in their way.

3015. True Identity (1991, Touchstone-Buena Vista, 92m, c). D Charles Lane, P Carol Baum & Teri Schwartz, W Andy Breckman, Will Osborne & Will Davies (based on the *Saturday Night Live* sketch by Breckman), PH Tom Ackerman, ED Kent Beyda, M Marc Marder, PD John DeCuir, Jr., AD Geoff Hubbard, SD Karen A. O'Hara.

LP Lenny Henry (Miles Pope), Frank Langella (Frank Luchino/Leland Carver), Charles Lane (Duane), J.T. Walsh (Craig Houston), Anne-Marie Johnson (Kristi Reeves), Andreas Katsulas (Anthony), Michael McKean (Harvey Cooper), Peggy Lipton (Rita).

Henry is a black passenger on a plane that appears doomed. Thinking he is about to die, the mobster in the seat next to him unloads on Henry, telling him of his life of crime. When the plane doesn't crash, the mobster decides Henry knows too much to live. To escape, Henry turns to a special effects friend and is done up in "whiteface."

3016. True Lies (1994, 20th Century–Fox, 141m, c). D & W James Cameron, P Cameron & Stephanie Austin, PH Russell Carpenter, ED Conrad Buff, Mark Goldblatt, Richard A. Harris, Shawn Broes & Scott Michael Keppler, M Brad Fiedel, PD Peter Lamont, AD Robert Laing & Michael Novotny, SD Joseph Hodges & Cindy Carr.

LP Arnold Schwarzenegger (Harry Tasker), Jamie Lee Curtis (Helen Tasker), Tom Arnold (Gib), Bill Paxton (Simon), Tia Carrere (Juno Skinner), Charlton Heston (Spencer Trilby), Art Malik (Aziz), Eliza Dushku (Dana Tasker), Grant Heslov (Faisil), Marshall Manesh (Khaled).

As far as his wife Curtis knows, Schwarzenegger is a simple computer salesman. In reality he's a secret agent to rival 007. While Arnie is battling baddies Malik and beauteous Carrere, naive Curtis is taken in by Paxton.

He leads her to believe that he's a secret agent who needs her help. What he really wants is to help himself to her. The secrets hubby and wife keep from each other land them both in the middle of a struggle to save the free world, in which many villains bite the dust before the sensational if absurd climatic special effects battle between good and evil.

3017. *True Romance* (1993, Morgan Creek–Warner Bros., 119m, c). D Tony Scott, P Samuel Hadida, Steve Parry & Bill Unger, W Quentin Tarantino, PH Jeffrey L. Kimball, ED Michael Tronick & Christian Wagner, M Hans Zimmer, PD Benjamin Fernandez, AD James J. Murakami, SD Thomas L. Roysden.

LP Christian Slater (Clarence Worley), Patricia Arquette (Alabama Whitman), Dennis Hopper (Clifford Worley), Val Kilmer (Elvis, unc.), Gary Oldman (Drexl Spivey), Brad Pitt (Floyd, Dick's Roommate), Christopher Walken (Vincenzo Coccotti), Bronson Pinchot (Eliot Blitzer), Samuel L. Jackson (Big Don), Michael Rapaport (Dick Ritchie), Saul Rubinek (Lee Donowitz).

For geeky comic book salesman Slater and cute whore Arquette it's love at first sight. Slater sees it as his duty to separate her from her life and pimp Oldman. Slater pumps Oldman full of lead and gathers together Arquette's belongings, accidentally picking up a suitcase filled with cocaine. The lovers make a quick stop at the preacher's and blow out of town in a purple Cadillac. The owners of the cocaine are in hot pursuit. It's difficult not to laugh at this violent film — but what are we laughing about?

3018. *Truly, Madly, Deeply* (1991, U.K., Samuel Goldwyn, 105m, c). D & W Anthony Minghella, P Robert Cooper, PH Remi Adefarasin, ED John Stothart, M Barrington Pheloung, PD Barbara Gasnold.

LP Juliet Stevenson (Nina), Alan Rickman (Jamie), Bill Paterson (Sandy), Michael Maloney (Mark), Jenny Howe (Burge), Carolyn Choa (Translator), Christopher Rozycki (Titus).

Stevenson can barely stand her grief when her lover Rickman drowns. His ghost returns to comfort her and brings with him an assortment of other spirits. This is not quite the kind of "life" Stevenson hoped to share with Rickman. The two leads are outstanding in this humorous but melancholy love story.

3019. *The Truman Show* (1998, Paramount, 102m, c). D Peter Weir†, P Scott Rudin, Andrew Niccol, Edward S. Feldman & Adam Schroeder, W Niccol†, PH Peter Biziou, ED William Anderson & Lee Smith, M Burkhard Dallwitz, PD Dennis Glassner, AD Richard L. Johnson, SD Nancy Haigh.

LP Jim Carrey (Truman Burbank), Laura Linney (Meryl), Noah Emmerich (Marlon), Natascha McElhone (Truman's Mother), Ed Harris† (Christof), Brian Delate (Truman's Father), Una Damon (Chloe), Blair Slater (Young Truman).

Carrey slowly discovers that his entire life is just a really big TV series. Unbeknownst to him, his entire life has been the subject of an extremely popular 24-hour-per-day TV show. If you think of the TV series *The Prisoner*, starring Patrick McGoohan, given a light touch, you have a taste for the film. It's a welcome change of pace for Carrey. Apparently, he doesn't always have to play a "dumb and dumber" role. Unaware and trusting will be enough.

3020. *Trust* (1991, Fine Line Features/Republic, 90m, c). D & W Hal Hartley, P Bruce Weiss, PH Michael Spiller, ED Nick Gomez, M Phil Reed, PD Daniel Ouellette, AD Julie Fabian.

LP Adrienne Shelly (Maria Coughlin), Martin Donovan (Matthew Slaughter), Merritt Nelson (Jean Coughlin), John McKay (Jim Slaughter), Edie Falco (Peg Coughlin), Marko Hunt (John Coughlin).

Pregnant obnoxious cheerleader Shelly and deranged computer whiz Donovan team up in an intriguing look at their mundane but touching lives.

3021. *Trusting Beatrice* (1993, Castle Hill Prods., 91m, c). D & W Cindy Lou Johnson, P Mark Evan Jacobs & Johnson, PH Bernd Heinl, ED Camilla Toniolo, M Stanley Myers, PD Cynthia Kay Charette, AD Philip Messina, SD Robert Kensinger.

LP Mark Evan Jacobs (Claude Dewey), Irene Jacob (Beatrice de Lucio), Charlotte Moore (Mrs. Dewey), Pat McNamara (Al Dewey), Steve Buscemi (Danny).

Landscaper Jacobs takes Frenchwoman Jacob, stranded in America without a green card, home to his eccentric family.

3022. *The Truth About Cats and Dogs* (1996, 20th Century–Fox, 97m, c). D Michael Lehmann, P Cari-Esta Albert, W Audrey Wells, PH Robert Brinkman, ED Stephen Semel, M Howard Shore, PD Sharon Seymour, AD Jeff Knipp, SD Maggie Martin.

LP Uma Thurman (Noelle), Janeane Garofalo (Abby), Ben Chaplin (Brian), Jamie Foxx (Ed), James McCaffrey (Roy), Richard Coca (Eric).

What should a guy trust — his eyes or his ears? British photographer Chaplin becomes intrigued listening to Garofalo, the host of a popular radio call-in show for pet lovers. While asking her for help with his Great Dane, he asks her for a date. Quite insecure, Garofalo describes her tall, beautiful roommate Thurman when Chaplin asks what she looks like. Then begins a strange three-way romance when both women fall for Chaplin. He likes what he sees of Thurman but, when together, what he hears isn't anything like what really gets to him when he listens to or talks to Garofalo by phone. How will it all come out?

3023. *Truth of Consequences, N.M.* (1997, Triumph Releasing, 101m, c). D Kiefer Sutherland, P J. Paul Higgins, Kevin J. Messick & Hilary Wayne, W Brad Mirman, PH Ric Waite, ED Lawrence Jordan, M Jude Cole, PD Anne Stuhler, AD Roswell Hamrick, SD Les Boothe.

LP Vincent Gallo (Raymond Lembecke), Mykelti Williamson (Marcus Weans), Kiefer Sutherland (Curtis Freley), Kevin Pollak (Gordon Jacobson), Kim Dickens (Andy Monroe), Grace Phillips (Donna Moreland).

Just out of prison, Gallo wants nothing more than to escape his past and find happiness with Dickens, but he's without funds. Believing that just one final caper will put him on easy street and let him achieve his dream, he becomes involved in a botched drug heist in which people get killed. Fleeing to Mexico with former prisonmate Sutherland and undercover narcotics agent Williamson, they end up in Truth or Consequences, New Mexico, where the story peters out.

3024. *Tumbleweeds* (1999, First Line Features, 102m, c). D Gavin O'Connor, P. Lisa Bruce, W O'Connor & Angela Shelton (based on a story by Shelton), PH Dan Stoloff, ED John Gilroy, M David Mansfield, PD Bryce Holtshousen.

LP Janet McTeer† (Mary Jo Walker), Kimberly Brown (Ava Walker), Gavin O'Connor (Jack Ranson), Jay O. Sanders (Dan Miller), Lois Smith (Ginger), Laurel Holloman (Laurie Pendelton), Michael J. Pollard (Mr. Cummings).

McTeer makes it a habit of skipping town with her 12-year-old daughter Brown after each failed romance. The film opens with one more escape, this time to San Diego. There it seems that both mother and daughter just might find reasons to stay put. The story and the film aren't much, but McTeer and Brown are both quite wonderful.

3025. *The Tune* (1992, October Films, 69m, c). D & P Bill Plympton, W Plympton, Maureen McElheron & P.C. Vey, PH John Donnelly, ED Merril Stern, M McElheron.

LP Voices: Daniel Nieden (Del), Maureen McElheron (Didi), Marty Nelson (Mayor/ Mr. Mega/Mrs. Mega), Emily Bindiger (Dot), Chris Hoffman (Wiseone/Surfer/Tango Dancer/ Note).

In Plympton's first feature length cartoon, the central character is a struggling songwriter who just can't come up with the final line for his "hit" song. He finds himself magically transported to Flooby Nooby Land where he learns to use his artistic talents.

3026. *Tune in Tomorrow* (1990, Cinecom, 108m, c). D Jon Amiel, P John Fiedler & Mark Tarlov, W William Boyd (based on the novel *Aunt Julia and the Scriptwriter* by Mario Vargas Llosa), PH Robert Stevens, ED Peter Boyle, M Wynton Marsalis, PD Jim Clay.

LP Barbara Hershey (Aunt Julia), Keanu Reeves (Martin Loader), Peter Falk (Pedro Carmichael), Bill McCutcheon (Puddler), Patricia Clarkson (Aunt Olga), Jerome Dempsey (Sam/Sid), Peter Gallagher (Richard Quince), Dan Hedaya (Robert Quince), Buck Henry (Fr. Serafim), Hope Lange (Margaret Quince), John Larroquette (Dr. Albert Quince), Elizabeth McGovern (Elena Quince).

Twenty-one-year-old Reeves is in love with Hershey, his older aunt by marriage. He is given instructions on making his passion work for him by wacky soap opera writer Falk, who echoes their affair in his radio show. It's the kind of role in which Falk has frequently found himself, a far-out kook who sees himself and the strange things he does or that happen to him as totally normal. Fun for the audience.

3027. *Tunnel Vision* (1996, Australia, Triboro Ent., 100m, c). D & W Clive Fleury, P Phil Avalon, PH Paul Murphy, ED John Scott, M David Hirschfelder & Ric Formosa, PD Phil Warner.

LP Patsy Kensit (Kelly Wheatstone), Robert Reynolds (Frank Yanovitch), Rebecca Rigg (Helena M. Yanovitch), Gary Day (Steve Doherty), Shane Briant (Kevin Bosey), Justin Monjo (Craig Breslin), David Woodley (David DeSalvo).

Cop Kensit and her partner Reynolds investigate a series of ritual killings of beautiful girls. All the clues point to Reynolds as the killer and Kensit as a potential victim.

3028. *Turbo: A Power Rangers Movie* (1997, 20th Century–Fox, 99m, c). D David Winning & Shuki Levy, P Jonathan Tzachor, W Levy & Shell Danielson, PH Ilan Rosenberg, ED Henry Richardson & B.J. Sears, M Levy, PD Yuda Ako.

LP Jason David Frank (Tommy/Red Ranger), Steve Cardenas (Rocky/Blue Ranger), Johnny Yong Bosch (Adam/Green Ranger), Catherine Sutherland (Katherine/Pink Ranger), Nakia Burrise (Tanya/Yellow Ranger), Jon Simanton (Lerigot).

Warning! This film is aimed at kids. Adults should avoid it. Kids should avoid it. The legendary Mighty Morphin Power Rangers are pitted against a crew of space pirates. Parents, watch what your kids are watching on TV. Pull the plug, quickly, before it's too late.

3029. *Turbulence* (1997, MGM/UA, 103m, c). D Robert Butler, P Martin Ransohoff & David Valdes, W Jonathan Brett, PH Lloyd Ahern II, ED John Duffy, M Shirley Walker, PD Mayling Cheng, AD Donald B. Woodruff, SD Donald Kraft.

LP Ray Liotta (Ryan Weaver), Lauren Holly (Teri Halloran), Hector Elizondo (Detective Aldo Hines), Brendan Gleeson (Stubbs), Rachel Ticotin (Rachel Taper), Jeffrey DeMunn (Brooks), Catherine Hicks (Maggie).

Murderer Liotta, believing he has nothing to live for and nothing to lose, hijacks a plane which he plans to crash. He doesn't count on plucky stewardess Holly eventually bringing the plane down safely.

3030. *Twelfth Night* (1996, U.K./U.S., Fine Line, 125m, c). D & W Trevor Nunn (based on the play by William Shakespeare), P Stephen Evans & David Parfitt, PH Clive Tickner, ED Peter Boyle, M Shaun Davey, PD Sophie Becher, AD Ricky Eyres, SD Marianne Ford.

LP Helena Bonham Carter (Olivia), Richard E. Grant (Sir Andrew Aguecheek), Nigel Hawthorne (Malvolio), Ben Kingsley (Feste), Mel Smith (Sir Toby Belch), Imelda Staunton (Maria), Toby Stephens (Orsino), Imogen Stubbs (Viola/Cesario), Steven Mackintosh (Sebastian).

Shakespeare's romantic comedy has been moved from the 1600s to the 1890s. Stubbs and her look alike brother Mackintosh are aboard a ship wrecked off the coast of Illyria. Stubbs is washed ashore and, believing her brother dead, disguises herself as a boy. She enters the service of Stephens, who sends "him" to press his suit for Bonham Carter, in mourning for her recently dead father and brother. Bonham Carter has pledged not to have contact with men for seven years, but she becomes interested in Stubbs as a boy. In the meantime, the latter has fallen for Stephens. When Mackintosh shows up alive the triangle becomes even more complicated.

3031. *Twelve Monkeys* (1995, U.S./U.K./Germany/Japan/France, Universal, 130m, c). D Terry Gilliam, P Charles Rosen, W David Peoples & Janet Peoples (based on the film *La Jette* by Chris Marker), PH Roger Pratt, ED Mick Audsley, M Paul Buckmaster, PD Jeffrey Beecroft, AD William Ladd Skinner, SD Crispian Sallis.

LP Bruce Willis (James Cole), Madeleine Stowe (Kathryn Railly), Brad Pitt† (Jeffrey Goines), Christopher Plummer (Dr. Goines), Jon Seda (Jose), David Morse (Dr. Peters), Frank Gorshin (Dr. Fletcher), Irma St. Paule (Poet).

Forty years after a plague has wiped out 99 percent of the population of the world and forced the survivors to move underground, scientists send convict Willis back in time to discover the source of the virus. The trail leads him in the wrong direction, but he takes some comfort with beautiful psychologist Stowe.

Pitt wins an Oscar nomination for his believable nutzoid performance. The plot is so convoluted that it is difficult to be certain what's what, but it is entertaining.

3032. Twenty Bucks (1993, Triton Pictures, 90m, c). D Keva Rosenfeld, P Karen Murphy, W Endre Bohem & Leslie Bohem, PH Emmanuel Lubezki, ED Michael Ruscio, M David Robbins, PD Joseph T. Garrity, AD Rando Schmook, SD Linda Allen.

LP Linda Hunt (Angeline), David Rasche (Baker), George Morfogen (Jack Holiday), Sam Jenkins (Anna Holiday), Brendan Fraser (Sam), Concetta Tomei (Sam's Mother), Elisabeth Shue (Emily Adams), Steve Buscemi (Frank), Christopher Lloyd (Jimmy).

Based on a story written by Endre Boehm in 1935 and revised by his son Leslie, the film follows the life of a $20 bill as it passes from one hand to another.

3033. The 24 Hour Woman (1999, Gallery–Artisan Ent., 93m, c). D Nancy Savoca, P Richard Guay, Larry Meistrich & Peter Newman, W Savoca & Guay, PH Teresa Medina, ED Camilla Toniolo, M Louis Vega & Kenny Gonzalez, PD Bob Shaw, AD Sarah Frank, SD Caroline Ghertler.

LP Rosie Perez (Grace Santos), Marianne Jean-Baptiste (Madeline Labelle), Patti LuPone (Joan Marshall), Karen Duffy (Marge Lynn), Diego Serrano (Eddie Diaz).

In this terrible movie, Perez portrays a hysteria-prone single woman who finds it difficult juggling motherhood and a high-paying job as the producer of a TV chat show. This is news? Try it with several kids and a low-paying job, Rosie.

3034. Twentyfourseven (1997, U.K., October Films, 96m, c). D Shane Meadows, P Imogen West, W Meadows & Paul Fraser, PH Ashley Rowe, ED William Diver, M Boo Hewerdine & Neill MacColl, PD John-Paul Kelly.

LP Bob Hoskins (Alan Darcy), Jimmy Hynd (Meggy), Mat Hand (Fagash), Danny Nussbaum (Tim), Karl Collins (Stuart), James Hooton (Knighty), Darren Campbell (Daz), Justin Brady (Gadget), James Corden (Tonka).

This film is the tale of Hoskins' efforts to form a boxing club in a dreary town in the English Midlands to give the young men of the town something to do and keep them out of trouble. For his performance Hoskins was named the best European Actor at the 1997 European Film Awards.

3035. 29th Street (1991, 20th Century–Fox, 101m, c). D & W George Gallo (based on the story by Frank Pesce, Jr. & James Franciscus), P David Permut, PH Steven Fierberg, ED Kaja Fehr, M William Olvis, PD Robert Ziembicki, AD Dayna Lee, SD Hugh Scaife.

LP Danny Aiello (Frank Pesce, Sr.), Lainie Kazan (Mrs. Pesce), Anthony LaPaglia (Frank Pesce, Jr.), Robert Forster (Sgt. Tartaglia), Frank Pesce, Jr. (Vito Pesce), Donna Magnani (Madeline Pesce).

This film is based on the true story of a New York actor, played by LaPaglia, who wins six million dollars in the New York State Lottery. The film deals with the effects, positive and negative, of his windfall on his close-knit Italian-American family.

3036. Twenty-One (1991, U.K., Triton Pictures, 101m, c). D Don Boyd, P Morgan Mason & John Hardy, W Boyd & Zoe Heller, PH Keith Goddard, ED David Spiers, M Michael Berkeley, AD Terrie Wixon.

LP Patsy Kensit (Katie), Jack Shepherd (Kenneth), Patrick Ryecart (Jack), Maynard Eziashi (Baldie), Rufus Sewell (Bobby), Sophie Thompson (Francesca), Susan Wooldridge (Janet).

Kensit is frank and charming as she delivers voice-over soliloquies on her array of lovers in this contemporary coming-of-age story.

3037. Twilight (1998, Paramount, 94m, c). D Robert Benton, P Arlene Donovan & Scott Rudin, W Benton & Richard Russo, PH Piotr Sobocinski, ED Carol Littleton, M Elmer Bernstein, PD David Gropman, AD David Bomba, SD Beth Rubino.

LP Paul Newman (Harry Ross), Susan Sarandon (Catherine Ames), Gene Hackman (Jack Ames), Reese Witherspoon (Mel Ames), Stockard Channing (Verna), James Garner (Raymond Hope), Giancarlo Esposito (Reuben), Liev Schreiber (Jeff Willis), M. Emmet Walsh (Lester Ivar).

An excellent cast of aging stars show they still know how to entertain. Newman, a former cop, now a private-eye, retrieves Witherspoon, the 17-year-old daughter of wealthy Hackman. She's run away with sleazy boyfriend Schreiber.

Once popular movie star Hackman is dying of cancer. His wife Sarandon, also a former movie star, sleeps with Newman but remains loyal (in her fashion) to her husband. To move the story along, there is a bit of blackmail, a murder and suspicion about the apparent suicide and mysterious disappearance of Sarandon's first husband years earlier. It doesn't make a lot of sense, but it's fun to watch all the old pros go through their paces.

3038. *Twin Falls Idaho* (1999, Sony Pictures Classics, 110m, c). D Michael Polish, P Marshall Persinger, Rena Ronson & Steven J. Wolfe, W Mark & Michael Polish, PH M. David Muller, ED Leo Trombetta, M Stuart Matthewman, PD Warren Alan Young, AD Grace Li, SD Alysia D. Allen.

LP Michael Polish (Francis Falls), Mark Polish (Blake Falls), Michele Hicks (Penny), Jon Gries (Jay), Patrick Bauchau (Miles), Garrett Morris (Jesus).

Real-life brothers Michael and Mark Polish star as Siamese twins, one of whom is very ill. The other falls in love with prostitute Hicks. The two brothers are fascinating to watch as they move together.

3039. *Twin Peaks: Fire Walk with Me* (1992, New Line Cinema, 135m, c). D David Lynch, P Francis Bouygues & Gregg Fienberg, W Lynch & Robert Engels, PH Ron Garcia, ED Mary Sweeney, M Angelo Badalamenti, PD Patricia Norris, SD Leslie Morales.

LP Sheryl Lee (Laura Palmer), Ray Wise (Leland Palmer), Moira Kelly (Donna Hayward), Kyle MacLachlan (Special Agent Dale Cooper), David Bowie (Phillip Jeffries), Chris Isaak (Special Agent Chester Desmond), Harry Dean Stanton (Carl Rodd), Dana Ashbrook (Bobby Briggs), Kiefer Sutherland (Sam Stanley).

This film chronicles the events leading up to to the murder of doomed nymphet Lee, whose death was the starting point for the inventive and very original TV series. If one has not seen the TV series *Twin Peaks*, one's reaction to the explanation of what happened before its inception may be akin to being the only one who doesn't get an inside joke.

3040. *Twin Town* (1997, U.K., Gramercy Pictures, 99m, c). D Kevin Allen, P Peter McAleese, W Allen & Paul Durden, PH John

Mathieson, ED Oral Norrie Otley, M Mark Thomas, PD Pat Campbell, AD Jean Kerr.

LP Dougray Scott (Terry Walsh), Dorien Thomas (Greyo), Rhys Ifans (Jeremy Lewis), Llyr Evans (Julian Lewis), William Thomas (Bryn Cartwright), Sue Roderick (Lucy Cartwright), Rachel Scorgie (Adie Lewis).

In this black comedy, the Lewis twins are not really twins, just brothers who are unemployed and perpetually stoned. They enjoy riding around town in stolen cars and making life hell for local contractor Thomas. He has a thing for the lads' sister, Scorgie, a hooker working for a massage parlor. Then there is Scott, a really ambitious thug. The film is often hilarious, if raunchy.

3041. *Twisted* (1997, Leisure Time Features, 100m, c). D & W Seth Michael Donsky (based on the novel *Oliver Twist* by Charles Dickens), P Adrian Agromonte & Bernard Arbit, PH Hernan Toro, ED Tom McArdle & Donsky, M Q Lazzarus & Danny Z, PD Scott Bailey.

LP William Hickey (Andre), Anthony Crivello (Eddie), Keiven McNeil Graves (Lee), David Norona (Angel), Jean Loup (Fine Art), Billy Porter (Shiniqua), Elizabeth Franz (Social Worker), Ray Aranha (Can Man).

In this loose adaptation of Dickens' *Oliver Twist*, 10-year-old orphan Graves is picked up by male hustler Loup after Graves' protector, blind street singer Aranha, is murdered. Loup takes the lad to a brothel, run by Hickey, where young boys are made available to those with the price. Crivello is a violent drug dealer, standing in for Bill Sykes, and Dickens' Nancy is represented by Crivello's abused boyfriend Norona. When Graves is sent out on his first job, his john turns out to be an undercover cop. Fearful that Graves will talk and his brothel will be raided, the Fagan-like Hickey convinces Crivello to guarantee that the boy keeps his silence. The story, which takes place in Manhattan's lower east side, upgrades Dickens' story by dealing with the problems facing youngsters left unprotected on a city's mean streets. The dialogue is very poor and several of the performances are definitely second-rate.

3042. *Twisted Justice* (1990, Hero/Brode, 90m, c). D, P & W David Heavener, PH David Hue, ED Gregory Schorer, AD Dian Skinner.

LP David Heavener (James Tucker), Erik Estrada (Cmdr. Gage), Jim Brown (Morris), James Van Patten (Kelsey), Shannon Tweed (Hinkle), Don Stroud (Pantelli), Karen Black (Mrs. Granger).

In the year 2020 cop Heavener is handicapped in pursuing a ruthless killer when he must surrender his gun.

3043. Twisted Obsession (1990, LIVE, 107m, c). D Fernando Trueba, P Andres Vicente Gomez, W Trueba & Manolo Matji, PH Jose Luis Alcaine, ED Carmen Frias, M Antoine Duhamel, AD Pierre-Louis Thevenet.

LP Jeff Goldblum (Dan Gillis), Miranda Richardson (Marilyn), Anemone (Marianne), Dexter Fletcher (Malcolm), Daniel Ceccaldi (Legrand), Liza Walker (Jenny), Jerome Natali (Danny).

Expatriate writer Goldblum's obsession for nymphet Walker leads to a murder. Doesn't it always?

3044. Twister (1996, Warner Bros., 117m, c). D Jan De Bont, P Kathleen Kennedy, Ian Bryce & Michael Crichton, W Crichton & Anne-Marie Martin, PH Jack N. Green, ED Michael Khan, M Mark Mancina, PD Joseph Nemec III, AD Dan Olexiewicz, SD Ron Reiss.

LP Bill Paxton (Bill Harding), Helen Hunt (Jo Harding), Cary Elwes (Dr. Jonas Miller), Jami Gertz (Melissa), Lois Smith (Aunt Meg), Alan Ruck (Dusty), Philip Seymour Hoffman (Rabbit).

Don't mess with Mother Nature, because Mother will always win. Scientist Hunt leads a team that chases through Oklahoma hoping to place a robotic mechanism inside a tornado so that it may give information that will make predicting new tornados more accurate. The plot isn't much but the winds really blow.

3045. Two Bits (1995, Miramax, 93m, c). D James Foley, P Arthur Cohn, W Joseph Stefano, PH Juan Ruiz-Anchia, ED Howard Smith, M Carter Burwell, PD Jane Musky, AD Tom Warren, SD Robert J. Franco.

LP Al Pacino (Grandpa), Mary Elizabeth Mastrantonio (Luisa), Jerry Barone (Gennaro), Alec Baldwin (Narrator), Patrick Borriello (Tullio), Andy Romano (Dr. Bruna), Donna Mitchell (Mrs. Bruna), Joanna Merlin (Gwendolina).

The time is the Depression. The place is South Philadelphia. The hero is 12-year-old Barone. The conflict is his desire to raise the two-bit admission price to a new movie house. The lad is poor but determined and willing to try any number of schemes to achieve his goal. Pacino is his dying grandfather who gives him no money but lots of advice.

3046. 2 Days in the Valley (1996, MGM/UA, 105m, c). D & W John Herzfeld, P Jeff Wald & Herb Nanas, PH Oliver Wood, ED Jim Miller & Wayne Wahrman, M Anthony Marinelli, PD Catherine Hardwicke, AD Kevin Constant, SD Gene Serdena.

LP Danny Aiello (Dosmo Pizzo), Greg Cruttwell (Allan Hopper), Jeff Daniels (Alvin Strayer), Teri Hatcher (Becky Foxx), Glenne Headley (Susan Parish), Peter Horton (Roy Foxx), Marsha Mason (Audrey Hopper), Paul Mazursky (Teddy Peppers), James Spader (Lee Woods), Eric Stoltz (Wes Taylor), Charlize Theron (Helga Svelgen), Keith Carradine (Detective Creighton).

In a violent film, no doubt inspired by *Pulp Fiction*, Aiello is left for dead by his partner. In trying to survive he gets caught up in the lives of several crazy amoralists.

3047. Two Deaths (1996, U.K., Castle Hill, 102m, c). D Nicolas Roeg, P Carolyn Montagu & Luc Roeg, W Allan Scott, PH Witold Stok, ED Tony Lawson, M Hans Zimmer, PD Don Taylor, AD Charmian Adams.

LP Michael Gambon (Daniel Pavenic), Sonia Braga (Ana Puscasu), Patrick Malahide (George Buscan), Ion Caramitru (Carl Dalakiss), Nickolas Grace (Marius Vernescu).

Four friends gather for a yearly reunion in 1989 Romania. Civil War rages outside their host's home, but inside they entertain each other by swapping secrets. The best of these is why beautiful housekeeper Braga endures host Gambon's abuse.

3048. Two Girls and a Guy (1998, Fox Searchlight, 92m, c). D & W James Toback, P Edward R. Pressman & Chris Hanley, PH Barry Markowitz, ED Alan Oxman, PD Kevin Thompson, SD Alisa Grifo.

LP Robert Downey, Jr. (Blake Allen), Heather Graham (Carla), Natasha Gregson Wagner (Lou), Angel David (Tommy), Frederique Van Der Wal (Carol).

Compulsive liar and womanizer Downey has "exclusive" relationships with both Graham and Wagner. They team up to teach him a lesson.

3049. 200 Cigarettes (1999, Paramount, 101m, c). D Risa Bramon Garcia, P Betsy Beers, David Gale & Van Toffler, W Shana Larsen, PH Frank Prinzi, ED Lisa Zeno Churgin, M Bob & Mark Mothersbaugh, PD Ina Mayhew, AD Judy Rhee, SD Paul Weathered.

LP Ben Affleck (Bartender), Casey Affleck (Tom), David Chappelle (Disco Cabbie), Guillermo Diaz (Dave), Janeane Garofalo (Ellie), Kate Hudson (Cindy), Courtney Love (Lucy), Jay Mohr (Jack), Martha Plimpton (Bridget), Christina Ricci (Val), Paul Rudd (Kevin).

A hip young ensemble cast appears in this '80s-nostalgia film about several young New Yorkers making their way to the same East Village New Year's Eve party held by Plimpton. Most of the talk among the characters is in regard to their sex lives and romantic involvements, coming or going.

3050. Two If by Sea (1996, Morgan Creek–Warner Bros., 97m, c). D Bill Bennett, P James G. Robinson, W Denis Leary & Mike Armstrong (based on their story), PH Andrew Lesnie, ED Bruce Green, M Nick Glenne-Smith & Paddy Moloney, PD David Chapman, AD Mark Haack, SD Stephen Shewchuk.

LP Denis Leary (Frank), Sandra Bullock (Roz), Stephen Dillane (Evan Marsh), Yaphet Kotto (O'Malley), Mike Starr (Fitzie), Jonathan Tucker (Todd), Wayne Robson (Beano).

After stealing a valuable painting, small-time thief Leary and his girlfriend Bullock hole up in a Cape Cod mansion to await the arrival of a mysterious stranger who has offered to buy the art work.

3051. The Two Jakes (1990, Paramount, 138m, c). D Jack Nicholson, P Robert Evans & Harold Schneider, W Robert Towne, PH Vilmos Zsigmond, ED Anne Goursaud, M Van Dyke Parks, PD Jeremy Railton & Richard Sawyer, AD Richard Schreiber, SD Jerry Wunderlich.

LP Jack Nicholson (Jake Gittes), Harvey Keitel (Jake Berman), Meg Tilly (Kitty Berman), Madeleine Stowe (Lillian Bodine), Eli Wallach (Cotton Weinberger), Ruben Blades (Mickey Nice), Frederic Forrest (Newty), David Keith (Loach), Richard Farnsworth (Earl Rawley), Tracey Walter (Tyrone Otley), Joe Mantell (Walsh), James Hong (Khan), Perry Lopez (Capt. Escobar).

Sequels usually aren't able to capture the magic of a memorable film, and this one is no exception. Ten years have passed since the events of *Chinatown* (1974), and Nicholson is still in the private investigation business, specializing in divorce cases. Faye Dunaway is long dead, but being forced to return to Chinatown due to the murder of a man who is having an affair with Tilly, the wife of real estate executive Keitel, rakes up painful memories. Stowe, wife of the deceased, who just happens to be Keitel's business partner, offers Nicholson some solace. Sure enough, Nicholson is once again the unwilling accomplice in a carefully planned murder for profit scheme. The cast is excellent and the dialogue shares some of the crispness of the earlier film, but ultimately the story isn't as captivating.

3052. Two Much (1996, Spain/U.S., Touchstone–Buena Vista, 118m, c). D Fernando Trueba, P Cristina Huete, W Fernando Trueba & David Trueba (based on the novel by Donald E. Westlake), PH Jose Luis Alcaine, ED Nena Bernard, M Michael Camilo, PD Juan Botella, AD Carlos Arditti, SD Barbara Peterson.

LP Antonio Banderas (Art/Bart), Melanie Griffith (Betty Kerner), Daryl Hannah (Liz Kerner), Danny Aiello (Gene Paletto), Joan Cusack (Gloria), Eli Wallach (Sheldon).

In this disappointing attempt at a screwball comedy, Banderas is bowled over by Griffith; but when he meets her sister Hannah, he also falls hard for her and must invent a twin brother to handle both ladies.

3053. Twogether (1995, Dream Catcher Entertainment Group, 122m, c). D & W Andrew Chiaramonte, P Emmett Alston & Chiaramonte, PH Eugene Shlugleit, ED Todd Fisher & Chiaramonte, M Nigel Holton, PD Philip Michael Brandes, AD Phil Zarling.

LP Nick Cassavetes (John Madler), Brenda Bakke (Allison McKenzie), Jimmy Piven (Arnie), Jim Beaver (Oscar), Tom Dugan (Paul), Damian London (Mark Saffron).

Talented painter Cassavetes meets Bakke,

and their sexual attraction is too much for them. The next morning they wake up in Las Vegas, hung over and married. Deciding the marriage was a mistake, they get a quick divorce and celebrate the end of their marriage with hot sexual action that leaves Bakke pregnant. The two agree to stay together until the baby comes but plan no romantic future together. Can this divorce be saved?

3054. *U Turn* (1997, Columbia TriStar, 125m, c). D Oliver Stone, P Dan Halsted & Clayton Townsend, W John Ridley (based on his book *Stray Dogs*), PH Robert Richardson, ED Hank Corwin & Thomas J. Nordberg, M Ennio Morricone, PD Victor Kempster, AD Dan Webster, SD Merideth Boswell.

LP Sean Penn (Bobby Cooper), Nick Nolte (Jake McKenna), Jennifer Lopez (Grace McKenna), Billy Bob Thornton (Darrell), Powers Boothe (Sheriff Potter), Claire Danes (Jenny), Joaquin Phoenix (Toby N. "TNT" Tucker), Jon Voight (Blind Man).

Stone unashamedly borrows from many films to put together this tale of cross and double-cross, murder and mayhem, in a small Arizona town. On the run with some money he owes to mobsters, Penn must stop in the town of Superior when his car breaks down. This brings him into contact with pretty Lopez and her husband-rapist-father Nolte, who hires Penn to kill Lopez. But she ups the ante, so Penn kills Nolte. Leaving town, the two are stopped by sheriff Boothe, who is Lopez's lover. When she becomes annoyed with what he tells Penn about her and Nolte, she shoots and kills the sheriff. Still miffed, she pushes Penn off a cliff into a canyon and attempts to drive away only to realize that Penn has the keys. She climbs down to him. He strangles her. He manages to get back to the car, but when he starts it, it (and he) blows up.

3055. *The Ugly* (1998, New Zealand, Essential Films, 93m, c). D & W Scott Reynolds, P Jonathan Dowling, PH Simon Raby, ED Wayne Cook, M Victoria Kelly, PD Grant Major, AD Gary Mackey.

LP Paolo Rotundo (Simon Cartwright, the Killer), Rebecca Hobbs (Dr. Karen Schumacher, the Interviewer), Jennifer Ward-Lealand (Evelyn Cartwright, Simon's Mother), Roy Ward (Dr. Marlowe, the Warden), Cath McWhirter (Helen Ann Miller).

Psychiatrist Hobbs arrives at a mental hospital to interview serial killer Rotundo in preparation for a sanity hearing. Rotundo refers to himself as "The Ugly." In flashbacks we learn of his childhood, which may have contributed to his antisocial behavior. He claims he is spurred on in his murderous rage by the ghosts of his past victims. By the end of the film Hobbs will have a deadly nightmare about her patient.

3056. *Ulee's Gold* (1997, Orion, 113m, c). D, P, W & ED Victor Nunez, PH Virgil Marcus Mirano, M Charles Engstrom, PD Robert "Pat" Garner, AD Debbie Devilla, SD Charles Kulsziski.

LP Peter Fonda (Ulee Jackson), Patricia Richardson (Connie Hope), Jessica Biel (Casey Jackson), J. Kenneth Campbell (Sheriff Bill Floyd), Christine Dunford (Helen Jackson), Steven Flynn (Eddie Flowers), Dewey Weber (Ferris Dooley), Tom Wood (Jimmy Jackson).

Fonda's performance and appearance certainly put audiences in mind of his father Henry. Florida beekeeper Fonda has seen some difficult times. He was the sole survivor of his unit in Vietnam. His wife died unexpectedly six years before the time of the film. His son Wood is in prison. His drug-addicted daughter-in-law, Dunford, took off and left Fonda to care for her children, rebellious teen Zima and young Biel. The latter is looking to make a connection with Fonda. In addition, he faces financial ruin unless he can get a specialty honey in from the hives. And then things get worse. For the rest of his Job-like problems, do yourself a favor and see the movie. See why the critics raved about the movie, its story and Fonda's greatest performance, one to rival that of his talented relatives.

3057. *Ultimate Desires* (1992, Canada, North American Pictures, 93m, c). D Lloyd Simandl, P Simandl & John Curtis, W Ted Hubert, PH Danny Knovak, ED Derek Whelan, M Braun Farnon & Robert Smart, AD Scott Richardson.

LP Tracy Scoggins (Samantha Stewart), Marc Singer (Jonathan), Brion James (Wolf), Robert Morrison (Arthur Kettner), Marc Bennet (Pierce), Suzy Joachim (Vicky).

Public defender Scoggins poses as a prostitute to solve a murder mystery. Good upward career move!

3058. *Ultraviolet* (1992, Concorde, 80m, c). D Mark Griffiths, P Catherine Cyran, W Gordon Cassidy, PH Gregg Heschong, ED Kevin Tent, M Ed Tomney, PD Carlos Barbosa, AD Richard Brunton, SD Tamara Murphy.

LP Esai Morales (Nick), Patricia Healy (Kristen), Stephen Meadows (Sam).

A sadistic madman harasses a reconciling couple in Death Valley.

3059. *The Unbelievable Truth* (1990, Miramax, 90m, c). D & W Hal Hartley, P Bruce Weiss & Hartley, PH Michael Spiller, ED Hartley, M Jim Coleman, Wild Blue Yonder & The Brothers Kendall, PD Carla Gerona, SD Sarah Stollman.

LP Adrienne Shelly (Audry Hugo), Robert Burke (Josh Hutton), Christopher Cooke (Vic Hugo), Julia Mueller (Pearl), Mark Bailey (Mike).

In this quirky black comedy, cynical model Shelly lives in a town where a bizarre murder occurs. Suspicion falls on ex-con and mechanic Burke.

3060. *The Unborn* (1991, Califilm, 83m, c). D & P Rodman Flender, W Henry Dominic, PH Wally Pfister, ED Patrick Rand, M Gary Numan & Michael R. Smith, PD Gary Randall.

LP Brooke Adams (Virginia Marshall), Jeff Hayenga (Brad Marshall), James Karen (Dr. Richard Meyerling), K. Callon (Martha), Jane Cameron (Beth).

In this tasteless B-movie an infertile wife is inseminated at an unorthodox clinic. She finds herself carrying a monstrous fetus.

3061. *The Unborn II* (1994, Concorde, 84m, c). D Rick Jacobson, P Mike Elliott, W Mark Evan Schwartz & Daniella Purcell (based on a story by Rob Kerchner), PH Mike Gallagher, ED John Gilbert, M John Graham, PD Robin Nixon, AD J. Michael Gorman.

LP Michelle Greene (Catherine Moore), Scott Valentine (John Edson), Robin Curtis (Linda Holt), Leonard O. Turner (Briggs), Brittany Powell (Sally Anne).

One dose of a blood-craving baby wasn't enough, apparently. This time baby-sitters make suitable victims for the "little one."

3062. *Under Siege* (1992, Warner Bros., 100m, c). D Andrew Davis, P Steven Reuther, Arnon Milchan & Steven Seagal, W J.F. Lawson, John Mason & Michael Rae, PH Frank Tidy, ED Robert A. Ferretti, Dennis Virkler, Don Brochu & Dov Hoenig, M Gary Chang, PD Bill Kenney, AD Bill Hiney, SD Rick Gentz.

LP Steven Seagal (Casey Ryback), Damian Chapa (Tackman), Patrick O'Neal (Captain Adams), Gary Busey (Commander Krill), Bernie Casey (Commander Harris), Tommy Lee Jones (William Strannix), Erika Eleniak (Jordan Tate).

Here's another film in which one extremely confident man is able not only to almost single-handedly (he does have some help from buxomy ex-playmate Eleniak) take on an army of bad guys but vanquish them as well. This time its a "navy of bad guys," and Seagal is working as a chef on a ship that is shanghaied by Busey and Jones. Too bad for them. Mindless fun.

3063. *Under Siege 2: Dark Territory* (1995, Warner Bros., 100m, c). D Geoff Murphy, P Steven Seagal, Arnon Milchan & Steve Perry, W Richard Hatem & Matt Reeves (based on characters created by J.F. Lawton), PH Robbie Greenberg, ED Michael Tronick, M Basil Poledouris, PD Albert Brenner, AD Carol Wood, SD Kathe Klopp.

LP Steven Seagal (Casey Ryback), Eric Bogosian (Travis Dane), Katherine Heigl (Sarah Ryback), Morris Chestnutt (Bobby Zachs), Everett McGill (Penn), Kurtwood Smith (General Stanley Cooper), Nick Mancuso (Tom Breaker), Andy Romano (Admiral Bates), Brenda Bakke (Gilder).

Returning to his role as a Navy Seal, Seagal combines a bit of *Die-Hard* with *Speed*. The bad guys, led by maniacal Bogosian, hijack a moving train and a satellite. Too bad for them, Seagal and his daughter are passengers. This time a porter helps the wooden one save the day. What's next, a zeppelin?

3064. *Under Suspicion* (1992, U.K./U.S., Columbia, 99m, c.) D & W Simon Moore, P Brian Eastman, PH Vernon Layton, ED Tariq Anwar, M Christopher Gunning, PD Tim Hutchinson, AD Tony Reading, SD Stephenie McMillan.

LP Liam Neeson (Tony Aaron), Kenneth Cranham (Frank), Maggie O'Neill (Hazel), Alan Talbot (Powers), Malcolm Storry (Waterston),

Martin Grace (Colin), Kevin Moore (Barrister), Alphonsia Emmanuel (Selina), Laura San Giacomo (Angeline).

In 1959 England, Neeson makes his living as a seedy private eye who sets up phony adulteries for divorce-seekers. Things take a bad turn when one of his clients is murdered and he's the number one suspect.

3065. *Under the Boardwalk* (1990, New World, 102m, c). D Fritz Kiersh, P Steven H. Charnin & Gregory S. Blackwell, W Robert King (based on a story by Matthew Irmas & King), PH Don Burgess, ED Daniel Gross, M David Kitay, PD Maxine Shepard, AD Corey Kaplan, SD Gina Scoppitici.

LP Keith Coogan (Andy), Danielle Von Zemeck (Allie), Richard Joseph Paul (Nick Rainwood), Hunter Von Leer (Midas), Tracey Walter (Bum), Steve Monarque (Reef), Brian Wimmer (Cage), Roxana Zal (Gitch).

In a *West Side Story* wannabe, two gangs are pitted against each other at a 1980s California beach. Coogan and Von Zemeck are the young Romeo and Juliet of the story. Surfing and Shakespeare don't mix.

3066. *Under the Hula Moon* (1996, Periscope Pictures, 96m, c). D Jeff Celantano, P Stacy Codikow, W Celantano & Gregory Webb, PH Phil Parmet, ED Donald Likovich, M Hidden Faces, PD Randal Earnest, AD David Fitzpatrick, SD Brent Bye.

LP Stephen Baldwin (Buzz), Emily Lloyd (Betty), Chris Penn (Turk), Musetta Vander (Maya Gundinger), Pruitt Taylor Vance (Bob).

Luckless couple Baldwin and Lloyd live in a trailer camp in Arizona. They both have dreams of something better. For Baldwin it's moving to Hawaii. For Lloyd it's having a baby. Both dreams are jeopardized by the arrival of Baldwin's brother Penn, who has broken out of prison and murdered a motorist.

3067. *Under the Skin* (AKA: *Iris and Rose*; *Skin*) (1997, U.K., Strange Dog Prods., 83m, c). D & W Carine Adler, P Kate Ogborn, PH Barry Ackroyd, ED Ewa J. Lind, M Ilona Sekacz, PD John-Paul Kelly, AD Niall Moroney.

LP Samantha Morton (Iris Kelley), Claire Rushbrook (Rose), Rita Tushingham (Mum), Stuart Townsend (Tom), Christine Tremarco ("Vron" — Veronica), Matthew Delamere (Gary).

Morton gives a sparkling performance as a 19-year-old who is jealous of her older sister Rushbrook, whom Morton believes their mother Tushingham always preferred because Rushbrook was married, pregnant and conventional. With Tushingham's death, Morton truly lets loose, impulsively quitting her job, breaking up with her boyfriend, having casual sexual encounters and continuing her rivalry with her sister.

3068. *Undercover Blues* (1993, MGM, 89m, c). D Herbert Ross, P Mike Lobell, W Ian Abrams, PH Donald E. Thorin & John Stephens, ED Priscilla Nedd-Friendly, M David Newman, PD Ken Adam, AD William J. Durrell, Jr., SD Jeff Haley & James Bayliss.

LP Kathleen Turner (Jane Blue), Dennis Quaid (Jeff Blue), Fiona Shaw (Novacek), Stanley Tucci (Muerte), Larry Miller (Detective Sergeant Halsey), Obba Babatunde (Sawyer).

In this comedy caper Turner and Quaid are a married couple who just happen to be espionage agents. Having taken time off to have a baby, the couple and their 11-month-old child are in New Orleans on vacation when they are called back into action to take on an old adversary who is behind a munitions snatch.

3069. *The Underneath* (1995, Populist Pictures–Gramercy, 99m, c). D Steven Soderbergh, P John Hardy, W Sam Lowry & Daniel Fuchs (based on the screenplay *Criss Cross* by Fuchs, from the novel by Don Tracy), PH Elliot Davis, ED Stan Salfas, M Chris Martinez, PD Howard Cummings, AD John Frick, SD Jeanette Scott.

LP Peter Gallagher (Michael Chambers), Alison Elliott (Rachel), William Fichtner (Tommy Dundee), Adam Trese (David Chambers), Joe Don Baker (Clay Hinkle), Paul Dooley (Ed Dutton), Elisabeth Shue (Susan), Anjanette Comer (Mrs. Chambers).

In this remake of the film noir favorite *Criss Cross*, chronic gambler Gallagher returns home for his mother Comer's marriage to Dooley. He foolishly tries to rekindle the spark between himself and his ex-wife Elliott, who is now linked to ruthless nightclub owner Fichtner. To save his hide, Gallagher has to come up with a robbery scheme.

3070. *Understanding Jane* (1998, U.K., DMS Films/Flash Point Pictures, 97m, c). D

Caleb Lindsay, P Nik Powell, W Jim Mummery, PH Christian Koerner, ED Lindsay.

LP Kevin McKidd (Elliot), Amelia Curtis (Dallas), John Simon (Oz), Louisa Milwood Haigh (Popeye).

For a lark, London friends McKidd and Simon answer a dating ad and end up with Curtis and Haigh. The two gals make a career of scamming men for free meals and cash.

3071. *The Undertaker's Wedding* (1998, U.S./Canada, Cabin Fever Ent., 85m, c). D & W John Bradshaw, P Nicolas Stiliadis, PH Edgar Egger, ED Ron Wisman, M VaRouje, PD Michael Close, SD Mayuko Udea.

LP Adrien Brody (Mario Bellini), Jeff Wincott (Rocco), Kari Wuhrer (Maria), Burt Young (Alberto), Holly Gagnier (Louise), Nicholas Pasco (Michael Caprelli).

Funeral director Brody is forced to hide mob boss Young's hotheaded brother Wincott. The latter's death has been faked to defuse a gang war. Wincott doesn't like to be cooped up and makes quite a bit of trouble for his host. Young sends over Wuhrer, Wincott's sexy wife, to calm him down. It doesn't, but it certainly sets Brody's blood a-boiling. When Wincott gives Brody some advice on how to win over his reluctant girlfriend Gagnier, it only sends her into Wincott's arms.

3072. *Undertow* (1996, Weintraub/Kuhn Prods., 92m, c). D Eric Red, P Tom Kuhn & Fred Weintraub, W Red & Kathryn Bigelow, PH Geza Sitkovics, ED Claudia Finkle, M John Frizzell, PD Bill Brodie, AD Galius Klicius, SD Bronius Galvydius.

LP Lou Diamond Phillips (Jack Ketcham), Charles Dance (Lyle Yates), Mia Sara (Willie).

Drifter Phillips is stranded during a torrential rainfall at the cabin of violent survivalist Dance and his abused and frightened wife Sara. The two men play numerous macho games with each other to impress Sara.

3073. *Underworld* (1997, Trimark, 95m, c). D Roger Christian, P Robert Vince & William Vince, W Larry Bishop, PH Steven Bernstein, ED Robin Russell, M Anthony Marinelli, PD John Ebden, AD Doug Byggdin, SD Mark Lane.

LP Denis Leary (Johnny Crown/Johnny Alt), Joe Mantegna (Frank Gavilan/Richard Essex), Annabella Sciorra (Dr. Leah), Larry Bishop (Ned Lynch), Abe Vigoda (Will Cassidy), Robert Costanzo (Stan), Traci Lords (Anna).

Released after seven years in prison, Leary is out to avenge his father's murder at the hands of mobsters. The latter had been attacked and rendered brain dead by Bishop, a cold-blooded killer for hire who, unhappy with his work, visited the comatose man in his hospital room and shot him through the head. Leary manages to kill all responsible for the dastardly deed.

3074. *The Unearthing* (1994, Prism Pictures, 85m, c). D, P & W Wrye Martin & Barry Poltermann, PH James Zabilla, ED Poltermann, M Ken Brahmstedt, AD Margot Czulewicz.

LP Norman Moses (Peter Null), Tina Ona Paukstelis (Katrina), Mildred Nierras (Cupid), Jamie Jacobs Anderson (Claire), Flora Coker (Olive).

A young unwed pregnant girl accepts the offer of marriage from a wealthy man. He claims it will allow his mother to die happily. The family has a taste for the blood of the unborn.

3075. *Unforgettable* (1996, MGM/UA, 111m, c). D John Dahl, P Dino De Laurentiis & Martha De Laurentiis, W Bill Geddie, PH Jeffrey Jur, ED Eric L. Beason, M Christopher Young, PD Rob Pearson, AD Doug Byggdin, SD Elizabeth Wilcox.

LP Ray Liotta (David Krane), Linda Fiorentino (Martha Briggs), Peter Coyote (Don Bresler), Christopher McDonald (Stewart Gleick), David Paymer (Curtis Avery), Duncan Fraser (Michael Stratton), Kim Cattrall (Kelly).

Medical examiner Liotta has barely escaped prosecution for the brutal murder of his wife. He turns to scientist Fiorentino, an expert in memory transference, in hopes of discovering the identity of the killer. It's not an exact science, you know.

3076. *Unforgiven** (1992, Warner Bros., 130m, c). D Clint Eastwood* P Eastwood*, W David Webb Peoples†, PH Jack N. Green†, ED Joel Cox*, M Lennie Niehaus, PD Henry Bumstead†, AD Rick Roberts & Adrian Gorton, SD Janice Blackie-Goodine†.

LP Clint Eastwood† (William Munny), Gene Hackman* (Sheriff "Little Bill" Daggett), Morgan Freeman (Ned Logan), Richard

Harris (English Bob), Jaimz Wolvett (The "Schofield Kid"), Saul Rubinek (W.W. Beauchamp), Frances Fisher (Strawberry Alice), Anna Thomson (Delilah Fitzgerald).

Former gunslinger Eastwood, who has given up his killing ways to raise his children after the death of his wife, is in need of money. He accepts the invitation of Wolvett to take a crack at the reward for killing two men who cut up the face of a prostitute. It seems her colleagues have taken a portion of their earnings to supply the bounty. The girls were not satisfied by the punishment, a beating, inflicted by sadistic Sheriff Hackman on the brutes. Old friend Freeman joins the crusade, but it costs him his life. Before Eastwood and Wolvett earn the reward, Eastwood also has to kill Hackman. The role fits Eastman perfectly, but Hackman walked off with the Oscar.

3077. Unhook the Stars (1996, Miramax, 105m, c). D Nick Cassavetes, P Rene Cleitman, W Cassavetes & Helen Caldwell, PH & PD Phedon Papamichael, ED Petra Von Oelffen, M Steven Hufsteter, SD Barbara Ward.

LP Gena Rowlands (Mildred), Marisa Tomei (Monica), Gerard Depardieu (Big Tommy), Jake Lloyd (J.J.), Moira Kelly (Ann Mary Margaret), David Sherrill (Ethan).

Desperate for someone to watch her son while she earns a living and has a life, single mother Tomei invades the lonely world of Rowlands. The film is an excellent character study but not a great story.

3078. Uninvited (1993, Imperial Ent. Corp., 90m, c). D & W Michael Derek Bohusz, P Larry Kaster & David Kleinman, PH Brett Webster, M Rick Kraushaar & Ed Tobin.

LP Jack Elam (Grady), Christopher Boyer (Jackson), Erin Noble (Cecilia), Bari Buckner (Emma).

Mysterious old Elam leads a group of misfits to a sacred Indian burial ground at the top of a mountain, promising them a treasure of gold. They are uninvited, you see.

3079. Universal Soldier (1992, TriStar, 98m, c). D Roland Emmerich, P Craig Baumgarten, Allen Shapiro & Joel B. Michaels, W Richard Rothstein, Christopher Leitch & Dean Devlin, PH Karl Walter Lindenlaub, ED Michael J. Duthie, M Christopher Franke, PD Holger Gross, AD Nelson Coates, SD Alexander Carle).

LP Jean-Claude Van Damme (Luc Devreux), Dolph Lundgren (Andrew Scott), Ally Walker (Veronica Roberts), Ed O'Ross (Colonel Perry), Jerry Orbach (Dr. Gregor), Leon Rippy (Woodward).

Reporter Walker discovers a plot to use the bodies of dead soldiers, including Van Damme and Lundgren, to manufacture perfect robosoldiers. The only thing that lets her escape with her life and the information is that Van Damme has flashbacks to his past.

3080. Universal Soldier: The Return (1999, Sony Pictures Ent.–TriStar, 82m, c). D Mic Rodgers, P Craig Baumgarten, W William Malone & John Fasano (based on characters created by Richard Rothstein, Christopher Leitch & Dean Devlin), PH Michael A. Benson, ED Peck Prior, M Don Davis, PD David Chapman, AD John Frick, SD Donnasu Sealy.

LP Jean-Claude Van Damme (Luc Deveraux), Michael Jai White (SETH), Heidi Schanz (Erin), Xander Berkeley (Dylan Cotner), Justin Lazard (Capt. Blackburn), Kiana Tom (Maggie).

Fans of Van Damme know what to expect of his films, and those who saw the original *Universal Soldier* in 1992 or the made-for-cable sequels — *Universal Soldier II: Brothers in Arms* and *Universal Soldiers III: Unfinished Business*, both with Matt Battaglia — are doubly warned. For the uninitiated, Van Damme is forced to take on a super computer, White and an army of cyborgs, angry that the government program supporting them is being shut down to save funds.

3081. The Unknown Cyclist (1998, Dream Vision Ent.–Trident, 96m, c). D Bernard Salzman, P Matthew Carlisle & Betsy Pool, W Howard Skora, Pool & Carlisle, PH Salzman & Mike Fash, ED Irit Raz, PD Stewart Campbell.

LP Lea Thompson (Melissa Cavatelli), Vincent Spano (Frank Cavatelli), Danny Nucci (Gaetano Amador), Stephen Spinella (Doug Stein), Michael J. Pollard (Gabe Sinclair), Lainie Kazan (Rachel).

Four survivors participate in an AIDS bike race to honor a deceased friend's last wish.

3082. Unlawful Entry (1992, 20th Century–Fox, 111m, c). D Jonathan Kaplan, P

Charles Gordon, W Lewis Colick (based on the story by Colick, John Katchmer & George D. Putman), PH Jamie Anderson, ED Curtiss Clayton, M James Horner, PD Lawrence G. Paull, AD Bruce Crone, SD Rick Simpson.

LP Kurt Russell (Michael Carr), Ray Liotta (Officer Pete Davis), Madeleine Stowe (Karen Carr), Roger E. Mosley (Officer Roy Cole), Ken Lerner (Roger Graham), Deborah Offner (Penny).

When their home is broken into, Russell and his wife Stowe make a mistake and call the police. This brings Liotta into their lives, and he's more than a little bit unstable. He lusts for Stowe and Russell's life. He's willing to forget which side of the law he's supposed to be on to get both.

3083. *Unstrung Heroes* (1995, Hollywood Pictures–Buena Vista, 93m, c). D Diane Keaton, P Donna Roth, Susan Arnold & William Badalato, W Richard LaGravenese (based on the book by Franz Lidz), PH Phedon Papamichael, ED Lisa Churgin, M Thomas Newman†, PD Garreth Stover, AD Chris Cornwell, SD Larry Dias.

LP Andie MacDowell (Selma Lidz), John Turturro (Sid Litz), Michael Richards (Danny Lidz), Maury Chaykin (Arthur Lidz), Nathan Watt (Steven/Franz Lidz), Kendra Krull (Sandy Lidz), Joey Andrews (Ash).

Young Watt's mother MacDowell is dying of cancer. His nutty-professor father Turturro refuses to accept the illness. Watt is sent to live with his very eccentric but understanding oddball uncles, Richards and Chaykin. This appealing film is based on the autobiography of Franz Lidz, Franz being the new name his uncles gave him.

3084. *Untamed Heart* (1993, MGM, 102m, c). D Tony Bill, P Bill & Helen Buck Bartlett, W Tom Sierchio, PH Jost Vacano, ED Mia Goldman, M Cliff Eidelman, PD Steven Jordan, AD Jack D.L. Ballance, SD Cliff Cunningham.

LP Christian Slater (Adam), Marisa Tomei (Caroline), Rosie Perez (Cindy), Kyle Secor (Howard), Willie Garson (Patsy), James Cada (1st Bill), Gary Groomes (2nd Bill).

Shy busboy Slater, who has a heart condition, saves Tomei, the waitress he admires from afar, from a pair of would-be rapists. This encounter leads to love. The performances of Slater, Tomei and Perez are charming in this very decent romantic comedy.

3085. *Up Close and Personal* (1996, Touchstone–Buena Vista, 124m, c). D Jon Avnet, P Avnet, Dick Nicksay & Jordan Kerner, W Joan Didion & John Gregory Dunne (suggested by the book *Golden Girl* by Alanna Nash), PH Karl Walter Lindenlaub, ED Debra Neil-Fisher, M Thomas Newman, PD Jeremy Conway, AD Mark W. Mansbridge & Bruce Alan Miller, SD Dorree Cooper.

LP Robert Redford (Warren Justice), Michelle Pfeiffer (Tally Atwater), Stockard Channing (Marcia McGrath), Joe Mantegna (Bucky Terranova), Kate Nelligan (Joanna Kennelly), Glenn Plummer (Ned Jackson), James Rebhorn (John Merino), Scott Bryce (Rob Sullivan), Dedee Pfeiffer (Luanne Atwater).

Michelle Pfeiffer desperately wants to break into broadcasting. She gets her chance at a Miami TV station where veteran reporter and producer Redford first becomes her mentor and then her lover. Her climb up the media ladder messes up their romance. The cast is good but the film is disappointing. It would have been perhaps a better story if it had more closely followed the tragic career of NBC reporter Jessica Savitch, which suggested it.

3086. *Urban Crossfire* (1994, Concorde–New Horizons, 95m, c). D Dick Lowry, P Lowry & Ann Kindburg, W T.S. Cook, PH Frank Beascoechea, ED Anita Brandt-Burgoyne, PD Guy Barnes.

LP Mario Van Peebles (Raymond Williamson), Peter Boyle (Dan Riley), Ray Sharkey (Victor Tomasino), Courtney B. Vance (Justis Butler), Michael Boatman (Robert Dayton).

Veteran white police detectives Boyle and Sharkey are aided by black patrolman Van Peebles in taking down a gang leader responsible for the killing of Van Peebles' partner.

3087. *Urban Legend* (1998, TriStar, 100m, c). D Jamie Blanks, P Neal H. Moritz, Gina Matthews & Michael McDonnell, W Silvio Horta, PH James Chressanthis, ED Jay Cassidy, M Christopher Young, PD Charles Breen, AD Benno Tutter, SD Cal Loucks.

LP Jared Leto (Paul), Alicia Witt (Natalie), Rebecca Gayheart (Brenda), Michael Rosenbaum (Parker), Loretta Devine (Renee), Joshua

Jackson (Damon), Robert Englund (Professor Wexler).

At a fictitious college, a group of students debate the truth of the campus legend about a grotesque student massacre by a deranged professor which took place 25 years earlier. Before long some lunatic starts a new killing spree on campus.

3088.　U.S. Marshals (1998, Warner Bros., 133m, c). D Stuart Baird, P Arnold and Anne Kopelson, W John Pogue (based on characters created by Roy Huggins), PH Andrzej Bartkowiak, ED Terry Rawlings, M Jerry Goldsmith, PD Mather Ahmad, AD Bruce Alan Miller & Mark Worthington, SD Gene Serdena.

LP Tommy Lee Jones (Chief Deputy Marshal Sam Gerard), Wesley Snipes (Mark Sheridan), Robert Downey, Jr. (John Royce), Kate Nelligan (U.S. Marshal Walsh), Joe Pantoliano (Deputy Marshall Cosmo Renfro), Irene Jacob (Marie).

Ninety-nine and ninety-nine percent of the time the sequel to a box-office hit is inferior. This film, featuring Jones in his role from *The Fugitive*, is no exception. It's not just that the movie misses the presence of Harrison Ford. Missing also is a credible story to thrill audiences. This times Jones and his team of marshals are pursuing Snipes, accused of murdering two top agents. Is this another case of an innocent man on the run to prove his innocence? Could be.

3089.　Used People (1992, 20th Century-Fox, 120m, c). D Beeban Kidron, P Peggy Rajski, W Todd Graff (based on his play *The Grandmother Plays*), PH David Watkin, ED John Tintori, M Rachel Portman, PD Stuart Wurtzel, AD Gregory Paul Keen, SD Hilton Rosemarin.

LP Shirley MacLaine (Pearl), Marcello Mastroianni (Joe), Kathy Bates (Bibby), Marcia Gay Harden (Norma), Jessica Tandy (Frieda), Sylvia Sidney (Becky), Bob Dishy (Jack).

This film has a distinguished cast, including Oscar winners MacLaine, Bates and Tandy, playing members of a Jewish family. Into their lives comes Italian restaurant owner Mastroianni, who has long carried a torch for MacLaine. Now that her husband has died, he feels the time is right to court her. Shirley is at first not interested, not so much because of their background differences but because she has enough on her hands heading a family of unhappy women, including daughters Bates and Harden. The former suffers the angst of overweight women with no willpower or self-esteem, and the second is a kook who likes to play out romantic scenes from movies with her male admirers. In addition, the next generation is without guidance or role models from their parents.

3090.　The Usual Suspects (1995, Gramercy, 96m, c). D Bryan Singer, P Singer & Michael McDonnell, W Christopher McQuarrie† PH Newton Thomas Sigel, ED & M John Ottman, PD Howard Cummings, AD David Lazan, SD Sara Andrews, FX Roy Downey.

LP Stephen Baldwin (McManus), Gabriel Byrne (Dean Keaton), Benicio Del Toro (Fenster), Kevin Pollak (Hockney), Kevin Spacey† (Roger "Verbal" Kint), Chazz Palminteri (Kujan), Pete Postlethwaite (Kobayashi), Suzy Amis (Edie), Giancarlo Esposito (Jack Baer), Dan Hedaya (Sgt. Rabin).

We're not sure we have all the answers to our questions about this slick modern film noir. But then neither does Customs Agent Palminteri, who is investigating a $91 million heist. No matter, it certainly is an intriguing film. It also introduces a new film buzz word, "Keyser Soze," which sounds like some exotic desert but is in fact the name of a dangerous and mysterious crime boss who is never seen in the film — or is he? The film is filled with violence, suspense and fine acting, especially from Spacey, one of five temperamental criminals hired for the big job by the big boss. The others include ex-cop Byrne, explosives expert Pollak and two hot-headed hooligans, Baldwin and Del Toro. Postlethwaite is excellent as Keyser Soze's contact with the gang.

3091.　Utz (1993, U.K./Italy/Germany, Castle Hill, 98m, c). D George Sluizer, P John Goldschmidt, William Sargent & Albert Schwinges, W Hugh Whitemore (based on the novel by Bruce Chatwin), PH Gerard Vandenberg, ED Lin Friedman & Eberhard Scharfenberg, M Nicola Piovani, PD Karel Vacek.

LP Armin Mueller-Stahl (Baron Kaspar Von Utz), Brenda Fricker (Marta), Peter Riegert (Marius Fisher), Paul Scofield (Doctor Vaclav Orlik), Miriam Karlin (Grandmother Utz).

Elderly and dying Baron Mueller-Stahl has

been a life-long collector of women and porcelain figures. When art dealer Riegert arrives for a visit he discovers the figures are missing, as is the Baron's housekeeper Fricker. She has long suffered from unrequited love for her employer. Riegert teams with the Baron's old friend Scofield to find out what's been going on.

3092. *The Vagrant* (1992, Brooksfilms, 91m, c). D Chris Walas, P Gillian Richardson, W Richard Jeffries, PH John J. Connor & Jack Wallner, ED Jay Ignaszewski, M Christopher Young, PD Michael Bolton, AD Eric Fraser, SD Andrew Bernard.

LP Bill Paxton (Graham Krakowski), Michael Ironside (Lieutenant Ralf Barfuss), Marshall Bell (The Vagrant), Mitzi Kapture (Edie Roberts), Colleen Camp (Judy Dansig).

When yuppie executive Paxton purchases a house, he finds it is already occupied by Bell, an ugly, diseased hobo. Paxton has the bum arrested and moves into his home. Like a cat that one can't get rid of, the vagrant returns and constantly harasses Paxton.

3093. *Valerie Flake* (1999, I.E. Films Prods., 88m, c). D John Putch, P Julie Philips, W Robert Tilem, PH Mark Putnam, ED Audrey Evans, M Alexander Baker & Clair Marlo.

LP Susan Traylor (Valerie Flake), Jay Underwood (Tim Darnell), Christina Pickles (Meg Darnell), Peter Michael Goetz (Douglas Flake), Rosemary Forsyth (Irene Flake).

In this film, embittered young widow Traylor deals with her grief by insulting her family and friends who dare offer her condolences. In addition, she drinks heavily and hops from one man's bed to another to forget. Don't think Traylor's sarcastic kiss-offs are limited to those who know her — strangers get the same sweet treatment. It's an interesting character study.

3094. *Vampire in Brooklyn* (1995, Paramount, 103m, c). D Wes Craven, P Eddie Murphy & Mark Lipsky, W Charles Murphy, Christopher Parker & Michael Lucker (based on a story by Charles Murphy, Eddie Murphy & Vernon Lynch), PH Mark Irwin, ED Patrick Lussier, M J. Peter Robinson, AD Gary Diamond & Cynthia Charette, SD Robert Kensinger.

LP Eddie Murphy (Maximillian/Professor Pauley/Guido), Angela Bassett (Rita), Allen Payne (Justice), Kadeem Hardison (Julius), John Witherspoon (Silas), Zakes Mokae (Dr. Zero), Joanna Cassidy (Dewey), Simbi Khali (Nikki).

Murphy takes the vampire legend for a comedy ride. He's a Caribbean bloodsucker who, in order to perpetuate his race, tries to convince Brooklyn cop Bassett to be the mother of his little suckers.

3095. *The Vampire Journals* (1997, Full Moon Studios, 81m, c). D & W Ted Nicolaou, P Vlad Paunescu, PH Adolfo Bartoli, ED Gregory Sanders, M Richard Kosinski, PD Valentin Calinescu, AD Viorel Ghenea, SD Ica Varna.

LP Jonathan Morris (Ash), David Gunn (Zachary), Kirsten Cerre (Sofia), Starr Andreeff (Iris), Ilinka Goya (Cassandra), Dan Condurache (Anton), Rodica Lupu (Rebecca).

Hoping to appeal to Anne Rice fans, this film offers plenty of nudity, violence and sex. Ever since he killed his beloved Lupu, Gunn, a "vampire with a human soul," has dedicated his existence to destroying those of his kind. In his crusade he is pitted against Morris, who presides over a group of bloodsuckers in Eastern Europe. They fight over Cerre, who, Morris initiates into vampirism.

3096. *Vampirella* (1997, Concorde–Sunset Films International, 76m, c). D Jim Wynorski, P Paul Hertzberg & Wynorski, W Gary Gerani (based on a story by Forrest J Ackerman), PH Andrea Rossotto, ED Richard Gentner, M Joel Goldsmith.

LP Talisa Soto (Ella/Vampirella), Roger Daltry (Vlad/Jamie Blood), Richard Joseph Paul (Adam Van Helsing), Brian Bloom (Demos), Corrina Harney (Sallah).

This film is a cheesy production drawn from the comic book series. Soto has had a thirty-century struggle with evil Dalton and his bloodsucking followers. She trails him to modern-day Las Vegas where she plans to enact her revenge for his slaughter of her stepfather, an elder of the planet Drakulon.

3097. *Vampire's Kiss* (1990, Hemdale, 105m, c). D Robert Bierman, P Barbara Zitwer & Barry Shils, W Joseph Minion, PH Stefan Czapsky, ED Angus Newton, M Colin Towns, PD Christopher Nowak.

LP Nicolas Cage (Peter Loew), Maria Conchita Alonso (Alva Restrepo), Jennifer Beals (Rachel), Elizabeth Ashley (Dr. Glaser), Kasi Lemmons (Jackie).

Obnoxious literary agent Cage becomes convinced that vamp Beals has turned him into a vampire. Cage's performance is way, way over the top, but that's nothing new.

3098. The Van (AKA: *Fish & Chips*) (1997, U.K./U.S./Ireland, BBC Films, 96m, c). D Stephen Frears, P Lynda Miles, W Roddy Doyle (based on his novel), PH Oliver Stapleton, ED Mick Audsley, M Eric Clapton & Richard Hartley, PD Mark Geraghty, AD Fiona Daly.

LP Colm Meaney (Larry), Donal O'Kelly (Bimbo), Ger Ryan (Maggie), Caroline Rothwell (Mary), Neili Conroy (Diane), Ruaidhri Conroy (Kevin), Brendan O'Carroll (Weslie), Stuart Dunne (Sam).

This film is set in 1990 when Ireland advanced to the semifinals of the World Cup. It is the story of two unemployed friends, Meaney and O'Kelly, who buy a piece of mobile junk from which they hope to sell burgers and fish & chips to hungry football fans. The humor of the film is about as amusing as four flat tires on their van.

3099. The Vanishing (1993, 20th Century–Fox, 110m, c). D George Sluizer, P Larry Brezner & Paul Schiff, W Todd Graff (based on the novel *The Golden Egg* by Tim Krabbe), PH Peter Suschitzky, ED Bruce Greene, M Jerry Goldsmith, PD Jeannine C. Oppewall, AD Steve Wolff, SD Anne Ahrens & Richard Yanez.

LP Jeff Bridges (Barney), Kiefer Sutherland (Jeff), Nancy Travis (Rita), Sandra Bullock (Diane), Park Overall (Lynn), Maggie Linderman (Denise), Lisa Eichhorn (Helene), George Hearn (Arthur Bernard).

Bullock disappears at a highway rest stop. Her boyfriend Sutherland is obsessed with finding out what happened to her. Three years later it appears that mysterious Bridges has the answers, but to get them Sutherland must experience what happened to Bullock.

3100. Vanya on 42nd Street (1994, Sony Picture Classics, 119m, c). D Louis Malle, P Fred Berner, W David Mamet (based on the play *Uncle Vanya* by Anton Chekhov), PH Declan Quinn, ED Nancy Baker, M Joshua Redman, PD Eugene Lee.

LP Wallace Shawn (Vanya), Julianne Moore (Yelena), Brooke Smith (Sonya), Larry Pine (Dr. Astrov), George Gaynes (Serybryakov), Lynn Cohen (Maman).

A group of actors rehearse a workshop production of Chekhov's Uncle Vanya in a rundown New York Theater. There are good performances all around in this filming of the complex Russian play.

3101. Varsity Blues (1999, Paramount, 104m, c). D Brian Robbins, P Tova Laiter, Mike Tollin & Robbins, W W. Peter Iliff, PH Charles Cohen, ED Ned Bastille, M Mark Isham, PD Jaymes Hinkle, AD Keith Donnelly, SD Tad Smalley.

LP James Ven Der Beek (Jonathan "Mox" Moxon), Jon Voight (Coach Bud Kilmer), Paul Walker (Lance Harbor), Ron Lester (Billy Bob), Scott Caan (Tweeter), Tiffany C. Love (Collette Harbor).

This film shows the abuses in fielding winning Texas high school football teams. Voight is a hissable coach, and TV's *Dawson Creek* heartthrob Van Der Beek is his star player.

3102. Vegas in Space (1993, Troma, 85m, c/b&w). D & P Phillip R. Ford, W Doris Fish, Miss X & Ford, PH Robin Clark, ED Ford & Ed Jones, M Bob Davis, AD Fish.

LP Doris Fish (Captain Dan Tracy/Tracy Daniels), Miss X (Vel Croford/Queen Veneer), Ginger Quest (Empress Nueva Gabor), Ramona Fischer (Mike/Sheila).

Four male astronauts are on a secret mission to the all-female planet of Clitoris. In order to infiltrate where men are forbidden to go they take a gender-changing pill. Cheap trash!

3103. Vegas Vacation (1997, Warner Bros., 94m, c). D Stephen Kessler, P Jerry Weintraub, W Elisa Bell (based on a story by Bell & Bob Ducsay), PH William A. Fraker, ED Seth Flaum, M Joel McNeely, PD David L. Snyder, AD Tom Valentine, SD Chris Spellman.

LP Chevy Chase (Clark W. Griswold), Beverly D'Angelo (Ellen Griswold), Randy Quaid (Cousin Eddie), Wayne Newton (Himself), Wallace Shawn (Marty — Dealer), Ethan Embry (Rusty Griswold), Marisol Nichols (Audrey Griswold), Miriam Flynn (Cousin Catherine), Christie Brinkley (Mystery Ferrari Beauty).

The Griswold family vacations are becoming a bit of a bore. Chase in particular seems no longer interested. Fortunately, Quaid reprises his popular role of Cousin Eddie. The family is in Las Vegas where Chase loses everything, wife d'Angelo is pursued by Newton and the kids get into fairly innocent trouble.

3104. *The Velocity of Gary* (1998, Cineville Prods., 100m, c). D Dan Ireland, P Dan Lupovitz, W James Still (based on his play), PH Claudio Rocha, ED Luis Colina, PD Amy Ancona, AD Rachel Kamerman, SD Melissa Levander.

LP Salma Hayek (Mary Carmern), Vincent D'Onofrio (Valentino), Thomas Jane (Gary), Olivia d'Abo (Veronica), Chad Lindberg (Kid Joey), Lucky Luciano (The King).

When bisexual D'Onofrio falls for studdish Jane, his spitfire waitress sweetheart Hayek is more than a bit put off. She and Jane put aside their differences when D'Onofrio contracts AIDS and slowly dies.

3105. *Velvet Goldmine* (1998, U.K./U.S., Miramax, 123m, c). D & W Todd Haynes (based on a story by Haynes & James Lyons), P Christine Vachon, PH Maryse Alberti, ED Lyons, M Carter Burwell, PD Christopher Hobbs, AD Andrew Munro.

LP Ewan McGregor (Curt Wild), Jonathan Rhys Meyers (Brian Slade), Toni Collette (Mandy Slade), Christian Bale (Arthur Stuart), Eddie Izzard (Jerry Devine), Emily Woof (Shannon), Michael Feast (Cecil).

Borrowing from *Citizen Kane*, the film follows reporter Bale, who is given the assignment in 1984 of discovering what happened to glitter rock star Meyers. The latter's career crashed when he faked his own killing onstage to fulfill his prophecy that he would be assassinated while performing. Bail interviews numerous people in Meyers' life, and through flashbacks we learn Meyers' story. Is this a fictionalized version of rock star David Bowie? You better believe it. And McGregor is Iggy Pop.

3106. *The Venice Project* (1999, Austria/U.S., Terra Film, 86m, c). D Robert Dornheim, P Norbert Biecha & Kara Meyers, W Nicholas Klein, PH Hannes Drapal, Dan Gilham & Maurizio dell'Orco, ED Klaus Hundsbichler, M Harald Kloser, PD Christian Marin.

LP Lauren Bacall (Countess Camilla Volta), Dennis Hopper (Roland/Salvatore), Linus Roach (Count Jacko/Count Giaccomo), Ben Cross (Rudy Mestry/Bishop Orsini), Stuart Townsend (Lark/Gippo the Fool), Hector Babenco (Danilo Danuzzi), Dean Stockwell (Senator Campbell), John Wood (The Viscount), Stockard Channing (Chandra Chase), Parker Posey (Myra).

It only took three weeks to film this project, which became a last-minute entry at the Venice Film Festival. If one looks at the story, dealing in a playful way about the past and future of art by jumping back and forth between 1699 and 1999, the film does appear to be a hurried project. But some of the individual parts and performances are memorable.

3107. *Venice/Venice* (1992, International Rainbow Pictures, 108m, c). D & W Henry Jaglom, P Judith Wolinsky, PH Hanania Baer.

LP Nelly Alard (Jeanne), Henry Jaglom (Dean), Suzanne Bertish (Carlotta), Daphna Kastner (Eve), David Duchovny (Dylan).

Filmmaker Jaglom portrays a filmmaker at the Venice Film Festival. He meets and becomes involved with French journalist Alard. The romance continues in his home of Venice, California, thus the title.

3108. *Venus Rising* (1996, Cyberfilms, Inc., 91m, c). D Leora Barish & Edgar Bravo, P Thomas Small, Johnna Levine & Albert Dickerson III, W Barish (based on a story by Barish & Henry Bean), PH John Thomas, ED James Fletcher & Bravo, M Deborah Holland, PD Kathleen McKernin, SD Katie Lipsitt.

LP Audie England (Eve), Costas Mandylor (Vegas), Billy Wirth (Nick), John Kerry (Man in Lifeboat), Richard Vidan (Lujan), Ivory Ocean (Wyndham).

This film, set in the not-too-distant future, is the story of England and Mandylor, who have escaped from a near-impregnable prison. Warden Ocean convinces lifer Wirth to help him recapture the escapees. The world into which England and Mandylor try to disappear is controlled by drugs and virtual reality.

3109. *Very Bad Things* (1998, Polygram, 100m, c). D & W Peter Berg, P Michael Schiffer, Diane Nabatoff & Cindy Cowan, PH David Hennings, ED Dan Lebental, M Stewart Copeland, PD Dina Lipton, AD Michael Atwell.

LP Christian Slater (Robert Boyd), Cameron Diaz (Laura Garrety), Daniel Stern (Adam Berkow), Jeanne Tripplehorn (Lois Berkow), Jon Favreau (Kyle Fisher), Jeremy Piven (Michael Berkow), Leland Orser (Charles Moore).

In a black comedy, five friends, Slater, Piven, Favreau, Stern and Orser, participate in a wild bachelor party in Las Vegas that leads to two grisly deaths.

3110. *A Very Brady Sequel* (1996, Paramount, 90m, c). D Arlene Sanford, P Sherwood Schwartz, Lloyd J. Schwartz & Alan Ladd, Jr., W Harry Elfont, Deborah Kaplan, James Berg & Stan Zimmerman (based on a story by Elfont & Kaplan, and characters created by Schwartz), PH Mac Ahlberg, ED Anita Brandt-Burgoyne, M Guy Moon, PD Cynthia Charette, AD Troy Sizemore, SD Bob Kensinger.

LP Shelley Long (Carol Brady), Gary Cole (Mike Brady), Christopher Daniel Barnes (Greg Brady), Christine Taylor (Marcia Brady), Paul Sutera (Peter Brady), Jennifer Elise Cox (Jan Brady), Jesse Lee (Bobby Brady), Olivia Hack (Cindy Brady), Henriette Mantel (Alice), Tim Matheson (Roy Martin/Trevor Thomas).

While the original parody of the once popular family TV comedy was rather campy and fun, the sequel demonstrates just how little there is to kid. Still looking like their TV counterparts, the Brady family and Alice must deal with the arrival of Long's ex-husband, a growing lust between Barnes and Taylor, Cox's envy of her pretty, popular sister, and assorted other problems of no consequences.

3111. *V.I. Warshawski* (1991, Hollywood–Buena Vista, 89m, c). D Jeff Kanew, P Jeffrey Lurie, W Edward Taylor, David Aaron Cohen & Nick Thiel (based on the novels by Sara Paretsky), PH Jan Kiesser, ED C. Timothy O'Meara & Debra Neil, M Randy Edelman, PD Barbara Ling, AD Larry Fulton, SD Anne H. Ahrens.

LP Kathleen Turner (V.I. "Vic" Warshawski), Jay O. Sanders (Murray), Charles Durning (Lt. Mallory), Angela Goethals (Kat), Nancy Paul (Paige), Frederick Coffin (Horton), Charles McCaughan (Trumble), Stephen Meadows (Bernard "Boom-Boom" Grafalk).

For those who felt that Turner was quite a dish and a talented actress to boot, this choice of roles will certainly tarnish her acting image.

She's a tough, leggy private eye investigating the killing of a hockey player. The plot is absolutely nothing.

3112. *Vice Academy III* (1991, Prism Ent., 88m, c). D, P & W Rick Sloane, PH Robert Hayes, M Alan Dermarderosian.

LP Ginger Lynn Allen (Holly), Elizabeth Kaitan (Candy), Julia Parton (Melanie/Malathion), Jay Richardson (The Commissioner), Joanna Grika (Miss Devonshire), Steve Maeto (Prof. Kauffinger).

Female Hollywood vice cops battle a toxic villainess. Ho hum!

3113. *Vicious Circles* (1997, Trimark, 90m, c). D Alexander Whitelaw, P Nik Powell, Stephen Woolley & J. Eivind Karlsen, W Stephen O'Shea & Whitelaw, PH Roman Winding, ED Jon Costelloe, M Robert Lockhart, PD Franck Benezech & Luc Chalon, AD Pierre Queffelean.

LP Carolyn Lowery (Andy Hunt), Paul Hipp (Dylan), Jerome Davis (Asher), Ben Gazzara (March), Tom Gilroy (Jack Morton), Masaya Kato (Morri), Marianne Borgo (Madame).

Lowery is forced into prostitution by a mysterious man in order to make money to free her brother, who is in prison on drug-possession charges. There's plenty of kinky situations, nudity and violence for those that demand it.

3114. *Village of the Damned* (1995, Universal, 99m, c). D John Carpenter, P Michael Preger & Sandy King, W David Himmelstein (based on the novel *The Midwich Cuckoos* by John Wyndham, and the 1960 screenplay by Stirling Silliphant, Wolf Rilla & George Barclay), PH Gary B. Kibbe, ED Edward A. Warschilka, M Dave Davies & John Carpenter, PD Rodger Mann, AD Christa Munro, SD Don De Fina.

LP Christopher Reeve (Alan Chaffee), Kirstie Alley (Dr. Susan Verner), Linda Kozlowski (Jill McGowan), Michael Pare (Frank McGowan), Meredith Salenger (Melanie Roberts), Mark Hamill (Reverend George).

A strange force has impregnated the women of quiet Midwich, California, producing disturbing albino children with telepathic powers and bright red and orange eyes. This is a tame remake of the superior 1960 British horror film of the same name.

3115. Vincent and Theo (1990, U.K./Fr./ U.S., Hemdale, 138m, c). D Robert Altman, P Ludi Boeken, W Julian Mitchell, PH Jean Lepine, ED Francois Coispeau & Geraldine Peroni, M Gabriel Yared, PD Stephen Altman, AD Dominique Douret, Ben Van & Jan Roelfs, SD Pierre Siore.

LP Tim Roth (Vincent Van Gogh), Paul Rhys (Theodore Van Gogh), Jip Wijngaarden (Sien Hoornik), Johanna Ter Steege (Jo Bonger), Wladimir Yordanoff (Paul Gauguin), Jean-Pierre Cassel (Dr. Paul Gachet).

This film examines the increasing madness that infects both painter Roth and his gallery owner brother Rhys. The latter loves his brother's work but can't get anyone interested in buying any of his paintings.

3116. The Virgin Suicides (1999, American Zoetrope, 97m, c). D & W Sofia Coppola (based on the novel by Jeffrey Eugenides), P Francis Ford Coppola, Julie Costanzo, Chris Haney & Dan Halsted, PH Edward Lachman, ED James Lyon & Melissa Kent, M Air, PD Jasna Stefanovic.

LP James Woods (Mr. Lisbon), Kathleen Turner (Mrs. Lisbon), Kirsten Dunst (Lux), John Hartnett (Trip Fontaine), Hannah Hall (Cecilia), Chelse Swain (Bonnie), Danny De-Vito (Dr. Hornicker), A.J. Cook (Mary), Leslie Hayman (Therese), Giovanni Ribisi (Narrator).

In her directorial debut, Sofia Coppola tells the disturbing tale of a disintegrating family of five teenage girls. They see suicide as a feasible solution to their various problems.

3117. Virtuosity (1995, Paramount, 105m, c). D Brett Leonard, P Gary Lucchesi, W Eric Bernt, PH Gale Tattersall, ED B.J. Sears & Rob Kobrin, M Christopher Young, PD Nilo Rodis, AD Richard Yanez-Toyon, SD Jay Hart.

LP Denzel Washington (Parker Barnes), Kelly Lynch (Madison Carter), Russell Crowe (Sid 6.7), Stephen Spinella (Lindenmeyer), William Forsythe (William Cochran), Louise Fletcher (Elizabeth Deane), William Fichtner (Wallace).

Ex-cop Washington is released from prison in order to pursue computer-generated killer Crowe. The latter's personality is made up of some 200 serial killers and criminal minds. Who would produce such a monster, you ask, and for what purpose? Good question.

3118. Virus (1996, Vidmark, 90m, c). D Allan A. Goldstein, P Damian Lee, W Les Standiford (based on his novel *Spill*), PH Nicolas Von Sternberg, ED Evan Landis, M Larry Cohen, PD Tim Boyd, AD Barry Isenor, SD Mary Wilkinson.

LP Brian Bosworth (Ken Fairchild), Leah Pinsent (Larraine Keller), David Fox (George Skanz), Daniel Kash (Ripley), Eric Peterson (Eric Black), Stephen Markle (President John L. Wheeler).

Secret service agent Bosworth attempts to prevent the president from entering a national park where biological warfare chemicals have leaked. Not worth a glance.

3119. Visual Sexuality (1999, U.K., Columbia TriStar, 93m, c). D Nick Hurran, P Christopher Figg, W Nick Fisher (based on the novel by Chloe Rayban), PH Brian Tufano, ED John Richards, M Rupert Gregson-Williams, PD Chris Edwards, AD Humphrey Bangham.

LP Laura Fraser (Justine), Rupert Penry-Jones (Jake), Luke de Lacey (Chas), Kieran O'Brien (Alex), Marcelle Duprey (Fran), Natasha Bell (Hoover).

Seventeen-year-old Notting Hill virgin Fraser is ready to give up the designation — but who is the right fellow for the job? She seeks advice from her black soul-friend Duprey and nerdy de Lacey on how to enlist the aid of school stud O'Brien. The film, despite much sexual confusion on the parts of the teens, could use more humor.

3120. Vital Signs (1990, 20th Century–Fox, 103m, c). D Marisa Silver, P Laurie Perlman & Cathlen Summers, W Larry Ketron & Jeb Stuart (based on Ketron's story), PH John Lindley, ED Robert Brown & Danford B. Greene, M Miles Goodman, PD Todd Hallowell, AD Dan Maltese, SD Keith Burns.

LP Adrian Pasdar (Michael Chatham), Diane Lane (Gina Wyler), Jack Gwaltney (Kenny Rose), Laura San Giacomo (Lauren Rose), Jane Adams (Suzanne Maloney), Tim Ransom (Bobby Hayes), Lisa Jane Persky (Bobby), William Devane (Dr. Chatham), Jimmy Smits (Dr. David Redding).

Medical students romp together in sexual situations yet still have a bit of time for hospital patients.

3121. *Volcano* (1997, 20th Century–Fox, 105m, c). D Mike Jackson, P Neal H. Moritz & Andrew Z. Davis, W Jerome Armstrong & Billy Ray (based on a story by Armstrong), PH Theo Van de Sande, ED Michael Tronick & Don Brochu, M Alan Silvestri, PD Jackson DeGovia, AD Scott Rittenour, Tom Reta, William Cruse & Donald Woodruff, SD K.C. Fox.

LP Tommy Lee Jones (Mike Roark), Anne Heche (Dr. Amy Barnes), Don Cheadle (Emmitt Reese), Gaby Hoffman (Kelly Roark), Keith David (Lt. Fox), Jacqueline Kim (Dr. Jaye Calder), John Corbett (Norman Calder).

A volcano erupts in the middle of Los Angeles. What? You want a description of the plot too? What plot? Special effects star, while Jones and his daughter Hoffman battle nature's monster, with some assistance from Heche.

3122. *Voodoo Dawn* (1991, Academy Ent., 83m, c). D Steven Fierberg, P Steven Mackler, W John Russo, Thomas Rendon, Jeffrey Delman & Evan Dunsky, PH James McCalmont, ED Keith Reamer, M Taj, PD Stephen McCabe.

LP Raymond St. Jacques (Claude), Theresa Merrit (Madame Daslay), Tony Todd (Makoute), Gina Gershon (Tina), Kirk Baily (Kevin).

Two college buddies travel south to visit an old chum. He turns out to be the latest victim in a series of horrible voodoo murders and is in the process of being transformed into a zombie.

3123. *Wag the Dog* (1997, New Line, 105m, c). D Barry Levinson, P Jane Rosenthal, Robert de Niro & Levinson, W Hilary Henkin† & David Mamet† (based on the novel *The American Hero* by Larry Beinhart), PH Robert Richardson, ED Stu Linder, M Mark Knopfler, PD Wynn Thomas, AD Mark Worthington, SD Robert Greenfield.

LP Dustin Hoffman† (Stanley Moss), Robert De Niro (Conrad Breen), Anne Heche (Winifred Ames), Denis Leary (Fad King), Willie Nelson (Johnny Green), Andrea Martin (Liz Butsky), Kirsten Dunst (Tracy Lime), William H. Macy (Mr. Young), Craig T. Nelson (Senator Neal), Woody Harrelson (Sgt. William Schumann).

In comparison to another movie of the same year about an American president, *Air Force One*, this funny film is more creditable. When the president is threatened by a sex scandal, White House insiders hire political fixer De Niro to find a way to divert attention from the scandal. He hires Hollywood filmmaker Hoffman to manufacture a war. Hoffman is a pure delight. Unfortunately for his character, he wants to take credit for his masterpiece — a political no-no.

3124. *Wagons East!* (1994, TriStar, 100m, c). D Peter Markle, P Garry Goodman, Barry Rosen, Robert Newman & Jeffrey Silver, W Matthew Carlson (Jerry Abrahamson), PH Frank Tidy, ED Scott Conrad, M Michael Small, PD Vince J. Cresciman, AD Hector Romero, SD Miguel Angel Gonzalez & Enrique Estevez.

LP John Candy (James Harlow), Richard Lewis (Phil Taylor), John C. McGinley (Julian), Ellen Greene (Belle), Robert Picardo (Ben Wheeler), Ed Lauter (John Slade), Rodney A. Grant (Little Feather).

In his last film, Candy appears as an incompetent wagonmaster who leads a wagon train back East for pioneers who decide the Wild, Wild West is too wild for them.

3125. *Wait Until Spring, Bandini* (1991, Belgium/Fr./U.S., Zoetrope Films, 100m, c). D & W Dominique Deruddere (based on the novel by John Fante), P Tom Luddy, Fred Roos & Erwin Provoost, PH Jean Francois Robin, ED Ludo Troch, M Angelo Badalamenti, Paolo Conte & Tom Waits, PD Robert Ziembicki, AD Roger Crandall, SD Lisa Dean.

LP Joe Mantegna (Svero Bandini), Ornella Muti (Maria Bandini), Faye Dunaway (Mrs. Effie Hildegarde), Burt Young (Rocco Saccone), Michael Bacall (Arturo Bandini), Renata Vanni (Donna Toscana, Maria's Mother).

An Italian immigrant family faces both a harsh winter in Colorado in 1925 and the scheming ways of temptress Dunaway, who has her eyes on the father, Mantegna. The film, based on an autobiographical novel, is seen through the eyes of the young son, Bacall.

3126. *Waiting for Guffman* (1997, Castle Rock Ent., 84m, c). D Christopher Guest, P Karen Murphy, W Guest & Eugene Levy, PH Roberto Schaefer, ED Andy Blumenthal, PD Joseph T. Garrity, AD John Frick, SD Jenny C. Patrick.

LP Christopher Guest (Corky St. Clair),

Eugene Levy (Dr. Allan Pearl), Fred Willard (Ron Albertson), Catherine O'Hara (Sheila Albertson), Parker Posey (Libby Mae Brown), Bob Balaban (Lloyd Miller).

Guest directs a musical show celebrating the 150th anniversary of Blaine, Missouri. He hopes to ride it to success on Broadway. It's amusing, but there's not much to it.

3127. *Waiting to Exhale* (1995, 20th Century–Fox, 121m, c). D Forest Whitaker, P Ezra Swerdlow & Deborah Schindler, W Terry McMillan & Ronald Bass (based on McMillan's novel), PH Toyomichi Kurita, ED Richard Chew, M Kenneth "Babyface" Edmonds, PD David Gropman, AD Marc Fisichella, SD Michael W. Foxworthy.

LP Whitney Houston (Savannah), Angela Bassett (Bernadine), Loretta Devine (Gloria), Lela Rochon (Robin), Gregory Hines (Marvin), Dennis Haysbert (Kenneth), Mykelti Williamson (Troy), Michael Beach (John, Sr.), Leon (Russell).

Four black women, Houston, Bassett, Devine and Rochon, have nothing but bad times with their jerky men. It's a feel-good film for black women, but not black men — or any men for that matter.

3128. *A Wake in Providence* (1999, Mister P. Prods.–Gladiator Pictures, 94m, c). D Rosario Roveto, Jr., P William Redner, Vincent Pagano, Roveto & Patrick Coppola, W Billy Van Zandt, Jane Milmore, Vincent Pagano & Mike Pagano, PH Mark Kohl, ED Gareth O'Neil, M Ed Alton, PD Bonita Flanders, AD Deborah Davis.

LP Vincent Pagano (Anthony), Victoria Rowell (Alissa), Mike Pagnano (Frankie), Adrienne Barbeau (Aunt Lidia), Micole Mercurio (Aunt Elaine), Lisa Raggio (Claudia).

Vincent Pagnano is an aspiring actor. He lives with girlfriend Rowell, a paralegal. When his grandfather dies, he returns home to Rhode Isalnd with Rowell. What a surprise for his family. He never told them she was black. It's a winning comedy.

3129. *Waking Ned Devine* (1998, U.K., Fox Searchlight, 91m, c). D & W Kirk Jones, P Glynis Murray & Richard Holmes, PH Henry Braham, ED Alan Strachan, M Shaun Davey, PD John Ebden, AD Mark Tanner.

LP Ian Bannen (Jackie O'Shea), David Kelly (Michael O'Sullivan), Fionnula Flanagan (Annie O'Shea), Susan Lynch (Maggie), James Nesbitt (Pig Finn), Maura O'Malley (Mrs. Kennedy), Robert Hickey (Maurice), Paddy Ward (Brendy).

Waking Ned Devine scores as the most charming film of the year. When it is announced that the only winning lotto ticket was bought in a tiny Irish town, Bannen, his wife Flanagan and his life-long friend Kelly set out to discover the winner and become his closest friend. They discover that the shock of winning was too much for Ned Devine, who died holding his lotto ticket. Bannen convinces the town to go along with the plan that Devine is not dead, and then each member of the village will share in the winnings. However, a lotto official arrives in town to verify that things are the way they should be, and Kelly is forced to assume the identity of the deceased.

3130. *A Walk in the Clouds* (1995, 20th Century–Fox, 103m, c). D Alfonso Arau, P Gil Netter, David Zucker & Jerry Zucker, W Robert Mark Kamen, Mark Miller & Harvey Weitzman (based on the 1942 screenplay *Quattro Passi Fra le Nuvole* by Piero Tellini, Cesare Zavattini & Vittorio de Benedetti), PH Emmanuel Lubezki, ED Don Zimmerman, M Maurice Jarre, PD David Gropman, AD Daniel Maltese, SD Denise Pizzini.

LP Keanu Reeves (Paul Sutton), Aitana Sanchez-Gijon (Victoria Aragon), Anthony Quinn (Don Pedro Aragon), Giancarlo Giannini (Alberto Aragon), Angleica Aragon (Marie Jose Aragon), Evangelina Elizondo (Guadelupe Aragon).

Shortly after WWII ends, vet Reeves is reluctantly on his way home to an unhappy marriage and a job he hates. He meets unmmarried, pregnant Sanchez-Gijon and agrees to pose as her husband when she goes to her Napa Valley home to break the news to her family. Papa Giannini is outraged, not about the baby but the "marriage." The two young pretenders fall in love and, after some difficult times, everything works out for the best, just like in a movie.

3131. *A Walk on the Moon* (1999, Miramax, 107m, c). D Tony Goldwyn, P Dustin Hoffman, Goldwyn, Jay Cohen, Neil Koenigsberger, Lee Gottsegen & Murray Schisgal, W Pamela Gray, PH Anthony Richmond, ED

Dana Congdon, M Mason Daring, PD Dan Leigh.

LP Diane Lane (Pearl Kantrowitz), Liev Schreiber (Marty Kantrowitz), Anna Paquin (Alison Kantrowitz), Viggo Mortensen (Walker Jerome), Tovah Feldshuh (Lilian Kantrowitz), Bobby Boriello (Bobby Kantrowitz).

In 1969, Lane is a seemingly happily married woman with two children, rebellious teen Paquin and little Boriello. But secretly she resents the fact that she missed the do-your-own-thing decade. When her husband Schreiber is unable to leave the city to be with them at their vacation cabin in the Catskills, she makes up for lost time with blouse salesman Mortensen. The effect of Lane's adultery makes up the film's second half. Lane, Paquin and Feldshuh are superb as women of three generations. Schreiber is a good guy whose only crime is that he's all-too-familiar and predictable. Mortensen makes a fine free spirit who allows Lane to briefly fly. There are no villains here. The film is a little gem.

3132. *Walking and Talking* (1996, Miramax, 83m, c). D & W Nicole Holofcener, P Ted Hope & James Schamus, PH Michael Spiller, ED Alisa Lepselter, M Billy Bragg, PD Anne Stuhler, AD Roswell Hamrick.

LP Catherine Keener (Amelia), Anne Heche (Laura), Liev Schreiber (Andrew), Todd Field (Frank), Kevin Corrigan (Bill), Randall Batinkoff (Peter).

The approach of Heche's marriage threatens to pull apart her long-time friendship with Keener. It's an interesting character study and examination of a friendship.

3133. *The Walking Dead* (1995, Savoy Pictures, 89m, c). D & W Preston A. Whitmore II, P Frank Price, George Jackson & Douglas McHenry, PH John Demps, ED William C. Carruth & Don Brochu, M Gary Chang, PD George Costello, AD Joseph M. Altadonna, SD Bill Cimino.

LP Allen Payne (PFC Cole Evans), Eddie Griffin (Pvt. Hoover Blanche), Joe Morton (Sgt. Barkley), Vonte Sweet (PFC Joe Brooks), Roger Floyd (Cpl. Pippins), Ion Overman (Shirley Evans).

There hasn't been a *Lost Patrol* film recently, so those of you clamoring for one — here it is. A squad of Marines in Vietnam must hack their way through the jungle, avoid the enemy and get back to safety.

3134. *The War* (1994, Universal, 127m, c). D Jon Avnet, P Avnet & Jordan Kerner, W Kathy McWhorter, PH Geoffrey Simpson, ED Debra Neil, M Thomas Newman, PD Kristi Zea, AD Jeremy Conway, SD Karen O'Hara.

LP Elijah Wood (Stu), Kevin Costner (Stephen), Mare Winningham (Lois), Lexi Randall (Lidia), Latoya Chisholm (Elvadine), Christopher Fennell (Billy), Charlotte Julius (Amber).

In a film attempting to teach peace and tolerance to youngsters, Costner is a Vietnam vet tortured by memories of the war. He has a tough time trying to teach his son to learn to live peacefully with a family of bullies rather than fight them.

3135. *The War at Home* (1996, Touchstone–Buena Vista, 124m, c). D Emilio Estevez, P Estevez, Brad Krevoy, Steve Stabler & James Duff, W Duff (based on his play *Home Front*), PH Peter Levy, ED Craig Bassett, M Basil Poledouris, PD Eve Cauley, SD Jeanette Scott.

LP Emilio Estevez (Jeremy Collier), Kathy Bates (Maurine Collier), Martin Sheen (Bob Collier), Kimberly Williams (Karen Collier), Corin Nemec (Donald), Ann Hearn (Music Teacher).

Estevez's family finds it impossible to deal with the fact that the boy who went off to war in Vietnam is forever changed. And Estevez has as much — or more — trouble dealing with his family's difficulty in accepting that he has changed.

3136. *The War Zone* (1999, U.K., Film Four, 98m, c). D Tim Roth, P Sarah Radclyffe & Dixie Linder, W Alexander Stuart (based on his novel), PH Seamus McGarvey, ED Trevor Waite, M Simon Boswell, PD Michael Carlin.

LP Ray Winstone (Dad), Tilda Swinton (Mum), Lara Belmont (Jessie), Freddie Cunliffe (Tom), Kate Ashfield (Lucy), Aisling O'Sullivan (Carol).

This depressing film is the story of a working-class family torn apart by incest and parental abuse. It is told from the point of view of 15-year-old Cunliffe. He discovers the terrible secret of his abusive father Winstone and his elder sister, the beautiful Belmont. Director

Roth maintains suspense as the film marches towards inevitable tragedy.

3137. *Warlock* (1991, Trimark, 102m, c). D & P Steve Miner, W David Twohy, PH David Eggby, ED David Finfer, M Jerry Goldsmith, PD Roy Forge Smith, AD Gary Steele, SD Jennifer Williams.

LP Ricard E. Grant (Giles Redferne), Julian Sands (The Warlock), Lori Singer (Kassandra), Kevin O'Brien (Chas), Mary Woronov (Channeller).

Just moments before powerful warlock Sands is to be executed in 1691, he's whisked (along with witchhunter Grant) three hundred years into the future. The two crash-land in Singer's Los Angeles home. Will justice finally be served?

3138. *Warlock: The Armageddon* (1993, Trimark Pictures, 98m, c). D Anthony Hickox, P Peter Abrams & Robert Levy, W Kevin Rock & Sam Bernard, PH Gerry Lively, PD Steve Hardie, AD John Chichester, SD David Koneff.

LP Julian Sands (Warlock), Christopher Young (Kenny Travis), Zach Galligan (Douglas), Joanne Pacula (Paula Dare), Paula Marshall (Samantha Ellison), Steve Kahan (Will Travis).

Well, Sands survived the first film. In this one he seeks six Druidic stones. They have the power to summon Satan's emissary if they land in the wrong hands — or to thwart the Devil if in the right hands. The keepers of the stones are a sect in a small California town.

3139. *Warriors of Virtue* (1997, MGM/UA, 103m, c). D Ronny Yu, P Dennis Law, Ronald Law, Christopher Law, Jeremy Law & Patricia Ruben, W Michael Vickerman & Hugh Kelley, PH Peter Pau, ED David Wu, M Don Davis, PD Eugenio Zanetti, AD Joseph P. Lucky & Deborah Ginsberg.

LP Angus MacFadyen (Komodo), Mario Yedidia (Ryan Jeffers), Marley Shelton (Elysia), Chao-Li Chi (Master Chung), Dennis Dun (Ming), Jack Tate (Yun), Doug Jones (Yee), Don W. Lewis (Lai/Major Keena).

It's the fantasy story of the struggle between good and evil which, because of its cinematic shortcomings, isn't likely to find much of an audience.

3140. *Washington Square* (1997, Hollywood Pictures–Buena Vista, 117m, c). D Agnieszka Holland, P Roger Birnbaum & Julie Bergman Sender, W Carol Doyle (based on the novel by Henry James), PH Jerzy Zielinski, ED David Siegel, M Jan A.P. Kaczmarek, PD Allan Starski, AD Alan E. Muraoka, SD William A. Cimino.

LP Jennifer Jason Leigh (Catherine Sloper), Albert Finney (Dr. Austin Sloper), Ben Chaplin (Morris Townsend), Maggie Smith (Aunt Lavinia Penniman), Judith Ivey (Aunt Elizabeth Almond), Betsy Brantley (Mrs. Montgomery).

This version of the Henry James novel has an excellent cast, all of who give fine performances. Still, those who believe that the performance of Olivia De Havilland in *The Heiress* (1949) was among the most Oscar-worthy efforts in film are bound to judge this film by that standard and find it somewhat wanting. But the James story of a wealthy, unattractive young woman, lacking in confidence and social skills, who finds a handsome young man courting her is still fascinating. Her father, a prominent physician, rightly suspects her beau is a fortune hunter and cruelly lets her know that no decent man would want her. From somewhere the young woman finds the character to punish both men who have so mistreated her.

3141. *Watch It* (1993, Skouras Pictures, 103m, c). D & W Tom Flynn, P Thomas J. Mangan IV, John C. McGinley & J. Christopher Burch, PH Stephen M. Katz, ED Dorian Harris, M Stanley Clarke, PD Jeff Steven Ginn, AD Barbara Kahn Kretschner, SD Martha Ring.

LP Peter Gallagher (John), John C. McGinley (Rick), Suzy Amis (Anne), Lili Taylor (Brenda), Jon Tenney (Michael), Cynthia Stevenson (Ellen).

Gallagher returns to Chicago and moves in with three self-absorbed buddies who play stupid post-adolescent games. As these escalate they turn nasty. Gallagher falls in love with veterinarian Amis but can't commit to her.

3142. *The Waterboy* (1998, Touchstone–Buena Vista, 88m, c). D Frank Coraci, P Robert Simonds & Jack Giarraputo, W Tim Herlihy & Adam Sandler, PH Steven Bernstein, ED Tom Lewis, M Alan Pasqua, PD

Perry Andelin Blake, AD Alan Au, SD Barbara Paterson.

LP Adam Sandler (Bobby Boucher), Kathy Bates (Mama Boucher), Henry Winkler (Coach Klein), Fairuza Balk (Vicki Vallencourt), Jerry Reed (Red Beaulieu), Larry Gilliard, Jr. (Derek Wallace).

Playing his usual socially retarded character, Sandler is the waterboy for a Louisiana college football team. It is discovered he has a special talent for tackling when he uses his pent-up anger. Sandler can live with the fact that many critics believe that his films are trash, since there are plenty of folks willing to pay cash to see the trash.

3143. The Waterdance (1992, Samuel Goldwyn Company, 106m, c). D Neal Jiminez & Michael Steinberg, P Gale Anne Hurd & Marie Cantin, W Jiminez, PH Mark Plummer, ED Jeff Freeman, M Michael Convertino, PD Bob Ziembicki.

LP Eric Stoltz (Joel Garcia), Wesley Snipes (Raymond Hill), William Forsythe (Bloss), Helen Hunt (Anna), Elizabeth Pena (Rosa), William Allen Young (Les).

This film deals unsentimentally with young novelist Stoltz who, after a hiking accident, becomes a paraplegic. He learns to adjust to his new limitations in a multi-ethnic rehabilitation center. The film will remind some of *The Men* (1950), starring Marlon Brando. The title refers to paraplegic Snipes' dream of dancing on water.

3144. Waterland (1992, U.K./U.S., Fine Line Features, 95m, c). D Stephen Gyllenhaal, P Katy McGuinness & Patrick Cassavetti, W Peter Prince (based on the novel by Grahm Swift), PH Robert Elswit, ED Lesley Walker, M Carter Burwell, PD Hugo Luczyc-Wyhowski, AD Helen Rayner.

LP Jeremy Irons (Tom Crick), Ethan Hawke (Mathew Price), Sinead Cusack (Mary Crick), John Heard (Lewis Scott), Grant Warnock (Young Tom), Lena Headley (Young Mary), David Morrissey (Dick Crick), Peter Postlethwaite (Henry Crick).

If a teacher in just about any school ever shared with his class all of the dark secrets of his troubled past, including incest, madness and murder, as does Irons in this film, he would surely be fired for not teaching what he was hired to teach. Perhaps the exposing of himself is therapeutic for the teacher, but shouldn't some space exist between instructor and students?

3145. Waterworld (1995, Universal, 134m, c). D Kevin Reynolds, P Charles Gordon, John A. Davis & Kevin Costner, W David Twohy, Peter Rader & Joss Whedon (uncredited), PH Dean Semler, ED Peter Boyle, M James Newton Howard, PD Dennis Gassner, AD David Klassen, SD Nancy Haigh.

LP Kevin Costner (Mariner), Dennis Hopper (Deacon), Jeanne Tripplehorn (Helen), Tina Majorina (Enola), Michael Jeter (Gregor), Gerard Murphy (Nord), R.D. Call (Enforcer).

Each year films compete for worst picture of the year. Most can be excluded from consideration because their aspirations are low and they achieved same. Any time Costner takes it upon himself to try to recapture the glory of *Dances with Wolves* (1990) by directing and starring in a film of his choosing, he puts himself in the running for the dubious honor, since he seems to believe he is making some kind of classic with an important message. This film is a classic stinker, with Costner giving another wooden performance, matched in ineptness by Tripplehorn. Hopper, seeing himself in a turkey, goes further over the edge than usual. The story, such as it is, takes place after the polar ice caps have melted, forcing surviving humans to live on water. Is it a myth or is it true that somewhere on the watery surface of the earth there is Dryland? Costner, as a mutant man-fish, may know, and the evil Hopper intends to find out.

3146. Wavelength (1995, Paramount–Dove Ent., 94m, c). D & W Benjamin Fry, P Fry & Andre Burgess, PH Chris Middleton, ED Clive Barrett, M Michael Storey, PD Caroline Greville-Morris, AD Rebecca Gillies & Steve Hudson.

LP Jeremy Piven (Paul Higgins), Kelli Williams (Claire Higgins), Liza Walker (Lucy Amore), James Villiers (James Mallinson), James Faulkner (Eric Amore), Byrne Piven (President), Richard Attenborough ("The Visitor").

Oxford professor Piven has a lovely wife, Williams, and a fun girlfriend, Walker. The pressures of his work and keeping two women satisfied is quite a strain. The only person he can turn to for help and understanding is mysterious Attenborough.

3147. *Wayne's World* (1992, Paramount, 95m, c). D Penelope Spheeris, P Lorne Michaels, W Mike Myers, Bonnie Turner & Terry Turner (based on characters created by Myers), PH Theo Van De Sande, ED Malcolm Campbell, M J. Peter Robinson, PD Gregg Fonseca, AD Bruce Miller, SD Jay Hart.

LP Mike Myers (Wayne Campbell), Dana Carvey (Garth Algar), Rob Lowe (Benjamin Oliver), Tia Carrere (Cassandra), Brian Doyle-Murray (Noah Vanderhoff), Lara Flynn Boyle (Stacy).

Based on a *Saturday Night Live* skit, the film follows the adventures of zany Myers and Carvey, two not-very-cool guys. They manage to endear themselves to audiences with their peculiar sayings about "babes" and various bodily functions. The film was a huge box-office hit. The story is of very little consequence.

3148. *Wayne's World 2* (1993, Paramount, 94m, c). D Stephen Surjik, P Lorne Michaels, W Mike Myers, Terry Turner & Bonnie Turner, PH Francis Kenny, ED Malcolm Campbell, M Carter Burwell, PD Greg Fonseca.

LP Mike Myers (Wayne Campbell), Dana Carvey (Garth Algar), Tia Carrere (Cassandra), Christopher Walken (Bobby Cahn), Heather Locklear (Herself), Ralph Brown (Del), Kevin Pollak (Jerry Segal), Olivia D'Abo (Betty Jo), Kim Basinger (Honey Hornee).

In this sequel, Myers and Carvey are back with their sophomoric but pleasant humor. Myers' girlfriend Carrere falls for slimy record producer Walken, as Wayne and Garth plan a major concert, "Waynestock." Look for Charlton Heston in a funny cameo.

3149. *Wedding Band* (1990, IRS Media, 82m, c). D Daniel Raskov, P John Schouweiler & Tino Insana, W Insana, PH Christian Sebaldt, ED Jonas Thaler, M Steve Hunter, PD Tori Nourafchan, AD Michael Thomas, SD Lucie Munoz.

LP William Katt (Marshall Roman), Joyce Hyser (Karla Thompson), Tino Insana (Hugh Bowmont), Lance Kinsey (Ritchie), David Bowe (Max).

A rock 'n' roll band plays at a series of weddings. It's a modest comedy.

3150. *Wedding Band* (1999, Bird Wolf Prod., 95m, c). D & W Martin Guigui, P Bill Henne, PH Massimo Zeri, ED Mark Grossman, M Charlie Midnight.

LP Deborah Gibson (Lisa Weinstein), Joey Scherr (Bobby Benigni), Martin Guigui (Max Tune), Kelly Bishop (Sylvia Weinstein), Les Shenkel (Irving Weinstein), Dom DeLuise (The Priest), Bernard Sanders (The Rabbi).

At the Jewish-Italian wedding of Gibson and Scherr, the bridal party, the guests and even the wedding singer share a lot of guilty secrets about the bride and groom.

3151. *Wedding Bell Blues* (1997, BMG Independents/Legacy Releasing, 111m, c). D Dana Lustig, P Ram Bergman, Mike Curb, Lustig & Carole Curb Nemoy, W Annette Goliti Gutierrez (based on a story by Gutierrez & Lustig), PH Kent L. Wakeford, ED Caroline Ross, M Tal Bergman & Paul Christian Gordon, PD Shay Austin, SD Lori Noyes.

LP Paulina Porizkova (Tanya), Illeana Douglas (Jasmine), Julie Warner (Micki), John Corbett (Cary), Jonathan Penner (Matt), Charles Martin Smith (Oliver), Richard Edson (Tom), Debbie Reynolds (Herself).

Roommates Porizkova, Douglas and Warner have all had bad experiences with men. Deciding they are sick of their circumstances, and wanting revenge on the male sex, they decide to head to Las Vegas, find three guys, marry them and immediately divorce 'them, all in the same day. Yeah, that'll show 'em!

3152. *The Wedding Gift* (GB: *Wide Eyed and Legless*) (1994, U.K., Miramax, 90m, c). D Richard Loncraine, P David Lascelles, W Jack Rosenthal (based on the books *Diana's Story* and *Lost for Words* by Deric Longden), PH Remi Adefarasin, ED Ken Pearce, M Colin Towns, PD Tony Burrough, AD Peter Findley.

LP Julie Walters (Diana Longden), Jim Broadbent (Deric Longden), Thora Hird (Deric's Mother), Sian Thomas (Aileen Armitage), Andrew Lancel (Nick Longden).

Convinced that her mysterious illness is going to take her life, Walters sets out to find a new wife for her husband Broadbent. Despite the tragedy in the story, the film has a great deal of charm and humor.

3153. *The Wedding Singer* (1998, New Line Cinema, 96m, c). D Frank Coraci, P

Robert Simonds & Brad Grey, W Tim Herlihy, PH Tim Suhrstedt, ED Tom Lewis, M Teddy Castellucci, PD Perry Andelin Blake, AD Alan Au, SD Lisa Deutsch.

LP Adam Sandler (Robbie Hart), Drew Barrymore (Julia Sullivan), Christine Taylor (Holly), Allen Covert (Sammy), Mathew Glave (Glen Gulia), Ellen Albertine Dow (Rosie), Angela Featherstone (Linda), Alexis Arquette (George), Jon Lovitz (Jimmie Moore), Steve Buscemi (David).

This is Sandler's best comic venture to date. Of course, that's only a matter of relativity. In this picture he tones down his usual imbecilic behavior. Sandler's occupation is given in the film's title. He saves Barrymore from the tragic mistake of marrying boorish womanizer Glave. Well, it's the least he can do after being stood up at his own wedding. The team of Sandler and Barrymore are no Tom Hanks and Meg Ryan, but they mesh rather nicely in this modest romantic farce.

3154.   *Weekend at Bernie's II* (1993, Tri-Star, 89m, c). D & W Robert Klane, P Victor Drai & Joseph Perez, PH Edward Morey III & Frank M. Holgate, ED Peck Prior, PD Michael Bolton, AD Eric Fraser, SD Scott Jacobson & Beth Kushnick.

LP Andrew McCarthy (Larry Wilson), Jonathan Silverman (Richard Parker), Terry Kiser (Bernie Lomax), Troy Beyer (Claudia), Barry Bostwick (Hummel), Tom Wright (Charles), Steve James (Henry), Novella Nelson (Mobu).

Kiser died in the 1989 *Weekend at Bernie's*, but his cadaver is as lively in this sequel as it was in the original. Now let's take a poll to see who cares. Get buried Bernie, you're dead.

3155.   *Welcome Home, Roxy Carmichael* (1990, Paramount, 98m, c). D Jim Abrahams, P Penney Finkelman Cox, W Karen Leigh Hopkins, PH Paul Elliott, ED Bruce Green, M Thomas Newman, PD Dena Roth, AD John Myhre, Rosemary Brandenburg & Nina Ruscio, SD Richard G. Huston & James A. Gelarden.

LP Winona Ryder (Dinky Bossetti), Jeff Daniels (Denton Webb), Laila Robins (Elizabeth Zaks), Thomas Wilson Brown (Gerald Howells), Frances Fisher (Roshelle Bossetti), Graham Beckel (Leo Bossetti), Dinah Manoff (Evelyn Whittacher), Ava Fabian (Roxy Carmichael).

When it's announced that beautiful, glamorous Hollywood actress Fabian is returning to her small Ohio home town, everyone is quite excited. None more so than moody teen Ryder, who fantasizes that the star is her mother. Few bothered to visit this film during its theatrical release — and for good reason.

3156.   *Welcome to Hollywood* (1998, Stone Canyon Ent., 89m, c). D Tony Markes & Adam Rifkin, P Zachary Matz & Markes, W Shawn Ryan & Markes, PH Kramer Morgenthau, Rob Bennett, Nick Mendoza & Howard Wexler, ED Jane Kurson, M Justin Reinhardt.

LP Tony Markes (Anton Markwell, aka Nick Decker), Adam Rifkin (Adam Rifkin), Angie Everhart (Angie Everhart), David Andriole (David Lake), Cameoes by Nicolas Cage, Jeff Goldblum, John Travolta, Laurence Fishburne, Will Smith, Cuba Gooding.

The premise is that real-life director Rifkin is going to make a documentary about the career of a real-life actor as he rises from obscurity to stardom. In this occasionally amusing comedy, his leading man is Markes.

3157.   *Welcome to Sarajevo* (1997, U.K./U.S., Miramax, 100m, c). D Michael Winterbottom, P Graham Broadbent & Damian Jones, W Frank Cottrell Boyce (based on the book *Natasha's Story* by Michael Nicholson), PH Daf Hobson, ED Trevor Waite, M Adrian Johnson, PD Mark Geraghty.

LP Stephen Dillane (Michael Henderson), Woody Harrelson (Flynn), Marisa Tomei (Nina), Emira Nusevic (Emira), Kerry Fox (Jane Carson), Goran Visnjic (Risto), James Nesbitt (Gregg), Emily Lloyd (Annie McGee).

Inspired by the experiences of a British journalist, this film brilliantly examines the relationship between jaded reporters and the brave people of Sarajevo under siege in 1992. The inhabitants desperately attempt to find some normality in their lives. The reporters wait for the next episode of death and carnage. The reporters, as represented by Dillane and Harrelson, find that remaining unflappable and professionally uninvolved is impossible. TV newsman Dillane risks his life and career to smuggle young Nusevic out of the country and to his home in England. It's a stunning work, both tragic and uplifting.

3158. Welcome to the Dollhouse (1996, Sony Pictures Classics, 87m, c). D, P & W Todd Solondz, PH Randy Drummond, ED Alan Oxman, M Jill Wisoff, PD Susan Block, AD Lori Solondz.

LP Heather Matarazzo (Dawn Wiener), Brendan Sexton, Jr. (Brandon McCarthy), Daria Kalinina (Miss Wiener), Matthew Faber (Mark Wiener), Angela Pietropinto (Mrs. Wiener), Eric Mabius (Steve Rodgers), Bill Buell (Mr. Wiener).

Awkward, unattractive 11-year-old Matarazzo suffers mistreatment at school and at home. She is convinced that her parents prefer her siblings. She's not very likeable, but she has a certain toughness to her that allows her to survive.

3159. Welcome to Woop Woop (1997, U.K./Australia, Goldwyn Films–MGM, 103m, c). D Stephan Elliott, P Finola Dwyer, W Michael Thomas (based on the book *The Dead Heart* by Douglas Kennedy), PH Mike Molley, ED Martin Walsh, M Stewart Copeland, PD Owen Paterson, AD Colin Gibson.

LP Jonathan Schaech (Teddy), Rod Taylor (Daddy O), Susie Porter (Angie), Dee Smart (Krystal), Barry Humphries (Bling Wally), Richard Moir (Reggie), Mark Wilson (Duffy), Paul Mercurio (Midget).

New York con man Schaech travels to a remote Australian outback town to escape his troubles. Along the way he meets sexy hitchhiker Porter. At the community of Woop Woop the alcoholic residents make dog food from kangaroos. Everyone is welcomed to the community, but none may leave.

3160. We're Back! A Dinosaur's Story (1993, Universal, 78m, c). D Dick Zondag, Ralph Zondag, Phil Nibbelink & Simon Wells, P Stephen Hickner, W John Patrick Shanley (based on the children's book *We're Back* by Hudson Talbott), M James Horner, AD Neil Ross.

LP Voices: John Goodman (Rex), Blaze Berdahl (Buster), Rhea Perlman (Mother Bird), Jay Leno (Vorb), Rene LeVant (Woo), Felicity Kendal (Elsa).

In this animated feature, a pack of revived dinosaurs return to their old stomping ground, which presently is New York City. The dinos are taught how to survive in the canyons of the city by a couple of kids.

3161. We're Talkin' Serious Money (1992, CineTel Films, 104m, c). D James Lemmo, P Paul Hertzberg, W Lemmo & Leo Rossi, PH Jacques Haitkin, ED Steve Nevius, M Scott Grusin, PD Dins Danielson, AD Susan Benjamin, SD Mary Buri.

LP Leo Rossi (Charlie), Dennis Farina (Sal), Fran Drescher (Valerie), John LaMotta (Gino the Grocer), Peter Iacangelo (Frankie the Beast), Catherine Paolone (Rosemarie), Robert Costanzo (Michael).

Two small-time con men borrow $10,000 from the mob to run a scam. When it goes sour, they have both the mob and the FBI on their trail.

3162. Werewolf (1997, A-Pix Ent., 95m, c). D & P Tony Zarindast, W Zarindast & Brad Hornbacher, PH Robert Hayes & Dan Gilman, ED Peter Taylor, M Keith Bilderbeck, PD George Pierson.

LP George Rivero (Yuri), Fred Cavalli (Paul Niles), Adrianna Miles (Natalie Burke), Richard Lynch (Professor Noel), Joe Estevez (Joel).

An archaeological team, led by Lynch, unearths the skelton of an anient native creature, similar to a werewolf, with predictable results.

3163. Wes Craven's New Nightmare (AKA: *Nightmare on Elm Street 7*) (1994, New Line, 112m, c). D & W Wes Craven, P Marianne Maddelena, PH Mark Irwin, ED Patrick Lussier, M J. Peter Robinson, PD Cynthia Charette, AD Troy Sizemore & Diane McKinnon, SD Stephen Alesch & Ruby Guidara.

LP Robert Englund (Himself/Freddie Krueger), Heather Langenkamp (Herself), Miko Hughes (Dylan), David Newsom (Chase Porter), Jeffrey John Davis (Freddy's Hand Double), Matt Winston (Chuck), Rob LaBelle (Terry), Wes Craven (Himself).

With this movie-in-a-movie, Craven is able to reunite cast members of the earlier *Nightmare on Elm Street* films with the movie's fictional character Freddie Krueger, who, through supernatural force, is able to pass from the reel to the real. The ghoulish feast has all the violence and terror the fans of the series have come to expect.

3164. Wet and Wild Summer (1993, Australia, Trimark Pictures, 95m, c). D Maurice Murphy, P & W Phillip Avalon, PH Martin McGrath, M John Capek.

LP Christopher Atkins (Bobby McCain), Elliott Gould (Mike McCain), Lois Larimore (Mrs. McCain), Richard Caret (Al Eastman), Rebecca Cross (Julie).

Lifeguard hunks and sexy resort guests frolic at a topless beach.

3165. What About Bob? (1991, Touchstone–Buena Vista, 97m, c). D Frank Oz, P Laura Ziskin, W Tom Schulman (based on a story by Alvin Sargent & Ziskin), PH Michael Ballhaus, ED Anne V. Coates, M Miles Goodman, PD Les Dilley, AD Jack Blackman, SD Anne Kuljian.

LP Bill Murray (Bob Wiley), Richard Dreyfuss (Doctor Leo Marvin), Charlie Korsmo (Siggy Marvin), Julie Hagerty (Fay Marvin), Kathryn Erbe (Anna Marvin), Tom Aldredge (Mr. Guttman), Susan Willis (Mrs. Guttman).

When his psychiatrist (Dreyfuss) goes on vacation, helplessly neurotic Murray follows and almost drives the Doc to mayhem against his patient. To make matters worse for the shrink, his wife and children think Murray is quite sweet. Lightweight stuff.

3166. What Becomes the Broken Hearted? (1999, New Zealand, Polygram Filmed Ent., 102m, c). D Ian Mune, P Bill Gavin, W Alan Duff (based on his novel), PH Allen Guilford, ED Michael Horton, M David Hirschfelder, PD Brett Schwieters.

LP Temuera Morrison (Jake Heke), Clint Eruera (Sonny Heke), Nancy Brunning (Tania Rogers), Pete Smith (Apelman), Lawrence Makoare (Grunt).

This powerful film deals with gang warfare among New Zealand's Maori population. Actually, it could be of gang wars just about anywhere.

3167. What Dreams May Come (1998, Polygram Films, 113m, c). D Vincent Ward, P Stephen Simon & Barnet Bain, W Ron Bass (based on the novel by Richard Matheson), PH Eduardo Serra, ED David Brenner & Maysie Hoy, M Michael Kamen, PD Eugenio Zanetti†, AD Thomas Voth & Christian Wintter, SD Cindy Carr†.

LP Robin Williams (Chris Nielsen), Cuba Gooding, Jr. (Albert), Annabella Sciorra (Annie Nielsen), Max Von Sydow (The Tracker), Jessica Brooks Grant (Marie Nielsen), Josh Paddock (Ian Nielsen), Rosalind Chao (Leona).

This film takes place in the "after-life." Deceased Williams won't accept the fact that because his depressed wife Sciorra committed suicide after his death and those of their children, they can't be together for eternity. The film came in and went out of theaters so quickly that most missed it — probably intentionally.

3168. What Happened Was... (1994, Samuel Goldwyn, 90m, c). D & W Tom Noonan (based on his play), P Robin O'Hara & Scott Macaulay, PH Joe DeSalvo, ED Richard Arrley, M Lodovico Sorret, PD Dan Ouelette, SD Andra Kanegson.

LP Tom Noonan (Michael), Karen Sillas (Jackie).

In this two-person drama, paralegal Noonan and law secretary Sillas get together for their first date, and before the evening is out they bare their souls.

3169. Whatever (1998, Sony Pictures Classics, 112m, c). D & W Susan Skoog, P Ellin Baumel, Michelle Yahn, Kevin Segalla & Skoog, PH Michael Barrow & Michael Mayers, ED Sandi Guthrie, PD Dina Goldman.

LP Liza Weil (Anna Stockard), Chad Morgan (Brenda Talbot), Kathryn Rossetter (Carol Stockard), Frederic Forrest (Mr. Chaminsky), Gary Wolf (Eddie).

Weil does a nice job portraying a teen about to make the transition from adolescence to adulthood.

3170. Whatever Happened to Harold Smith? (1999, U.K., UIP, 94m, c). D Pete Hewitt, P Ruth Jackson & David Brown, W Ben Steiner, PH David Tattersall, ED Martin Walsh, M Rupert Gregson-Williams, PD Gemma Jackson, AD David Warren.

LP Tom Courtenay (Harold Smith), Stephen Fry (Dr. Peter Robinson), Michael Legge (Vince Smith), Laura Fraser (Joanna Robinson), Lulu (Irene Smith), David Thewlis (Nesbit).

This film unsuccessfully attempts to blend two stories. In one teenager Legge practices his John Travolta Saturday Night Fever impersonation. But he is too shy to ask Fraser out on a date, despite his strong lust for her. The other is about Courtenay, Legge's father, who unexpectedly develops kinetic brain powers that cause him a great deal of trouble.

3171. What's Eating Gilbert Grape? (1993, Paramount, 117m, c). D Lasse Hallstrom, P Meir Teper, Bertil Ohlsson & David Matalon, W Peter Hedges (based on his novel), PH Sven Nykvist, ED Andrew Mondshein, M Alan Parker & Bjorn Isfalt, PD Bernt Capra.

LP Johnny Depp (Gilbert Grape), Juliette Lewis (Becky), Leonardo DiCaprio† (Arnie Grape), Mary Steenburgen (Betty Carver), Crispin Glover (Bobby McBurney), John C. Reilly (Tucker Van Dyke), Darlene Cates (Momma).

In this offbeat film, Depp is the titular head of a dysfunctional family consisting of his mother Cates, who weighs more than 500 pounds, his mentally retarded 17-year-old brother DiCaprio and two constantly fighting teenage sisters. Depp is having an affair with married Steenburgen, but is quickly hooked by Lewis when she is stranded in their small Midwestern town. It's a strange, sad story, but the performances save the film from its going-nowhere story.

3172. What's Love Got to Do with It (1993, Touchstone–Buena Vista, 120m, c). D Brian Gibson, P Doug Chapin & Barry Frost, W Kate Lanier (based on the autobiography *I, Tina* by Tina Turner & Kurt Loder), PH Jamie Anderson, ED Lisa Day, Stuart Pappe, Dave Rawlins, Michael J. Hill & Thomas G. Finnan, M Stanley Clarke, PD Stephen Altman, AD Richard Johnson, SD Rick Simpson.

LP Angela Bassett† (Tina Turner), Laurence Fishburne† (Ike Turner), Jenifer Lewis (Zelma Bullock), Phyllis Yvonne Stickney (Alline Bullock), Rae'ven Kelly (Young Anna Mae).

Tina Turner is one sexy woman with a powerful voice. Basset does a superb job in this biopic. She is discovered by Fishburne, in an impressive portrayal of Ike Turner. His initial charm grows chilling, leading to an abusive relationship from which the singer finally escapes and moves on to even more show business glory.

3173. When a Man Loves a Woman (1994, Touchstone–Buena Vista, 125m, c). D Luis Mandoki, P Jordan Kerner & Jon Avnet, W Ron Blass & Al Franken, PH Lajos Koltai, ED Garth Craven, M Zbigniew Preisner, PD Stuart Wurtzel, AD Steven A. Saklad, SD Kara Lindstrom & Stan Troop.

LP Andy Garcia (Michael Green), Meg Ryan (Alice Green), Ellen Burstyn (Emily), Tina Majorino (Jess Green), Mae Whitman (Casey Green), Lauren Tom (Amy), Philip Seymour Hoffman (Gary).

Ryan is married to loving husband Garcia, has two sweet young daughters and a hidden alcohol problem. Garcia learns that her problem is just as much his, while she tries to return to sobriety.

3174. When Night Is Falling (1995, Canada, October Films, 94m, c). D & W Patricia Rozema, P Barbara Tranter, PH Douglas Koch, ED Susan Shipton, M Lesley Barber, PD John Dondertman, SD Megan Less & Rob Hepburn.

LP Pascale Bussieres (Camille), Rachael Crawford (Petra), Henry Czerny (Martin), David Fox (Reverend DeBoer), Don McKellar (Timothy).

Bussieres, a Toronto professor of mythology, is engaged to theologian Czerny. She meets Crawford, a trapeze artist with a traveling circus. The two women fall in love. Now she must decide what and who she wants in her life.

3175. When the Party's Over (1993, Strand Releasing, 115m, c). D Matthew Irmas, P Ann Wycoff & James Holt, W Wycoff (based on the story by Wycoff & Irmas), PH Alicia Weber, ED Dean Goodhill & Jerry Bixmai, M Joe Romano, PD John Gary Steele.

LP Elizabeth Berridge (Frankie), Rae Dawn Chong (M.J.), Sandra Bullock (Amanda), Kris Kamm (Banks), Brian McNamara (Taylor), Fisher Stevens (Alexander).

Three women and a gay man share a house and each others' empty lives.

3176. When Time Expires (1998, Regent Ent.–Evergreen, 93m, c). D & W David Bourla, P Larry Estes, PH Dean Lent, ED Bruce Wescott, M Todd Hayden, PD Stuart Blatt, SD Melissa Levander.

LP Richard Grieco (Travis Beck), Cynthia Geary (June Kelly), Mark Hamill (Bill Thermot), Tim Thomerson (Rifkin Koss), Ron Masak (TV Evangelist).

Space traveler Grieco must intervene in the past to prevent a nuclear war.

3177. *Where Angels Fear to Tread* (1992, U.K., Fine Line Features, 112m, c). D Charles Sturridge, P Derek Granger, W Tim Sullivan, Granger & Sturridge (based on the novel by E.M. Forster), PH Michael Coulter, ED Peter Coulson, M Rachel Portman, PD Simon Holland, AD Luigi Marchione & Marianne Ford.

LP Helena Bonham Carter (Caroline Abbott), Judy Davis (Harriet Herriton), Rupert Graves (Philip Herriton), Giovanni Guidelli (Gino Carella), Barbara Jefford (Mrs. Herriton), Helen Mirren (Lilia Herriton).

Based on Forster's first novel, this film is the story of repressed sexuality breaking loose. Fortyish British widow Mirren travels to Italy at the urging of her in-laws. There she dallies with and then marries 21-year-old Guidelli — with disastrous consequences. The performances, especially that of Bonham Carter as Mirren's traveling companion, are more impressive than the story and its presentation. Bonham Carter seems born to appear in costume pictures of times gone by.

3178. *Where Sleeping Dogs Lie* (1993, TriStar, 89m, c). D Charles Finch, P Mario Sotela & Finch, W Finch & Yolande Turner, PH Monty Rowan, ED B.J. Sears & Gene M. Gemaine, M Hans Zimmer & Mark Mancina, PD Eve Cauley, AD Lisa Snyder, SD Anthony Stabley.

LP Dylan McDermott (Bruce Simmons), Tom Sizemore (Eddie Hale), Sharon Stone (Serena Black), Joan Chen (Sara), Kristen Hocking (Marlee), William Edward Lewis (Short Man/Dwarf).

Struggling writer McDermott moves into the abandoned home where five years earlier a wealthy family was murdered. His investigation of the case gets a boost when stranger Sizemore comes along and reveals things that only the murderer could know.

3179. *Where the Day Takes You* (1992, New Line Cinema, 92m, c). D Mark Rocco, P Paul Hertzberg, W Michael Hitchcock, Kurt Voss & Rocco, PH King Baggot, ED Russell Livingstone, M Mark Morgan, PD Kirk Petrucelli.

LP Dermot Mulroney (King), Lara Flynn Boyle (Heather), Balthazar Getty (Little J.), Sean Astin (Greg), James LeGros (Crasher), Ricki Lake (Brenda), Kyle MacLachlan (Ted), Peter Dobson (Tommy Ray).

Mulroney is the slightly older leader of a group of runaways trying to survive on Hollywood Boulevard. He tries to protect the younger kids and prevent them from becoming involved in the violence and drugs that they live among. He falls for newcomer Boyle, but their romance hasn't much of a chance due to the squalid conditions in which they live.

3180. *Where the Heart Is* (1990, Touchstone–Buena Vista, 94m, c). D & P John Boorman, W John Boorman & Telsche Boorman, PH Peter Suschitzky, ED Ian Crafford, M Peter Martin, PD Carol Spier, AD James McAteer & Susan Kaufman.

LP Dabney Coleman (Stewart McBain), Uma Thurman (Daphne McBain), Joanna Cassidy (Jean McBain), Crispin Glover (Lionel), Suzy Amis (Chloe McBain), Christopher Plummer (Homeless Gent), David Hewlett (Jimmy McBain).

Wealthy demolitions expert Coleman decides to teach his family the value of money. He forces them out onto the streets to join the homeless. Well-intentioned, but a big disappointment.

3181. *Where the Red Fern Grows, Part 2* (1994, VCI Communications, 93m, c). D & P Jim McCullough, W Samuel Bradford, PH Joe Wilcots, M Robert Sprayberry.

LP Doug McKeon (Billy Coleman), Wilfrod Brimley (Grandpa Will), Chad McQueen (Rainie Pritchard), Lisa Welchel (Coleman), Adam Faraizl (Wilson).

This sequel to the very popular family movie of 1974 stars Brimley as a wise grandfather. Set deep in the Louisiana woods, it's the sweet coming-of-age story of McKeon, a veteran who lost a leg in WWII.

3182. *Where the Rivers Flow North* (1994, Caledonia Pictures, 111m, c). D Jay Craven, P Bess O'Brien, W Craven & Don Bredes (based on the novel by Howard Frank Mosher), PH Paul Ryan, ED Barbara Tulliver, PD David Wasco, SD Sandy Wasco.

LP Rip Torn (Noel Lord), Tantoo Cardinal (Bangor), Bill Raymond (Wayne Quinn), Michael J. Fox (Clayton Farnsworth), Treat Williams (Champ's Manager), Amy Wright (Loose Woman).

In 1927 Vermont, logger Torn is at odds with his housekeeper-lover Cardinal over selling his land to the power company. She wants them to take the money and move on. He's reluctant to change the only life he's ever known.

3183. *While You Were Sleeping* (1995, Hollywood Pictures–Buena Vista, 100m, c). D Jon Turtelaub, P Joe Roth & Roger Birnbaum, W Daniel G. Sullivan & Fredric Lebow, PH Phedon Papamichael, ED Bruce Green, M Randy Edelman, PD Garreth Stover, AD Chris Cornwell, SD Larry Dias.

LP Sandra Bullock (Lucy Moderatz), Bill Pullman (Jack), Peter Gallagher (Peter), Peter Boyle (Ox), Jack Warden (Saul), Glynis Johns (Elsie), Michael Rispoli (Joe, Jr.), Jason Bernard (Jerry), Ally Walker (Ashley Bacon).

Lonely token-seller Bullock has a thing for handsome commuter Gallagher. When he is mugged on the train platform she rescues him. Since he's unconscious, she goes with him to the hospital. There she is mistaken for his fiancée. She meets Gallagher's family who, saddened by Gallagher's coma, are nevertheless delighted to meet his lover. The exception to this is Pullman, Gallagher's brother, who suspects things are not what they seem. As he probes into his brother's relationship with Bullock he falls for her himself. What will happen when Gallagher comes out of the coma? Do we have to draw you a picture?

3184. *Whispers* (1990, Canada, Cinepix–ITC Ent., 93m, c). D Douglas Jackson, P John Dunning & Don Carmody, W Anita Doohan (based on the novel by Dean R. Koontz), PH Peter Benison, ED Jacques Jean, M Fred Mollin, PD Charles Dunlop.

LP Victoria Tennant (Hilary Thomas), Jean Leclerc (Bruno Clavell), Chris Sarandon (Sergeant Tony Clemenza), Linda Sorenson (Kayla).

When L.A. writer Tennant is unexpecetedly and viciously threatened by landowner Leclerc, a man she barely knows, she is forced to kill him. But the police don't believe her when sources place Leclerc hundreds of miles away at the time. Sure enough, he's not dead.

3185. *Whispers in the Dark* (1992, Paramount, 107m, c). D & W Christopher Crowe, P Martin Bregman & Michael S. Bregman, PH Michael Chapman, ED Bill Pankow, M

Thomas Newman, PD John Jay Moore, SD Justin Scoppa, Jr.

LP Annabella Sciorra (Ann Hecker), Jamey Sheridan (Doug McDowell), Anthony LaPaglia (Detective Morgenstern), Jill Clayburgh (Sarah Green), John Leguizamo (Fast Johnny C.), Deborah Unger (Eve Abergray), Anthony Heald (Paul), Alan Alda (Leo Green).

Psychiatrist Sciorra discovers that two of her patients, Leguizamo, an ex-con with a violent nature towards women, and art gallery saleswoman Unger, have been engaging in kinky sexual experiences. Then Unger is murdered. Leguizamo looks like a likely suspect, but there are many others.

3186. *White Fang* (1991, Walt Disney–Buena Vista, 104m, c). D Randal Kleiser, P Marykay Powell, W Jeanne Rosenberg, Nick Thiel & David Fallon (based on the novel by Jack London), PH Tony Pierce-Roberts, ED Lisa Day, M Basil Poledouris, PD Michael Bolton, AD Sandy Cochrane, SD Brian Kasch.

LP Klaus Maria Brandauer (Alex), Ethan Hawke (Jack), Seymour Cassel (Skunker), Susan Hogan (Belinda), James Remar (Beauty), Bill Mosely (Luke), Clint B. Youngreen (Tinker), Pius Savage (Grey Beaver).

In Alaska during the Gold Rush, young Hawke befriends a wolf-dog. It's the third film version of the Jack London classic tale.

3187. *White Fang 2: Myth of the White Wolf* (1994, Walt Disney–Buena Vista, 106m, c). D Ken Olin, P Preston Fischer, W David Fallon, PH Hiro Narita, ED Elba Sanchez-Short, M John Debney, PD Cary White, AD Glen W. Pearson, SD Tedd Kuchera.

LP Scott Bairstow (Henry Casey), Ethan Hawke (Jack, uncredited), Charmaine Craig (Lily Joseph), Al Harrington (Moses Joseph), Anthony Michael Ruivivar (Peter), Alfred Molina (Rev. Leland Drury), Geoffrey Lewis (Heath).

White boy Bairstow and his wolf-dog lead a starving Native American tribe to food during the Alaskan Gold Rush.

3188. *White Hunter, Black Heart* (1990, Warner Bros., 112m, c). D & P Clint Eastwood, W Peter Viertel, James Bridges & Burt Kennedy (based on the novel by Viertel), PH Jack N. Green, ED Joel Cox, M Lennie Niehaus, PD

John Graysmark, AD Tony Reading, SD Peter Howitt.

LP Clint Eastwood (John Wilson), Jeff Fahey (Pete Verrill), Charlotte Cornwell (Miss Wilding), Norman Lumsden (Butler George), George Dzundza (Paul Landers), Edward Tudor Pole (Reissar).

This film is inspired by writer Viertel's experiences with John Huston during the location shooting of *The African Queen* (1951). Eastwood is a movie director more interested in shooting an elephant than in shooting his picture.

3189. *White Light* (1991, Academy Ent., 96m, c). D Al Waxman, P Anthony Kramreither, W Ron Base, PH Burt Dunk, ED David Nicholson, M Paul Zaza, AD Ray Lorenz, SD Csaba Kertesz.

LP Martin Kove (Sean Craig), Allison Hossack (Rachel Rutledge), George Sperdakos (David Ramon), Martha Henry (Ella Wingwright), James Purcell (Bill Dockerty).

After a near-death experience in which he encounters beautiful blonde Hossack, Kove tries to find out who she is or was.

3190. *White Man's Burden* (1995, Savoy Pictures, 89m, c). D & W Desmond Nakano, P Lawrence Bender, PH Willy Kurant, ED Nancy Richardson, M Howard Shore, PD Naomi Shohan, AD John Ivo Gilles, SD Evette F. Siegel.

LP John Travolta (Pinnock), Harry Belafonte (Thaddeus), Kelly Lynch (Marsha), Margaret Avery (Megan), Tom Bower (Stanley), Andrew Lawrence (Donnie).

How would you like it if you were white in a society in which the blacks have the power and wealth, and whites are treated by the dominating blacks like, well, like blacks are treated by whites in the real world. Filled with all kinds of reverse stereotypes, the film is too contrived to adequately sell its message.

3191. *White Men Can't Jump* (1992, 20th Century–Fox, 115m, c). D & W Ron Shelton, P Don Miller & David Lester, PH Russell Boyd, ED Paul Seydor & Kimberly Ray, M Bennie Wallace, PD Dennis Washington, AD Roger Fortune, SD Robert R. Benton.

LP Wesley Snipes (Sidney Deane), Woody Harrelson (Billy Hoyle), Rosie Perez (Gloria Clemente), Tyra Ferrell (Rhonda Deane), Cylk Cozart (Robert), Kadeem Hardison (Junior).

Black Snipes and white Harrelson team up to hustle some bucks on playground basketball courts. If basketball isn't your thing and you don't care for a steady stream of obscenities, there's not much here for you.

3192. *White Palace* (1990, Universal, 103m, c). D Luis Mandoki, P Mark Rosenberg, Amy Robinson & Griffin Dunne, W Ted Tally & Alvin Sargent (based on the novel by Glenn Savan), PH Lajos Koltai, ED Carol Littleton, M George Fenton, PD Jeannine Claudia Oppewall, AD John Wright Stevens, SD Lisa Fischer.

LP Susan Sarandon (Nora Baker), James Spader (Max Baron), Jason Alexander (Neil Horowitz), Kathy Bates (Rosemary Powers), Eileen Brennan (Judy), Steven Hill (Sol Horowitz), Rachel Levin (Rachel Horowitz).

Widowed young Jewish lawyer Spader develops a yen for older, less educated hamburger waitress Sarandon. Let's see, what is the romance up against? Age. Religion. Education. Social Status. Good thing Sarandon supplies Spader with plenty of hot sex.

3193. *White Sands* (1992, Warner Bros., 101m, c). D Roger Donaldson, P William Sackheim & Scott Rudin, W Daniel Pyne, PH Peter Menzies, Jr., ED Nicholas Beauman, M Patrick O'Hearn, PD John Graysmark, AD Michael Rizzo, SD Michael Seriton.

LP Willem Dafoe (Ray Dolezal), Mary Elizabeth Mastrantonio (Lane Bodine), Mickey Rourke (Gorman Lennox), Samuel L. Jackson (Greg Meeker), Mimi Rogers (Molly), M. Emmet Walsh (Bert Gibson).

When sheriff Dafoe finds a dead stiff at a remote Indian reservation clutching a gun and a briefcase containing half-a-million dollars, he decides to take the dead man's identity and see where it leads him. It takes him to wealthy Mastrantonio, who buys black market weapons. FBI agent Jackson uses Dafoe as bait to catch Rourke, an ex–CIA agent turned arms dealer. It's a confusing mess.

3194. *White Squall* (1996, Hollywood Pictures–Buena Vista, 128m, c). D Ridley Scott, P Mimi Polk Gitlin & Rocky Lang, W Todd Robinson, PH Hugh Johnson, ED Gerry Hambling, M Jeff Rona, PD Peter J. Hampton & Leslie Tomkins.

LP Jeff Bridges (Christopher Sheldon), Caroline Goodall (Dr. Alice Sheldon), John Savage (McCrea), Scott Wolf (Chuck Gieg), Jeremy Sisto (Frank Beaumont), Ryan Phillippe (Gil Martin), David Lascher (Robert March), Eric Michael Cole (Dean Preston).

Bridges is put on trial for criminal incompetence when several of his young charges are killed in a sudden storm in the Caribbean. It's based on the true story of the adventures of 13 young men who were students at Ocean Academy. The curriculum consisted of a year-long adventure aboard the brigatine Albatross.

3195. White Tiger (1996, Keystone Pictures, 94m, c). D Richard Martin, P Robert Vince & William Vince, W Don Woodman, Gordon Melbourne & Roy Sallows (based on a story by Bey Logan), PH Gregory Middleton, ED Kerry Uchida, M Graeme Coleman, AD Don MacAulay.

LP Gary Daniels (Mike Ryan), Matt Craven (John Grogan), Cary Hiroyuki-Tagawa (Victor Chow), Julia Nickson (Jade), Lisa Langlois (Joanne Grogan), George Cheung (Fong).

When his partner is killed by a Chinese gang leader, DEC agent Daniels takes the law into his own hands to exact revenge. With so many such film plots, is it any wonder that certain troubled and sick young people feel that they can and should address their problems with violence?

3196. Whiteboys (1999, Fox Searchlight, 92m, c). D Marc Levin, P Henri Kessler, Richard Stratton & Ezra Swerdlow, W Garth Belcon, Danny Hoch, Levin & Stratton, PH Mark Benjamin, ED Emir Lewis, M Che Guevara, PD Carolyn Greco.

LP Danny Hoch (Flip), Dash Mihok (James), Mark Webber (Trevor), Piper Perabo (Sara), Eugene Bird (Khalid), Bonz Malone (Darius).

Living in Iowa doesn't do it for teen Hoch. He is heavy into rap, and finally convinces himself that he is actually black. His biggest dream is to relocate to a housing project in Chicago so he can groove with his homies, deal in drugs and become a hip hop artist.

3197. Who Shot Patakango? (1992, Castle Hill Prods., 104m, c). D & PH Robert Brooks, P Halle Brooks, W & ED Robert & Halle Brooks, AD Lionel Driskill.

LP David Knight (Bic Bickham), Sandra Bullock (Devlin Moran), Kevin Otto (Mark Bickham), Aaron Ingram (Cougar), Brad Randall (Patakango).

This coming-of-age story is set in Brooklyn during the 1950s. Knight is the leader of a "clean-living" gang of seniors at a vocational high school. Good music of the period.

3198. The Whole Wide World (1996, Sony Pictures Classics, 105m, c). D Dan Ireland, P Carl-Jan Colpaert, Kevin Reidy, Ireland & Vincent D'Onofrio, W Michael Scott Myers (based on the novel *One Who Walked Alone* by Novalyne Price Ellis), PH Claudio Rocha, ED Luis Colina, M Hans Zimmer & Harry Gregson-Williams, PD John Allen Frick, SD Terri L. Wright.

LP Renee Zellweger (Novalyne Price), Vincent D'Onofrio (Robert E. Howard), Ann Wedgeworth (Mrs. Howard), Harve Presnell (Dr. Howard), Benjamin Mouton (Clyde Smith).

Set in Texas in the 1930s, this film is based on the real-life relationship between pulp fiction writer Robert E. Howard, the creator of Conan the Barbarian, here effectively played by D'Onofrio, and schoolteacher/aspiring writer Novalyne Price, played by Zellweger.

3199. Whore (1991, Trimark Pictures, 85m, c). D Ken Russell, P Ronaldo Vasconcellos & Dan Ireland, W Russell & Deborah Dalton (based on the play *Bondage* by David Hines), PH Amir Mokri, ED Brian Tagg, M Michael Gibbs, PD Richard Lewis, AD Naomi Shohan, SD Amy Wells.

LP Theresa Russell (Liz), Benjamin Mouton (Blake), Antonio Fargas (Rasta), Sanjay (Indian), Elizabeth Morehead (Katie), John Diehl (Derelict).

Beautiful prostitute Russell finds the street life to be very dangerous. It's no use knocking a working girl.

3200. Whore 2 (AKA: *Bad Girls*) (1994, Castle Hill, 85m, c). D & W Amos Kollek, P Julian Schlossberg, PH Ed Talavera, ED Dana Cogdon, AD A. Lars Bjornlund.

LP Amos Kollek (Jack), Maria Sucharetza (Lori), Mari Nelson (Mary Lou), Gilbert Giles (Vernon), Jessica Sager (Susan), Alicia Miller (Tina).

Russell's gone, replaced by some other beauties who make their living catering to men's sexual needs.

3201. *Who's the Man?* (1993, New Line Cinema, 85m, c). D Ted Demme, P Charles Stettler & Maynell Thomas, W Seth Greenland (based on a story by Greenland, Dr. Dre & Ed Lover), PH Adam Kimmel, ED Jeffrey Wolf & John Gilroy, M Michael Wolff, PD Ruth Ammon, SD Susan Raney.

LP Dr. Dre (Himself), Ed Lover (Himself), Jim Moody (Nick Crawford), Badja Djola (Lionel Douglas), Denis Leary (Sgt. Cooper), Richard Bright (Demetrius), Karen Duffy (Officer Day).

Hip-hop stars Dr. Dre and Ed Lover portray two fast-talking workers at a Harlem barbershop. They are recruited by the police to investigate a murder.

3202. *Why Do Fools Fall in Love* (1998, Warner Bros., 115m, c). D Gregory Nava, P Paul Hall & Stephen Nemeth, W Tina Andrews, PH Ed Lachman, ED Nancy Richardson, M Stephen James Taylor, PD Cary White, AD John Chichester, SD Clare Scarpulla & Michael Bernard.

LP Halle Berry (Zola Taylor), Vivica A. Fox (Elizabeth Waters), Lela Rochon (Emira Eagle), Laurenz Tate (Frankie Lymon), Paul Mazursky (Morris Levy).

This film is based on the life of doo-wop singer Frankie Lymon. After his death three women step forth to claim his estate, each believing herself to have been his only wife. The young singer's biggest hit, the title song was made when he was 13. He died when he was only 25.

3203. *Why Me?* (1990, Triumph, 88m, c). D Gene Quintano, W Donald E. Westlake & Leonard Mass, Jr. (based on Westlake's novel), PH Peter Deming, ED Alan Blesam, M Basil Poledouris, PD Woody Grocker.

LP Christopher Lambert (Gus Cardinale), Christopher Lloyd (Bruno), Kim Greist (Jane Cardinale), J.T. Walsh (Inspector Mahoney), Michael J. Pollard (Ralph).

In this slapstick caper film, jewel thieves Lambert and Lloyd get away with an enormously valuable but cursed ring. It seems the Turkish government, the Armenian Liberation Army, the CIA and assorted other groups all want the missing gem.

3204. *Wicked* (1998, Frankenstein Ent., 96m, c). D Michael Steinberg, P Frank Bed-dor, W Eric Weiss, PH Bernd Heinl, ED Daniel Gross, M Eri Martinez, PD Dominic Watkins.

LP Julia Stiles (Ellie Christianson), William R. Moses (Ben Christianson), Patrick Muldoon (Lawson Smith), Vanessa Zima (Inger Christianson), Michael Parks (Det. Boland), Chelsea Field (Karen Christianson), Louise Myrback (Lena, the au pair), Linda Hart (Mrs. Potter).

This amusing thriller will probably be shown on cable during the middle of the night. Fourteen-year-old Stiles gets her chance to play house with her father, Moses, when her cheating mother, Field, is murdered.

3205. *Wide Awake* (1998, Miramax, 88m, c). D & W M. Night Shyamalan, P Cary Woods & Cathy Konrad, PH Adam Holender, ED Andrew Mondshein, M Edmond Choi, PD Michael Johnston, SD Andrea Fenton.

LP Joseph Cross (Joshua Beal), Timothy Reifsnyder (Dave O'Hara), Dana Delany (Mrs. Beal), Denis Leary (Mr. Beal), Robert Loggia (Grandpa Beal), Rosie O'Donnell (Sister Terry).

This film deals with young Cross' adjustment to the death of his beloved grandfather Loggia.

3206. *Wide Sargasso Sea* (1993, Fine Line Features, 100m, c). D John Duigan, P Jan Sharp, W Sharp, Carole Angier, Duigan, Shelagh Delaney & Bronwyn Murray (based on the novel by Jean Rhys), PH Geoff Burton, ED Anne Goursaud & Jimmy Sandoval, M Stewart Copeland, PD Frankie Drago, AD Susan Bolles, SD Ron Von Blombert.

LP Karina Lombard (Antoinette Cosway), Nathaniel Parker (Rochester), Rachel Ward (Annette Cosway), Michael York (Paul Mason), Martine Beswicke (Aunt Cora), Claudia Robinson (Christophene), Huw Christie Williams (Richard Mason), Casey Berna (Young Antoinette).

Set in the 1840s on an island that was once a British slave colony, this something of a prequel to Charlotte Brontë's *Jane Eyre* seethes with eroticism. Proper Englishman Parker marries the tragic Ward (the poor unfortunate whom he has to lock in an attic in the Brontë story). It's one hot, tragic film.

3207. *Widow's Peak* (1994, U.K./U.S., Fine Line, 101m, c). D John Irvin, P Jo Manuel, W Hugh Leonard (based on his story),

PH Ashley Rowe, ED Peter Tanner, M Carl Davis, PD Leo Austin, AD David Wilson & Richard Elton.

LP Mia Farrow (Miss Catherine O'Hare), Joan Plowright (Mrs. Doyle Counihan), Natasha Richardson (Edwina Broom), Adrian Dunbar (Godfrey), Jim Broadbent (Clancy), Anne Kent (Miss Grubb), John Kavanagh (Canon).

Here's a delightful film concerning an elaborate plot to take revenge on the well-to-do ladies of an Irish village. When Richardson arrives in town, Farrow seems to have it in for the new arrival. The performances are extraordinary, even if the story is rather farfetched.

3208. *The Wife* (1996, Artistic License, 101m, c). D & W Tom Noonan (based on his play), P Scott Macaulay & Robin O'Hara, PH Joe DeSalvo, ED Richmond Arrley, M Ludovico Sorret, PD Dan Ouellette, AD Sarah Lavery.

LP Julie Hagerty (Rita), Tom Noonan (Jack), Wallace Shawn (Cosmo), Karen Young (Arlie).

In an interesting talkfest, therapists Hagerty and Noonan are visited one evening by their patient Shawn and his emotionally disturbed wife Young.

3209. *Wilbur Falls* (1999, Vexations Films, 95m, c). D & W Juliane Glantz (based on a story by Jim Halfpenny), P David L. Dellman, PH Kurt Brabbee, ED John Gilbert & Duncan Burns, M Halfpenny, AD David Dowdy.

LP Danny Aiello (Phil Devereaux), Sally Kirkland (Roberta Devereaux), Shanee Edwards (Renata Devereaux), Jeff Daurey (Arnie), Cheril Hayres (Jodi Baker).

At her high school graduation, valedictorian Edwards reveals her involvement in the disappearance of one of her classmates who was among the many who taunted her when she first arrived in town. In flashbacks we learn more.

3210. *Wild America* (1997, Morgan Creek–Warner Bros., 105m, c). D William Dear, P James G. Robinson, Irby Smith & Mark Stouffer, W David Michael Wieger, PH David Burr, ED O. Nicholas Brown, M Joel McNeely, PD Steven Jordan, AD Jack Balance, SD Heather McElhatton.

LP Jonathan Taylor Thomas (Marshall), Devon Sawa (Mark), Scott Bairstow (Marty), Frances Fisher (Agnes), Jamey Sheridan (Marty, Sr.), Tracey Walter (Leon), Don Stroud (Stango).

Based on a true adventure, three brothers trek across America in 1967 to film wild animals in their natural habitats. If you are a staunch animal lover, you may be able to overlook the lack of much of a story.

3211. *Wild at Heart* (1990, Samuel Goldwyn Pictures, 126m, c). D & W David Lynch (based on the novel by Barry Gifford), P Monty Montgomery, Steve Golin & Joni Sighvatsson, PH Frederick Elmes, ED Duwayne Dunham, M Angelo Badalamenti, PD Patricia Norris.

LP Nicolas Cage (Sailor Ripley), Laura Dern (Lula Pace Fortune), Diane Ladd (Marietta Pace), Willem Dafoe (Bobby Peru), Isabella Rossellini (Perdita Durango), Harry Dean Stanton (Johnnie Farragut), Crispin Glover (Dell), Grace Zabriskie (Juana).

Lovers Cage and Dern are on the run from her vicious mother Ladd. This Gothic romance has everything that David Lynch fans have come to expect and enjoy — sex, violence, humor and quirkiness. It's a bit like the *Wizard of Oz*, but definitely not for the kiddies.

3212. *Wild Bill* (1995, MGM/UA, 98m, c). D & W Walter Hill (based on the novel *Deadwood* by Peter Dexter, and the play *Fathers and Sons* by Thomas Babe), P Richard D. Zanuck & Lili Fini Zanuck, PH Lloyd Ahern, ED Freeman Davies, M Van Dyke Parks, PD Joseph Nemec III, AD Daniel Olexiewicz, SD Gary Fettis.

LP Jeff Bridges (James Butler "Wild Bill" Hickok), Ellen Barkin (Calamity Jane), John Hurt (Charley Prince), Diane Lane (Susannah Moore), David Arquette (Jack McCall), Keith Carradine (Buffalo Bill Cody).

Shown mostly in flashback, this story of frontiersman Wild Bill Hickok and manly Calamity Jane isn't much like the heroic film *The Plainsman* (1937) starring Gary Cooper and Jean Arthur. Much more realistic, and sans romantic nonsense, it is nevertheless an intriguing Western.

3213. *Wild Hearts Can't Be Broken* (1991, Walt Disney–Buena Vista, 89m, c). D Steve Miner, P Matt Williams, W Williams & Oley

Sassone, PH Daryn Okada, ED Jon Poll, M Mason Daring, PD Randy Ser, SD Jean Alan.

LP Gabrielle Anwar (Sonora Webster), Cliff Robertson (Doctor Carver), Dylan Kussman (Clifford), Michael Schoeffling (Al Carver), Kathleen York (Marie).

In this film, based on a true story, Anwar runs away from home to join a traveling carnival. She becomes a horse-diver — that is, she rides a horse as it jumps off a high tower into a tank of water. She has an accident and is blinded, but she recovers to mount once again and resume her career.

3214. Wild Orchid (1990, Vision, 100m, c). D Zalman King, P Mark Damon & Tony Anthony, W Patricia Louisianna Knop & King, PH Gale Tattersall, ED Mark Grossman & Glenn A. Morgan, M Geoff MacCormack & Simon Goldenberg, PD Carlos Conti, AD Alexandre Meyer, Yeda Lewinsohn & Jane Cavedon, SD Leonardo Haertling.

LP Mickey Rourke (James Wheeler), Jacqueline Bisset (Claudia Lirones), Carre Otis (Emily Reed), Assumpta Serna (Hanna Minch), Bruce Greenwood (Jerome MacFarland), Oleg Vidov (Otto Minch), Milton Goncalves (Flavio).

In a silly if sensuous movie, mysterious millionaire Rourke is involved with both Bisset and Otis in Rio De Janeiro. Rourke likes to push the sexual envelope. The film contains very explicit love scenes. Allegedly, in one scene (which one? which one?) Rourke and Otis take their acting all the way to completion. The film is only slightly more interesting than a triple-X pornographic film.

3215. Wild Orchid 2: Two Shades of Blue (1992, Triumph Releasing, 107m, c). D Zalman King, P David Saunders & Rafael Eisenman, W King & Patricia Louisiana Knop, PH Mark Reshovsky, ED Marc Grossman & James Gavin, M George Clinton, PD Richard Amend, AD Randy Eriksen, SD Chance Reardon.

LP Nina Siemaszko (Blue), Tom Skerritt (Ham), Robert Davi (Sully), Brent Fraser (Josh), Christopher McDonald (Senator Dixon), Wendy Hughes (Elle), Liane Curtis (Mona), Joe Dallesandro (Jules).

This film has nothing to do with Wild Orchid. When her jazz musician and drug addict father Skerritt dies from some bad stuff, Siemaszko is sold into prostitution. She runs away, finds true love with high school football star Fraser and reforms. Some may miss Rourke.

3216. Wild Things (1998, Sony Pictures/Columbia, 108m, c). D John McNaughton, P Rodney Liber & Steven A. Jones, W Stephen Peters, PH Jeffrey L. Kimball, ED Elena Maganini, M George S. Clinton, PD Edward T. McAvoy, AD Bill Hiney, SD Bill Cimino.

LP Kevin Bacon (Ray Duquette), Matt Dillon (Sam Lombardo), Neve Campbell (Suzie Toller), Theresa Russell (Sandra Van Ryan), Denise Richards (Kelly Van Ryan), Daphne Rubin-Vega (Gloria Perez), Bill Murray (Ken Bowden), Robert Wagner (Tom Baxter), Carrie Snodgress (Ruby).

In this sexy thriller, teen Richards cries rape when her advances to guidance counselor Dillon are ignored. Things look bad for Dillon when another sexy teen, Campbell, comes forth with the same accusation. However, Dillon's lawyer, Murray, is able to break down Campbell's story and she confesses that the two girls had hatched a plot to ruin Dillon. But that's not all there is to it — not by a long shot. Otherwise there would be little for cop Bacon to investigate.

3217. Wild Wild West (1999, Warner Bros., 107m, c). D Barry Sonnenfeld, P Jon Peters & Sonnenfeld, W S.S. Wilson, Brent Maddock, Jeffrey Price & Peter S. Seaman (based on a story by Jim Thomas & John Thomas), PH Michael Ballhaus, ED Jim Miller, M Elmer Bernstein, PD Bo Welch, AD Tom Duffield, SD Patrick Sullivan, Maya Shimoguchi, Gerald Sullivan & Mariko Braswell.

LP Will Smith (James West), Kevin Kline (Artemus Gordon/President Grant), Kenneth Branagh (Dr. Arliss Loveless), Salma Hayek (Rita Escobar), Ted Levine (General McGrath), M. Emmet Walsh (Coleman), Bai Ling (Miss East), Sofia Eng (Miss Lippenreider).

Once again Hollywood visits the "Vast Wasteland" of television series rather than come up with an original idea. The TV series of 1964–68 starring Robert Conrad and Ross Martin was only interesting during the episodes that dwarf Michael Dunn showed up as a small but dangerous villain. The big screen version has an admirable cast, but even they can't make a silk purse out of a sow's ear. For those who insist on being told the plot, black special government agent Smith, teamed with his resourceful partner Kline, are pitted against Southern white villain and military genius Branagh, who is motivated by a desire to take revenge for his personal and political setbacks during the Civil War.

3218. Wilde (1998, U.K., Sony Pictures Classics, 116m, c). D Brian Gilbert, P Marc Samuelson & Peter Samuelson, W Julian Mitchell (based on the biography *Oscar Wilde* by Richard Ellmann), PH Martin Fuhrer, ED Michael Bradsell, M Debbie Wiseman, PD Maria Djurkovic, AD Martyn John.

LP Stephen Fry (Oscar Wilde), Jude Law (Lord Alfred Douglas), Jennifer Ehle (Constance Wilde), Vanessa Redgrave (Lady Speranza Wilde), Gemma Jones (Lady Queensberry), Judy Parfitt (Lady Mount-Temple), Michael Sheen (Robert Ross), Tom Wilkinson (Marquis of Queensberry).

Fry bears a remarkable resemblance to Wilde and gives an extraordinary performance. This third film biography of the legendary Irish wit is the first to candidly deal with his homosexuality. From the very beginning Wilde was attracted to men, but he married and had children (as that was the thing expected of him); but all along he had affairs with males. The love of his life was Lord Alfred Douglas, played nicely by Law, but this affair proves to be his downfall.

3219. Wilder Napalm (1993, TriStar, 109m, c). D Glenn Gordon Caron, P Barry Levinson, Mark Johnson & Stuart Cornfeld, W Vince Gilligan, PH Jerry Hartleben, ED Artie Mandelberg, PD John Muto, AD Dan Webster, SD Mark Garner & Les Bloom.

LP Debra Winger (Vida), Dennis Quaid (Wallace Foudroyant), Arliss Howard (Wilder Foudroyant), M. Emmet Walsh (Fire Chief), Jim Varney (Rex).

Brothers Quaid and Howard both have pyrokinetic abilities. The lads have been at odds for years. The rivalry is in part because Quaid is in love with Howard's wife Winger, but mostly because Quaid wants to use their power to become rich and famous and Howard doesn't.

3220. Wildest Dreams (AKA: *Bikini Genie*) (1990, Vestron, 80m, c). D & P Chuck Vincent, W Craig Horrall (based on a story by Vincent), PH Larry Revene, ED James Davalos, M Joey Mennonna, AD Mark Hammond.

LP James Davies (Bobby Delaney), Deborah Blaisdell (Joan Peabody), Heidi Paine (Dancee), Ruth Collins (Stella), Jill Johnson (Rachel Richards), Jeanne Marie (Isabelle).

When Davies releases sexy genie Paine from a bottle she works overtime putting love spells on beautiful women in order to find just the right one for her master.

3221. William Shakespeare's A Midsummer Night's Dream (1999, Fox Searchlight, 116m, c). D & W Michael Hoffman (based on the play by William Shakespeare), P Leslie Urdang & Hoffman, PH Oliver Stapleton, ED Garth Craven, M Simon Boswell, PD Luciana Arrighi, AD Maria Teresa Barbasso & Andrea Gaeta, SD Ian Whittaker.

LP Kevin Kline (Nick Bottom), Michelle Pfeiffer (Titania), Rupert Everett (Oberon), Stanley Tucci (Puck), Calista Flockhart (Helena), Anna Friel (Hermia), Christian Bale (Demetrius), Dominic West (Lysander), David Strathairn (Theseus), Sophie Marceau (Hippolyta).

Is it a commentary on the literary experience of American film audiences that the makers of this movie felt the need to identify it as *William Shakespeare's A Midsummer Night's Dream*? Whose other "Midsummer Night's Dream" would it be? Rather than the prominent cast assembled for this production, the director would have been better off with an ensemble cast who worked together. Individually, the stars and would-be stars emote adequately, but things seldom work as intended when they interact with each other. It's a lush production — but give us the 1935 Hollywood version or even Woody Allen's *A Midsummer Night's Sex Comedy*.

3222. William Shakespeare's Romeo & Juliet (1996, U.S./Australia/Canada, 20th Century–Fox, 113m, c). D Baz Luhrmann, P Gabriella Martinelli & Luhrmann, W Luhrmann & Craig Pearce (based on the play by William Shakespeare), PH Don McAlpine, ED Jill Bilcock, PD Catherine Martin†, AD Doug Hartwick, SD Brigitte Broch†.

LP Leonardo DiCaprio (Romeo), Claire Danes (Juliet), John Leguizamo (Tybalt), Paul Rudd (Dave Paris), Jesse Bradford (Balthasar), Harold Perrineau (Mercutio), Dash Mihok (Benvolio), Diane Venora (Gloria Capulet), Paul Sorvino (Fulgencio Capulet), Brian Dennehy

(Ted Montague), Miriam Margoyles (The Nurse), Pete Postlethwaite (Father Laurence).

Set in present day Miami, this updated version of Shakespeare's tragic romance uses his words and story. The young leads DiCaprio and Danes almost make it work, but the rest of the cast don't pull their weight.

3223. Wind (1992, TriStar, 123m, c). D Carroll Ballard, P Mata Yamamoto & Tom Luddy, W Rudy Wurlitzer, Mac Gudgeon & Larry Gross (based on the story by Jeff Benjamin, Howard Chelsey, Kimball Livingston & Roger Vaughan), PH John Toll, ED Michael Chandler, M Basil Poledouris, PD Laurence Eastwood.

LP Matthew Modine (Will Parker), Jennifer Grey (Kate Bass), Cliff Robertson (Morgan Weld), Jack Thompson (Jack Neville), Stellan Skarsgard (Joe Heiser), Rebecca Miller (Abigail Weld).

Modine chooses the chance to be on the America's Cup team over his girlfriend Grey. He makes a technical error that causes his team to lose. Undaunted, he seeks out Grey and her new boyfriend, engineer Skarsgard, and convinces them to design the ultimate racing boat for the next set of races.

3224. The Wind in the Willows (1997, U.K., Columbia, 87m, c). D & W Terry Jones (based on the novel by Kenneth Grahame), P John Goldstone & Jake Eberts, PH David Tattersall, ED Julian Doyle, M John Du Prez, Jones, Andre Jacquemin & David Howman, PD James Acheson, AD Keith Pain, SD Anna Pinnock.

LP Steve Coogan (Mole), Eric Idle (Rat), Terry Jones (Toad), Anthony Sher (Chief Weasel), Nicol Williamson (Badger), John Cleese (Mr. Toad's Lawyer), Stephen Fry (Judge), Bernard Hill (Engine Driver), Michael Palin (The Sun).

It's a live-action version of Kenneth Grahame's children's classic. The story is of Toad and his friends united against the evilness of the weasels. Director Jones had to work very hard, perhaps too hard, to expand the story to a feature length. Still, it has its moments.

3225. Wing Commander (1999, 20th Century–Fox, 100m, c). D Chris Roberts, P Todd Moyer, W Kevin Droney (based on a story and character by Roberts), PH Thierry Arbogast, ED Peter Davies, M Kevin Kiner, PD Peter Lamont, AD Charles Lee, SD Michael Ford.

LP Freddie Prinze, Jr. (Chris Blair), Saffron Burrows ("Angel" Devereaux), Matthew Lillard ("Maniac" Marshall), Tcheky Karyo (Paladin), Jurgen Prochnow (Gerald), David Suchet (Sansky), David Warner (Tolwyn).

Rather than see this movie, audiences should wait for the video game. Oh, you say, the film is based on a popular video game. Well, then those not into a hodge-podge of ideas borrowed from many much better science-fiction films would be better served reading a Ray Bradbury story.

3226. The Wings of the Dove (1997, Miramax, 102m, c). D Iain Softley, P Steven Evans & David Parfitt, W Hossein Amini† (based on the novel by Henry James), PH Eduardo Serra†, ED Tariq Anwar, M Ed Shearmur, PD John Beard, AD Andrew Sanders, SD Joanne Woollard.

LP Helena Bonham Carter† (Kate Croy), Linus Roache (Merton Densher), Alison Elliott (Millie Theale), Elizabeth McGovern (Susan Stringham), Michael Gambon (Lionel Croy), Charlotte Rampling (Aunt Maude), Alex Jennings (Lord Mark).

In one of the better films of the year, Bonham Carter excels as a penniless woman who must depend upon the "kindness" of her wealthy, snobbish, domineering aunt Rampling. The latter, who runs the younger woman's life, does not intend seeing her niece make the same "mistake" as did her sister, who married a poor man for love. The marriage ended in Bonham Carter's mother's death and her father's fall into alcoholism and drug addiction. The catch is that Bonham Carter has already fallen in love with handsome journalist Roache — who, you guessed it, is quite poor. The aunt breaks up the young lovers and sends Bonham Carter to Venice where she meets and becomes best friends with the "world's richest orphan," Elliott. The latter is seriously ill. When Roache shows up, Bonham Carter plays down their past relationship and pushes him into Elliott's arms. Her plan is for Roache to marry Elliot, who will shortly die, leaving everything to him, and then he will be able to marry Bonham Carter. The resolution of the plot lines does great justice to the Henry James novel.

3227. *The Winner* (1997, LIVE Ent. 90m, c). D Alex Cox, P Kenneth Schwenker, W Wendy Riss (Based on her play *A Darker Purpose*), PH Denis Maloney, ED Carlos Puente, PD Cecilia Montiel.

LP Rebecca DeMornay (Louise), Vincent D'Onofrio (Philip), Frank Whaley (Joey), Delroy Lindo (Kingman), Michael Madsen (Wolf), Billy Bob Thornton (Jack), Richard Edson (Frankie), Saverio Guerra (Paulie).

Depressed D'Onofrio has found a reason to live, what with a five Sunday winning streak at the tables of a Las Vegas casino. His success attracts a number of seedy characters, including DeMornay, who hopes to get him to marry her so she can pay off her large debt to Lindo, the owner of the casino. It's an offbeat morality story.

3228. *The Winslow Boy* (1999, U.K., Sony Pictures Classics, 104m, c). D & W David Mamet (based on the play by Terence Rattigan), P Sarah Green, PH Benoit Delhomme, ED Barbara Tulliver, M Alaric Jans, PD Gemma Jackson, AD Andrew Munro, SD Trisha Edwards.

LP Nigel Hawthorne (Arthur Winslow), Jeremy Northam (Sir Robert Morton), Rebecca Pidgeon (Catherine Winslow), Gemma Jones (Grace Winslow), Guy Edwards (Ronnie Winslow), Matthew Pidgeon (Dickie Winslow).

Rattigan's 1946 play about the case of a 13-year-old boy who is expelled from his military academy for allegedly stealing a classmate's pocket money was brilliantly filmed in 1948. In it Sir Cedric Hardwicke, as a retired bank manager, risks his funds and health to vindicate his son. Robert Donat portrays a prominent barrister who takes the boy's case to parliament to "Let right be done." This current production is well-made with a fine cast. Its audience will be limited to those who can appreciate the fuss that some are willing to make and the extent of their efforts to right a wrong.

3229. *The Winter Guest* (1997, U.K./U.S., Fine Line Features, 110m, c). D Alan Rickman, P Ken Lipper, Edward Pressman & Steve Clark-Hall, W Sharman MacDonald & Rickman (based on the play by MacDonald), PH Seamus Garvey, ED Scott Thomas, PD Robin Cameron Don.

LP Phyllida Law (Elspeth), Emma Thompson (Frances), Gary Hollywood (Alex), Arlene

Cockburn (Nita), Sheila Reid (Lily), Sandra Voe (Chloe), Douglas Murphy (Sam), Sean Biggerstaff (Tom).

Real-life mother and daughter Law and Thompson beautifully portray an estranged mother and daughter. They spend an unexpected weekend together when meddlesome Law comes to visit her recently widowed and withdrawn daughter and the latter's son, Hollywood.

3230. *The Wisdom of Crocodiles* (1998, U.K., Zenith Prods./Goldwyn Films, 98m, c). D Po Chih Leong, P David Lascelles & Carolyn Choa, W Paul Hoffman, PH Oliver Curtis, ED Robin Sales, M John Lunn & Orlando Gough, PD Andy Harris, AD Ben Scott.

LP Jude Law (Steven Griscz), Elina Lowensohn (Anna Levels), Timothy Spall (Inspector Healey), Kerry Fox (Maria Vaughan), Jack Davenport (Detective Roche).

Law is a researcher with a great appetite for blood. The things a talented young actor must do on his way to an Oscar nomination for *The Talented Mr. Ripley*.

3231. *Wishmaster* (1997, LIVE Ent., 90m, c). D Robert Kurtzman, P Pierre Clark Peterson & Noel A. Zanitsch, W Peter Atkins (based on a story by Pierre David), PH Jacques Haitkin, ED David Handman, M Harry Manfredini, PD Dorian Vernacchio & Deborah Raymond.

LP Tammy Lauren (Alexandra Amberson), Andrew Divoff (The Djinn/ Nathaniel Demerest), Tony Todd (Johnny Valentine), Kane Holder (Merritt's Guard), Robert Englund (Raymond Beaumont), Wendy Benson (Shannon Amberson), Tony Crane (Josh Aickman).

When a drunken longshoreman causes a statue to break open, the Djinn within it escapes into a large semiprecious gem. Through a series of events the gem is brought to gemologist Crane, who is killed by the violent spirit. His colleague Lauren is shocked and determined to find out what has happened and why. Her adversary is a genie who offers people their wildest wishes but grants them in twisted and deadly ways.

3232. *The Witches* (1990, U.K./U.S., Warner Bros., 91m, c). D Nicolas Roeg, P Mark Shivas, W Allan Scott (based on the book by Roald Dahl), PH Harvey Harrison,

ED Tony Lawson, M Stanley Myers, PD Andrew Sanders, AD Norman Dorme, SD Robin Tarsnane.

LP Anjelica Huston (Mrs. Ernst/Grand High Witch), Mai Zetterling (Helga), Jasen Fisher (Luke), Rowan Atkinson (Mr. Stringer), Bill Paterson (Mr. Jenkins), Brenda Blethyn (Mrs. Jenkins), Charlie Potter (Bruno Jenkins).

Nine-year-old Fisher thwarts evil Grand High Witch Huston, who plans to change all children into mice. Too scary for very young kids.

3233. With Friends Like These... (1998, Parkway/Quadrant Prod., 105m, c). D & W Philip Messina, P Robert Greenhut, PH Brian J. Reynolds, ED Claudia Finkle, M John Powell, PD Beth DeSort, SD Joanna Venszky.

LP Adam Arkin (Steve Hersh), Robert Costanzo (Johnny DiMartino), Beverly D'Angelo (Theresa Carpenter), Elle Macpherson (Samantha Mastandrea), Laura San Giacomo (Joanne Hersh), David Strathairn (Armand Minetti), Jon Tenney (Dorian Mastandrea).

The movie follows the efforts of four small-time actors to win the same important role in Martin Scorsese's upcoming gangland picture.

3234. With Honors (1994, Warner Bros., 103m, c). D Alek Keshishian, P Paula Weinstein & Amy Robinson, W William Mastrosimone, PH Sven Nykvist, Ed Michael R. Miller, M Patrick Leonard, PD Barbara Ling, AD Bill Arnold & Carl Sprague, SD Cricket Rowland, Suzan Wexler & Bobbie Frankel.

LP Joe Pesci (Simon Wilder), Brendan Fraser (Monty Kessler), Moria Kelly (Courtney Blumenthal), Patrick Dempsey (Everett Calloway), Josh Hamilton (Jeff Hawkes), Gore Vidal (Professor Philip Hayes Pitkannan).

Harvard Honors student Fraser loses his Honor's thesis. Quick-witted homeless man Pesci finds it and blackmails Fraser into giving him a place to stay. It's trite — but expected — that Fraser will eventually learn more important lessons about life from the bum than he does from his snobbish thesis advisor Vidal. We doubt that clever Harvard students would ever allow themselves to be in the position of choosing to fulfill a dying man's wishes over finishing the most important papers in their young lives.

3235. With or Without You (1999, U.K., Miramax, 90m, c). D Michael Winterbottom, P Andrew Eaton, W John Forte, PH Benoit Delhomme, ED Trevor Waite, M Adrian Johnson, PD Mark Tildesley.

LP Christopher Eccleston (Vincent Boyd), Dervia Kirwan (Rosie Boyd), Yvan Attal (Benoit), Julie Graham (Cathy), Alun Armstrong (Sammy), Lloyd Hutchinson (Neil).

This appealing romantic triangle features ex-cop Eccleston working somewhat unhappily in the window-repair business of his father-in-law. His wife Kirwan is a receptionist at an art center. They have been married ten years but are unable to conceive a child. Into this situation steps Attal, Kirwan's former pen pal whom she has never met. This didn't stop the two from falling in love via the mail. The correspondence stopped when Kirwan met Eccleston and Attal married, but now he's divorced and in Belfast to see if he can revive his romance with Kirwan.

3236. Within the Rock (1996, A-Pix Ent., 88m, c). D & W Gary J. Tunnicliffe, P Stanley Isaacs, Scott McGinnis & Robert Patrick, PH Adam Kane, ED Roderick Davis, M Rod Gammons & Tony Fennell, PD Dorian Vernacchio & Deborah Raymond.

LP Xander Berkeley (Ryan), Caroline Barclay (Dr. Dana Shaw), Bradford Tatum (Cody Harrison), Brian Krause (Luke Harrison), Barbara Patrick (Samantha "Nuke-em" Rogers).

Earth is threatened by a meteor headed on a collision course with the planet. Miners are sent into space to intercept the meteor and change its course. They discover a very unfriendly alien at the center of the meteor, just awakened from a million-year sleep.

3237. Without Limits (1998, Warner Bros., 117m, c). D Robert Towne, P Paula Wagner & Tom Cruise, W Towne & Kenny Moore, PH Conrad L. Hall, ED Claire Simpson & Robert K. Lambert, M Randy Miller, PD William Creber, AD William Durrell, Jr., SD Roberta Holinko.

LP Billy Crudup (Steve Prefontaine), Donald Sutherland (William Bowerman), Monica Potter (Mary Marckx), Jeremy Sisto (Frank Shorter), Gabe Olds (Don Kardong), Judith Ivey (Barbara Bowerman).

This film followed by one year the Disney film *Prefontaine* about professional runner

Steve Prefontaine. He led a crusade against the dictatorial Amateur Athletic Union. Despite fine performances from Crudup as the runner and Sutherland as his coach, the film is only marginally interesting.

3238. *Wittgenstein* (1993, U.K., Zeitgeist, 71m, c). D Derek Jarman, P Tariq Ali, W Jarman, Terry Eagleton & Ken Butler, PH James Welland, ED Budge Tremlett, M Jan Latham Koenig, AD Annie Lapaz.

LP Karl Johnson (Ludwig Wittgenstein), Michael Gough (Bertrand Russell), Tilda Swinton (Lady Ottoline Morrell), John Quentin (John Maynard Keynes), Kevin Collins (Johnny), Clancy Chassay (Young Wittgenstein), Nabil Shaban (Martian).

The story of eccentric Viennese-born philosopher Ludwig Wittgenstein is told in a series of blackout sketches featuring several very prominent individuals, including Bertrand Russell and John Maynard Keynes.

3239. *Wolf* (1994, Columbia, 125m, c). D Mike Nichols, P Douglas Wick, W Jim Harrison & Wesley Strick, PH Giuseppe Rotunno, ED Sam O'Steen, M Ennio Morricone, PD Bo Welch, AD Tom Duffield & Tom Warren, SD Linda DeScenna†.

LP Jack Nicholson (Will Randall), Michelle Pfeiffer (Laura Alden), James Spader (Stewart Swinton), Kate Nelligan (Charlotte Randall), Christopher Plummer (Raymond Alden), Richard Jenkins (Detective Bridger), Om Puri (Dr. Vijay Alezias), Eileen Atkins (Mary).

Manhattan book editor Nicholson isn't able to cope with the power plays within his company until his car hits a wolf on a country road and the animal bites him. Soon Nicholson notices some changes in his hairy appearance and his behavior. He becomes a ruthless animal in the business world and attracts beautiful Pfeiffer in the bargain. It's a clever, if not totally satisfactory, combination of horror story, social commentary and character study.

3240. *The Wolves of Kromer* (1998, U.K., Discodog Prod., 82m, c). D Will Gould, P & W Charles Lambert (based on his play, adapted by Lambert & Matthew Read), PH Laura Remacha, ED Carol Salter, M Basil Moore-Asfouri, PD Mark Larkin.

LP Lee Williams (Seth), James Layton (Gabriel), Rita Davies (Fanny), Kevin Moore (The Priest), Angharad Rees (Mary), Leila Lloyd-Evelyn (Polly), Margaret Towner (Doreen).

This film is a parable about homosexuality and outsider status. The stereotypical town of Kromer is filled with hypocritical people who piously parade their churchgoing status while maintaining a mean-spirited attitude towards a transient local wolf group. It consists of attractive young men who run around the countryside barefooted in long fur coats and are quite physical with each other.

3241. *Woman, Her Men, and Her Futon* (1992, Republic Pictures, 90m, c). D & W Mussef Sibay, P Dale Rosenbloom & Sibay, PH Michael Davis, ED Howard Heard, M Joel Goldsmith, PD Peter Raubertas, AD Florina Roberts, SD Richard Way.

LP Jennifer Rubin (Helen), Lance Edwards (Donald), Grant Show (Randy), Michael Cerveris (Paul), Duane Michel (Gail).

Rubin tests the water to find her perfect lover, but all the candidates she turns up are lacking in some way or another.

3242. *A Woman Undone* (AKA: *Joshua Tree*) (1996, Rehme Prods–Lancaster Prods., 91m, c). D Evelyn Purcell, P David Lancaster, W William Mickleberry, PH Toyomichi Kurita, ED Stan Salfas & Quincy Gunderson, M Dan Licht, PD Steven Legler, AD Nanci B. Roberts, SD Barbara Cassel.

LP Mary McDonnell (Teri Hansen), Randy Quaid (Allen Hansen), Sam Elliott (Ross Bishop), Benjamin Bratt (Jim Mercer), Charles Noland (Trim), Cheryl Anderson (Nina).

McDonnell is found cowering in a dry gulch after her husband Quaid is discovered burned to death in the family car. She is arrested for murder. Flashbacks detail the troubled marriage of McDonnell and Quaid, his extreme jealousy and her steamy affairs. McDonnell is unable to explain or remember anything about the six bullets found in Quaid's charred remains.

3243. *A Woman's Tale* (1991, Australia, Orion Classics, 93m, c). D Paul Cox, P Cox & Santhana Naidu, W Cox & Barry Dickins, PH Nino Martinetti, ED Russel Hurley, M Paul Grabowsky, PD Neil Angwin.

LP Sheila Florance (Martha), Gosia Dobrowolska (Anna), Norman Kaye (Billy), Chris Haywood (Jonathan), Ernest Gray (Peter), Myrtle Woods (Miss Inchley).

In a simple but beautiful story, elderly Florance, dying of cancer, wishes to live out her final days with the same dignity and independence that she has demonstrated all her life.

3244. Women Talking Dirty (1999, U.S./ U.K., Rocket Pictures, 94m, c). D Coky Giedroye, P David Furnish & Polly Steele, W Isla Dewar (based on her novel), PH Brian Tufano, ED Budge Tremlett, M Elton John, PD Lynne Whiteread, AD Tim Ellis.

LP Helena Bonham Carter (Cora), Gina Mckee (Ellen), Richard Wilson (Ronald), Eileen Atkins (Emily Boyle), Kenneth Cranham (George), James Nesbitt (Stanley).

If viewers enter the theater expecting to hear actress Bonham Carter and others talking dirty, they will be disappointed. The only dirty talking may come from members of the audience who wasted the price of admission in order to see a series of flashbacks from a postdivorce party which are far from entertaining or revealing.

3245. The Wonderful Ice Cream Suit (1998, Walt Disney Pictures–Buena Vista, 77m, c). D Stuart Gordon, P Roy E. Disney & Gordon, W Ray Bradbury (based on his short story and play), PH Mac Ahlberg, ED Andy Horvitch, M Mader, PD Stuart Blatt, AD Randy Eriksen, SD Ellen Brill.

LP Joe Mantegna (Gomez), Esai Morales (Dominguez), Edward James Olmos (Vamenos), Clifton Gonzalez Gonzalez (Martinez), Gregory Sierra (Villanazul), Liz Torres (Ruby Escadrill), Sid Caesar (Sid Zellman), Howard Morris (Leo Zellman).

Five L.A. Barrio men each pony up $20 in order to buy a gorgeous white suit that they wear in hour-long shifts one balmy Friday night. The suit changes each of their lives.

3246. Wonderland (1999, U.K., Universal/ Polygram, 108m, c). D Michael Winterbottom, P Michelle Camarda & Andrew Eaton, W Laurence Coriat, PH Sean Bobbitt, ED Trevor Waite, M Michael Nyman, PD Mark Tildesay.

LP Shirley Henderson (Debbie), Gina McKee (Nadia), Molly Parker (Molly), Ian Hart (Dan), John Simm (Eddie), Stuart Townsend (Tim), Kika Markham (Eileen), Jack Shepherd (Bill).

This film covers four days in London in rainy November. It examines the lives of three sisters and their parents as they attempt to deal with unpromising circumstances or futures. The story is bleak but the performances are winning.

3247. Woo (1998, New Line Cinema, 84m, c). D Daisy V.S. Mayer, P Beth Hubbard & Michael Hubbard, W David C. Johnson, PH Jean Lepine, ED Nicholas Eliopoulos & Janice Hampton, M Michel Colombier, PD Ina Mayhew, AD Vlasta Svoboda.

LP Jada Pinkett Smith (Woo), Tommy Davidson (Tim), Duane Martin (Frankie), Michael Ralph (Romaine), Darrel M. Heath (Hop), Dave Chappelle (Lenny), Paula Jai Parker (Claudette).

This less-than-stellar comedy pits gorgeous and conceited extrovert Smith with insecure, straitlaced law student Davidson. The mismatched couple brought together on a blind date don't hit it off—but they will.

3248. The Wood (1999, Paramount–MTV Films, 107m, c). D Rick Famuyiwa, P Albert Berger, Ron Yerxa & David Gale, W Famuyiwa & Todd Boyd, PH Steven Bernstein, ED John Carter, M Robert Hurst, PD Roger Fortune & Maxine Shepard, AD Richard Haase.

LP Omar Epps (Mike), Sean Nelson (Young Mike), Taye Diggs (Roland), Trent Cameron (Young Roland), Richard T. Jones (Slim), Duane Finley (Young Slim), Malinda Williams (Young Alicia), Sanaa Lathan (Alicia).

This earnest attempt to depict the coming of age of three friends in Inglewood, California (i.e. "The Wood"), is short on story. Although it offers an assortment of opportunities for minority filmmakers and actors, we are not sure this is what the NAACP had in mind when it protested the lack of racial diversity in films and TV series.

3249. The World Is Not Enough (1999, MGM–Enos Prods., 125m, c). D Michael Apted, P Michael G. Wilson & Barton Broccoli, W Neal Purvis, Robert Wade & Bruce Fierstein, PH Adrian Biddle, ED Jim Clark, M David Arnold, PD Peter Lamont, AD Neil Lamont, SD Simon Wakefield.

LP Pierce Brosnan (James Bond), Sophie Marceau (Elektra), Robert Carlyle (Renard), Denise Richards (Christmas Jones), Robbie

Coltrane (Valentin Zukovsky), Judi Dench (M), Desmond Llewelyn (Q), John Cleese (R), Maria Grazia Cucinotta (Cigar Girl), Samantha Bond (Moneypenny).

Goody, goody, it's time for another visit from 007, with Brosnan filling the role quite nicely. As is usual in these films the villains are power-hungry maniacal types and the women are drop-dead beautiful. These almost make up for the overly wild story crammed with way too many ingredients. The film begins with an exhilarating 15 minute prologue that is worth the price of admission. Unfortunately, the film goes downhill from there. Brosnan takes up with Marceau, who is to inherit vast holdings, including an unfinished oil pipeline from Asia to Istanbul. Their romance is interrupted by her old tormenter Carlyle, a terrorist with a bullet lodged in his brain that will eventually kill him but presently allows him to feel no pain. Add to the mix Richards, dressed like a hooker but in fact, if you can believe it, a nuclear scientist. It's all very silly if you think too much about it, so it is best not to do so and just sit back and enjoy the show. Some critics argue that 007 should be once and for all retired because the movies featuring him are so repetitive, both in plot and in spectacular scenes. This is probably one of the reasons the films continue to do big box office business.

3250. *Woundings* (1998, U.K., Muse Prods., 102m, c). D & W Roberta Hanley (based on the play by Jeff Noon), P Chris Hanley & Bradford L. Schiel, PH Alun Bollinger, ED Andrew Marcus, M Wendy Carlos, PD Chris Roope, AD Tim Ellis.

LP Julie Cox (Angela), Sammi Davis (Denise Jones), Twiggy Lawson (Viv), Emily Lloyd (Kim Patterson), Charlie Creed-Miles (Stanley Jardine), Guy Pearce (Jimmy Compton).

Set sometime in the future, when Britain is engaged in a civil war, the movie examines the psychological scars caused by occupation. The government sends a group of recruited young women to one bleak outpost to make conditions more palatable for the occupation forces. But the place is not the exotic and romantic location the women were led to believe.

3251. *Wrestling Ernest Hemingway* (1993, Warner Bros., 122m, c). D Randa Haines, P Joe Wizan & Todd Black, W Steve Conrad, PH Lajos Koltai, Ed Paul Hirsch, M Michael

Convertino, PD Waldemar Kalinowski, AD Alan E. Muraoka, SD Florence Fellman & Carlos Arditti.

LP Robert Duvall (Walt), Richard Harris (Frank), Piper Laurie (Georgia), Sandra Bullock (Elaine), Shirley MacLaine (Helen), Micole Mercurio (Bernice), Marty Belafsky (Ned Ryan).

Boozy Irish ex-sea captain Harris and Cuban barber Duvall have nothing in common, save being elderly and lonely in Florida. This is enough to begin a friendship which, if not overly satisfactory, is better than none at all. Duvall has an old man's innocent letch for waitress Bullock; but Harris has more carnal interests. The title comes from Harris' claim that he once wrestled Ernest Hemingway. Not a great story or movie, but the male leads give fine performances.

3252. *Wrongly Accused* (1998, Warner Bros., 85m, c). D & W Pat Proft (based on characters created by Roy Huggins), PH Glen MacPherson, ED James R. Symons, M Bill Conti, PD Michael Bolton, AD Sandy Cochrane, SD Lin MacDonald.

LP Leslie Nielsen (Ryan Harrison), Richard Crenna (Lt. Fergus Falls), Kelly LeBrock (Lauren Goodhue), Melinda McGraw (Cass Lake), Michael York (Hibbing Goodhue), Sandra Bernhard (Dr. Fridley), Aaron Pearl (One-Armed, One-Legged, One-Eyed Killer).

Nielsen's brand of parody seems to be wearing thin. For this comedy, think *The Fugitive*. Classical violinist Nielsen takes up with LeBrock, wife of his benefactor York. The latter is murdered by Pearl, a one-armed, one-legged, one-eyed man. The killing is made to look like Leslie's doing. He escapes and goes on the lam, with U.S. Marshall Crenna close behind.

3253. *Wyatt Earp* (1994, Warner Bros., 195m, c). D Lawrence Kasdan, P Jim Wilson, Kevin Costner & Kasdan, W Kasdan & Dan Gordon, PH Owen Roizman†, ED Carol Littleton, M James Newton Howard, PD Ida Random, AD Gary Wissner, SD Cheryl Carasik.

LP Kevin Costner (Wyatt Earp), Dennis Quaid (John "Doc" Holliday), Gene Hackman (Nicholas Earp), David Andrews (James Earp), Linden Ashby (Morgan Earp), Jeff Fahey (Ike Clanton), Joanna Going (Josie Marcus), Mark Harmon (Sheriff Johnny Behan),

Michael Madsen (Virgil Earp), Catherine O'Hara (Allie Earp), Bill Pullman (Ed Masterson), Isabella Rossellini (Big Nose Kate), Tom Sizemore (Bat Masterson), JoBeth Williams (Bessie Earp), Mare Winningham (Mattie Earp).

The main defect of this film is its length, but that's not the only problem. The story of Earp and Doc Holliday has been told so often that it's difficult to maintain an interest in this retelling. The filmmakers seemed to believe that a great deal of violence would pull in audiences, but it didn't.

3254.   The X-Files (1998, 20th Century–Fox, 120m, c). D Rob Bowman, P Chris Carter & Daniel Sackheim, W Carter (based on a story by Carter & Frank Spotnitz), PH Ward Russell, ED Stephen Mark, M Mark Snow, PD Christopher Nowak, AD Gregory Bolton & Hugo Santiago, SD Jackie Carr.

LP David Duchovny (Agent Fox Mulder), Gillian Anderson (Agent Dana Scully), Martin Landau (Dr. Alvin Kurtzweil), Armin Mueller-Stahl (Conrad Strughold), Blythe Danner (Jana Cassidy).

Devotees of the continuing and unusual television series, like trekkies before them, see so much in their favorite show that they can stand it if now and then one of the episodes is not as fascinating as the others. Novices who walk into a theater to see what the fuss is all about may come away shaking their heads wondering what is supposed to be the appeal. The story of this film, despite three startling and suspenseful scenes which take up the first 20 minutes of the movie, is routine and familiar. When FBI agents Duchovny and Anderson are unable to prevent a threatened Oklahoma City–like bombing of the Federal building at Dallas, they are blamed. It seems that persons unknown, for reasons unknown, are intent on breaking up the successful team.

3255.   Xtro 2: The Second Encounter (1991, North American Pictures, 92m, c). D & P Harry Bromley Davenport, W John A. Curtis, Edward Kovach & Lister Steven, PH Nathaniel Massey, ED Derek Whelan, M Braun Farnon & Robert Smart, PD Glenn Patterson.

LP Jan-Michael Vincent (Dr. Ron Sheperd), Paul Koslo (Dr. Alex Summerfield), Tara Buckman (Dr. Julie Casserly), Jano Frandsen (McShane), Nicholas Lea (Baines).

A research facility, experimenting with dimension travel, sends three researchers to a parallel dimension, but only one returns. He's carrying a biohazardous creature which escapes into the air shafts and threatens to kill everyone at the facility.

3256.   Year of the Comet (1992, Castle Rock–Columbia, 89m, c). D Peter Yates, P Yates & Nigel Wooll, W William Goldman, PH Roger Pratt, ED Ray Lovejoy, M Hummie Mann, PD Anthony Pratt, AD Desmond Crowe & Chris Seagers, SD Stephenie McMillan.

LP Penelope Ann Miller (Maggie Harwood), Timothy Daly (Oliver Plexico), Louis Jourdan (Philippe), Art Malik (Nico), Ian Richardson (Sir Mason Harwood), Ian McNeice (Ian).

In this amusing romantic comedy Miller and Daly compete for a rare Lafitte 1811 bottle of wine. They must team up when thieves put in their claim for the prize.

3257.   Year of the Gun (1991, Triumph, 111m, c). D John Frankenheimer, P Edward R. Pressman, W David Ambrose & Jay Presson Allen (based on the book by Michael Mewshaw), PH Blasco Giurato, ED Lee Percy, M Bill Conti, PD Aurelio Crugnola, AD Luigi Quintili, SD Franco Fumagalli.

LP Andrew McCarthy (David Raybourne), Valeria Golino (Lia Spinelli), Sharon Stone (Alison King), John Pankow (Italo Bianchi), Mattia Sbragia (Giovanni), George Murcell (Pierre Bernier).

American journalist McCarthy is in Italy to write a novel on the political instability of the country. In his draft he uses real names. Photojournalist Stone wants to collaborate, and the Red Brigade wants to kill anyone associated with or mentioned in the book.

3258.   You Can Thank Me Later (1998, Canada, Cinequest Films, 110m, c). D Shimon Dotan, P Dotan & Netaya Anbar, W Oren Safdie (based on his play *Hyper-Allergenic*), PH Amnon Salomon, ED Anbar, M Walter Christian Rothe, PD Michael Devine.

LP Ellen Burstyn (Shirley Cooperberg), Amanda Plummer (Susan Cooperberg), Ted Levine (Eli Cooperberg), Mark Blum (Edward

Cooperberg), Mary McDonnell (Diane), Genevieve Bujold (Joelle), Jacob Tierney (Simon Cooperberg).

This film is mostly set in a hospital room where members of a wealthy Montreal Jewish family await the results of the father's surgery. The dysfunctional family exchange recriminations and abuse in a comedy drama which is neither as comical nor dramatic as one might like.

3259. ***Young Guns II*** (1990, Morgan Creek–20th Century–Fox, 104m, c). D Geoff Murphy, P Irby Smith & Paul Schiff, W John Fusco (based on characters created by Fusco), PH Dean Semler, ED Bruce Green, M Alan Silvestri, PD Gene Rudolf, AD Christa Munro, SD Andy Bernard.

LP Emilio Estevez (William H. Bonney), Kiefer Sutherland (Doc Scurlock), Lou Diamond Phillips (Jose Chavez y Chavez), Christian Slater (Arkansas Dave Rudabaugh), William Petersen (Pat Garrett), Alan Ruck (Hendry French), James Coburn (John Chisum).

In this sequel to the sophomoric 1988 film, Estevez, as Billy the Kid, and his buddies are back. It's just another excuse for some horse play with loads of lead flying.

3260. ***The Young Poisoner's Handbook*** (1996, U.K./Germany/France, CFP Distribution, 99m, c). D Benjamin Ross, P Sam Taylor, W Jeff Rawle & Ross, PH Hubert Taczanowski, ED Anne Sopel, M Robert Lane & Frank Strobel, PD Maria Djurkovic, AD Mark Stevenson.

LP Hugh O'Conor (Graham), Antony Sher (Dr. Zeigler), Ruth Sheen (Molly), Roger Lloyd Pack (Fred), Charlotte Coleman (Winnie), Paul Stacey (Dennis), Samantha Edmonds (Sue), Charlie Creed-Miles (Berridge).

In this film, based on a true story, O'Conor is obsessed with chemistry and fed up with his mother. He comes up with a concoction which he adds to her chocolates, killing her. He is sent to a prison for the criminally insane, where he is put under the care of Sher. Eight years later, on the recommendation of Sher, O'Conor is released, but he reverts to his poisoning ways and lays low eight more victims before being put away for good. The death throes of his victims are horrifying.

3261. ***Your Friends and Neighbors*** (1998, Gramercy Pictures, 99m, c). D & W Neil LaBute, P Steve Golin & Jason Patric, PH Nancy Schreiber, ED Joel Plotch, M Metallica, PD Charles Breen, SD Jeffrey Kushon.

LP Amy Brenneman (Mary), Aaron Eckhart (Barry), Catherine Keener (Terri), Nastassja Kinski (Cheri), Jason Patric (Cary), Ben Stiller (Jerry).

Other than the rhyming names, what else is cute about this black comedy? Well, it isn't that the male characters are charming creatures. They view the woman as merely toys in this comic exploration of misogyny. It's difficult to care what happens to any of the six characters.

3262. ***You've Got Mail*** (1998, Warner Bros., 119m, c). D Nora Ephron, P Nora Ephron & Lauren Shuler Donner, W Nora & Delia Ephron (based on the screenplay *The Shop Around the Corner* by Samson Raphaelson, from the play *Parfumerie* by Miklos Laszlo), PH John Lindley, ED Richard Marks, M George Fenton, PD Dan Davis, AD Ray Kluga & Beth Kuhn, SD Susan Bode.

LP Tom Hanks (Joe Fox), Meg Ryan (Kathleen Kelly), Parker Posey (Patricia Eden), Greg Kinnear (Frank Navasky), Jean Stapleton (Birdie), Steve Zahn (George Pappas), David Chappelle (Kevin Scanlon), Dabney Coleman (Nelson Fox).

Sometime before or after viewing this movie, moviegoers should watch Ernst Lubitsch's masterful 1939 romantic comedy *The Shop Around the Corner*, one of the most charming movies ever made. The present version of the story of two people who can barely tolerate each other in person but find each other perfect soul mates through anonymous communications is special in its own way. Hanks is about the closest actor we have to James Stewart. Both actors seem at home in almost any genre. We would not be at all surprised one day to see Tom, like Jimmy, star and shine in a Western. Ryan, while a completely different type than the fragile Margaret Sullivan, is most appealing. Hanks' character needs all the charm he can muster to get Ryan to fall in love with him in person after unknowingly falling in love with him in an exchange of e-mails. As the scion of a large bookstore chain, he succeeds in putting her small and special bookstore out of business. If you can believe that destroying a person's dreams and livelihood can still lead to love, you will thoroughly enjoy this picture.

3263. *Zandalee* (1991, Electric Pictures, 100m, c). D Sam Pillsbury, P William Blaylock & Eyal Rimmon, W Mari Kornhauser, PH Walt Lloyd, ED Michael Horton, PD Michael Corenblith, SD Merideth Boswell.

LP Nicolas Cage (Johnny Collins), Judge Reinhold (Thierry Martin), Erika Anderson (Zandalee Martin), Joe Pantoliano (Gerri), Viveca Lindfors (Tatta), Aaron Neville (Jack).

Bored sexy Anderson has an affair with Cage, her husband Reinhold's friend. Graphic sex scenes are offered instead of a plausible story.

3264. *Zebrahead* (1992, Triumph Releasing, 100m, c). D & W Anthony Drazan, P Charles Mitchell, Jeff Dowd & William F. Willett, PH Maryse Alberti, ED Elizabeth Kling, M Taj Mahal, PD Naomi Shohan, AD Dan Whifler, SD Penny Barrett.

LP Michael Rapaport (Zack Glass), Kevin Corrigan (Dominic), Lois Bendler (Dominic's Mother), Dan Ziskie (Mr. Cimino), DeShonn Castle (Dee Wimms), N'Bushe Wright (Nikki), Marsha Florence (Mrs. Wilson).

This film is a tepid story of young interracial love. Rapaport is white and Wright is black. How will they resist the various pressures of parents, friends and society? The performances by the youngsters are admirable.

3265. *Zero Effect* (1998, Sony Pictures/Columbia Pictures, 115m, c). D & W Jake Kasdan, P Lisa Henson, Janet Yang & Kasdan, PH Bill Pope, ED Tara Timpone, M The Greyboy Allstars, PD Gary Frutkoff, AD Philip J. Messina, SD Maggie Martin.

LP Bill Pullman (Daryl Zero), Ben Stiller (Steve Arlo), Ryan O'Neal (Gregory Stark), Kim Dickens (Gloria Sullivan), Angela Featherstone (Jess).

Millionaire O'Neal hires Pullman, the world's greatest and most private, private detective, to put an end to a longstanding extortion scheme. With the help of sarcastic Stiller, the eccentric sleuth sets up an elaborate sting operation to flush out the perpetrator. It looks like the guilty party is Dickens. Pullman compromises his investigation by falling for her. The offbeat comedy ultimately disappoints by trying to be just too hip.

3266. *Zero Patience* (1994, Canada, Cinevista, 100m, c). D & W John Greyson, P Louise Garfield & Anna Stratton, PH Miroslav Baszak, ED Miume Jan, PD Sandra Kybartas, SD Armando Sgrignuoli.

LP John Robinson (Sir Richard Burton), Normand Fauteux (Patient Zero), Dianne Heatherington (Mary), Richardo Keens-Douglas (George), Bernard Behrens (Dr. Placebo).

Fauteux is the Canadian flight attendant reputed to have carried the AIDS virus to North America. Now dead, his ghost pleads for someone to tell his story. His cause is taken up by English explorer Sir Richard Burton. Would you believe this is a musical?

3267. *Zeus and Roxanne* (1997, MGM/UA, 98m, c). D George Miller, P Frank Price, Gene Rosow & Ludi Boeken, W Tom Benedek, PH David Connell, ED Harry Hitner, M Bruce Rowland, PD Bernt Capra, AD Alfred Kemper, SD Beth Kushnick.

LP Steve Gutenberg (Terry Barnett), Kathleen Quinlan (Mary Beth Dunhill), Arnold Vosloo (Claude Carver), Dawn McMillan (Becky), Miko Hughes (Jordan Bennett), Majandra Delfino (Judith Dunhill).

This film for the kiddies features a dog and a dolphin who become fast friends. The friendship leads to a romance between the dog's owner Gutenberg and marine biologist Quinlan, who is studying dolphin behavior.

3268. *Zooman* (1995, Manheim Company–Logo Productions, 95m, c). D Leon Ichaso, P James B. Freydberg & Michael Manheim, W Charles Fuller (based on his play *Zooman and the Sign*), PH Jeffrey Jur, ED Gary Karr, M Daniel Licht, PD Richard Hoover, AD Keith Cox, SD Sandy Struth.

LP Louis Gossett, Jr. (Reuben Tate), Charles S. Dutton (Emmett), Cynthia Martells (Rachel), Khalil Kain (Zooman), Hill Harper (Victor), CCH Pounder (Ash), Vondie Curtis Hall (Davis), Alyssa Ashley Nichols (Jackie).

Kain is the violent title character who accidentally kills little Nichols. Her grief-stricken father Gossett can't believe that there are no witnesses to the crime. He puts up a sign on his house which reads "The killers of our Jackie are free because our neighbors will not identify them." Indeed they will not; they are afraid of getting involved and fearful of the violence Kain would visit on them if they opened their mouths. Meanwhile, Harper, the dead girl's brother, having learned that the killer's name is Zooman, gets a gun and goes looking for the unrepentant killer.

Index

References are to entry numbers

609

Index

Index

Index

Index

Index